DATE DUE

Soviet Criminal Justice under Stalin is the first comprehensive account in any language of Stalin's struggle to make criminal law in the USSR a reliable instrument of rule.

Using recently declassified archives, *Soviet Criminal Justice under Stalin* reveals the story of nonpolitical justice, on the local scene as well as in the center. Contrary to conventional wisdom, Peter Solomon emphasizes the initial weakness of the Soviet state and the limits of the dictator's capacity to rule. In the first decades of Soviet power, most judges, procurators, and investigators were not jurists but temporary recruits. Erratic and willful, they responded more to local politicians than to central authorities. When Stalin extended the criminal law or made it unusually severe, they resisted enforcement of the decrees. Near the end of his life and rule, Stalin made Soviet legal officials more compliant by developing judicial careers and strict assessment of the occupants' performance. The result, Solomon shows, was the flowering of an accusatorial bias that outlasted the Stalin era.

Solomon's study also offers new perspectives on the collectivization of the peasantry and the Great Terror, as well as on the politics of abortion and the disciplining of the labor force.

Written in a clear and direct manner, *Soviet Criminal Justice under Stalin* should appeal to anyone interested in the political, social, or legal history of the USSR, the reform of justice in post-Soviet states, law in authoritarian regimes, or comparative legal development.

SOVIET CRIMINAL JUSTICE UNDER STALIN

Cambridge Russian, Soviet and Post-Soviet Studies: 100

CAMBRIDGE RUSSIAN, SOVIET AND POST-SOVIET STUDIES

Series list continues after index

Soviet Criminal Justice under Stalin

Peter H. Solomon, Jr.

University of Toronto

CAMBRIDGE
UNIVERSITY PRESS

PUBLISHED BY THE PRESS SYNDICATE OF THE UNIVERSITY OF CAMBRIDGE
The Pitt Building, Trumpington Street, Cambridge CB2 1RP, United Kingdom

CAMBRIDGE UNIVERSITY PRESS
The Edinburgh Building, Cambridge CB2 2RU, United Kingdom
40 West 20th Street, New York, NY 10011–4211, USA
10 Stamford Road, Oakleigh, Melbourne 3166, Australia

First published 1996

Printed in the United States of America

Typeset in Palatino

Library of Congress Cataloguing-in-Publication Data
Solomon, Peter H., Jr.
   Soviet criminal justice under Stalin / Peter H. Solomon, Jr.
      p.   cm. – (Cambridge Russian, Soviet and post-Soviet studies : 100)
   Includes biographical references and index.
   ISBN 0 521 40089 9 hardback
   ISBN 0 521 56451 4 paperback
   1. Criminal justice, Administration of – Soviet Union – History. 2. Criminal
law – Soviet Union – History. 3. Political questions and judicial power – Soviet
Union – History. 4. Soviet Union – Politics and government – 1936–1953. I.
Title. II. Series.
KLA 1572.S65   1996
364.947 – DC20   96-3884
                                                                                 CIP

A catalogue record for this book is available from
the British Library

ISBN 0 521 40089 9 hardback
ISBN 0 521 56451 4 paperback

To the memory of my parents, Peter Herman Solomon, 1918–1988, and Barbara Miller Solomon, 1919–1992

Contents

Illustrations

Preface

Like most works of history this book reflects the time when it was written. The last years of Soviet power saw the breakdown of governmental restrictions on historical discourse, and in Russia the investigation of the Stalinist past became not only respectable but also a cause. Almost overnight there emerged historians and journalists who shared my interest in criminal justice under Stalin. At the same time, the new era produced a revolution in sources, as Soviet authorities and their successors made available to scholars a large part of the archival record, including material used in this book.

My interest in the development of criminal justice under Stalin began well before the opening of history in Russia. More than fifteen years ago, during the Brezhnev era, I examined crime and punishment in the 1920s and 1930s, and even before the accession of Gorbachev I had begun investigating criminal policy and the administration of justice under Stalin. When I decided to write this book, I assumed that the relevant archival material would remain off-limits. Between 1984 and 1989 I read widely and deeply in the printed record, especially journals and newspapers, while at the same time conducting interviews with former Soviet legal officials in emigration.

To my surprise and delight, the archives of the Soviet government and the Communist party of the Soviet Union did start to open in 1990, and each year thereafter offered new and more secret documents on the legal agencies. For five years I pursued archival research before deciding to invoke closure.

It is a pleasure to acknowledge the help of friends, colleagues, and institutions. To start, I wish to thank Eugene Huskey, Robert Sharlet, Yoram Gorlizki, and Susan Gross Solomon for thoughtful readings of the manuscript at various stages. Successive cohorts of students in my seminars also read draft chapters, urging me to keep them accessible.

In both the conduct of research and the testing of ideas I had much help – from research assistants, especially Gennady Ozernoi and Todd Foglesong, and from Robert W. Davies, Sheila Fitzpatrick, Levon Grigorian, James Harris, Julie Hessler, Peter Juviler, Oleg Khlevniuk, Vsesolod Kuritsyn, Harry Leich, Yuri Luryi, Peter Maggs, Viktor Mani-ichuk, Elena Naumova, Joan Neuberger, Dina Nokhotovich, Marina Rebrova, William Rosenberg, Raia Rozina, Louise Shelley, Lewis Siegel-baum, Robert Tucker, Arkady Vaksberg, and William Wagner. Above all, I am indebted to Eugene Huskey, with whom I spent many hours puzzling over the politics of criminal justice in the 1930s and my "com-rades on the archival front," Gabor Rittersporn and Yoram Gorlizki, who generously shared with me so many of their discoveries.

The staff of the following archives and libraries facilitated my re-search and earned my gratitude: (1) in Russia: the Lenin Library, the Institute of Scientific Information in the Social Sciences (INION), the libraries of the Institute of State and Law and of the Procuracy Institute, the State Archives of the Russian Federation (GARF) – and at both of its predecessors the Central State Archive of the October Revolution (TsGAOR) and the Central State Archive of the Russian Federation (TsGA), and at the Russian Center for the Preservation and Study of Documents of Current History (RTsKhIDNI), the former Central Party Archive (TsPA); and (2) in North America: the Harvard Law Library, the Library of Congress, and the Robarts Library of the University of Toronto, especially its microtext reading room (Iqbal Wagle and Joan Links), the office of interlibrary loans, and the order department (Mary Stevens).

My colleagues at the University of Toronto influenced this study in ways they may not know. The Center of Criminology and its core faculty over the years (Tony Doob, Richard Ericson, Clifford Shearing, and Philip Stenning) helped to shape my thinking about crime and criminal justice. The Centre for Russian and East European Studies, and particularly my partners in the Stalin Archives Project (Robert Johnson, Ron Pruessen, Susan Solomon, Lynne Viola) kept the larger issues of interpreting Soviet history firmly in view. My home base, the Depart-ment of Political Science, offered a culture of civility rare in university life and a broad understanding of political science that facilitated a fruitful marriage of teaching and research.

Others further away also contributed to this project. The Institute of State and Law of the Russian Academy of Sciences served as my home away from home, the base for five research stays in Moscow. Colleagues at the Institute who helped me included Aleksandr M. Iakovlev, Sofiia Kelina, Vladimir Kudriavtsev, Igor Petrukhin, Valery Savitskii, and Viliam Smirnov. For support and encouragement over the years I also wish to thank Harold Berman, Sheila Fitzpatrick, John Hazard, Leon Lipson, Sir Leon Radzinowicz, and Robert Sharlet.

In the production of this book I have benefited from the cheerful, efficient and accurate typing of Hyla Levy, Jana Oldfield, and Marian Reed; and from the editorial scrutiny of Cynthia Benn, Holly Johnson, and Frank Smith of Cambridge University Press.

Over the decade of work on this book I received financial support from a variety of sources: for the conduct of interviews and research at the early stages from the Lady Davis Foundation of Jerusalem, Israel, and the Soviet Interview Project of the University of Illinois; for research travel to the USSR from the International Research and Exchanges Board and the Association of Universities and Colleges of Canada; for occasional research from the Centre of Criminology of the University of Toronto (drawn from a grant from the Ministry of the Solicitor General of Canada), the Law Faculty of the University of Toronto (drawn from a grant from the Connaught Foundation), and the Office of Research Administration of the University of Toronto; for major support of research and writing throughout the project (in three separate grants) from the Social Sciences and Humanities Research Council of Canada; and for support during a critical year of writing from the John Simon Guggenheim Memorial Foundation. I am grateful to all of these benefactors.

Needless to say, my wife Susan has done the most to support and encourage me over the years. To our children, Raphael and Rachel, who are now old enough to read this book, I offer thanks for forcing me to enjoy a rich life beyond its creation.

An earlier version of Chapter 7 appeared in the *Slavic Review*, 46:3/4 (1987), 391–413, as "Soviet Criminal Justice and the Great Terror." A longer version of the third part of Chapter 4 appeared in William G. Rosenberg and Lewis H. Siegelbaum, eds., *Social Dimensions of Soviet Industrialization* (Bloomington: Indiana University Press, 1993), 223–247, under the title "Criminal Justice and the Industrial Front."

Glossary

aktiv a set (often a list) of active members of an organization (e.g., the Communist party)

All-Russian Central Executive Committee (*VTsIK*) legislature of the RSFSR

babki older women who performed abortions underground

batrak a peasant employed by another private peasant

cassation review in the USSR the first and mandatory (upon request) review by a higher court of the conduct and outcome of a criminal trial

Central Control Commission top party body for the discipline of party members

Central Committee refers to both the elected body of the Communist party and the staff or apparatus that served its chiefs (known as secretaries)

Central Executive Committee (*Tsentralnyi Ispolnitelnyi Komitet*) the legislature of the USSR, 1924–1938; replaced by the Supreme Soviet

Cheka the political police, 1918–1922 (literally, Extraordinary Commission)

commissar minister in the first decades of Soviet power

commissariat equivalent of a ministry

Communist Academy a body of research institutes in social sciences and humanities emphasizing a Marxist or proletarian approach

compulsory work a noncustodial sanction requiring the recipient to perform work designated by local government authorities; from 1933 called "corrective work"

comrades' courts lay courts organized in factories or residences to adjudicate minor infractions and disputes

corrective work see "compulsory work"

Council of People's Commissars (Sovnarkom)   the cabinet of the Soviet government; became Council of Ministers in 1946

county court (*uezd sud; okruzhnoi sud*)   an intermediate court that existed only in the early years of Soviet power; eliminated in 1930

district (*raion*)   basic territorial administrative unit (from 1930), covering especially rural areas, equivalent of a county in the United States

Eser   Socialist Revolutionary

GPU   the political police, 1922–1923 (literally, State Political Administration)

hooliganism   rowdy (usually drunken) behavior in a public place

kolkhoz   collective farm

kolkhoznik   collective farm member

Komsomol   Communist Youth Organization

kulak   in Bolshevik class analysis a "rich" peasant, usually employing other peasants

Narkomiust   People's Commissariat of Justice. Until 1936 existed only on the republican level. In 1946 renamed Ministry of Justice

NEP   New Economic Policy (1921–1928)

Nepman   a derogatory term for traders and private business persons in the 1920s

nomenklatura   lists of posts in government and party bodies whose filling required at least confirmation by a party official; *and* from this, persons who occupy such posts, i.e., important persons

NKVD   People's Commissariat of Internal Affairs. The all-union version of this agency, formed in 1934, absorbed the OGPU and acted as its successor

oblast   see region

OGPU   the political police, 1923–1934 (literally, United State Political Administration)

people's court (*narodnyi sud*)   the basic, regular court in the USSR from 1920. Staffed by full-time paid judges. *Not* a lay court.

plenum   a session attended by all members of a body. Thus, a plenum of the USSR Supreme Court was a meeting attended by all the judges of that court

procuracy   agency responsible for both the conduct of prosecutions and the supervision of legality in public life. Until 1933 there was no USSR procuracy and republican bodies were subordinate to the commissariats

procurator   legal official responsible for both the conduct of prosecutions and the supervision of legality in public life

Rabkrin   Commissariat of Workers' and Peasants' Inspection

raion see "district"

region (*oblast*) the main administrative unit between the cities and districts (*raiony*) below and governments of the republics above. Replaced the province (*guberniia*) in 1929. In size the region resembles a state in the United States

regional court (*oblastnoi sud*) the court at the regional level. Replaced the provincial court in 1930. Performs both trial work (for the more serious cases) and cassation reviews of cases heard in people's courts

review in supervision (*nadzor*) the second and discretionary review of the outcome of a criminal case already heard by a cassation panel

RSFSR Russian Union of Federated Socialist Republics

seredniak middle peasant

Shakhty trial 1928 trial of engineers and foreign specialists used by Stalin to launch persecution of bourgeois specialists

Stakhanovite a worker who, often with the help of his peers and bosses, exceeded norms of productivity by wide margins (named after the coal miner Aleksei Stakhanov)

territory (*krai*) a large administrative unit in remote, especially northern, parts of the RSFSR, embracing several regions (*oblasti*)

territorial court (*kraisud*) similar to a regional court, but corresponding to a "territory"

25,000er an industrial worker enrolled in a special program to help in collectivization of the countryside

wrecking conduct undermining the normal operation of state industry, trade, or commerce. Treated as a political crime

Introduction

This book presents a history of Soviet criminal justice in the years of Stalin's rule (1924–1953). No doubt some readers find the juxtaposition of Stalin and "justice" strange, even oxymoronic. They associate Stalin with terror – extralegal, sometimes arbitrary repression – and do not picture courts in the USSR administering criminal law in a remotely normal fashion. Of course, Stalin's political police did achieve extraordinary power, and its agents applied force against many citizens, especially in 1937–1938. But terror was not the only or even the main form of social control used by Soviet leaders before 1953.

During the 1930s and 1940s Stalin and his colleagues overcame Bolshevik ambivalence about law and embraced the criminal sanction as an instrument of rule. In the process they wrestled with and resolved such issues as whether legal procedures mattered, what functions the criminal law should perform, what shape legal institutions should take, what sort of persons should staff them, and how much autonomy those persons should have from their political masters. These decisions produced a system of criminal justice that outlasted Stalin and his terror. To be sure, that system had serious flaws, which included an accusatorial bias and the intrusion of bureaucratic and political pressures. But they did not derive from the terror.

Western Sovietological literature has paid relatively little attention to the history of criminal justice in the USSR. Individual scholars (for example Berman, Huskey, Juviler, Sharlet, Oda, and Rittersporn) have dealt with aspects of the story, as have a handful of scholars in the USSR and post-Soviet Russia.[1] But none of them has attempted a comprehen-

---

[1] Harold Berman, *Justice in the USSR* (Rev. ed., Cambridge, Mass., 1963); chaps. 1–2; Peter Juviler, *Revolutionary Law and Order* (New York, 1976), chaps. 1–2; Eugene Huskey, *Lawyers and the Soviet State: The Origins and Development of the Soviet Bar, 1917–1939*

sive study. In undertaking such an inquiry I hope to enrich knowledge of government and society in the Stalin era, especially the relationship between the policies of leaders and actual patterns of administration. At the same time, I believe, familiarity with the checkered history of Soviet criminal justice under Stalin will promote understanding of the challenge of legal reform in post-Soviet states.

In investigating the history of criminal law and its administration in the USSR, I have used a distinct methodology, one that differs from that used in previous studies of the subject. While continuing to pay close attention to the role of the tyrant and the central bureaucracy, I focus equally on people and institutions – asking how their perspectives, interests, and conduct shaped the administration of justice and influenced the formation of legal policies. This approach reflects traditions within criminology and criminal justice history.[2] It also complements the work of historians of Soviet Russia whose marriage of political and social history has invigorated their field.[3]

(Princeton, N.J., 1988); Huskey, "Vyshinsky, Krylenko, and the Shaping of the Soviet Legal Order," *Slavic Review*, 46:3/4 (1987), 414–428; Robert Sharlet, "Stalin and Soviet Legal Culture," in Robert Tucker, ed. *Stalinism* (New York, 1977); Robert Sharlet and Piers Beirne, "In Search of Vyshinsky: The Paradox of Law and Terror," *International Journal of the Sociology of Law*, 12 (1984), 153–177; Gabor Tamas Rittersporn, "Soviet Officialdom and Political Evolution: Judiciary Apparatus and Penal Policy in the 1930s," *Theory and Society* 13 (1984), 211–237; Rittersporn, *Stalinist Simplifications and Soviet Complications: Social Tensions and Political Conflicts in the USSR: 1933–1953* (Chur, Switzerland, 1991), esp. chap. 5; Hiroshi Oda, "Revolutionary Legality in the USSR, 1928–1930," *Review of Socialist Law*, 6:2 (1980), 141–151; Oda, "The CPSU and the Procuracy on the Eve of the Revolution from Above," in D.A. Loeber, ed., *Ruling Communist Parties and Their Status under Law* (Dordrecht, 1986).

M.V. Kozhevnikov, *Istoriia sovetskogo suda, 1917–1956* (Moscow, 1957); G.V. Shvekov, *Pervyi sovetskii ugolovnyi kodeks* (Moscow, 1970); V.M. Kuritsyn, *Perekhod k NEPu i revoliutsionnaia zakonnost* (Moscow, 1972); V. Bukov, *Sud i obshchestvo v sovetskoi Rossii: u istokov totalitarianizma* (Moscow, 1992); Oleg V. Khlevniuk, *1937-i: Stalin, NKVD i sovetskoe obshchestvo* (Moscow, 1992).

2 See, for example, James Q. Wilson, *Varieties of Police Behavior: The Management of Law and Order in Eight Communities* (Cambridge, Mass., 1969); James Eisenstein and Herbert Jacob, *Felony Justice. An Organizational Analysis of Criminal Courts* (Boston, 1977); Richard Ericson and Patricia Baranek, "Criminal Law Reform and Two Realities of the Criminal Process," in Anthony Doob and Edward Greenspan, eds., *Perspectives in Criminal Law: Essays in Honour of John Ll.J. Edwards* (Aurora, Ont., 1985), 255–276; Leon Radzinowicz and Roger Hood, *The Emergence of Penal Policy in Victorian and Edwardian England* (London, 1986); David Rothman, *Conscience and Convenience; The Asylum and Its Alternatives in Progressive America* (Boston, 1982); and Lawrence Friedman and Robert Percival, *The Roots of Justice: Crime and Punishment in Alameda County, California, 1870–1910* (Berkeley, Calif., 1981).

3 Moshe Lewin, *The Making of the Soviet System: Essays in the Social History of Interwar Russia* (New York, 1985); Sheila Fitzpatrick, *Education and Social Mobility in the Soviet Union 1921–1934* (Cambridge, 1979); Ronald Suny, "Toward a Social History of the

This study deals with not only criminal justice but also the role of law in the Soviet order. The assumptions held by Soviet leaders about the law and its relationship to politics helped to shape the history of criminal justice. In focusing upon the criminal law, I can tell only a part of the story of how Soviet leaders accepted and interpreted the utility of law. But that part is important. As a domain of public law, the criminal realm supplied the locus for struggle over the uses and role of law.

The development of law and criminal justice in the USSR started with handicaps that were not easily overcome. To begin, legal tradition in Russia was weak.[4] As in other autocracies, so in tsarist Russia, the ruler stood above the law. Moreover, while law served the tsars as an instrument of rule, it was not the main one, and some areas of public administration fell outside of legal regulation. In the last decades of tsarism officials in the government in St. Petersburg recognized how law could help them gain leverage over local officials, but as of 1917 their legal institutions reached only a minority of the population.[5]

Bolshevik attitudes toward law reinforced its low status in Russian political culture. Following Marxist analysis, they treated the law as wholly instrumental, a tool in the hands of rulers rather than a good in itself. In addition, some revolutionaries questioned whether law could serve a proletarian state and adopted a nihilistic attitude toward legal forms and procedures.

Not only was support for law in Russian and Bolshevik cultures weak, but legal institutions had only started to take root in tsarist Russia. To be sure, in the last decades before the Revolution officials had organized a new system of courts and legal procedures that reflected contemporary European models. Moreover, they had support from an attentive public in the major cities.[6] Nonetheless, the administration of criminal justice in the late tsarist period failed to reach much of the public. Even courts at the lowest rung of the hierarchy, the justice of the peace court (*mirovoi sud*), were located only in cities, and left most of the countryside untouched. Rather than deal with courts some days' journey away, rural dwellers often ignored them. Many peasants dealt only

October Revolution," *American Historical Review*, 88:1 (1983), 31–52; Lynne Viola, "The Campaign to Eliminate the Kulak as a Class: Winter, 1929–1930," *Slavic Review*, 45:3 (Fall 1986), 503–524; Graeme Gill, *The Origins of the Stalinist Political System* (Cambridge, 1990); and J. Arch Getty and Roberta T. Manning, eds., *Stalinist Terror: New Perspectives* (Cambridge, 1993).

4 Harold Berman, *Justice in the USSR* (Rev. ed., New York, 1963), part two.
5 George Yaney, *The Systematization of Russian Government* (Urbana, Ill., 1973).
6 Samuel Kucherov, *Courts, Lawyers, and Trials under the Last Three Tsars* (New York, 1953); William Wagner, "Tsarist Legal Policies at the End of the Nineteenth Century: A Study in Inconsistencies," *Slavonic and East European Review*, 54:3 (July 1976), 371–394.

with the lay courts established in rural districts and known as *volost* courts, the land captains (*zemskie nachalniki*), and agents of administrative bodies (police, tax collectors, timber inspectors). It remained for the Bolsheviks to build a unified legal order for the country as a whole.[7]

The goals of the Bolshevik leaders went further. After the Revolution they tried to replace tsarist legal institutions with new socialist alternatives. In addition, the Bolsheviks decided to staff their legal agencies not with lawyers trained under the old regime but with their own people, politically trustworthy amateurs who had joined the Bolshevik party. Despite expectations, this strategy failed to produce a reliable body of legal officials, ready to implement party policies, let alone the will of the leader. In due course, Stalin would insist that officials in the legal realm obtain legal education as well as party membership and would encourage them to make careers in the legal agencies. His associates would also find ways to make those legal officials conform to the dictates of their bureaucratic superiors.

The Soviet effort to develop new legal institutions and cultivate trustworthy legal officials was retarded and distorted by the turbulent course of Soviet history. The law and criminal justice did not develop in a vacuum. They were to a large extent dependent variables, acted upon and reflecting the major events of the times. Thus, the collectivization drive, the Great Terror of 1937–1938, and the buildup to World War II influenced the criminal law and its administration, as did the conservative shift in Soviet social policy in the mid-1930s and the bureaucratization and professionalization of public life in the late 1940s. To write about the history of criminal justice in the USSR calls for investigation of these events, albeit from a particular perspective.

Finally, the political system that emerged under Stalin posed another set of challenges for Soviet legal officials and jurists. One of these was Stalin himself, the dictator whose immense authority cast a shadow over the legal realm. From the early 1930s Stalin made Soviet criminal law his own. Virtually every change bore the mark of his hand, and he used the criminal law for many purposes – to squeeze grain out of hungry peasants, to pressure and scapegoat his officials, to reverse the decline in the birth rate, to inculcate labor discipline in the workforce – as well as to deter juvenile delinquency, hooliganism, and theft. In the process, Stalin extended the scope of the criminal law beyond its usual functions and made punishments unusually severe. Accommodating,

---

[7] Peter H. Solomon, Jr., "Criminalization and Decriminalization in Soviet Criminal Policy, 1917–1941," *Law and Society Review*, 16:1 (1981–1982), 9–44. On the practices of the *volost* courts, see George Yaney, *The Urge to Mobilize: Agrarian Reform in Russia, 1861–1930* (Urbana, Ill., 1982), 21–35.

avoiding, and resisting these innovations in the criminal law occupied much of the energy of legal officials at all levels of the hierarchy during the 1930s and 1940s.

Another troublesome feature of the political system was the role of the Communist party as coordinator and supervisor of public life. Provincial and local party officials treated judges, procurators, and investigators as they did other officials, and it would require prolonged struggle to establish a semblance of normal relations between political and legal authorities.[8] Even extreme concentration of authority in the hands of central legal officials did not stop local politicians from intervening in the work of the courts and procuracy to serve their own and the regime's purposes.

The presence alongside the legal agencies of a powerful political police represented yet another aspect of the Stalinist political system that threatened the development of criminal justice. The eventual compartmentalization of the legal and extralegal spheres was an achievement of the Stalin era that made the ordinary functioning of criminal law possible. But, as we shall see, this compartmentalization did not come without cost to practitioners of ordinary justice.

In analyzing and interpreting the history of Soviet criminal justice, I speak to not only students of the Soviet experience but also colleagues in the history and sociology of law. The story of criminal justice in the USSR relates to a number of questions in the study of legal development.

One of these questions is the limits of the criminal sanction in authoritarian states. In a now classic study Herbert Packer argued that at least in democracies the overuse and misuse of criminal law had costs.[9] Even more important, Packer continued, using the criminal law where enforcement was problematic produced especially bad effects, including the arbitrary use of discretion by officials and decreased public respect for the law. As a result, leaders faced constraints in the way that they could use the criminal law with profit. Packer developed his argument on the basis of the experience of Western democracies, but this does not mean that it has to be limited to them. Did the constraints on the use of the criminal law faced by democratic leaders apply as well to the leaders of authoritarian regimes? The example of Joseph Stalin should help answer this question, for that dictator regularly pushed the criminal law in the USSR beyond its normal scope and range of punishment. Furthermore, there were indications that legal officials and other would-be enforcers of the law did not always act as Stalin bade them.

[8] On relations between party politicians and public administration in the provinces, see Jerry F. Hough, *The Soviet Prefects* (Cambridge, Mass., 1969).
[9] Herbert Packer, *The Limits of the Criminal Sanction* (Stanford, Calif., 1968).

As we shall see, they evaded and resisted the enforcement of some laws and application of some punishments.

Another question of broad concern is the meaning and limits in the modern state of nonprofessional forms of justice.[10] For more than two decades Soviet authorities attempted to operate a modern system of criminal justice with intricate procedures using as staff persons who lacked not only higher legal education but even general secondary education. Moreover, many of those who served as prosecutors or judges left their posts quickly, to be replaced by new and equally unprepared colleagues. In short, in the 1920s and 1930s being a judge, procurator, or investigator in the USSR involved neither commitment to a career nor preparation. The Soviet system, however, did not constitute a form of lay justice, because its officials did consist of full-time paid personnel, but it did represent an unusual kind of nonprofessional or amateur justice. At the same time, the Soviets experimented with lay justice, but at no time were the lay tribunals (such as comrades' court and rural social courts) more than an appendage to formal legal institutions.

Finally, there is the question of the forms that criminal justice can take within authoritarian states. As a rule, authoritarian rulers do not submit to the discipline of law. Yet, while rejecting its constraints, they often recognize the law's utility as an instrument of rule. Typically, they treat the law as their tool and use it unconstrained by institutions or a societal commitment to rule of law. In the process, though, they may discover that it is hard to gain compliance with laws when rulers stand above them. By failing to submit to legal regulation, rulers may erode the legitimacy and diminish the effectiveness of their own laws. This tension between the desire to make law work and the desire to avoid its constraints forms a core dilemma for authoritarian rulers.[11] How they resolve it varies with the country and the time, but the variations may follow patterns. In times of revolutionary change, for example, leaders may tend to reject law as a constraint on their freedom of action, while in times of regime consolidation they may embrace law to define the new order. In ordinary times, leaders may allow some areas of public life to operate largely according to law, while in other realms reserving for themselves the prerogative to intervene against or beyond the law. The history of Soviet criminal justice offers examples of each of these solutions.

---

[10] Doris Marie Provine, *Judging Credentials: Nonlawyer Judges and the Politics of Professionalism* (Chicago and London, 1986).

[11] Roberto Unger, *Law in Modern Society* (New York, 1976), 64–66, makes a similar argument about the tensions in what he calls "bureaucratic law."

Illustrations

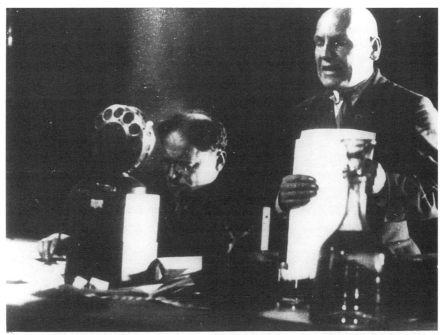

1. Nikolai Krylenko, prosecuting at a trial (late 1920s). Courtesy of The David King Collection, London

2. Andrei Vyshinskii in 1933. Courtesy of The David King Collection, London

3. Joseph Stalin, ca. 1935. Courtesy of The David King Collection, London

4. Aron Solts (second from left), in the late 1920s. Others in the group include: on the far left, Viacheslav Molotov; seated in the center, Mikhail Kalinin; and beside him, seated, A.S. Eunikidze. Courtesy of The David King Collection, London

5. A court in session in the early 1920s (probably a provincial court). Courtesy of The David King Collection, London

6. The USSR Supreme Court in regular session, 1929. Courtesy of The David King Collection, London

7. The Shakhty trial of 1928, a show trial before the USSR Supreme Court meeting in an auditorium. The newspaper heading reads: "In the presence of the Supreme Court." Courtesy of The David King Collection, London

8. Ivan T. Goliakov, Chairman,
USSR Supreme Court, 1938–1948.
Courtesy of *Rossiiskii
gosudarstvennyi arkhiv
kinofotodokumentov*
(The Russian State Archive of Film
and Photographic Documents),
Moscow

9. Nikolai M. Rychkov, USSR
Minister of Justice, 1938–1948.
Courtesy of *Rossiiskii
gosudarstvennyi arkhiv
kinofotodokumentov*
(The Russian State Archive of Film
and Photographic Documents),
Moscow

10. Grigorii N. Safonov, USSR
Procurator-General, 1948–1953.
Courtesy of *Rossiiskii
gosudarstvennyi arkhiv
kinofotodokumentov*
(The Russian State Archive of Film
and Photographic Documents),
Moscow

11. Anatolii A. Volin, Chairman,
USSR Supreme Court, 1948–1957.
Courtesy of *Rossiiskii
gosudarstvennyi arkhiv
kinofotodokumentov*
(The Russian State Archive of Film
and Photographic Documents),
Moscow

12. At the Kremlin in 1948: Joseph Stalin, Lavrentii Beriia, Anastas Mikoyan, and Georgii Malenkov. Courtesy of The David King Collection, London

PART I

The first phase

1   The design of an experiment

At the end of the Civil War Bolshevik leaders faced the questions of what to include in their criminal law, who should administer it, and how. In answering these questions the central concern of the Bolsheviks was making the criminal law serve socialism. Consequently, they regarded their mission as special. Their task was to design an experiment, the first system of criminal justice that would discriminate for the toiling classes rather than against them and that would replace the formal and remote institutions of bourgeois justice with socialist variants that would be simple and accessible. The solution that Bolshevik leaders fashioned in the early years of the New Economic Policy (NEPs 1921–1928) involved choices about three issues – the content of the law, the people who would execute it, and the institutions and procedures for its administration. In this chapter we shall examine all of these.

Before doing so, we pause to consider the attitudes of the Bolsheviks toward the law and their experience in administering justice during the Civil War. The ideas that the revolutionaries brought with them about law were far from consistent and soon generated ambivalence and tensions that made the NEP solution to the design of criminal justice suspect from the start.

The Bolsheviks, the law, and courts

Shortly after the Revolution most Bolshevik leaders adopted an instrumental view of law. Without enshrining law as a value and always stressing the subordinate status of the law, Lenin and his colleagues used the law as a tool for implementing their policies. This approach to law was consistent with the autocratic tradition of the tsars and had roots in the ideas and assumptions of Russian Marxism as well. Paradoxically the same Marxist tradition that supported an instrumental view of law also prompted doubts about the role of law in the new socialist state.

In Marxist culture law represented the instrument through which the ruling bourgeoisie defined and defended its capitalist order, especially the system of property. A communist revolution, most Bolsheviks assumed, would destroy the bourgeois state and its laws, leaving the workers free to administer themselves without the restraints of private law. Under communism, much of law and legal institutions would prove unnecessary and be subject to elimination. But the Bolshevik Revolution had brought Russia not to the doorstep of communism but to the start of a transition period of undetermined length and character. The nature of law and legal institutions in the new Soviet state would depend, at least in theory, upon how Soviet leaders understood this period of transition. As individual party members differed about this latter issue, so among the Bolsheviks there emerged a spectrum of views about the law, whose midpoint shifted with the times.[1]

Among the first acts of the Bolsheviks upon coming to power was the elimination of tsarist law and courts, and in the heady days of postrevolutionary fervor few Bolsheviks were ready for the restoration of private or civil law. Many hoped that as they were building communism in the factories and soviets, so they could manage without resorting to the tool of the capitalists. Their leader V.I. Lenin shared this point of view, but political realist that he was, quickly realized that the new regime needed at least public law. Lenin used criminal law in particular as a weapon for dealing with a panoply of problems. At the same time, early Bolshevik jurists, like Peter Stuchka, justified Lenin's actions. According to Stuchka, for the period of transition from capitalism to socialism Soviet law had to exist to serve the interests of the new rulers, the working class.[2]

Lenin agreed with Stuchka that a proletarian law, designed to serve socialism, was necessary and desirable. Lenin also insisted that Soviet

---

[1] Major discussions of Lenin's views on law are found in Harold Berman, *Justice in the USSR* (Rev. ed., New York, 1963), 13–32; Ivo Lapenna, "Lenin, Law and Legality," in Leonard Schapiro and Peter Reddaway, eds., *Lenin: The Man, the Theorist, the Leader* (New York, 1967), 235–264; Piers Beirne and Alan Hunt, "Law and the Construction of Soviet Society: The Case of Comrade Lenin," in Piers Beirne, ed., *Revolution in Law: Contributions to the Development of Soviet Legal Theory, 1917–1938* (Armonk and London, 1990), 61–98; Jane Burbank, "Lenin and the Law in Revolutionary Russia," *Slavic Review*, 54:1 (Spring 1995), 23–44.

[2] "Editors' Introduction" in Piers Beirne and Robert Sharlet, eds., *Pashukanis: Selected Writings on Marxism and Law* (London, 1980), 20–22. See also Petr Stuchka, "Proletarskoe pravo," in Stuchka, *12 let borby za revolutsionno-marksistkuiu teoriiu prava* (Moscow, 1931); and Stuchka, "Revolutsionnaia zakonnost," ibid., 102–104.

law be simple and popular and above all avoid the bureaucratic defor-
mations that he had encountered in his short career as a lawyer under
the tsars. But the more functions Lenin attributed to the law, the more
difficult it would prove to keep it simple. By spring 1918 Lenin expected
that the criminal law would serve not only to combat the former exploit-
ers and the problems he associated with them, but also to discipline and
educate the workers, who had proven too unruly to be trusted with
self-management. And, as the Civil War set in, Lenin insisted that to
accomplish all of these functions the laws set by the Soviet state would
have to be observed. By the fall of 1918 "revolutionary legality" had
emerged as one of Lenin's slogans.

In promoting the observance of laws by provincial and local officials
and citizens throughout the realm, Lenin was not seeking to restrain
proletarian power. In fact, the leader had no difficulty authorizing the
broad use of extralegal coercion (terror) as yet another instrument of the
young state for the battle against its opponents. Already in February
1918 the Cheka (the political police of Lenin's Russia) gained the authority not only to investigate but also to judge and punish counterrevolu-
tionaries. To be sure, the Bolsheviks had also established special courts
for dealing with political enemies, revolutionary tribunals modelled
loosely after those of the French Revolution. But to the Cheka leader
Felix Dzherzhinski and his followers the young, embattled state could
not rely even upon the tribunals to deliver blows to its enemies. However summary their proceedings, the tribunals remained a kind of
court, and in practice their judges acquitted some of those on trial and
gave lenient sentences to others.

During 1918 the Cheka expanded its use of extrajudicial coercion to
respond to offenses not usually regarded as political and it emerged as
a major competitor for the courts and tribunals.[3] In response, justice
officials and judges from the revolutionary tribunals attacked the broad
powers of the Cheka and sought its subordination to provincial justice
agencies. In January 1919 the Moscow party organization followed the
advice of Narkomiust official Nikolai Krylenko and endorsed depriving
the Cheka of the right to adjudicate. Anti-Cheka backlash led Bolshevik
leaders to limit the sentencing power of the Cheka officials to parts of
the country under martial law or rebellion. But this legal restriction had
little impact upon the conduct of terror. To avoid the revolutionary

[3] George Leggett, The Cheka: Lenin's Political Police (Oxford, 1981), 41–61, 172–175; N.
Polianskii, "Revoliutsionnye tribunaly," Pravo i zhizn, 1927, no. 8–10, 67–79; M.V.
Kozhevnikov, Istoriia sovetskogo suda 1917–1956 gody (Moscow, 1957), 86; V.P. Portnov
and M.M. Slavin, Stanovlenie pravosudiia Sovetskoi Rossi (1917–1922 gg.) (Moscow, 1990),
53–71.

tribunals, Cheka officials transferred suspects to areas under martial law.[4]

The use of terror by Lenin and the Bolsheviks against their political enemies (real or imagined) took the Soviet state a step beyond its tsarist predecessor. In the 1880s, after courts with juries created by the Judicial Reform of 1864 had acquitted assassins of tsarist officials, authorities created a separate sphere of political justice. By directing political cases either to the Senate or military tribunals, the regime ensured that the judges would deliver the appropriate verdicts.[5] In separating political from regular criminal justice, the tsars followed a classic course for embattled authoritarian regimes. The Bolsheviks went further and applied force directly without judicial hearings. The antilaw strain in Bolshevik theory may have facilitated the use of terror, but for many Bolsheviks no justification was needed. For them terror represented the appropriate and necessary weapon for defending the Revolution. And, it was a tool used by their opponents as well.[6]

At the same time as Lenin sanctioned the terror applied by the Cheka, he also supported the development of courts and criminal law. One of the Bolsheviks' first decrees established the courts in Soviet Russia, and the new regime promulgated a long series of laws governing their operation. To manage the courts the Bolsheviks established the Commissariat of Justice (Narkomiust), and from summer 1918 that agency's jurists began drafting legal codes, a process that lasted throughout the Civil War. From the start Narkomiust officials gathered information about the conduct of justice at the local level, and their perceptions of that early experience influenced the design of criminal justice after the Civil War.[7]

---

4 Leggett, The Cheka, 138–151; "Zhurnal plenarnykh zasedanii vtorogo vserossiiskogo s'ezda oblastnykh i guberskikh komissarov iustitsii, 2–6 iiuliia 1918 goda, g. Moskvy," Materialy Narkomiusta, 3 (1918), 14–17; "Iz istorii vzaimootnoshenii chrezvychainykh komissii i revoliutsionnykh tribunalov," Voprosy istorii, 1990, no. 7, 155–163.

5 William G. Wagner, "Tsarist Legal Policies at the End of the Nineteenth Century: A Study in Inconsistencies," Slavonic and East European Review, 54:3 (July 1976), 371–394; N. Polianskii, "Tsarskie voennye sudy," Sotsialisticheskaia zakonnost (hereafter SZ), 1937, no. 12, 64–75.

6 Moshe Lewin, "The Civil War: Dynamics and Legacy," in Diane P. Koenker et al., eds., Party, State and Society in the Russian Civil War (Bloomington, Ind., 1989), 406.

7 For a comprehensive collection of early Soviet decrees on the courts and analysis of their development, see Nikolai V. Krylenko, Sudoustroistvo RSFSR (lektsii po teorii i istorii sudoustroistva) (Moscow, 1923).

   On Narkomiust's role in drafting codes, statutes, and decrees, see Kozhevnikov, Istoriia sovetskogo suda, 105–113; G.V. Shvekov, Pervyi sovetskii ugolovnyi kodeks (Moscow, 1970); and O.I. Chistiakov, "Organizatsiia kodifikatsionnykh rabot v pervye gody Sovetskoi vlasti (1917–1923)," Sovetskoe gosduarstvo i pravo (hereafter SGiP), 1956, no. 5.

The actual administration of justice before 1921 offered much to please the many Bolsheviks who were suspicious of formal laws and institutions. Tsarist courts were dismantled, and at least officially tsarist law discarded as well. The new Soviet people's courts came under the control of local government (soviets), and they were staffed with persons loyal to the Revolution. Criminal law and the law of criminal procedure developed slowly and partially. Where the law did not supply guidance, judges were instructed to rely upon their "revolutionary consciousness."

To Soviet justice officials in Moscow this situation was far from satisfactory. They recognized how little leverage they had over the conduct of judges and lower justice officials and how decentralized and even anarchic was the overall shape of Soviet justice. As a result, the chiefs of Narkomiust began promoting a series of mechanisms for creating a judicial system and establishing the power of their agency. The goals of Narkomiust's officials included administrative subordination of local justice agencies to the commissariat, independence of judges from local politicians, and codified laws.

For at least the first year after the Revolution, courts in Soviet Russia were the creatures of local authorities. The decree of November 17, 1917, issued by the government in Moscow authorized the formation of local courts, but soviets at various levels, county (*uezd*) congresses of soviets, and even meetings of provincial justice officials assumed responsibility for the actual establishment of courts, selection of judges, and setting of rules of operation. Reflecting their local origins, the first Soviet courts bore many names: "people's courts," "temporary people's courts," "revolutionary courts," "temporary revolutionary courts," "people's public courts." Most provincial governments established their own "commissariats of justice" (the term did not yet refer to the equivalent of a ministry), and those provincial justice bodies struggled both to gain leverage over the local courts and to maintain autonomy vis-à-vis Narkomiust in Moscow.[8]

For the Commissariat in Moscow the challenge lay in developing a uniform structure of courts and gaining authority over particular courts. By mid-1919 Narkomiust had gone a long way toward accomplishing these ends. It had established a common structure and nomenclature for the courts under its jurisdiction. And it had subordinated the provincial justice commissariats, transforming them into provincial departments of

---

[8] "O sude," Dekret SNK 24 noiabria 1917, in I.T. Goliakov, ed., *Sbornik dokumentov po istorii ugolovnogo zakonodatelstva SSSR i RSFSR 1917–1952 gg.* (Moscow, 195), 15–16, *Materialy Narkomiusta*, 1–3 (1918), passim.

justice.[9] From 1919 to 1922 the courts themselves (with the exception of military justice and special tribunals on the railroads) fell into a two-tiered system. On the bottom were the people's-courts (*narodnye sudy* or *narsudy*), the local court that had replaced the justice of the peace court (*mirovoi sud*) of the tsarist period. The people's courts differed from their predecessors in the extent of their jurisdiction and in hearing cases by a mixed panel of a judge and two lay assessors, but they often borrowed rules of operation from the peace courts. Appeals from the people's courts went to a province (*guberniia*) level congress of people's court judges (analogous to the former congress of peace court judges) but no further.[10] The revolutionary tribunals, designed originally for political cases, occupied the upper tier of the court system. Organized at the province level, the jurisdiction of the revolutionary tribunals included the most serious nonpolitical offenses (speculation, bribery), and in practice they heard other criminal cases as well that belonged to the jurisdiction of the people's courts. In 1920, more than 80% of their cases were *nonpolitical*. Moreover, the tribunals acquitted or otherwise dropped cases against nearly one-third of its defendants, and gave noncustodial or suspended sentences to 60% of those whom they convicted; 3.5% received the death penalty.[11] Although the revolutionary tribunals (like the people's courts) usually heard cases quickly without defense counsel or prosecution and without formal procedures, their decisions were subject to review in Moscow by the Cassation Tribunal attached to the All-Russian Central Executive Committee (VTsIK).[12]

[9] For a detailed account of the process of standardization and subordination, see John N. Hazard, *Settling Disputes in Soviet Society* (New York, 1960), chaps. 3 and 4.

[10] Iu.S. Tokarev, "Dokumenty narodnykh sudov (1917–1922 gg.)," *Voprosy istoriografii i istochnikovedeniia istorii SSSR* (Moscow, 1963), 143–175; Portnov and Slavin, *Stanovlenie pravosudii*, 14–52; Kozhevnikov, *Istoriia sovetskogo suda*, 62–77.

[11] M.N. Gernet, *Prestupnost za granitsei i v SSSR* (Moscow, 1931), 74; G.E. Petukhov, *Sovetskii sud i stanovlenie revoliutsionnoi zakonnosti v gosudarstvennom upravlenii* (Kiev and Odessa, 1982), 67–68; Kozhevnikov, *Istoriia sovetskogo suda*, 86; E. Tarnovskii, "Dvizhenie prestupnosti v predelakh R.S.F.S.R. po svedenii mestnykh sudov za 1919–20gg." *Proletarskaia revoliutsiia i pravo*, no. 15 (1921), 1–13.

[12] Eugene Huskey, *Russian Lawyers and the Soviet State. The Origins and Development of the Soviet Bar, 1917–1939* (Princeton, N.J., 1986), 63–71; Portnov and Slavin, *Stanovlenie pravosudiia*, 81–85. According to archival sources used by Portnov and Slavic, the Cassational Tribunal of VTsIK in 1920 reviewed 1,420 verdicts of a total of 23,325 rendered by the revolutionary tribunals in 1920. It canceled 268, mainly because of procedural irregularities such as failure to present the accusation to the accused, an illegally constructed bench, or incomplete investigation. Note that the caseload of the revolutionary tribunals represented 2% of all criminal cases heard by Soviet courts in 1920. The *narsudy* heard 84%, and the revolutionary military tribunals 14%. The latter dealt especially with cases of desertion from the army. Tarnovskii, "Dvizhenie prestupnosti," 12–13.

The establishment of a uniform typology of courts and a framework for their administration did not produce consistency in sentencing or verdicts. In the absence of codes or laws defining the parameters of judicial action, judges either listened to other masters or acted entirely on their own. Narkomiust officials accepted neither of these outcomes.

In the first years after the Revolution most judges were subordinate to local political officials. To begin, local soviets and congresses of soviets had issued ordinances defining the shape of courts, their powers, and procedures, in some cases retaining for themselves the right to review decisions of the courts! After Narkomiust had established a single court structure, local officials still treated judges as their charges, giving them instructions in particular cases and removing from office those who did not comply. In an attempt to sever the bond between county officials and judges, Narkomiust staff placed in the 1920 statute on courts the requirement that the provincial executive committees (*gubispolkom*) give consent to all recalls of judges. By 1922 some leading Bolshevik jurists wanted to go further and award the Soviet people's court judge's tenure in office (as tsarist judges in the county and higher courts had had). Thus, Krylenko, Slavin, and other Narkomiust officials argued that only long-term (or life) appointments would protect judges from local politicians and raise the authority of the courts. This argument contradicted the earlier rejection of "judicial independence" as a bourgeois irrelevance both by the Commissar of Justice Kurskii and Marxist legal theorists Stuchka and Reisner – a position still supported by Narkomiust's Lisitsyn.[13]

In identifying the damage done to the administration of justice by the dependence of judges on local authorities, Krylenko and his colleagues showed perspicacity and foresight. As we shall see, neither the organizational mold of Soviet courts that crystallized in 1922–1923 nor any future reorganizations or reforms succeeded in severing the ties between judges and local politicians. Local power would remain a prime force shaping the administration of criminal justice in the USSR throughout its history. We shall return to it often.

Finally, the absence of a criminal code (or the equivalent) gave judges more discretion – or power – than the chiefs of the Justice Commissariat

---

[13] N. Polianskii, "Sovetskoe zakonodatelstvo o sudoustroistve v ego osnovnykh momentakh (obshchie sudebnye uchrezhdenii)," *Pravo i zhizn*, 1927, no. 8–10, 91–94; "Protokoly III Vserossiiskogo s'ezda deiatelei sovetskoi iustitsii," *Materialy Narkomiusta*, no. 11–12 (1921), 38; Portnov and Slavin, *Stanovlenie pravosudiia*, 40–41; V.M. Kuritsyn, *Perekhod k NEPu i revoliutsionnaia zakonnost* (Moscow, 1972), 108. Kuritsyn argued that interference in trials by local officials (from the *ispolkomy*) was justified during the Civil War because of the political unreliability of many judges. Once the War was over, he insisted, the practice became intolerable.

were willing to accept. At a meeting of justice officials in 1920, the agency's representatives announced their strong support for a traditional criminal code that defined punishments as well as crimes and general principles.[14] For some of them this position represented a big change. In 1918 the official in charge of drafting criminal legislation, M. Kozlovskii, had denounced codification as a "useless effort," unnecessary since the Bolsheviks were determined to give the revolutionary masses a chance to create their own law (*pravotvorchestvo*). Writing a year later, the justice commissar Dmitrii Kurskii registered approval of the way judges had thus far used their discretion in convicting and punishing persons accused of familiar (but not yet proscribed) crimes. Yet, by 1920 these officials had changed their position on the need for a criminal code.[15]

Why? What else had changed in the interim? For one thing, Narkomiust had gathered fuller information about judicial behavior in the absence of defined crimes and punishments. As of mid-1919 the edicts of the Bolsheviks defined only political, service (*dolzhnostnye*), and economic crimes, but nothing more, and they did not specify the punishments. Left on their own, however, Soviet judges proved unwilling to simply follow revolutionary consciousness. Indeed, for most ordinary crimes – thefts, assault, murder, drunkenness, insults – judges of the people's courts and revolutionary tribunals used *tsarist* law. The reliance was not just implicit; "everywhere" (*splosh i riadom*), the justice officials now realized, judges were citing the Criminal Statute (*Ugolovnoe ulozhenie*) of 1845! Moreover, in choosing punishments, judges operated independently and inconsistently. The only common thread in sentencing was extreme leniency![16]

Not only did Narkomiust officials recognize and disapprove of inconsistent and overly lenient sentencing, but they had come to regard this pattern of behavior as a symptom of a more vital problem – the weak authority of the government in Moscow and especially of the Commissariat of Justice. The same Kozlovskii who in 1918 had spoken of giving law-making power to the masses had changed his tune by

---

14 "Protokoly III Vserossiiskogo s'ezda," 73–80.
15 M. Kozlovskii, "Proletarskaia revoliutsiia i ugolovnoe pravo," *Proletarskaia revoliutsiia i pravo*, 1918, no. 2, 21–28; D. Kurskii, "Novoe ugolovnoe pravo," ibid., 1919, no. 2–4, 23–34. In contrast, Iakov Berman of the Commissariat sought full codification in early 1919. See Ia. Berman, "K voprosy ob ugolovnom kodekse sotsialisticheskogo gosduarstva," ibid., 35–39. A condensed version of the Kozlovskii article was published in English in Michael Jaworskyj, ed., *Soviet Political Thought. An Anthology* (Baltimore, 1967), 69–71.
16 Shvekov, *Pervyi sovetskii*, 67–100; "Protokoly III Vserossiiskogo s'ezda"; Tarnovskii, "Dvizhenie prestupnosti."

June 1920. At a conference of justice officials, he stated sharply, "We cannot let each judge decide about this or another crime. We have such variation now . . . for speculation some give a small fine, others always deprivation of freedom. . . . In the interests of centralization of authority we must issue a code." Without codes, Kozlovskii went on, the center could not give direction to the periphery, and absent such direction "there would be no state, just nomadic hordes." Joining Kozlovskii was Nikolai Krylenko, the future justice commissar. In resolving the question of a criminal code, Krylenko explained, "I would begin by declaring that socialist legal consciousness, not the old law, is the starting point. But socialist legal consciousness does not mean the consciousness of one or another judge, rather the cumulative experience." To be sure, Krylenko opposed the matching of punishments to particular crimes. This idea was to become a fixation for Krylenko and a position that he tried to impose on Soviet criminal law during the late 1920s and early 1930s. However, in 1920, Krylenko joined Kozlovskii and others from the Commissariat in supporting the standardization and centralization that a criminal code implied.[17] Not everyone on the scene agreed with Narkomiust's position. Just a few weeks earlier a congress of judges from the revolutionary tribunals had taken a resolution denouncing the plans for a code defining crimes and punishments. Kozlovskii displayed special venom for these and other opponents of his (new) views. "We have no doubt (about the need for a code), nor should any sensible person in government, even the anarchist and the person who fears the old code, which in fact . . . still governs us."[18]

The association of law – by Narkomiust's leaders – with centralized authority should not go unnoticed, for this too was a theme that would recur later on. As we shall see, from the mid-1930s Stalin himself promoted the authority of the laws issued by the Soviet state, and Stalin did so as a means of centralization and combatting the power of local political officials.

What contribution did the experience of Bolshevik rule before 1922 make to the later development of Soviet criminal justice? First, I would argue, the very attainment of power by the Bolsheviks ensured the victory of the instrumental view of law over the other competing Bolshevik conception, the eliminationist or antilaw view. The victory, however, was far from complete. The antilaw view remained a strong part

---

17 "Protokoly III Vserossiiskogo s'ezda."
18 Ibid. Months later a congress of justice workers in Petrograd joined the tribunal judges in opposing a criminal code. A rapporteur insisted that "proletarian law would lose a lot" if a code were promulgated; and the resolution of the congress opposed even the setting of minimum and maximum punishments for particular crimes. Shvekov, *Pervyi sovetskii*, 129.

of Bolshevik political culture and continued to influence the administration of criminal justice during the Civil War and for decades to come. Second, the struggle of the Bolsheviks to hold onto power (including the Civil War) gave birth to a parallel system of terror or extralegal coercion that competed with the justice agencies and assumed responsibility for repressing political (counterrevolutionary) offenders. The agencies of terror were to outlast the time when the Bolsheviks were under siege. To be sure, the Cheka's immediate successor, the GPU (State Political Administration) lost the authority to adjudicate and punish, but it regained it in 1924. Under Stalin the OGPU (United State Political Administration) grew into the superagency for terror for which Stalin and Stalinism are best known. Finally, the actual experience of justice officials in administering the courts generated strong support within the Commissariat of Justice from 1920 for a uniform and centralized system of justice that included traditional criminal and civil codes. Without such codes, the officials had concluded, neither the autonomy of the courts nor authority of central legal agencies could develop.

The declaration of the New Economy Policy (NEP) in 1921 gave the Narkomiust officials a quicker and more resounding victory than they might otherwise have had.[19] Their cause was furthered by the new role of law that the decisions in economic policy implied. The partial restoration of capitalist institutions, including the market and private property, gave the law new legitimacy and functions. The immediate consequences included the decision to revive civil law and accelerate work on codification. For the designers of criminal justice, especially in Narkomiust, the restoration supported their platform of grounding the administration of the criminal law in traditional institutions and procedures, albeit with special features. On a larger plane, the new status of law under NEP represented a victory for the instrumental view of law over the eliminationist approach.

This particular victory, however, left some Bolsheviks uneasy. NEP law, like its economy, bore too great a resemblance to the old order. Traditional institutions and procedures might be easy to set in motion (and the element of tradition might account for the long-range viability of the system of justice designed in the early 1920s), but to some contemporary Bolsheviks they smacked of defeat. Some jurists were forthright in expressing these concerns. A.G. Goikhbarg, one of the founders

---

[19] I agree with Nikolai Krylenko that the core of Soviet criminal justice developed before NEP and NEP only hastened its full expression. Krylenko was taking issue with Kurskii's claim that NEP was the driving force behind Soviet justice. According to Krylenko, Kurskii's claim was valid only for *civil* law. Krylenko, *Sudoustroistvo RSFSR*, 157–160. John Hazard gave an eloquent restatement of Krylenko's case in *Settling Disputes*, 485–486.

of Soviet civil law, warned lest the reestablishment of law might bring with it a revival of the ideology of law. To avoid this disaster, he called for the conduct of antilaw propaganda, not, as he put it, to encourage disobedience to the laws established by Soviet authority, but to strip legal norms of their "halo" of sanctity.[20]

Despite the status law achieved under NEP, the tension between using law and eliminating it persisted in the minds and hearts of Bolsheviks. To be sure, open attacks on law (such as were made in the first year of Soviet power) ceased, and criticism of law per se tended to be muted. But the bias of some Bolsheviks against law showed. It appeared in the openly expressed prejudices of politicians against professional lawyers, in the Marxist jurisprudence created by a circle of leading jurists, and in the struggle against the complexity of the new laws that dominated criminal policy in the later years of NEP. At the end of the 1920s when the continuation of NEP itself was called into question, the antilaw, eliminationist point of view had a resurgence and for a time influenced the administration of justice in the USSR.

The content of the law

The Criminal Code of 1922 – on which all later Soviet codes have been based – represented a distinct blend of tradition and novelty. In its structure, many of its orienting concepts, specification of crimes, and penal arsenal Soviet criminal law borrowed much from the past. At the same time, certain categories of crime, the approach to punishment, and the central principles embodied in the code were original and gave the code a socialist flavor.

The drafting of the code, while in the minds of some of its authors "rushed," extended over a number of years. To be sure, the actual code that was promulgated was composed during spring and summer of 1921, then reviewed by the Institute of Soviet Law, and finally discussed and revised by the 4th Congress of Judicial Workers (January 1922); a commission appointed by the Council of People's Commissars (February-April 1922); and the All Russian Central Executive Committee (VTsIK) (May 1922). The latter devoted four plenary and three committee sessions to the code.[21] Before this year of intensive work, however, there had been much effort expended on the code. Serious

20 A.G. Goikhbarg, "Justice, the Ideology of Law, and Revolution," in Jaworskyj, *Soviet Political Thought*, 121–134.
21 Stennogrammy IV Vserossiiskogo S'ezda Deiatelei Sovetskoi Iustitsii (26–30 ianvaria 1922 g.), *Materialy Narkomiusta*, 16–17 (Moscow, 1922), 22; Shvekov, *Pervyi sovetskii*, 137–159; *III sessiia VTsIK IX sozyva (12–17 maia 1922 g.)*, Biulleteni nos. 3, 4, 8, 9, and 10.

work began in Narkomiust in 1919, and by 1921 three competing drafts had come into circulation. Furthermore, all of the drafting groups had the opportunity to consult the draft criminal code of 1903, itself a special resource. Although never passed into law, the 1903 code marked the culmination of twenty years of discussions and was by all accounts one of the finest codes in Europe. Based on a careful comparison of criminal law throughout the Western world, it had served as a model for law reform in Germany and Austria.[22] While Bolshevik jurists displayed ambivalence about borrowing from this "bourgeois code" (which the Socialist Revolutionary Commissar of Justice Steinberg had made the basis of his draft criminal code in 1918), it offered answers to some theoretical problems that were too useful to reject.[23] And, it was not tsarist law.

At the heart of the new criminal code stood the offenses that are criminal almost everywhere, what a leading criminologist has called "the constant core of crimes." Crimes against the person – from assault to murder – were defined in accordance with the 1903 draft code. Offenses against personal property – theft, robbery, etc. – drew upon the intricate (and partly unworkable) distinctions of tsarist law itself (the 1845 Criminal Statute).[24] But there were three categories of crime that the Bolsheviks shaped to suit their interests and that helped make their code distinctive: counterrevolutionary crimes, economic crimes, and crimes by officials.

Like other absolutist rulers, the tsars had featured crimes against the state in their criminal law. Moreover, they defined those offenses broadly enough to encompass most challenges to their authority. The Soviet draftsmen not only built upon this tradition but carried it further. To protect the young Soviet state that had just emerged from Civil War, they devised a long list of political offenses that they dubbed "counterrevolutionary," and defined them in broad language. In so doing, they gave the political section of the code such elasticity that authorities could politicize almost any crime.[25]

When the 1922 Criminal Code came into operation, all cases of counterrevolutionary crimes had to be heard in the courts. The GPU

---

[22] Shvekov, *Pervyi sovetskii*, 115–142; N.S. Timasheff, "The Impact of the Penal Law of Imperial Russia on Soviet Penal Law," *American Slavic and East European Review*, 10:4 (1953), 442–444.

[23] Shvekov, *Pervyi sovetskii*, 105–112; Timasheff, "The Impact of the Penal Law, 442–462.

[24] Leon Radzinowicz and Joan King, *The Growth of Crime: The International Experience* (London, 1978), chap. 5; Timasheff, "The Impact of the Penal Law," 455–469.

[25] Ibid.; Edward Hallett Carr, *Socialism in One Country, 1924–1926* ([originally London, 1959]; paperback, Baltimore, 1970), vol. 2, 453–459; "Ugolovnyi kodeks RSFSR" (1922), Goliakov, *Sbornik dokumentov*, no. 154.

had inherited from the Cheka neither the right to mete out summary sentences nor the power to confine political offenders through administrative exile. Moreover, the revolutionary tribunals had been scheduled for elimination. Within months, however, the GPU had begun regaining some of these powers. Supplementary legislation gave the new political police agency the power to exile abroad and inside the USSR any participant in "counterrevolutionary activity" (August 1922) and to place in a camp for three years activists of the former political parties that had competed with the Bolsheviks (October 1922).[26] The return of the political police into the repression of state crimes did not remove the courts from the domain of political prosecutions; it led to a rough division of labor. During NEP the courts heard a substantial number of cases of terrorism against Soviet officials (committed mainly by peasants) and of opposition to the Revolution by former tsarist "officials" (half of whom turned out to be peasants).[27] The OGPU dealt extrajudicially with such offenses as treason and espionage.

Another type of crime that the Bolsheviks defined to suit their needs was "economic crime." To establish an economic order with much of industrial capacity removed from the hands of private owners required a battery of new offenses. Characteristic was the new crime of speculation, defined in its original version after the Revolution as "buying and selling to make a profit" (*s tseliu sbyta*). The partial restoration of the market under NEP led to a narrower definition: "artificial raising of prices of products through an agreement of traders among themselves or through keeping products off the market" (any trading in hard currency remained a crime).[28] The most widely prosecuted economic crimes in the first years of NEP consisted of misdeeds that Soviet lawmakers had upgraded from administrative violations (under the tsars) to crimes – homebrewing and marketing homebrew; and violating the rules on the felling of timber. However, the criminal code included as well a list of offenses designed to police the boundaries of the mixed economy. These included nonfulfillment of contracts (especially with state agencies); violations of the state monopoly (in industry); violation by an employer of labor laws and rules of collective contracts; and failure to pay taxes. Although these offenses were not prosecuted often, their place in the code signified that Soviet leaders regarded the crimi-

---

26 Leggett, *The Cheka*, 344–346; A.P. Kositsyn, ed., *Istoriia sovetskogo gosudarstva i prava*, 2 (Moscow, 1968), 580. This chapter was written by V.P. Portnov.

27 A. Rodnianskii, "Karatelnaia politika gubernskikh sudov po kontrrevolutsionnym prestupleniiam v 1926," *ESIu*, 1927, no. 33, 1009–1011.

28 "O spekuliatsii," Dekret SNK ot 22 iulia 1918, in Goliakov, *Sbornik dokumentov*, no. 41; "Ugolovnyi kodeks RSFSR" (1922), Article 137.

nal law as a tool for regulation of the economy well before the Stalin Revolution.[29]

The third category of crime to which the Bolshevik draftsmen devoted special attention was crimes by officials (that is, service, or *dolzhnostnye*, crimes). Subjecting misdeeds by public officials to the criminal sanction was part of the European tradition and it had been reflected in the 1903 draft criminal code. Whereas the 1903 draft code contained a skimpy section on crimes in service that highlighted only the most serious offenses, the Soviet code outlined a whole range of offenses. As Commissar of Justice Dmitrii Kurskii explained, these crimes would assume importance under the Soviets because state ownership of industry would swell the number of public officials. Some of the crimes by officials would be familiar to the Western reader, including those most frequently prosecuted during NEP – taking bribes and embezzlement of state property (the latter would be treated as a property crime later on). The code also included such offenses as exceeding one's authority, misusing one's power, and criminal negligence. These offenses would become weapons of choice in some of the regime's battles in the 1930s.[30]

The punishments adopted in the Criminal Code of 1922 represented a sharp break from the tsarist past. For most offenses the range of sentencing options revealed a leniency that was new to Russian law. In place of the short prison terms that tsarist law used for lesser crimes, the Bolsheviks used noncustodial sanctions. Even for serious crimes, the terms of imprisonment rarely exceeded a few years. At first, the maximum term of confinement was ten years, and the death penalty was reserved for serious political crimes by "class enemies." This new leniency brought Russia into the orbit of Western European penal practice, where in the preceding few decades progressive ideas of penal reform had taken hold. Consistent with this tradition was the adoption by the Bolsheviks of the noncustodial "compulsory work" and their genuine desire to use confinement in prison to rehabilitate offenders. The Bolshevik jurists designed this system of punishment to deal with criminal offenders from the "toiling classes"; for "class enemies" they continued to show little mercy.[31]

---

[29] Peter H. Solomon, Jr., "Criminalization and Decriminalization in Soviet Criminal Policy, 1917–1941," *Law and Soviet Review*, 16, no. 1 (1981), 9–43; "Ugolovnyi kodeks RSFSR (1922)," Articles 146–141; Shvekov, *Pervyi sovetskii*, 194–199.

[30] B.S. Utevskii, *Obshchee uchenie o dolzhnostnykh prestupleniiakh* (Moscow, 1948), 171–271; Timasheff, "The Impact of the Penal Law," 460–461; D.M. Kurskii, "K voprosu ob izdanii Ugolovnogo Kodeska," *Materialy Narkomiusta* 13 (1921), 12; "Ugolovnyi kodeks RSFSR (1922)," Articles 105–118.

[31] For more detail, see Solomon, "Soviet Penal Policy," 196–203.

The goal of making the criminal law serve socialism affected not only the definition of crimes and the penal arsenal, it influenced as well the principles embodied in the criminal code. While many of the technical legal principles drew their definition from earlier models (such as the 1903 draft code) the 1922 criminal code enshrined three new principles that lay at the core of Bolshevik conceptions of the criminal law: analogy, judicial discretion, and class favoritism. All three, however, provoked controversies.

Soviet jurists and politicians alike divided on the question of analogy. Was it sufficient to provide judges with a list of crimes (some broadly defined), or did judges need as well the power to convict a person who committed an act that went against the interests of the new ruling class and was merely analogous to a proscribed act? Tsarist law, like the law of many European autocracies, had contained the principle of analogy and left no place for its opposite, *nullem crimen sine lege*; but the reformers who composed the 1903 draft code decided to eliminate analogy. The first three Bolshevik draft codes presented a spectrum of positions. While the draft of Narkomiust (in 1920) included analogy, the draft prepared by the Institute of Soviet Law eliminated the principle. The draft of the consultative group went to the further extreme of eliminating any specification of crimes (conviction was to be based upon the "dangerous state" of the accused).[32] In defending the inclusion of analogy, one of the drafters of the first version of the 1922 code claimed that analogy was a necessary expedient because "we cannot anticipate all crimes" and because "a detailed code (that listed all crimes) would take several years to prepare and we need one now."[33] But when the Special Commission appointed by the Council of People's Commissar reviewed the draft code, it rejected analogy and inserted *nullem crimen sine lege* in its place. This forced Commissar Kurskii and his colleague Nikolai Krylenko to plead with the delegates to the All-Russian Central Executive Committee to restore analogy to the code. Krylenko repeated the argument that the young state could not anticipate all of the crimes that its enemies would devise and therefore judges needed the extra flexibility. His voice carried the day, and analogy became a part of Soviet criminal law, to remain so until 1958. Within months of the code's promulgation, Narkomiust issued an interpretation that restricted analogy to use in exceptional circumstances, but

---

[32] Timasheff, "The Impact of the Penal Law," 448–449; Shvekov, *Pervyi sovetskii*, 130–137, 144.

[33] "Stennogrammy IV Vserossiiskogo S'ezda," 17–18. The Soviet Criminal Code of 1922 contained 227 articles as opposed to 687 in the 1903 *proekt* and 1711 in the 1885 "shortening" of the 1845 Statute. See Timasheff, "The Impact of the Penal Law."

there was a larger symbolic issue at stake.[34] Supporters of analogy wanted to ensure that the criminal law never interfered with the defense of the young socialist state. Not even temporarily was the law to be converted from a weapon of the new ruling class (the proletariat) into an obstacle to the fulfillment of its interests.

The most important principle permeating the new criminal code was judicial discretion. Most of the articles defining crimes gave judges a broad choice of sanctions – including at least a spectrum of terms of custody and other noncustodial options as well, such as the characteristically Soviet punishment "compulsory work." The code instructed judges to choose in accordance with their "socialist legal consciousness," and, in case the range of punishments indicated for a particular offense was too restrictive, judges were granted the authority to sentence "below the minimum" stipulated for the particular crime. (In an early draft they had the option of going above the maximum as well!)[35] In explaining this system of sanctions, Commissar Kurskii used a technical term from Western penology, "relatively determined sanctions." To Professor Grodzinskii of the Ukraine the system derived from the ideas of the German master Professor Liszt, thus representing the "advanced principles" of social defense.[36] But to most politicians and justice officials in the USSR the rationale for the adoption of judicial discretion was to keep a place for the revolutionary consciousness of judges in the administration of Soviet justice. In the words of a chairman of a revolutionary tribunal, "we stand between two worlds" and in order not to return to the old we must continue to rely upon the revolutionary consciousness of judges, rather than the letter of the law.[37] To be sure, many justice officials in the provinces disagreed and called for the specification of exact penalties to fit particular crimes, but some of their colleagues objected that such a listing "would deprive the court of the possibility of choosing punishments in accordance with their revolutionary legal consciousness."[38] In short, Bolshevik distrust of the limitations of formal law translated into a fixation upon the discretion of judges, who, they believed, would ensure that the practice of criminal justice continued to serve the cause of the Revolution, as it had done during the years of Civil War.

[34] Kuritsyn, *Perehkod k NEPu*, 95–97; Shvekov, *Pervyi sovetskii*, 147, 152–155, 170; *III sessiia VTsIK IX sozyva*.

[35] "Ugolovnyi kodeks RSFSR (1922)," Articles 9 and 28; "Stennogrammy IV Vserossiiskogo S'ezda," 25.

[36] III sessiia VTsIK, Biulleten 3, 27–30; "Stennogrammy IV Vserossiiskogo S'ezda," 23–24, 28.

[37] Ibid., 28.

[38] Kuritsyn, *Perekhod k NEPu*, 96.

A third, and especially controversial principle that the Bolsheviks enshrined in their criminal law was class bias. At first, discrimination by class appeared in muted form. The 1922 criminal code promised to defend the government of the toilers from counterrevolutionary crimes that had a class color (actions against the working class; agitation to help the international bourgeoisie). The code also included on its list of mitigating circumstances the commission of a crime "because of hunger or need." In contrast, the Fundamental Principles of the Criminal Legislation, issued in October 1924, expanded class bias in Soviet criminal law. The Principles made the connection of a convicted offender, past or present, to a class that exploits labor grounds for a more severe penalty and conversely the status of an offender as a worker or "toiling peasant" grounds for a more lenient sanction.[39] This open adoption of class bias reflected criticisms of the 1922 code and the horror of Bolshevik politicians like Aron Solts at discovering that the jails of Moscow were filled with poor, unemployed persons who had gained sustenance through illegal trade in spirits.[40]

No sooner had Bolshevik politicians and jurists adopted the principle of discrimination by class than they began to have second thoughts. In summer 1925, after a revival of the slogan "revolutionary legality," the RSFSR Supreme Court took a stand against class discrimination, especially in the form of leniency for workers who committed crimes. By the fall the same Solts who two years earlier had worried about the large number of toilers in the prisons insisted that the choice of penalty should not depend upon affiliation with a particular class, a view that gained support from Nikolai Bukharin. When a new criminal code was issued in 1926 the words supporting discrimination by class remained in place, but in 1927 they were removed both from the Fundamental Principles and the Criminal Code.[41]

The idea of a criminal justice based upon class distinctions did not go away. It remained in the intellectual baggage of many Bolsheviks ready

[39] "Ugolovnyi kodeks RSFSR (1922)," Articles 5, 67, 70, 25; "Osnovnye nachala ugolovnogo zakonodatelstva SSSR i Soiuznykh Respublik," in Goliakov, ed., *Sbornik dokumentov*, no. 213, Articles 31b and 32b.

[40] "Stennogrammy IV Vserossiiskogo S'ezda," 30; A. Solts, "Nasha karatelnaia politika (Obsledovanie Moskovskikh tiurem)," *Pravda* (Aug. 22, 1923), 1; A. Solts and S. Fainblit, *Revoliutsionnaia zakonnost i nasha karatelnaia politika* (Moscow, 1925); Solomon, "Criminalization and Decriminalization," 16–17.

[41] Carr, *Socialism in One Country*, vol. 2, 465–469; "Ugolovnyi kodek RSFSR Redaktsii 1926 goda," Goliakov, ed., *Sbornik dokumentov*, no. 266, articles 47b and 48b; "Ob izmenii osnovnykh nachal ugolovnogo sakonodatelstva SSSR i Soiuznykh Respublik," Post. TsIK SSSR ot 25 fevralia 1927 g., ibid., no. 225.

to be retrieved and given new form when the political context changed and warfare among the classes resumed.

The people of the law

However much they argued about the law's content, Bolshevik politicians and jurists agreed about the people of the law. The judges and the procurators had to be members of the Communist party and hail largely from the ranks of the toiling classes. It went without saying that for the criminal law to serve socialism it had to be administered by "our own people" (nashi liudi). Only Communists and workers could be expected to be inspired with "revolutionary consciousness" and counted on to use the discretionary powers afforded by the criminal law in the interests of the new regime.[42]

Bolshevik leaders acted upon this belief. In recruiting staff for the legal system, they sought out Communists and quickly achieved a high level of party saturation among legal officials.[43] By 1923, 78.9% of procurators held party cards (97.6% at the provincial level); 63% of people's court judges belonged to the party (76% of provincial court judges and 100% of their chiefs). By 1928, 100% of procurators were party members, and 85.6% of judges at the people's courts. Even among investigators 54.1% had joined the party by 1928.[44]

The other side of the coin was that few of the political trustees who

---

[42] This point was implicit in one of the first Bolshevik statements about law. In "Revoliutsiia i sud," (Pravda, Dec. 1, 1917), A. Lunacharskii explained that the Revolution called for a new law based upon the "intuition of the people." This law would require new judges.

Leading jurists participating in the Third Congress of Judicial Activists (June 1920) referred to "our communist-judges." One of them (A.S. Lisitsyn) was explicit. "We will have no professional judges. The court must be communist in its content and its work." The best preparation for judicial work would not be legal education but a reading of Bukharin's ABC of Communism! "Protokoly III Vserossiiskogo S'ezda," 13. A judge of three years' standing insisted that for the main task of trials – determining the truthfulness of witnesses – professional judges were "the worst of all." With this "truth," he went on, "almost all legislators and theoreticians agree." Sergei Simson, "Spornye voprosy deistvuishchego ugolovnogo protsess," Materialy Narkomiusta 13 (Moscow, 1921), 29–38.

[43] As of 1921 only 35% of judges at the people's courts were Communists (members of the Bolshevik party), but during 1922 and 1923 major efforts were made to recruit more Communists into the legal agencies. Narkomiust, Otchet k Vserossiiskomu S'ezdu Sovetov (Moscow, 1921), 25–27; Kuritsyn, Perekhod k NEPu, 111.

[44] A.S. Pankratov, "Kadry sovetskoi prokuraturyi," Na strazhe sovetskikh zakonov (Moscow, 1972), 135; God raboty pravitelstva RSFSR. Materialy k otchety pravitelstva za 1927–1928 (Moscow, 1929), 185–189; M.V. Kozhevnikov, Istoriia sovetskogo suda, 1917–1956 (Moscow, 1957), 105–186.

served as judges and procurators came armed with legal education. In fact, the majority of legal officials in the 1920s and 1930s had not even completed high school. Arguably, the Bolsheviks had little choice. There was a shortage of trained lawyers remaining in the USSR after the Revolution and Civil War and few of them had the political credentials required for a post of procurator or judge. The small corps of jurists who were Communists or allowed to join the party the Bolshevik leaders placed in key positions in the central legal agencies and to a lesser extent in provincial government. In so doing, they favored the procuracy over the courts (as of 1923, 26.7% of provincial procurators had higher legal education and 17.5% other higher education as opposed to only 18.9% of members of provincial courts).[45] Since procurators were supposed to supervise the legality of the acts of government agencies, knowledge of the law was for them indispensable. Still, more than half of them, even at the province level, lacked this qualification.

The shortage of Communist lawyers may have forced the Bolsheviks to staff their legal agencies with persons lacking legal training, but this did not bother most of them. Suspicious of lawyers from the start, many Bolsheviks stood ready to give politically trusted amateurs a chance to administer the law. For nearly two decades Soviet politicians took the low educational level of their legal cadres for granted and did almost nothing to change it. To be sure, the heads of the legal agencies tried to expose their subordinates to practical training in law. By the mid-1920s most provincial courts were sponsoring a short course in law (usually three months) for some of their court and procuracy officials. In 1926 the Commissariat of Justice in Moscow gained authorization to establish the Higher Legal courses that provided a year of legal education to a handful of talented legal officials. However inadequate academically, the various courses did supply a substantial number of legal officials with rudimentary knowledge about the law. As of 1932, 35% of the people's court judges had participated in this form of judicial preparation.[46]

The courses were hardly the equivalent of higher legal education. But Bolsheviks did nothing to promote that enterprise. During the 1920s the production of lawyers averaged a mere 500 per year in the RSFSR, a fraction of the number graduating in the last year of the tsars.[47] In the

45 Pankratov, "Kadry"; Kozhevnikov, *Istoriia*, 186.
46 Pankratov, "Kadry," 137; Kozhevnikov, *Istoriia*, 265.
47 Pankratov, "Kadry," 138: In the last years of the tsars, law was a popular subject at universities. 37.9% of all students at the major universities were enrolled in law. Even with a dropout rate of 15% per year, over 2,000 of the 4,171 students enrolled in law at Moscow University in 1914 would graduate – more than the total number of lawyers produced by that institution in the first ten years of the Soviet period. See A.F. Shebanov, *Iuridicheskie vysshie uchebnye zavedeniia* (Moscow, 1963), chap. 1.

1930s, the figure dipped to the mid 300s, and in 1933 only 180 lawyers graduated.[48] Most of the new lawyers headed not for posts in the legal agencies but for better paid and more prestigious jobs in economic agencies. Those with political ambitions were more likely to be made chairman of a district executive committee than a judge.[49]

The failure of Bolsheviks to promote legal education, at a time when higher education in the technical sciences expanded dramatically, calls for explanation. In part, it stemmed from the belief held by many party members that law would lose its significance in the socialist order and lawyers become redundant. More important, one suspects, was the view among politicians that the administration of justice did not differ from other areas of public administration and required no specialized expertise. If the officials of city and provincial government and party did not require higher education, why should judges? Their task, after all, was at its core a political one, and for this political credentials and consciousness should be sufficient.

The decline in the production of lawyers and use of this scarce commodity outside the legal realm led to a falling off in the educational level of procurators and judges. Among procurators in the USSR, the percentage who had completed higher legal education dropped from 29% in 1923 to 11–12% in the early 1930s. The share of people's court judges with higher legal education fell from 8.4% in 1923 to 4.2% in 1935. As of 1935, 84.6% of these judges had completed nothing more than elementary school. By definition, defense lawyers had completed legal education, but most of those practicing in 1930 had received that education under the tsars.[50]

[48] N. Aleksandrovich, "Povyshenie kvalifikatsii kadrov rabotnikov organov iustitsii – vazhneishaia zadacha," ZaSZ, 1935, no. 1, 29–30. The drop in the number of lawyers graduated in the early 1930s had not been planned. According to the plan approved by the Kollegium of Narkomiust in 1929, the reduction of lawyers was to continue at a rate of 500 per year, with the hope of returning to a norm of 10% of justice officials having higher education. Pankratov, "Kadry," 138.

[49] According to Kozhevnikov, in 1928, 52 of the 315 graduates of the law faculty of Moscow University went to work in the agencies of Narkomiust (courts and procuracy); in 1929, 40 of 315. In the country as a whole not more than half of the graduates in law stayed in legal work. M.V. Kozhevnikov, "Puti razvitiia sovetskoi prokuratury," part 2, Uchenye zapiski MGU, vyp. 147, Trudy iuridicheskogo fakultet, kn. 5 (Moscow, 1950), 45. As of 1933, only 25–30% of the law graduates were absorbed into the procuracy and courts; Gaishpuit, "Reorganizatsiia pravovykh vuzov i postanovka dela podgotovki kadrov rabotnikov iustissiia," Organy iustitsii na novom etape (5oe soveshchanie rukovodiaschikh rabotnikov iustitsii iun 1931) (Moscow, 1931), 108. Kozhevnikov, "Nashi kadry," SIu, 1935, no. 35, 4–6.

[50] Pankratov, "Kadry," 135; Sostav rukovodiashchikh rabotnikov i spetsialistov SSSR (Moscow, 1936), 304–315; Kozhevnikov, Istoriia, 185; ibid., "Puti razvitiia," 44; ibid., "Nashi kadry," 4; Huskey, Russian Lawyers and the Soviet State, 100.

The capacity of Soviet legal personnel to administer criminal justice was further aggravated by the manner of their selection and the high rate of turnover among their ranks. On paper, the scheme for selecting judges and procurators was well designed. No candidate could attain either of these posts without passing the scrutiny of both legal and political officials. Thus, nomination for election (unopposed) as a people's court judge called for support both from a party committee (at first at the provincial, later the district level) and the provincial court. Selection as district procurator depended upon the consent of legal and party authorities at the provincial level.[51] In practice, however, neither sort of authority used its powers of scrutiny. In proposing candidates for jobs in the legal agencies, party secretaries paid little heed to qualities of character or mind appropriate to the posts, treating the positions of judge and procurator as no different from other patronage appointments. When provincial court officials reviewed the candidates proposed by party secretaries, they could not afford to be fussy, for in most provinces there was a shortage of talent available for government work and many posts in the judicial agencies lay vacant.[52]

Careless and unconsidered recruitment of judges, procurators, and investigators took its toll. The performance of some of the new officials was so weak that they had to be removed from office and transferred to other work. Thus, among judges in the late 1920s the rate of turnover was 24%, and of these persons 35% were fired for misdeeds and 25% for displaying qualities inappropriate for a judge. Turnover among investigators in the procuracy was also high, averaging 40% in the early 1930s.[53]

Not only the weakest legal officials left their posts but also some of the strongest. Judges and procurators who proved especially successful in their work were susceptible to transfer by party authorities to more prestigious posts in local government. This was easy to effect, for judges were paid abysmally low salaries and there was no provision for increases due to either seniority or merit. A few might be promoted eventually to the provincial court, but for most the alternative was promotion up and out of the legal system.[54]

51 For details see Peter H. Solomon, Jr., "Local Political Power and Soviet Criminal Justice, 1922–41," *Soviet Studies* 36, no. 3 (July 1985), 306–309.

52 N. Bogomolov, "O raspreditelnoi rabote mestnykh partorganizatsii (K postanovleniiu TsK ot 27 iunia 1927 g.)," *Izvestiia TsK*, 1927, no. 30–31, 1–3; Solomon, "Local Political Power," notes 13 and 14.

53 A. Stelmakhovich, "Chistka organov iustitsii, ee tseli i zadachi," *ESIu*, 1929, no. 26, 594–595; F. Niurina, "K voprosam sledstvii," *ZaSZ*, 1936, no. 4–6.

54 M. Fokin-Belskii, "Pokonchit s uravnilovkoi v organakh iustitsii," *SIu*, 1931, no. 34, 23; S. Kostin, "Uravnilovka i tekuchest rabotnikov v organakh iustitsii," *SIu*, 1932, no. 14, 25–26.

For the USSR high rates of turnover of legal officials proved especially damaging. In the administration of justice, as in other walks of life, experience might serve as a substitute for formal education. But the high rates of turnover assured that the majority of Soviet legal officials had neither attribute.

All the same, the situation with Soviet legal officials was not uniformly bad. To be sure, from the mid-1920s to the mid-1930s the bulk of those officials (60–65%) consisted of uneducated and inexperienced cadres whose membership was constantly changing. But there were also two other categories: a small layer of cadres who had higher legal education (averaging in the procuracy around 10% and in the judiciary 5%); and a substantial minority with at least a few years' experience in the justice agencies and often some practical training. The officials with higher legal education tended to be concentrated in Moscow and in provincial centers (where they still made up a small minority of the officials). But those with some experience were distributed more broadly throughout the country.

The courts and procuracy had far more talent than other law enforcement agencies. In the late 1920s police chiefs and heads of detective units consisted mainly of peasants with elementary education alone (over 90%). Less than 1 in 1,000 had higher education. Turnover rates among district police chiefs stood at 58% in 1929 and only a quarter had any training for their jobs.[55]

To the historian of criminal justice the readiness of the Bolsheviks to rely upon uneducated political trustees to administer their justice agencies stands out as the distinguishing feature of their attempt to create a socialist legal order. Whether or not they understood it, the Bolsheviks were conducting an experiment on a grand scale. Unlike any previous national authority, they tried to operate a modern legal system, whose institutions and procedures were as complex as those found elsewhere, with cadres lacking in qualifications, training, and education. Soviet legal officials were not laymen – for they held full-time jobs – but neither were they professionals, since they lacked the education and the corporate identity that marks that status. Most legal officials in the USSR, like most local politicians, were amateurs, ordinary people performing strange and wonderful new roles.

---

[55] *God raboty Pravitelstva za 1927–28*, 187–189; *Administrativnye organy v novykh usloviiakh* (Moscow, 1930), 24–30; "Sostoianie i rabota mestnykh organov NKVD," *Administrativnyi vestnik*, 1930, no. 4, 29–49. See also Neil Weissmann, "Policing the New Order: The Soviet Militsiia, 1917–1928," unpublished paper.

Procedures and institutions

Of the features of "bourgeois justice," the Bolsheviks especially disliked its formality. As they saw it, complicated procedures did less to protect workers and peasants than to mystify and confuse them. In contrast most Bolsheviks hoped to create in the new state legal procedures that would be simple and legal institutions accessible to ordinary people. This goal dovetailed with the commitment to staffing the courts with their own people, most of whom had little education legal or otherwise. Nevertheless, in 1922 Soviet authorities promulgated a code of criminal procedure that established a formal and full-fledged set of procedures. At first glance, this action seems puzzling.

Why resurrect the code of criminal procedure? One reason was the strongly held view of the Commissar of Justice D.M. Kurskii that procedural rules mattered. Already in 1919 he wrote: "We have a right to demand that every court, in rendering its sentences, observe the forms of procedure decreed by Soviet power." Another reason was the realization on the part of some jurists that the existing laws on procedure left unresolved a number of key issues and that taken as a group those laws were far from simple. With the rules of procedure scattered in the different statutes and decrees judges devoted too much time to determining how they should proceed. And their uncertainty about procedures lowered the image of justice in the eyes of the public.[56] What tipped the balance in favor of a new code was the announcement of NEP and with it the revival of the role of law in regulating the economy. The new status of law put opponents of legal procedure on the defensive and allowed its supporters to argue that procedural codes were no longer just an option but a pressing necessity.[57]

Not all Bolshevik jurists agreed with this argument. A judge of three years' standing, for example, insisted that the existing procedural laws handled all the issues that came up in the practice of the courts and had the virtue of avoiding the "scholastic complexity" of the tsarist procedural law. Even Nikolai Krylenko, chairman of the commission charged with drafting the new code of criminal procedure, voiced concern about

---

[56] D.M. Kurskii, "O edinom narodnom sude," *Proletarskaia revoliutsiia i pravo*, 1919, no. 1, 18; A.S. Tager, "Spornye voprosy deistvuiushchego ugolovnogo protsessa," *Materialy Narkomiusta*, 9 (M., 1921), 3–17.

[57] A resolution taken at the eleventh conference of the Bolshevik party stressed the place of law in the new economy. "New forms of relations created in the process of revolution and on the basis of the economic policy conducted by the authorities must be fully expressed in law and defended in the courts . . . the courts of the Soviet republic must be raised to a corresponding level." Cited in N.N. Polianskii, *Ocherk razvitiia sovetskoi nauki ugolovnogo protsessa* (Moscow, 1960), 22. For discussion of the effects of NEP on the role of law, see Kuritsyn, *Perekhod k NEPu i revoliutsionnaia zakonnost*, chap. 1.

the dangers of returning to complicated procedure. Nonetheless, his commission proceeded in the fall of 1921 to draft an intricate code with 450 articles, many of them informed by consultation with legal scholars who had prerevolutionary experience. While introducing the draft code at the Fourth Congress of Judicial Workers, an embarrassed Krylenko shrugged off the code as a collection of technical rules that was unworthy of discussion.[58] But Chairman of the All-Russian Central Executive Committee Mikhail Kalinin expressed what was for the moment the official view – that procedures were important because of the new role of law and the courts under NEP. As Kalinin put it, observance of procedures was bound to strengthen the respect of the masses for the courts. Just as "they [the bourgeois governments] developed respect for the court in the consciousness of the masses through the implementation of procedures," so the Bolsheviks might as well.[59]

It was hard to speak out against Kalinin's argument at a time when Lenin was leading the retreat from the revolutionary excesses and disorder of the Civil War period. But some Bolshevik jurists continued to hold principled objections to formal procedures. Within months they started to criticize the new code (Krylenko himself was at it in 1923), and soon they gained support from other jurists for whom the issue was less one of principle than of practicality. One or another of the rules set down in the Criminal Procedure Code was proving too difficult for Soviet legal officials to handle or had become an unnecessary obstacle in the way of efficient performance.[60] Later in the decade, as we shall see, simplification of procedure became a central issue in the politics over reform of criminal justice.

In designing institutions for the administration of justice, Bolshevik politicians and jurists displayed a similar ambivalence. To establish public respect for the law and restore its function as regulator of economic relations, the Bolsheviks opted for traditional institutions. At the same time, to give those institutions a socialist flavor they gave them

58 Sergei Simson, "Spornye voprosy deistvuiushchego ugolovnogo protsessa;" Hazard, *Settling Disputes*, 33Off.; O.I. Chistiakov, "Organizatsiia kodifikatsionnykh rabot v pervye gody sovetskoi vlasti (1917–1923 gg.)," *SGiP*, 1965, no. 5, 7.
59 "Rech Presedatelia VTsIK tov M.I. Kalinina," *ESIu*, 1922, no. 5, 6–7. Also "Stenogrammy IV Vserossiiskogo S'ezda," 95–96.
60 Hazard, *Settling Disputes*, 340. Lisitsyn, "Nuzhno uprostit sudoproizvodstvo," *ESIu*, 1922, no. 43, 1–3.
    "Tezisy doklada A.A. Vyshinskogo po p. 5 povestki dnia V Vserossiiskogo s'ezda deiatelei sovetskoi iustitsii: 'Voprosy ugolovno sudebnogo protsessa,' " *ESIu*, 1924, no. 12–13, 299–300. Note that the introduction to a 1925 commentary on the Criminal Procedure Code written by the chairman of the Leningrad provincial court, Nakhimson, stated that "not all norms of the Criminal Procedure Code are obligatory." Polianskii, *Ocherk razvitiia*, 28.

special features, many of which would take on increased significance after the era of the NEP.

In 1922 the leaders opted for a hierarchy of courts that started with the people's courts (*narsud*) as its lowest rung and added above them provincial courts (*gubsud*), to be replaced in the 1929 by territorial and regional courts (*kraisud* and *oblsud*), and republican courts (including the RSFSR Supreme Court). The revolutionary tribunals were eliminated, and in 1924 the USSR Supreme Court was established. The people's and provincial courts heard almost all of the trials, while the provincial (later regional) and republican courts handled the appeals. In the 1920s the USSR Supreme Court dealt mainly with constitutional issues and jurisdictional conflicts; its appellate jurisdiction was limited to military justice. At trial in people's and provincial courts alike a panel of three persons – a judge and two lay assessors – decided the verdict and sentence.[61] While in the mid-1920s most serious cases were reserved for the provincial courts (around 8%), the jurisdiction of the people's courts expanded at the end of the decade to include many serious nonpolitical crimes.[62]

The function of prosecution at trial was vested in a newly independent agency, the procuracy. But the procuracy had another function of such moment that the conduct of prosecutions quickly receded to second place. The principal function of the Soviet procuracy was general supervision, that is monitoring the legality of actions of local and provincial governments and to a lesser extent field units of central agencies as well. Before 1864 a version of general supervision had numbered among the functions of the tsarist procuracy (itself a part of the Ministry of Justice). The revival of this watchdog function had prompted Lenin to insist that the procuracy agencies in the provinces and localities be subordinated only to the central government and not also to the corresponding local authorities. At the same time, the responsibility for scrutinizing the legality of public administration occupied most of the time and energy of procurators and their assistants, so that they paid relatively little atten-

---

[61] N.V. Krylenko, *Sudoustroistvo RSFSR* (Moscow, 1923); Hazard, *Settling Disputes*. Samuel Kucherov, *The Organs of Soviet Administration of Justice: Their History and Operation* (Leiden, 1970). In Germany a mixed bench that combined representatives of the public and a judge in the rendering of verdicts had been adopted for lesser crimes in 1877, and in 1924 it was extended to serious crimes. It was considered superior to the jury by many Continental jurists. Gerhard Casper and Hans Zeisel, "Lay Judges in the German Criminal Courts," *Journal of Legal Studies*, 1 (Jan. 1972), 135–141.

[62] The decentralization of the jurisdiction of the courts was gradual. In 1928 newly formed circuit (*okrug*) courts assumed responsibility for a large share of the criminal cases handled at the provincial court. When the circuit courts were eliminated in 1930, most of their caseload was passed down to the people's court; Kozhevnikov, *Istoriia sovetskogo suda*, 195–197, 227.

tion either to conducting trials or to other functions relating to criminal justice, such as supervising the investigators and appealing decisions.[63]

District level procurators and their assistants rarely appeared in court. In 1927, 1.6% of trials at the people's court had a procurator in attendance. At the provincial courts, where the cases were more serious, a representative of the procurator appeared in 30% of trials in the Russian Union of Federated Socialist Republics (RSFSR) in 1927 (in Moscow only 11.6% and in Saratov nearly all). Usually, it was an assistant procurator (*pomoshchnik prokurora*), though sometimes an investigator filled in.[64] As a result, at most trials the judge conducted the proceedings. One factor, apart from shortage of manpower, that may have limited procuracy participation in trials was the availability of defense counsel. When a procurator appeared in court, conduct of the defense by an attorney became mandatory. Although there was a sizable defense bar in Moscow, most provincial cities had a shortage of lawyers (there were hardly any in the countryside) and they were engaged mainly with civil matters.

To conduct the pretrial investigation, a central part of inquisitorial criminal procedure, the Bolsheviks established the position of "investigator," a legal official, not a police detective. Investigators had the duty to question the accused and the witnesses and record their testimony (usually done after police detectives had completed their work), gather and evaluate material evidence, solicit expertise, and summarize the results in an act of accusation. The package of materials resulting from the "preliminary investigation" (usually a large tome) was admitted as evidence at trial and served as the basis for its proceedings. Following the French model of the "examining magistrate," the Soviets placed the investigator in the offices of the courts and made judges responsible for their conduct. At the same time, though, the operational work of the investigators in making cases came under the supervision of the procurator. This dual subordination of investigation, a characteristic of the late same period as well, provoked controversy throughout the 1920s until finally in 1928 the investigators were moved to the exclusive domain of the procurator. In practice, though, investigators in most

---

63 R.A. Rudenko, "Leninskie idei sotsialisticheskoi zakonnosti i printsipy organizatii i deiatelnosti sovetskoi prokuratury," *Na strazhe sovetskikh zakonov*, 5–19; Glenn G. Morgan, *Soviet Administrative Legality. The Role of the Attorney General's Office* (Stanford, Calif., 1962); Kozhevnikov, "Puti razvitiia sovetskoi prokuratury," 38; Sergei Kazantsev, *Istoriia tsarskoi prokuratury* (St. Petersburg, 1993), chap. 3.

64 M. Polevoi-Genkin, "Deiatelnost nizovoi (uezdnoi i raionnoi) prokuratury," *ESIu*, part 2, 1927, no. 38, 1176–1178; P.I. Kudriavtsev, "Prokurorskii nadzor za rassmotrenie ugolovnykh del v sude," *Na strazhe sovetskikh zakonov*, 285; Huskey, *Russian Lawyers and the Soviet State*, 95, 127–142.

parts of the country already were serving as assistants to the procurator. Shorthanded themselves, procurators began recruiting investigators for a variety of tasks (such as screening of complaints from citizens), so that as much as three-quarters of the time of investigators was taken up with work other than the preparation of criminal cases.[65]

A pretrial investigation was mandatory for some serious crimes and an option for many others where an inquest conducted by the police would normally suffice. In practice, the investigators did not bother to conduct preliminaries for cases outside their mandatory jurisdiction. As a result over 90% of criminal cases in the 1920s and early 1930s arrived at court without a preliminary investigation. Moreover, of those cases that had formally passed through this stage, many had not received thorough examination, for the investigators were authorized to waive active inquiries and proceed to compose the accusatory act whenever they considered the evidence compiled by the police sufficient for conviction. As a rule, investigators took this shortcut most often in crimes of violence and concentrated their investigative work on economic and official crimes.[66]

Investigators also had responsibility for composing the accusatory act in cases of more serious crimes that had been investigated by the police alone. This duty was meant to ensure that investigators screened cases coming from the police and held its officials to some reasonable standards, but it failed on both counts. More often than not, investigators simply copied the evidence supplied by the police onto the forms required for the accusatory act and sent the cases to the courts.[67]

Even before the movement to simplify criminal procedure had its effects, there were in the practice of Soviet criminal justice two distinct models of the criminal process. The first was the intricate model consisting of an elaborate pretrial investigation conducted by an investigator and a trial at which procurators and defense attorneys argued the case before judge and assessors. The second was a much simpler alternative, in which preliminary investigation was replaced by a police inquest, and the trial was conducted without prosecution and usually without defense as well. (Apart from trials where prosecution was present or the accused was a minor or had a physical defect, defense was admitted

65 Judah Zelitch, *Soviet Administration of Criminal Law* (Philadelphia, 1931), 128–138; Zhogin, "Nadzor za rassledovaniem prestuplenii," *Na strazhe sovetskikh zakonnov*, 238–241; M. Kozhevnikov, "Za sozdanie edinogo apparata po rassledovaniia prestuplenii," *ESIu*, 1928, no. 12, 353–354. *Sorok let sovetskogo prava*, 1 (Leningrad, 1957), 581–590.
66 Filin, "Gde obiazatelno predvaritelnoe sledstvie" *ESIu*, 1927, no. 50, 1531–1532; Kozhevnikov, "Za sozdanie edinogo apparata"; M. Polevoi-Genkin, "Deiatelnost nizovoi (uezdnoi i raionnoi) prokuratury," part one, *ESIu*, 1927, no. 37, 1143–1144.
67 Polevoi-Genkin, "Deiatelnost nizovoi," parts one and two.

only at the discretion of the judge.) During the 1920s the overwhelming majority of criminal cases followed the simple model. The attack on the complexity of criminal procedure focused upon the first model, but that model applied only to a minority of serious cases, heard in the main at the provincial courts.

On the surface, the practice of criminal justice in the USSR in the 1920s resembled that of eighteenth-century England, where magistrates courts staffed by laymen (albeit educated) handled the bulk of criminal cases without counsel or elaborate pretrial activities. As long as the people's courts heard mainly minor cases and serious crimes were handled at the provincial courts, the comparison has validity. But by 1930 the jurisdiction of the people's courts had expanded to the point where many serious crimes came under their sway. And, there was no increase either in the use of preliminary investigations before trials or in the participation of counsel. If anything, both of these practices decreased in the early 1930s.

While establishing traditional institutions and procedures for the administration of criminal justice, Bolshevik politicians and jurists still wanted to avoid recreating justice agencies that were formal and remote from ordinary people. To bring the courts close to the population, they promoted the use of demonstration or show trials and developed channels for the participation of members of the public in the administration of justice.

The demonstration trial represented a form of court hearing on circuit. Much like their English counterparts two centuries before, Soviet judges were expected to conduct a portion of their trials away from their home building and in the towns closer to where the claimants resided.[68] In 1926, 17.1% of all criminal cases had their trial at a "visiting session"; and for serious cases the proportion was even higher. Of criminal cases heard by the provincial courts 44.1% were tried at visiting sessions, mostly in small cities or towns. The Soviet innovation was to take some of these trials even closer to the people. In 1926, 15.7% of the trials on circuit were held in factories or villages, and these were known as "demonstration trials." At the factory such trials were often held between shifts so that as many of the workers as possible would be instructed in the consequences of wrongdoing.[69]

---

[68] Norma Landau, *Justices of the Peace, 1679–1760* (Berkeley, Calif., 1984).

[69] Narkomiust actively promoted visiting sessions and demonstration trials by requiring judges to report on the number of such trials that they staged. See "O poriadke, formakh i srokakh predstavleniia statisticheskoi otchetnosti v statisticheskii otdel NKIu . . . ," *Sbornik tsirkuliarov Narkomiusta RSFSR za 1922–1925* (Moscow, 1926), 24–37. On English justice on circuit, see Sidney and Beatrice Webb, *English Local Government: Parish and the County* (London, 1906).

To achieve their educational effect the demonstration trials (*prokazatelnyi protsess*) had to be conducted in a simple and direct way and to produce conviction and sentence according to plan. Otherwise, these "trial-lectures" (as one observer called them) would not serve as a form of agitation. But it was clear that there were costs. Defense counsel were discouraged from pursuing their cases too vigorously and convictions were almost certain. Sentences at demonstration trials tended to be harsher than usual. One commentator suggested that this was inevitable, since the public would consider the usual penalties to be too soft.[70] Taking issue with this conclusion, a judge agreed that the masses preferred harsh penalties, but he insisted that this was no reason to mete them out. "We must not be led by the masses, but vice versa; those listening to the sessions (at demonstration trials) should receive a lesson in citizenship." Apparently, some trials in factories and villages turned rowdy and disorderly as the public in attendance found ways of "participating" in the shows to which they were privy. The same judge pointed out that it was the responsibility of judges to create an atmosphere of calm deliberation, so that the effect of the sentence would not be retributive![71] The absence of acquittals and prevalence of harsh sentences at demonstration trials led a leading politician to condemn the institution. Speaking at the Fifteenth Party Congress, Aron Solts dubbed it "the most unjust kind of trial" and "nothing like what Lenin had in mind" when he promoted show trials for political cases.[72]

But the demonstration trial in factory and village was the analogue for ordinary cases of the show trial for political ones (the Russian word for both was the same). Between 1921 and 1924 a series of political show trials of former oppositionists had been held in Moscow and given wide coverage in the national press. Their purpose was to educate the Soviet public and deter its members from oppositional activity.[73] In like manner, the demonstration criminal trials in factories received special attention from the press, both local and national. While ordinary demonstration trials displayed a prosecutorial bias, the outcomes of

70 "O vyezdnykh sessiakh gubsudov i narsudov," Instruktivnoe pismo NKIu no. 2–13 noiabria 1927 g., *ESIu*, 1927, no. 47, 1484–1485; Elifamov, "O pokazatelnykh protsessakh," *Rabochii sud*, 1925, no. 19–20, 831–832; see also Huskey, *Russian Lawyers and the Soviet State*.

71 Z.M. Brodianskii, "O pokazatelnkh protsessakh," *Rabochii sud*, 1925, no. 27–28, 1104–1105.

72 *Piatnadtsatyi s'ezd VKP(b). Dekabr 1927 goda. Stenograficheskii otchet*, 1 (M., 1961), 605.

73 Some of these cases (mainly those in which the prosecution speech by Krylenko was included in a collection of his speeches) were described in Aleksandr Solzhenitsyn, *The Gulag Archipelago, 1918–1956* 1–2 (New York, 1973), chap. 9. See also *Protsess predatelia-provokatora Okladskogo Petrovskogo v Verkhovnom Sude* (Leningrad, 1925).

political show trials were often predetermined by politicians and in the 1930s the charges contrived. While political show trials occurred only in particular periods (1921–1924, 1928–1933, 1936–1938), the demonstration criminal trials remained part of Soviet justice throughout the 1920s and most of the 1930s.

Until 1928 members of the public could participate in the administration of justice in two ways. Either they served as lay assessors or they appeared as public accusers at trial. Later, between 1928 and 1933, new forms of public involvement would be developed partly in response to the revival of antilaw, eliminationist sentiment. These forms included lay courts, assistance groups for the procuracy, and "socialist replacements."[74]

The post of lay assessor was the most important channel for public participation at all times. Every criminal trial required the presence on the bench of two lay assessors; without the assessors the trial would not be legal. Consequently, provincial and local justice officials made the recruitment of assessors a priority and went out of their way to ensure that the pools of assessors represented the appropriate mixture of social classes. Where feasible, potential assessors were also exposed to a few hours of instruction in legal affairs. The more assessors understood the law, the more likely they were to operate independently of the judge with whom they rendered the verdict and issued the sentence.[75]

In the 1920s the other role for members of the public at trial was that of public accuser. Public accusers were ordinary citizens who "volunteered" to speak at trial on behalf of the public or their public organization, so establishing a "link between the procuracy and the masses." But it proved difficult to recruit people for this task. Peasants feared persecution by fellow villagers, and workers the loss of pay for time away from the job. (As a rule, factory directors refused to compensate their employees for time spent in court.) In 1927 the financial obstacle was removed, and expenses and payments provided for public accusers. With this boost, the organizers of public accusations succeeded in arranging 18,000 appearances at trial in a year. This was still only a few percent of trials, and these numbers obscured regional variation. In some places public accusers appeared in most serious cases (and especially in demonstration trials); in others, hardly at all.

74 F. Niurina, "Organy iustitsii na novom etape," *SGiRP*, 1932, no. 5–6, 133–151.
75 Stelmakhovich, "Itogi kampanii po perevyboram narzasedatelei i obshchestvennaia rabota suda," *Proletarskii sud*, 1927, no. 1–2, 1–4; N. Lagovier, *Narodnye zasedateli* (Moscow and Leningrad, 1926); ibid., "Demokratiia v sovetskom sude," *Sovetskoe stroitelstvo*, 1929, no. 3, 27–40. In 1928 and 1929 the journal *Rabochii sud* published a supplement, "Sputnik narodnogo zasedatelia." It discussed the social makeup, preparation, and election of assessors.

The quality of the appearances also varied. Not infrequently, public accusers appeared at trials where no procurator was in attendance and without advance preparation and they did not always perform according to plan. At the Stalingrad provincial court, for example, one public accuser reportedly conceded, "You judges know better how to judge than I, an inexperienced person"; and in another case, the accuser refused to support the charge, stating that he agreed with the defense![76]

Conclusion

In its initial design Soviet criminal justice did constitute a socialist experiment. In staffing legal agencies with uneducated workers and peasants loyal to the Communist party and entrusting them with vast discretion in applying the laws and a mandate to bias their decisions in favor of the toiling classes, the Bolsheviks broke with the tsarist past. In the definition of crimes, the mounting of demonstration trials, and the recruitment of the public into the administration of justice, they added further elements of novelty.

At the same time, Bolsheviks also embraced traditional institutions and forms of procedure that appeared suspect to some members of their ranks. The choice was both rational and shrouded in a cloak of legitimacy. The NEP that Lenin had introduced heralded an era of consolidation for which purpose the leader himself had stressed the importance of law and legal procedures. The adoption of the NEP, however, was viewed by some Bolsheviks as a tactical retreat (even Lenin had said so at one time), and there were jurists who believed that NEP legal institutions, like NEP itself, would be temporary, replaced sooner or later by less formal, simpler, and more flexible approaches to the prosecution and sentencing of offenders.

In short, the experiment did not cohere, at least for some of its key players. Criticism by some Bolshevik jurists was never far from the surface during NEP; and when the opportunity arose, they spoke out against the traditional forms.

Still, the greatest source of vulnerability for Soviet criminal justice lay less in the disagreements about its shape than in its governing principle of instrumentality. The commitment of politicians to legal institutions and procedures was contingent. Their bets were hedged. As long as

[76] N. Lagovier, "Prokuratura i obshchestvennye obviniteli," *ESIu*, 1922, no. 42, 8–9; idem, "Obshchestvenyye obviniteli," *ESIu*, 1925, no. 14, 351–356; idem, "Novyi etap v razvitii instituta obshchestvenykh obvinitelei," *ESIu*, 1927, no. 35, 1085–1087; idem, "Institut obshchestvennykh obvinitelei v 1927 god," *Rabochii sud*, 1928, no. 15, 1136–1138; N. Porm-Koshitsk, "Obshchestvennye obviniteli v derevne," *ESIu*, 1927, no. 41, 1283; L.I. Urakov, *Obshchestvennoe obvinenie i obshchestvennaia zashchita* (Moscow, 1964), 10–18.

laws and legal procedures served the cause they would continue more or less unharmed. But when politicians adopted more radical goals and perceived the utility of law in new ways, there was nothing to protect legal values and institutions against encroachments from all sides, including the critics within the legal community itself.

2 Criminal justice under NEP

In any country the practice of criminal justice goes beyond what is set down in the rules of criminal law and procedure. The conduct of legal officials is bound to reflect factors other than the law, among them organizational demands, personal values, and local cultures. In the USSR during NEP the differences between the expectations of law-maker and the results achieved in practice were especially great, but they were not surprising. One reason for the differences was the mis-match between the capabilities of justice officials and the demands placed upon them. Another reason was the cultural gap between the world of the capital city and much of provincial Russia.

To understand the practice of criminal justice under NEP and how Soviet politicians reacted to it, it is useful to examine that practice from two perspectives. The first is that of the central legal officials. Struggling to make subordinates meet their standards of efficiency, central officials formed an image of practice from the reports submitted by the provincial and local agencies and inspectors of the local scene. Central legal officials recognized the mismatch between the personnel and the legal procedures they were expected to follow and made it urgent issue for policymakers to address.

The second perspective is that of legal officials. Judges, procurators, and investigators alike had to cope with the demands from Moscow, but they felt an equally pressing need to fulfill obligations to patrons on the local and provincial scenes and to pay heed to the customs of the communities in which they worked. Moreover, as political appointees lacking background in the law, they stood ready to respond to political messages, whether central or local in origin, even in disregard of legal norms.

This chapter depicts the operations of procuracy and courts, first as they appeared to the central legal officials, and then from the vantage point of local officials. Finally, it examines in some depth how central

politicians and officials reacted to the performance of the legal agencies
and how they struggled to reform them in the last years of NEP.

The experiment in practice: The view from the center

During the first months of 1927 the Commissariat of Workers' and
Peasants' Inspection (Rabkrin) investigated the operations of the justice
agencies. Under the direction of Viktor Radus-Zenkevich, a member of
the Praesidium of the Central Control Commission of the Bolshevik
party, surveyors from Rabkrin's legal department, with the help of
outside consultants, analyzed the data contained in reports submitted
to Narkomiust and added to them the results of their own inquiries in
the field.[1] Not only did the Rabkrin investigation provide a fine over-
view of the practice of justice agencies, but it also encapsulated the view
central officials took of it and served as a starting point for their discussion of reform in 1927 and 1928.

The most striking finding of Rabkrin was the large proportion of
criminal cases started by the police that did not end in convictions. To
begin, many cases were stopped during pretrial investigation. Of cases
whose inquiries were handled by the police in 1926, 64% were dropped
by procuracy investigators at the police's request (74% in 1927). Of cases
handled directly by the investigators, the latter sent less than half to the
courts. These particular figures reflected rules whereby the police registered and started cases for every complaint received, regardless of
whether there was evidence that a crime had been committed or, if it
had been, about the identity of its perpetrator.[2]

---

[1] For an account of the survey, see S.N. Ikonnikov, *Sozdanie i deiatelnost ob'edinennykh
organov TsKK-RKI v 1923–1934 gg.* (Moscow, 1971), 271–276. The main publication of its
findings were V. Zenkovich, "Nizovaia set suda, sledstviia i prokuratury" (po materialam NK RKI SSSR), in two parts: *ESIu*, 1927, no. 35, 1078–1083 and no. 36, 1109–1114.
M. Polevoi-Genkin, "Deiatelnost nizovoi (uezdnoi i raionnoi) prokuratury" (po materialam obsledovaniia NKRKI SSSR), in two parts: *ESIu*, 1927, no. 37, 1142–1145, and no.
38, 1176–1178; "Postanovlenie ob'edinennogo zasedaniia Kollegii NK RKI SSSR i NK
RKI RSFSR po teme plana NK RKI SSSR 'Nizovaia set sudebno-sledstvennykh organov
i prokuratury,' " in two parts: *ESIu*, 1927, no. 39, 1222–1225, and no. 40, 1255–1257; V.
Radus-Zenkovich, "Sudebnaia sistema; prokuratury (Sistema postroeniia, raboty, rukovodstva)" (po materialam NK RKI SSSR), in two parts: *ESIu*, 1928, no. 30, 829–832, and
no. 31, 853–856. Zenkovich, "Nizovaia set suda, sledstviia i prokuratury" (K reorganizatsii sudebnogo dela), *Izvestiia* (Oct. 11, 1927), 6. See also the study by a consultant to
Rabkrin, A.A. Gertsenzon, *Borba s prestupnostiu v RSFSR* (Moscow, 1928).

[2] A. Rodnianskii, "Rabota organov doznanii v 1927 goda" (po otchetam gubprokurorov),
ESIu, 1928, no. 36–37, 991–997; Kozhevnikov, "Za sozdanie edinogo apparata po rassledovaniia prestuplenii," *ESIu* 1928, no. 12, 353–354; Judah Zelitch, *Soviet Administration
of Criminal Law* (Philadelphia, 1931), 348.

But this did not mean that the work of investigation, by police or investigators, was adequate. Of the cases from the police that the investigators did forward to the court – on the assumption that they had prepared a prosecution – the judges discarded a large number at pretrial review. During the "distribution sessions" people's court judges dropped 32.5% of the criminal cases coming before them. Judges at the provincial courts, reviewing the more serious cases that had been prepared by senior investigators, stopped 49.3%![3] The high share of cases stopped before trial indicated not only that police and investigators did not understand the requirements for evidence but also that screening of cases by investigators and procurators was minimal. The procedural law required that investigators review the evidence and compose the accusatory statement for all cases investigated by police that could result in a year's imprisonment. Rather than assess the police files, however, investigators routinely copied their conclusions onto new forms. Procurators were supposed to screen cases prepared by investigators, but they rarely paid attention to these cases, even when they had to argue them in trial.[4]

As if this were not enough, of those cases that went to trial in the mid and late 1920s, a quarter ended in acquittals (25% in the people's courts and 26% in the provincial courts).[5] Acquittals were given in all kinds of cases, even political cases involving peasants who had acted on the wrong side during the Civil War or even later found ways of opposing Soviet power.[6] (By the standards of tsarist justice, however, these rates of acquittal were not high.)

Combining the figures on cases stopped by judges at the distribution sessions and acquittals, one finds that less than 40% of the cases forwarded by investigators to the courts ended in convictions. This record was particularly egregious for an inquisitorial system, where the pretrial inquiry were supposed to establish a sound case documented in written form.

Whether all of the acquittals were deserved is far from certain. Hardly ever did procurators protest an acquittal to higher authorities during the NEP years, and the appeals launched by defense counsel against convictions showed that many judges paid little heed to the requirements of evidence or procedural norms.[7] Some of the unre-

---

3 Radus Zenkovich, "Sudebnaia sistema," part two.
4 Polevoi-Genkin, "Deiatelnost nizovoi," part one.
5 Zenkovich, "Nizovaia set," part one; Zelitch, *Soviet Administration of Criminal Law*, 353.
6 A. Rodnianskii, "Karatelnaia politika gubernskikh sudov po kontrrevolutsionnym prestupleniiam v 1926 g.," *ESIu*, 1927, no. 33, 1009–1011.
7 Polevoi-Genkin, "Deiatelnost nizovoi," part two.

viewed acquittals may also have reflected extraneous considerations (such as bribes or political favors).

The Rabkrin survey also produced data on the performance of judges that struck many observers as almost as weak as that of the police and investigators. Careful examination suggests, however, that, as recorded in the official data, judicial behavior did not fall below the standards of the tsarist era.

When a trial ended in a verdict of guilty, it was likely that the convict would receive a lenient, usually noncustodial sanction. During the first years of NEP 80% of persons convicted in court received a sentence of compulsory work, to be organized by local authorities. In assigning this penalty judges took into account the petty quality of many offenses that came before them (e.g., illegal homebrewing or timber felling), the predominance of peasants and workers in the docket (sometimes unemployed), and the guidelines of Soviet penal policy, which stressed the use of noncustodial alternatives to prison. But in many places local authorities proved incapable of organizing tasks for the convicts (all the more difficult in a time of unemployment), and in order to avoid giving what amounted to meaningless sentences, judges began using short terms of imprisonment instead of compulsory work. By 1926, 40% of convicts received terms in prison, usually numbering in months; the rest still received a noncustodial sentence. The shift from 20% to 40% custodial sanctions was sufficient to produce overcrowding in the prisons. Although the 1926 criminal code gave judges the opportunity to use noncustodial alternatives for a wider variety of offenses, they continued to favor short terms in prison for crimes that they considered deserving of punishment (e.g., hooliganism).[8] The stubborn insistence of judges on giving prison terms for all "real crimes" was an object of criticism in the Rabkrin report and would, as we shall see, cause trouble for the judges later on.[9]

The principal indicator of quality in the work of trial judges, one favored by Soviet scrutineers in the 1920s and later on, was the record of verdicts and sentences appealed to higher courts. Soviet law allowed at least one mandatory review of the outcome of trial in what the Soviets called "cassation." This term quickly proved to be a misnomer, for, whatever limitations on the grounds for appeal had been intended, in practice the cassation review in the USSR turned into a full appeal, in which not only procedure but also the evidence and sentence were reviewed. As of 1924 cassation panels had the right not only to cancel

[8] Peter H. Solomon, Jr., "Soviet Penal Policy, 1917–1934: A Reinterpretation," *Slavic Review*, 39:2 (June 1980), 195–208.
[9] Zenkovich, "Nizovaia set," part two.

the verdict and remand for a new trial but also to lower the punishment or throw the case out entirely.[10]

The composite data on the fate of criminal cases in cassation appeal were as follows. In 1926 nearly 20% of convictions at the people's courts and more than 30% of those at the provincial courts were taken up on appeal. The cassation panels reviewing these appeals left intact 57.3% of the decisions from the former and 71% of those from the latter (this in 1927). In all of the other cases reviewed, the cassation panels of the provincial courts (for cases from the people's courts) and of the RSFSR Supreme Court (for cases from the provincial courts) lowered the sentence or overruled the conviction (sometimes with remand to new trial). In considering appeals, the review panels relied upon the written record of the case (appearances by counsel on either side were exceptional) and introduced changes largely because the documents failed to support the verdict or sentence.[11] Procedural violations sometimes served as grounds for changes, but, according to a Supreme Court directive, only when they affected the quality of the evidence.[12]

If one goes a step further and combines the data on the frequency of appeals and their results, one learns that of the total number of convictions appeals produced a change in verdict or sentences in 9.1% of convictions from trials at people's courts and 10% of those from the trials at provincial courts. To most contemporary observers these figures seemed high and indicators of poor work by trial judges. But, as the veteran statistician E. Tarnovskii showed, these data were consistent with tsarist practice. In 1914 a total of 9% of the decisions of the trial courts (justice of the peace and circuit) were changed in either "cassation" or "appeal."[13] The meaning of the figures might differ in the Soviet context. For one thing, the new reliance on noncustodial sanctions (as opposed to the tsarist practice of relying almost entirely upon prison) might have changed the likelihood of appeals. If one could assume that convicts receiving term of confinement were most likely to appeal, then in the Soviet period one of every two such persons might have appealed and one of every four with some success. Whether reasoning of this sort is warranted is uncertain, because rates of appeal

10 A.S. Tager, "Osnovnye problemy kassatsii v sovetskom ugolovnom protsesse," *Problemy ugolovnoi politiki*, 4 (1937), 67–68; Zelitch, *Soviet Administration of Criminal Law*, 271–320.

11 Ibid.; K. Gailis, "Doklad o rabote Ugolovno-Kassatsionnoi Kollegii Verkhovnogo Suda za 1928 g.," *Sudebnaia praktika*, 1929, no. 10, 8–14, and no. 11, 3–6; Radus-Zenkovich, "Sudebnaia sistema," part two.

12 M. Chelyshev, "Piat let raboty UKK Verkhsuda RSFSR," *Rabochii sud*, 1928, no. 8–9, 677–684.

13 Cited in Zelitch, *Soviet Administration of Criminal Law*, 316.

varied from one part of the country to another.[14] Moreover, rates of appeal might have been related to the presence or absence of defense counsel at trial. the procedure for requesting appeal, however, was simple, requiring only the verbal indication by the accused and no special form.

To complete the picture of the systems of appeals one must add the final stage of "supervisory review." Of the 180,000 cases heard in cassation in the RSFSR in 1926, the RSFSR Supreme Court chose to reconsider in a supervisory review (*nadzor*) some 2,000 cases and it introduced changes in most of them.[15] This was to be expected, since in accepting cases for review, either a member of that Court or a senior procurator had already identified grounds for reconsideration. Supervisory reviews were also undertaken by the plenums and *praesidia* of the provincial courts, but I have no data on their frequency or results. The Supreme Court's own plenum and praesidia reviewed a handful of decisions from the Court's Criminal Collegium.

To the Rabkrin investigators who compiled or analyzed these data the administration of justice required urgent attention. The various statistical indicators and the practices that they described suggested that the work of police, investigators, and judges – while not necessarily unfair – was at least inefficient and wasteful. Before seeing how the investigators and their political masters proposed to deal with the problem, let us examine the practice of legal officials from another perspective.

The practice of criminal justice: a view from below

At the provincial and local levels most investigators, procurators, and judges were ordinary persons of worker-peasant backgrounds who had received posts in the legal agencies through political patronage. While many took their jobs seriously, they remained a part of their local scenes. As a result, they responded in varying degrees to the politicians upon whom their jobs depended and the culture and concerns of their locales.

The lines of dependence between justice officials and provincial and local politicians strengthened during the 1920s. As I have explained in

---

[14] In Leningrad, where some judges at the people's courts had legal education, only 8.7% of their decisions were appealed in 1926 (and of these 73.3% were confirmed). In Kharkov, in the same year 42% of decisions from the people's courts were appealed. F.M. Nakhimson, "Rabota sudebno-sledstvennykh organov Leningradskoi gubernii za 1926 god," *Rabochii sud*, 1927, no. 4, 258–260; "Sorok sem tysiach nerazreshennykh sudebnykh del," *Pravda*, October 27, 1926, 4.

[15] Gailis, "Doklad o rabote . . . za 1928," part one, 10.

detail elsewhere, party officials at the provincial level had a decisive voice in appointment of people's court judges up to 1928; then, that power shifted to county politicians, and in 1930 to district (*raion*) bosses. By 1926 judges depended upon county (*uezd*, later *okrug*) authorities for budgetary allocations; and later upon district chieftains. Although the absence of dual subordination was meant to shield procurators from local influence, party officials still had leverage over them (through consultation in appointments and supplementary budgetary appropriations).[16]

As cliques and networks of officials gained power in particular provinces and localities, they often drew justice officials under their sway, thereby gaining protection against the unmasking and prosecution of their own misdeeds.[17] Traditionally, political office in provincial Russia brought with it a variety of perks and privileges. The same became true in the Soviet period, as the newcomers to power readily took advantage of their positions. From the start of NEP Soviet authorities in the center struggled against the misdeeds and corruption of their officials. The first years of NEP witnessed two major campaigns, one against bribe-taking, and the other against embezzlement of state funds, and through periodic reviews the control commissions purged the party of many miscreants.[18] These efforts did not prevent local cliques from pursuing their interests for extended periods of time. A good example was Smolensk province where the scandal of 1928 led to the firing of the province's political establishment and leading officials in some of its regions besides. Among other things, politicians had condoned and protected factory management and rural officials implicated in criminal activity. Whether through direct intervention with police and investigators or through the screening of cases at the control commissions, politicians had dealt with their protégés "in a family way."[19]

Not only might legal officials be asked to cooperate with local politicians in protecting their friends from prosecution, they might also be tempted to take personal advantage of their offices. Peasant judges of

---

16 Peter H. Solomon, Jr., "Local Political Power and Soviet Criminal Justice, 1922–1941," *Soviet Studies*, 37:3 (July 1985), 306–310.

17 On political cliques in the provinces, see T.H. Rigby, "Early Provincial Cliques and the Rise of Stalin," *Soviet Studies*, 33:1 (Jan. 1981), 3–28.

18 B.S. Utevskii, *Obshchee uchenie o dolzhnostnykh prestupleniiakh* (Moscow, 1948), 257–269; A.A. Gertsenzon, "Osnovnye tendentsii dinamiki prestupnosti za desiat let," *Sovetskoe pravo*, 1928, no. 1, 69–85; *Sbornik tsirkuliarov narkomiusta RSFSR za 1922–1926 gg.* (Moscow, 1927), 267ff.

19 "O polozhenii v Smolenskoi organizatsii," Postanovlenie TsKK soglasovannoe s TsK VKP(b)," *Izvestiia TsK*, 1928, no. 16–17, 15–16. See also Daniel Brower, "The Smolensk Scandal and the End of NEP," *Slavic Review*, 45:4 (Winter 1986), 689–706.

the prerevolutionary rural lay (*volost*) courts had a reputation for accepting bribes, and at least the Asiatic parts of the USSR still featured social structures in which exchange relations predominated. Anticipating the problem, Soviet lawmakers included in the 1922 and 1926 criminal codes a special article making it a crime for judges to allow "mercenary considerations" to influence the outcomes of trials.[20] Prosecutions of judges, however, were infrequent, as it was difficult to prove charges of corruption. One reported case (in 1926) ended in acquittal when the accused showed that his denouncer had borne him a personal grudge. Five other cases (in 1928–1929) however, ended in convictions. In one of them authorities succeeded in showing that the judge in question had received visitors in his apartment, drank with them, and took their "presents," which were as likely to include food and goods as money. The most dramatic case of judicial corruption during NEP involved some two dozen judges, procurators, investigators, and defense counsel in Riazan. The center of this extensive and effective operation was the secretary of the provincial court (a former tsarist clerk) who reputedly "could do anything." Defense attorneys in Riazan understood that through this court secretary came access to most of the judges of the provincial court, many people's court judges, the assistant procurator of the province who prosecuted most serious cases, and some investigators. The investigation of the scandal revealed that the provincial chief of police also took payoffs from local merchants to ignore violations of regulations and laws. Similar machinations were taken uncovered at the provincial court in Tver.[21]

Not a few judges were open to influence. Levels of pay of all legal officials were low, and some judges sought ways of supplementing their incomes. They improvised well. Judges faced reprimands at the disciplinary tribunals in the mid-1920s for working as underground lawyers on the side, for using material evidence for their own needs,

---

[20] Anatole Leroy-Beaulieu, *The Empire of the Tsars and the Russians* (New York, 1894), 270–291; Donald Wallace, *Russia* (London, 1912), 542–544; Peter Czap, Jr., "Peasant Class Courts and Peasant Customary Justice in Russia, 1861–1912," *Journal of Social History*, 1:2 (Winter 1967). "Ugolovnyi kodeks RSFSR" (1922), Article 111, and "Ugolovnyi kodeks RSFSR (1926), Article 114 – both in I.T. Goliakov, ed., *Sbornik dokumentov po istorii ugolovnogo zakonodatelstva SSSR i RSFSR, 1917–1952* (Moscow, 1954), 116ff. and 256ff.

[21] Lib, "Lozhnyi donos," *Pravda*, Nov. 5, 1926, 6; Lib, "Diskreditirovanie vlasti," ibid., Jan. 12, 1928, 6; K. Digarov, "Sudia – vziatochnik," *Krestianskii iurist*, 1928, no. 23, 2; Lib, "Razlochivshiesia," *Pravda*, March 5, 1929, 5; "Sudi, kuplennye banditami," ibid., March 23, 1929, 5. Lib, "Dela riazanskikh sudebnykh rabotnikov," ibid., March 12, 1928, 6, and March 21, 1928, 6; L. Govorov, "Vopiisuchie bezobraziia v Tserskom gubsude," ibid., Jan. 19, 1929, 3; L. Govorov, "Sudebnyi apparat tverskoi gubernoi nuzhdaetsia v generalnoi chistke," ibid., Feb. 2, 1929, 4.

and for organizing paid admissions to trials! Other judges were censured for taking on cases in which they had a personal interest in the
outcome. In addition, the records of the Narkomiust indicated that each
year 8% of judges in the RSFSR were fired for "crimes, association with
alien types, and excessive drunkenness." As a rule, the discovery of
misconduct came during the periodic but infrequent checkups that
higher authorities made on their subordinates, and clever and lucky
judges probably succeeded in covering up their peccadilloes.[22]

Attempts to bribe judges in criminal cases may have been limited
by the ease that offenders had in dealing with the police. According
to official data, 1,400 policemen each year were convicted of crimes
(bribery and theft), and many more were subjected to disciplinary proceedings.[23] In Smolensk where the party and governmental establishment underwent a corruption investigation by officials from
Moscow, the whole detective force was reportedly on the take. The
detectives in Smolensk sold releases from jail, dropped cases for "large
sums, acquisition of stolen goods, and sex," engaged in drunken orgies
with criminals, stopped persons on the street without cause to extract
money from them, and ran a private detective bureau that took money
from the victims of crimes to pursue their cases. There is no reason to
assume that all police and detective squads fell to this level of deprav-
ity (though the chief detectives of Leningrad and Astrakhan were
caught covering up cases in 1929).[24] But one must remember that
Smolensk was an ordinary Russian provincial city, neither a city with
a local tradition of shady dealings (like Odessa) nor one with an Asiatic
profile.

The Tatar republic provided another variant of the corruption of
judicial agencies. In a large rural area a gang of horse thieves (partly
clan-based) assumed power and kept all local authorities, including
police and legal officials, under its sway. Cases brought against members of the gang either failed to leave the police station or fell apart at
trial. In one case, the judge arranged a conditional sentence in return for
getting to keep the stolen horse! When local citizens tried to unmask the
gang, they risked attack. When after some years higher authorities

22 N. Nemtsev, 'O ditsiplinarnykh prostupkakh nashikh sudei," *Rabochii sud*, 1925, no.
    47–48, 1755–1758; A. Stelmakhovich, "Chistka organov iustitsii, ee tseli i zadachi,"
    ESIu, 1929, no. 26, 594–595.
23 A. Rodnianskii, "Rabota organov doznanii v 1927 godu" (po otchetam gubprokuro-
    rov), *ESIu*, 1928, no. 36–37, 991–997.
24 Mikh. Tipograf, "Protsess byvshykh sotrudnikov Smolenskogo ugolovnogo rozyska
    (po materialm predvaritelnogo i sudebnogo sledstviia)," *Sud idet*, 1929, no. 6, 303–305;
    "Arest nachalnika Leningradskogo oblastnogo ugrozyska," *Pravda*, Jan. 30, 1929, 2;
    "Arest nachalnika Astrakhanskogo ugolovnogo rozyska; ibid., June 27, 1929, 4.

intervened and restored order, criminal charges were brought against seventy-eight persons and the cases were heard by the RSFSR Supreme Court on circuit.[25]

The local perspective of Soviet judges was not limited to involvement in provincial cliques and openness to improper influences. It also meant adjusting their conduct to the values of their communities and to their own sense of priorities and rationality. In assigning punishments, for example, judges displayed a strong independence from central direction and used the sanctions that made sense to them and their constituents. Thus when judges came in the mid-1920s to rely more and more upon short terms of imprisonment in place of the noncustodial sanction compulsory work, they were responding not to policy directions from the center (which quickly went in the opposite direction). Rather, the judges were using their discretion to sentence in a way that made sense in their world. According to one knowledgeable observer, in the "peasant milieu" noncustodial sanctions had no meaning at all. When judges failed to impose confinement, they appeared powerless, all the more since the noncustodial sanction was not implemented.[26]

The crime for which judges insisted upon prison terms in the mid-1920s was hooliganism (75% of sentences in 1926), and this practice reflected genuine social concern about disorder on the streets of cities and villages.[27] With the help of journalists, public fear about disorder intensified and focused around the vaguely defined phenomena of "hooliganism," which became synonymous with both drunken disorder and violent crime.[28] During 1926 police created many cases of hooliganism (a directive of December 1925 gave them authority to go after anyone drunk in a public place, give fines if they refused to leave, and book them if they refused to pay); and judges responded by handing out "real punishments."[29] In this particular campaign central

---

[25] Lib, "Derevnia Chutei," *Pravda*, Oct. 23, 1926, 6.

[26] "Doklad Narodnogo Komissara Iustitsii RSFSR tov. Iansona – Otchet NKIu RSFSR," *ESIu*, 1929, no. 9–10, 193–212.

[27] B. Briskin, "Nekotorye itogi borby s khuliganstvom," *ESIu*, 1928, no. 16, 491–494; Neil Weissman, "The Soviet Campaign against Hooliganism in the 1920s," paper delivered at 1986 meeting of the American Historical Association.

[28] At the height of the panic (Sept.-Oct. 1926) a group rape of a woman in Leningrad was treated by the press as a case of hooliganism. Later coverage of the case dropped this designation. "Obvinitelnoe zakliuchenie po delu sorok khuliganov," *Pravda*, Oct. 14, 1926, 3; "Prigovor po Chubarovshom delu," *Pravda*, Dec. 29, 1929, 5.

[29] "O merakh borby s ulichnym khuliganstvom, beschinstvom na pochve pianstva," Tsirk. NKIu No. 252 and NKVD no. 677 ot 14 Dek. 1925, *Sbornik tsirkuli ov narkomiusta RSFSR*, 277–279.

authorities entered late in the day, increasing the formal penalties for hooliganism long after judges had done so on their own.[30]

Judges and other legal officials in the localities sometimes took a casual approach to laws and directives from the center. To a degree this was to be expected of the young Communist judges and investigators for whom the technicalities of the law seemed foreign and mysterious, if not downright unnecessary (and they were encouraged in this view, as we shall see, by some of their leaders). But disdain for the law was not a universal phenomenon, and many of the new legal officials tried to do their jobs well. In so doing, however, they faced handicaps. First, there were far too many laws and directives imposed by central authorities. Second, the system of distributing laws, administrative orders, and court decisions was inadequate, and many failed to reach the backwaters. Third, when the directives arrived and the officials could understand them, they had trouble organizing and remembering them. And with the high levels of turnover among legal officials (especially in the provinces and localities), many investigators and judges were unaware of laws and orders from the recent past. It was enough for most legal officials to try to keep track of basic documents, the codes, and the orders reprinted in handbooks (when they were available).[31]

For central officials trying to guide their subordinates the most effective instrument was reports. Throughout the decade they bombarded their charges with new requirements and forms, and they stressed the completion of reports within the allotted time frames.[32] Thirty percent of judges subjected to proceedings at the disciplinary court faced the charge of failing to complete the reports.[33] For their part, the legal officials learned how to present their work in the best light, to adjust to the norms about caseloads and movement of cases. When the central authorities wanted to highlight a particular offense (i.e., start a campaign) or stress the use of a particular penalty, they invariably required a special report.[34]

---

[30] "O meropriiatiakh po borbe s khuliganstvom," Postanovlenie SNK ot 29 oktiabria 1926 g. *Biulletin NKVD*, 1926, no. 28, 279.

[31] N. Nemtsev and D. Kornitskii, "Revizionnye zametki," *ESIu*, 1928, no. 40–41, 1055–1057.

[32] *Sbornik tsirkliarov narkomiusta RSFSR za 1922–1925*, 24–57; "Perechen otchetnykh svedenii polezhashchikh predstavlenii mestnamyi organami iustitsii v NKIu," *ESIu*, 1929, no. 398–399.

[33] Nemstev, "O ditsiplinarnykh prostupkakh nashikh sudei."

[34] In the embezzlement campaign of 1925 Narkomiust required a special monthly report. "O meropriiatiakh po borbe s rastratami," Tsikuliar ot 26 avgusta 1925 no. 167 in *Sbornik tsiruliarov narkomiusta*, 267.

Campaigns have played a part in law enforcement in many countries as a way for leaders to gain compliance of local officialdom for a change in policy without raising the stakes high. Campaigns also played a special part in the Soviet order more generally, as Bolshevik authorities struggled to get various messages across to the Soviet population (become literate, stop drinking, etc.). And, with collectivization, mobilization techniques in law enforcement, as other realms, would take on a new degree of intensity and significance. For the meantime, though, under NEP campaigns against crime were by and large of the traditional variety.[35] One of them, the hooliganism campaign of 1926, did not even begin at government initiative; authorities joined later in the effort to control a genuine social panic. The campaigns against bribery and embezzlement were typical campaigns in which central authorities assigned priorities to local officials, and instructed them to prosecute where possible and punish more severely. Although lacking the stridency of tone of the Stalinist campaigns of the 1930s, these campaigns shared with them one characteristic. They derived from governmental policies outside the realm of criminal justice, in this case the effort to improve the quality of public administration.

Politicians and criminal justice

Throughout the 1920s the discussion and development of policies for law enforcement and justice in the USSR was dominated by a group of politicians who served as the leading officials of the relevant central agencies – the RSFSR Commissariat of Justice (Narkomiust) and its administrative subordinates; the RSFSR Procuracy and RSFSR Supreme Court; the RSFSR Commissariat of Internal Affairs (Narkomvnudel); and the USSR Commissariat of Workers' and Peasants' Inspection (Rabkrin). This group included Nikolai Krylenko, Aron Solts, Peter Stuchka, Dmitri Kurskii, N.M. Ianson, Viktor Radus Zenkevich, Iakov Brandenburgskii, and Evsei Shirvindt. Top-level politicians and the Politburo itself were involved only intermittently, and the court of decision on conflicts among the agencies and the approval of legislative initiatives was often the RSFSR Council of People's Commissars (Sovnarkom). This pattern appears to have typified policy realms that were not top political priorities.[36] The Politburo did retain an interest in particular criminal cases of extraordinary political significance. In Sep-

---

[35] On campaigns in Soviet experience see Peter Kenez, *The Birth of the Propaganda State. Soviet Methods of Mass Mobilization 1917–1929* (Cambridge, 1985).

[36] T.H. Rigby, "Stalinism and the Monoorganizational Society," in Robert Tucker, ed., *Stalinism (New York, 1977), 53–76.*

tember 1926 it established a Commission on Political (Court) Cases to review on behalf of the Politburo the accusatorial acts in cases referred to it by local party secretaries. (At the end of the decade the Commission shifted to reviewing death sentences.)[37]

Although most of these leading officials in justice and law enforcement had a stake in the system, they did not act merely of defenders of the agencies. They approached the practice of criminal justice not only as its managers but also as revolutionary critics continuing the struggle to create socialist justice. For half a decade (1922–1926) they showed considerable patience. By and large the politicians in the justice realm regarded the system they had created as an experiment to be watched, assessed, and adjusted in response to experience. Fine-tuning the system represented the core of justice policy in these years. Moreover, the adjustments were introduced in the main through changes in legislation, which the top justice officials regarded as the main instrument for guiding justice officials. By 1927 the strategy of fine-tuning no longer seemed sufficient. A variety of operational problems – some of them already "crises" – had accumulated to the point where most leading justice officials agreed that it was time to consider reforming institutions and procedures.

Whatever the eventual content of the reforms, Bolshevik officials did not want to abandon any of the features that made their legal institutions socialist. Their goal was to make the experiment work. In scrutinizing the practice of criminal justice in 1927 and 1928 and debating how to reshape its institutions, Bolshevik legal authorities agreed upon the importance of two values. The first was the need to continue relying on Communist cadres. No matter what, the legal agencies had to be staffed and run by "our people," that is, by Communist, proletarian officials and not by the lawyers who had dominated the bourgeois courts before the Revolution. Since judges and procurators held positions of power and authority, they had to be "red" and not necessarily "expert." To be sure, the authorities recognized that the absence of legal qualifications influenced the quality of the work of investigators and judges. In 1926 Narkomiust went so far

---

37 According to the Statute on the Commission of the Politburo on Political (Court) Cases, the party officials in the localities were to submit documents on any cases they deemed politically significant and or cases for which they wanted to hold demonstration or show trials. The commission was supposed to pass to the Politburo itself materials on the most important cases. The Statute stressed that local party bodies were not to give directions to courts or procuracy offices in these cases without clearance from the Politburo. As of September 1928, the commission consisted of the Commissar of Justice N.M. Ianson as chair; V.R. Menzhinskii, head of the OGPU; and M.F. Shkiriatov, member of the party control commission. "Polozhenie o komissii TsK VKP9B) po polit(icheskim) (sudebnym) delam" (utv. Politburo TsK VKP(b) 23 IX 26g) in O.V. Khlevniuk et al., comp. *Stalinskoe Politbiuro v 30-e gody Sbornik dokumentov* (Moscow, 1995), 58.

as to convince the Council of People's Commissars to provide funds for remedial legal courses (of three-month duration) for some of its cadres. But Narkomiust's leaders did not want to make their investigators and judges into lawyers. Nor could they have succeeded in so doing, for anti-lawyer sentiment was reviving. The emergence of adversarial oratory in a handful of well-publicized trials at the provincial courts offended some Bolsheviks. It aroused both Ianson and Solts of Rabkrin to criticize Soviet justice at the Fifteenth Party Congress (in 1927) for displaying a "professional legal deviation"![38]

Nor did the legal chieftains show much concern about the low level of general education among their cadres. In a system of justice that stressed written documentation, the inability of many investigators and judges to write adequate prose could harm its operations. But in the 1920s top legal officials adopted a stance of quiet tolerance toward what they regarded as the "externals." A certain degree of crudeness and incompetence in writing was an acceptable price of using "our people" to staff the legal agencies. As long as the judges did not disgrace Soviet power by appearing drunk in court, and as long as they met minimal standards of efficiency as measured in quantitative indicators, their work was considered satisfactory. This was what Ordzhonikidze meant when he observed at the Fifteenth Party Congress that "we do not expect much from our judges."[39]

The second value that top legal officials held dear was efficiency. Maximizing efficiency in public administration had emerged in the mid-1920s as a cause throughout Soviet government, a cause expressed in the movements for rationalization, scientific organization of labor, and the "regime of economy."[40] The cause had much support among politicians worried about the revival of bureaucracy and red tape that the Soviet order had spawned. The legal realm shared these traits, and it became a natural target for the guardians of efficiency in Soviet government, the officials of Rabkrin. In the context of the larger governmental campaign for efficiency, even the heads of Narkomiust agreed

[38] "Sovet Narodnykh Komissarov RSFSR ob ocherednykh zadachakh NKIu," ESIu, 1926, no. 30, 913–916; "V Sovnarkome" (Rezoliutsiia SNK RSFSR po otchetnomu dokladu Narkomiusta); ibid., 927–281; Piatnadtsatyi s'ezd VKP(b). Dekabr 1927 goda. Stenograficheskii otchet (Moscow, 1961), vol. 1, 527.

[39] Ibid., 613.

[40] Kendall Bailes, "Revolution, Work and Culture: The Controversy over Scientific Management in the Soviet Union, 1920–1924," Soviet Studies, 29:3 (July 1977), 373–394; Edward Hallett Carr, Foundations of a Planned Economy 1926–1929 (London, 1971), vol. 2, 306–324; N. Lagovier, "Zadachi organov iustitsii v sviazi s provedeniem rezhima ekonomii," ESIu, 1926, no. 34, 1009–1012; "V Kollegii NKIu: Meropriatii po rezhimu ekonomii v organakh NKIu," ESIu, 1926, no. 54, 1239.

with their scrutineers from Rabkrin that combatting waste should be a central task for the legal agencies. There was also a personal connection. The head of the Rabkrin team investigating the justice agencies in 1927 Radus Zenkevich had worked as Krylenko's assistant in the procuracy (head of general supervision) from 1923 to 1925.[41]

As we have seen, the portrait of legal practice provided in the reports of Narkomiust and the Rabkrin survey suggested a good deal of "waste." At least to contemporary observers, the frequency of cases stopped, acquittals, and verdicts and sentences changed at higher instances suggested a less than efficient operation. (It was also seen as "unfair" to the persons "dragged into the legal process," only to be exonerated later on.[42]) The politicians in the legal realm recognized that at the root of the problems lay the misfit between the qualifications of legal officials and the demands of their jobs. But the leaders assumed – without question – that it was the latter rather than the former that ought to be changed. To narrow the gap between the capabilities of the ordinary, untrained persons who served as investigators and judges and the complicated formal rules and procedures that they were expected to follow, one had to change the rules and procedures. Reform, especially in the form of the simplification of procedures, was the appropriate response to inefficiency and weak performance of the procuracy and courts.

The question at the heart of the politics of Soviet criminal justice in 1927 and 1928 was how best to simplify. During these years the leaders of the justice agencies debated this issue and adopted a series of reforms. In the process they revealed a broad spectrum of opinion about what changes were needed. Underlying their disagreements were fundamental divisions about the place of law under socialism. Already present at the time of the Revolution, these decisions had been muted by Lenin's adoption of NEP and the return to traditional legal institutions. Did all laws have to be observed by those who implemented them, or could judgments based upon expediency take precedence over law? How important were formal rules of procedure? How could one ask legal officials to follow rules without making them into unfeeling bureaucrats and losing the revolutionary quality in Soviet justice? These dilemmas continued to plague Soviet legal authorities, and their doubts about the legal order of NEP kept bubbling to the surface despite the official policy that supported law and laws. In 1925, for example, the national press published an attack by Aron Solts on officials whose

---

[41] *Iuridicheskii kalendar na 1923* (Moscow, 1923), 225. In 1925 Radus Zenkovich became chairman of TsIK and Commissar of Rabkrin for Belorussia. Ikonnikov, *Sozdanie i deiatelnost*, 66.
[42] Zenkovich, "Nizovaia set."

unfeeling, rigid attachment to the laws led to poor decisions. The RSFSR Procurator Krylenko answered that it was dangerous to allow any young official to act outside the law in the name of revolutionary consciousness.[43] Again, at the Fifteenth Party Congress a number of speakers questioned the importance of formal rules and procedures, in this case for judges. Rather than following the letter of the law, they should follow their "revolutionary instinct" in the handling of particular cases. Again, it was up to Nikolai Krylenko to defend the importance of legality and the functioning of the legal system.[44]

There is irony in Krylenko's defending legal institutions in 1927 against this volley of cynical attacks, for this was the same Krylenko who had just initiated a far-reaching reform of criminal law and procedure whose main purpose was simplification. Among authorities in the legal realm Krylenko's position was one of the most radical. In this instance (as before and after) Krylenko spoke differently in political forums from the way he did among jurists. But he was not alone in inconsistency of posture. Aron Solts, of Rabkrin's Legal Department and the RSFSR Supreme Court, would attack legal formalism whenever it produced results he thought were unfair and defend legal procedures when their nonobservance led to injustices. Solts personified the ambivalence that ran through the whole group of legal authorities. This sharp-tongued, choleric revolutionary wanted a justice system that was fair – that is, consistent, class sensitive, or right according to Solts's own views (at a given moment) – but, at the same time, unbureaucratic and informal. For Aron Solts this unsolved, perhaps unsolvable, dilemma (faced earlier by Lenin himself) remained a burning issue. Solts insisted upon having the benefits of law without its costs.[45]

---

43 A. Solts, "O revoliutsionnoi zakonnosti," *Pravda*, Nov. 25, 1925, 4; N. Krylenko, "Po povodu 'filosofskikh razmushlenii tov. Soltsa o revoliutsionni zakonnosti', o starom' i 'novom' prave, i o prakticheskoi smysle ego predlozhenii," *Pravda*, Dec. 8, 1925, 4. A. Solts, "Prokurorskaia kritika," *Pravda*, Dec. 16, 1925, 4.

44 *Piatnadtsatyi s'ezd VKP(b)*, 577–598.

45 At the Fifteenth Party Congress, Solts criticized the Procuracy for failing to pursue local political authorities for their violations of legality. At the same time he lambasted the police and courts for prosecuting too many workers and peasants for trifles (through their formal and overzealous application of laws on hooliganism and theft) and for conducting "demonstration trials" that were biased against the accused. Ibid., 601–606. During the NEP period Solts aimed most of his arrows at the injustices perpetrated by legal officials who followed the letter of the law too closely or got caught up in the red tape of their bureaucratic procedures. During collectivization, in contrast, Solts found more injustices flowing from the violations of "revolutionary legality" on the part of local officials and plenipotentiaries and fought to make observance of the law more common. See, for example, Solts, "Nasha karatelnaia politika (obsledovanie Moskovskikh tiruem)," *Pravda*, Aug. 22, 1923, 1; A. Solts, "Nelepoe delo," *Pravda*, Jan. 2, 1928, 2; "Ulushchit kachestvo raboty sudov," *Sovetskaia iustitsiia (SIU)*, 1931, no. 24,

Throughout the public discussion of the role of law and the tension between legality and flexibility lay ambiguity about one important point. Just who did a particular writer or orator expect either to observe the laws of the revolutionary state or exercise his own revolutionary consciousness? Was it simply judges (and other legal officials) or all public officials? Was the issue simply one of consistency and discipline within the legal system or was it a question of using law to promote these qualities throughout the public administration? As a rule, in the mid-1920s the supporters of the strict observance of law took the latter, broader perspective. To this camp – which included not only legal officials but also politicians like Mikhail Kalinin, Lazar Kaganovich, and Nikolai Bukharin – law represented a bulwark against the tendencies of officials to be lazy (not bothering to know the rules), dependent upon "local considerations," and downright arbitrary.[46] According to one writer, the slogan "revolutionary expediency" became an excuse to allow any young official to act on his own. There was nothing "revolutionary," not to speak of "legal," about this sort of conduct. Rather it replicated the old tsarist tradition, according to which each official thought himself "tsar and God" and executed the laws accordingly.[47] Some critics of revolutionary legality (who asked what could be "revolutionary" about the observance of laws) also addressed this broader terrain of public life as a whole, but they often confused the issue by arguing against formal application of law in general while drawing illustrations of its irrationality from the world of justice.[48]

The distinction between the observance of laws by legal officials and officialdom in general may seem academic. It is difficult to promote law for one sphere without doing so for another; and hard to maintain a coexistence of spheres of public life that are and are not regulated according to law. But much of Soviet history has been characterized by just such a coexistence, however uneasy or imperfect. What changed was the relative size and shape of these spheres. Even more important for our story, the inclinations of Soviet leaders to promote either legality or flexibility at a given time might be grounded in concerns about either the legal system or loss of control over officialdom. Whatever the motivations, decisions taken to address one concern could have implications for the other.

13–16; "Zadachi sovetskogo suda v novoi obstanovke (Iz doklada t. Soltsa na Vsezoiuznom partsoveshchanii po voprosam sudebnoi rabote)," *SIu*, 1933, no. 10, 1–3.

[46] Edward Hallett Carr, *Socialism in One Country, 1924–1926* (Baltimore, 1970), vol. 2, 498–501.

[47] P. Zaitsev, "Revoliutsionnaia zakonnost ili revoliutsionnaia tselesoobraznost," *ESIu*, 1925, no. 51, 1573–1575; N. Nekhamkin, "Revoliutsionnaia zakonnost na mestakh," *ESIu*, 1926, no. 2, 33–34.

[48] For example, Solts, "O revoliutsionnoi zakonnosti."

The politics of reform

During 1927 and 1928 the leaders of Soviet justice debated a series of reforms in criminal justice that they hoped would alleviate its problems, simplify its procedures, and make it work more efficiently. Some proposals were adopted quickly, others put on hold and adopted later on, still others rejected entirely. The implementation of almost all of the changes came only in 1929 when the political context had changed, and with it often the meaning of the changes as well. All the same, the reforms had been conceived and adopted as responses to the difficulties of criminal justice under NEP, and it is important to understand their origins as well as their consequences (often unintended).

The reforms may be divided into two categories – responses to overcrowding in the courts and prisons; and responses to the complexity of procedures for processing of criminal cases, before and during trial.

Responses to overcrowding

The Rabkrin officials who assessed the justice agencies in 1927 had shown dismay at the many cases that reached the courts only to be stopped or end in acquittals. Not only did this seem wasteful, but the large volume of unproductive cases was partly responsible for the failure of most courts to move cases expeditiously. This was not the first time that the new Soviet courts had become congested. To deal with this same problem Aron Solts and Shmuel Fainblit had proposed in 1924 the transfer to administrative hearings of most cases of the common petty offenses – homebrewing, timber felling, and petty hooliganism – cases that together made up 40% of criminal trials. This suggestion was adopted by Soviet lawmakers and implemented in 1925, but the dockets of the courts quickly refilled. Once again, they were dominated by pretty cases, this time personal disputes among peasants, which produced civil as well as criminal cases. To the Rabkrin surveyors of 1927 these petty disputes did not deserve consideration by the courts, and their inclusion in the courts' purview slowed and weakened the courts' performance in more important cases. Again the solution was decriminalization. To handle petty disputes, Viktor Radus Zenkevich of Rabkrin proposed founding lay courts both in the villages and the factories.[49]

---

[49] Peter H. Solomon, Jr., "Criminalization and Decriminalization in Soviet Criminal Policy, 1917–1941," *Law and Society Review*, 16:1 (1981–1982), 15–21; Zenkovich, "Nizovaia set," part one.

Some jurists greeted the idea of establishing informal "comrades' courts" and "rural lay courts" as a move away from formal legal structures in the direction of more socialist revolutionary ways of resolving disputes. But the participatory dimension of the proposal also provoked opposition. Some voices insisted that justice meted out by peasants was bound to be less consistent than that offered at the people's court, and probably also corrupt, like the rural lay courts (*volost* courts) of the tsarist period. Others objected that comrades' courts in the factories would make trade-union officials into disciplinarians as opposed to defenders of the workers. (This shift was about to occur regardless of the fate of the comrades' courts.) Most legal officials ultimately accepted the idea of lay courts as a convenient way to relieve the courts of the petty disputes that clogged its dockets. In March 1928 the Sovnarkom adopted the proposal and approved the creation of lay courts as an experiment.[50]

The promotion by the regime in 1928–1929 of Cultural Revolution, with its emphasis upon radical schemes and its encouragement of the antilaw eliminationist views, helped the lay courts develop from a mere experiment in 1928 to a component part of the Soviet legal order by 1930. As I have argued elsewhere, the rural courts proved more viable than the comrades' courts in the factories. The irony was that even as the court dockets were relieved of petty disputes, they were quickly refilled with new kinds of cases generated by the collectivization drive.[51]

In 1927, when the Rabkrin undertook its survey of the justice agencies, more than the courts suffered from congestion. The prisons were also overcrowded, and addressing that issue had become part of a nasty conflict between justice officials in Narkomiust and the penal authorities of the RSFSR Commissariat of Internal Affairs (Narkomvnudel). At the root of what was known as the "prison crisis" lay the failure of local government authorities to implement the noncustodial sanction of compulsory work. Lacking the financial, human, and organizational capacity to arrange work projects for convicts (especially difficult in a time of unemployment), most local authorities ignored the referrals from the courts. For their part the judges quickly realized that without implementation their sentences to compulsory labor lacked meaning and, even worse, undermined the authority of the court. As a result, for most offenses that they considered consequential (e.g., hooliganism), judges began in 1925 using short terms of imprisonment in place of the noncustodial alternatives. As the prisons became overcrowded, penal authorities increased the application of conditional early release and resorted

[50] Solomon, "Criminalization and Decriminalization."   [51] Ibid., 27–34.

as well to frequent amnesties of prisoners. These practices infuriated the judges and their superiors in Narkomiust, who argued that penal authorities misused their discretion to undermine the sentencing policy of the courts.

As officials in the two commissariats traded charges, the RSFSR Council of People's Commissar (Sovnarkom) took up the issue. Hearing reports from both of the disputants and from Rabkrin (in the fall of 1927), the Sovnarkom tried to effect a compromise. In its edict of March 1928 the Sovnarkom asked Narkomiust to get judges to replace short-term imprisonment with compulsory work wherever it was legally possible and the Commissariat of Internal Affairs to temper its application of early release and amnesties. The council gave both commissariats the task for developing plans for improving the execution of compulsory work.

But the commissariats in Moscow found no way to get local politicians to organize compulsory work, and judges refused to cooperate with requests that they hand out a sanction that they considered unreal. In fact, throughout 1928 judges in the RSFSR ignored directives from Narkomiust that asked them to use compulsory work instead of short-term imprisonment. Penal authorities continued to regulate prison congestion through early releases. To cut through this roadblock (and also enhance its imperialistic designs to acquire control of the prisons), Narkomiust's leaders issued a Directive in January 1929 threatening judges with criminal prosecution if they did not comply with the new "policy." Comply they did, and the noncustodial sanction of compulsory work resumed its old position of dominance in the penal arsenal of Soviet courts, a position it would retain into the mid-1930s. Ironically, the prisons got no relief, for the increased levels of repression during collectivization kept them full to the brim, while at the same time supplying business for the OGPU's newly organized camps.[52]

The resolution of the "prison crisis" had a larger significance. It represented the first major effort by politicians and bureaucrats to develop and implement criminal policy outside of the framework of legislation. Until March 1928 this happened rarely. To be sure, during the campaign against embezzlement Narkomiust instructed judges to give severe sentences; and the Council of People's Commissars advised the agency to pay special attention to this crime. But as a rule, authorities tried to shape the practice of criminal justice by making changes in the law. For example, to encourage judges to make more use of noncustodial sanctions, the authorities saw that the 1926 Criminal Code gave them more opportunity to use those sanctions than

---

[52] Solomon, "Soviet Penal Policy, 1917–1934," 204–208.

had the 1922 version.[53] Until March 1928 meetings of the Council of
People's Commissars dealt more with the financial and organization
sides of the administration of justice than issues of policy.[54] And up
to 1928, when Soviet scholars wrote about criminal or penal *policy*,
they recorded how Soviet judges sentenced, not the line on sentencing
handed out by some authority.[55]

With the March 1928 edict this pattern stopped. This time the Council of People's Commissars did not propose changes in the law but
called upon Narkomiust to instruct judges how to use the discretion
conferred upon them by the law. And to gain compliance with his
instructions, the Commissar of Justice himself, Nikolai Ianson, saw fit
in January 1929 to threaten uncooperative judges with criminal prosecution. Ianson's action was condemned by some jurists as "hooliganistic," but it was a harbinger of things to come.[56] In the future, politicians
and legal officials in the center would often direct criminal policy without adjusting the law. Studies of criminal policy would focus upon the
initiatives of leaders and authorities in whatever form – be they laws,
edicts, bureaucratic directives, speeches, or editorials.

Simplifying procedure

The debate of 1927–1928 about the simplification of procedures investigation and trial centered on the new draft criminal procedure code
advanced by the Deputy Commissar of Justice Nikolai Krylenko. Some
of Krylenko's proposals aroused such bitter opposition that the actual
adoption of the draft was put off, as one after another governmental
body insisted upon yet another revision. Key parts of that code, however, did gain official backing, some through changes in the law, others
by administrative decree. The reforms that were adopted separately
were not the personal hobbyhorses of Krylenko that evoked so much
controversy but rather ideas that had been proposed earlier by the
Rabkrin investigators. Moreover, they were also changes that had support from significant constituencies.

Viktor Radus-Zenkevich, M. Polevoi-Genkin, Aleksei Gertsenzon,
and the other Rabkrin surveyors of Soviet criminal justice had been dis-
mayed by the waste. One of its worst symptoms was the large proportion

53 V. Shiraev, "Ugolovnyi kodeks RSFSR redaktsii 1926 g.," *Pravo i zhizn*, 1927, no. 2, 51–59.
54 For example, "V Sovnarkome."
55 See, for example, E. Shirvindt, "Perspektivy ugolovnoi politiki i lishenie svobody,"
     Problemy prestupnosti, 3 (Moscow, 1928), 3–16.
56 "O karatelnoi politike i sostoianii mest zakliuchenii," Postanovlanie VTsIK i Sovnark-
     oma RSFSR ot 26 marta 1928 g. po dokladam NKIu i NKVD, *ESIu*, 1928, no. 15,
     417–419; "Doklad Narodnogo Komissara Iustitsii," 209.

(and number) of criminal cases that were started and allowed to proceed through inquest or investigation only to be stopped at court in the distribution session or end in acquittal at trial. The Rabkrin team was well aware that neither the police nor the investigators conducted pretrial investigations satisfactorily. The observers also recognized that none of the screening mechanisms between the completion of the inquiry and the arrival of cases at the court had any effect. While investigators stopped the cases already designated by the police as dead, they rubber-stamped all the indictments in cases that the police deemed ready for trial. Procurators did the same with the cases prepared by the investigators.

The only solution, the scrutineers believed, was to force investigators and procurators to assume responsibility for the screening of cases by eliminating the distribution sessions at the courthouse. Such a move would leave investigators and procurators wholly responsible for pretrial screening of cases, and, if successful, save the time of judges and assessors freed from the duty of reviewing cases before trial.[57]

The elimination of the distribution session was a key plank in the Rabkrin program for reforming the legal process. But the reformers also called for further changes in the work both of investigation and courts. While supporting the claim of the Procuracy for full control of the investigations, the Rabkrin group also wanted to cut down on unnecessary, repetitive paperwork. In this spirit, it proposed that whichever agency (police, procurator investigator, or otherwise) conducted the pretrial inquiry should also compose the act of accusation. In other words, for the bulk of cases in which the police conducted the inquiry, the documents compiled by the police would not have to be copied onto different forms by the investigators. The latter would be responsible merely for checking them.[58] In addition, Rabkrin was ready to mount a full-scale reform of the division of responsibilities among judicial bodies, involving decentralization of both trials and the cassation appeals. More than half of the cases then heard at provincial courts (8% of total criminal cases) would be taken down to the new county (*okrug*) court or the people's court (*narsud*); and cassation appeals were to be handled for all cases in court no higher than the provincial court, leaving the RSFSR Supreme Court free to develop its supervisory role.[59]

57 Zenkovich, "Nizovaia set," both parts; "Postanovlenie ob'edinnego zasedaniia." Note that the petty cases that passed directly from the police to court without a pro forma review by an investigator (per Article 105:2 of the Criminal Procedure Code) would henceforth be screened by a judge sitting alone.

58 Zenkovich "Nizovaia set," part 2, 1110–1111; Polevoi-Genkin, "Deiatelnost nizovoi," part one.

59 "Postanovlenie ob'edinnego," 1223; Radus-Zenkovich, "Sudebnaia sistema i prokuratura," parts one and two.

In the summer and fall of 1927 when Rabkrin was circulating these proposals, RSFSR Procurator Nikolai Krylenko started to promote a new code of criminal procedure. The first draft of the code included proposals for changes similar to the ones from Rabkrin, but it served as well as a vehicle for the advancement of Krylenko's personal agenda. Throughout the draft code Krylenko attacked both the adversarial element in trials and the binding legal authority of procedural rules. The controversy over these radical blows at legal standards drew fire from Krylenko's colleagues, practitioner and scholar alike.[60]

Acting on a long-festering dissatisfaction with the complex formal trials as conducted at the provincial courts that sometimes ended in victory for the defendants, Krylenko announced that it was time to cut back on the adversary process at trial. Any rules that protected the accused and gave his or her defender resources that might save an enemy of the revolution from punishment had to be eliminated. The Criminal Procedure Code of 1922, Krylenko kept insisting, had represented a compromise between the approach of the revolutionary tribunals of the Civil War, which had facilitated the repression of enemies, and the rules of bourgeois adversarial procedure (as found in the tsarist Court Statute of 1864). To undo the compromise, Krylenko proposed making the presence of defense counsel at trial wholly contingent upon the judge's consent (unless a procurator were present, the accused were a minor, or a trade union came to his support). As if this were not enough, Krylenko was ready to undermine counsel's participation in trials to which he was admitted by enlarging the powers of the judge to control the proceedings. The draft code granted judges the powers to stop the questioning of any witness at any time, to stop the whole judicial inquiry at any time and to skip the judicial inquiry entirely in a case where the accused had confessed (proceeding straight to sentence).[61]

As if this were not enough, Krylenko attacked the legal status of procedural rules. Under socialism, he insisted, criminal procedure

[60] N. Krylenko, "Pora," *Revoliutsiia prava*, 1927, no. 4, 84–91. "Tezisy o reforme UPK, Postanovlenie kollegii Narkomiusta RSFSR ot 9 iuniia 1927 g., *ESIu*, 1927, no. 47, 1471–1473; N. Krylenko, "K proektu novogo UPK," *ESIu*, 1927, no. 47, 1457–1459; "Proekt Ugolovnogo Protsessualnogo Kodeks RSFSR s postateinym nakazom NKIu o poriadke priozvodstva ugolovnykh del v sudebnykh uchrezhdeniiakh RSFSR," *ESIu*, 1927, no. 47, 1473–1481, and no. 48, 1510–1520; "Reforma sovetskogo ugolovnogo protsessa: Doklad N. Krylenko i sodoklad A.Ia. Estrina," *Revoliutsiia prava*, 1928, no. 1, 99–119.

[61] Earlier at the Fifth Congress of Judicial Workers in 1924 A.Ia. Vyshinskii had proposed bypassing the court inquiry in cases where the accused had confessed. Vyshinskii had also criticized the complexity of the Procedural Code in general. "Tezisu doklada A.Ia. Vyshinskogo," *ESIu*, 1924, no. 12–13, 299–300.

should be treated as not law but "technique," and its rules should not be obligatory. In place of the long, intricate code with more than 400 articles, legal officials should have at their disposal a short code (eighty-three articles in the first draft) that defined the structure of operations. This code would be supplemented by an administrative decree (*nakaz*) that supplied technical rules to guide officials at the moment, rules that would serve as "orientation" rather than as binding obligations. Krylenko was not the first to draw this distinction. Already in 1925, while serving as a procurator at the RSFSR Supreme Court, Aron Solts wrote in a preface to a commentary on the 1922 Code of Criminal Procedure that "not all norms of the Criminal Procedure Code are obligatory. Only some are; others are really instructions that lack the force of law."[62] But Krylenko's adoption of this point of view had special significance. Its advocacy by the Deputy Commissar of Justice gave it both legitimacy and the potential for attaining the status of policy.

As soon as it was made public, the Krylenko draft code became the center of debate and left the Rabkrin proposals in the background. The debate focused on the controversial ideas that Krylenko had added to the agenda of simplification already in the air.[63]

Hardly any of Krylenko's colleagues, officials and scholars alike, accepted his plan for a short code supplemented by an administrative decree. To be sure, some loyal officials on the procuracy side of Narkomiust (e.g., Nikolai Lagovier) helped Krylenko gain the support of the Commissariat's Collegium, but meetings of the Moscow provincial procuracy, the Moscow provincial court, and the Plenum of the RSFSR Supreme Court objected to the form of the code, as did most of the Marxist jurists who belonged to the legal section of the Communist Academy.[64] For some of them, the issue was one of principle – that the status of procedure should not be downgraded. For others, the consideration was practical. Replacing one document with two would complicate rather than simplify the work of legal practitioners. In deference to this strong opposition, Krylenko quickly abandoned the scheme in the

---

62　N.N. Polianskii, *Ocherki razvitiia sovetskoi nauki ugolovnogo protsessa* (Moscow, 1960), 28.

63　The two sessions of formal discussions at the Communist Academy were summarized in A.L. "K reforme ugolovnogo protsessa (Disput v. Kommunisticheskoi Akademii)," *ESIu,* 1928, no. 2, 45–49, and I.S. "V Kommunisticheskoi Akademii: Disput o reforme UPK," *ESIu,* 1928, no. 4, 115–119. Fuller transcripts were provided in "Reforma sovetskogo ugolovnogo protsessa: Preniia po dokladu N. Krylenko i zackliuchitelnoe slova N.V. Kryleno i A. Ia.Estrina," *Revoliutsiia prava,* 1928, no. 2, 67–93.

64　N. Lagovier, "Perspektivy uproshcheniia nashego ugolovnogo protsessa," *ESIu,* 1928, no. 3, 72074; "Plenum Verkhsuda RSFSR o proekte UPK," *ESIu,* 1928, no. 8, 240–241; "Reforma sovetskogo ugolovnogo protsessa: Preniia."

next version of the draft procedure code.[65] One suspects that he did so reluctantly, for experimenting with the form of codes indulged Krylenko's revolutionary spirit. His colleagues had little use for such eccentricity. Not only did they condemn the form of the draft Criminal Procedure Code but they also rejected with equal vigor Krylenko's plan for a strange new criminal code that would eliminate the listing of crimes and corresponding punishments, replacing them with groups of crimes matched with sentencing options.[66]

Of all the proposals in the draft Criminal Procedure Code, those reducing the role of defense counsel aroused the greatest controversy. At a meeting of the legal section of the Communist Academy, Krylenko's attack on the adversarial process met fierce opposition. A.Ia. Estrin, head of the criminal section of the Institute of Soviet law (and also a procurator) argued that an adversarial contest was essential in order to have a *legal* trial and that to deny "accused toilers" a defense would represent a "left deviation." The chairman of the RSFSR Supreme Court, Peter Stuchka, contended that the adversary process and the principles associated with it (such as inviolability of the person, openness, and right to counsel) represented not bourgeois institutions ready for discard but "cultural achievements" of mankind that had to be preserved. He agreed that they should be readily available "to help our toilers," adding that there was no reason for the Soviets to wait 100 years like the French to offer full protection to their citizens at trial. (Stuchka was referring to the reform of criminal procedure in France in

---

65 "Proekt Ugolovno-Protsessualnogo Kodeksa RSFSR," *ESIu*, 1928, no. 28, 799–803, and no. 29, 818–824; A. Iodkovskii, "Proekt UPK," *ESIu*, 1928, no. 29, 781–784, and no. 29, 905–808.

66 Krylenko claimed that in eliminating doses of punishment, he was removing from the criminal code the bourgeois principle of "equivalence," a principle tied to the psychology of the market. When colleagues objected that doses were necessary for the law to deter potential offenders, Krylenko insisted that nothing more than self-defense should serve as the motive for punishments. The most trenchant critique of Krylenko's plan to eliminate equivalence came from the scholar who had most developed this concept in the Marxist analysis of legal relations. While agreeing with Krylenko that deterrence did not require specification of punishments to match crimes (and disliking the idea of equivalence in general), E.V. Pashukanis asked whether doses could be removed from *judicial* repression. "Judicial repression is different from administrative. It operates on the basis of norms that are known and predictable." For administrative agencies there may be broad discretion and no hard rules, and even courts can rule administratively. "But if a court decides one thing today and changes its mind tomorrow, it is not a court." This argument made by Pashukanis at the beginning of 1929 supports Eugene Huskey's contention that Pashukanis did not deserve the reputation as a legal nihilist later attached to him by Vyshinskii. N.V. Krylenko, "Osnovy peresmotra U.K. RSFSR," part 2 (with debate), *Revoliutsiia prava*, 1929, no. 2, 105–130 (quotation at 117–118); Huskey, *Russian Lawyers and the Soviet State*, 172.

1897 through which defense counsel were finally admitted to the pre-liminary examination.[67]) On this issue, however, Krylenko did have support. Despite the passionate views of its chairman, Stuchka, the Plenum of the RSFSR Supreme Court voted to support Krylenko's restrictions on the defense, as did a majority of members the Moscow provincial court (over the objections of its chairman.[68]) But Stuchka and Estrin may have been more in tune with popular opinion on the issue. Through a survey of members of the trade unions in the old capital the Leningrad provincial court found strong support for the defense bar and its role in court.[69] Members of the government who were not jurists also were chary about the wisdom of emasculating the institution of the defense. Members of a commission appointed by the Council of People's Commissars to review a later draft (1928) and then the inner council (*malyi sovnarkom*) (in 1929 and 1930) insisted upon changing provisions regarding *access* of defense, whittling them down to the point where the restrictions vanished entirely (in 1931). Still, the right of judges to curtail the activities of defense at trial remained a part of the third Krylenko draft code of 1931.[70]

The Krylenko draft code of criminal procedure never did become law. The issue of access of defense counsel helped derail the adoption of the code by forcing extra reviews and revisions in 1929 and 1930. By 1931, although Krylenko did not stop trying to get the code adopted, it was too late. The unsettled conditions of the war against the peasantry made it impossible to get any code of law promulgated and by the time relative calm returned (in 1934), the policy of simplification embodied in the Krylenko code had become obsolete.

67 "Reforma sovetskogo ugolovnogo protsessa: Doklad"; "Tezisy P.I. Stuchka o reforme UPK," *Revoliutsiia prava*, 1928, no. 1, 120–125.
68 "Plenum Verkhsuda RSFSR"; "Proekt UPK na plenumakh gubsudov i soveshchani-iakh prokurorov," *ESIu*, 1928, no. 8, 242–246; A. Stelmakhovich, "K problemam nashego sudoustroistva," *Proletarskii sud*, 1928, no. 1–2, 2–9. The Moscow provincial court was ready to eliminate defense counsel from trials entirely. The issue in this sharp form had been the subject of a public debate in April 1928, under the patronage of Aron Solts. Huskey, *Russian Lawyers and the Soviet State*, 146.
69 "Uproshchenie subdebnogo protsessa, i rol zashchitnika v sude (Mnenie rabotnikov suda, prokuratury, i profsoiuzov)," *Rabochii sud*, 1928, no. 3, 253–255; Huskey, *Russian Lawyers and the Soviet State*, 148–149.
70 First, mandatory participation of defense counsel at trial was added for accused who were too illiterate to handle their own defense. Then, the right of the judge to refuse admission of defense was limited to cases that were "simple and clearcut." Finally, in yet another version, the admission of defense counsel to trial became itself obligatory and the provision of court-appointed counsel mandatory in the case of illiterates. V. Undrevich, "Ugolovno-protsessualnyi kodeks RSFSR," *Ezhegodnik sovetskogo stroitel-stva i prava* (Moscow, 1931), 379–393; Zelitch, *Soviet Administration*, 375–380; Huskey, *Russian Lawyers and the Soviet State*, 174–175.

The controversy over Krylenko's attack on the adversary process must not be allowed to hide the other elements in his draft code that did gain support and were adopted as official policy, whether in law or administrative regulation. First, Krylenko joined Radus Zenkevich and Rabkrin in advocating the elimination of the distribution sessions at court and the shift of pretrial screening to the procuracy. Although the plenum of the RSFSR Supreme Court joined its chairman, Stuchka, in opposing this measure, their arguments had little effect once it had been decided to transfer the investigators to the exclusive domain of the procurator. Almost everywhere, procurators and investigators supported the move, and in October 1929 it became law.[71] No longer would cases be screened by the court before trial; unless the judge in chambers saw something seriously wrong with a file (and called for a preparatory session), the case would go straight to trial. This reform called for a change in the work of investigators and procurators who were solely responsible for screening cases passing their desks. The new system of prosecutorial screening might have worked, if procuracy offices had had competent staff and case loads had remained at normal levels. By the time this reform was instituted neither of these conditions obtained.

Krylenko also supported some of Rabkrin's other ideas for streamlining pretrial procedures – the equalization of the status of investigating agencies and the elimination of paperwork. Both of these proposals were included in the draft criminal procedure code, gained support in procuracy circles, and were adopted first in a Narkomiust directive of June 1929 and then in a law in October 1929.[72] The elimination of the difference in status between the police inquest and the investigation conducted by the investigator of the procuracy made it possible to relieve investigators of the onerous duty of reviewing the materials submitted by the police and then composing the act of accusation. Henceforth, the police would compose the act directly and investigators check the materials before court. To the legal theorist, this step represented the final step in the dilution of the system of evidence.[73] It was customary in inquisitorial procedure to admit at trial evidence estab-

71 "Proekt Ugolovno-Protsessualnogo Kodeksa" (1927) and (1928); "Plenum Verkhsuda RSFSR o proekte UPK: "Tezis P.I. Stuchka"; V. Undrevich, "Ugolovno-protsessualnyi kodeks RSFSR." In Belorussia the distribution sessions were eliminated in April 1929, six months before the RSFSR. Istoriia gosudarstva i prava Belorusskoi SSR I (1917–1936) (Minsk, 1970), 442.
72 "Proekt Ugolovno-Protsessualnogo kodeks" (1927); "O rabote organov rassledovaniia i nadzore za nimi (Rezoliutsiia tretego soveshchaniia prokurorskogo nadzora utverzhdennaia kollegii NKIu 9 aprelia 1928 g.)," ESIu, 1928, no. 15, 420–422; Undrevich, "Ugolovno-protsessualyi kodeks."
73 Zelitch, Soviet Administration, 138–139.

lished at the preliminary examination or investigation, without detailed examination, on the ground that it was compiled by a neutral officer of the court rather than by an administrative agency like the police. Even as of the mid-1920s this principle had been compromised, when investigators came under operational subordination to the procuracy. Their full transfer to the procuracy in 1928 delivered yet another blow, but there was still sufficient difference in theory between the quality of case preparation of investigators (who were legal officers) and that of the police to justify treating them differently in court. In practice, though, the low quality of the conduct of investigators reduced that difference almost to nil. The quality of pretrial investigations even of senior investigators was such that 49% of their products were stopped at court; and the investigators' contribution to the cases coming to them from the police had been minimal. As long as police detectives and procuracy investigators alike remained at a low level of competence, the equalization of their status made little practical difference. All evidence arriving in court was composed by officials of police and prosecution and none was screened, let alone verified by a neutral party.[74]

Finally, Krylenko joined with the Rabkrin surveyors in supporting a restructuring of the jurisdictions within the court hierarchy. The thrust of this reform was decentralization and simplification. The Krylenko code called for enlarging the jurisdiction of the people's court, at the expense both of the provincial courts and the newly established county courts. Since trials at the people's court rarely featured participation of counsel, this shift would help accomplish Krylenko's goal of increasing the number of judicial hearings unspoiled by a contest of adversaries. Second, he agreed with Rabkrin that some minor offenses deserved neither a trial with assessors nor review in cassation. For such offenses as refusal to appear for military service, a single judge might make a final decision.[75] Circumstances were to favor Krylenko's proposals. Decentralization became a trend throughout Soviet government in the late 1920s and the legal realm was no exception. In 1930, with the elimination of the county and its courts, most of its trial jurisdiction was assumed by the people's courts. At the same time, the right of cassation appeal was denied to all offenders convicted and sentenced to less than three months' corrective work or a fine under 100 rubles.[76]

---

74 For details on the new system of inquiry and investigation, see V.L. Gromov, *Predvaritelnoe rassledovanie v sovetskom ugolovnom protsesse. Rukovodstvo dlia organov rassledovaniia* (5th rev. ed.; Moscow, 1931).
75 "Ugolovno-protsessualnyi kodeks" (1928).
76 Kozhevnikov, *Istoriia sovetskogo suda*, 195–197; Undrevich, "Ugolovno-protsessualnyi kodeks."

These changes represented only a part of the barrage of measures adopted by various authorities to simplify investigation, trial, and appeal in the era of collectivization. As we shall see, in 1929 and 1930 legal officials would be directed to cut so many corners in the processing of some types of cases that it became unclear which rules remained in force.

The reforms discussed here show that the idea of simplifying procedures and many reforms adopted in its name had their origins as prescriptions for the maladies of criminal justice under NEP. Had the NEP remained, those reforms might not have taken on new meanings and might have served their original purpose of adjusting criminal justice in the USSR to the capability of its administrators.

PART II

The years of collectivization

3   Campaign justice

In 1929 the political context of Soviet justice changed dramatically. Stalin and colleagues replaced the NEP, which had nurtured law, with breakneck industrialization and agricultural policies that were tantamount to a war against the peasantry. The latter had grave implications for law and criminal justice. Already in the winter of 1928 Stalin had authorized seizure of grain as his answer to peasants who refused to sell at low prices. By the second half of 1929 such administrative methods had replaced the market as the principal means of getting food to the fast-growing cities. At the same time, collectivization of the peasantry joined grain procurement as a political priority. These two struggles formed the core of a civil war, in which officials and plenipotentiaries from the towns tried to divide and conquer the peasants.

The war against the peasantry transformed the administration of justice. To begin, it drastically reduced the volume of civil litigation. The laws of property became obsolete, and the disruption of the lives of peasants made formalized divorce a luxury. The fate of criminal law differed. Rather than lose relevance, the criminal sanction became a weapon for use in the struggle. As we shall see, legal officials spent months in villages helping to prosecute and convict peasants who failed to cooperate with regime policies. Under pressure from local politicians to act decisively, legal officials often abandoned the procedures of the law, so that their activities resembled the coercion of the OGPU.

Collectivization affected law in two other important ways. First, the struggle encouraged disregard for law among local politicians and officials. The extraction of grain, squeezing of peasant households, and organization of collective farms (*kolkhozy*, plural of *kolkhoz*) required so much extra legal coercion that legal procedures became obstacles to the accomplishment of political goals. Second, the mobilization of legal officials to spend months on the campaign trail produced a deterioration in the administration of ordinary criminal justice in the towns.

Until most of the peasantry gave up resisting and joined the *kolkhozy* (after the Famine of 1932–1933), Soviet leaders did little to stop the repression or restore the status of law. To be sure, each spring officials in the center condemned the leftist excesses of the previous harvest campaign and blamed misguided enthusiasm of local officials for the most egregious outrages. A few top legal officials and agencies promoted "revolutionary legality" as a means of restraining the warriors and reaffirming the values of law. However, Stalin himself supported reviving the authority of law only in 1934, after he had declared that the war against the peasantry had been won and the restoration of order assumed primary status.

The era of collectivization represented a low point in the history of Soviet criminal justice. Chapters 3 and 4 deal with this era. Chapter 3 focuses on campaign justice, that is, the activities of legal officials in the villages. The chapter examines the origins of campaign practices in 1928 and 1929, their dynamics, the political pressures (local and central) that shaped them, and the role of law, however limited, as a restraint and corrective. Chapter 4 starts by analyzing the consequences of campaign practices for administration of justice: the ultimate deterioration of legal standards during the Famine of 1932–1933 and the practice of ordinary justice throughout 1929–1933. It goes on to examine the use of the criminal sanction in industry from 1929–1935 and explore the symbolic dimension of prosecutions.

The transition to campaign justice

The growth of coercion in the countryside and the mobilization of legal officials to the grain front did not happen all at once. The collectivization campaign of winter 1930 made these processes universal, but both of them were well underway in some localities. Wherever and whenever district (*raion*) authorities implemented orders to collect grain, the outlines of campaign "justice" began to emerge. The growth of campaign justice paralleled the spread of grain procurement.

The first grain procurement campaign, that of winter 1928, exhibited characteristics of the coming syndrome. To begin, political authorities in the center called for criminal prosecutions against persons opposing their policies and in the process expanded the criminal law without bothering to rewrite it. Thus, through a directive in February 1928 the party Politburo declared that kulaks (supposed rich peasants) who held back grain surpluses from the collectors should be prosecuted as "speculators."[1] Moreover, in practice local officials and activists extended coercion beyond limits of law and party policy. Party guidelines called for the extraction of grain only from kulaks. The grain was meant to be surplus grain, for which a minimal price was supposed to be paid. Yet, in a county near Odessa the commission formed by the district party secretary imposed delivery obligations on not only kulaks but also middle and poor peasants. Members of the commission proceeded to search the premises of these peasants and to seize as much grain as they liked, usually without payment.[2] For this particular "distortion of the party line" some of the participants faced the criminal charge of "discrediting Soviet power." No such fate awaited most local authorities who had used illegal force to take grain.

During 1929, as grain procurement assumed top political priority, the observance of legal rules in the taking of grain became increasingly irrelevant. Bold procurators and judges who tried to prosecute those who used excessive force risked losing their jobs; and *Pravda* warned legal officials not to place formal legality ahead of the political line.[3]

This did not mean that legal officials stood idly on the sidelines. Rather than impose legal standards on the officials and activists seizing grain, investigators, procurators, and judges were expected to help them. To begin, there was the problem of resistance. Peasants did not take kindly to coercion. In resisting the collection of grain and first attempts at dekulakization and forced collectivization (summer 1929), some peasants resorted to arson and physical attacks on officials and activists in the countryside, including rural correspondents (*selkory*) and officials of the rural Soviet (*selsovety*). Acts that used to be treated as ordinary offenses (arson, assault, murder) police and judges started qualifying as political crimes (e.g., terrorism). As coercion in the countryside grew, so did peasant reaction. While in 1928 the judicial agencies in the RSFSR recorded 144 cases of terrorism, in 1929 they processed more than 1,000. The largest increase came in the Lower Volga region, where collectivization was well underway.[4]

District level OGPU staff joined regular police in the investigation of incidents of terrorism, but as a rule the security police passed the cases on to the courts. Initially, in the first part of 1929, judges continued the old practice of applying moderate terms of imprisonment (three to five

1 *Pravda*, Feb. 15, 1928, 1; Hiroshi Oda, "The Communist Party of the Soviet Union and the Procuracy on the Eve of the Revolution from Above," in Dietrich André Loeber, ed., *Ruling Communist Parties and Their Status under Law* (Dordrecht, 1986), 120.
2 "Prestupleniia khlebozagotovitelei v Blagoevskom raione," *Pravda* (May 6, 1928), 5.
3 Oda, "The Communist Party," 124–125.
4 D. Shepilov. "Terroristicheskie akty klassovogo vraga," in E.G. Shirvindt, ed., *Klassovaia borba i prestupnost* (Moscow, 1930), 36–70, esp. 38 and 54.

years), but under pressure from attacks in the press on their leniency (a "right deviation"), most judges shifted gears, sentencing these "political" offenders to terms of eight to ten years. In early 1930, two-thirds of persons convicted of terrorism got eight to ten years and another sixth the death penalty.[5]

Keeping cases of peasant resistance in the courts rather than encouraging the OGPU to process them summarily enabled authorities to publicize the trials. Through coverage in the national and local press and demonstration trials held in factories and villages, the regime dramatized the conflicts and propagated its version of events. The Shakhty trial of 1928, though based upon contrived charges, had explained the regime's attack on bourgeois specialists. Similarly, accounts in *Pravda* in 1929 of a series of trials dealing with real resistance of peasants helped to establish the image of the kulak as an enemy of regime policies in the countryside. The evil status of the NEPman – the privateer who rivaled the kulak in the mythology of the day – found confirmation in a fall 1929 trial that was presented to readers of *Pravda* on a daily basis. The operators of private fishing firms in Astrakhan had bribed more than fifty officials of the taxation and financial offices. The trial of the Astrakhan case took place in a theater and lasted for two and a half months.[6]

In addition to confronting opposition, legal officials had the even more daunting task of using the law to help implement the seizure of grain and the bankrupting of peasant households (to encourage collectivization). One line of attack involved prosecutions for speculation against peasants found to have "hoarded grain." From summer 1929 the most commonly used weapon was a charge according to Article 61 – "refusing to fulfill tasks imposed by the government." The tasks in question were obligations to deliver grain that individual households had assumed either in the form of hard quotas or contracts. According to rules developed in the spring and summer of 1929, agricultural officials could impose these obligations upon kulaks and better-off middle-class peasants; failure to deliver was interpreted as "refusal to fulfill tasks." In its June 1929 version Article 61 stipulated for first-time offenders a fine of up to five times the obligation that was unfulfilled and for a second conviction a year of compulsory work or prison.[7]

5 E.G. Shirvindt, "Obostrenie klassovoi borby i ugolovnaia repressiia," ibid., 8.
6 Kamochkin (Khoperskii okrug), "Klassovaia borba v kazachem tsentre i uchastie v nei organov suda," *SIu*, 1929, no. 47, 1110–1112; "Delo Atrakhanskikh vreditelei," *Pravda* (Aug. 30, 1929), 4, and continuing coverage throughout September and October (final article on Oct. 29).
7 Goliakov, *Sbornik dokumentov*, 314. See also R.W. Davies, *The Socialist Offensive: The Collectivization of Soviet Agriculture* (Cambridge, Mass., 1980), chap. 2.

To apply Article 61 and help with the process of grain collection and collectivization required the physical presence of legal officials in the villages. Visits to the countryside were not a novelty for Soviet judges or procurators. Since the beginning of NEP judges had conducted circuit sessions in villages (usually at the location of a major crime), and procurators had made periodic tours of the countryside to check on the legality of actions of rural officials and hear complaints. Still, at the beginning of 1928 the Third Conference of Procurators concluded that the countryside received insufficient attention from district and city officials. In the future, the resolution stated, procurators had to do better than make "episodic visits" to the villages, where they appeared to the inhabitants as actors on tour ("*gastrolery*"). Instead, procurators should "actively interfere on the side of poor peasants and hired hands (*batraks*) in the ongoing class war" by establishing ties with the local *aktiv* and meeting the peasants.[8] Pious resolutions of conferences did not change the conduct of procurators in the countryside, but mobilization by the local political bosses to take part in campaigns acted like a bolt of lightning.

From 1929 until 1933, 1934, or 1935 (depending on the location) the focus of the battle in the countryside was campaigns. The most important of these were based upon the agricultural cycle – the spring sowing campaign, during which contractual obligations were set (lasting about six weeks), and the fall procurement campaign (lasting two to three months). Naturally, the timing and duration of these campaigns varied with the location, and in warmer climates where a calendar year might include two harvests, the campaigns multiplied accordingly. In addition, there were occasional electoral campaigns that were used by local officials to assess the legal and class status of peasant households.

During 1929 legal officials began taking part in all of these campaigns.[9] Their participation required minor adjustments. For one thing, weeks, even months, away from the office inevitably affected the fulfillment of their regular duties. A procurator from the Lower Volga, where the campaign cycle started early, complained that he had only 30% of his time remaining for regular work.[10] Even more serious were

8 I. Dragunskii, "Rabota prokuratury v dervene v 1927 godu," *SIu*, 1928, no. 49–50, 1251–1256 and no. 51–52, 1285–1288; M. Sanin, "Nedochety raboty prokuratury v derevne," *SIu*, 1928, no. 36–37, 975–976; "Rezoliutsii tretego soveshchanii prokurorskogo nadzora," ibid., 1928, no. 14, 419.
9 See, for example, S. Golunskii, "Prokuratura i posevnaia kampaniia," *ESIu*, 1929, no. 12, 262–263; "Ob usilenii uchastiia organov iustitsii v peredybornoi kampanii," Direktivnoe pismo NKIu kraevym . . . sudam, prokuroram . . . ot 20 iavariia 1929," *ESIu*, 1929, no. 4, 95.
10 "Doklad Narkomiusta RSFSR tov. Iansona," *ESIu*, 1929, no. 9–10, 214–215.

the pressures of the campaign itself. On the one hand, legal officials faced demands from politicians and plenipotentiaries alike to act quickly and ruthlessly in the conduct of their duties. Quick inquiries, trials on the spot, convictions without fail were expected from procurators and judges who were serving the cause. Sometimes, politicians even instructed their legal troops about charges and sentences.[11] On the other hand, legal officials were obliged to go beyond their duties as procurators and judges and take a direct part in the conduct of campaigns. The euphemism that described this extra involvement was "administrative work." By fall 1929 legal officials were complaining about the need to perform it.[12]

While the most direct pressures that shaped campaign justice in its initial phase came from provincial and local political establishments, Narkomiust in Moscow also instructed its charges to cooperate. In a major circular issued in the summer of 1929 the chiefs of Narkomiust directed legal officials to give top priority to cases related to grain procurement and target kulaks and speculators in grain. At the same time, Narkomiust condemned "criminally passive, bureaucratic formalism on the part of procurement agencies and local authorities" and told legal officials to prosecute officials who failed to bring in the grain or pursue peasants who failed in their contracts. This was the first time that procurators and judges were told to prosecute rural officials, using the charges of abuse of authority and negligence. Another directive later in the summer advised procurators to organize assistance groups in the villages (aktivy) who would give signals about troublemakers and help procurators conduct focused "surveys" when they arrived in the village.[13]

By the fall of 1929 it was apparent to observers in Moscow that legal officials not only failed to respond to the illegal actions of zealots on the campaign front but were themselves committing excesses. The Second All-Russian Conference of Procuracy-Court Officials that convened in November aired this problem. The delegates confirmed that in violation of law and the policy of class differentiation, prosecutions did not focus upon kulaks and well-to-do middle peasants. Ordinary

[11] Oda, "The Communist Party;" Davies, *The Socialist Offensive*, 133; Lynn Viola, *The Best Sons of the Fatherland* (Oxford, 1986), 28.
[12] "Doklad Narkomiusta," N., "Na vtorom soveshchanii mestnykh sudebno-prokurorskikh rabotnikov," *ESIu*, 1929, no. 48, 1126; "Rabotniki iustitsii o sebe (Na vserossiiskom s'edze rabotnikov iustitsii)," *Pravda*, Feb. 23, 1929, 5.
[13] "O delakh, sviazannykh s khlebozagotovitlenoi kampanii," Tsirkular NKIusta, no. 104 ot 26 avgusta 1929, *ESIu*, 1929, no. 34, 808; "Direktivnoe pismo o sistematicheskoi proverke sobliudeniia revoliutsionnoi zakonnosti," Tsirkular Narkomiusta no. 112 ot 23 sent. 1929, *ESIu*, 1929, no. 39, 926–927.

middle and even poor peasants were assigned contracts (illegally) and convicted for nonfulfillment, not to speak of speculation. Conference discussions also revealed that all too often the convictions were based upon nothing more than accusations. Investigators had not stopped to gather evidence nor judges to examine it. Some of the top legal officials reacted sharply to these facts. The "conscience of the party," Aron Solts (member of the RSFSR Supreme Court and Head of the Legal Department of Rabkrin) denounced procurators who deferred to local power and allowed excesses of these kinds to occur. Even Deputy Commissar Nikolai Krylenko promised that Narkomiust would "try again" to keep its subordinates from acting too boldly.[14] But the voices of caution fell like straws in the wind. Just before the Conference Stalin had announced the all-out drive for collectivization (based on the spontaneous actions of the peasantry). Whatever their concerns, legal officials had to swallow hard and support the policy of the day. The control of excesses took second place in the speeches and resolutions of the Conference to denunciation of right deviations and calls for the development of "fighting tempos." The slogan adopted by the conference was "minimum of form and maximum of class content, in cases that concern our class enemy."[15]

The coldest juxtaposition of expediency and legality came days after the Conference. Writing in the journal of Narkomiust, the head of Moscow regional court, Nikolai Nemtsov, advocated disregard for legal procedures. An Old Bolshevik from Siberia, who served as party secretary of Narkomiust in addition to his judicial duties, Nemtsov stated that in cases of counterrevolutionary activity in the countryside on the part of kulaks, procedural norms got in the way. "They objectively, despite our intentions, play the role of defender of the class enemy." After all, the stories of the events in question were usually well known to the local *aktiv*, with which the procuracy and court officials were connected, and as a result detective work was easy to complete. However, the norms for pretrial investigation and the trial itself – with "all their loopholes" – enabled kulak elements to counterpose their own versions of events and tie cases up in red tape, rendering the eventual blows against them late and ineffective.[16] It was not uncommon to hear arguments of this kind among local party secretaries for whom legal proceedings constituted an obstacle. But for a leading justice official to argue in this manner was – in the words of one of his critics – "throwing

---

14 "Na vtorom soveshchanii," 1123–1134.
15 Ibid.; Mikhailovskii, "O naplevatelskom otnoshenii k zakonu," *SIu*, 1930, no. 1, 1–2.
16 N. Nemtsov, "Revolutsionnaia zakonnost i rabota suda v rekonstruktivnom periode," *ESIu*, 1929, no. 47, 1101–1102.

fat on the fire."[17] Nemtsov's quintessential expression of legal nihilism drew criticism from a number of legal officials and scholars, including the young Mikhail Strogovich (who was to become a leading specialist in criminal procedure), but in a final comment the editors of Narkomiust's journal supported Nemtsov's stance. They conceded that a left deviation in which officials took a wholly condescending view of revolutionary legality was unacceptable. But legal officials were justified, according to the organ of the Commissariat of Justice, in ignoring laws that they considered outdated, as long as they did so "in an orderly fashion."[18]

This editorial comment appeared in *Sovetskaia iustitsiia* during January 1930, when the campaign for total collectivization was in full swing. Events were running ahead of the theoreticians and bureaucrats alike. The period of transition was over.

The nature of campaign justice

From November 1929 until at least 1934, campaigns in the villages assumed a dominant place in the work of district and city justice officials. To be sure, in the spring of 1930 Stalin himself attacked the brutality of the collectivization campaign that he had sponsored, and some legal officials shared the responsibility for excesses with their colleagues.[19] But the fate of the unfortunate scapegoats did not change the course of campaign justice.[20] New sowing and harvesting campaigns came with the seasons, and with them new struggles to eliminate kulaks and collectivize the peasantry. Each time local political authorities mobilized legal cadres to serve the cause. Campaigns led to the formation of "brigades" of investigators, procurators, and judges that would sweep into the villages to conduct "raids" (*reidy*) or "attacks" (*nastupleniia*), sometimes on horseback, other times on foot. Once in the village, legal officials indicted, prosecuted, tried, and sentenced peasants and village officials whose actions held back the

---

17 Mikhailovskii, "O naplevatelskom," 2; N. Khover, "Kak khoroshie stremleniia inogda provodiat k nepravilnym prakticheskim vyvodam," *SIu*, 1930, no. 1, 4–6; M. Strogovich, "Revoliutsionnaia zakonnost i sud," *SIu*, 1930, no. 2, 12–13.
18 "O sotsialisticheskoi rekonstruktsii revolutsionnoi zakonnosti i borbe na dva fronta," *SIu*, 1930, no. 5, 1–3.
19 I. Stalin, "Golovoorkruzhenie ot uspekhov," in Stalin, *Voprosy Leninisma*, 11th ed. (Moscow, 1952), 331–336.
20 See, for example, "Postnanovlenie oblKK VKP (b) po dokladu o rezultatakh obsledovaniia Bobrovskoi raiKK-RKI," *Kontrol mass*, 1931, no. 5–6, 38–40. As this edict put it, "The lessons of the excesses of 1930 were not learned in Bobrovsk."

campaigns. Party bosses also used legal officials as plenipotentiaries, and on occasion courts held sessions "to liquidate the kulaks."[21]

On the campaign trail legal officials were not alone. They joined a motley assortment of officials and activists from the towns, many of whom used force and made arrests. To confiscate property or deport peasants, however, usually required the participation of some law enforcement authority. The most important alternative to the legal officials was the staff of the OGPU. In the dispossession and deportation of kulaks officials of the OGPU played a leading role, but as of 1930 this agency lacked the personnel in the countryside to act on its own. Its agents – like the legal officials – relied on a variety of helpers, plenipotentiaries, and assistants deputized for particular actions.[22]

During collectivization the OGPU grew in size, as the government authorized new enrollments and the agency found retiring army personnel to swell its ranks. Not only did this agency have to manage a growing network of camps and exile points, but it also did some of the policing of the countryside.[23] In most districts regular police faced both a shortage of cadres and a crisis of quality aggravated by constant turnover. Regular police also were drawn into campaign work, for which they were ill equipped.[24] A district inspector complained that during the winter of 1930 he faced kulak agitation against entering a kolkhoz in one place; priests and their supporters protecting the closing of a church in another; kulaks and priests resisting dekulakization in a third; the killing of young calves in the fourth, and disturbances in timber felling in a fifth. All this, he moaned, and without a horse! (His superiors in the county police, he complained, provided only "paper circulars.")[25] Still, police participated in the campaigns to the extent possible. The Ural provincial police sent out nearly 3,000 persons, including students and mounted police reserves, to pursue kulak elements.[26]

Our concern here is with legal officials, not their company on the campaign trail, and with how they administered justice. We shall now

[21] P.S. Stuchka, "Doklad ob obshchikh direktivakh Verkhovnogo Suda po kulatskim delam," *Sudebnaia praktika*, 1931, no. 7, 4–7.
[22] The best material on the OGPU in 1930 came from the Smolensk Archive. See Merle Fainsod, *Smolensk under Soviet Rule* (New York, 1958), chap. 8.
[23] A. Aldekeev, *Na strazhe zakonnosti (Stanovlenie i razvitie prokuratury Kazakhskoi SSR)* (Alma-Ata, 1981), 84.
[24] "Sostoianie i rabota mestnykh organov NKVD (po materialam s 1/X 29 g. po 1/II j30 g.)," *Administrativnyi vestnik*, 1930, no. 4, 60–61.
[25] S.K., "V raione sploshnoi kollektivizatsii," *Administrativnyi vestnik*, 1930, no. 4, 60–61.
[26] I.I. Kizilov, *NKVD RSFSR (1917–1930)* (Moscow, 1969), 149.

examine the content and forms of campaign justice that were characteristic from 1930 to 1934.

Prosecutions and trials in the villages focused almost exclusively upon helping grain collection and collectivization. The major functions performed during the "raids" consisted of

1. squeezing peasants to obtain grain and bankrupt farm households. This entailed prosecuting kulaks and middle peasants (*seredniaks*) as well for nonfulfillment of hard quotas (Article 61, sections 1–3 – or 61^{1-3} as in the Russian original) and to a lesser extent speculation (Article 107).
2. pressing village officials (such as chairmen of *selsovety* or *kolkhozy*) with prosecutions for misuse of authority and criminal negligence (Articles 109 and 111) – first to get them to comply with the orders of district officials, especially regarding procurements, and second to provide scapegoats for failures.
3. confronting resistance to collectivization such as burning collective property (arson, Article 58^9, or wrecking, Article 58^7), speaking out against collectivization (antisoviet agitation, Article 58^{10}), killing livestock or horses (Art. $79^{1 \text{ and } 3}$), and spoiling machinery (Article 79^2).
4. defending "allies of the regime" from attack or persecution, including village officials, rural teachers, rural correspondents (*selkory*), and 25,000ers (threatening an official, Article 73^1, or terrorism, Article 58^8).

To help identify culprits, legal officials established ties with the local *aktiv*, recruiting villagers to serve in "assistance groups." Members were supposed to signal procurators and investigators about their neighbors' wrongdoings and help officials when they arrived in the village.

Legal officials of the Central Black Earth Region provided a quantitative record of their campaign activities. Between January 1 and March 15, 1930 (defined here as the "spring sowing campaign"), 53 brigades of judicial officials made 347 trips to the countryside, held 253 meetings of peasants, and gave 1,158 reports. They convicted 51 persons of terrorism, 117 of counterrevolutionary agitation, 1,544 for killing cattle, 2,115 for nonfulfillment of the sowing plan, and 753 officials for negligence or abuse of power. The next fall, during the harvest campaign court and procuracy workers spent 8,409 man days in the countryside, convicting 7,347 peasants for nonfulfillment of hard quotas, 1,414 for speculation or hiding grain, 3,066 officials for negligence or abuse of power.[27] In winter 1930–1931, a brigade was sent from Narkomiust in Moscow to help the regional court in the Central Black Earth Region that was itself overburdened with cases, among them 8,000 on appeal from the harvest campaign.[28]

While gross numbers speak to the scope of the operation, they say nothing about its haphazard, improvisatory quality. According to a report from the Far Eastern Territory describing the harvest campaign of 1929–1930, "Brigades were organized and went out to find cases. . . . In 14 days we covered 31 villages and decided 62 cases; there was no concern for quality, and the court became an administrative predator of the worst type, wandering about with no knowledge of local conditions."[29] When the brigades arrived at particular villages, they gained information from informants (peasant members of the *aktivy*), formed posses and moved against private farmers thought to have grain. As a rule, the brigades processed cases of nonfulfillment of hard quotas without delay. According to an authoritative report, 52% of these cases were decided on the day of the crime (that is of its uncovering) and 33% more within five days.[30] The trials might be held outdoors, in the village square or in a field. One group of trials was held in front of the hut occupied by the Kruglitsii rural soviet (in Orgezhskii district). The whole village attended. At first, the folk were quiet, but when the accused started giving excuses the audience replied with accusations and taunts. "Who traded in homebrew? Who told us not to enter the collective farms? Who agitated against the grain contracts?" Every sentence in the case "brought a roar from the crowd." The court session ended with the singing of the "International."[31]

Legal officials in the villages had responsibility for enforcing new crimes added to the code to help the cause of collectivization. In January 1930 it became a crime for a person to kill one's own cattle (rather than face confiscation); in November of that year it became a crime for collective farms to kill pregnant livestock or stock of breeding age, and in April 1932 for anyone to kill a horse without permission of a veteri-

[27] Ia. Gurevich, "Organy iustitsii TsChO na khlebzagotovitelnom fronte," *SIu*, 1931, no. 9, 22–24; "Rabota sudebnykh organov po vesennei posevnoi kampanii," *SIu*, 1930, no. 16, 13–15.

[28] N., "Na chetvertom soveshchanii (iz zala soveshchanii)," part 1: *SIu*, 1930, no. 16, 13–15.

[29] N., "Na tretem soveshchanii sudebno-prokurorskikh rabotnikov RSFSR (Iz zala zasedanii)," part 2: *SIu*, 1930, no. 22–23, 15.

[30] N. Lagovier, "Iz praktiki sudebno-prokurorskoi raboty na khlebzagotovitelnom fronte," *Sud idet*, 1931, no. 21, 3–8.

[31] A. Gruzintskii, "Sud v poliakh," *Sud idet*, 1931, no. 18, 11–14.

narian. In March 1931 "spoiling a tractor" joined the arsenal of criminal offenses.[32]

Nonetheless, the bulk of the prosecutions conducted in the villages involved not new crimes but old, already existing offenses. These fell into three key categories: political crimes (Article 58, including terrorism, counterrevolutionary agitation, and wrecking), nonfulfillment of hard quotas (Article 61), and negligence or misuse of office (Articles 111 and 109).

During the campaign of the winter of 1929–1930 the number of political prosecutions in the courts rose dramatically, continuing the trend from the previous year, but the number of such prosecutions still represented a tiny fraction of the total.[33] The severity of sentences for these convictions (eight to ten years for most offenders, death penalty for some) gave these cases special significance. Qualification as a political offense required inquiry into the motives, circumstances, and class background of those involved. But few judges made the necessary distinctions or treated these cases with care. This pattern held whether the cases of political offenses were heard by county courts in the villages or panels of the regional courts in the cities.[34] The steady trickle of rulings and directives from the RSFSR Supreme Court on cases of counterrevolutionary crime suggests that legal officials continued to use charges of Article 58 during 1931 and 1932, but at levels well below that reached in 1930.[35] In late 1932 a new political crime, theft of socialist property according to the Law of August 7, 1932, replaced terrorism and counterrevolutionary agitation as the most serious offense.

During the campaigns of 1930 and 1931 the most common charge was nonfulfillment of hard quotas, that is, obligations to deliver grain (Article 61). Even large fines stipulated for first offenders forced peasants to yield grain kept for personal use, if not to sell their property. In practice, judges also used the more serious penalties provided for repeat offenders for first-timers. While the application of imprisonment or

---

[32] Goliakov, *Sbornik dokumentov*, 350, 359, 362–363.

[33] Cases of counterrevolutionary crimes went up from 1,111 in 1928 to 4,612 in 1929; and of terrorism from 184 to 2,175. A. Estrin, "Ugolovnaia politika i ugolovnoe zakonodatelstovo v 1929 i 1930 i reforma UK," *Ezhenedelnik sovetskoi iustitsii*, 394, 399.

[34] "Vyvody iz doklada o kontrrevoliutsionnykh prestupleniiakh (utverzhendo plenumom Sibkraisuda v zasedanni ot 19–20 aprelia 1930g)," *Sudebnaia praktika*, 1930, no. 11, 11–12; "Iz praktiki po kontrrevoliutsionnym prestpleniiam," ibid., 1931, no. 7, 18–19.

[35] *Sbornik raz'iasnenii Verkhovnogo Suda RSFSR*, 3rd ed. (Moscow, 1932) and *Sbornik raz'iasnenii Verkhovnogo Suda RSFSR*, 4th ed. (Moscow, 1935), passim.

The number of convictions for state crimes (Article 58) rendered by general courts in the RSFSR (excluding military tribunals and transport courts) dropped from 6,822 in 1930 to 1,666 in 1931 and 1,779 in 1932 (GARF, f.9492sch, op.29, d.42, 126).

banishment to these offenders contradicted the law, the practice gained approval from the RSFSR Supreme Court, "as long as it was applied only to kulaks."[36] During the harvesting campaign in the Central Black Earth Region only 12% of convicts under Article 61 received fines (often with confiscation of property), 15.9% suffered terms of imprisonment, 24.7% banishment from the village (permitted since January 1930 as a substitute for imprisonment of up to one year), and 45.9% terms of corrective work. While in the towns where most offenders had employment corrective work led to a deduction from salary, its meaning in the countryside was unpredictable. When rural soviets had to organize work assignments, they often ignored the duty, and sometimes with inducements from the convict, supplied fake documents about the implementation of punishment. When town-based corrective-labor bureaus administered the penalty, they might assign peasant offenders to "mass work in remote places," even though their terms of corrective work were too short to qualify for such assignments.[37]

Whatever the penalty assigned, the chances were good that conviction according to Article 61 would lead eventually to the destruction of a peasant's household. Almost any family farm was vulnerable. Although the hard quotas were meant for kulaks and well-to-do peasants, procurement officials had to assign quotas to a sizable portion of the peasants in each village. Often, the kulaks of previous years had left the scene, having suffered deportation or wisely "self-dekulakized," by joining the kolkhoz or fleeing to the towns. Under the circumstances the agricultural officials had little choice but to assign quotas to persons classified as middle and even poor peasants. When these unfortunates failed to fulfill the quotas, they faced prosecution, and the result sooner or later was usually breakup of the farm or bankruptcy, forcing the victims who were not imprisoned or deported to join the kolkhoz or leave the village.

The other central focus of legal officials on campaign in the village was crimes by officials, especially misuse of power and criminal negligence. These charges gave the district leaders the weapons with which to blame village authorities or emissaries from the district center for foul-ups in the taking of grain or collectivization. During winter 1930–1931, 1,409 officials were convicted in Ivanovo-Industrial Region. Of these, 27.3% were chairmen or deputy chairmen of a rural soviet, 8.4% chairmen of region, 28.5% worked in cooperatives, and 6.3% came

---

36 "Vyvody po doklade o rabote sudapparate Sibiri v khlebzagotovitelnom kampanii 1929/1930 goda, utverzh. plenumom kraevogo suda 17 ianvaria 1930 goda," *Sudebnaia praktika*, 1930, no. 3, 19–20. The publication of this ruling of the Siberian provincial court in the journal of the RSFSR Supreme Court indicated the latter's approval.
37 Gurevich, "Organy iustitsii TsChO"; N.V. Krylenko, ed., *Sovetskaia ugolovnaia repressiia* (Moscow, 1934), 179–181; 103–104.

from the district executive committee. The grounds for prosecution were often trivial, and the acts or omissions that prompted them unavoidable. Prosecutions did not spare new and inexperienced officials. For example, the chairman of a rural soviet who had held his post for a mere twenty-four days and received no guidance from district authorities was convicted of criminal negligence and sentenced to six months' corrective work. His sins included "tardiness in assigning hard quotas, failing to provide the villages with a sowing plan, disturbing the organization of the seed fund, failing to stop illegal felling of timber, and not firing activists who collected too little grain."[38] Prosecutions of this kind contributed to the high rates of turnover among rural officialdom. While most of those convicted received a noncustodial sanction, many lost their jobs as a result.[39]

The mindless prosecution of rural officialdom continued into the mid-1930s. The target shifted from the staff of rural soviets and cooperatives to kolkhoz chairmen, and the rate of prosecutions grew each year until 1936. Throughout the period prosecutions served the interests of politicians in the district, providing scapegoats for failures and pressuring villages officials to fulfill their obligations. Some prosecutions also enabled village or kolkhoz notables to protect themselves from attack by blaming others. Thus, criminal charges might help one set of local potentates undermine the positions of rivals. In Chapter 4 we will examine the struggle of central authorities to stop counterproductive prosecutions of rural officials.

In conducting prosecutions and trials in the villages, legal officials failed to observe the most elementary of legal rules. Critical observers, such as the chairmen of the RSFSR Supreme Court, identified four major shortcomings: the breakdown of procedural norms and standards of evidence; the failure to distinguish the class position of the accused and, if relevant, the victim; the escalation of political charges; and sentencing above the limits prescribed in the criminal code.

[38] "Iz rezoliutsii Ivanovo-Promyshlennogo oblsuda o sudebnoi praktike po dolzhnostnym prestupleniia, sviazannym s khozaistvenno-politicheskimi kampaniiama na sele" (30 maia), *Sudebnaia praktika*, 1931, no. 13, 13–14. See also "Itogi izucheniia del narsudov po dolzhnostnym prestupleniiam sviaznnym s provedeniem khoz-polit. kampaniiami" (Iz protokola Glavsuda TaSSR ot 19 iuniia 1931 g.), ibid., 1931, no. 14, 15.

In the RSFSR, according to official data, 77,576 persons were convicted under Article 61 in 1930, 195,843 in 1931, and 90,777 in 1932. GARF, f.9492sch, op.25, d.42, 129.

[39] Viola, *Best Sons of the Fatherland*, 8. Convictions for misuse of authority, exceeding authority, and negligence (Articles 109–111) in the RSFSR were registered at 153,261 in 1930, 204,790 in 1931, and 181,141 in 1932. These figures were produced by subtracting the data on convictions for bribery, embezzlement, and faking documents for money (Articles 116–120) from the total number of convictions for "official crimes." GARF, f.9492sch, op.2s, d.42, 133–134.

Under the pressure of the campaigns, legal officials all but abandoned procedural norms and standards of evidence. A well-documented example comes from the work of the Tiumen county court. While on circuit in the villages during the first collectivization campaign (1929–1930), members of this court handed out sentences of capital punishment for counterrevolutionary crimes to some seventy-seven persons. When the RSFSR Supreme Court surveyed the results, it found that in three-quarters of these cases trials had taken place in the absence of any witnesses or victims; that documents on the social position of the accused had not been supplied; and, sometimes, that there had been no court inquiry at all. In its cassation reviews the Ural regional court had not only failed to correct these mistakes, but also compounded them by issuing directives of its own to hear cases without witnesses.[40] Though perhaps an extreme case, the experience of the Tiumen court was not unique. A view of counterrevolutionary cases in Siberian courts for 1930 discovered "an intolerable simplification of trials, involving hearings without witnesses and denying the accused the right to present evidence that might acquit." Moreover, in the name of efficiency Siberian authorities often joined unrelated cases for trial (in one instance fifty kulaks charged with counterrevolutionary offenses).[41] Likewise, a scrutineer of judicial practice in Smolensk province during the first ten days of September 1930 found that judges often refused to accept evidence from the defense. Some judges also denied convicts their legal right to request a review in cassation before the implementation of sentence. These practices led the observer to conclude: "Judges have moved from simplification to maximum simplification or annihilation."[42]

The breakdown of procedural norms and standards of evidence went well beyond the simplifications that Krylenko had promoted and Narkomiust endorsed. No doubt the message from central legal authorities contributed to the low quality of campaign justice, but it was not responsible for it. After all, the central authorities had endorsed simplification not abandonment of procedures. Narkomiust's directives authorized simpler documents not their elimination; shorter lists of witnesses, not hearings without witnesses. Peter Stuchka and the RSFSR Supreme Court had directed judges to stop the review at trial of non-controversial issues, not to refuse hearing testimony from the defense.[43]

---

40 "O rabote Tiumenskogo okrsuda," Postanovlenie Verkhsuda RSFSR ot 18 ianvariia 1930 G., *Sudebnaia praktika*, 1930, no. 3, 3–4.
41 "Vyvody iz doklada o kontrrevoliutsionnykh."
42 A. Kon, "Khlebozagotovitelnaia kampaniia v sudebnoi praktike," *SIu*, 1931, no. 3, 27–28.
43 Undrevich, "Ugolovno-protsessualnyi kodeks;" "O nekotorykh peregibakh v sudebnoi rabote," *SIu*, 1930, no. 9, 1–13.

Despite the significance of class for the qualification of crimes, legal officials in the villages rarely bothered to determine the social position of the accused or the victim, say by checking his or her property holdings or whether he or she had employees. Not only would such inquiries have been onerous, but they had no relevance to local authorities served by legal officials. Take the example of opposition to collectivization, a political offense only if the accused were a kulak. To an official trying to move peasants into kolkhozy any person who opposed his efforts deserved the status of kulak, whatever his economic situation. Not surprisingly, in the North Caucasus "under the influence of the local 'hurrah collectivization mood' some judges used naked administrative methods in conducting the campaigns and convicted middle and poor peasants groundlessly for agitation against collectivization." All they had done was "to express their views at meetings or refuse to enter the kolkhoz."[44] The territorial court in the North Caucasus reversed many of these convictions. Similarly, a territorial court in Siberia stopped 57.3% of Article 58 cases launched against middle peasants in 1930 and mistakes in "class policy" led to the changes in half of the political convictions in the Far Eastern Territory.[45]

At the same time, agricultural officials routinely assigned hard quotas to middle peasants, even though the law allowed such assignments only to kulaks and well-to-do peasants. For their part, legal officials did not hesitate to indict and punish those middle peasants who failed to deliver.[46] An official in Smolensk reported that his colleagues had trouble distinguishing a middle peasant from one that was well-to-do. But the exercise was of no consequence, he reported, once the grain collection campaign went into high gear. In November 1930, after a couple of months of trying to observe the rules, officials in Smolensk "began committing excesses against the middle peasants that included sentences to prison, confiscation of property, and large fines that in reality liquidated the farms."[47] For many of the campaigners this result was wholly satisfactory. According to veteran observers from Narkom-

---

44 "O borbe s peregibami voznikshim v sudakh v sviazi s kolkhoznym dvizheniem," Iz Tsirkuliari, no. 6, 1930 g. Severno-Kavakazskogo kraisuda, *Sudebnaia praktika*, 1930, no. 7, 20.
45 "Vyvody iz doklada o kontrrevoliutsionnykh"; "Na tretem."
46 For example: "O borbe s peregibami," "V Kollegii NKIu," *SIu*, 1933, no. 19, 22–23. In some villages, officials assigned hard quotas to the bulk of the inhabitants (30% of households in 18 rural soviets in Chermankhovskii district in East Siberian territory; 53% and 80% in particular rural soviets in the Middle Volga). M.M. Braginskii and N. Lagovier, *Revoliutsionnaia zakonnost i prokurorskii nadzor v selskokhoziaistvennykh politicheskikh kampaniiakh* (Moscow, 1933), 65.
47 Kon, "Khlebozagatovilenaia kampaniia."

iust, "some lower agricultural workers regard hard quotas applied to poor and middle-class peasant households as a peculiar method of forcing them into the kolkhozy."[48] When grain had to be delivered and kolkhozy formed, the mythology of class vanished.

Another defect of campaign justice that flowed from the first two was improper escalation of ordinary criminal cases into political ones. The regime's policy mandated escalation of charges when members of alien or hostile classes attacked the regime's officials or allies out of political motives. Thus, were a kulak to assault, kill, or burn down the house of a rural soviet official or a rural correspondent, a qualification of terrorism (rather than assault, murder, or arson) was appropriate. The problem was that investigators and judges did not ensure that the motives for such acts were political or check the class of those involved. To the disgust of members of the RSFSR Supreme Court and staff at Narkomiust, legal officials commonly prosecuted as terrorism assaults on rural (village) officials that stemmed entirely from personal conflicts, often drunken brawls.[49] Arson might have been conflated to terrorism without signs of a political motive. Occasionally, the victims of assault or arson made false claims to be public officials or appointed themselves "social activists" so as to bring the full wrath of the law against their rivals.[50] Rural officials enjoyed charging with counterrevolutionary agitation any peasants who criticized them, whatever their status or the pretext.

Finally, in assigning punishments at trials held in the villages, judges often failed to observe the norms of the criminal code. As we have seen, one common improvisation during winter 1930 was applying penalties provided for a second offense of nonfulfillment of hard quotas to first-time offenders, thereby assuring the imprisonment or deportation (banishment) of many peasants. Following their political instincts paid off for these judges, when the RSFSR Supreme Court approved the practice.[51] More often, though, central legal officials deplored failures to observe the law on sentencing. They repeatedly criticized judges who confused the sanction "confiscation of property" with dekulakization and ordered the seizure of farms as well as movable property or who confused banishment and exile and used them for crimes to which they

---

48 Braginskii and Lagovier, *Revoliutsionnaia zakonnost*.

49 "O nekotorykh peregibakh v sudebnoi rabote," *Sbornik raz'iasnenii Verkhognogo Suda RSFSR*, 2nd ed. (Moscow, 1931), 372–375.

50 Ibid., "O rassledovanii del o kontrerevoliutsionnykh prestupleniiakh," Instruktivnoe pismo vsem kraevym . . . prokurorum . . . ,Tsirkuliar no. 61, *SIu*, 1930, no. 16, 27–30.

51 By publishing in its bulletin this directive of the Siberian provincial court, the RSFSR Supreme Court gave its tacit approval to the practice. See "Vyvody po dokladu o rabote sudapparata Sibiri."

did not apply (e.g., criminal negligence).[52] Some improvisations bordered on the preposterous. A judge sent two officials accused of negligence and sentenced to corrective work to serve as plenipotentiaries in the grain campaign![53]

One effect of these sentencing practices was a gradual rise in the average severity of punishments, particularly in cases related to campaigns. To be sure, in 1930 – after the ban on short-term imprisonment came into effect – only 10% of court sentences in the RSFSR were custodial. Most sentences featured corrective work or a fine. However, by 1933, 29% of sentences prescribed imprisonment, and to terms much longer than those used in the 1920s, when 40% of punishments were custodial. While some of the increase in prison sentences replaced exile and banishment, which were no longer in favor, most of the increase came at the expense of more lenient noncustodial alternatives.[54]

The sources of campaign justice

The most immediate and influential source of campaign justice – both the unlawful conduct of legal officials and their disregard for the illegalities of others – was pressure from local politicians. "Why do court-procuracy workers lose their distinctiveness (*litso*)?" asked a procurator from Smolensk. "Exclusively because there is too much local influence on these workers and too great is their fear of 'deviation.' From these acts comes the basis for excesses and the ignoring of revolutionary legality."[55] Many central legal officials joined in blaming local officials, but the former were not blameless. Especially Nikolai Krylenko and some of his colleagues at Narkomiust encouraged investigators and judges to put political goals ahead of legal forms.

Local politicians (at the district or city level) gave instructions to legal officials directly and in person, rather than through the remote medium of paper circulars. The officials had reasons to pay heed. Procurators and judges depended on party bosses in the locality for their jobs, financial support and a variety of perks. Between 1930 and 1932 the district party committee (*raikom*) not only shared responsibility for hiring judges, but it also had the authority to fire judges at its own initiative (after 1932 the recall of judges required consent from the regional executive committee [*oblispolkomy*]. Until 1935 courts received their budgets entirely from the

---

52 *Sbornik raz'iasnenii Verkhovnogo Suda*, 2, 354, 361.
53 P.T., "Soveshchanie narsudei Moskvy," *SIu* 1930, no. 29, 18.
54 M.D. Shargorodskii, *Nakazanie po sovetskomu ugolovnomu pravu* (Moscow, 1958), esp. 74–75.
55 Kon, "Khlebozagotovitenaia kampaniia," 28.

corresponding executive committee (after 1930, this meant that of the district for people's courts). Accordingly, most judges depended upon the district bosses for adequate accommodation (not always provided), funds for secretaries, and travel expenses (both treated as luxuries), and clearances on personal matters (permission to take a vacation). In theory the exclusive subordination of procurators to their organizational superiors shielded them from dependency on local politicians. In practice, procurators also fell partly under the sway of the locals. The appointment of new procurators – a responsibility of the procuracy itself – still required consent from the local party officials. While the latter could not fire a procurator, they could complain to his superiors. Likewise, while the operating funds for the procuracy offices came from the budget of the republican procuracy, local authorities often supplied extra funds. Forging good relations with these authorities might also protect procurators from an overload of special assignments.[56]

For the district party chiefs the execution of political tasks took precedence over observance of law. Many of them believed in their missions and conducted the war against the peasantry with enthusiasm.[57] All of them felt pressure from their superiors to get the grain collected and the farmsteads collectivized. Failure at either task might lead to firing (immediately or in a later purge) and threatened criminal prosecution as well.

Local politicians accepted articles of the criminal code that helped the collection of grain and collectivization. But they resented all legal rules and procedures whose observance impeded the fulfillment of those tasks. Their disdain was reflected in the consistent antilaw bias in the local press, which criticized right deviations far more often than left excesses.[58] (By the early 1930s the district and city newspapers were subordinate to party officials.) Moreover, local party bosses regularly fired judges and procurators alike (sometimes illegally) for "sluggishness" or showing a "right deviation." One judge whose "sluggish tempos" brought him a charge of criminal negligence mended his ways by passing judgment on sixty cases in a single day. Forty of them failed to stand on appeal.[59]

Some of the legal officials at the local level shared the outlook of the politicians. Cast from the same mold, they too were young party members of humble origins possessing limited formal education and an ele-

---

[56] Solomon, "Local Political Power."

[57] Viola, *Best Sons of the Fatherland.*

[58] N.L., "Organy iustitsii na khlebozagotovitlenom fronte," *SIu,* 1931, no. 4, 28. My reading of *Molot* for 1929 and 1933 confirms the observations of N.L. (Lagovier).

[59] "Na tretem;" "V Kollegii NKIu;" Gurevich, "Organy iustitsii TsChO."

mentary knowledge of the law. At least some of them were more impressed by the social transformation they were effecting than the law they were supposed to execute. The procurator of the Far Eastern Territory justified the excesses committed in his vast province on the grounds that "the tempos were maintained and grain quotas filled." Another procurator warned that the legal agencies would lose out to the OGPU the prize of handling political crimes, if they did not stop delaying the implementation of sentences with appeals.[60] The procurator of the Chechen Ingush Region told his helpers: "Don't listen to the law; listen to me." The police chief of the Central Black Earth Region announced that in Kursk "the laws (especially the criminal procedure code) have grown obsolete and we can no longer be guided by them in our work."[61]

Whether or not they had qualms, procurators and judges usually cooperated with local politicians, both by putting policies ahead of law and responding to particular requests. Some forms of cooperation we have already examined. Rarely did procurators hold to account plenipotentiaries and activists who violated the law. Mindlessly, judges convicted middle and poor peasants for nonfulfillment of quotas meant to be applied only to their better-off neighbors, and rural officials disregarded procedural rules and neglected to consider evidence that might lead to acquittals.

One indication of legal officials' deference to their political masters was a readiness to circumvent the appeals process. Local politicians resented the obligatory cassation reviews. Not only did the appeals process delay the implementation of sentences, but it might even change a sentence or verdict. Either way, the process frustrated the political goals that lay behind prosecution, by putting off or stopping the seizure of grain or bankruptcy of farms. To avoid such outcomes, procurators ordered, illegally of course, the execution of some sentences before the cassation hearing. Thus a peasant might suffer confiscation of his horse only to discover after a successful appeal that the animal in question could not be retrieved. In the absence of such confiscation, though, the convict might have sold or eaten the animal, thereby frustrating the implementation of sentences should the verdict and sentence be upheld. Another ploy to avoid the effects of appeal was for judges to lower sentences or corrective work to three months, in order to place the case in a category not subject to appeal.[62]

---

[60] "Na tretem," part one: *SIu*, 1930, no. 21, part two.
[61] "Za nezbleymost sovetskogo zakona, za sotsialisticheskoe pravosoznanie," *ZaSZ*, 1934, no. 8, 1–4.
[62] Kon, "Khlebozagotovitelnaia kampaniia," 28; "Postanovlenie Kollegiia NKIu o delakh, ne podlezhashchikh kassatsionnomu obzhalovaniiu," *SIu*, 1931, no. 27, 5–6.

The death penalty posed a special problem. After the winter of 1930 when judges had awarded capital punishment "frivolously," the RSFSR Supreme Court had required that implementation of the death penalty be held off until its own members had conducted a review and staff of the All-Russian Central Executive Committee had heard an application for pardon. (In addition, according to secret rules, republican level procurators were supposed from December 1929 to inform the Politburo's Commission on Court Cases of all sentences of capital punishment to enable it to conduct reviews.) But legal officials in the localities (not to speak of their political masters) found it hard to wait. Judges from the regional courts bombarded the Supreme Court of the Republic with telegrams about particular cases. A few procurators disregarded "categorical prohibitions" and ordered convicts executed "because seventy-two hours had passed since the telegram had gone to the Supreme Court."[63]

Legal officials also paid heed to the suggestion of district party officials regarding particular criminal cases. Typically, politicians tried to use the courts to pursue grudges, say against rural correspondents who criticized them or "25,000ers" who meddled in their affairs. Not only did the authorities initiate cases, they also tried to dictate outcomes. Thus, the chief of the organization department of the Danilovskii district party committee directed a judge to convict two 25,000ers for criminal negligence and sentence them to two years, "so that they won't try to come around here again."[64] Or, consider a case from the Black Earth Region, in winter 1930. A teacher who regularly criticized the local bosses tried to get electoral rights removed from a kulak already convicted of bribery. The kulak in question, however, was the drinking partner of the chairman of the district soviet. As reward for his interference, the teacher received an order from the district party committee to leave the region and a notice of criminal prosecution. The charges against the teacher consisted of "stealing the protocol of a meeting at which poor peasants had defended him" and "exploiting a hired hand," that is, the woman who washed his shirts and cooked his cabbage soup. It was "characteristic," reported the narrator, an official from the regional court that reviewed the case, "that the local investigators and procurators complied in pressing these ridiculous charges."[65]

---

63 *Sbornik raz'iasnenii Verkhovnogo Suda*, 3, 341; *Sbornik raz'iasnenii Verkhovnogo Suda*, 4, 35; Khlevniuk, "Rol Politbiuro," 3–4.

64 I.N., "Bolshe chutkosti vnimaniia k kolkhoznym kadram," *Za tempy, kachestvo, proverku*, 1931, no. 1, 42.

65 Rusakov, "Neveroiatno, no fakt," *Slu*, 1930, no. 11, 6–12.

In addition to constant pressure from local politicians to help them execute political tasks, legal officials also received signals from central legal officials. The speeches, editorials, directives, and instructions from Narkomiust, the republican procuracy and the USSR and RSFSR, Supreme Courts often reinforced the directions from the locality by placing political tasks ahead of the observance of legal norms. To be sure, the messages from the center were mixed ones, varying with the time and author. But many Bolshevik legal officials shared the commitments of the regime and recognized the need to subordinate law to their achievement.

Central legal officials faced a dilemma. While accepting larger regime commitments, they also cared about the maintenance of elementary levels of legality and the quality of the administration of justice. As jurists (most of the central officials had legal education), they worried about the contradictions built into the current policies. For example, both policy and law limited application of hard quotas to kulaks and well-to-do peasants; yet practice of grain procurement involved quotas for middle peasants. For example, Narkomiust, which had earlier encouraged procurators to participate fully in the campaigns, now insisted that they review criminal cases handled incorrectly. To help these officials make trips of two months to the "worst localities," Commissar of Justice Ianson requested a special allocation of 100,000 rubles from the Council of People's Commissars. That body granted the agency 30,000 for this purpose.[66]

What should legal officials do, after the fact, about the most egregious examples of arbitrary and legal coercion? Should they hold plenipotentiaries and their deputies to account? This question was not easy for central legal officials to answer, for many of them must have sensed that the excesses of local officials were usually approved by the political leadership before or after the fact, if they were not also sponsored by it. Through the early 1930s, top legal officials disagreed in their approach to excessive coercion, and many of them changed their positions on this issue more than once.

Not surprisingly, the shifting postures of top legal officials reflected fluctuations in policies of the regime. In spring 1930, after Stalin's public attack on excesses, central legal officials unanimously called for the punishment of overzealous activists and the observance of "revolutionary legality" in the future. From the summer of 1930, however, with the

[66] "Ob otpuske iz rezervnogo fonda SNK RSFSR 100,000 R. na raskhody po kommandirovkam rabotnikov prokuratury dlia likvidatsii i ispravleniia peregibov, dopushchennykh mestnymi organami vlasti pri kollektivizatsii selskogo khoziastva i likvidatsii kulachestva," SNK RSFSR, 5-4-1930, WKP 525, 195–196.

mounting of new campaigns, the focus upon restraint receded. At the height of the harvest and sowing campaigns, political goals took precedence; at the most, a directive might speak of avoiding deviations to the left and the right. After the grain had been collected, it was easier to criticize the excesses of the campaign, including violations of the law. But never after spring 1930 does one encounter a consistent line among central legal officials about the observance of legal restraints in agricultural campaigns.

In the middle period of collectivization – from summer 1930 to summer 1932 – central legal agencies and their chiefs divided in their approach to legality. As we shall see, the RSFSR Supreme Court and Rabkrin paid the most attention to legality and emerged as defenders of restraint. In contrast, Narkomiust and especially its leader, Krylenko, kept reminding legal officials that larger political goals took precedence. They did this first of all by supplying guidelines about the formation of brigades, the foci of campaign activity, and the tempos of work. More important, Narkomiust required detailed reporting about campaign justice from each region, which meant that the district officials had to supply their region superiors with a record of achievements in the villages. The reports included the number of man days spent in the villages, the numbers and types of cases started there, the tempos of case processing and the sentences imposed, not to speak of the number of speeches given and persons enrolled in the *aktivy*.[67] To be sure, the guidelines issued by Narkomiust might include elements of restraint – cautions to avoid left excesses and exhortations to follow the class policy or collect better evidence. But these were balanced with warnings about right deviations, and the editorials and articles in the journal of the Commissariat stressed the achievement of political goals.

Whatever balance characterized the message of Narkomiust to legal officials, the speeches of its leader Nikolai Krylenko tended to offset. Highly committed to regime policies, Krylenko was slow to condemn excess. Unlike acting Commissar of Internal Affairs Evsei Shirvindt (who spoke out in March 1930) or Peter Stuchka of the RSFSR Supreme Court (who complained in January), Krylenko first condemned excesses only in May and even that summer he promoted revolutionary legality half-heartedly. Moreover, Krylenko remained on the radical wing of the spectrum of central legal officials. In June 1931, at a conference of legal officials where the problem of excesses occupied center stage,

---

67 On general reporting requirements as of mid-1929, see "Perechen otchetnykh svedenii podezhashchikh predstavlenii mestnym organam iustitsii v NKIu," *ESIu*, 1929, no. 398–399. For an example of report data on campaigns see Gurevich, "Organy iustitsii TsChO."

Krylenko's speech failed to mention the subject. Reacting to criticism of the omission, Krylenko then mocked the "schematicism" of colleagues who advocated "not touching middle peasants under any circumstances."[68] Similarly in the winter of 1932 Krylenko stressed "finishing off the class enemy" when others bewailed violations of class policy.[69]

In addition to the directives and speeches from the central legal officials, local procurators and judges also received orders from regional level procurators and judges. The messages from the regional officials were just as ambiguous as those from the center. In directives to district level subordinates, provincial judges and procurators might encourage achievements in a current campaign, or criticize excesses from an earlier one. Cassation panels of provincial courts regularly changed verdicts in cases handled poorly by judges of the people's courts, but did so inconsistently. Moreover, the conduct of trials at the regional courts was often no better than at the people's courts, forcing the RSFSR Supreme Court to change many of their decisions.[70]

The law as restraint

While Narkomiust and Nikolai Krylenko told procurators and judges to help make campaigns successful, two other central agencies and their leaders emphasized the need for legal officials to maintain "revolutionary legality." Those agencies were the RSFSR Supreme Court and the Legal Department of the Commissariat of Workers' and Peasants' Inspection (Rabkrin). Charged with hearing appeals from court decisions and complaints about the actions of officials, these agencies had responsibility for dealing with breaches of legality. But their activities reflected even more the character of the men who ran them.

Peter Stuchka, chairman of the RSFSR Supreme Court, and Aron Solts, head of the Legal Department of Rabkrin, had many years' experience in the struggle to develop a socialist legal order. As Old Bolsheviks, their view of socialist law stressed class bias, and they paid special

---

68 N.V. Krylenko, "Iz itogov sibirskikh vpechatlenii," *SIu*, 1930, no. 15, 1–3; "O khlebzagotovkakh," Doklad tov N.V. Krylenko na 3 soveshchanii sudebno-prokurororskikh rabotnikov, *SIu*, 1930, no. 22–23, 1–7. "O revoliutsionnoi zakonnosti," Rech T. Krylenko na XVI partinom s'edze, *SIu*, 1930, no. 24–25, 20–21. Note that at the party congress, where Krylenko represented legal officialdom as a whole, the commissar took a more positive stand on revolutionary legality than he did in forums for legal officials.

69 P. T-khov, "Piatoe soveshchanie rukovodiashchikh rabotnikov organov iustitsii . . . ," *SIu*, 1932, no. 5, 1–3; "Doklad N.V. Krylenko," ibid., no. 6, 13–26.

70 N. Lagovier, "Na shestom soveshchanii rukovodiashchikh rabotnikov iustitsii . . . ," *SIu*, 1932, no. 5, 1–3; "Doklad N.V. Krylenko," ibid., no. 6, 13–26.

attention to the treatment of the toilers. When the full force of grain procurements struck ordinary peasants who did not match their image of kulaks, Stuchka and Solts registered shock. In an intensely personal statement (spring 1930) Stuchka denounced the treatment of the peasantry. Stressing his credentials as a revolutionary, he wrote, "I am for the revolution, but here is class excess, and I raise my voice against class excess."[71] Aron Solts, the fiery orator who had stood for flexibility in the administration of justice, was no less horrified at the fate of the peasantry, whose treatment seemed to violate elementary principles of fairness. The main contribution of the RSFSR Supreme Court to holding coercion in check came in its reviews of the work of lower courts. Both through instructions and individual case decisions the judges reaffirmed the requirements of determining the class of the accused, gathering evidence, providing some kind of hearing, and using punishments properly. The Court adopted this position during the winter 1930 campaign. Already in January, one of its edicts denounced the sloppy performance of the Tiumen county (okrug) court, particularly its sentencing offenders to death on the basis of empty charges without examining witnesses or checking the social position of the accused.[72] From this point on, the Court displayed tough standards on reviewing appeals, regularly reversing verdicts or changing sentences when evidentiary and procedural rules had been disregarded. The journal of the Court reported a stream of such cases.

In its cassation reviews of political (Article 58) convictions, especially when the death penalty was imposed, the Supreme Court usually had guidance from the Politburo's Commission on Political Cases. According to a Politburo resolution of December 1929 judges hearing political cases were to send the record of sentence to the Commission for review. The Commission's decision was to be forwarded to the court body hearing the cassation review, typically the RSFSR Supreme Court. Through its commission the Politburo kept control, for a time, of the implementation of the death penalty and acted to mitigate excessive harshness below. But by keeping its role a secret, the Politburo left the credit for dispensing "mercy" to the Supreme Court.[73]

---

[71] P. Stuchka, "Revoliutsiia i revoliustsionnaia zakonnost," *Sovetskoe gosudarstvo*, 1930, no. 3, 15–22.

[72] "O rabote Tiumenskogo okrsuda," Postanovlenie Verkhsuda RSFSR ot 18 ianvaria 1930 g., *Sudebnaia praktika*, 1930, no. 3, 3–4.

[73] In 1932 the Politburo commission was headed by Mikhail Kalinin, whose main post was chairman of the Central Executive Committee, or head of state. The members included Pavel Postyshev, the Central Committee secretary in charge of legal affairs; Matvei Shkiriatov, member of the Central Control Commission; the Commissar of Justice of the RSFSR Nikolai Krylenko; Ivan Akulov, deputy chairman of the OGPU

Most of the cases reviewed by the Russian Supreme Court involved neither political cases nor the death penalty, and most of the actions of the court aimed at curbing illegalities came at its own initiative. To reach a broader range of judges, especially at the people's courts, the RSFSR Supreme Court issued a barrage of instructions and resolutions. Based upon cases reaching the Court and special surveys and studies undertaken by its staff, the resolutions touched on many of the illegal practices associated with campaign justice. These included the need to determine the class of the accused, the misuse of political charges and inappropriate procedural shortcuts (such as reducing the term for appeals). The edict also dealt with fresh issues including the criminal liability of persons who returned illegally from banishment, and the appropriateness of applying hard quotas to juveniles. The Court encouraged judges to protect 25,000ers and shield rural officials from senseless prosecutions for negligence. The Court also discouraged the misuse of penal sanctions, including the confiscation of property, banishment, and the death penalty.[74] We have already seen how this Court reserved the right to review all sentences of execution and how some procurators resisted. In 1932 the Court threatened with criminal prosecution any official who did not observe this ruling.[75]

The message from the RSFSR Supreme Court reached legal officials at all levels. At least this body insisted that legal officials observe important legal rules and it stood ready to change verdicts that reflected violations.

The impact of the Supreme Court on the conduct of collectivization was limited, for it could influence only investigators and judges. It had no leverage over the excesses committed by other officials and activists, nor could it force procurators to deal with them. But this limitation did not stop the Chairman of the RSFSR Supreme Court, Peter Stuchka, from railing against other sorts of illegality. In a speech in the spring of 1930 Stuchka denounced all local initiatives that set aside the law. These included the Moscow regional court's setting aside a whole body of NEP law and the claims of other legal officials that "revolutionary legality was a thing of the past, if not a right deviation." Stuchka also

and member of the Ukrainian Politburo, soon to be named procurator-general; P.A. Kameron from the USSR Supreme Court; and A.P. Egorov from the RSFSR Supreme Court. During the harvest campaign of 1932–1933, various shortcuts in the review of death sentences were introduced, some in connection with the Law of August 7, 1932, others to enable OGPU *troiki* to implement their death sentences without review by the Commission of the Politburo. See Khlevniuk, *Stalinskoe Politbiuro v 30-e gody*, 58–66.

[74] See *Sudebnaia praktika*, 1930–1931, passim, and *Sbornik raz'iasnenii Verkhovnogo Suda RSFSR*, 2 and 3, passim.

[75] *Sbornik raz'iasnenii*, 3, 341.

condemned all instances of individual arbitrariness, including those that made up "the fantastic sea of illegality" existing in the localities and perpetrated in the main against middle and poor peasants.[76] A year later, in a report on cases dealing with kulaks, Stuchka again raged against excesses, including the liquidation of kulaks outside of collectivization campaigns.

In contrast to the RSFSR Supreme Court, the Supreme Court of the USSR contributed little to the restraint of excesses and promotion of legality. The main reason was the limited jurisdiction of the Court. Until 1933 the USSR Supreme Court had no relationship to the republican Supreme Courts. It could not hear appeals from those courts or courts subordinate to them, but only from the small network of USSR courts (military tribunals and later railroad and water courts). In 1931 the Court did gain the right to conduct surveys of the work of lower courts on behalf of the Praesidium of the Central Executive Committee and investigated the conduct of judges during the agricultural campaigns of 1931 and 1932. Neither the results nor the edicts based upon those surveys were published.[77]

The other central agency struggling against excesses by legal agencies was the Legal Department of Rabkrin. Headed by Aron Solts and including other Old Bolsheviks like Shmuel Fainblit, this group of crusaders examined individual cases and conducted surveys of the justice agencies in particular places. The Moscow headquarters acted as troubleshooters, taking on claims of injustice from many sources and using its moral and political authority to rectify them. Some cases came from Rabkrin's Department of Complaints or provincial Rabkrin units, others directly from the parties concerned. When Solts, Fainblit, or a subordinate decided that a court had acted improperly, he protested to the procuracy or a higher court and often succeeded in getting the decision reconsidered and reversed. Complaints about actions of plenipotentiaries and activists also reached Rabkrin's Department of Complaints, and

76 Stuchka, "Revoliutsiia i revoliutsionnaia zakonnost"; P.S. Stuchka, "Doklad ob obshchikh direktivakh Verkhsuda po kulatskim delam," *Sudebnaia praktika*, 1931, no. 7, 4–7.

77 The chairman of the USSR Supreme Court, A. Vinokurov, resented the limited jurisdiction of his tribunal. Feeling "that the main flow of life was passing by the Supreme Court of the Union . . . and that because of its competence it could not take part as needed in socialist construction and the fight with opportunism . . . ," Vinokurov called in 1930 for the transformation of the Court into a "type of directive agency" with full authority over lower courts. This request was fulfilled but only in 1938. See L. Smirnov, ed., *Vysshyi sudebnyi organ SSSR* (Moscow, 1984), 45; T.N. Dobrovolskaia, *Verkhovnyi sud SSSR* (Moscow, 1964), 33–37; Peter H. Solomon, Jr., "The USSR Supreme Court: History, Functions and Future Prospects," *American Journal of Comparative Law* 38:1 (1990).

on occasion it addressed the complaint, even prompting prosecution of the responsible officials.[78]

The key to getting a wrong redressed was reaching the central office in Moscow. Lower levels in the agency's hierarchy were both over-whelmed with business and powerless to deal with officialdom at their own level. Thus, the office of Rabkrin in the Central Black Earth Region received 10,000 complaints a year from kulaks, private owners, and workers concerning abuse of power by officials. Though the staff tried to deal with some of them, its reach was limited. Often, it was too late ("the house was destroyed"). District level Rabkrin officials, often working individually, were both overburdened and loath to confront local power. Frequently, they reviewed 150 to 200 complaints in one evening and stamped all of them with the resolution "deny."[79] There were exceptions. In spring 1931 (the season for dealing with excesses), a Rabkrin team from Bobrovsk district made 25 trips to the villages to hear 426 complaints and managed to satisfy one-fifth.[80]

In addition to protesting individual cases, the Legal Department of Rabkrin in Moscow conducted surveys of the work of justice agencies in the Caucasus, Belorussia, the Ukraine, Central Asia, and parts of the RSFSR. Unusually thorough in character, these surveys offered vivid, critical portraits of campaign practices in particular regions and districts. Each survey served as the basis for edicts through which Rabkrin tried to reshape the work of both its subordinate officials and the justice agencies.

Throughout the early 1930s, the driving force of Rabkrin's Legal Department remained its chief, Aron Solts. Old Bolshevik, a leading member of the party's Central Control Commission, fiery orator, out-spoken champion of causes, Aron Solts was for most of the 1920s the top party activist concerned with legal affairs. Known as the "conscience of the party," Solts had considerable personal authority. His views carried so much weight that his report on the peasant homebrewers in Moscow's jails (1923) led almost immediately to legislation de-

---

[78] S. Fainblit, "V borbe za ukreplenie revoliutsuionnoi zakonnosti" (Iz opyta iurtotdela TsKK-RKI), *Za tempy, kachestvo, proverku*, 1932, no. 15–16, 85–86; "Bolshe vnimaniia k liudiam" (Iz tekushikh del iurotdela TsKK-RKI), ibid., no. 17–18, 77–78. In his novel *Children of the Arbat* (New York, 1988), Anatoli Rybakov described a personal appeal to Comrade Solts. In the story Solts used his authority to right a wrong perpetrated against a young man by a party organization.

[79] "Usilit borbu za revoliutsionnuiu zakonnost" (Doklad t. Ermolaeva na sentiabrskom plenume oblKKK VKP (b)), *Kontrol mass*, 1932, no. 10–11, 9–12.

[80] "Postanovlenie oblK VKP (b) po dokladu o rezultatakh obsledovaniia Bobrosvskoi raiKK-RKI," *Kontrol mass*, 1931, no. 5–6, 38–40.

criminalizing that offense.[81] Comrade Solts's outrage in 1930–1932 at the unfair and "uncommunist" treatment of middle peasants and other toilers had a similar bite, but Solts was no longer in a position to have an immediate impact. Nonetheless, he tried. Solts's attitude toward formal law had changed from the 1920s to the 1930s, but not in the direction of most of his peers. Whereas during NEP Solts saw the law as the source of wrongs that he abhorred, during collectivization he viewed law as the main bulwark against arbitrary coercion. Solts could never abide the manner in which collectivization was conducted. In a speech at the funeral of Stuchka in 1932, Solts argued that one could be flexible with the law without going so far as to violate it; and that while it was necessary to promote "socialist construction" (i.e., collectivization), one must never lose sight of the purpose of that construction (that is, a good life for the toilers). Later that year at a session of the Supreme Court Solts went on to denounce the "overpoliticization of criminal cases."[82] As we shall see, Solts became one of the main critics of the excesses associated with the Famine of 1932–1933.

It is unlikely that the speeches of Solts and Stuchka or the directives of their agencies actually restrained legal officials. Most procurators and judges on campaign had little choice other than to resume the patterns of conduct that local politicians demanded. However, the decisions that the RSFSR Supreme Court made on appeal and the initiatives of Rabkrin to secure such reviews did make a difference to the individual persons involved. In 1930–1931, one-quarter of all criminal cases had a cassation review by a higher court. Since the number of sentences to imprisonment, exile, banishment or death totaled 12.3% in 1930 and 16.7% in 1931, one can infer that the bulk of cases ending in these serious sanctions were reviewed, along with a substantial number of other cases involving hard quotas.[83]

The cassation reviews for most of these cases were held at the regional courts and resulted in a change in verdict of sentence one-third of the time. The more serious cases that had trials at the regional courts were reviewed at the RSFSR Supreme Court (along with other cases received there in supervision). According to the official data, that court changed 90% of the sentences that it reviewed in the first part of 1931!

[81] Fainblit, "V borbe za ukreplenie;" S. Fainblit, "Sud i prokuratury pod kontrol partii i mass," Za tempy, 1931, no. 4, 19–21; S. Fainblit, "KK-RKI dolzhny udeliat bolshe vnimaniia rabote suda" (Kak rabotaiut sud i prokuratura v BSSR), ibid., 1932, no. 2, 54–56. See Solomon, "Criminalization and Decriminalization."

[82] "Traurnoe zasedanie planuma Verkhovnogo Suda RSFSR posvetaiushchei pamiati P. I. Stuchki," SIu, 1932, no. 9, 39–40. "Voprosy sudebnoi politiki na rasshirennom Plenume Verkhovnogo Suda," ibid., no. 10, 40.

[83] "Ulushchit kachestvo raboty sudov," SIu, 1931, no. 24, 13–16. Shargorodskii, Nakazanie.

The reviews by the Supreme Court included most convictions for political crimes (Article 58). Thus, nearly 60% of convictions for counterrevolutionary agitation in 1930 were overruled on the grounds that the accused were middle peasants. Finally, all sentences to the death penalty required confirmation by the RSFSR Supreme Court (and through it by the Politburo Commission on Political Cases). The Court insisted that the punishment be justified. Of the seventy-six death sentences imposed by the Tiumen county court during the first collectivization campaign the Supreme Court set aside forty-six; only nine of the remainder were implemented.[84]

The clearest sign that appeals affected the outcomes of campaign cases was the resentment of local politicians. We have seen how appeals threatened to undermine the fulfillment of political tasks, and how local authorities pressed judges and procurators to find ways of avoiding the bad effects of appeals.

One should not exaggerate the impact of appellate court decisions. The conduct of the cassation panels on the regional courts was often shoddy (still based upon inadequate documentation). Many of the appeals it denied may have been justified. Moreover, many weak court decisions were not reviewed at all. At the same time, the rampant violations of legality on the part of local officials and plenipotentiaries remained unchecked. Some of those actions were perpetrated by officials of the OGPU, on whom there were no visible restraints after 1930.[85] In reviewing decisions of trial courts, higher courts could help individuals, but they could not stem the tide of arbitrary coercion.

However limited the impact of the RSFSR Supreme Court and Rabkrin on the state of legality on the countryside, the activities of those bodies had a larger significance. By holding some judicial decisions to legal standards, they helped maintain the framework of law and the self-respect of those who directed its administration. Had central legal officials failed entirely to respond to the denigration of legal procedures by legal officials, there would have been little basis for the reconstruction of the administration of justice after collectivization.

---

[84] "Ulushchit kachestvo;" "O rabote Tiumenskogo okrsuda."

[85] In March 1930 the procurator of the Western Region complained in writing to the chief of the provincial OGPU about the actions of an operative who, without the knowledge of the county level, OGPU had mobilized and subordinated to himself the investigators of the region. He told them (and the police chief) to "go into the countryside, seize kulaks and launch without fail a criminal case according to Article 58-10 against all of them." The OGPU man then ordered a judge to rush to the villages to hear the cases. The regional procurator called for the firing of this OGPU official and the initiation of criminal proceedings against him. "Nachalnik OGPU tov. Zalinu ot Prokurora Zapadnoi oblasti Kulikova ot 24/III, 1930g." Smolensk Party Archive, WKP 260, 44.

4   The decline of legality

The winter of 1933 marked a low point in the history of Soviet criminal justice. The extraction of grain from peasants fighting starvation required even more force than the earlier harvest campaigns. Despite misgivings and initial resistance many procurators, investigators, and judges took part in this repression by implementing Stalin's harsh law on theft. But there was more to the decline of legality. In the early 1930s ordinary criminal justice in the towns suffered from neglect and as a result fell below the simple standards of the NEP period. At the same time, the Stalinist leadership succumbed to the temptation to use the criminal sanction to supply scapegoats for failures in state-owned industry and trade. All of these developments contributed to the deterioration in both the quality of the administration of justice and the authority of law and legal procedures. Together, they form the subject of Chapter 4.

The campaign of 1932–1933

In July 1932 Stalin and associates decided to take grain from the Soviet peasantry in amounts bound to produce starvation and death. The leaders knew about the shortfalls of the previous harvest, due largely to the inadequacy of kolkhoz organization. They had also received warnings from Ukrainian party leaders that some villages had little grain and meeting the new targets would cause starvation. But Stalin chose to pursue and stay a reckless course through ten months of hunger, repression, and breakdown of order. The campaign of 1932–1933 turned out to be the decisive round in Stalin's virtual war against the peasantry.[1]

---

[1] See Robert Conquest, *The Harvest of Sorrow. Soviet Collectivization and the Terror-Famine* (Oxford, 1986); and Moshe Lewin, *The Making of the Soviet System* (New York, 1985), chap. 6.

Conducting this war required confronting the mounting theft of grain, an act of self-defense and preservation that was becoming widespread.[2] On August 7, 1932, the Soviet government promulgated an extraordinary new law making theft of public property, including from collective farms, subject to the death penalty or in the presence of mitigating circumstances to a minimum term of ten years' imprisonment! Initiated and virtually written by Stalin himself, the new law declared that public property was "the basis of the Soviet system and therefore holy and inviolable." Persons making attempts on this property were to be treated as "enemies of the people." Although the declarative part of the law condemned theft of all kinds of public property, the law singled out theft of cargo on railroads and ships and theft from collective farms and cooperatives, especially "harvest in the fields, public storage, and cooperative warehouses." From the start the bulk of cases launched in the Law of August 7 concerned theft of grain in the countryside.[3] Two weeks later another new law made speculation in consumer goods (including grain) worth five to ten years "in concentration camps."[4] But it was the Law of August 7 that dominated judicial practice. As a weapon for activists trying to collect grain, the Law received special publicity. Not only the national press, but also provincial party journals highlighted the new law, giving it more attention than earlier laws, including the edict of June 25, 1932, "On Revolutionary Legality."[5] Issued to mark the tenth anniversary of the Procuracy, that earlier edict (to be discussed in Chapter 5) had set curbs on the illegal coercion associated with the campaigns. The Law of August 7 and the mission it served eclipsed the edict on revolutionary legality and rendered it impotent for nearly a year.

Stalin personally played the leading role in both the development of the Law of August 7 and its presentation to the world. The leader

2 Theft of public property was on the rise in the first part of 1932. Thus, in Taganrog (in the North Caucasus) convictions in the courts reached 243 cases between January 1 and August 15, 1932 – i.e., before the campaign associated with the Law of August 7 – in comparison with a mere 16 cases in the same months of 1931. I-n., "Bespochchadnyi otpor raskhititelem obshchestvennoi sobstvennosti," *Put Sovetov* (Rostov-na-donu), 1932, no. 19–20, 43–47.

3 Goliakov, *Sbornik dokumentov*, 335–36; A. Shliapochnikov, "Zakon 7 avgusta ob okhrane obshchestvennoi sobstvennosti," *SGiRP*, 1933, no. 5, 21–31. Because of its extreme sanctions, a major treatise on political crimes included a chapter on the Law of August 7. See A.A. Gertsenzon et al., *Gosudarstvennye prestupleniia (Ugolovnoe pravo, Osobenniaia chast)* (Moscow, 1938), 95–109.

4 Goliakov, *Sbornik dokumentov*, 336.

5 Ibid., 333–334. I compared the coverage of the Edict on Revolutionary Legality and the Law of August 7 in the following journals: *Put Sovetov* (Rostov); *Partrabotnik Severnogo Kavkaza*; *Kommunist* (Samara); *Na Sovetskom postu* (Western Siberia).

explained his idea for a new law on theft in three letters to Kaganovich and Molotov, all written between July 20 and 26, 1932. The first letter noted the rash of thefts from railroad cars and collective farms "organized in the main by kulaks, dekulakized persons, and other antisocial elements trying to shatter our new structure." According to existing law, Stalin went on, "these gentlemen [*gospoda*]" were treated as ordinary thieves who received two to three years in prison of which they served six to eight months. This situation, Stalin inferred, only "encourages them to go on with their counterrevolutionary 'work'." Therefore, he "suggested" a minimum term of ten years, and "as a rule the death penalty. Without these and similar draconian socialist measures [*sic*] it is impossible to establish a new social discipline and without this discipline it is impossible to strengthen our new order." In the second letter Stalin elaborated on the Law's rationale. If people object, he wrote to his henchmen, tell them that capitalism could not have destroyed (*razbit*) feudalism, "if it had not made private property holy and punished in the harshest way violators of its interests. . . . So too socialism cannot finish off (*dobit*) and bury capitalist elements and the individual self-seeking habits and traditions that serve as the basis for stealing . . . if it does not announce that public property (cooperative, kolkhoz, and state) is holy and inviolable . . . and if it does not protect that property 'with all its forces.' " In the third letter Stalin argued that to deter and stop thefts repression had to be well publicized and legally grounded. Under these circumstances stern measures would not only work, but they would even gain the respect of the population "because the peasant (*muzhik*) loves legality (*zakonnost*)." Stalin paid personal attention to the publicity accorded the new Law. Shortly after its issuance he asked Kaganovich to arrange a Central Committee directive on its implementation, and days later he complained to the same aide that *Pravda* had given it inadequate coverage. What was needed, Stalin told Kaganovich, was "a long and systematic campaign."[6]

For the heads of the legal agencies the Law of August 7, 1932, posed special problems. They knew that judges would need guidance and support in applying such draconian punishments. In a series of directives issued shortly after the Law's promulgation the Collegium of Narkomiust, the USSR Supreme Court, the Praesidium of the Central Executive Committee, and the OGPU set ground rules. To begin, the rules distinguished two categories of accused, those who deserved the

---

6 "Pismo Stalina Kaganovichu i Molotovu," 20 iiuliia 1932; "Pismo Stalina Kaganovichu i Molotovu," n.d. (late July 1932); "Pismo Stalina Kaganovichu," 26 iiuliia 1932; "Pismo Stalina Kaganovichu," 4 avgusta 1932; "Pismo Stalina Kaganovichu," 11 avgusta 1932; "Pismo Stalina Kaganovichu," 17 avgusta 1932.

death penalty and those for whom ten years' imprisonment was appropriate. Capital punishment, according to the instructions, was reserved for persons convicted of organized and serious thefts, for kulaks and class-hostile elements (absent extenuating circumstances), and for kulaks who stole grain from kolkhozy. When kolkhozniki or simple private peasants stole grain, they were to receive ten years' imprisonment, as long as there were no aggravating circumstances. Even the most minor thefts of grain, the legal chieftains stressed, were to be heard by real courts and treated as serious crimes. The rural lay courts (*selskie obshchestvennye sudy*) lost jurisdiction over these cases. This new practice contrasted with the factory setting, where the comrades' courts (also lay bodies) were encouraged to deal with all thefts worth under fifty rubles. Only in the rural setting did the top legal officials envisage the use of the Law of August 7 for petty thefts. The inclusion of petty thefts in the countryside within the scope of the Law assured that judges would be tempted to use Article 51 of the RSFSR Criminal Code, the provision authorizing sentences below the lower limit for a given crime. Through Article 51 judges could assign sentences under ten years of imprisonment. But Narkomiust RSFSR set out an unequivocal policy of reserving Article 51 for exceptional cases. Whenever a judge used the Article, he was to report the occurrence to a higher court. To ensure supervision of judicial practice with such severe punishments, the authorities also established obligatory cassation review of sentences under the Law – by the RSFSR Supreme Court for capital punishment and the regional courts for imprisonment. In addition, Narkomiust directed all courts to provide telegram reports on their practice with the Law at ten-day intervals.[7]

Finally, the RSFSR Commissariat of Justice extended the jurisdiction for cases under the Law to the people's courts. Since the elimination of county courts in 1930, charges that could bring capital punishment could be heard only at a regional or supreme court. But Russian legal officials believed that regional courts could not handle the new caseload. In permitting judges of the people's courts to hear cases under the Law of August 7, the Commissariat stressed that they could *not* apply the death penalty! Whenever a case involved a kulak as the accused or a large-scale organized theft – that is, had the characteristics that made capital punishment a possibility – the case was still to be heard at a regional court. The people's courts were to try cases under the Law only when the accused was a toiler *and* the size of the theft

[7] GARF, f.8131sch, op.27s, d.21, 5–6 (Postanovlenie Kollegii Narkomiusta ot 21 avgusta 1932); f.353s, op.16, d.11, 101–106; d.16, 4–5 (Instruktsiia po primeneniiu . . .); f.8131, op.27, d.21, 5–18.

moderate or small. This distinction introduced by Narkomiust RSFSR drew sharp criticism from the procurator of the USSR Supreme Court, Peter Krasikov. Krasikov accused Narkomiust of having created two separate out laws of the Law of August 7, 1932 – one with a maximum of ten years' imprisonment; the other, the death penalty. He repeatedly urged higher authorities to deprive people's courts of jurisdiction in any cases relating to the Law, but his pleas were ignored.[8]

Allowing people's courts in the RSFSR to hear cases under the Law had two consequences. First, it enabled the courts of Russia to handle a large volume of cases of persons accused under the Law. In the Ukrainian Republic, where cases under the Law remained in the exclusive jurisdiction of the regional courts, there were half as many cases tried per capita as in Russia.[9] Second, the judges at the people's courts in Russia tended to assign more lenient punishments than their colleagues at the regional courts. To a degree, this reflected differences in the nature of the cases heard by the two courts. But it also reflected the unwillingness of many of the young party members who served as judges in the people's courts to apply the harsh provisions of the Law of August 7. For these judges the use of Article 51 and with it assignment of punishments *below* ten years' imprisonment was not an exception but the rule! According to Commissar of Justice Krylenko, in the remaining months of 1932, judges in Russia used Article 51 in 40% of their decisions. Moreover, a secret resolution of the Commissariat indicated that more than 80% of convicts sentenced under Article 51 had received noncustodial sanctions![10] The same resolution drew the obvious conclusion: many courts were directly violating Narkomiust's instructions on the use of Article 51. There was also regional variation in punishments. In Moscow Region, judges used Article 51 in half of their decisions; in Leningrad Region, 84%, in the Lower Volga, 89%, and in

8 GARF, f.8131sch, op.27s, d.21, 8–18.
9 GARF, f.9474sch, op.16s, d.80, 24–25.
10 RTsKhIDNI (TsPA), f.17, op.2, d.514, vyp.2, 20; GARF(TsGA), f.353sch, op.16s, d.11, 127–128. In fall 1932 and winter 1933, central legal agencies had an especially difficult time collecting statistical data, material from the localities was incomplete and inaccurate. GARF, f.353sch, op.16s, d.11, 174–174ob. As a result, the composite data cited by various official reports showed discrepancies, sometimes severe ones. The 40% figure cited by Krylenko for use of Article 51 by people's court judges up to Jan. 1, 1933, came out as 36% in a report by RSFSR Supreme Court Chairman Bulat. More striking were the different figures for the use of Article 51 during the first three months of the Law. The November resolution of Narkomiust's collegium set the figure at 24.9% (below Krylenko's 40%), but Krylenko himself at a meeting in 1934 recalled the judges gave Article 51 in 60% of cases in that first period. I. Bulat, "God borby za okhranu sotsialiticheskoi sobstvennosti," *SIu*, 1993, no. 15, 1–2; GARF, f.353sch, op.16s, d.11, 127–128; "O zadachakh organov iustitsii, doklad t. Krylenko," *SIu*, 1934, no. 9, 3.

the Urals, 90%. Another way legal officials coped with the excessive harshness of the Law was ignoring it. Some investigators and judges continued during the fall of 1932 to prosecute persons who stole from kolkhozy under Article 162 of the RSFSR Criminal Code, which provided much milder punishments. This approach was especially pronounced in the Western Region, in Gorkii Region, in Leningrad Region, and in the Chechen Republic (where in some districts the Law of August 7 was not used at all).[11]

The efforts by judges to soften or bypass the Law of August 7 were matched by "silent opposition" to the Law on the part of Russian society. Even politically active persons, according to historian Oleg Khlevniuk, often failed to cooperate in the Law's enforcement. Thus, Komsomol members who witnessed thefts pretended not to have seen them, and members of party *aktivy* failed to join in the struggle against theft. For their part, officials tried to suppress reports on thefts in institutions.[12]

To combat resistance to the Law on the part of people's court judges, the Collegium of Narkomiust decided on November 17 to deprive those judges of the right to use Article 51 in cases under the Law. Instead, they could make representations to the regional courts and ask permission to use the Article in particular cases but not apply it on their own. In exceptional circumstances, where the poverty of the accused had prompted a small theft, courts were to consider dropping the case entirely (through Article 6 of the Criminal Code) rather than convicting and applying Article 51. Despite this new prohibition, most people's court judges went right on using Article 51, at least for the rest of the year. The Article's use declined sharply only after Stalin's speech of January 7, 1933.[13]

The resistance of judges to the Law, in spite of its political significance, reflected unwillingness to violate their personal sense of justice. As one judge told Krylenko, "I will not raise my hand to lock up a person for ten years for stealing four ears." Krylenko told the Central

[11] Bulat, "God borby;" Shliapochnikov, "Zakon 8 avgusta." In Leningrad Region, judges used Article 162 for 90% of relevant thefts. V. Maslov and N. Chistiakov, "Stalinskiie repressii i sovetskaia iustitsiia," *Kommunist*, 1990, no. 10, 106–107.

[12] O.V. Khlevniuk, *1937-i: Stalin, NKVD. i sovetskoe obshchestvo* (Moscow, 1992), 25.

[13] GARF, f.353sch, op.16s, d.11, 127–133 (Postanovlenie Kollegii Narkomiusta ot 17 noiabria 1932g.); A.S. Shliapochnikov, "Okhrana obshchestvennoi (sotsialisticheskoi) sobstvennosti," ZaSZ, 1935, no. 1, 14–17. Composite data cited by Procurator-General Vyshinskii in April 1933 (through March) suggests no decline in the use of Article 51 before Jan. 1 (GARF, f.8131sch, op.27s, d.21, 32), but in a 1934 speech Krylenko claims that the decline began in late November after the Narkomiust resolution ("O zadachakh organov iustitsii").

Committee in January 1933 that this attitude represented a widespread and stubborn mindset. "We are dealing," he reported, "with deep prejudices bred with mother's milk, with traditions of old forms of bourgeois legal thought, the idea that one must judge not from the political directives of party and government but from considerations of a 'higher justice.' "[14]

Judges at higher courts also avoided the full force of the Law. Although regional court judges heard the more serious cases that could lead to capital punishment, they limited death sentences to 4% of total convictions under the Law. Moreover, the Russian Supreme Court reversed nearly half of those sentences (without guidance from the Politburo Commission on Court Cases), and the Praesidium of the Central Executive Committee pardoned still more. According to Krylenko, the total number of persons actually executed under the Law in the RSFSR as of January 1 did not exceed 1,000.[15]

Soviet judges had good reason to react skeptically to many of the cases that reached them. For one thing, the vast majority of cases under the Law involved small or petty thefts committed by peasants. For another, the quality of case preparation had reached a nadir even for Soviet conditions. In mid-November, before the grain collection campaign went into high gear, most cases under the Law were investigated by police, who ignored the relevant circumstances and failed to observe elementary

---

14 RTsKhIDNI, f.17, op.2, d.514, vyp.2, 17–21 (Rech Krylenko). A legal official from the North Caucasus gave the same observation a positive interpretation. To him judges had manifested "judicial conscience" in finding ways to curb the impact of the Law of August 7. "Na vosmon rashirenom," *SIu*, 1933, no. 7, 7.

15 RTsKhIDNI, f.17, op.2, d.514, vyp.2, 19–21; GARF, f.353sch, op.16s, d.11, 127–128. According to a Politburo instruction of Sept. 16, 1932 the RSFSR Supreme Court (and other top courts) engaged in reviews of death sentences issued under the Law of August 7, 1932, were to conduct their reviews within forty-eight hours of receipt of the case files. Their decisions were to be final and, when positive, implemented as soon as possible. This procedure was to replace the established procedures for review of death penalties, thereby implying that the Politburo Commission would not participate. See Khlevniuk, *Staliniskoe Politbiuro*, 61–62. Note that this instruction says nothing about the process of pardoning, and other evidence (e.g. Krylenko's speech to the 1933 January Plenum) indicates that the Central Executive Committee continued issuing pardons in cases of the Law of August 7. RTsKhIDNI, f.17, op.2, d.514, vyp. 2, 21.

Data on the number of death sentences issued in 1932 according to the Law of August 7, 1932, show some variation, reflecting no doubt the weakness of reporting on crime and punishment during these difficult times. Thus, according to one source in the USSR, as a whole there were 5,320 sentences (in the general courts of the RSFSR, 2,686; of Ukraine 1,297, of Belorussia 83; of Uzbekistan, 56; of Turkmenistan 27; of Tadzhikistan 27; of Azerbaizhan 115; of Armenia 7; and in the transport courts 812 and military tribunals 208) and another source sets the total at 6,833. GARF, f.9474, op.17, d.30, 170,222; op.1, d.76, 110. These sources give no exact data on the implementation of sentences.

demands of procedure. "Intolerable simplifications" were widespread. For their part, judges were also careless, sometimes combining into one trial unrelated cases. Some judges at the people's courts assigned the death penalty despite the prohibition; and some applied the Law retroactively in cases that lacked the political significance to justify it.[16]

The changes in the larger political context during winter 1932–1933 assured that the Law of August 7 would be used even more frequently, severely, and carelessly. The breakdown of legality and fanning of repression took particularly extreme forms in the major grain producing areas where the famine had begun. "In virtually every kolkhoz and settlement we have dozens, hundreds of cases of theft of wheat," reported the North Caucasus party secretary Sheboldaev, "and especially all over the Kuban." And various rural officials (kolkhoz chairmen included) committed the sins of holding back grain for their starving members or failing to extract the last morsels from them.[17] The emergency plan to confront this kulak sabotage identified three settlements (*stanits*) for special attention, and to each of these city authorities of Krasnodar sent a team of investigators, procurators, and judges. The legal officials stood ready to deal on the spot with thefts of grain or resistance to grain collection by rural officials. Already by the end of November the three settlements alone had generated thirty-three cases against rural officials who either "hid grain," "resisted the procurement plan," or "sold grain to the peasants."[18] At the end of the year, another fifteen settlements were added to the blacklist and received similar treatment. According to the historian Viktor Danilov, nearly half of the Communist officials were "purged" and in most cases prosecuted as well. There were also instances of the deportation of whole villages, in which the OGPU played a greater part than legal officials.[19]

This attack on rural officials was directed from the Politburo, which dispatched special commissions to force the collection of grain. Stalin ordered his colleagues to use criminal prosecutions toward this end.

[16] Ibid., 129–133; S. Botvinnik, "Organy iustitsii v borbe za provedenie zakona 7 avgusta," *SIu*, 1934, no. 24, 1–4.

[17] B. Sheboldaev, "Slomit sabotazh seva i khlebozagotovok, organizirovannyi kulachestvom v raionakh Kubani," *Partrabotnik severnogo kavkaza*, 1932, no. 25–26, 3–12.

[18] Liburkin (procurator from Krasnodar), "V borbe za khled i sev," *SIu*, 1933, no. 2–3, 28–29; "O khode chistki selskikh partiinykh organizatsii," Postanovlenie obed inenogo zasedaniia biuro Sev-Kav.kraikoma i prezidium KraiKK VK (b) ot 24 noiabria 1932, *Partrabotnik severnogo kavkaza*, 1932, no. 27–28, 42–45.

[19] V.P. Danilov and N.A. Ivnitskii, "Leninskii kooperativnyi plan i ego osushchestvlenie s SSSR," in Danilov, ed., *Ocherki istorii kollektivizatsii selskogo khoziaistva v Soiuznykh respublikakh* (Moscow, 1963), 155; Nobuo Shimotamai, "A Note on the Kuban Affair: the Crisis of Kolkhoz Agriculture in the North Caucasus," *Acta Slavica Iaponica* 1 (1983), 46–47.

Furious that local authorities in a district near Dneprpetrovsk had allowed *kolkhozy* to hold back grain for seeding, Stalin declared that "deceivers of the party and swindlers, carrying out a kulak policy under the flag of agreement with the general line of the Party," these villains "should be arrested immediately, freed from their posts, and given five to ten years each" (this under another section of the Law of August 7). The result was a series of trials of local officials for "criminally frustrating grain deliveries" and "organizing kulak sabotage."[20]

Only in early January, at a Plenum of the Central Committee of the Bolshevik party, did Stalin publicly vent his rage about theft. In a widely publicized speech he called theft of socialist property "a counterrevolutionary outrage" and declared that the Law of August 7 represented "the basis of revolutionary legality at this time." At the same meeting, Justice Commissar Krylenko responded to his master by calling for more executions of thieves. Krylenko condemned the USSR Supreme Court and Praesidium of the Central Executive Committee for overturning death sentences and awarding pardons. He even proposed that judges at the people's courts be given the right to impose capital punishment. Krylenko repeated his tough stance a week later at a meeting of the Collegium of Narkomiust, but met resistance from some of his colleagues.[21]

Stalin's speech had a dramatic effect on implementation of the Law of August 7. Over the next few months prosecutions under the Law increased fourfold, and most convicts received the full ten-year term of imprisonment, despite the fact that they were peasants who had stolen small amounts of grain. The awarding of penalties below the legal limit (through Article 51) fell sharply to the level of 10% (according to most sources) or 20% (in data cited by Procurator-General Vyshinskii). The proportion of convicts who received the death penalty rose from 4% to 5%.[22] In short, under sufficient pressure most judges yielded. Stalin's personal intervention and the threat of sanctions that accompanied it prompted Soviet judges to deliver widespread convictions and severe punishments under the Law of August 7 even though they violated the judges' personal sense of justice. But gaining the compliance of judges came at a price – the price of excess and suspension of personal responsibility that accompanies the worst kind of campaigns.

---

[20] A. Ilin, "Kollektivizatsiia: Kak eto bylo," *Pravda*, Sept. 16, 1988, 3: Conquest, *Harvest of Sorrow*, chap. 12; United States Congress, Commission on the Ukrainian Famine, *Report to Congress* (Washington, D.C., 1988), xv.

[21] I. Stalin, "Itogi pervoi piatiletki," in Stalin, *Voprosy Leninizma*, 11th ed. (Moscow, 1952), 427–429; RTsKhIDNI, f.17, op.2, d.514, vyp.2, 20.

[22] Botvinik, "Organy iustitstii;" A. Shliapochnikov, "Okhrana obshchestvennoi (sotsialisticheskoi) sobstvennosti," *ZaSZ*, 1935, no. 1, 14–17; Shliapochnikov, "Zakon 7 avgusta." GARF, f.8131sch, op.27s, d.21, 32.

In prosecuting cases of theft during the winter of 1933 legal officials in the villages all but abandoned legal procedures. Most cases (90% according to one report) received their "investigation" from the police; and procurators did not bother to give them a rubber-stamp. Rudimentary at best, the investigations by police and investigators alike commonly failed to establish the fact of the theft, when it occurred, whether it was serious, the circumstances and social background of the prime offenders, and the participation of other suspects. The investigations did meet the demand for "good tempos." In the Ivanovo Industrial Region (late fall 1932), one-half of the investigations were completed in a day and another quarter in three days. In the Ukraine most cases were completed in one or two days. Under the circumstances there was little chance to protect the rights of the accused. Indulging in what critics called "the crudest simplifications of procedural rules," investigators failed to present the accused with the charge and give him access to the file before the trial.[23] Trials were no better. Despite the seriousness of the charges, in Russia judges at people's courts heard most of the cases under the Law of August 7. In Zvenigorod district, they did so without witnesses and 45% were canceled on appeal. In another district in the Middle Volga, hearings were so flawed that 87% of the verdicts were cancelled. In many places persons other than judges performed judicial duties. Thus, in the Middle Volga a bailiff heard seventy cases. In Belorussia, a procurator reported in March 1933, grain procurements were fulfilled but only "by mobilizing others [sic] to help with investigations and trials." An official from Gorkii Territory reported that his territorial court had just confirmed twenty-two "spare" members of the court and distributed them to handle cases. Their quality proved low, for, "there exists the view . . . that anyone can judge." This was no doubt true, if judges followed the direction of one regional court judge. He instructed the judges of his people's courts, "You have eyes. Read the accusation of the police. They do not write for nothing. . . . There is such a Law of August 7. Take it, read it, and fire off ten years."[24]

The disappearance of a semblance of legality in the actions of legal officials in the villages fanned the flames of arbitrary repression. The repression included beatings of peasants who refused to work for the kolkhoz (ordered by district officials) and midnight seizures of property

[23] N. Lagovier, "Nedochety predvaritelnogo rassledovaniia po delam o khishcheniiakh sotsialisticheskoi sobstvennosti," *SIu*, 1932, no. 35–36, 8–9; "Orhan iustytsii v boroba za khlib," *Revoliutsiine pravo*, 1933, no. 1, 1–5; "Na vosmom rashirennom," part 2, *SIu*, 1933, no. 8, 5–12; "Rassledovanie del o khishcheniiakh," *SIu*, 1933, no. 4, 6–9.

[24] "Na vosmom rashirennom," part one; N. Krylenko, "Praktika primeneniia Zakona ot 7 avgusta 1932 g.," *ZaSZ*, 1934, no. 6, 1–10, at 7.

without warrants or inventories.[25] But above all, there was a rise in arrests, with and without grounds, by all sorts of unauthorized persons, or as Stalin put it in May, "by anyone who felt up to it." To be sure, groundless arrests and pretrial detention that exceeded the rules were nothing new; they had been part of campaign practice since fall 1929.[26] By all accounts, the situation in 1933 was worse than before. To procurators examining cases of abuse later in the year, the actions of activists making arrests sometimes resembled the "vigilantism" (*samosudy*) perpetrated by peasant resisters. At the initiative of Procurator-General Vyshinskii, the Supreme Court of the USSR directed judges to qualify vigilante actions by officials as instances of "exceeding authority" (Article 110 of the RSFSR Criminal Code).[27]

The state of illegality in the Ukraine rivaled that in the worst parts of Russia, but prosecutions according to the Law of August 7 during winter 1933 stood at half the rate per capita as that recorded in the RSFSR. The lower rate reflected the fact that in the Ukraine only regional courts could hear cases according to the Law and not also people's courts as in Russia. All the same, the convictions by regional courts in the Ukraine consisted mainly of petty thefts, a head of cabbage or handful of ears of wheat – 89.5%, as opposed to 51.5% in the RSFSR. When higher courts reviewed convictions according to the Law after the Instruction of May 8 had called a halt to mindless prosecutions, they left intact only 43.6% of the sentences of Ukrainian courts as opposed to 54.2% from courts in Russia.[28]

The deterioration of the conduct of the procuracy and courts during winter 1933, especially in the application of the Law of August 7, called for a response from central legal officials. Most of them just waited for the storm to pass. They were loath, if not also afraid, to criticize policies and practices that Stalin himself had promoted. But there was one exception, and that was Aron Solts, Old Bolshevik and self-appointed conscience of

---

25 "V Kollegii NKIu," *SIu*, 1933, no. 19, 22–23.

26 "O primeneniiu repressivnykh mer v otnoshenii kulakov i drugikh sryvaiushchikh zagatovki i sbor nalogov i platezhei," Pismo Zam. Prok. oblasti vsem okruzhnym prokuroram zapadnoi oblasti ot 26 okt. 1929, WKP 261, 22–23; "O borbe s nezakonnymi arestami," Tsirkuliar no. 51 Narkomiusta ot 24 aprelia 1930 g., *SIu*, 1930 no. 12, 32; A. Aldekeev, *Na strazhe zakonnosti (Stanovlenie i razvitie prokuratury Kazakhskoi SSR)* (Alma-Ata, 1981), 87. See also Lynne Viola, "L'ivresse de succès: Les cadres Russes et le pouvoir Soviétique," *Revue d'Etudes Slaves*, 64:1 (1992), 75–101.

27 GARF, f.8131sch, op.27s, d.24, 108–112; "O kvalifikatsii samosudov," Postanovlenie 45 Plenuma ot 23 oktiabria 1933, in A.N. Vinokurov, ed., *Sbornik postanovlenii, raz'iasnenii i direktiv Verkhovnogo Suda SSSR deist. na 1 aprelia 1935 g.* (Moscow, 1935), 97.

28 GARF, f.9474sch, op.16s, d.80 (Shliapochnikov, "Prestupnost v SSSR"), 24–25; f.8131sch, op.27s, d.21, 12–13; A. Vyshinskii "XVII parts'ezd i nashi zadachi," *SIu*, 1934, no. 9, 6–13.

the party in the legal realm. In his twin roles as member of the Russian Supreme Court and the head of Rabkrin's Department of Legal Affairs, Solts knew about the implementation of the Law in the countryside. Within days of the January Plenum he began pressing to limit use of the Law. On the basis of a survey (*reviziia*) conducted by his Department, Solts called for a return to the use of Article 162 of the Criminal Code for most theft cases – a position that Commissar Krylenko criticized at a meeting of Narkomiust's Collegium on January 19. But Solts was not inhibited. He responded by telling other high legal officials that it was their duty to go to the Central Committee and tell Stalin about the realities of the Law in practice. Solts himself did precisely that. On February 1, 1933, he "put the question" to the leadership – presumably at the meeting of the Politburo which Solts did attend – and it responded with a secret Politburo resolution that directed judges to separate out (*otseiatsia*) the cases of petty theft committed out of need or lack of consciousness (and not by recidivists) and apply to them Article 162 instead of the Law of August 7.[29] This decision promised to stop many of the egregious injustices associated with the Law. According to Krylenko, no less than 40% of rural thefts would qualify for removal from the scope of the Law. Despite his earlier misgivings, Krylenko quickly followed the new line emanating from the leadership. On February 14 the Collegium of Narkomiust issued its own resolution repeating the Politburo resolution and adding that for petty thefts that still did not qualify for Article 162 judges should go back to using Article 51 within the limits established by earlier Narkomiust directives or drop the cases.[30]

But this change in policy had little effect in practice. In the context of famine and the extraordinary campaign against the peasantry, most legal officials observed neither Narkomiust's February resolution nor the Central Committee instruction that had inspired it.[31] The secret status of the two documents could not have helped their diffusion. Neither was ever discussed in the press or any journal. Moreover, Solts's argument that the Law of August 7 was overused got almost no public support during February or March. A notable exception was a fellow Rabkrin official, Shmuel Fainblit, whose report on legal practice in the Lower Volga criti-

---

[29] GARF, f.353sch, op.16s, d.11, 159–164; f.8131sch, op.27s, d.40 (Stenogramma Pervogo Vsesoiuznogo soveshchaniia sudebno-prokurorskikh rabotnikov, preniia), 119–120; f.8131sch, op.27s, d.21, 12; RTsKhIDNI, f.17, op.163, d.554, 8. For the protocol of the Politburo meeting of February 1, 1993, see Khlevniuk, *Stalinskoe Politbiuro*, 224.

[30] GARF, f.8131sch, op.27s, d.21, 12–15; 40–50 (Postanovlenie Kollegii NKIu . . . ot 14 II 1933); f.353sch, op.16s, d.11, 166–174.

[31] Data on convictions under the Law of August 7 broken down by quarters show substantially more cases heard by judges in the second quarter of 1933 than the first quarter. See Shliapochnikov, "Okhrana obshchestvennoi."

cized the many cases of small thefts under the Law, as well as the "race for numbers of cases." The main reason why judicial practice did not change lay elsewhere. Trial court judges, especially in the grain-producing areas, remained under extraordinary pressure from local politicians to continue using the Law of August 7 as Stalin had directed at the January Plenum. As a result, the main effect of the February resolution of Narkomiust came not at trials but in appellate hearings, as cassation panels converted convictions under the Law to Article 162.[32]

But Comrade Solts did not give up the fight. Under the auspices of his agency, Rabkrin, he organized in mid-March an All-Union Party Meeting on Court Work. This unique gathering convened 167 delegates from the control commissions, courts, and procuracy offices, corrective-labor institutions, lay courts, economic organizations, the army, press, and Komsomol; and included representatives from most republics and regions. The conference heard speeches by Krylenko, Vyshinskii, and Solts and included four days of debate, during which delegates reported on the deterioration of legal practice. The reports and resolutions of the conference were "confirmed," but none was published.[33] What did reach print, however, both in the journal of Rabkrin and eventually in that of Narkomiust, was an extract from the speech of Aron Solts.

Nearly two months before the Instruction of May 8, in which Stalin quietly called a halt to mass prosecutions in the countryside, Solts openly advocated restraint. To begin, Solts contended that the Law of August 7 was overused. The Law's purpose, he reminded listeners, was to confront the organizers of thefts that undermine socialist construction; the law was not meant to be used for everyday petty thefts or against the "toilers." The burden of choice, Solts claimed, lay with the judges. Each judge should avoid a formal approach, distinguish types of theft, and listen to his or her conscience. "Every judge must think and check what he has done so that there will be fewer of these cases." "Better less, but better"; "it is not the quantity but the quality that counts." Moreover, Aron Solts insisted, "This is not a law for a longer period of time. It must deliver its blow so that the situation will change." Solts's characterization of the Law contrasted with that of Stalin's henchman Lazar Kaganovich, who a day or two before had

32 S. Fainblit, "Nado pretvoriat direktivy v zhizne" (Rabota organov iustitsii Nizhne Volzskogo kraia), *Za tempy, kachestvo, proverku*, 1933, no. 6, 38–40; Krylenko, "O zadachakh organov iustisii," A. Shliapochnikov. "Organy iustitsii RSFSR v borbe za okhrany obshchestvennoi (sotsialisticheskoi) sobstvennosti," *SIu*, 1934, no. 2, 10.

33 "Informatsionnoe soobshchenie," *SIu*, 1933, no. 6, inside cover. Although the debates were not published, one may assume that they were no less frank than those at the Eighth Conference of Justice Workers of the RSFSR, which was held directly after the Party Conference. For a summary of parts of those discussions, see "Na vosmom rasshirennom," parts one and two.

jokingly announced to a congress of high-performing kolkhozniki (shockworkers) that "such laws live for decades, even centuries."[34]

Shortly after the Conference Aron Solts's advocacy of restraint in the use of the Law of August 7 gained further official support. On March 27 a meeting of the Praesidium of the Central Executive Committee discussed the matter and issued its own (secret) resolution repeating the earlier restrictions on the use of the Law set out in the Politburo resolution of February 1. Once again, the leadership repeated its new stance that the Law of August 7 was to be reserved for serious actions by class-hostile elements. In cases of petty thefts by peasants, committed out of need or lack of consciousness, judges were to apply Article 162. Although this resolution did eventually become the authoritative guideline for use of the Law of August 7, it had no impact until after Stalin's Instruction of May 8.[35]

Another voice against repression and illegality in the areas of the Famine belonged to the writer M.S. Sholokhov. In April 1933, Sholokhov sent two letters to Stalin, documenting the horrors in the Kuban (North Caucasus) and calling for investigation from Moscow. Stalin responded by ordering the dispatch of supplementary grain to the two districts whose desperate straits Sholokhov had bemoaned and agreeing to send Matvei Shkiriatov from the Central Control Commission to investigate the situation. (This investigation would lead in due course to a Politburo meeting on June 4, 1933, with Sholokhov in attendance, at which a number of local party officials from the districts in question would be fired for "committing excesses".) Still, Stalin was unwilling to accept Sholokhov's criticisms of his policies at face value. In a handwritten reply to the writer (dated May 6, 1933) Stalin agreed that there was no justification for "outrages." Nonetheless, the leader insisted, "you see only one side of the matter. The grain growers in your region (and not only yours) are conducting sabotage and leaving the Red Army without grain. [They are waging] a war with Soviet power."[36]

Even as Stalin answered Sholokhov so bluntly, the leader must already have had concerns about the repression. For two days later Stalin told his subordinates that the time had come to cut down on coercion and revive the authority of law enforcement agencies. In the secret,

---

[34] A. Solts, "Zadachi sovetskogo suda v novoi obstanovke" [Iz doklada na Vsesoiuznom partsoveshchanii po voprosam sudebnoi raboty], *Za tempy, kachestvo, proverku,* 1933, no. 7–8, 27–32, and *SIu,* 1933, no. 10, 1–3; "Surovo karat vragov narodov," *Izvestiia* (March 16, 1933), 1.

[35] GARF, f.353sch, op.16s, d.13, 27–29; f.9474sch, op.16s, d.79, 14–15.

[36] "Rech tovarishcha N.S. Khrushcheva," *Pravda,* March 10, 1963, 1–3; RTsKhIDNI, f.558, op.1, d.3459, 1–6; *Pisma I.V. Stalina V.M. Molotovu, 1926–1936 gg. Sbornik dokumentov* (Moscow, 1995), 245–246. See also "Sholokhov i Stalin, Perepiska nachala 30-kh godov," *Voprosy istorii,* 1994, no. 3, 3–25.

though much cited, Instruction of May 8, 1933, addressed to all party and soviet workers and all agencies of the OGPU, courts and procuracy, Stalin and Molotov ordered: (1) an end to arrests by persons other than law enforcement officials and the confirmation of all pretrial detentions by the procurators; (2) the end of the resettlement of whole villages; and (3) reduction by half, from 800,000 to 400,000, of the number of persons held in prisons and colonies (excluding camps).

Stalin and Molotov's diagnosis of the situation was grave. "We know," they wrote, "that mass arrests continue, and they are made by persons without the authority to do so – kolkhoz chairmen, chairmen of rural soviets, party secretaries, district and territorial authorities. They arrest whomever they see fit, and this in turn incites the proper agencies to make arrests without grounds, acting on the principle 'first arrest, then look into the matter.' " In revealing that the prisons (and the small network on agricultural and juvenile colonies) held at least 800,000 inmates (many of them awaiting trial), the leaders were telling informed persons how far things had gone. The prisons of the USSR (dating from tsarist times) had an official capacity of about 175,000. Within two months a massive release of prisoners (*razgruzka*) did occur, so that in July the official head count stood at 397,284.[37]

The Instruction of May 8 also had special significance for law and criminal policy. First, in justifying the changes, the leaders declared that the era of extraordinary repression had ended and the battle against theft had run its course. "The three-year war in the countryside is over. The victory has been won; the kolkhoz has conquered. An important part of that victory was the battle of 1932 against theft." To central legal officials these words signaled that the Law of August 7 should be reserved for the most serious, large-scale thefts. Even thefts connected with the spring harvest campaign – a Narkomiust directive indicated – were to be qualified under Article 162 and middle and poor peasants given terms in prison only when their acts reflected mercenary motives. Narkomiust did not supply this interpretation on its own initiative, but based its directive on a joint resolution of the Central Executive Committee and Council of People's Commissars SSSR.[38] However, the orders of central agencies, legal and governmental, still influenced practice only gradually. District-level political officials in many areas continued to press for wide use of the Law of August 7 and went so far as to fire judges who refused to use it as an instrument of repression. As

---

[37] "Instruktsiia vsem partiino-sovetskim rabotnikam i vsem organam OGPU, suda, i prokuratury," (sekretno) ot Predsedatelia SNK V. Molotov (Skriabin) i Sekretaria TsK VKP (b) I. Stalin, ot 8 maia 1933, WKP 178, 135–136; GARF, f.353sch, op.16s, d.13, 78–79.
[38] "Instruktsiia vsem;" GARF, f.353sch, op.16s, d.13, 44–46.

a result, Aron Solts complained in October 1933, old patterns of conduct continued. Some judges still gave long terms of prison to peasants convicted of stealing trifles. Illegal arrests and vigilante actions remained commonplace. There were places where the substitution of Article 162 for the Law had not begun and where judges continued to misapply the death penalty, despite the fact that the Russian Supreme Court overruled most of these sentences.[39] On the global level, however, prosecutions in rural theft cases did move from the Law of August 7 and back to Article 162 of the Criminal Code of the RSFSR. In the second half of 1933 convictions according to the Law fell to less than half of the number recorded in the first half of the year, while prosecutions using Article 162 rose even more. During 1934 and 1935 the use of the Law plummeted further, reaching in 1936 a mere 4,262 persons for the whole RSFSR (as opposed to 103,388 in 1933). In the Ukraine the drop was even more precipitous.[40] Second, in spelling out the rules and regula-

---

[39] Ibid., 78–79.

[40] Convictions under the Law of August 7, 1932, in the general courts of the RSFSR were recorded as follows:

1932	22,347
1933	103,388
1934	37,729
1935	12,827
1936	4,262
1937	1,177
1938	858
1939	241
1940	346

During World War II, use of the Law revived and reached at its height 4,190 in 1944. *Source:* GARF, f.9492sch, op.2s, d.42 (Dvizhenie osuzhdennykh obshchimi sudami RSFSR za 1927–1946 gg.), 127.

The pattern of convictions under the Law and Article 162, Sections g and d, in the general courts of the RSFSR and the equivalents in the Ukraine (i.e., excluding transport courts and military tribunals) was as follows:

RSFSR		Law of August 7th	Article 162 g/d
1933	I	69,523	54,903
	II	33,865	97,236
1934	I	19,120	70,480
	II	14,609	68,720
1935	I	6,706	45,035
Ukraine			
1933		12,767	65,504
1934		2,757	34,489
1935		730	32,364

Source: GARF, f.9474sch, op.16s, d.80, 24–25.

tions for the making and sanctioning of arrests, the Instruction of May 8, 1933, gave new authority to procuracy bodies and conferred on legal procedures an importance that they had lacked since the onset of collectivization. In the course of 1933 and 1934 politicians and jurists seeking to restore the authority of law and bring normalcy to the administration of justice would cite this instruction, along with the earlier edict of June 25, 1932, "On Revolutionary Legality," as sources for a new policy.

But Stalin and Molotov's announcement that legal procedures mattered did not end mass repression in the countryside, any more than it stopped prosecutions according to the Law of August 7. Despite the self-congratulatory phrases in the Instruction, the process of collectivization was yet to be completed in some parts of the USSR, and local officials condoned and even encouraged the continuation of abuses. In the Western Region, observers reported in the fall of 1934, self-directed searches and arrests, beatings of detainees, and vigilante acts perpetrated by rural officials, while procurators and judges stood on the sidelines and watched. Similar repressions were observed in Central Asia, parts of the Ukraine, Western Siberia, Cheliabinsk, and Voronezh regions. According to the procuracy of the Far Eastern Territory, the Instruction of May 8 did not reach all party officials in the periphery. As a result, some of them were unaware of their responsibility for curtailing repression and thought that this was a matter only for procurators and investigators.[41]

Moreover, excessive and groundless prosecutions of kolkhoz chairmen and other rural officials had emerged as a tool of rural administration, and, at least until the Great Purge, a substitute for regulation and supervision. As a rule, district officials had no regular contract with the villages. Communication by mail or telephone was unreliable. The periodic visits by district level personnel (every few months at most) turned into moments for uncovering mistakes and reacting to shortcomings, real or imaginary. Criminal charges were laid on the slightest pretext: discovery of some spoiled potatoes or missing fodder; the presence of a sick horse; or a shortfall in the harvest. Laying the charges, usually of negligence, were either plenipotentiaries or the police; by 1935 involvement by district procuracy officials had become rare.[42] Contemporary

---

[41] "O sudebnoi praktike po delam, sviazannym s uborkoi i gospostavkami 1934 goda," Postanovlenie 49 Plenuma Verkhovnogo Suda SSSR ot 28 dekabria 1934, SZ, 1935, no. 2, 58–59; "Rabota organov suda i prokuratury Zapadnoi oblasti," Postanovlenie Narkomiusta RSFSR ot 11/X 1934, SIu, 1934, no. 29, 4–5; Popov, "Gosudarstvennoi terror;" RTsKhIDNI, f.17, op.165, d.47, 50.

[42] R. Rausov, "Organy iustitsii–na borbu za ulushchenie pochotovo-telegrafnoi i telefonnoi sviazi," SIu, 1933, no. 9, 19; Mitrichev, "Dolzhnostnye prestupleniia v kolkhozakh Venevskogo raiona Moskovskoi oblasti," SIu, 1935, no. 2, 4–5; Gusev, "Gorkovskaia

observers recognized the role that criminal prosecutions played in rural administration. One wrote, "The sword of a Damocles stands over the head of all kolkhoz chairmen." In fact, he went on, "a conveyor policy" was in effect, whereby rural officials were charged and prosecuted on a routine basis and then fired or rotated out of positions of authority.[43]

By mid-1935 Stalin decided to take new steps to reduce repression and arbitrary prosecutions in the countryside. One such measure was the issuance of two new secret decrees of the Central Committee and Sovnarkom that condemned unauthorized arrests and sought to make mandatory screening of arrests by the procuracy a reality (edicts of June 17, 1935, and December 19, 1935).[44] Another measure was the amnesty or at least review of convictions for many of the victims of repression in the early 1930s. One decree (June 29, 1935) provided for an amnesty for all current members of kolkhozy who had convictions for crimes bringing no more than five years' imprisonment. Many rural officials of 1932–1934 had been sentenced to noncustodial sanctions and while losing their posts had been allowed to remain members of their collective farms. They were eligible for this amnesty as long as they had good work records. A second decree called for the release of any former officials, regardless of current status, who had been convicted of specific offenses (such as sabotage of the grain campaign).[45] Finally, a third decree (January 16, 1936), this one secret, authorized a review of all convictions according to the Law of August 7, 1932 registered before January 1, 1935. This review came at the initiative of Andrei Vyshinskii, who wrote to the Politburo in December 1935 that the Law of August 7 was still being misapplied. According to a member of the USSR Su-

prokuratura," E.G. Lependi, "Praktika privlechenii k ugolovnoi otvetsvennosti predsedatelei kolkhozov po Gorkovskomu kraiu i 'vyvikhi' v rabote sledstviia," *SIu*, 1935, no. 21, 14–15; Tseliev, "Nado pokonchit."
43 Mitrichev, "Dolzhnostnye prestupleniia."
44 "O poriadke soglasovaniia arestov," Postanovlenie SNK SSSR i TsK VKP(b) ot 17 iiunia 1935 goda, RTsKhIDNI, f.17, op.3, d.965, 75;
45 "Postanovlenie TsIK i SNK SSSR o sniatii sudimosti s kolkhoznikov ot 29 iuliia 1935," *ZaSZ*, 1935, no. 8, 53; "Ob osvobozhdenii ot dalneishego otbyvaniia nakazaniia, sniatii sudimost i vsekh pravoogranichenii, sviazannykh so osuzhdeniem riada dolzhnostnykh lits, osuzhdennykh v svoe vremia v sviazi s sabotazhem khlebozagatovki i vypuska trudovykh zaimov i bon i prochikh denezhnykh surrogatov," Postanovlenie TSiK SSSR ot 11 avgusta 1935, *Za SZ*, 1935, no. 9, 63.
   Implementation of the first decree was placed in the hands of district level commissions, whose members toured the countryside holding ceremonies of purification in the villages. The pardoned kolkhozniki were forced to make appearances, describe their crimes and punishments, and show appropriate contrition. See D. Kokorev, "Sniatie sudimosti s kolkhoznikov Voronezhskoi oblasti," *SIu*, 1936, no. 3, 7. In addition, many of the candidates for this amnesty failed to apply – "evidently because they did not know about the decree" – and the Politburo was forced to extend the period for applications. RTsKhIDNI, f.17, op.163, d.553, 57.

preme Court in 1937, 97% of eligible convictions were reassessed and in over 80% the result was requalification of the charge, mainly to Article 162 (ordinary theft). Sentences were lowered for one-third of the convicts and many were released at once.[46]

Through the case reviews and amnesties Stalin signaled *in public* that the political need for repression in the Soviet countryside was past and that in the new kolkhoz order criminal prosecutions were to play a reduced role. How quickly his message influenced legal practice in rural areas is difficult to determine. For once the rural scene lost its special political significance, the officials of the central procuracy and justice agencies paid less attention to rural prosecutions in their journals, reports, and recorded discussions. The reality was that grain collection campaigns still called for special measures by Procuracy officials well into the 1940s and prosecution of kolkhoz chairmen reached unacceptably high levels again in 1946 and early 1947. I suspect that the continuing role of legal officials in rural administration depended upon the pressures exerted by local politicians and as a result varied with the district and the time.

Ordinary criminal justice during collectivization

In normal times (such as the NEP) the investigation and prosecution of murders, assaults, and hooliganism had high priority in the work of Soviet legal officials. During the years of collectivization the confrontation with all but the most serious crimes of violence took second place to campaign justice. Any legal work unconnected with the agricultural campaigns remained for legal officials to handle after they had contributed to the tasks of the day.

The time available for legal officials to pursue their ordinary duties was in short supply. Campaign responsibilities took most district level (and many regional level) investigators, procurators, and judges away from their offices or courtrooms for months, leaving them empty or operating with reduced staff. In the Western Region in 1930–1931,

[46] GARF, f.9474, op.1, d.109, 12; RTsKhIDNI, f.17, op.163, d.554, 5–8. According to GARF, f.3316, op.84, d.1837, 88–89, 40,879 persons convicted under the Law of August 7, 1932 gained immediate release from confinement as a result of the decree of Jan. 16, 1936. (This citation supplied by Gabor Rittersporn.) Moreover, in a secret resolution on Oct. 23, 1937, the Politburo ordered the Procuracy and Commissariat of Justice to review more cases from the countryside, especially those involving former officials and minor offenses on the part of members of collective farms. The result was further releases and reductions of sentences. Oleg Khlevniuk, "The Objectives of the Great Terror, 1937–1938," in Julian Cooper et al., eds., *Soviet History, 1917–53: Essays in Honour of R.W. Davies* (London, 1995), 168–169.

judges and procurators spent 40% of their time in the villages; and in Tiumen the courtrooms closed.[47] At the same time, local and regional politicians imposed on procurators a variety of administrative tasks unrelated to their legal functions, including the conduct of surveys about the conditions of transport and bridges, shops and bazaars, and so forth. The more time procurators spent away from legal duties, the more investigators working in procuracy offices assumed responsibility for duties of the procurators.[48]

Few of the legal officials in the provinces and localities were prepared to handle the double burden of campaign work and regular duties. The task would have challenged the most qualified and experienced legal officials, but most investigators and judges lacked these attributes. Low salaries and new competition from other sectors like industry and agriculture made it increasingly difficult in the 1930s for the legal agencies to recruit competent staff. Authorities compromised on the already minimal qualifications, and the educational profile of the legal agencies plummeted below the low levels of the 1920s.[49] In some provincial backwaters the cadres problem took extreme forms; in Daghestan, for example, local bosses hired staff for legal agencies "from the streets." Many of those hired did not stay long on the job. Turnover rates for investigators in the early 1930s reached 40% a year. At all times, a portion of the posts in the procuracy and courts remained vacant.[50]

The assumption of time-consuming campaign work forced officials of the short and weakly staffed legal agencies to make adjustments that hurt the conduct of ordinary justice. Investigators abandoned preliminary investigation of serious, nonpolitical crimes, and relied on the police to conduct pretrial inquiries. Judicial officials encouraged the diversion of additional cases to lay courts and administrative procedure and recruited for work in the courts and procuracy a variety of lay

[47] N., "Na chetvertom soveshchanii (Iz zala soveshchanii): part one: *SIu*, 1931, no. 3, 22; "O rabote Tiumenskogo okrsuda."

[48] N., "Na vtorom soveshchanii mestnykh sudebno-prokurorskikh rabotnikov (Nabroski)," *ESIu*, 1929, no. 48, 1126; S. Fainblit, "KK-RKI dolzhny udeliat bolshie vnimaniia rabote suda" (Kak rabotaiut sud i prokuratura v BSSR), *Za tempy, kachestvo proverku*, 1932, no. 2, 55; A.Ia. Vyshinskii, *Sudoustroistvo v SSSR*, 3rd ed. (Moscow, 1936), 205–207.

In August 1933 a circular of Narkomiust forbade procurators from assigning to investigators duties not associated with their jobs. *Sbornik tsirkuliarov i raz'iasnenii Narkomiusta RSFSR* (Moscow, 1934), 15–17.

[49] A.S. Pankratov, "Kadry sovetskoi prokuratury," *Na strazhe sovetskikh zakonov* (Moscow, 1972), 137–151; Kozhevnikov, *Istoriia sovetskogo suda, 1917–1956*, 265–267. *Sostav rukovodiashchikh rabotnikov spetsialistov soiuza SSR* (Moscow, 1936), 308–311.

[50] "Pervoe vsesoiuznoe soveshchanie subdebno-prokurorskikh rabotnikov," *SZ*, 1934, no. 5, 21–25.

substitutes. Finally, legal officials of all stripes reacted to pressure by seeking further ways of cutting corners and rushing proceedings at trial. Each of these adjustments by legal officials contributed to a deterioration of the quality of the administration of justice in ordinary cases.

The police had always played a large role in pretrial inquiries. Most lesser crimes, such as hooliganism, simple theft, and homebrewing, did not call for preliminary investigation. The law stipulated just a brief inquiry by the police. Only more serious crimes – political offenses, crimes by officials, major crimes of property or violence – required a preliminary investigation by an investigator from the procuracy.[51] During the 1920s these legal rules were usually observed. In 1926 procuracy investigators handled nearly 150,000 cases, including the most serious in all categories. Many of these pretrial investigations went to investigators at the provincial level, for serious offenses belonged to the exclusive jurisdiction of the provincial courts. But in 1930 most serious cases were transferred to the people's court, so that the burden of investigation fell to the district procuracy offices, where staff was in shorter supply.[52] Moreover, this shift coincided with the mobilization of district level investigators and procurators onto the campaign trail. Lacking the capacity to handle the investigation of crimes other than political (including all campaign cases), procuracy offices handed over to the police the tasks of gathering evidence and preparing serious criminal cases.

As a result the police assumed an expanded role in pretrial inquiries about ordinary crime. There was a tendency, wrote an official from Narkomiust, for the police to investigate all crimes of violence no matter how complicated, even though they lacked the technology to photograph the bodies of murder victims or expertise in fingerprinting. In Leningrad Region the procurator issued an order (in December 1931) to his district procurators to send the most complicated, nonpolitical cases to the police. Consistent with this order, a study of cases of theft of socialist property in Leningrad Region (in 1932) revealed that investigators handled only 14% of the cases. Most received pretrial inquiries from the police, and some from the OGPU.[53]

---

51 "Ugolovno-protsessualnyi kodeks RSFSR" (1923) in S.A. Golunskii, ed., *Istoriia zakonodatelstva SSSR i RSFSR po ugolovnomu protsessu i organizatsii suda* (Moscow, 1955), 261–262. With the shift of serious crimes to the people's courts a list of crimes requiring a preliminary investigation was provided. Ibid., 489.

52 *Otchet prokuratury RSFSR Prezidiumu VTsIK za 1926 g.* (Moscow, 1927), 111; "O reorganizatsii mestnykh organov iustitsii v sviazi v likvidatstii okrugov," Golunskii, *Istoriia zakonodatelstva*, 521–522.

53 M. Fokin-Belskii, "Sledovatel ili militsiia," *SIu*, 1932, no. 13, 21–22; M. Alperin and G. Sheinin, "Metodika rassledovaniia del o khishchenii obshchestvennoi (sotsialisticheskoi) sobstvennosti," *Voprosy sovetskoi kriminalistiki* (Leningrad, 1933), 13–15.

During the tough campaign of 1932–33 the police also assumed a major share of the pretrial work in cases related to the campaign. In Moscow Region (not even a grain-producing area) 90% of the cases prosecuted according to the Law of August 7 received a police inquiry rather than an investigation.[54]

The substitution of police inquiry for an investigation conducted by an investigator from the procuracy had grave implications. However low the quality of the investigators and whatever shortcuts they took, the capabilities and performance of the police were worse. Composed largely of "chance folk" (*sluchainye liudi*), police units experienced extraordinary turnover, in 1929–1930, nearly 60% of district chiefs and 100% of ordinary policemen. No more than a quarter of the chiefs had received the two-month training course, and hardly any of their subordinates, including the one or two detectives assigned to each district department.[55] Many of the police officials investigating cases neither respected nor understood rules of evidence and forms of procedure. In the name of "simplification," they often failed to compose the required documents and to check with witnesses. When procurators reviewing case files insisted that the police produce more evidence to support their charges, the police grumbled about "interference on the side of the defendant." In one instance, police branded a procurator who had held them to account "an as yet unexposed defender of the class enemy."[56]

Not only investigators but also judges as well required relief from their usual duties in dealing with ordinary, nonpolitical (noncampaign-related) crime. A common response to overload in criminal justice is the shifting of categories of cases to bodies outside the regular courts. By the time the collectivization campaigns were underway, Soviet authorities were using this device. They had started diverting cases during the last years of NEP as a way of reducing court calendars overcrowded with civil and minor criminal cases. Through legislation passed in 1928, they transferred cases of personal insults and petty hooliganism to administrative proceedings (fines applied by the police) and newly established lay bodies, the rural lay courts in the villages, and comrades' courts in the factories. In practice, this move did keep many potential criminal cases from the courts, allowing more time for cam-

---

54 "Na vosmom rasshirennom soveshchanii raabotnikov iustitsii RSFSR," part two: *SIu*, 1933, no. 8, 11.

55 N. Bardulin, "Militsiia i ugolrozysk nuzhdaiutsia v korennoi chistke," *SIu*, 1930, no. 15, 13–16; E.G. Shirvindt, ed., *Administrativnve organy v novykh usloviiakh* (Moscow, 1930), 24–30.

56 L. Skorniakov, "Kak my uprostili protsess rassledovaniia," *SIu*, 1930, no. 28, 12–13; A.Ia. Vyshinskii, "Nashi zadachi," *ZaSZ*, 1935, no. 5, 13; Sirin, "Za sobliudenie protsessualnykh norm, *SIu*, 1935, no. 34, 10.

paign-related cases. Take the example of hooliganism. In 1928 cases of hooliganism made up 40.7% of criminal trials in the RSFSR; in 1933 only 9.7% despite the fact that there had been no decline in rowdy behavior.[57]

Even relief from cases of personal insults and petty hooliganism and the decline in civil cases during the first years of collectivization proved insufficient for judges. The demands of campaign work left them overworked and courthouses understaffed. Local authorities tried to cope with the situation by shifting even more cases to the alternative venues. For example, party bosses in Stalingrad complained in December 1931 that their judges were distracted by "everyday cases" and that these should be heard administratively or by comrades' courts.[58] There are indications that rural lay courts were sometimes pressed by authorities to take on cases that exceeded their jurisdiction. During 1933 Narkomiust even received inquiries about which cases of theft those bodies might hear.[59] The answer was firm: only petty theft and when authorized by a court. Additional, even illegal diversions of criminal cases, from the courts, may have relieved a small part of the pressure of the collectivization period.

More significant in facilitating the work of the courts was the attraction of laymen to assist in their work. The vehicle for this recruitment was the program of "socialist substitutions" launched by authorities in late 1929. Utopian in character, the program had the goal of bringing trusted workers from the factories on a part-time basis into public administration. The program flourished in the realm of justice, where the agencies needed help. Between 1930 and 1933 about 40% of the socialist substitutes worked for the justice agencies.[60]

According to the plan, the workers selected by their enterprises would work alongside of the regular judges (and also procurators). The substitutes would help judges, not take over their responsibilities. Thus, in Moscow eight workers had the opportunity to serve on panels of the RSFSR Supreme Court (each giving up one work day of every ten). In a number of territorial courts in early 1931, workers helped to fill out appeals panels. However, local officials extended "socialist substitu-

---

[57] See Chapter 2. A.A. Gertsenzon, "Klassovaia borba i perizhitki starogo byta," *SIu*, 1934, no. 1, 16–17.

[58] "O perestroike organov iustitsii g. Stalingrada," Postanovlenie biuro Stalingradskogo gorkoma VKP (B) ot 31 dek. 1931, *SIu*, 1932, no. 8, 23.

[59] "Dela o khishchenii sotsialisticheskoi sobstvennosti . . . " Tsiruliar Narkomiusta no. 125 ot 26 iuniia 1933, *SIu*, 1933, no. 15, 6.

[60] F. Niurina, "Opyt sotsialisticheskogo sovmestitelstva v organakh iustitsii," *Za tempy*, 1931, no. 7, 95–97; "Pervoe Vsesoiuznoe soveshchanie sudebno-prokurorskikh rabotnikov: Prenie po dokladam . . . " *SZ*, 1934, no. 6, 34.

tions" well beyond their design. District politicians in the Urals started appointing their own "public judges" and "public procurators," and the idea soon spread to other parts of the country. The problem with "substitutions" of this kind was that the participants had to take over the responsibilities of people's court judges or assist procurators. Public judges at the people's courts heard trials alone, without the guidance of a real judge, and assumed the task of directing the lay assessors! The Narkomiust official in charge of lay participation, Fanni Niurina, criticized this practice and in 1931 her agency issued guidelines limiting the numbers of public judges and calling for their close supervision. But these imprecations had little effect. By 1933–1934 substitutes played a major role at some courts. In the Western Region in 1933 substitute judges in 27 districts conducted 257 circuits and on their own handled 2,340 cases. Similar patterns obtained in the Middle Volga and Stalingrad.[61]

Substitutes did not take part in the work of every court. A study in 1934 of nine regions revealed that in 70% of the districts no public judges at all had been appointed. Overall, there were 774 substitutes for 1,583 people's courts. The uneven distribution assured that in some places there were two or three public helpers for each judge, and these might handle as many as 40 to 50 cases per month. Their quality also varied. While many were party members and some performed well enough to graduate to posts in the judicial agencies, others "had been given too much responsibility too soon." Substitutes also worked in the procuracy. In 1934 they constituted 23% of all assistant procurators. In the city of Moscow 20 of 27 investigators had "substitutes" working at their sides.[62]

The wide use of substitutions in the administration of justice helped to undermine the significance of proper appointments and encouraged justice officials themselves to improvise. In February 1931, for example, Narkomiust authorized the appointment of some people's court judges as "spare members of the regional court," ready for secondment when the need arose. When 22 spares were appointed in Gorkii territory in 1932–1933 and sent to the countryside, the results were so poor that one-fifth of them had to be relieved. At the local level legal officials substituted for one another. In the Far Eastern Territory when a judge fell sick, the procurator went out to the villages to hear trials. Later, he

---

61 *Sbornik tsirkuliarov narkomiusta RSFSR* (1931), 16. Niurina, "Opyt sotsialisticheskogo;" P.G. Volodarskii, *Sotsialisticheskoe sovmestitelstvo v organakh iustitsii* (Moscow, 1934), 13; Moskvichev, "Sotssovmestitelstvo v organakh iustitsii Srednei Volgi," *SIu*, 1934, no. 7, 14–15.

62 Volodarskii, *Sotsialisticheskoe sovmestitelstvo*, 17, 60; "Pervoe vsesoiuznoe soveshchanie: Prenie," *SIu*, 34; 60.

claimed that the local politicians had pressured him. In Azerbaizhan and Armenia, investigators acted as judges. In the Middle Volga, a judge deputized his bailiff to hear 70 cases.[63]

Another kind of improvisation pursued by legal officials in ordinary criminal cases was the adoption of shortcuts. One unauthorized device was to channel cases into the so-called "duty chambers" (*dezhurnye kamery*), courtrooms that provided assembly-line treatment for simple cases that required no preparation. Duty chambers were meant only for these simple cases; and at the sessions judges were supposed to observe elementary standards of procedure. But in the early 1930s duty chambers heard serious cases, including many that involved young offenders. The cases were rushed through the day in court without discussion of motives and often resulted in a sentence of imprisonment. Typically, the hearings at duty chambers produced no protocols – in the case of Rostov-na-Donu on orders of the territorial court![64]

When cases went to a full trial, judges wanted to move them along quickly, and regarded the activities of defense counsel as an obstacle to efficiency. In the early 1930s, even more than before, judges expressed their dislike of counsel and even harassed them during trials. At the same time, some judges displayed close ties with the procurator (when there was one in court) and sometimes gave the impression that everything had been decided in advance. This was not the case in all courtrooms, for the level of acquittals at trial remained constant during the early 1930s at 8–10%, the same level as in the 1920s.[65]

All of these practices – the expanded role of the police in investigations, excessive reliance on administrative procedures and lay courts, the use of socialist substitutions, and the pursuit of shortcuts in the courts – suggest a decline in quality of ordinary justice. The pressure that campaign work placed on the legal agencies took its toll in the performance of normal duties, as well as in the campaigns themselves.

During the early 1930s the number and percentage of weak decisions by courts in the USSR probably increased. While this deterioration might have been offset by changes in appellate practice, it appears that this was not the case. Examination shows that during the early

63 *Sbornik tsirkuliarov Narkomiusta* (1931); "Na vosmom rashirennom," 10; "Pervoe vsesoiuznoe soveshchanie: Prenie," *SIu*, 12; 32.
64 *Sbornik raz'iasnenii Verkhovnogo Suda RSFSR 4* (Moscow, 1935), 340ff.
65 "Pervoe vseosoiuznoe soveshchanie sudebno-prokurorskikh rabotnikov: Doklad Vyshinskogo," *SZ*, 1934, no. 5, 30; "Pervoe vsesoiuznoe soveshchanie sudebno-prokurorskikh rabotnikov: Prenie po dokladam," *SZ*, 1934, no. 6, 38–40; Huskey, *Russian Lawyers and the Soviet State*, 176–178.
   In 1935 the rate of acquittals in the RSFSR was 10.2%. Kozhevnikov, *Istoriia sovetskogo suda*, 283.

1930s neither the percentage of cases appealed nor the proportion changed in cassation increased. In 1931 defendants requested a cassation review (mandatory upon request) in a quarter of criminal cases, and 35% of the reviews led to a change in sentence or verdict. As a result, about 9% of cassation reviews introduced a change in trial decisions, about the same as the rate in 1926 (9.1% of decisions from the people's courts). Moreover, the quality of some of these changes was open to question, as the RSFSR Supreme Court changed the results in almost all of the cassation decisions that it reviewed in supervision. A more serious problem was that defendants failed to appeal many bad decisions from trial.[66]

The deterioration of the administration of criminal justice in ordinary cases came at an unfortunate time. It coincided with the migration of millions of peasants into the cities, some to assume jobs in industry, others to fill seasonal posts. With this massive shift of population and the disruption it produced came a dramatic increase in crimes of violence. Many, if not most, of the incidents fell under the heading of hooliganism.[67]

The increase in acts of hooliganism does not appear in the data on the courts, for by 1932 the police were handling most cases of hooliganism in administrative procedure (90%). Combining data from courts and police, one learns that the number of cases of hooliganism processed by authorities in 1931 stood at twice the level of 1926; and in 1932 at three times! As if this were not enough, the acts defined as hooliganism had become more serious. While in the 1920s nearly half of the charges involved nothing more than personal insults, in the early 1930s even cases handled by the police (supposedly "petty" in nature) commonly involved physical assaults or weapons. By 1932–1933 more than half of the cases of hooliganism that reached the courts came under the charge of "malicious hooliganism." The situation was especially bad in Moscow, where groups of ruffians reportedly terrorized the population in broad daylight. Hooliganistic activity also became in the early 1930s the leading source of murders, replacing "jealousy." (Overall, though, cases of murder decreased.)[68]

[66] "Ulushchit kachestvo raboty sudov," *Slu*, 1931, no. 24, 13–16; "Pervoe vsesoiuznoe soveshchanie: Prenie," *SZ*, 29–31.
[67] L. Vul, "Khuliganstvo v Moskve i borba s nim" *ZaSZ*, 1935, no. 8, 18–21; Peter Juviler, *Revolutionary Law and Order* (New York, 1976), 57–58.
[68] S. Bulatov, "Khuliganstvo i mery borby s nim v rekonstruktivnom periode," *SGiRP*, 1933, no. 4, 63–74; A. Shliapochnikov, "Prestupnost i repressiia v SSSR" (kratkii obzor), *Problemy ugolovnoi politiki*, 1 (1935), 75–100; A. Gertsenzon, "Organy iustitsii v borbe s khuliganstvom," *SZ*, 1935, no. 2, 14–19; A. Gertsenzon and Z. Vyshinskaia, "Okhrana lichnosti i borba s ubiistvami (obzor)." *Problemy ugolovnoi politiki*, 3 (1937), 70, 72.

In addition to hooliganism, crimes by juveniles were also on the rise in the early 1930s. To begin, the disruptions in the countryside caused by deportations and famine produced a new wave of homeless children, to which authorities responded heroically during 1933. Of more lasting significance was the formation of a large cohort of young troublemakers still blessed with a parent. Typically, they consisted of ne'er-do-wells who had quit or been kicked out of school and whose parent(s) lacked means of supervision. Observers thought that the increase in female participation in the workforce contributed to the problem.[69]

Public recognition of the problems of hooliganism and juvenile crime and the attempts to confront them came only in 1934 and 1935, after the adoption by the regime of a policy of restoring the authority of law and legal procedures.

Criminal law, scapegoating, and industry

Collectivization was not the only political cause of the late 1920s and early 1930s. The Soviet regime also waged another war on the industrial front, to expand industry and industrial production at breakneck pace. Since the factories, new and old, were owned and managed by the state, the criminal sanction was readily available as a tool of management. In fact, the criminal law offered a natural supplement to the disciplinary sanctions available to the owners and managers of private firms in other countries, especially when the man in charge of the industrialization drive was Joseph Stalin.

Stalin favored the use of the criminal sanction in the economy. Repeatedly he tried to shape the conduct of the economy's managers through the threat of punishment. Even when the deterrent effect was minimal, Stalin employed the criminal sanction as a means of displacing blame. An example already familiar to the reader is the mass prosecution of the chairmen of kolkhozy for failures in the delivery of grain, a practice that Stalin decided to curtail only in 1935. In fact Stalin had a special penchant for scapegoating, for displacing blame for shortcomings not only in the eyes of others but in his own eyes as well.[70] This feature of Stalin's personality contributed to the broad use of the criminal sanction in the management of the Soviet economy.

---

69 "Rasshirennyi plenum detkomissii VTsIK (3–6 marta, 1934)," *Sbornik po voprosam okhrany detstva*, 1934, no. 2–3, 6–38. "Borba s detskoi prestupnostiu," *Sbornik po voprosam okhrany detstva*, 1935, no. 2, 33–35; V. Tadevosian, "Prestupnaia sreda i nesovershennoletniki," *SIu*, 1935, no. 31, 9–11.

70 Robert Tucker, *Stalin in Power: The Revolution from Above, 1928–1941* (New York and London, 1990), 166.

Scapegoating flourished in the USSR of the early and mid-1930s not only because of Stalin's inclinations but also from the logic of the situation that he created. During the collectivization and industrialization drives, officials in all areas of the economy worked under intense pressure to perform tasks that were often impossible to complete. At all levels in the hierarchies officials were being held personally liable for shortcomings, and it was in their interests to try to shift the blame onto others.

It is important to distinguish what was novel about the industrial prosecutions that occurred during the industrialization drive. The punishment of managers who engaged in such dishonest actions as stealing from their firms, cheating the government or accepting large bribes was not new. All of these practices had been subject to prosecution during the 1920s, more só than in the 1930s. The novelty lay in the use of the criminal sanction as a response to poor performance by a factory or its employees. Thus, in 1929–1931, a dizzying number of circulars (from the Council of People's Commissars, Narkomiust, or other agencies) instructed justice officials to prosecute wayward officials for failing to observe the rules of accounting, disregarding passport regulations by hiring employees without the right documents, delaying the unloading of railroad cars, and other omissions.[71] Likewise, an interpretation of the law issued in 1929 by Narkomiust made it a crime for the managers of a state firm to produce or deliver defective or substandard goods![72] Finally, at the same time the authorities especially encouraged the prosecution and punishment of administrators blamed for accidents and the breakdown of production. Just as "spoiling tractors" had become a criminal offense in the countryside in 1930, so "spoiling machines" and "disorganizing production" became grounds for criminal prosecutions in industry.[73]

The legal tools for these prosecutions consisted of two types of criminal offenses – crimes of service or crimes by officials (*dolzhnostnye prestupleniia*) and state crimes.

The tsarist government shared in the European tradition of regulating the conduct of its officials with the threat of prosecution and had special tribunals for this purpose. The Bolsheviks continued this tradition by

---

[71] *Sbornik tsiruliarov i raz'iasnenii Narkomiusta RSFSR deistvuiushchikh na 1 maia 1934 g.* (Moscow, 1934), 95–216.

[72] *Sbornik tsirklulairov Narkomiusta RSFSR deistvuiushchikh na 1 iiunia 1931 g.* (Moscow, 1931), 81; Ark. Lipkin, "Vnimanie voprosam kachestva produktsii," *SIu*, 1931, no. 2, 21–22.

[73] Although the use of Article 111 in accident cases became widespread in 1929, the circulars of Narkomiust regulating the practice came mainly in early 1931. See F.L. Nakhimson et al., eds., *Sud i prokuratura na okhrane proizvodstva i truda* (Moscow, 1931), 338–360; and *Sbornik tsirkuliarov Narkomiusta* (1931), 84–88.

including in their criminal codes a whole section of "service crimes" (*dolzhnostnye prestupleniia*) and establishing special disciplinary courts to handle some prosecutions. (These courts were soon abolished.) Service crimes included not only dishonest actions such as swindling or bribe-taking but also breaches of duty such as "exceeding or misusing one's authority," and "negligence." Interpreted in a narrow way and applied only to responsible officials, these crimes did not go beyond the tsarist approach to disciplining government officials. But in a state-owned economy there was always the potential for broader application. Starting in 1929, directives of the USSR Council of People's Commissars, the Procuracy, and Narkomiust demanded the application of misuse of authority (Article 109 of the 1926 criminal code) and negligence (Article 111) to officials in industry, trade, and transport for a wide variety of mistakes, accidents, and failures in performance. Moreover, the range of persons treated as "officials" for purposes of prosecution quickly broadened to include not only management but also shop foremen and heads of small railway depots, and sometimes simple employees. Worst of all, these persons could be held criminally responsible not only for actions performed but also for omissions, accidents, failures that were not intentional and often not even the fault of the accused. In the 1930s the most commonly prosecuted service crime became "criminal negligence," that is (in paraphrase) the failure by a person in authority to act or fulfill a duty or the manifestation by such a person of a careless attitude toward service through red tape or slow performance of his duties.[74]

Soviet authorities also created another, sharper weapon for use against wayward officials – a charge of a political offense. Already in the 1920s Soviet criminal law provided that when misuse of office or negligence was committed by a person of "alien social origin" for the purpose of harming the Soviet state, his acts could be qualified as a political charge, especially as "wrecking" (Article 58.7). But this charge was rarely used in part because the courts required a showing of intent to harm the state (as well as of the harmful consequences of the act). Charges of wrecking became much easier to prosecute in January 1928 when the USSR Supreme Court ruled – probably on Stalin's orders – that a showing of "counterrevolutionary intent" was no longer required for a prosecution of "wrecking," only intent to commit the act.[75] This

---

74 Utevskii, *Uchenie o dolzhnostnykh*, esp. 386–394; *Sbornik tsirkuliarov* (1931); Goliakov, *Sbornik dokumentov. On the prosecution of service crimes through 1927, see A.A. Gertsenzon, Borba s prestupnostiu v RSFSR* (Moscow, 1928).

75 "O priamom i kosvennom umysle pri kontrrevoliutsionnom prestuplenii," Raz'iasnenie 18 plenuma Verkhovnogo suda SSSR ot 2 ianvaria 1928 g., *Sbornik postanovlenii, raz'asnenii i direktiv Verkhovnogo Suda SSSR deistvuiushchikh na 1 aprelia 1935g* (Moscow, 1935), 100.

change coincided with the initiation by Stalin of a campaign of repression and intimidation against the "bourgeois specialists," those industrial managers and engineers who were not Bolsheviks. The campaign featured not only the mounting of contrived prosecutions (such as those in the famous Shakhty and Industrial Party show trials), but also the escalation of charges of negligence and abuse of authority into charges of wrecking. The high-pitched atmosphere of 1928–1930 led journalists and even jurists to describe ordinary cases of negligence in political terms. Thus, spoiling machines through ignorance of how to operate them became "petty wrecking."[76]

The industrialization drive that brought the criminal sanction into industry might have led to mass prosecutions of managers. The reckless expansion of old enterprises and construction of new ones produced both a rash of accidents and marked decline in the quality of production. Failures of comparable scope had led to the prosecution and conviction of many kolkhoz chairmen and other rural officials. Yet, while industrial prosecutions received much coverage in the press, the actual volume of these cases – especially after 1930 – was small. There were two main reasons – a shortage of enforcers of the law and Stalin's policy from 1931 of "protecting specialists."

In the early 1930s the main initiators of prosecutions for negligence and abuse of authority in the enterprise were procurators, especially those who worked in the new industrial departments of the regional procuracy offices. Procuracy offices at the district level lacked the staff to pay much attention to industry, especially during the frequent campaigns in the villages, and were likely to do little more than respond to serious accidents.[77] But the criminal law could not serve industrialization if procurators simply "followed the flow of cases." According to the RSFSR Commissar of Justice Krylenko, procuracy officials needed to take an active role, establishing relationships with the staff of important factories and visiting them regularly. Once on the site, procurators were to check for interruptions in production, low-quality output, and accidents. They were also expected to establish assistance groups among the workers to provide signals to the procuracy when troubles arose.

---

[76] F. Kamenskii, "Posobniki vreditelei (porcha oborudovaniia na pische-bumazhnoi fabrike im Zinoveva v Leningrade)," *Sud idet*, 1929, no. 7, 357–360; I. Sadovnikov, "Zadachi prokuratyrai i suda v stroitelnom sezone," *SIu*, 1930, no. 13, 19; Vs. Luppov, "Kak rabotaiut organy iustitsii promyshlennykh raionov Urala," ibid., 1931, no. 19, 24–26.

[77] B. Sakhov, "Organy iustitsii v borbe za kachestvo produktsii i vypolnenie planov kapitalnogo stroitelstva," *SIu*, 1931, no. 1, 14–16; "Borba s iavleniiami vyzyvaiushchimi proryvy v vypolnenii promfinplana mashinostroenii," Postanovlenie Kollegii NKIu ot 1/X 1931 g., *SIu*, 1932, no. 2, 15–16.

The conduct of these on-site visits to factories, known colloquially as "surveys" or "mass check-ups" or "raids," became part of the procuracy's function of general supervision.[78] Instead of focusing upon reviews of the legality of local administrative ordinances and regulations, procurators targeted industry.

To ensure performance of this added responsibility, authorities established industrial departments in the regional and republican procuracies. But the new departments were small (consisting on average of five to six investigators and assistant procurators) and their staff of weak quality. As a result, the departments could supervise no more than a fraction of the factories on their territories and these only superficially.[79] One of the best industrial departments, that of the Leningrad regional procuracy, managed to visit a mere seventy-seven enterprises during 1931, most of them twice. While raiding factories, the Leningrad procuracy officials did take steps to improve production, forcing one director to address problems of safety and sanitation and helping another to obtain raw materials. They also launched prosecutions (between April 1932 and March 1933, against 1,581 persons, including dozens of top officials in the enterprises), but the quality of these prosecutions was especially low. As a result, judges dropped many charges (35% of those from machine-building plants), many trials ended in acquittal (up to 25%), and many more convictions were reversed on appeal. Finally, the punishments assigned in production cases in Leningrad (that is, those relating to accidents and defective production) rarely exceeded a fine or term of corrective work. Only in a handful of cases, involving drunken workers who destroyed machines, did judges resort to imprisonment.[80]

Procurators supervising industry got some help from other officials. Until its demise in 1934 the offices of Rabkrin performed similar supervision of some industrial plants. And OGPU officials rushed to the

---

78 "Rol i zadachi prokuratury po okhrane truda i proizvodstvu" (Tesizy k dokladu tov. Krylenko na 4-om soveshchanii rukovodiashchikh rabotnikov organov iustitsii kraev [obl.] [RSFSR]), *SIu*, 1932, no. 2, 5–8.

79 "O novoi strukture organov prokuraturov," *SIu*, 1931, no. 24, 31–32; *Sbornik tsirkuliarov Narkomiusta* (1931), 40; M.V. Kozhevnikov, "Puti razvitiia sovetskoi prokuratury," part 2; *Uchenye zapiski MGU*, vyp. 147, *Trudy iuridicheskogo fakulteta*, 5 (Moscow 1950), 55.

80 M. Alperin et al., "Perestroika organov iustitsii v borbe za promfinplan," in B.S. Mankovskii and V. Undrevich, eds., *Klassovaia borba i prestupnost na sovremennom etape*, 1 (Leningrad, 1933), 104–141; Albitskii et al., "Kak Leningradskaia prokuratura perestraevaet po-novomu rabotu v promyshlennosti," *SIu*, 1931, no. 2, 17–20. For more detailed analysis of the work of the industrial department of the Leningrad procuracy, see Peter H. Solomon, "Criminal Justice and Soviet Industrialization," in Lewis Siegelbaum and William Rosenberg, eds., *Social Dimensions of Soviet Industrialization* (Bloomington, Ind., 1993), 223–247.

scene of serious accidents (ever vigilant for signs of sabotage or wreck-ing). Overall, though, the Soviet government lacked the capacity to police industry for failures in the production process.

The other obstacle to widespread prosecutions against industrial managers was the policy of protecting specialists adopted by Stalin in 1931. Before that time – from spring 1928 to early 1931 – Stalin had sponsored the persecution of engineers and managers who lacked party credentials or the appropriate class origins. But in 1930 Ordzhonidikze and other top industrial officials fought this policy and by spring 1931 convinced Stalin to end specialist baiting. In May, Narkomiust issued a detailed directive cautioning procurators and judges against unjustified prosecution of managers and specialists and stipulating new proce-dures for vetoing these cases. In June, Stalin made the new line his own explaining in public that specialists had become loyal to the Soviet regime and deserved respect. The RSFSR Supreme Court then an-nounced that it would hold procurators and judges criminally respon-sible for unfounded prosecution of specialists.[81]

The new policy of protecting specialists (instead of persecuting them) led to a precipitous drop in prosecutions against executives in industry.[82] It also removed pressure from justice officials, who had found it difficult to conduct prosecutions against managers who had protection from local politicians or the central agencies. Even before the new line on protecting specialists, prosecutions for defective goods had targeted middle level officials rather than the bosses. From 1931 to 1936 (when the Great Terror revived prosecutions against manag-ers), middle and lower level "officials" (shop foremen, supervisors of railway depots) received the brunt of industrial prosecutions – not just

---

[81] Kendall Bailes, *Technology and Society under Lenin and Stalin* (Princeton, N.J., 1978), chap. 5 and 6; Nicholas Lampert, *The Technical Intelligentsia and the Soviet State* (London, 1979), chap. 3 and 4, 99ff.; "O poriadke privlechenii k ugolovnoi otvetstvennosti khoziaistvennikov i spetsialistov," Tsirk, *NKIu* no. 58 krai (obl) prok. ot 22 maia 1931, *SIu*, 1931, no. 16, 15; *Sbornik raz'iasnenii Verkhovnogo Suda RSFSR*, 3 (Moscow, 1931), 238–241.

[82] Thus, in Moscow Region, instead of the cases tried against 2,500 accused persons in the third quarter of 1931 (the indictments dating in the main from before Stalin's speech), only 56 specialists appeared in the courts of Moscow in the fourth quarter. Similar declines were observed in the Urals and the regional court of the Central Black Earth Region; only in Leningrad Region was there some stability. By spring 1932 the chair-man of the Moscow regional court complained that specialists were getting too much protection. One of them had received a year's corrective work for the rape of a 14-year-old maid, as the judge put it, "so as to avoid a break from production." N. Nemtsov, "Sudebnaia praktika Moskovskogo oblastnogo suda po delam, sviazannym s ohkraniem prav spetsialistov," *SIu*, 1931, no. 12, 1–6; Ark. Lipkin and P. Krasnopet-sev, "Itogi proverki vypolnenii direktiv NKIu o spetsialistakh," ibid., 6–9.

defective goods, but for accidents, production breaks, and other mishaps.[83]

The two most common pretexts for prosecutions against officials in industry during the 1930s were accidents and the production of defective goods. The records of both show how prosecutions were used to displace blame for mishaps away from the leadership and its policies and onto the shoulders of middle and lower level officials. Some of the leaders seem also to have believed that prosecutions could prevent accidents and reduce substandard production, but if either were so, the infrequency and low quality of prosecutions would have mitigated the effect.

There was nothing unusual about the Soviet government's assuming responsibility for trying to reduce accidents. In nineteenth-century England, during a period of expansion in private industry, the government used criminal prosecutions to protect its public from private entrepreneurs responsible for unsafe working conditions or transport. Like other Western governments, however, Great Britain came to emphasize prevention through regulation over prosecution and punishment.[84] This option, however, was unavailable to Soviet authorities. As long as they pursued reckless expansion of industry and pressured managers to produce at almost any cost, it was impossible to reduce accidents through regulation. Of course, criminal prosecutions were no substitute, since they did not prevent accidents. But they did shift the blame from the shoulders of politicians (like Stalin) to employees in the enterprises.

In the USSR of the early and mid-1930s any major accident (with loss of life or limb) was likely to produce a prosecution. Responses to less serious accidents were sporadic and inconsistent, since there were insufficient procurators and investigators to do more. Moreover, the quality of prosecutions in accident cases was low. According to a Leningrad criminologist, either the investigator questioned a few people and drew conclusions without checking documents; or, having heard the accused, "fully ignored their explanations and sent the case on to court."[85]

---

[83] B. Sakhov, "Organy iustitsii v borbe za kachestvo produktsii i vypolnenie planov kapitalnogo stroitelstva," *SIu*, 1931, no. 1, 14–16; Utevskii, *Uchenie o dolzhnostnykh*, 386–394.

[84] For discussion and references, see Solomon, "Criminal Justice and Soviet Industrialization"; also P.W.J. Bartrup and P.T. Fenn, "The Evolution of Regulatory Style in the 19th Century British Factory Inspectorate," *Journal of Law and Society*, 10:2 (Winter 1983), 201–222.

[85] See, for example, "Vzryv na shakhte 'Mariia' na Donbasse," *Sud idet*, 1930, no. 17, 17–18; "Sud nad vinovnikam avarii na zavode im. Stalina," *Pravda*, April 6, 1933, 4; "Borba s iavleniiami"; Alperin et al., "Nedochety v rassledovanii dolzhnostnykh i khoziaistvennykh prestuplenii v promyshlennosti," *Voprosy sovetskoi kriminalistiki* (Leningrad, 1933), 32–40.

Accidents on public transport produced even more cases than those in industry – because the police were close at hand and because they led often to injuries. Accidents on trams (in the city of Moscow, there were fifty injuries a month) generated prosecutions, as did accidents on railroads and ships.[86] For the latter special line courts were established in 1931, and OGPU staff often joined procuracy officials in handling these nonpolitical cases. However, OGPU investigators prepared cases no better than their colleagues in the procuracy.[87]

Naturally, criminal prosecutions did not reduce the frequency of accidents in Soviet industry or transport. This fact disappointed those leaders who believed that punishment could deter accidents. As Lazar Kaganovich complained in 1935 with what one observer described as "classical clarity," "procurators accuse, judges judge, and the number of crashes rises."[88] No other result was possible when workers and drivers lacked training, had to use poorly maintained machines, and worked under pressure. But the prosecutions did displace the blame for accidents from makers of the policy of rapid industrialization onto the shoulders of those who implemented it.

Another consequence of overly rapid industrialization was a sharp drop in the quality of production, especially of consumer goods; and the lasting priority that Soviet planning gave to quality of production made defective goods a characteristic feature of Soviet industry. As early as December 1929 Soviet leaders tried to address substandard goods by announcing that their production made managers subject to charges of criminal negligence. But procurators started few cases, because of the difficulty in establishing direct responsibility and a reluctance to prosecute important persons. In the first months of 1933 Stalin mounted a campaign to expand prosecutions for production of defective goods. When the campaign failed, he issued a new law.[89]

---

86 I. Gural, "Borba s prestupnostiu na mestnom transporte v Moskve," *ZaSZ* 1935, no. 9, 26–28; Ia. Vitbaum, "Na borbe s avariiami na gorodskom transporte," *SIu*, 1933, no. 23, 10.

87 Kozhevnikov, *Istoriia sovetskogo suda*, 346–347; V. Odintsev, "Kak rabotaiut linenye zheleznodorozhnye sudy Moskovskogo oblastnogo suda," *SIu*, 1931, no. 9, 17–20; "Leninggradskii oblastnoi sud v borbe za pererstroiku zheleznodorozhnogo transporta," ibid., no. 23, 2, 11–13; A.M. Lipkin, "Prokuratura v borbe s krusheniiami," *Za SZ*, 1934, no. 5, 5–6.

88 G. Segal, "K itogam maiskogo soveshchaniia sudebno-prokurorskikh rabotnikov zheleznodorozhnogo transporta," *Za SZ*, 1935, no. 7, 7–9.

89 Goliakov, *Sbornik dokumentov*, 250; Sakhov, "Organy iustitisii;" N. Chekalov, "V borbe za kachestvo produktsii, *SIu*, 1931, no. 30; P.P. "Borba za kachestvo produktsii. Opyt Leningradskih organov iustitsii v 1933 g.," *SIu*, 1933, no. 20, 2–3; Volodarskii, "Moskovskii reid po borbe za kachestvo produktsii shirpotreba," *SIu*, 1933, no. 21, 13–14.

The edict of December 8, 1933, made directors and other top managers of enterprises personally liable for the production of substandard or incomplete goods and subject to a minimum punishment of five years in prison.[90] This harsh law proved difficult to execute because of vague language. Did directors had to have acted so as to directly cause poor production? Need their actions have been intentional? Laws from Stalin's mouth or hand rarely met standards of legal draftsmanship.

But Stalin did care about his new law on defective goods, and it was accompanied by an intensive, though short-lived, campaign. The ambitious Andrei Vyshinskii, by this time the Deputy Procurator-General of USSR, took personal charge of the campaign. Within a month of promulgation of the law, Vyshinskii had coauthored a lengthy directive on implementation that required completion of investigations within ten days; spoke about the law at a research institute; reported on the law to a meeting of the Procuracy's Collegium; and organized a two-day radio broadcast about the low quality of production featuring top officials from Narkomiust and leading factory directors, in all a total of 100 participants.[91] When these efforts produced a mere 90 prosecutions in the first two months, Vyshinsky raised the stakes. After confirming the dismal results of the initial implementation of the law at a meeting of regional procurators in late January, he organized a closed circuit radio hook-up for industrial procurators and at regional courts judges around the RSFSR. For the whole day of February 13, these legal officials heard speeches by such luminaries as Procurator-General Ivan Akulov, USSR Supreme Court Chairman A. Vinokurov, RSFSR Commissar of Justice Nikolai Krylenko, and his deputy, Fanni Niurina. Moreover, the procurators and judges on the line had to answer questions. Vyshinskii personally quizzed them about particular cases, among other things complaining about the tendency to lower charges in cases of production of defective goods due to negligence (Article 111) in order to avoid giving harsh sentences.[92]

The pressure from Vyshinskii had the desired effect. Following the broadcast, procurators "in every province and republic" held meetings about defective goods, and in March and April they launched hundreds of new cases. The quality of the investigation in these cases that were concocted on demand fell below the usual low standards.[93] To their

[90] Goliakov, *Sbornik dokumentov*, 340.
[91] *Slu*, 1934, no. 3, 12–13; "Proizvodstvennyi pokhod organov iustitsii imeni XVII part'ezda," ibid., no. 1, 110–111.
[92] R. Orlov, "Prokuratura v borbe za provedenie zakona ot 8 dekabria," *Slu*, 1934, no. 9, 16–17; "Kak my boremsia za kachestvo produktsii," *Za SZ*, 1934, no. 19–15.
[93] Ibid.; "O rabote organov iustitsii po primeneniiu zakona 8 dekabriia 1933 g.," Postanovlenie 48 Plenuma Verkhovnogo Suda SSSR, *Za SZ*, 1934, no. 10, 33.

credit judges proved unwilling to convict or punish without legal grounds. Both trial judges (at the regional level) and the RSFSR Supreme Court introduced restrictive interpretations of the law. It applied only to finished goods, not to spare parts or repairs. It required a showing of intent, or at least a causal connection. Its applicability to subordinate employees in a firm was limited.[94] For these and other reasons trial courts threw out or requalified more than a quarter of the cases that they heard with charges according to the law of December 8, 1933. Many other convictions were overruled by the RSFSR Supreme Court. For the whole of 1934 the 747 prosecutions registered in the RSFSR produced only 163 convictions that stood up at trial and on appeal.[95] In making cases, the procurators had found it difficult to focus on heavy industry (as the law stipulated); only 27% of the cases came from this sector, and few of these ended in convictions. Among other things, the Commissariat of Heavy Industry kept petitioning for the dropping of prosecutions against "this or that manager." Nor did the prosecutions focus mainly upon managers. While one-third of the accused comprised top figures in the enterprise (director, deputy director, or chief engineer), the rest of those indicted came from the middle or lower ranks of officialdom.[96]

Like most campaigns of an hysterical type, this one ran its course quickly. By the fall of 1934 the number of new prosecutions for production of defective goods had slowed to a mere trickle. In 1935 it leveled off; only 92 prosecutions were started in the whole of the RSFSR.[97]

If the only function performed by prosecutions was to provide scapegoats for the low quality of production, a larger number of prosecutions may have been unnecessary. If the leaders sought to actually frighten managers into improving the performance of industry (regardless of whether this was possible), then the implementation of the 1933 law was inadequate. At least one leader continued to harbor such delusions, and it was none other than Joseph Stalin. Stalin tried one more time. In June 1940 the Soviet government issued yet another law on defective goods. The law did not change the punishment – it merely replaced "no

---

94 "Kak Leningradskii oblastnoi sud provodit v zhizn zakon 8 dekabria," *Za SZ*, 1934, no. 3, 43–44; "God borby Moskovskoi prokuratury za kachestvo produktsii," ibid., no. 12, 7–10; S. Prigov, "Zakon 8 dekabria v praktike prokuratury Saratovskogo kraia," ibid., 1935, no. 12, 7–14: *Sbornik raz'iasnenii Verkhovnogo Suda RSFSR*, 4 (Moscow, 1935), 299–301.

95 R. Orlov and L. Chernov, "God zakona 8 dekabria," *Za SZ*, 1934, no. 11, 15–18; F. Niurina, "Dva goda zakona 8 dekabria," ibid., 1935, no. 12, 5–6.

96 Orlov and Chernov, "God zakona;" G. Roginskii, "Praktika primeneniia zakona 8-go dekabriia," *Za SZ*, 1934, no. 6, 11–17.

97 Niurina, "Dva goda."

less than five years' deprivation of freedom with "from five to eight years' imprisonment." It also raised the rhetoric by declaring that the production of substandard goods was "an antigovernment crime equivalent to wrecking." Needless to say, the implementation of the 1940 law was no better than that of the laws of 1933.[98]

Industrial prosecutions could provide scapegoats for accidents, defective goods, and other consequences of Stalin's industrialization policy only if the public knew about the trials. Accordingly, from 1929 production-related trials received extraordinary publicity. Many took the form of demonstration trials, and the accounts in newspapers provided drama at its best.[99] For example, *Pravda* reported a series of trials of traders in food and cooks at factory cafeterias.[100] During collectivization the quality of the diet enjoyed by most Soviet citizens declined as meat and dairy products became scarce. The fault lay with repression and disorganization in the countryside, but trials in Moscow and Leningrad shone the spotlight elsewhere. Thus, a trial prepared by the OGPU in 1930 accused a group of traders of destroying the food supply for the city of Moscow. The traders on the dock included such obvious enemies of the Soviet order as a former landowner and an editor from the tsarist Ministry of Finance. According to the account in *Pravda*, the group had "consciously tried to create hunger and produce shortages of goods for workers."[101] Even more fantastic were the accusations leveled against cooks. More than one trial declared the cooks in factory cafeterias negligent after foreign objects such as nails, soap, ants, roaches, and boiled mice turned up on the plates of workers. In one such case the cook was convicted of wrecking. The case was unusual and intricate. The cook in question was a former kulak, who had escaped from prison and been implicated in a murder since his escape. By the time the investigation had

---

98 Goliakov, *Sbornik dokumentov*, 406; S. Livshits, "Sudebnaia praktika po delam o vy-puske nedobrokachestvennoi produktsii," *SIu*, 1941, no. 8, 3–6 and no. 9, 6–9.; G. Golst, "Borba s vypuskom nedobrokachestvennoi, nekompletnoi i nestandartnoi pro-duktsii," *SZ*, 1950, no. 6, 13.

99 "Rol i zadachi prokuratury"; *Sbornik tsirkuliarov Narkomiusta* (1931), 81–88. Sometimes trials were held in theaters. See "Sud nad vinovnikam katastrofii na Volge," *Pravda*, July 22–26, 1933. *Pravda*, 1930–1936, passim.

100 "Itogi vypolneniia postanovlenii chetvertoi soveshchanii rukovodiaschchikh rabot-nikov organov iustitsii RSFSR i ocherednye zadachi organov iustitsii," Doklad N.V. Krylenko na piatom soveshchanii rukovodiashchikh organov iustitsii RSFSR 5 iuniia 1931, *SIu*, 1931, no. 22, 7; Ark. Lipkin, "Vnimanie voprosam kachestva produktsii," ibid., 1932, no. 2, 21–22; M. Ravich, "Dela rabochego snabzheniia v Leningradskikh sudakh," *SIu*, 1932, no. 22, 13–18.

101 "Raskryta kontrrevoliutsionnaia organizatsiia vreditelei rabochego snabzheniia," *Pravda*, Sept. 22, 1930, 3–4.

been completed, he admitted that he was a "convinced Trotskyite" who had intentionally placed foreign objects in the food to harm the workers.[102]

For Stalin the explanatory function of criminal prosecutions equaled that of deterrence, but he still believed in the threat of prosecution. In 1934, for example, Stalin's government issued a new law requiring custodial sanctions for salespersons who cheated customers intentionally or accidentally through the use of weights and measures. The new law might well have restrained those salespersons who intentionally cheated their customers (as opposed to those who did so unwittingly because of faulty scales that they could not get repaired). But only if the law were properly implemented. However, most judges seem to have believed that custodial sanctions were too harsh a measure to be applied to ordinary salespersons, at least when their breaches were minor, if not unintentional. As a result, judges regularly avoided the mandatory term of imprisonment by requalifying the charges in cases of weights and measures to criminal negligence or abuse of power (Articles 111 or 109). In this way judges at the people's courts in Moscow managed to sentence to prison a mere 21.7% of persons charged with cheating customers.[103]

This was not the first time that judges in the USSR failed to assign harsh sentences that political leaders called for. As we have seen, judges resisted implementing the Law of August 7, 1932, and complied with it only after much pressure. Likewise, in cases of defective goods, judges insisted on tough standards of evidence. We will encounter more instances where judges used their legal discretion to avoid or at least mute the effects of harsh or overextended criminal laws, even when it was clear that they came from Stalin himself.

When seen in the light of later history, the industrial prosecutions of the first half of the 1930s had another kind of significance. They supplied an ingredient for the Great Terror. As we shall see in Chapter 7, a key part of the Terror was a campaign of vigilance, in which workers were encouraged to unmask those of their bosses whose actions had harmed production, or led to other mishaps. The campaign of vigilance of 1937–1938 had at its roots the tradition of holding industrial officials criminally responsible for failures in the plant. Both the practice of prosecutions and the metaphors for describing their

---

102 Lib, "Vrag ne dremlet," *Pravda*, July 9, 1933, 4, and July 10, 1933, 4; "Proletarskii sud nad vrediteliami obshchestvennogo pitannia," ibid., July 12, 1933, 4.

103 "Postanovlenie prezidiuma Verkhsuda RSFSR ot 8 dek. 1934 po dodkladu ob obsledovanii raboty sudov po delam ob omerivanii i obveshivaniiu pokupatelei i narushenii roznichnykh tsen," *SIu*, 1935, no. 1, 23; B. Babichev, "Kak boriutsia s obmanom potrebitelei organy iustitsii Novorossiiska," ibid., no. 2, 10.

sins had become familiar parts of popular culture in the USSR before 1937.[104]

Conclusion

In Chapters 3 and 4 we saw how collectivization and grain collection affected the administration of criminal justice. The mobilization of legal officials to pursue missions in the villages led to a decline in the observance of procedures in searches, arrests, trials, and sentencing, culminating in the breakdown of legality in the countryside during winter 1933. For the most part procurators and judges served as the agents of local politicians, as they pursued the larger goals of the regime. The emphasis on campaign justice through the early 1930s produced a corresponding neglect of ordinary criminal justice and the development of simplifications and substitutes that further discredited the administration of justice. At the same time, the criminal law served to deflect blame for some of the devastating consequences of the industrialization drive of the early 1930s.

Two developments made the mobilization of criminal law and breakdown of legality less devastating. The first was the resistance by legal officials to implementing the criminal law when it seemed unjust. The conduct of judges in muting the sharp edge of the Law of August 7, 1932, placed limits on that law's repressive potential. However many peasants actually received ten years in prison for stealing grain, their number would have been greater had judges not refused to implement the law as written, at least for the first four months. This example of resistance to Stalinist excess in criminal policy was one of many that we shall encounter in this book. Another force that checked illegalities to a small degree was the words and deeds of a few top officials brave enough to fight abuses, especially when perpetrated by legal officials. The names of Peter Stuchka, Evsei Shirvindt, I.L. Bulat, and Alexander Vinokurov deserve recognition, but above all it was Aron Solts who repeatedly complained in strident tones when injustices befell ordinary peasants and workers. Solts's finest hour came with his almost singlehanded campaign to convince Stalin to curtail broad use of the Law of August 7, 1932.

The efforts of these legal officials notwithstanding, the quality of criminal justice in the USSR did decline during collectivization and the

---

[104] Similarly, a mania with spies and enemies had also entered Soviet popular culture. See Gabor Rittersporn, "The Omnipresent Conspiracy: On Soviet Imagery of Politics and Social Relations in the 1930s," in Nick Lampert and Gabor Rittersporn, eds., *Stalinism: Its Nature and Aftermath. Essays in Honour of Moshe Lewin* (London, 1992), 101–120.

authority of legal forms and procedures with it. Stalin and Vyshinskii recognized these developments, and, we shall see, tried to rectify them when it became expedient. They did so by fostering a return to traditional legal order. Yet, to secure the authority of law would require as well checking the power of local political officials, and this goal would prove a formidable challenge.

PART III

The conservative shift

5   Returning to traditional
       legal order

The years 1934 to 1936, the very time Stalin was sharpening and starting to use the weapon of extralegal terror against enemies – mostly imagined – witnessed the start of a return to traditional legal order in the USSR. What began as an attempt to repair the damage to the authority of law wreaked by collectivization led to the abandonment of some Bolshevik features of criminal justice and the return to key aspects of the tsarist justice. The main purpose underlying these developments was to strengthen the criminal law and make it a reliable weapon for Stalin at a time when the main political challenge had become stabilization and consolidation rather than social change. On a larger plane, the policy of strengthening the authority of law represented Stalin's commitment, realized gradually during the last two decades of his life and rule, to building a strong and centralized Soviet state.

The process of the return to tradition was gradual and multifaceted and involved decisions and shifts in policy that could not be realized all at once. It began in 1934 with the rejection of simplified procedures in the administration of justice and the attempt to revive the authority of legal rules. This led within a few years to the rejection of the antilaw strain in Soviet legal theory. The process also included (1) decisions to reorganize the legal agencies to foster centralization of authority and enhance the power of the procuracy, the agency on which Stalin could best rely; (2) a fundamental shift in the attitude of Stalin and his top officials toward staffing of the legal agencies (rejecting uneducated cadres and promoting legal training for legal officials); and (3) the use of Soviet law to enhance the reputation of the Soviet state at home and abroad.

It is tempting to describe this process as an attempt to "restore" or "revive" law, but in so doing, one must take care to clarify what kind of law was at stake. What Stalin sought to cultivate was not the "rule of law" or even attachment to general legal principles but rather law in its

Russian autocratic sense, as a tool for the leader and instrument of his rule.[1] The Stalinist conception of law, like the tsarist and Bolshevik before, assumed that law was subordinate to political power. Moreover, it implied no restrictions on the use of extralegal coercion or terror. Reviving the authority of law meant sharpening this particular coercive tool by enhancing enforcement and compliance.

The timing of the attempt to restore the authority of law and develop a traditional legal order was not accidental. The process began in 1934 when Soviet economic policy came to emphasize the consolidation of the gains made during the collectivization and industrialization drives. Moreover, the strengthening of law represented part of the larger "conservative shift" that occurred in social policy and culture. Social policy in the mid-1930s featured among other things the criminalization of abortion and juvenile delinquency. As we shall see in Chapter 6, both of these changes involved abandonment of progressive approaches pursued in the 1920s and the return to tsarist practices (or worse). Likewise for Soviet culture, the mid-1930s represented a period of the specification of new official norms associated with "socialist realism" and their enforcement by creative unions. The keepers of cultural orthodoxy rejected modernism in form and substance and promoted instead the classical, the heroic, the accessible, and the chaste. At the same time, Soviet culture also displayed an increasingly anti-Western xenophobic strain that heralded the revival of Russian nationalism, another tradition that Stalin made his own. Add these developments to the return to traditional legal order and you get the syndrome described by the emigré sociologist Nicholas Timasheff as "the great retreat," his term for what I call the "conservative shift."[2]

Along with the "conservative shift" in social policy and culture went the first steps undertaken by Stalin to build a strong and centralized state. When Stalin became dictator in 1929, his state lacked these attributes. Even with party discipline and control over key appointments, the compliance of provincial and local officials with the policies of the center was not easy to ensure. Moreover, to accomplish collectivization

---

[1] The Stalinist conception of law bore the traits of what sociologist of law Roberto Unger called "bureaucratic law." Distinguished from customary law in its positive and public character and from legal order in its lack of generality and autonomy, bureaucratic law represented law imposed by the state to serve the interests of its masters. As such, bureaucratic law suffered "an inevitable conflict" over how to satisfy the twin imperatives of instrumentalism and legitimacy. See Roberto Unger, *Law in Modern Society* (New York and London, 1976), 50–51, 58–59, 65–66.

[2] Nicholas Timasheff, *The Great Retreat. The Growth and Decline of Communism in Russia* (New York, 1946); A. Kemp-Welch, *Stalin and the Literary Intelligentsia, 1928–1939* (London, 1991).

Stalin had encouraged local initiatives that fell outside of central directives. As the war with the peasantry came closer to a victory, Stalin showed increasing interest in curbing local initiative and creating a centralized political order. As articulations of central authority, the laws of the Soviet state assumed a new importance for the dictator. He made the point abundantly clear in his famous remarks to the Seventeenth Party Congress in January 1934, when he condemned provincial and local officials "who like feudal appanage princes think that the laws were written not for them but for fools."[3] For Stalin, the revival of the authority of law served to strengthen his own hand and centralize power. As we shall see, the reorganization of the legal agencies in the mid and late 1930s did centralize power within the legal realm to a new degree. Likewise, the shift to a policy of encouraging legal officials to acquire credentials and make careers in the legal agencies was to produce in the long run a more pliable and conformist body of judges, procurators, and investigators.

Symbolic of the conservative shift and the attempt to consolidate the political order was the promulgation in 1936 of the Stalin Constitution. That Constitution also played a major part in the unfolding of Stalin's new policy of using law to enhance the reputation of the Soviet state, even providing camouflage for illegalities perpetrated out of the limelight. The multiple meanings and uses of that Constitution receive attention at the end of the chapter.

The story of the return to traditional legal order in the mid-1930s is permeated with politics and struggle. Vyshinskii's famous battle with Krylenko played a major part in both the official rejection of legal nihilism and the emergence of the USSR Procuracy as a center of power.[4] Likewise, Stalin's personal distrust of Krylenko and many other old-guard leaders of the Bolshevik legal establishment led him to find or create pretexts for their replacement by a more servile cast of characters, before, during, and after the Great Purge.

Propaganda and political struggle aside, the attempt by Stalin and Vyshinskii to foster the strengthening of the criminal law as an instrument of rule was genuine. Not only did Stalin begin using the criminal sanction to deal with social and economic problems, but also the leadership began treating the courts as institutions whose performance warranted close scrutiny by party officials in the regions and localities.[5]

---

[3] I. Stalin, "Otchetnyi doklad XVII s'ezdu partii o rabote TsK VKP(b)," 26 ian 1934 g., in Stalin, *Voprosy Leninizma* (11th ed.; Moscow, 1952), 517.

[4] Eugene Huskey, "Vyshinskii, Krylenko, and the Shaping of the Soviet Legal Order," *Slavic Review*, 46:3–4 (Fall/Winter 1987), 414–428.

[5] RTsKhIDNI (formerly TsPA IML), f.17, op.120, d.171, 2–20; ibid., d. 170, 18–21, 53.

The change in the regime's position on the importance of legal training for procurators, investigators, and judges also reflected real concern over the low quality of the administration of justice.

The chapter begins by exploring the origins and meaning of the attempt to restore the authority of law in the spring of 1934. It proceeds to examine the struggles over the reorganization of the legal agencies that resulted in both centralization in all of them and a superior position for the Procuracy vis-à-vis the others; to analyze the shift in attitudes and policies toward the educational qualifications of legal officials; and, finally, to assess the meaning of the Stalin Constitution for Soviet criminal justice.

Restoring the authority of law

In the spring of 1934, under the public lead of Deputy Procurator-General Andrei Vyshinskii, Soviet authorities officially repudiated the negative attitude toward law that they had promoted during collectivization. They replaced that posture with a new policy of restoring the status of legal rules and procedures and supporting their observance.

Some of the authoritative public statements in 1934 seemed to promote the observance of law not only by legal agencies but also in public administration in general. At the Seventeenth Party Congress, Stalin criticized provincial and local officials who failed to observe "Soviet and party laws" and acted condescendingly toward directives from central authorities. An occasional speech by Vyshinskii or editorial in *Pravda* also called for a broad-ranging respect for laws. And, behind the scenes, at a meeting of Procuracy officials in August, Lazar Kaganovich, Central Committee secretary and Politburo member, insisted that the laws of Soviet power had to become obligatory (*byli by ob'izatelnym*) without exception for Communists and nonparty members alike and especially for all who occupied offices from the bottom to the top of the state apparatus. But the promotion of law in public life did not run deep. Neither the national press nor provincial party and government journals made legal regulation a cause.[6] Nor did any identifiable group of scholars or officials pursue this goal. The new policy toward legal rules applied mainly to the procuracy and courts.

The announcement of the new policy came at the First All-Union Conference of Court-Procuracy Workers in April 1934. Signs of the new

6 Stalin, "Otchetnyi doklad"; RTsKhIDNI, f.17, op.165, d.47, 2; *Pravda*, 1934–1935; *Molot*, 1934; *Partiinyi rabotnik Severenogo Kavkaza*, 1934–1936; *Partiinaia rabota* (Samara), 1936; *Partiinyi rabotnik* (Saratov), 1936.

approach, however, were visible months before the Congress, and the origins of the new line date back to 1932. Even then, respect for law was associated with Andrei Vyshinskii.

How could Andrei Vyshinskii of all people have been associated with the restoration of the authority of law? The very Vyshinskii who has gone down in history as the prosecutor and stage manager of the great show trials of the Stalin Purges, which featured forced confessions and fantastic plots. The apparent contradiction runs deeper still. As Stalin's procurator-general, Vyshinskii also managed the Purge in the Procuracy (which, as we shall see, devastated the agency), served as a member of the NKVD Special Board (which ordered the shooting of so many "enemies"), and created the jurisprudence of terror used to make the Terror seem legal. Yet, this same Vyshinskii served as the key promoter of the authority of law and reformer of the legal agencies in the years prior to the Purge, 1931–1936.

The paradox of Vyshinskii had deep roots. To a considerable degree, Vyshinskii personified the Bolshevik approach to law, which, as we have seen, treated law and legality in a highly instrumental fashion and generally tolerated the use of extralegal repression when it seemed expedient. At the core, though, of Vyshinskii's particular dual role as promoter of the restoration of the authority of law and participant in the Terror and Purge lay his relationship with Joseph Stalin.[7] Andrei Vyshinskii, former Menshevik admitted to the Bolshevik party in 1920 at Stalin's behest, pursued a career in the 1920s as prosecutor and judge, educational official, and legal scholar. At all times, he was Stalin's faithful servant; only as such could he have played the part of chief judge at the Shakhty trial in 1928. The key, though, was that this well-educated, dapper jurist, with brilliant command of rhetoric, understood before most others how Stalin would need and use law. As early as 1927 Vyshinskii distanced himself from the legal nihilists who were coming into vogue. While the exponents of the antilaw perspective saw criminal procedure as a set of technical rules headed for oblivion, Vyshinskii treated it as a system of legal norms. In 1930 Vyshinskii wrote that Soviet criminal law had the important function of defending the socialist state and its legal order from all encroachments.[8] This, before Stalin began speaking of the need for the strengthening of the state on the path to socialism.

---

[7] For an insightful account of this relationship, see Arkady Vaksberg, *Stalin's Prosecutor. The Life of Andrei Vyshinsky* (New York, 1990).

[8] Robert Sharlet and Piers Beirne, "In Search of Vyshinsky: The Paradox of Law and Terror," *International Journal of the Sociology of Law*, 12 (1984), 165; reprinted in Beirne (ed.), *Revolution in Law: Contributing to the Development of Soviet Legal Theory, 1917–1938* (Armonk, N.Y., and London, 1990), 136–156.

In the early 1930s Vyshinskii emerged as the key spokesman for law because he understood Stalin's growing interest in law in all its dimensions. On the one hand, Vyshinskii readily joined his master in hypocrisy and deceit. "Intelligent and wary, Vyshinskii understood the leader's insidiousness and took it as a key directive. And Stalin knew that he knew and that is what sealed the union." These eloquent words come from the pen of Arkady Vaksberg, legal journalist and biographer of Vyshinskii.[9] Vaksberg was referring to Stalin's sponsorship of law and democratic institutions for the benefit of appearances, to put a mask on extralegal coercion and terror. On the other hand, there is reason to believe that Vyshinskii – like Stalin – appreciated the utility of well-constituted legal authority for a strong centralized state. Law could serve not only to make terror less visible, but also as an instrument for its political master. Not every matter had to be relegated to the world of raw force.

Yes, the same Vyshinskii who helped Stalin perpetrate the terror also helped him to try to restore the authority of law and the effectiveness of the administration of justice. There was no real contradiction, for in both tasks, Vyshinskii was serving his master Stalin, a man who found uses for both varieties of coercion, legal and extralegal.

Here we start by examining Vyshinskii's postures in 1932–1933 and the changes in the political context that made the new line on the authority of law appropriate. Then, we analyze the Congress of Court and Procuracy workers of spring 1934, spell out the elements of the new policy toward the law and its implementors, and assess its consequences for the administration of justice in the mid-1930s.

Two political actions made the promotion of the observance of laws a plausible position for Vyshinskii to support. The edict of June 25, 1932, "On Revolutionary Legality," legitimized the use of legal restraints against officialdom when politically expedient. The Instruction of May 8, 1933, gave the blessing of Stalin and Molotov to the need for observance of laws to curb excesses in the countryside and create order that central authorities could control.[10]

To mark the tenth anniversary of the founding of the Procuracy, the USSR government (Central Executive Committee and Council of People's Commissars) issued the edict "On Revolutionary Legality." The edict of June 25, 1932, resembled the cautionary statements issued by the legal agencies each spring that criticized the excesses of the campaigns of the fall and winter, but there were differences. To begin, the edict bore the

---

9   Vaksberg, *Stalin's Prosecutor*, 64.
10   "O revoliutsionnoi zakonnosti," Postanovlenie TsIK i SNK SSSR ot 25 iiunia 1932, in Goliakov, *Sbornik dokumentov*, 333–334, "Ob okhrane imushchestva," ibid., 335–336.

pedigree of the government as a whole (not just particular agencies), thereby lending its message more authority. At the same time, unlike the usual statements that balanced criticism of left excesses and right deviations, the edict of June 25 emphasized excesses. Among other things, it called for the end of the misapplication of hard quotas, the prosecution of officials and plenipotentiaries responsible for illegal arrests and searches, and the observance of the laws governing kolkhozy. Recently two Soviet historians argued that the edict "On Revolutionary Legality" constituted a maneuver by Stalin to relieve the mounting tensions in society, as reflected in the mounting flow of letters of complaint.[11] The timing of the edict lends plausibility to this hypothesis, since each spring during collectivization Stalin focused public attention on the excesses of the previous fall's grain collection campaign and the punishment of those held responsible (the scapegoats). Nonetheless, top legal officials took the decree seriously. Within a month of its issuance, Krylenko and Narkomiust convened, ahead of schedule, the Seventh Conference of Russian Court-Procuracy Workers and made implementation of the decree the centerpiece of discussion. Krylenko, whose initial statements about the decree had been lukewarm, spoke about the need to mobilize justice officials to protect legality.[12] To Krylenko the decree of June 25 made curbing excesses in the implementation of agricultural policies first priority. He urged procurators to check every complaint, "every letter to *Pravda*," every inmate in prison. Shortly after the conference the RSFSR Supreme Court issued its own resolution instructing judges to observe revolutionary legality by fulfilling their legal obligations.[13]

Despite the initial efforts of the legal agencies, the decree "On Revolutionary Legality" hardly influenced the message received by rural

---

[11] Vasilii Maslov and Nikolai Chistiakov, "Staliniskie repressii i sovetskaia iustitsiia," *Kommunist*, 1990, no. 10, 102–112.

[12] "Doklad tov. Krylenko na torzhestvennom zasedanii 3 iiuliia 1932 g.," *SIu*, 1932, no. 20, 4–12; "Doklad tov. Krylenko na sobranii partaktiva g. Moskvy 8 iiuliia 1932 g.," ibid., no. 21, 1–4.

[13] "Doklad Narkoma iustitsii tov. N.V. Krylenko na iiulskom soveshchanii rukovodiashchikh rabotnikov iustitsii RSFSR," *SIu*, 1932, no. 24, 3–8; "Postanovlenie iiulskogo soveshchanii rukovodiashchikh rabotnikov iustitsii po dokladu N.V. Krylenko," ibid., no. 23, 11–13; GARF, f.353sch, op. 16s, d.12, 33–34 ("O vypolneniu postanovleniia . . . ot 25 iiuniia 1932 revoliutsionnoi zakonnosti," Prikaz Narkomiust ot 10 iiuliia 1932). "Postanovlenie Prezidiuma Verkhsuda po voprosu o meropriiatakh vytekuiushchikh iz postanovleniia TsIK i SNK SSSR o revoliutsionnoi zakonnosti," ibid., no. 22, 1–3.

The introduction to the Supreme Court resolution implies dissatisfaction with the measures adopted by Narkomiust and the conference. The difference was that Krylenko stressed the response of legal officials (procurators) to illegal actions by other officials, whereas Bulat and the Supreme Court emphasized making the conduct of legal officials themselves more fitting and in accordance with legal rules.

officials, let alone their conduct. Within less than two months the call for restraint became obsolete when the government issued the Law of August 7, making theft of grain subject to draconian punishment. Officials could not implement the new Stalinist law, an instrument for seizing grain from starving peasants, while respecting legal procedures. Legal officials had no trouble discerning which law took precedence. Whereas *Pravda* and *Izvestiia* gave the June decree just a few days' attention, they publicized the Law of August 7 for ten full days, coverage that included a mass of articles, letters from toilers, and editorials. Similarly, provincial party and government journals gave more attention to the Law of August 7 than to the June edict.[14]

The edict "On Revolutionary Legality" did help its principal author A.Ia. Vyshinskii identify with the promotion of law. In publicizing the edict, Vyshinskii explained in *Pravda* how the observance of laws would take on new significance in the future and argued against leftist positions. And, in an academic setting, he dubbed revolutionary legality a "creative force" that would help the toilers build socialism, and tried to dissuade his listeners that the concept was associated with NEP.[15]

Where Vyshinskii differed from Krylenko and other legal officials was in his reaction to the Law of August 7. While most officials quickly relegated revolutionary legality to the back burner, in favor of joining Stalin's new campaign against theft and the battle against peasants who tried to avoid starvation, Vyshinskii did not retreat. Naturally, he joined the other officials in praising the new law on theft, and identified the August law, along with the June decree, as a pillar of Soviet criminal policy. Unlike the others, Vyshinskii continued to call attention to the June edict. Even in his first article after the issuing of the Law of August 7, Vyshinskii went on promoting revolutionary legality. Moreover, in the fall of 1932 he allowed publication of his treatise "Revolutionary Legality in the Contemporary Era." In this work Vyshinskii did not place law above politics. Revolutionary legality, that is, the observance of laws, Vyshinskii insisted, was a method of the dictatorship of the proletariat. Nor did this method contradict the principles of "revolutionary expediency" or "socialist legal consciousness," but through some dialectic was to be combined with them. The correct balance of the

---

14 See *Pravda* and *Izvestiia* for June, July, and August, 1932, especially June 27 and 28, August 8 and 9, and August 20–25. The concentrated dose of materials on the Law of August 7 in the later part of August in both newspapers suggests that the editors were fulfilling instructions from a higher authority.

15 A. Vyshinskii, "Revoliutsionnaia zakonnost i nashi zadachi," *Pravda*, June 28, 1932, 2; "Revoliutsionnaia zakonnost na nyneshnem etape sotsialistichekogo stroitelstva," Doklad t. Vyshinskogo na otkrytom sobranii iacheik VKP(b) NKIu, *SIu*, 1932, no. 19, 2–8.

moment depended on political expediency. While Vyshinskii used clever rhetoric to protect himself against charges of heresy, his tract placed special emphasis upon the observance of law. Unlike other politicians in the legal realm, Vyshinskii openly condemned discussion of the withering of government, courts, and law as "leftist conversations and moods."[16] Vyshinskii's position contrasted with those taken after August 7 by Nikolai Krylenko, Commissar of Justice, Mikhail Kalinin, Chairman of the Central Executive Committee, and Pavel Postyshev, the Central Committee secretary in charge of justice agencies.[17]

Why Vyshinskii adopted this position is not clear. Was it a consequence of his duties as procurator of the RSFSR (his post from May 1931 to June 1933)? Was it a matter of conviction? Or did Vyshinskii have the nose to sense that in the future Stalin would embrace any and all instruments of dictatorship, including law?

Vyshinskii's posture on revolutionary legality sounded strange during the struggles of the winter 1932–1933, but it gained new relevance after Stalin and Molotov issued their Instruction of May 8. This widely distributed and much-cited secret instruction recognized that arbitrary coercion in the countryside had outlived its usefulness. The leaders warned that observing the laws on the making and sanctioning of arrests was now the order of the day, along with the release of many detained in prisons.[18]

Soon after issuing the Instruction of May 8, Stalin authorized the formation in June 1933 of a USSR Procuracy.[19] Vyshinskii assumed the post of deputy procurator-general of the USSR, but served under a quiet figurehead, Ivan Akulov. As a result, Vyshinskii moved from procurator of the RSFSR subordinate to the RSFSR Commissar of Justice Krylenko to a position of independence from that Commissariat and on a higher level in the political hierarchy. This position gave Vyshinskii the status and opportunity to resume the promotion of law.

Vyshinskii was the figure who made the first public statement in support of law in the summer following the Instruction of May 8. On August 23, 1933, *Pravda* and *Izvestiia* reprinted a speech delivered by Vyshinskii as prosecutor at a trial of officials charged with incomplete delivery of combines. The text appeared under the headline "Soviet law is strong and hard, a law that is unquestionable"; and "Iron discipline,

---

16 A. Vyshinskii, "Revoliutsionnaia zakonnost i okhrana obshchestvennosti sobstvennosti," *Izvestiia*, Aug. 21, 1932, 2; A.Ia. Vyshinskii, *Revoliutsionnaia zakonnost na sovremennom etape* (Moscow, 1932).

17 F. Starovoitov and A. Shliapochnikov, "Za ukreplenie revoliutsionnoi zakonnosti (obzor)," *SGiRP*, 1932, no. 11–12, 116–122.

18 "Instruktsiia vsem."

19 Golunskii, *Istoriia zakonodatelstva*, 510–511.

the most scrupulous observance of Soviet law is OBLIGATORY for all!" The text included such statements as: "The role of Soviet law and socialist legality is to demand from the whole population, from every citizen, exact and holy (sic) implementation of the laws. " 'Or,' as Lenin said, "We must learn to respect Soviet law as indestructible . . . and to understand that any ignoring of the demands of socialist legality is impermissible."[20] The language of this speech had a distinctive flavor, sounding as if Vyshinskii had just returned from a meeting with Stalin and reproduced his sentiments. Recall that Stalin had described property as "holy" in the Law of August 7. At the least, Vyshinskii was mimicking his leader.

Through fall 1933 and winter 1934 Vyshinskii continued to promote the observance of law. For example, in December the Central Executive Committee heard him condemn underestimation of Soviet law and rail against the simplification of procedure and the treatment of law as a "family affair." This, a month before Stalin condemned provincial and local officials for disregarding his laws.[21] At the same time, the staff of the All-Union Procuracy followed Vyshinskii's lead in highlighting the low quality of investigations and trials and the inadequate preparation of legal officials.[22] One veteran official of Narkomiust, recently transferred to Vyshinskii's Procuracy, offered a full-scale attack on simplification in legal proceedings that would have been impossible a year earlier.[23]

Neither the promotion of new standards by the Procuracy nor statements by Stalin and Vyshinskii improved the practice of justice. The agricultural campaigns of fall 1933 featured the same excesses and coercion as earlier ones, though in some places not as extreme as during the Famine. Both Narkomiust RSFSR and the USSR Supreme Court continued to mobilize the participation of legal officials in campaign justice. It would take a dramatic step to entrench the new approach as policy and give reform in the administration of justice a chance.[24]

The turning point came at the First All-Union Conference of Court-Procuracy Workers. Unlike previous meetings of legal officials, this

---

20 "Sotsialisticheskaia sobstvennost – nezyblemaia osnova sovetskogo stroia," *Pravda*, Aug. 7, 1933, 1.
21 "Za vysokoe kachestvo nashei raboty," Rech A.Ia. Vyshinskogo na vechernom zasedanii 30 dek. 1933 g., na tretii sessii TsIK SSSR VI sozyva, *SZ*, 1934, No. 1, 5–8; Stalin, "Otchetnyi doklad," 517.
22 *SIu*, 1933, no. 19, 17; no. 20, 18; and see A.S. Tager, "Osnovnye problemy kassatsii v sovetskom ugolovnom protsesse," *Problemy ugolovnoi politiki*, 4 (1937), 84–85.
23 A. Piatakov, "Za chetkoe primenenie zakona," *SZ*, 1934, no. 2, 39–40; N. Lagovier, "Vrednoe uproshchenstvo v sledstvennoii i sudebnoi rabote," *SIu*, 1934, no. 10, 7–8.
24 N. Kulagin, "Bolshe printsipalnost v borbe za sotsialisticheskuiu zakonnost," *SIu*, 1934, no. 7, 12–13; *SIu*, Fall 1933, passim; *Postanovleniia i raz'iasnenii Verkhovnogo Suda SSSR, 40–44 plenuma*, 23–26.

conference was organized by the Procuracy rather than Narkomiust. The setting gave Vyshinskii as deputy procurator-general the opportunity to seize the initiative and lay out a new program for criminal justice. The meeting began with a speech from Procurator General Akulov. Then it heard Krylenko give a searing account of the arbitrary coercion associated with the Law of August 7. Finally came the climax, Vyshinskii's own report on the Procuracy and the courts.[25]

In his presentation, Vyshinskii announced that the era of simplified procedures had ended. Henceforth all procedural rules would be mandatory. Instead of substituting "nose" – that is, intuition about what constituted revolutionary legal consciousness – for knowledge of the law (as Nemtsov had once suggested), Soviet legal officials would have to know and apply legal rules. Their task, in Vyshinskii's words, was to combine revolutionary legality expressed in rules with socialist legal consciousness, not to rely on the latter alone. Achieving this standard would require nothing less than an overhaul (*perestroika*) in the work of investigators, procurators, and judges, and Vyshinskii proceeded to outline what this overhaul would entail.

The investigators of the Procuracy, for example, would be expected to stop shirking their duties and giving short shrift to legal rules. They were to resume the conduct of investigations in serious cases; no longer could they allow police to act in their place. They were obliged to collect evidence conscientiously and thoroughly. At the close of their investigations they were to make case files available to the accused and counsel (according to the requirements of the Criminal Procedure Code).

Procurators drew more of Vyshinskii's fire. He condemned Procuracy offices for favoring activities associated with general supervision over work with criminal cases. The handling of these cases in investigation, trial, and appeal, he insisted, should become the main focus of the work of the procurators. Instead of an occasional office review of a convict's petition for appeal, procurators should actively supervise investigations, ensure that courts performed pretrial reviews of case files (at the so-called distribution sessions), appear personally at court for these sessions and at trials, and bring appeals of court decisions in cassation. Fulfilling these demands would require major adjustments for most Procuracy officials. The shift of focus would be easier for regional procuracy offices, where staff was greater and a reorganization along branch lines might facilitate a shift from supervisory to case work. But district procuracy offices, with but two or three procurators, would have to give up some of their current activities, at least the extra admin-

---

[25] "Pervoe vsesoiuznoe soveshchanie sudebno-prokurorskikh rabotnikov," *SZ*, 1934, no. 5, 7–41.

istrative duties imposed by local politicians and probably much of general supervision as well.

The shift in the main focus of the Procuracy from supervisory to prosecutorial functions was bound to enhance the power and prestige of the agency. In the 1920s while occupied mainly with checking the legality of acts of local governments and public administration, the Procuracy had become an agency of secondary importance. Its prime duty had infinite scope, and was impossible to perform well. There were other supervisory bodies competing with the Procuracy. And, the realities of political power limited what the procuracy official could achieve in curtailing abuses in the work of the agencies and local government. However, as a prosecutorial agency the Procuracy could perform well, especially if it were centralized and invested with additional powers, such as the right to supervise preliminary investigations and the legality of proceedings in court. A similar shift in the focus of the Procuracy from supervisory to prosecutorial work had occurred in 1864 as part of the judicial reform under Alexander II. As a result of that shift the Russian Procuracy became a more important and authoritative agency, even though it remained a part of the Ministry of Justice.[26] In the 1930s there was an additional reason why such a shift in function would enhance the power of the Procuracy, and that was Stalin's personal interest in criminal prosecutions, against ordinary and especially political offenders. Under Stalin, already in the early 1930s the agencies of coercion and law enforcement had assumed special prominence, and, as Vyshinskii no doubt anticipated, their significance was destined to grow. As the prestige and power of the Procuracy grew, so would that of its leader.

At the 1934 conference Vyshinskii also had hard words for judges. They should stop displaying "an accusatory deviation" and serving as toadies to law enforcement. Instead of acting as if cases had been decided, they should listen to the testimony of the accused at trial. Judges should stop harassing defense counsel either with jokes at their expense or intimidation. Moreover, Vyshinskii continued, judges needed to acquire attributes of culture. They should cease showing familiarity with procurators during trials – "Vasia, would you like a break?" – and learn how to write protocols and sentences. Too often the conclusions of judges "touched on all the important problems of the world, but did not indicate clearly who was guilty of what. They (the judges) think that by citing industrialization, the second five-year plan, class war, and imperialist intrigues, their sentences will prove politically sound."

---

[26] Sergei M. Kazantsev, *Istoriia tsarskoi prokuratury* (Saint-Petersburg, 1993), chap. 3.

Vyshinskii's report did more than provide a new program for justice agencies. It also offered an indictment of the way justice had been administrated during collectivization, and focused blame on those persons Vyshinskii chose to hold responsible. The speaker did not refer to the pressures that local politicians heading agricultural campaigns exerted on legal officials. Nor did he blame the shortage of qualified cadres for their weak performance.

Vyshinskii reserved the brunt of his attack for his colleagues at Narkomiust. The deterioration of the administration of justice stemmed from "an underestimation of the role of the courts and procuracy," itself a product of "leftist orientations." With circulars licensing legal officials to simplify procedures and invent shortcuts, officials of Narkomiust, especially his rival Krylenko, had encouraged poor attitudes toward the law. As the sponsor of simplified procedures in the past, Krylenko was vulnerable to attack, and Vyshinskii exploited this vulnerability with relish. Vyshinskii had the advantage over Krylenko. Vyshinskii's position was consistent with Stalin's current posture on the observance of law. That Krylenko's readiness to subordinate legal forms to political expediency had reflected the Leader's desires just a few years earlier the hypocritical Vyshinskii did not mention.

Vyshinskii's program received the blessing of the Conference. Its resolutions called for the full observance of procedural rules by legal officials, a new focus of procurators on the court, and new standards of conduct for judges. Within a few weeks the USSR Supreme Court lent its imprimatur to the program. In an edict of its own the Court called for the revival of the distribution sessions (for pretrial review of case files), and insisted on new standards for trials. Judges should ensure independent assessment of the evidence (usually with the testimony of witnesses), take responsibility for protocols, write good verdicts and sentences, and provide explanations for changes in cassation. The RSFSR Supreme Court not only approved the Conference resolutions but also added its own suggestions including budgetary provisions for court secretaries and the establishment of an examination for court officials.[27]

While there is no evidence that Vyshinskii's program gained explicit endorsement from the Politburo, its thrust did have the leadership's support. At a special meeting of procurators held at the Central Com-

---

[27] "Rezoliutsiia soveshchanii," *SIu*, 1934, no. 13, 31–34. "Raz'iasnenie 47 plenuma Verkhovnogo Suda SSSR po voprosu o neobkhodimosti strozhaishego sobliudeniia sudami ugolovno-protsessualnykh norm ot 7 iuaniia 1934 g.," *SIu*, 1934, no. 19, 2–3. "V Prezidiume Verkhsuda RSFSR," *SIu*, 1934, no. 15, 20–21.

mittee in August 1934 Kaganovich and Molotov spoke extensively about the need to improve the administration of justice and enhance respect for law. Ordzhonikidze, Iagoda, and Kalinin also took part in the proceedings.[28] Moreover, according to Kaganovich, the boss himself had become preoccupied with the weaknesses of the justice agencies. "For a long time," reported Kaganovich to another meeting in September, "literally every day he has insisted on the eradication of defects in investigations and the courts and asked about the struggles against arbitrary decisions and for socialist legality."[29]

Comments by Stalin's comrades also clarify that the leader's interest in strengthening the courts and procuracy related in part to his readiness to give them new responsibilities for political cases. When in July 1934 the OGPU was reorganized and included in a new all-union NKVD, the agency lost the right to hear (adjudicate) most political cases. As Kaganovich explained, "the reorganization of the OGPU means that, as we are in more normal times, we can punish [class enemies] through the court and not resort to extrajudicial repression as we have until now."[30] To handle political challenges through the courts and according to laws represented to Stalin the mark of a stable order, which, he believed or hoped, had arrived. The murder of Sergei Kirov in December 1934 would show this hope illusory and lead to renewed involvement of extrajudicial police tribunals not only in the adjudication of political charges but also in some operations relating to ordinary offenders. This later development, however, should not cast doubt on the intentions of Stalin and his colleagues in 1934.

In addition to generalized political support for improving the administration of justice, the Politburo also approved specific measures. In a secret resolution of July 10, 1934 (issued to establish the jurisdiction of the new special collegia of the regional and republican supreme courts), the Politburo endorsed a package of measures, including a special recruitment for the regional courts and procuracy offices largely from current staff of the OGPU and executive committees of regional soviets; pay raises for investigators (to match the salaries of judges) and technical staff of the courts (to the level of staff of the executive committee); and an expansion of remedial training for legal officials. By midfall the chiefs of the legal agencies had formulated a study program for

---

28 RTsKhIDNI, f.17, op.165, d.47, esp. 2–3, 37, 53, 158, 165.
29 "Vstuplenie tov. Kaganovicha na soveshchanii sudebno-prokurorskikh rabotnikov Moskovskoi oblasti," Sept. 21, 1934 (in a file of appearances by Kaganovich, L.M., for 1934), 47.
30 RTsKhINDI, f.17, op.165, d.47, 3.

legal officials that would prepare them to face a new examination called the "juridical minimum."[31]

Despite the rallying of support for Vyshinskii's program and the approval of supplementary measures to support the court and procuracy, one legal agency stayed on the sidelines. In contrast to the USSR Procuracy and the RSFSR Supreme Court, Narkomiust RSFSR did little to promote the program of renewal. To be sure, the journal of the Commissariat published a small but steady stream of articles on the quality of investigation and trials, including instructional materials and reports from local practice. Neither the journal nor the directives of the agency that published it contributed much to Vyshinskii's program of restructuring.[32] The passivity of Narkomiust might have reflected bureaucratic drift. During 1934 the work of the agency lacked clear focus, and in the fall Krylenko, the Commissar himself, was off the job, due either to illness or an extended vacation.[33] More likely, the posture of the Commissariat on restructuring stemmed from Krylenko's own distaste for it.

At a meeting of procurators held in August, Krylenko articulated his position on both the new status of law and Vyshinskii's program of reform. While accepting the former (as Stalin's new line), Krylenko quietly rejected much of the latter. Legality was more important in the current period than before, Krylenko conceded. But rather than turn their attention to the administration of justice – as Vyshinskii had ordered – procurators should pay more attention than ever to the supervision of public administration. Krylenko called this task "the obligatory function of the Procuracy, from which it could not withdraw." At the same time, he continued, legal officials ought to focus on the countryside, in order to finish off the struggle against class enemies. The difference between the current moment and the immediate past was that with socialism almost completed, a new constructive role for law had arisen. "We have now established the slogan of legal structure," Krylenko explained, "not in the sense that the preceding structure was not legal, but that the activities of Soviet institutions must be based on more exact foundations of the formal law."[34]

31 RTsKhIDNI, f.17, op.3, d.948, 95–98 (O rabote sudov i prokuratury); "V Sovnarkome SSSR," Pravda, July 26, 1934; 3; "Iuridicheskii minimum dlia prakticheskikh rabotnikov prokuratury i sledstviia," SIu, 1934, no. 28, 2; "Iuridicheskii minimum sdat ne pozdnee chem 1 apreliia 1935 g.," Prikaz no. 416 po NKIu RSFSR ot 16 sent. 1934, ibid., 3.

32 Sovetskaia iustitsiia, 1934, passim.

33 For much of fall 1934 the directives of Narkomiust were signed by Bulat or Niurina in the capacity of "acting" commissar.

34 Untitled extract from Krylenko's speech to procurators on August 2, 1934. SIu, 1934, no. 22, 1–2.

Krylenko's unwillingness to support Vyshinskii's approach to refocusing the Procuracy and articulation of his own view of the importance of broad supervisory work of that agency detracted from the force of Vyshinskii's message. Justice officials who attended conferences or read the journals of the Commissariat and the Procuracy recognized the differences among the two leading officials.

Even more detrimental was the petering out of top-level public patronage for strengthening law in the Soviet order. This did not happen at once. During the spring and summer of 1934 articles and editorials in *Pravda* underscored the new official status of law. On May 8 (anniversary of the Stalin/Molotov Instruction) an editorial hailed law as a source of good work habits. The toilers would give their all, confident that the unshakable Soviet law would protect their rights. In August, on the occasion of the liquidation of the OGPU Collegium, Vyshinskii contended that any wavering from Soviet law would help the class enemy. Two days later Aron Solts expounded on "socialist legality" and on August 7 (anniversary of the law on theft), another editorial contended that "Soviet law was a live and operational expression of the will of the party and government."[35] On August 1 and September 21 top officials of the Central Committee sponsored two conferences, one of Procuracy officials held right at the Central Committee, the other for court and Procuracy officials from the city of Moscow, and at both of these meetings Lazar Kaganovich communicated the leadership's commitment to the strengthening of law and the administration of justice.[36] From the fall of 1934, however, the cause of law lost its position of priority among the messages disseminated by the regime. Whether this was due to the failure of Stalin to return to the issue or the emergence of new concerns (e.g., with state security in the wake of the murder of Kirov) or to a new level of secrecy in Soviet politics is uncertain. The problem was that without persistent and public support from the highest level of political leadership, Vyshinskii's campaign to improve the administration of justice faced insurmountable odds. On the path to improving the practice of justice lay three obstacles: the nature of local power, continuation of agricultural campaigns, and the problem of cadres. To these would soon be added the autonomy and power of the political police.

---

[35] "Nezyblemost sovetskogo zakona – osnova sotsialisticheskogo pravosoznaniia," *Pravda*, May 8, 1934, 1; A. Vyshinskii, "O sotsialisticheskom pravosoznanii," ibid., Aug. 3, 1934, 2–3. A. Solts, "O sotsialisticheskoi zakonnosti," *Pravda*, Aug. 5, 1934, 6; "Na strazhe sovetskogo zakona," ibid., Aug. 7, 1934, 1.

[36] RTsKhIDNI, f.17, op.165, d.47 (Soveshchanie pri TsK VKP (b) rabotnikov Prokuratury ot 1 avgusta 1934 goda); "Vstuplenie tov. Kaganovicha na soveshchanii."

The program of restructuring the administration of justice had to be implemented in cities, provinces, and localities, where party officials continued to reign over all spheres of public life including justice. It remained commonplace for local bosses to direct legal officials in individual cases as well as in their style of work. As of the mid-1930s procurators and judges depended too much on their local political masters to resist their demands.[37] Corruption also infected local justice agencies. Examples included a massive bribery scam in Odessa, embezzlement by officials in the Ukrainian Narkomiust, and less shocking incidents in Daghestan and more "Asiatic" locations.[38]

At the same time, Stalin's announcement that the victory of socialism was at hand did not end the need to rely on campaigns to bring grain from the fields. In 1934 and 1935 at least the rhythm and requirements of agricultural campaigns still influenced the administration of justice. In the summer and fall of 1934 justice officials went to the villages armed with new directives defining proper conduct and urging them to avoid activities not tied to their legal tasks. The Politburo had even "suggested" in a secret resolution that regional party committees desist from "mobilizing" legal officials for the agricultural campaigns.[39] Yet, as we have noted, the conduct of the procurements often followed old patterns of repression.

Finally, the new commitment to improving the administration of justice was bound to run squarely into the problem of cadres. The challenge remained the same as in the 1920s. How could Bosheviks get uneducated, political trustees to understand and act the parts of investigators, procurators, and judges? Bolshevik jurists had always assumed that this was possible. But the actual performance of legal officials strained the faith even of zealots and crusaders. Krylenko him-

[37] See, for example, Portnoi and Mikhailenko, "A sudi kto?" *Pravda*, Sept. 17, 1934, 2; Mnukhin, "A prokuror molchit . . . " (Pismo nachalnika politotdela), ibid., Oct. 6, 1934, 4; RTsKhIDNI, f.17, op. 120, d.171, 16–17. For more examples and analysis see Solomon, "Local Political Power."

[38] D. Shten, "Odesskii oblsud zasoren chuzhdymi liudmi," *Pravda*, Aug. 29, 1933, 4; "O nezakonnom raskhodovanii i razbazarivanii sredstv v Narkomiuste Ukrainy," *Pravda*, Oct. 28, 1934, 2. E. Sh., "Kalenym zhelezom vyzhech politicheskoe i bytovoe razlozhenie," *Partiinoe stroitelstvo*, 1935, no. 14, 44–46; Sh. "Dagestan – k itogam chiski partorganizatsii NKIu," *ZaSZ*, 1935, no. 1, 56–57; RTsKhIDNI, f. 17, op 120, d. 171, 14, 141.

[39] G. Roginskii, "O rabote prokurorskogo nadzora po uborochnoi kampanii, 1934 g.," *SZ*, 1934, no. 7, 3–4; Zorin, "Zadachi prokuratury v uborochnoi kampanii," ibid., 4–7; V. Lebedinskii, A. Bolshakov, "Uroki o borbe prokuratury za urozhai i zernopostavki v 1933 g.," ibid., 7–9; "Ob uchastii sudebnykh organov v uborochnoi kampanii," Postanovlenie 48 Plenuma Verkhovnogo Suda SSSR," ibid., no. 11, 32–33; RTsKhIDNI, f.17, op.3, d.948, 98.

self reflected on the issue at the end of this speech to the Conference of April 1934. Citing evidence of indiscriminate arrests in the fall of 1933 (e.g., a teacher arrested eight kolkhozniki he suspected of theft, beat them, and placed them in a cold shed), the jurist shook his head in wonderment. How could things like this happen? "On the periphery," he reflected, "we have 96% party members in judicial work; 48% of worker origin. These are not stupid people (*durnye kadry*). . . . Party membership must be the best guarantee that we have a person who is conscious, who pays heed to the purpose of his work, who observes party discipline. . . . With such people, we should not have the facts that we do."[40] Not only legal chieftains like Krylenko and Vyshinskii but also the political leaders had begun to show concern about the low educational level of judges, procurators, and investigators. At the conference of procurators held at the Central Committee in August 1934 both Kaganovich and Molotov complained repeatedly about the problem. "You must show that you know jurisprudence," said Kaganovich. Right now "one cannot distinguish a procurator from a *raikom* secretary, but there must be a difference." "I would consider it ideal," Kaganovich said a month later, "if over the next four years procurators of districts, cities, and judges throughout the country had secondary or higher egal education." Molotov told the meeting of procurators that "we (i.e., the leadership) are exchanging views on the need to restore judicial faculties and create literate and responsible workers for the procuracy and the courts."[41] As we shall explain later in this chapter, the reevaluation of the experiment in staffing the legal agencies with uneducated cadres would unfold during 1935 and 1936, but it is clear from archival sources that this process originated in 1934.

In addition to these tangible obstacles to improvement in criminal justice there emerged an intangible one. The liquidation of the Collegium of the OGPU in summer 1934 and projected shift of political cases to the courts seemed to herald a decline in the coercive powers of the OGPU. But with the murder of Kirov in December the political police administration in the newly formed NKVD SSSR regained the right to try its own cases, using summary procedures that contrasted with the new emphasis on legal rules. At the same time, the police acquired a license to search out enemies and "socially dangerous persons," not just in the countryside but also in public administration everywhere. The growth in cases initiated and heard by police tribunals in 1935 and 1936

---

40 N.V. Krylenko, "Praktika primeneniia zakonov ot 7 avgusta 1932 g.," *ZaSZ*, 1934, no. 6, 1–10.
41 RTsKhIDNI, f.17, op. 165, d.47, 179–180; "Vstuplenie tov. Kaganovicha na soveshchanii," 63; RTsKhIDNI, ibid., 165.

was substantial and many of them apparently nonpolitical in nature, but the activities of the political police did not bear directly on the work of most judges and procurators at the local level.[42] Still, the rising tide of extrajudicial repression, itself justified by a peculiar jurisprudence, contradicted the message beamed at legal officials that an age of legality had arrived. The persistence and growth of extralegal coercion in 1935 and 1936 gave the earlier public statements of Stalin and Vyshinskii about the importance of law and legal procedures a hollow ring.

The decline in *public* promotion of the status and authority of law at the end of 1934 (to be revived only during the 1936 discussion of the Stalin Constitution) did not end the leadership's commitment to securing more effective administration of criminal justice. Rather, it marked a shift to deliberation behind the scenes and the consideration of secret measures. In May 1935 the Council of People's Commissars under the leadership of V.I. Molotov, Stalin's closest colleague, directed the Commission on Soviet Control to conduct an investigation of the practice of the courts. In the fall, the Commission delivered a scathing report, summarized in a memorandum addressed to Stalin and Molotov. Although, as we shall see, the investigation of the courts had political overtones (it was meant to embarrass Krylenko), the substantive message in the report did not get lost. In spring 1936, the staff of the Central Committee drafted a "closed letter" to party organizations about the work of court, procuracy, and investigatory agencies and an accompanying decree of the Central Committee as well. Not only did these documents repeat the sharp critique supplied by the Soviet Control Commission, but they also promised top level political support for the measures to improve the legal agencies. The second (and subsequent) of four drafts of the closed letter concluded with these words: "The Central Committee [read Stalin] thinks that the present condition of the court-procuracy agencies is intolerable, leads to the discrediting of Soviet courts and law, and undermines the authority of the Soviet court." The letter went on: "The Central Committee obliges territorial committees [regional committees, etc.] . . . without interference in operational work, to provide systematic supervision of the work of the justice agencies, to guarantee exact and undeviating observance by investigatory-procuracy agencies of the laws and procedures for protecting citizens. . . . "[43] In other words, members of the leadership proposed

42 Goliakov, *Sbornik dokumentov*, 347; V.P. Popov, "Gosudarstvennyi terror v sovetskoi Rossii, 1923–1953 (Istochniki i ikh interpretatsii)," *Otechestvennye arkhivy*, 1992, no. 2, 28; J. Arch Getty, Gabor T. Rittersporn, and Viktor N. Zemskov, "Victims of the Soviet Penal System in the Pre-War Years: A First Approach on the Basis of Archival Evidence," *American Historical Review*, 98:4 (Oct. 1993), 1032, 1034–1035.
43 RTsKhIDNI, f.17, op.120, d.171, 2–20; d.170, 18–21.

explicit elevation of the performance of the justice agencies into a major responsibility for party officials at the regional level, and by extension at the district and city levels as well. Previously, party officials in the provinces and localities had been responsible for appointments, promotions, and dismissals in the legal agencies and for occasional reviews of their performance at irregular intervals, usually in response to requests for information on the implementation of Central Committee edicts or signals of abuses. Moreover, a resolution of a party conference on courts and penal policy organized by the Central Control Commission in 1933 had recommended that judges and procurators make regular reports to party committees.[44]

The draft closed letter was neither adopted nor sent to regional party officials. Its approval by the leadership was delayed by the review of the draft Constitution, which officials expected would entail changes in the letter; and then derailed by the unfolding of terror and purge. To be sure, both Nikolai Krylenko, Commissar of Justice, in fall 1936, and then I.A. Piatnitskii, head of the political-organizational department of the Central Committee, in spring 1937, used the discovery of "Trotskyites" among court and procuracy workers as grounds to promoting the draft letter's approval and distribution but to no avail.[45] Still, other measures, including the reorganization of the legal agencies and the emphasis on courts in the new Constitution, would underscore Stalin's seriousness about reviving the authority of the judiciary and reinforce the trend toward increasing involvement of regional and local party officials in its supervision.

Not only Stalin but also other politicians and top legal officials felt frustration at the slow realization of the policies of reviving legal procedures and improving the administration of justice. During 1935–1936 the leaders developed two new strategies for overcoming the obstacles to these processes, each of which had long-term consequences for Soviet criminal justice. The first strategy focused on organization. It featured the reorganization of the legal agencies to produce a more centralized and

---

[44] Thus, in 1934 and 1935, some district party committees in Smolensk Region reviewed the progress of their courts and procuracy offices in implementing the restructuring demanded by Vyshinskii, and one investigated a court after its judge was denounced by an official of the OGPU. Early in 1936 the Smolensk regional committee issued a directive to district party officials asking them to pay more attention to filling vacancies in the courts. "Protokoly Nos. 8, 9, 11, and 21 Zasedanii Medynskogo raikoma VKP(b) ot 15 i 30 apreliia, 18 maia i 11 okt., 1934," WKP 80, 34–42; 140–143;. "Protokol no. 21 zasedaniia biuro Tumanovskogo raikoma VKP(b) ot 27 avgusta 1935," WKP 86, 157–163; "Ob ukreplenie narodnykh sudov i prokuratury," Vypiska ot protokola No. 77 zasedaniia Biuro Zapobkoma VKP(b) ot 8 marta 1936 g., WKP 237, 60. See also RTsKhIDNI, f.613, op.1, d.151, 94–96ob.

[45] RTsKhIDNI, f.17, op.120, d.244, esp. 37, 89, 119–127.

pliant administration of justice, with more power in the hands of the Procuracy. Centralization of power within the legal agencies might offset the dependence of legal officials in the provinces on local power and make the criminal sanction a more reliable weapon for the leader. The secondary strategy focused on the people of the law. What began as an attempt to fire the weakly prepared legal officials and provide remedial legal education for the rest led in 1936–1937 to more radical ideas, such as universal legal preparation for those officials, and the expansion of higher legal education and infusion of more lawyers into the ranks of legal officialdom. We shall examine both of these strategies in turn, paying particular attention to the politics involved in their adoption.

Reorganizing the legal agencies: Politics and power

In spring 1936, while deciding the content of the draft Constitution of 1936, Stalin approved a major reorganization of the legal agencies – the Procuracy, Supreme Court, and Commissariat of Justice. The reorganization centralized power within each of the agencies and redistributed their functions in a way that enhanced the power of the Procuracy. Stalin's devotion to strengthening the state made centralization inevitable. The shift in power to the Procuracy, however, might not have occurred had not Vyshinskii already prevailed over his rival Nikolai Krylenko in bureaucratic battles of 1934–1935.

Here we examine first the campaign of Andrei Vyshinskii to weaken Krylenko and Narkomiust and then the actual reorganization of the legal agencies – its origins, content, and implications.

The implementation during 1934 and 1935 of the policies of restoring the authority of the law and strengthening the administration of justice were intimately connected with political struggles. The conflicts were personal and institutional. On the other hand, they pitted Andrei Vyshinskii, the rising protégé of Stalin and instrument of his program for building reliable legal agencies, against Nikolai Krylenko, the leading justice official of the past and embodiment of the old former (but also Stalinist) policies of mobilizing legal officials to serve political causes and simplifying legal procedures and rules. On the other hand, institutional rivalry raged as well, especially between the new USSR Procuracy (Vyshinskii's agency) and the RSFSR Narkomiust (Krylenko's bailiwick).

We have already seen how the rivalry between Vyshinskii and Krylenko emerged in 1932, when Vyshinskii began promoting the observance of legal rules (revolutionary legality) at a time when Krylenko was emphasizing the contribution of legal officials to the battle against the peasants. The conflict became more pronounced in 1934 when Vyshinskii announced the new policy of restoring the authority of law and status of legal procedures and tried to detach legal officials from political campaigns.

The institutional rivalry also had a long history. The Procuracy began in Soviet Russia as an agency subordinated to the Commissariat of Justice (as the prerevolutionary Procuracy had been a part of the Ministry of Justice). At first, both the autonomy and power of the Procuracy vis-à-vis the Narkomiust were limited. Even though procurators in the provinces and localities stood in subordination only to higher level Procuracy agencies (and not to provincial justice agencies or governments), the RSFSR Procuracy as a whole remained part of Narkomiust and the republican procurator served as a deputy commissar of justice. Procuracy agencies began to emerge from their subordinate status in June 1933 with the establishment of the USSR Procuracy. This new agency stood on its own (for another three years there was no Narkomiust on the all-Union level). However, the republican-level procuracies still remained part of the republican commissariats of justice. Technically, republican procuracies fell into a state of dual subordination, that is to both the USSR Procuracy and the republican justice commissariats. The USSR Procuracy performed "general guidance" of the republican procuracies, while the justice commissariats handled their "operational direction."[46] In a secret resolution in July 1934 the Politburo declared it "expedient" to remove the republican procuracies from the justice commissariats, but this did not happen right away and Vyshinskii was to fight for exclusive control of lower procuracy office for two more years.

The failure to obtain full and exclusive control of lower procuracy agencies infuriated Vyshinskii. One reason was the resulting problems that his agency faced in dealing with provincial and local procuracy offices. The heads of the RSFSR Procuracy had their own views on issues, and with support from the RSFSR Narkomiust they delayed or blocked measures dictated by Vyshinskii. Thus, 1934, when Vyshinskii called for the reorganization of procuracy offices to correspond to sectors of public administration (as opposed to functions) – a reform that mimicked Stalin's new stance against functionally organized departments in general – Vyshinskii faced strong objections from the RSFSR Procuracy. There were also occasions when officials of the RSFSR office failed to transmit orders of the USSR Procuracy to regional and district level procurators.

---

[46] M.I. Kozhevnikov, "Puti razvitiia sovetskoi prokuratury," part three, Uchenye zapiski MGU, vyp.147, Trudy iuridicheskogo fakulteta, kn. 5 (Moscow, 1950), 56; A. Ia. Vyshinskii, *Sudoustroistvo v SSSR* (3rd ed.: Moscow, 1936), 201–204; P.I. Kudriavtsev, "Prokurorskii nadzor za rassmotreniem ugolovnykh del v sude," in *Na strazhe sovetskikh zakonov* (Moscow, 1972), 283–286; RTsKhIDNI, f.17, op.3, d.948, 95–96.

In mid-1935, Vyshinskii denounced such delays, making a particular fuss over the fate of one of his directives relating to juvenile cases.[47]

Another reason for Vyshinskii's resentment of the ambiguous position of the USSR Procuracy was the strong record of gains already made by procuracy agencies in their power vis-à-vis the courts. As we saw in Chapter 2, the Procuracy had gained full control of preliminary investigations in 1928, when the investigators were removed from dual supervision by courts and Procuracy bodies and placed fully under the sway of the Procuracy. Furthermore, the 1933 law establishing the USSR Procuracy gave to procurators the broad responsibility for "observing the correct and uniform applications of the laws by court institutions," with the right to demand case files at any stage. To be sure, since 1922, procurators had the right to protest courts' decisions both in cassation and through appeals in supervision. But the new language describing the power of the Procuracy in criminal cases was broader and gave that agency a position of superiority in the trial setting. The language in the Law on the USSR Procuracy initiated the doctrine that procurators in court were responsible at one and the same time for both the prosecution and the legality of the proceedings. This construction of the role of the procurator in court gained in significance in the mid and late 1930s as procurators began attending more trials and eventually shifted their focus to prosecutorial work.[48] The USSR Procuracy also obtained broader responsibilities vis-à-vis police agencies.[49]

As of the mid-1930s, procurators had become the dominant actors in the administration of criminal justice in the USSR. Controlling the preliminary investigation, with a broad power to supervise the legality of criminal proceedings while prosecuting cases, and with the right to appeal decisions of courts at any time, they stood above trial judges in power and prestige. Power in the courtroom found reinforcement in the rising political status of procurators. Since the 1920s procurators of the district, city, and region had developed close connections with local and

---

47 Kozhevnikov, "Puti razvitiia sovetskoi prokuratury," 59–62; V., "Nelzia li bez organizatsionnoi putanitsy plodiashchei volokitu," *ZaSZ*, 1935, no. 6, 36.

48 Kudriavtsev, "Prokurorskii nadzor," 284–285; "Polozhenie o Prokurature SSSR," 17 dekabria 1933 g., *SZ SSSR*, 1934, no. 1, st.2a and b.

49 Whereas the 1922 statute on the Procuracy gave its officials responsibility for supervising preliminary inquests and investigations, especially with regard to pretrial detention, the 1933 statute entrusted the Procuracy with the much broader task of "supervising the legality and correctness of the activities of the OGPU, police, and corrective-labor institutions." Even though the performance of these functions by procuracy offices became more formal than real in the late Stalin years, their presence in the Law on the Procuracy added to that agency's prestige. "Polozhenie o Prokurature SSSR"; M. Iu. Raginskii and G.A. Terekhov, "Razvitie zakonodatelstva o prokurorskom nadzore v SSSR," in *Na strazhe*, 217–228.

provincial politicians, manifested in a formal right to attend sessions of the executive committees (*ispolkomy*) and give advice. From the mid-1930s many procurators became members as well of party committees at the local or regional levels and sometimes even of their bureaus. As such, procurators solidified their position as part of the local political establishment. Only in the dual subordination of republican procuracies did the Procuracy experience weakness.[50]

The growing power of the Procuracy did not go unnoticed by the heads of other legal agencies. Early in 1934 the chairman of the RSFSR Supreme Court, I.L. Bulat, presided over a discussion at his court of the wisdom of removing investigators from Procuracy and putting them under the tutelage of Narkomiust. At the 1934 Congress of Court-Procuracy Workers, Vyshinskii rejected this proposal on the grounds that it would deprive investigators of a clear master and return them to the ambiguous position they had occupied from 1864 to 1928.[51]

During 1935 Andrei Vyshinskii embarked on a campaign to discredit Nikolai Krylenko and the agency over which he presided. Vyshinskii began the attack already in the winter, months before his promotion to procurator-general. He criticized his rival not only for positions on current issues but also for stances in the past.

One area of conflict was the drafting of a new criminal code. In 1929–1930 Krylenko had advanced a draft code of a radical type, which eliminated the matching of particular crimes with corresponding punishments and replaced it with two groups of crimes (more and less dangerous) and two lists of punishments from which judges could choose. Although Krylenko's draft code gained approval from the legal community in 1930, it never became law. And when a new drafting commission convened in late 1934, it rejected the Krylenko draft and over Krylenko's objections replaced it with a traditional draft criminal code. Afterwards, Krylenko joined in providing public support for the new version, but this made no difference to Vyshinskii. Sensing Krylenko's vulnerability, Vyshinskii attacked the latter's ideas as reflected in the 1930 draft code as well as his reluctance to abandon them in 1935.[52]

---

[50] Interviews.

[51] GARF, f.8131sch, op.27s, d.41, 64–67.

[52] See, for example, N. Krylenko, "Proekt novogo ugolovnogo kodeksa SSSR," *Problemy ugolovnoi politiki*, 1 (1935), 3–25; and A.Ia. Vyshinskii, "Rech tov. Stalin 4 maia i zadachi organov iustitsii," *SIu*, 1935, no. 18, 7. For detailed analysis of the debate over the draft criminal code (and references), see Hiroshi Oda, "Criminal Law Reform in the 1930s," in Ferri Feldbrugge, ed., *The Distinctiveness of Soviet Law*, and Huskey, "Vyshinskii, Krylenko," 422–423. Ironically, at some point in 1930–1931, Vyshinskii had lent support to Krylenko's draft criminal code, for which sin Vinokurov of the USSR Supreme Court reproached Vyshinskii in December 1936. GARF, f.9474, op.1, d.101, 158–166.

Vyshinskii also lambasted Krylenko for his stance in the late 1920s against adversarial conflict in the courtroom and his readiness to have trials conducted by judges sitting alone. In contrast, Vyshinskii called for the revival of the defense bar and even the admission of defense counsel to the preliminary investigation.[53]

Krylenko held up his side of the debate. Krylenko accused Vyshinskii of inconsistency and opportunism in supporting the edict following the murder of Kirov that introduced simplified procedures in cases of terrorism.[54] Krylenko was right that the degree contradicted Vyshinskii's recent stand in favor of a unified criminal procedure that would eschew all of the simplifications that Krylenko and Narkomiust had promoted during collectivization. Touché! In a debating tournament, score one for Nikolai Vasilich. But this was hardball politics, and once again Vyshinskii had shown the flexibility required to serve his master Stalin faithfully. By summer 1935 momentum of events favored Vyshinskii, and no arguments mounted by Krylenko mattered.

In addition to pursuing Nikolai Krylenko at conferences and on the pages of journals, Andrei Vyshinskii may also have tried to discredit the justice commissar behind the scenes. At least, others helped the procurator-general toward this end. In May 1935, at the orders of Molotov, head of the Council of People's Commissars, the Commission of Soviet Control undertook a detailed investigation of the work of the courts in ten regions and territories and a few republics. In scale this survey appeared to match the one performed in 1928 by Rabkrin (and described in Chapter 2). The results of the 1928 study were published openly, but in 1935 the Commission limited dissemination of its conclusions to two brief edicts, each of which condemned the performance of a particular territorial court and made scapegoats out of its leading figures. The Commission failed to make public either the scope of its investigation or the conclusions of the study. Instead, in November 1935 the chairman of the Commission delivered a secret report to Stalin and Molotov. That report not only catalogued the sins of judges but also blamed their weak performance on the Commissariat of Justice. It was Krylenko's commissariat that had failed to replace weak judges with better ones (as required by the secret Central Committee directive of July 10, 1934); Narkomiust that had failed to implement properly the reeducation program for judges (as mandated in a Council of People's Commissars decree of March 5, 1935); Narkomiust that allowed corrup-

53 Vyshinskii, "Nashi zadachi," *ZaSZ*, 1935, no. 5, 15; Huskey, "Vyshinskii, Krylenko," 421.
54 Krylenko, "Tochka nad 'i,' " *SIu*, 1935, no. 33, 8–11.

tion (bribery of judges and secretaries), red tape, violations of procedures, and groundless prosecutions and convictions.[55]

Already in August 1935 before the delivery of the Commission's report, Krylenko took the initiative and wrote Stalin. Nikolai Vasilevich tried to undercut the coming attack by personally uncovering shortcomings in the administration of justice and showing what his agency had accomplished. Thus, Krylenko noted progress made in remedial education for judges, but blamed the Sovnarkom for failing to provide money to expand the intake of students in law faculties. He complained about other budgetary problems, low pay for legal officials, and inadequate buildings, and asked the Central Committee (i.e., Stalin) for help. Krylenko also wrote another letter to Molotov (at the Sovnarkom) refuting the charges that he had not promoted legal education. The head of the Soviet Control Commission, Antipov, answered Krylenko's defense.[56]

Not only Krylenko but also the chairman of the RSFSR Supreme Court, I.L. Bulat, came under attack behind the scenes during 1935. The technique was the same. Again, the Commission on Soviet Control conducted an investigation. Its report on the RSFSR Supreme Court lambasted that body for delays in reviewing cases, distortion in penal policy (failing to change noncustodial sentences in speculation cases) and a "criminally irresponsible" attitude toward the protection of state secrets (many judges on the Court lacked security clearances). Like Krylenko, Bulat wrote a letter of defense to Stalin and Molotov. All the same, a draft resolution of the Central Committee in 1936 called for "reinforcement of the leadership of the RSFSR Supreme Court."[57]

The investigations of Narkomiust and the RSFSR Supreme Court (the most powerful Supreme Court at the time) were conducted on orders of Viacheslav Molotov, but Stalin probably knew about them.[58] How complicit was Vyshinskii in suggesting or promoting the investigations I do not know, but they served his purpose. The discrediting of his rival Krylenko (as well as of Bulat, head of another key legal agency) contributed to Vyshinskii's rise to the pinnacle of the legal world.

---

[55] RTsKhIDNI, f.17, op.20, d.171, 2–20; "O rabote sudov Severo-Kavkavskogo kraia," Postanovlenie komissii sovetskogo kontrolia pri sovnarkome SSSR, ot 11/VIII 1935, *SIu*, 1935, no. 25, 2–3; "O rabote sudov Kuibyshevskogo kraia," Postanovlenie komissii sovetskogo kontrolia pri SNK SSSR ot 5/X, 1935, ibid., no. 30, 1.

[56] RTsKhIDNI, f.17, op.120, d.171, 1–10, 21ff.

[57] Ibid., 31ff., 43–57.

[58] Until 1938 the USSR Supreme Court had a limited appellate jurisdiction; the bulk of cases had final review by the RSFSR Supreme Court. Peter H. Solomon, Jr., "The USSR Supreme Court: History, Role and Future Prospects," *American Journal of Comparative Law* (Winter 1990), 201–215.

The weakening of the position of Krylenko and Narkomiust coincided with the first meetings of a commission to revise the USSR Constitution. That commission appointed a set of subcommissions, and the subcommission on judicial affairs was charged with drafting sections of the court and procuracy that became part of the new Stalin Constitution.[59] It was in this context that the reorganization of the legal agencies was devised.

It was clear that centralization of power would be a dominant motif of changes in the structure and functions of the legal agencies. Still to be determined was the allocation of responsibilities and power among them. The Procuracy was to emerge the winner, but the victory for Vyshinskii came only at the last minute.

The subcommission on judicial affairs, headed by Andrei Vyshinskii himself, met once during summer 1935 to approve a draft submitted by Vyshinskii. The draft conferred upon the USSR Supreme Court "leadership of and supervision over the activity of all courts in the USSR," a phrase that suggested new appellate powers. (Previously, most appeals could go no higher that republican supreme courts.) The draft also gave the Procuracy exclusive power to supervise the legality of court actions and their correspondence with judicial policy.[60]

Away on vacation, Nikolai Krylenko failed to attend the meeting of the subcommission, but on his return wrote a critical response to Stalin and Vyshinskii. Krylenko reserved special condemnation for the plan to give the Procuracy exclusive supervisory power over the courts. Krylenko insisted that the function of supervising the legality of court actions be assigned to the Supreme Courts of the USSR and the republics, as well as to the Procuracy. The final version of the section of the Constitution on court-procuracy agencies incorporated Krylenko's suggestion.[61] Krylenko's victory, however, turned out to be pyrrhic.

---

[59] I.B. Berkhin, "K istorii razrabotki konstitutsii SSSR 1936 g.," in *Stroitelstvo Sovetskogo gosudarstva* (Moscow, 1972), 63–80; V.V. Kabanov, "Iz istorii sozdanii konstitutsii SSSR 1936 goda," *Istoriia SSSR*, 1976, no. 6, 116–127.

[60] GARF, f.3316, op.40, d.81 (Protokoly zasedanii konstitutionogo komiteta . . .) 9, 41–46.

[61] Krylenko also objected to Vyshinskii's plan for direct election not only of people's court judges but also of those serving in the regional courts. Once again, Vyshinskii accepted Krylenko's criticism and in the December draft proposed that regional court judges be elected by the corresponding executive committee of the soviet (*ispolkom*).

Perhaps the most interesting proposal included in the Vyshinskii draft of the section on courts and procuracy concerned the USSR Supreme Court. Vyshinskii proposed that this body be given the right to hear challenges to the constitutionality of laws and decisions taken by republican governments and all-union commissariats. The right to initiate such cases would have belonged only to the government of the USSR and the Procuracy of the USSR. Decisions or recommendations of the Supreme Court on constitutional issues would require confirmation by the legislature. The revival of this

To begin, at the meetings of the parent Constitutional Commission in spring 1936 Vyshinskii regained for the Procuracy a status superior to Narkomiust and by implication to the courts as well. Stalin decided to give the Procuracy the power of "supreme supervision over the exact fulfillment of the laws by *all* [emphasis added] commissariats and subordinate agencies. . . . " According to Vyshinskii, Krylenko rose to speak against vesting this power in the Procuracy, but dropped his objections after Stalin included it in the final draft (May 15, 1936).[62] To be sure, the final draft of the Constitution also reserved supervision of judicial activity of the courts for the USSR Supreme Court and did not mention the Procuracy in this connection. But in practice this made no difference. For the USSR Procuracy already had the right to appeal cases to any court and the obligation to supervise the legality of proceedings at all trials.

At the same time, Vyshinskii achieved his long-standing goal of ending the dual subordination of republican procuracy offices. The reorganization of the central legal agencies approved by Stalin in May 1936 (and announced in July) gave the USSR exclusive domain over the republican procuracies, now once and for all separated from the justice commissariats.[63]

As expected, the reorganization centralized power not only in the Procuracy but throughout the administration of justice. Through the draft Constitution and the draft Law on Court Organization (completed in May 1936 and promulgated in July 1938), the USSR Supreme Court gained the right to hear in supervision any case from any court. Whereas previously the USSR Supreme Court had appellate jurisdiction limited to cases from the transport courts, military collegia, and appeals of cases already heard by plenums and praesidia of republican courts, that jurisdiction grew to explicitly include any case whose trial was heard at a republican supreme court, regional or people's court in the small republic.[64] Neither the constitution nor the law on court organization laid out the Supreme Court's powers vis-à-vis cases heard at a people's court in the RSFSR, but the laws specified that the Court

limited power of constitutional review remained in the December draft, but was dropped (by Stalin) before the issuing of the final version of the draft Constitution. GARF, f.3376, op.40, d.81, 11.42–52.

[62] Kabanov, "Iz istorii," 120–125; A. Vyshinskii, "Stalinskaia konstitutsiia i zadachi organov iustitsii," *SZ*, 1936, no. 8, 19–20.

[63] "Ob obrazovaniia Narodnogo Komissariata Iustitsii SSSR," Postanovlenie TsIK i SNK SSSR ot 20 iuliia 1936, in Golunskii, *Istoriia zakonodatelstva*, 556; N. Krylenko, "Soiuzno-respublikanskii Narkomat Iustitsii," *Pravda*, July 27, 1936, 1.

[64] Kozhevnikov, *Istoriia sovetskogo suda*, 298–301; Vyshinskii, "Stalinskaia konstitutsiia," 19; Solomon, "The USSR Supreme Court."

exercised supervision over all courts and by 1939 the Court acted as if it could hear any and all cases in supervision.

Another reform ensured that the USSR Supreme Court would hear more cases in supervision. In order to cut back on the overall number of such reviews (and multiple reviews in particular cases) top legal officials decided to eliminate the praesidia and plenums of the regional courts. The corollary to this change, however, was confining reviews in supervision to Supreme Courts of the USSR and the three largest republics. Yet, without drastic improvement in the work of trial and cassation courts, reviews in supervision would continue in large numbers, in spite of the inconvenience for lawyers forced to travel to Moscow, Kiev, or Minsk.[65]

Finally, a new all-Union Narkomiust was formed right away with full authority over the parts of the republican justice commissariats that remained after the removal of republican procuracy offices. To the USSR Narkomiust went responsibility for legal education and the management of cadres, preparation of legislative suggestions and drafts, juridical publishing and supervising the regional bar organizations and the notaries. Moreover, the new USSR Narkomiust also assumed, at the expense of the USSR Supreme Court, responsibility for the administration of the courts.[66]

This reallocation of functions among the legal agencies was bound to displease many legal officials, and some dared to voice objections. These included three members of the USSR Supreme Court. One Supreme Court judge, Anton Antonov-Saratovskii, in an article in *Pravda*, mocked the idea of a Commissariat of Justice without procurators. What would remain, according to the judge, a mere Commissariat of Courts (Narkomsud) rather than of Justice. Better, Antonov-Saratovskii proposed, to reconstitute the Justice Commissariat by subordinating the USSR Procuracy to the new Narkomiust SSSR! In making this proposal, Antonov-Saratovskii was attacking the new superior position of the Procuracy and its leader Vyshinskii. Having served with Vyshinskii as a judge in two major political trials (of the Toiling Peasant party and the Industrial party) and more recently on the editorial board of Vyshinskii's journal *Sotsialisticheskaia zakonnost*, Antonov-Saratovskii probably understood the dangers of vesting too much power in Vyshinskii's hands.[67] Another

65 Krylenko, "Zadachi sudebnykh organov v sviazi s proektom konstitutsii," *SIu*, 1936, no. 26, 1–8; A. Vinokurov, "K voprosu o sudoustroistve Soiuza SSSR i soiuznykh respublik," *ZaSZ*. 1935, no. 1, 35–38; Kabanov, "Iz istorii."
66 "Polozhenie o Narodnom Komissariate Iustitsii SSSR," Postanovelnie TsIK i SNK SSSR ot 8 dek.1936, in Golunskii, *Istoriia zakonodatelstva*, 557–558.
67 A. Antonov-Saratovskii, "Narkomiust ili Narkomsud?" *Pravda*, June 29, 1936, 3. Krylenko answered the critique in "Narkomiust ili Narkomsud?" (Otvet tov. Antonovy-Saratovskomu), *Pravda*, July 8, 1936.

member of the USSR Supreme Court, I. Lebedev, also threatened the new power of the Procuracy by suggesting that republican and regional soviets gain the right to confirm appointments of their procurators. Finally, the Chairman of the USSR Supreme Court, A. Vinokurov, directed his fire against the powers lost by his agency. To retrieve some, he insisted that the Supreme Court's function of "judicial supervision" should be understood in a broad way to include not only review of particular cases but also studies of how lower courts implemented the law. And, in Vinokurov's view, Narkomiust should play no part in monitoring judicial performance. The Commissariat should be limited to checking that lower courts followed the directions of the USSR Supreme Court and performing administrative work.[68] An official close to Vyshinskii denounced Vinokurov's broad understanding of judicial supervision and at the same time predicted a lasting conflict between Narkomiust and the Supreme Court, as long as the meanings of the terms judicial supervision and judicial administration remained vague.[69]

The plan to reorganize the legal agencies announced in June and July of 1936 (and fully implemented only in 1938) represented an important first step in the centralization of authority in the administration of justice. For it subordinated republican procuracy agencies and commissariats of justice to all-Union masters and moved the review of many court cases into the USSR Supreme Court. What the reorganization did not do, however, was to enhance the authority of either central or republican authorities over legal officials of the region (*oblast*), district (*raion*), and city. It would take a variety of further measures, including the conversion of work in the legal agencies into a *career* and new ways of assessing performance, to make lower officials more responsive to their bureaucratic masters.

Cadres, education and careers: Questioning the experiment

Both the weak performance of legal officials and their readiness to ignore directions from their agencies reflected the problem of cadres, the predominance among judges, investigators, and procurators of uneducated amateurs not making careers in the administration of justice. Until the mid-1930s most politicians and top legal officials accepted this

---

68 A. Bazhanov, "Predlozheniia k glave IX proekta Stalinskoi Konstitutsii," *SZ*, 1936, no. 11, 21–26.

69 A. Vinokurov, "Proekt Konstitutsii SSSR i sudebnye organy," *SZ*, 1936, no. 9, 24–27; S. Golunskii, "Nuzhna iasnost," *SZ*, 1936, no. 11, 12–15. Conflicts of this sort were commonplace in many countries. They were to be expected in a country like the USSR where lines of responsibility among agencies were rarely well defined.

state of affairs as normal, if not desirable, in the new workers' state, and there was no attempt to change it. As we have seen, in 1934 Stalin and other top leaders began discussing the need for more educated legal officials. In 1935 the promotion of legal education for judges, procurators, and investigators gained broad support among the leadership, and by mid-1936 Stalin had approved plans to expand both the juridical preparation of legal officials and higher education to produce lawyers, some for posts in the legal agencies. In addition, the first steps were planned to encourage legal officials to make careers in the courts and procuracy. These developments reflected the exasperation of political leaders with the performance of the courts and procuracy and their realization that frequent replacement of incompetent legal officials did little to improve the administration of justice.

A new critical assessment of the performance of the courts and procuracy can be discerned in the journals of the central legal agencies. The assessors focussed in part upon the program announced in 1934 by Vyshinskii to raise the authority of legal procedures and institutions. To what extent, they asked, had the simplification of procedures been abandoned and replaced with strict observance of legal rules? Had the procuracy offices shifted the focus of their work from monitoring the legality of local government to prosecution of criminal cases at trial? Had judges revived preliminary sessions? Inquiry confirmed that progress had been made on all fronts. By 1935 some investigators had started compiling proper acts of indictment.[70] Regional procurators managed to send representatives to half of all trials held at the regional courts. In contrast, district procurators and their assistants attended a mere 3% of trials at the people's court (it was not easy for district procurators to resist continuing demands from local politicians to help in rural campaigns). Many judges, though far from all, had revived preliminary sessions for complicated criminal cases *and* had begun respecting the rights of defense counsel.[71] But this promising start at the realization of Vyshinskii's program did not satisfy the chiefs of the legal agencies, who, under pressure from politicians, demanded instant changes from past practices.

Apart from Vyshinskii's program, the assessors of the administration of justice in 1935 began holding legal officials to higher standards of performance than had obtained before the deterioration produced by

[70] Golunskii, "Pervye uspekhi v borbe za ulushchenie sledstviia," *SIu*, 1936, no. 10, 8–9; N. Lagovier, "Perestroika provoditsia slishkom medlenno i nereshitelno (o sudebno-nadzornoi praktike prokuratury)," *SIu*, 1935, no. 9, 5–6; "Preniia po dokladu prokurora Soiuza t. A. Ia. Vyshinskogo," *SZ*, 1936, no. 8, 41.

[71] Lagovier, "Podgotovitelnye zasedaniia suda," *SIu*, 1936, no. 1, 9; Antinov, "Odin iz luchshikh," ibid., no. 10, 16.

collectivization. There is no evidence that the performance of the procuracy and courts in the mid-1930s was worse than it had been in
1927–1928, but their political and bureaucratic masters judged it more
severely. For example, the critics complained of the wasted efforts of
investigators a substantial share of whose completed cases were
dropped by the procurators who reviewed them before trial or judges
at the preliminary sessions.[72] They complained as well of the habits of
procurators of giving cursory review to indictments coming from the
police (as opposed to investigators of their own agency), failing to
attend preliminary sessions of the courts, and coming to trial unprepared.[73] Judges received condemnation for conducting trials informally, writing verdicts ungrammatically, and, above all, rendering
verdicts that appellate instances would decide to change. Less than
two-thirds of court decisions survived review without change, but this
proportion was the same as had obtained in the 1920s.[74]

In short, in the assessments of practice produced by the central legal
agencies a sharp, critical tone replaced the more tolerant, tutelary approach of the 1920s. There was a good reason for the change, and that
was new pressure from the political leadership. From mid-1934 the
Central Committee of the Communist Party began regular involvement
in supervising the administration of justice, and in spring 1935
Viacheslav Molotov ordered the Soviet Control Commission to do the
investigation of the courts that we have already discussed. That investigation led to a series of secret decrees and directives addressed to the
courts and procuracy. To Stalin and his cronies both agencies stood
guilty of inefficiency, waste, and disorder, as manifested by the high
percentages of cases dropped at various stages, ending in acquittals, or
with verdicts changed on appeal.[75] Dropped charges, acquittals, reversals of decisions represented to Stalin not the proper working of legal
procedures meant to prevent punishment of the innocent, but rather
"unfounded prosecutions" and "unfounded convictions," that is, signs
of sloppy or defective work by investigators, procurators, or judges.

[72] S. Golunskii, "O vozbuzhdenii ugolovnogo presledovaniia," *ZaSZ*, 1936, no. 2, 38–42;
RTsKhIDNI, f.17, op.120, d.171, 2.
[73] I. Rostovskii, "Prokuratura Novonikolaevskogo raiona Stalingradskogo kraia ne per-
estroilas," *Slu*, 1935, no. 6, 8–11; N. Lagovier, "Perestroika prokoditsia slishkom
medlenno;" V. Zaitsev, "Kak rabotaiet prokuratura Zapadnoi oblasti," ibid., 1935, no.
24, 14–16; E. Livov, "O sudebnoi rabote prokuratury (zametki sudei), *ZaSZ*, 1935, no.
9, 12–24.
[74] "O rezultatakh oblesledovaniia raboty sudebnykh organov Cheliabkinsoi oblasti,"
Postanovlenie prezidiuma Verkhovnogo Suda RSFSR ot 34/ix, 1935," *Slu*, 1935, no. 29,
23–24; I. Bulat, "Kachestvo raboty sudov – na uroven trebovaniia Stalinskoi Konstitutsii," *Slu*, 1936, no. 24, 7–10.
[75] RTsKhIDNI, f.17, op.120, d.171, 2–9.

For Stalin, like most Soviet leaders, the simple and obvious solution to poor performance by officials of any kind was to replace them. Accordingly, along with Vyshinskii's program to raise standards of performance in the legal agencies came a Central Committee order (July 10, 1934) to review all judges and remove the incompetent. In this particular screening (or purge), hardly the first in Soviet history, 12% of judges were removed. But their replacements proved no better.[76] This was hardly surprising, since competent, literate, and respectable candidates for posts in the legal agencies were hard to find. For years, authorities had been forced to fire legal officials at any time, as reports of amoral conduct (drunken binges), malfeasance, or sheer incompetence reached their ears. In addition, many of the best judges and procurators chose to leave posts in the legal agencies for better paying and more prestigious jobs elsewhere. Overall, the annual rate of turnover among investigators and assistant procurators in 1936 reached 50%; and among judges in some parts of the country, 25%.[77] Often replacements could not be found at all. At the start of 1936, more than a year before the Great Purge, the vacancy rate among people's court judges stood at 12.4%, and among judges of the regional courts at 34%. In city and district procuracy offices 29.6% of posts lay vacant, as did 35% of those in regional procuracies.[78]

Despite the obvious futility of constant replacement of legal officials, Stalin did not abandon the search for "rotten apples." In 1936 the Central Committee planned another "review" of legal cadres. By the time it was conducted (late 1936–early 1937), this review assumed a political character not associated with the review of 1934. From the procuracy agencies alone, between August 1, 1936, and March 1, 1937, charges of "Trotskyite activity" led to the firing of 164, exclusion from the party of 137, and arrest of 39.[79] This was but a prelude to the massive purge of legal officials in 1937–1938.

Nevertheless, during the mid-1930s it became clear even to the Soviet leadership that actual improvement in the performance of judges, investigators, and procurators called for training and keeping some of the cadres already in place. Better educated cadres, making careers

---

[76] Ibid, d.170, 2–20.

[77] F. Niurina, "K voprosam sledstviia," ZaSZ, 1936, no. 5, 4–6; G. Roginskii, "Organizatsionnye voprosy perestroiki raboty organov Prokuratury v svete proekta Stalinskoi konstitutsii," SZ 1936, no. 8, 28–40; RTsKhIDNI, f.17, op. 120, d.170, 14–15.

[78] Ibid., 9–10.

[79] RTsKhIDNI, f.17, op.120, d.244 ("O meropriiatiiakh po ulushcheniem kachestva raboty sudebnykh, prokurorskikh i sledstvennykh organov," Proekt postanovlenie TsK VKP(b)), 22–35; Piatnitskii, "Spravka o polozhenii s kadrami v organakh prokuratury" (April 28, 1937), ibid., 122–127.

in the legal agencies, and with reasons to shoulder responsibility would provide the key ingredient in a more effective administration of justice.

Open dissatisfaction with the qualifications of legal officials emerged in 1935. Already that winter an official of the Procuracy criticized the small number of *lawyers* working in the legal agencies. That spring Vyshinskii told a meeting of justice workers that they neither felt like jurists nor spoke a common professional language.[80] How could Soviet legal officials feel or speak like jurists when most of them were not? Nearly two-thirds of investigators had no legal education of any kind (even short-term or remedial), and 60% had not gone beyond elementary school. Fully half of the judges lacked legal training, including 41 of 56 members of the RSFSR Supreme Court! Higher legal education was an attribute of 24.2% of judges at the regional courts and a mere 4.3% at the people's courts. The educational level of procurators was marginally better; 56.3% had no legal training.[81]

Recruitment of lawyers for posts in the legal agencies could not solve the problem, for the legal faculties and institutes were producing few graduates. Under the influence of the antilaw perspective, which foresaw the obsolescence of law, authorities had allowed enrollments to dwindle. In 1932 the total number of students in the USSR studying to become lawyers numbered 1,131 (in 1933 the figure was 1,276; and in 1934, 1,675). The number of graduates averaged 250 to 300 per year, this for a population of about 160 million. Moreover, most new lawyers took jobs outside the administration of justice. Many of the legal officials who had obtained higher legal education had done so through correspondence courses.[82] In February 1935 the government did approve modest expansion of higher legal education through the establishment of two new legal institutes (Kharkov and Tashkent). It also increased the study of law from three years to four; and established a new specialization in "court-procuracy-investigatory work," with the goal of producing 100 lawyers for the legal agencies in 1937.[83]

The only feasible way to improve the qualifications of legal officials in the short run was through provision of legal training for new recruits

[80] Vyshinskii, "Nashi zadachi," 5–6.
[81] Kozhevnikov, "Puti razvitiia sovetskoi prokuratury," 79; Kozhevnikov, "Nashi kadry," *SIu*, 1935, no. 35, 4–6; RTsKhiDNI, f.17, op.120, d.170, 11–12.
[82] N. Aleksandrovich, "Povyshenie kvalifikatsii kadrov rabotnikov organov iustitsii – vazhneishaia zadacha," *ZaSZ*, 1935, no. 7, 29–30; Kozhevnikov, "Nashi kadry," "Na soveshchanii rukovodiashchikh sudebnykh rabotnikov," *SIu*, 1936, no. 24, 10–14. As of 1937, the population of the USSR was about 162 million. Iu.A. Goliakov, ed., *Vsesoiuznaia perepis naseleniia 1937 g.* (Moscow, 1991), 22.
[83] I. Krastin, "Reorganizatsiia pravovogo obrazovaniia," *ZaSZ*, 1935, no. 4, 25–26.

and officials already on the job. It was not necessary to begin from scratch. Already in place was a small, but growing, Central Correspondence Institute of Soviet Law, which offered higher legal education by correspondence to legal officials who had completed secondary school. Also operating was a program of secondary-school legal training by correspondence, and a number of one-year juridical schools for new recruits and six-month courses for current officials.[84]

This first step in the new effort to improve the qualifications of legal officials was the announcement near the end of 1934 of a modest but obligatory study program for all officials of the courts and procuracy in preparation for an examination known as the "juridical minimum." During 1935 study circles were organized in many cities, but often the participating officials lacked access to the required readings. Almost no materials came in languages other than Russian. To compensate, central legal officials organized a series of radio lectures – Vyshinskii on criminal procedure (three hours), Krylenko on "revolutionary socialist legality and the tasks of justice agencies," Pashukanis on "the state" – but these lectures could be heard only on closed circuit within Moscow region. Stenographic reports were then prepared for broader circulation. The progress of the study circles was so slow that the date of the examination was put off until the end of 1935. When the test was finally administered, the grading standards were lax.[85]

In addition to the juridical minimum, political leaders also authorized a series of new opportunities for legal training. These included establishment of a Legal Academy offering a two-year course for potential leading cadres; expansion of the number of one-year juridical schools (from 15 in 1934 to 19 in 1935 to 32 in 1936); expansion of the six-month courses (from 14 in 1933 to 31 in 1935); and a new three-month course to train legal secretaries, bailiffs, and notaries.[86]

Making these programs succeed in improving legal cadres was not easy. Take, for example, the training provided in the six-month juridical courses. Not only was there a shortage of textbooks (for some subjects none had been published since the 1920s), but also the teachers lacked qualifications. Most were practicing lawyers with neither higher de-

---

84 Malsagov, "Zaochnoe iuridicheskogo obrazovanie," *SIu*, 1936, no. 29, 9–11; A.F. Shebanov, *Iuridicheskie vysshie uchebnve zavedeniia* (Moscow, 1963), 50–51.
85 Boldyrev, "Prokurory, sudi, sledovateli Zapadnoi oblasti za ucheboi," *ZaSZ*, 1935, no. 5, 49; Krasin, "Iuridicheskaia podgotovka sudebno-prokurorskikh rabotnikov," ibid., no. 8, 26–28; K. Maslov and P. Tarasev-Radionov, "Sdat iurminimum na otlichno," ibid., 29–31; M. Strogovich, "O iurminimume i iuridicheskoi gramatnosti," ibid., 1936, no. 7, 67–68.
86 Krastin, "Reorganizatsiia"; "Pismo ot Krylenko."

grees nor experience in teaching. Although many judges attended the courses, the preparation that they received was rudimentary. According to one critic, most graduates were prepared for little more than work as legal secretaries or bailiffs.[87] The All-Union Legal Academy to train the new judicial elite had trouble recruiting its students. The Academy was supplied with stipends for 250, but local authorities proved reluctant to release their employees for two years. The Moldavian government refused to send members of its republican Supreme Court. The territorial court of the North Caucasus recalled one member who was just starting the Academy to face criminal charges of careless work and proceeded to send him to work as a senior judge in a people's court! Many of the officials who reached the Academy required training in Russian language, mathematics, and geography, as well as in legal subjects.[88]

Spring 1936 marked a turning point in the approach of the top leadership toward legal education. In reaction to the dismal results of the investigation of the work of the legal agencies conducted by staff of the Commission on Soviet Control, the leaders approved a dramatic expansion of higher legal education and the intensification of measures to provide legal officials with preparation in law. To begin, the leaders decided to raise the intake of new students in law faculties and institutes to 2,455 in the fall of 1936, a measure that promised to double the number of students studying law. Moreover, the plan called for increasing new enrollments to 2,935 in 1938 and 3,550 in 1940. With a four-year program in place, these projections would yield 11,000 studying law in 1939, as opposed to 2,400 in 1935–1936. At the same time, the leadership also authorized a similar expansion of the forms of legal education suitable for legal officials, including both the one- and two-year juridical schools and correspondence education, higher and secondary.[89]

Most striking, though, was the "suggestion" in one draft edict that all judges who lacked legal preparation (there were more than 2,500) be required to complete the six-month course during 1936 or the first half of 1937.[90] The purges prevented this particular draft edict from being

---

[87] "Na soveshchanii;" Skliarskii, "Podgotovka i perepodgotovka sudei," *SIu*, 1937, no. 8, 10–11.

[88] I. Krastin, "Vsesoiuznaia pravovaia akademiia," *ZaSZ*, 1936, no. 1, 18–20.

[89] RTsKhIDNI, f.17, op.120, 22–35"; I. Krastin, "Stalinskaia Konstitutsiia i zadachi pravovogo obrazovaniia," *SZ*, 1936, no. 11, 27–30; M. Granovskii, "Organizatsiia sudov v tretei piatiletki," *SIu*, 1937, no. 12, 5–7.

[90] RTsKhIDNI, f.17, op.120, 22–35. According to Krastin, the leadership issued a joint party–state edict on legal education on June 23, 1936. Krastin, "Staliniskaia Konstitutsiia."

promulgated, but together with the measures adopted, it signaled the new attitude of the Soviet leadership toward legal education and its place in the preparation of legal officials. Weakly educated officials might remain in practice, but they were no longer considered acceptable, let alone desirable.[91]

The timing of the adoption of the new policy toward legal education gave it added significance. The decision coincided with other decisions taken by Stalin to reorganize the legal agencies and to offer to the public the draft Constitution of the USSR. As a result, the new policy represented a part of the program of returning to traditional legal order, the program Vyshinskii pursued on Stalin's behalf.

The shift in policy toward legal education gained immediate support from top legal officials and encouraged some of them to initiate further measures. At a conference in mid-1936 a member of the RSFSR Supreme Court, Iakov Berman, insisted that within a few years all juridical workers had to have legal education. Berman received warm support form other legal officials in attendance. In the fall, Krylenko himself supported the expansion of higher legal education, a process he was blamed for discouraging a few years earlier.[92] More surprisingly, in the public debate on the draft Constitution, two officials chose to go beyond the current line and propose making legal preparation a constitutional requirement for judges at people's courts. Chairman of the Criminal Collegium of the RSFSR Supreme Court F. Nakhimson spoke merely of "juridical preparation," leaving open what level of education would be required; but an assistant procurator from Alma-Ata used the words "legal education," a phrase that usually implied higher legal education. In either version the proposal was radical, for it would limit the recruitment of judges to persons who had already passed some course in law. The proposal did not go unopposed.[93] One district procurator from the Western region objected that requiring legal education would deprive the agencies of officials whose "experience, culture, and political judgment" outweighed their lack of "formal" education. Two other commentators insisted that it was unnecessary to make legal education for judges a constitutional requirement because the process of their nomination and election would

---

[91] Note that in 1938 authorities made secondary legal education by correspondence obligatory for all legal officials who lacked legal education. *Sbornik prikazov i instruktsii Narodnogo Kommissariata Iustitsii*, vyp. 1 (Moscow, 1940), 46.

[92] "Sodoklad t. Bermana;" N. Krylenko, "Narkomat iustitsii SSSR i ego zadachi," *Slu*, 1936, no. 23, 1–13.

[93] F. Nakhimson, "O narodnome sude i sudiiakh," *Izvestiia*, June 26, 1936, 3; Efim Prygov, "Kogo izbiratete narodnymi sudami," *Pravda*, June 18, 1926, 3.

make legal education a prime trait for those selected. This point of view seems to have held sway, for no educational requirement was introduced for judges into the Stalin Constitution.[94]

Improving the educational qualifications of legal officials would have little effect on their performance unless the high rates of turnover were eliminated and more judges, investigators, and procurators made work in the legal agencies a career. As of 1936 top officials in the legal agencies and staff of the Central Committee of the Communist Party recognized the need to start addressing some of the causes of high rates of turnover: the low pay and prestige of work in the legal agencies and the lack of opportunities for advancement in rank and salary. The same draft Central Committee edict (June 1936) that authorized the expansion of higher legal education also called for the introduction of differential levels of salary for procuracy and court workers based upon education and years of service. The edict also suggested the introduction of standard uniforms for legal workers and designated members of a commission to approve their design. Late that summer deputy Procurator-General Roginskii announced a plan for career development in the Procuracy. The plan would establish eight ranks of investigator and fourteen different ranks of procurator with different levels of pay for each. Promotion would depend on both seniority and performance. There would be no demotions, unless indicators of performance (*pokazateli*) were negative. The performance of each employee was to be reviewed periodically by attestation committees whose judgments would be passed to higher officials responsible for promotions. This system would operate throughout the now unified USSR Procuracy, to which all republican procuracies were now subordinate. Putting this plan into effect took more time than its sponsors had anticipated. As of spring 1938, no progress had been made, and Andrei Vyshinskii told a conference of procuracy officials that it was time to address a formal proposal on the subject to the Soviet government. The actual acceptance of such a proposal and introduction of ranks and differential pay (with corresponding uniforms and insignia) followed only in 1943.[95]

---

[94] P. Stelmakhov, "Dopolneniia tt. Prygova i Lenskogo oshibochnymi," *Pravda*, June 27, 1936, 2; Bazhanov, "Predlozheniia k glave IX,"

[95] RTsKhIDNI, f.17, op.120, d.244, 22–25; G. Roginskii, "Organizatsionnye voprosy perestroiki"; "Vsesoiuznoe prokurorskoe soveshchanie," *SZ*, 1938, no. 6, 8; "Ob ustanovlenii klassovykh chinov dlia prokurorsko-sledstvennykh rabotnikov organov prokuratury," Ukaz Prezidiuma Verkhvnogo Soveta SSSR ot 16 sent.1943, in G. Safonov, ed., *Spravochnik po zakonodatelstvu dlia sudebno-prokurorskikh rabotnikov*, 1 (Moscow, 1949), 81–85. On problems of implementing ranks within the Procuracy, see RTsKhIDNI, f.17, op.117, d.770, 111–121.

As we have seen, 1936 marked a turning point in the approach of the Soviet leadership toward legal education. Stalin and his colleagues committed the Soviet government to both the production of more lawyers and the provision of legal training to most legal officials. In so doing, the leadership recognized that effective administration of justice required that its officials have legal skills. But the leadership remained attached to the long-standing pattern of recruiting new legal officials through party channels and providing legal training *after* they had begun working in the agencies. We will discuss the persistence and implications of this pattern in later chapters.

The Stalin Constitution

To students of Soviet law the promulgation of the Stalin Constitution of 1936 symbolized the regime's commitment to the return to a traditional legal order and the restoration of the authority of law.[96] While correct, this view of the contribution of the Constitution to Soviet legal development requires qualification. First, it is worth stressing that the Constitution did not initiate this process. The decision to restore the authority of legal rules and procedures came in 1934, and the plans for the centralization of power within the legal agencies and enhancement of the legal preparation of legal officials developed in 1935 and 1936, alongside of the drafting of the Constitution. Their fulfillment did not require the Constitution. Second, the Constitution had further consequences for the development of criminal law and its administration in the USSR. To appreciate them calls for delineating the political meaning of the document.

The purpose of the Stalin Constitution was not, as Merle Fainsod so elegantly explained, to impose limits on Soviet government or its power. The concept of "constitutionalism" in a Western sense had no place in the authoritarian order represented by one-party dictatorship. Rather, in designing the new constitution, Stalin seemed to have had two main purposes: to present the USSR to the outside world as a democratic state; and to enhance the authority, legitimacy, and respectability of the Soviet state at home.[97]

The needs of foreign policy prompted Stalin to project a new image of the USSR to the outside world. The rise of Nazi Germany threatened the security of the USSR, and in 1935 Stalin shifted Soviet foreign policy to promote international alliances against Hitler and cooperation of

---

96 Berman; *Justice in the USSR*, Robert Sharlet, "Stalinism and Soviet Legal Culture," in *Robert Tucker, ed., Stalinism* (New York, 1977).

97 Merle Fainsod, *How Russia Is Ruled (Revised ed., Cambridge, Mass., 1963), 349–350.*

Communist parties in Europe with their socialist competitors through the formation of antifascist popular fronts. To achieve new alliances and partnerships required shedding the negative image of the USSR as violent and dictatorial and its replacement by one of normal, democratic government. The Constitution was meant to project that new image. Spokesmen for the USSR presented the Constitution as a democratic document and Stalin himself emphasized its "international significance."[98]

On its face the new Constitution did present the appearance of democratic order. The listing of the full panoply of political rights and freedoms helped to convey the image of democracy, as did the promises of laws made only by legislatures (and therefore stable) and of direct competitive elections. An attentive reader of the new Constitution might notice that freedom of speech, assembly, and the press were permitted only "in order to strengthen socialist society" and that, by implication, the freedom to criticize the regime was excluded.[99] But many readers were not attentive, and others only heard of the promises of freedoms without knowing about the qualification. Then too, few readers realized that in addition to "stable laws," the government of the USSR and the Communist party of the Soviet Union issued countless edicts, instructions, and directives, many secret and most with the authority of law. Nor would most readers have heard that in the fall of 1937 Stalin changed his mind about allowing multiple candidates to compete for posts in the upcoming elections.[100] Another element of democracy in the new Constitution was the guarantee of judicial independence, included in part to reassure the Western public about Soviet legality when extralegal terror was starting to rage. Ironically, the guarantee of judicial independence was to cause confusion at home, when some judges took it as authorization to ignore directions from local politicians.[101]

The democratic elements in the Stalin Constitution might also have enhanced the legitimacy of the Soviet state at home. But the Constitution served to strengthen the state in other ways as well. For one thing, it furthered the ongoing process of centralization of power in Soviet government. For another, it mobilized popular participation in public

---

[98] Arch Getty, "State and Society under Stalin," *Slavic Review*, 50:1 (Spring 1991), 18–25; I.V. Stalin, "O proekte konstitutsii Soiuza SSR," in Stalin, *Voprosy Leninizma*, 572.

[99] "Konstitutsiia (Osnovnoi zakon) SSSR," in *Sbornik zakonov SSSR i Ukazov Prezidisuma Verkhovnogo Soveta SSSR (1938-noiabr 1958 g.)* (Moscow, 1959), 15–17 (esp. Article 125); Stalin, "O proekte," 569.

[100] Getty, "State and Society," 29–31.

[101] See Chapter 8.

life, through both the well-managed but also revealing public discussion of the draft Constitution and the first elections to the USSR Supreme Soviet. Finally, and perhaps most important, by defining the structures of the state, the Constitution conferred upon them an aura of respectability that ordinary laws could not.[102]

Underlying both the foreign and domestic functions of the new constitution ran a common element that was new to Soviet law and destined to have profound implications for the future of criminal justice in the USSR. The common element was the importance of *appearances*. From 1937 until well after Stalin's death, Soviet politicians were preoccupied with the public image of their government in all its aspects and did their best to project, at home and abroad, an image of the Soviet order as normal and democratic. Appearance of normalcy, order, effectiveness, and even fairness mattered especially for the administration of justice, since performance in this area of government reflected on the public image of the USSR, as respecting legal and human rights, that was conveyed by the Soviet Constitution. Or, to put it differently, if the Constitution, the highest law, was supposed to project a positive image of Soviet government, so too was the rest of Soviet law subordinated to it.

The result was that from 1937 Soviet politicians came to expect from the administration of justice if not actual improvements, then at least *the appearance* of good performance. During the late 1930s the image of administration of justice operating normally could serve to mask and distract attention from extralegal coercion or terror. After World War II, the appearance of efficient, orderly, and fair criminal justice assumed additional importance. The establishment of the people's democracies in Eastern Europe made Soviet socialism into a model of an advanced political formation that the new states were supposed to emulate. This new role for Soviet socialism prompted Stalin to insist on the appearance of new levels of perfection in Soviet public administration, including criminal justice. How this demand produced distortions in the practice of the courts and procuracy will be discussed in Chapter 11.

---

[102] Ellen Wimberg, "Socialism, Democratism and Criticism: The Soviet Press and the National Discussion of the 1936 Draft Constitution," *Soviet Studies*, 44:2 (1992), 313–332; Fainsod, *How Russia Is Ruled*, 350.

The discussion of the draft Constitution, even in *Pravda*, included many complaints and queries of an embarrassing kind, inter alia about the judiciary, legal procedures, and the protection of rights. Gabor Rittersporn has hypothesized that what the leadership learned about popular resentments from the discussion of the draft constitution contributed to the decision to launch "mass operations" in 1937–1938. Gabor Tamas Rittersporn, *Stalinist Simplifications and Soviet Complications, Social Tensions and Political Conflicts in the USSR: 1933–1953* (Chur et al.: Harwood, 1991), 87–89, 160.

Once Stalin had decided to use the Constitution to legitimate the Soviet state and project its respectability abroad, he could no longer tolerate the continuation of the antilaw tendency in Soviet legal thought. The views on law espoused by Marxist legal scholars in the 1920s – such as of law as a temporary category likely to disappear with capitalist social relations; or procedural law as mere technique whose simplification was praiseworthy – sounded discordant, if not downright disloyal. For now these ideas tended to undermine the new myth of the constitutional basis of the Soviet political order.

Within Soviet legal discourse the ideas of the legal nihilists had lost currency long before, and by 1934 the official line had rejected all of their ideas. But their influence lingered on, in the teaching of law and in the hearts and minds of many party officials to whom the antilaw perspective had always appealed.

To destroy the remaining influence of the antilaw perspective and reinforce the new functions of Soviet law, Stalin engineered an attack on Pashukanis. In January 1937 a Central Committee functionary named Iudin denounced Pashukanis in *Pravda*. Not long after, Pashukanis was arrested, and Vyshinskii and others joined in a chorus of further denunciations and specification of the bad influence exerted by Pashukanis and his school on Soviet jurisprudence and legal practice.[103] The singling out of Pashukanis as a devil figure was grossly unfair. This distinguished legal theorist had not espoused many of the positions taken by particular legal nihilists. Moreover, he had changed his position on some key issues to accommodate new political times.[104] But Pashukanis remained the best known member of that group of Marxist legal scholars and as such personified the threatening doctrines associated with it. Stalin attacked Pashukanis and ultimately purged most of his associates to discredit the antilaw strain and eliminate any potential threat to the new political functions served by the Constitution and Soviet law.

Conclusion

The mid-1930s represented a turning point in the history of Soviet criminal justice. The criminal law remained an instrument serving Stalin, but the tasks served by the law changed. With collectivization nearly completed, Stalin sought to consolidate the new social order and create a strong centralized state. Such a state required respect for the laws that it issued, and it was not surprising that Stalin should decide to restore the authority of law and to create reliable, centralized agen-

---

[103] Sharlet, "Stalinism and Soviet Legal Culture," 168–178.
[104] Huskey, *Russian Lawyers and the Soviet State*, 172.

cies for its administration. Consistent with the return to a traditional legal order was the shift in the leaders' attitudes toward the education of legal officials and their pursuit of careers in legal agencies. The experiment of the 1920s in using uneducated, political trustees to staff the courts and procuracy had lost its glow because it produced legal officials who failed to meet the standards of a centralized bureaucratic organization. On the one hand, their performance was too inconsistent and unpredictable. On the other hand, too many of them showed an independence of mind and action that the leadership did not value. Finally, at the very time that Stalin turned the sword of terror against Soviet officialdom itself, he tried to present to the outside world a Soviet state that was normal. With the issuance of the new Constitution, law and legal institutions became part of the facade of the Soviet state, while remaining as well working parts of its administration.

These policy shifts of the mid-1930s would take many years to be fully realized, if only because of the interruptions of the Terror and the War. The centralization of the legal agencies, the development of a corps of educated career-oriented legal officials and the improvement, real and apparent, in the performance of these officials would continue to the end of Stalin's life. As a result, the struggle between leaders trying to use the criminal sanction in strange and harsh ways and legal officials trying to act according to their own values would also continue.

6   Stalin's criminal policy: from tradition to excess

In Chapter 5 we saw how Stalin encouraged the return to a traditional legal order to fashion the criminal law into a reliable instrument of rule. Chapter 6 deals with the way Stalin used that weapon in relation to ordinary, nonpolitical crimes in the mid and late 1930s.

During the years between collectivization and the outbreak of World War II Stalin ordered three major extensions of the criminal sanction. He criminalized juvenile delinquency (in 1935), abortions (in 1936), and finally infractions of labor discipline (in 1940). This chapter deals with the first two of these extensions. At the same time, the Soviet leadership approved measures that led to a gradual increase in the severity of sentences assigned by Soviet judges, especially for common offenses like hooliganism and theft. Stalin did not decide that punishments in general should be harsher, but some of his policies had that effect.

The criminalization of juvenile delinquency and abortions and the trend toward harsher punishments constitute parts of the conservative shift in Soviet domestic politics that characterized the mid-1930s. On the one hand, these changes represented a return to tradition, a partial restoration of tsarist policies and practices. Before 1917 both juvenile delinquency and abortion had been subject to criminal prosecutions; Stalin's actions in 1935 and 1936 recriminalized conduct that Bolshevik leaders had decriminalized shortly after the Revolution. Likewise, the punishments provided in tsarist law and applied by Russian courts were more severe than those promoted by the Bolsheviks for ordinary crimes in the late 1920s and early 1930s. Under the influence of Progressive penology from Western Europe, the authors of the criminal codes of 1922 and 1926 in Russia had emphasized noncustodial sanctions, in particular that Bolshevik creation "compulsory work" (from 1933 "corrective work"). For practical reasons (to reduce overcrowding and eliminate the revolving door of the prisons), Soviet leaders decided in

1928 to eliminate terms of imprisonment under one year. The result was that noncustodial sanctions came to dominate the practice of the courts in the early 1930s.

On the other hand, Stalin's return to past practices represented more than the mere turning back of the clock. For one thing, they reversed gains made during the revolutionary period that had moved Soviet judicial and penal practice either into the European mainstream (in the case of juvenile delinquency) or ahead of it (in the case of abortion). For another, some of the reversals had new meanings because of changes in the social context. Thus, in the crowded Soviet cities, filled with peasants fleeing collectivization and living in urban poverty, more people needed birth control than in the last tsarist period. The demand for abortions had multiplied precisely when Stalin chose to ban it. A further difference lay in the effects of prosecutions, for both juvenile crime and performance of abortions, upon those accused and convicted. While the overall number of young convicts sent to prison in the late 1930s did not exceed tsarist practice, most suffered longer terms of confinement. Likewise, the Stalinist ban on abortions produced greater enforcement than did its tsarist predecessor. Finally, the return to custodial sanctions during the 1930s for many common offenses corresponded to normal practices not only of tsarist but also of Bolshevik criminal justice in the 1920s. But, with terms under one year disallowed in the mid and late 1930s, some petty offenders had to endure longer terms of imprisonment than would have been normal in earlier times.

Chapter 6 also illustrates one theme of this book, that excesses, either in criminalization or punishment, tend to breed resistance on the part of law enforcement officials and judges and result in less implementation than the authors of the excesses sought. The reactions to the criminalization of juvenile delinquency and abortion illustrate this point. In Chapter 4 we encountered resistance to the harsh punishments stipulated by the Law of August 7, 1932, as well as to the decree on cheating customers with weights and measures. Resistance to extreme punishments became even more common in the period after World War II.

Juvenile crime

The edict of April 7, 1935, "On the Struggle against Juvenile Crime" lowered the minimum age of criminal responsibility from 14 (or 16) to 12 for a short list of common crimes: "theft; causing violence, bodily injury, mutilation; murder or attempted murder." The edict also stipulated that all youngsters accused of these crimes had to be judged in court and subjected to the same penalties as adults.[1]

The edict reversed previous Bolshevik policy of giving young offenders preferential treatment. After experimenting with a minimum age of criminal responsibility as high as 17 and lowering it by degrees, the Bolsheviks settled in 1922 upon 14 for some crimes and offenders and 16 for the rest. The minimum age of criminal responsibility in tsarist law – when it could be established that a crime had been committed "with reason" – stood at 10. The Soviet code also stipulated that punishments were not to be applied at all to juvenile offenders for whom the medical or pedagogical measures assigned by a Juvenile Affairs Commission proved sufficient; and that when punishments were needed, judges should apply a discount – to 14- to 15-year-olds of one-half of what an adult offender would receive for the same offense and for 16- to 17-year-olds one third. In no case was a person under 18 to receive more than half of the maximum term provided in the code.[2] Note that in setting the minimum age of responsibility at 14 the Bolsheviks had placed themselves on a par with European countries. England had raised its minimum to 14 only in 1908.[3]

During the 1920s and early 1930s most young offenders in the Soviet Union had their cases heard not in court but in sessions of the juvenile affairs commissions. In fact, no offense even by a 14- or 15-year-old could go to court except by referral from a commission. And once the commissions gained the right in 1929 to sentence young offenders directly to juvenile labor colonies, the referrals became rare. The edict of April 7, 1935, ensured that many of these same youngsters would go to court and that more of them would receive criminal punishments (as opposed to educational measures). In the RSFSR a companion edict (issued on November 25, 1935) disallowed sentencing discounts based on age.[4]

This harsh edict bore the mark of Stalin's hand. The simple, nonlegal language (the list of crimes made no sense to lawyers), the abandon-

---

[1] "O merakh borby s prestupnostiu sredi nesovershennoletnikh," Postanovlenie TsIK i SNK SSSR ot 7 aprelia 1935 g., in Goliakov, *Sbornik dokumentov*, 381–382.

[2] "Ugolovnyi kodeks R.S.F.S.R. (1922)"; V.I. Kufaev, *Iunye pravonarushiteli* (2nd ed., expanded; Moscow, 1922), 39–42. See also Peter Juviler, "Contradictions of Revolution: Juvenile Crime and Rehabilitation," in Abbott Gleason et al. eds., *Bolshevik Culture: Experiment and Order in the Russian Revolution* (Bloomington, Ind. 1985), 261–278.

[3] Leon Radzinowicz and Roger Hood, *The Emergence of Penal Policy in Victorian and Edwardian England* (Oxford, 1990), 629–633.

[4] Goliakov, *Sbornik dokumentov*, 314, 398–399. In late April, the Procuracy had explained that the new law had eliminated sentencing discounts (through Article 50 of RSFSR criminal code), but this was by no means clear, and the changes in law were necessary. See, GARF. f.8131sch, op. 28s, d.6, 73.

ment of the progressive approach in favor of a traditional Russian one, and the harshness itself testify to Stalin's personal role. Nonetheless, the edict did represent a response to real issues: the growth in juvenile delinquency (itself a part of a more general deterioration in public order) and a loss of confidence among the officials in the agencies handling delinquency. Those officials wanted reform, but not the abandonment of the Bolshevik approach to delinquency.

As we saw in Chapter 4, the mass migration to the cities – as peasants fled from collectivization and famine – produced a rise in hooliganism and in juvenile crime. New young workers, fresh from the countryside, often working in construction, drank and indulged in rowdy, violent conduct. At the same time, teenagers, typically with one parent, engaged in theft, pickpocketing, and hooliganism, thereby adding to the perception in the capital cities of a deterioration in public order. Already in 1934 the regime responded to the problem of hooliganism with a decree raising penalties for hooliganism on transport, a Komsomol edict exhorting its young activists to combat hooliganism, and finally, with a campaign. During winter 1935 court convictions for hooliganism in Moscow doubled, while administrative sanctions also rose by one and a half times. In March 1935 the Soviet government raised penalties for malicious hooliganism and made carrying a knife a criminal offense.[5]

The response to the rise in juvenile crime originated with the officials charged with confronting it. The main institution for both hearing cases of young lawbreakers and supervising them in the community was the juvenile affairs commission. In 1934 Moscow had a citywide commission, and subordinate to it ten district level commissions. The commissions' members saw the increase in juvenile crime up close. Commission data showed that the number of young offenders in Moscow rose from 5,108 in 1933 to 8,858 in 1934. Of these 69% were 14 or younger; more than 33% had been excluded from school, and half had only one parent to supervise them. Left on their own, the youngsters engaged in theft (65% of cases) – including pickpocketing – and in fights and roughhousing (26%), often qualified as hooliganism.[6]

The commission officials were alarmed not only by the rise in juvenile lawbreaking but also by their own inability to deal with the young

5 A. Gertsenzon, "Organy iustitsii v borbe s khuliganstvom," ZaSZ, 1935, no. 2, 14–18; L. Vul, "Khuliganstvo v Moskve i borba s nim," ibid., no. 8, 18–21; "O merakh borby s khuliganstvom," Postanovlenie TsIK i Snk SSSR ot 29 marta 1935 g., Goliakov, Sbornik dokumentov, 381.
6 V.K., "O detskoi prestupnosti (na soveshchanii prokuratury soiuza)," Slu, 1935, no. 13, 11–12; I. Averbakh and S. Bulatov, "Zakon 7 apreliia 1935 g. i borba s prestupnostiu nesovershennoletnikh," Problemy ugolovnoi politiki, 2 (1936), 33–54.

offenders. In 1934 the ten district commissions in Moscow had to service some 16,000 children – including the homeless as well as the lawbreakers. Each commission had a staff of two or three. According to the head of the city commission, the district commissions faced unmanageable tasks. Sessions of the three-person commissions (including the chairman, a doctor, and a judge, who was often absent) could order the removal of a child from his family, but there were usually no places available in the children's homes to implement the order. Likewise, the commissions could offer few employment opportunities. In 1934 they had available six workshops with a mere 400 places. For difficult children and young offenders not sent to a juvenile labor colony, the commissions could as a rule supply only supervision in the form of occasional home visits. With caseloads of 500 teenagers per staff member, these checkups could not be frequent.[7] In short, the juvenile affairs commissions had too large a workload and too few resources to respond to young offenders.

The solution favored by commission officials and the procurators who supervised the commissions was the establishment of children's courts. The idea received serious discussion at a meeting on juvenile crime convened by the USSR Procuracy on March 17, 1935. The chairman of the Moscow city commission, Faishevskaia, argued that children's courts would not only handle the most serious offenders better than the commissions but could lighten their workloads. The idea of juvenile courts was far from novel, but represented a return to tsarist practice. Before World War I juvenile courts in eleven Russian cities heard all cases with suspects under 14. The proposal to revive juvenile courts gained support not only from the representatives of the police who attended the meeting but also from the Procurator-General, Andrei Vyshinskii. Vyshinskii took the initiative in calling for changes in the criminal code to permit hearing in court of criminal cases involving juveniles without prior sanction of the commissions and the elaboration of a draft law on juvenile courts (with their own judges and investigators). There is no indication that the meeting on juvenile crime even considered lowering the age of juvenile responsibility. The new juvenile courts were supposed to hear cases involving 14- to 16-year-olds.[8]

---

[7] "Rasshirennyi plenum detkommisii VTsIK (3–6 marta, 1934)," *Sbornik po voprosam okhrany detstva* (izd. komisii po ulushchenii zhizni detei pri VTsIK), 1934, no. 2–3, 20–24; "Borba s detskoi prestupnostiu," ibid., 1935, no. 2, 33–35; I. Averbakh, "Zakon 7 apreliia i prestupnost nesovershennoletnikh," *Za*, 1935, no. 8, 10–15; Averbakh and Bulatov, "Zakon 7 apreliia."

[8] "Borba s detskoi prestupnostiu;" "Soveshchanie po borbe s detskoi prestupnostiu," *ZaSZ*, 1935, no. 4, 42; V.K., "O detskoi prestupnostiu."

Within days of the meeting, the chiefs of the USSR Procuracy went on to approve the proposal to revive juvenile courts and narrow the functions of the juvenile affairs commissions. Moreover, they asked republican procuracy offices to mount urgent studies of the state of juvenile crime and report back no later than April 25.[9] Clearly, the top Procuracy officials did not anticipate Stalin's intervention.

Just two weeks later – without warning – Stalin issued *his* edict. In addition to lowering the age of criminal responsibility to 12 for a list of common crimes, the edict sent all young persons accused of crimes to regular courts, subjected them to punishment (as opposed to medical-educational measures), and established criminal responsibility for adults who enticed minors into crimes (or prostitution and begging). Along with the edict, the leadership ordered the elimination of the juvenile affairs commissions. Archival evidence confirms that the edict on juvenile crime was Stalin's personal creation. A draft of the edict presented to Stalin by Vyshinskii a week before its issuance contained only two relatively modest changes in the law. It established the criminal responsibility for adults who enticed juveniles into crime; and for a short list of common crimes it eliminated the bias in the law favoring the use of medical-educational measures over punishments. In the future, the draft edict stipulated, in sentencing juveniles judges would have the right to choose between the two alternatives. But Stalin *in his own hand* "edited" the draft edict by (1) enlarging the list of crimes to which the edict applied to include murder and attempted murder and any theft at all (not just "systematic" ones); (2) eliminating the option of medical-educational measures and directing judges to apply to juveniles "all measures of criminal punishment"; and (3) adding the critical words that lowered the age of criminal responsibility from 14 to 12.[10]

This harsh and reactionary edict shocked Soviet jurists, and, as we shall see, challenged them to find ways to make its implementation palatable.[11] But it is important to correct a common misimpression of

---

9 GARF, f.8131sch, op.27s, d.55 (Protokol operativnogo soveshchaniia prokuratury SSSR), 26–28.

10 "O merakh borby s prestupnostiu sredi nesovershennoletnikh;" "O rabote ONO v sviazi s likvidatsiiu Komones," Prikaz Narkompros No.20/003 ot 15 iiuliia 1935, *Sbornik po voprosam okhrany detstva*, 1935, no. 4, 48–49, and *SIu*, 1935, no. 28, 23; RTsKhIDNI, f.17, op.163, d.522, 23, 27.

   Another sign of the suddenness of Stalin's decision was the issuance of the edict on juvenile crime a few weeks before the Politburo meeting that approved it. Discussion and approval of the edict of April 7, 1935, took place at the meeting of April 25, 1935. The sequence suggests that Stalin consulted his colleagues only indirectly through a survey vote (*opros*). RTsKhIDNI, f.17, op.3, d.962, 3.

11 Averbakh and Bulatov, "Zakon 7 apreliia, 1935 g.;" V. Tadevosian, "Zakon 7 apreliia 1935 g. i borba s prestupnostiu sredi nesovershennoletnikh," *SIu*, 1937, no. 10–11, 48–51.

the edict. The new law did not in practice subject young convicts to capital punishment.[12] To be sure, the law speaks of the application to juveniles of "all measures of criminal punishment"; and a circular of the Supreme Court and Procuracy of April 20, 1935, explained that the article in the criminal code that forbade application of the death penalty to juveniles (Article 22) had become obsolete. The same circular stressed, however, that the death penalty could be applied to juveniles "only in exceptional cases, heard by regional courts and cleared with the USSR Supreme Court and Procuracy."[13] But this did not mean that the death penalty was actually applied to juveniles. To begin, hardly any of the crimes listed in the new edict on juvenile crime subjected even adults to the death penalty. Murder did not become a capital offense in the USSR until 1950. The only kind of theft that could bring execution in 1935 was an incident serious enough for prosecution under the Law of August 7, 1932. A ruling of the USSR Supreme Court in December 1935 did clarify that the edict on juvenile crime encompassed not only ordinary thefts but also those qualified under the Law of August 7 (whose official minimum penalty was ten years' imprisonment). This ruling opened the door to prosecution of juveniles for a crime that could subject an adult to the death penalty. But it remained unlikely that a child would receive this punishment. First, by 1936 the Procuracy and higher courts were allowing the use of the Law of August 7 only for the most serious, large-scale thefts of state property (it was no longer the law of "seven ears"). In fact, in 1936 the courts of the RSFSR convicted a mere 4,300 persons under the Law (less than 1% of theft prosecutions) and sentenced to death only 44 persons. After 1936 the Law of August 7 fell into virtual disuse. Total convictions in the RSFSR numbered in 1937, 1,200; in 1938, 858; and in 1939, 241.[14] Moreover, official data on sentencing in cases with juvenile offenders heard under the law indicated that in 1936 and the first half of 1937 at least there had been no executions. The report included a column for capital punishment, but left it blank.[15] I should add that extensive reading in the archives (on my part and that of colleagues) revealed no examples of actual executions. To be sure, in June 1936 the chiefs of the legal agencies reported to Stalin and Molotov an incident in which eight young men (aged 15–18) had systematically raped schoolgirls under threat of arms, and the officials asked permission for the party leaders

[12] Alexander Orlov, *The Secret History of Stalin's Crimes* (New York, 1953), 38–41; Robert Conquest, *The Great Terror*, 86, 142.
[13] GARF, f.8131sch, op.28s, d.6, 47a.
[14] Tadevosian, "Zakon 7 apreliia 1935"; Popov, "Gosudarstvennyi terror," 26; GARF, f.9474, op.1, d.109, 8–9.
[15] GARF, f.8131sch, op.27s, d.533, 203.

to charge the offenders with "banditism" (Article 59.3) and apply the death penalty to the 16-year-old ringleader. (Note that "banditism" was not even a crime listed in the edict.) There is no record of Stalin and Molotov's reply, but the official data already cited suggest that they refused.[16]

A prominent source of the allegation that the edict on juvenile crime subjected young persons to the threat of capital punishment was the memoir of Alexander Orlov, a high-ranking official of the political police. Orlov reported that on the personal orders of Ezhov, the Commissar of Internal Affairs from mid-1936, investigators in political cases used to present the text of the edict to arrestees in order to pressure them into confession. The investigators allegedly told accused persons that the law had extended the death penalty to children and implied that their own offspring could be at risk should a case be concocted against them. Though second-hand (Orlov was already out of the USSR in 1936), Orlov's account of this cruel deception and blatant misuse of the law may be accurate.[17]

Through the edict of April 7, 1935, Stalin had spoken. Educational and legal officials were left to pick up the pieces. Their challenge lay in making the best of a bad situation by limiting the damage inflicted by the new edict and trying somehow to improve the handling of delinquents.

The elimination of the juvenile affairs commissions gave new responsibilities to educational officials. According to a companion decree in May 1935, the officials at provincial and city offices of public education assumed responsibility for the supervision and placement of difficult children who had not been convicted of crimes. These officials had to perform these duties of the former commissions without their experience or additional staff. The same decree also reorganized the institutions for young troublemakers (homes, labor colonies), but instead of improving them called upon republican authorities to increase financial support.[18]

---

[16] GARF, f.8131sch, op.27s, d.72, 7. I am grateful to Dr. Gabor Rittersporn for sharing this reference. Note that a recent and critical Soviet study of the history of juvenile justice in Russia omits mention of the possibility of capital punishment for children. See E.V. Melnikova, *Pravosudie po delam nesovershennoletnikh: istoriia i sovremennost* (Moscow, 1990), esp. 45–51.

[17] Orlov, *The Secret History*.

[18] "O likvisdatsii detskoi besprizornosti i beznadzornosti," Postanovlenie SNK SSSR i TsK VKP(b) ot 31 maia 1935, *Sobranie zakonov i rasporiazhenii*, 1935, no. 32, 473–477; "Rabota otdelov narodnogo obrazovaniia." The government of the RSFSR did allocate an additional 24.6 million rubles to the provincial governments for measures to deal with homeless and unsupervised juveniles. But these funds at best replaced cuts introduced by the provincial executive committees. See *Sbornik po voprosam okhrany detstva*, 1935, no. 5, 25, and no. 4, 1–2.

Legal officials faced even greater burdens. Investigators and judges had to deal not only with new caseload but also with a new sort of offender. Investigators who followed their usual perfunctory routines often failed to establish the age of offenders (except by sight or word of mouth), questioned young witnesses uncritically, and failed to summon adult guardians for interrogation. At the same time, judges tended to neglect procedural norms, such as the holding of preliminary sessions and the provision to young suspects of defense counsel. Within a few months the USSR Supreme Court and Procuracy reacted with a ruling that juvenile cases called for higher standards than adult ones. These included the designation of investigators to specialize in cases involving juveniles, mandatory representation by defense counsel, and strict observance of procedures at trial. Moreover, in their joint decree the chiefs of the central legal agencies encouraged judges to avoid punishment wherever possible and use social-educational measures in their stead (that is placement in homes or the assignment of guardians).[19]

The most important improvisation for dealing with the new caseload was the establishment of juvenile courts. In his first public statement on the April edict Procurator-General Vyshinskii repeated his earlier support for the idea of juvenile courts.[20] Rather than wait for the drafting and approval of a new law, judicial officials moved ahead quietly on their own. In Moscow, within weeks of Stalin's edict (on May 11, 1935) special juvenile chambers of the city court began hearing cases. Housed in the old Danilovskii monastery (where the Moscow commission on juvenile affairs used to meet!) the new juvenile chambers set an example for the rest of Russia. The trial sessions were closed to the public. The judges heard only four cases a day (as opposed to the usual twenty in regular courts), used teachers and doctors as regular consultants, and saw that the accused received special legal counsel. Presiding over the chambers was a calm and sensitive lady, Comrade Makarova of the Moscow city court. The juvenile chambers heard all cases where the accused was under 17 (unless an adult were also charged). Within a month the chambers operated two courtrooms. (The chambers concentrated on cases against the youngest offenders. Two-thirds of the accused in the first months were between

19 "O merakh borby s prestupnostiu sredi nesovershennoletnikh," Direktivnoe pismo Verkhovnogo Suda i Prokuratury SSSR ot 23 iiulia 1935 g. no. 36/71, *Sbornik* 70–73; and in V.S. Tadevosian, *Rassledovanie del o prestupnostiu nesovershennoletnikh* (Moscow, 1946), 46–51.
20 A.Ia. Vyshinskii, "Borba s prestupnostiu sredi nesovershennoletnikh," *Izvestiia*, April 10, 1935, 1.

12 and 14 years old.) Most were charged with pickpocketing or other forms of theft.[21]

With this model in mind, the RSFSR Supreme Court ordered (in September 1935) the establishment of juvenile chambers at the people's courts of Moscow, Leningrad, Rostov, Sverdlovsk, Gorkii, Novosibirsk, and Stalingrad. Had all of these cities established chambers, Soviet authorities would have returned to the situation just before the Revolution, when nine Russian cities had juvenile courts. The record in practice proved mixed. Saratov and Kharkov joined Moscow in establishing good juvenile courts in 1935; Leningrad had done so by 1937; but Rostov and Voronezh never did.[22]

Even where there was no juvenile chamber, some judges found ways of responding to the needs of the accused teenagers. A senior judge in Kaluga avoided convictions and prison sentences by taking cases of juveniles accused of theft or beatings to "specialist conferences" of teachers and parents and applying educational measures. Another judge in the Mari ASSR organized informal meetings with parents and succeeded in dropping before trial 27 of the 34 cases involving 12- to 16-year-olds that had reached his courtroom in 1937. Criminologists of the 1990s would call these practices "diversion"![23]

Still, the cities with good juvenile courts or creative judges ready to divert juvenile cases stood as exceptions to the rule. In most places juvenile cases received no better handling than adult ones. Investigators routinely failed to establish evidence or explore the roots of the crimes. Parents were not summoned; the clearances from procurators not obtained; preliminary hearings avoided; and the trials rapid and mechanical. Occasionally children under 12 were tried and convicted, though

21 A. Bendik, "O rabote narodnykh sudov po borbe s nesovershennoletnimi prestupnikami v g. Moskve," SZ, 1935, no. 8, 15–17; B. Faivush, "Dela nesovershennoletnikh v narodnykh sudakh," Sbornik po voprosam okhrany detsva, 1936, no. 1, 4–10; B.I. Faivush, "Iz istorii spetsializirovannykh sudebnykh organov po delam nesovershennoletnikh v 1935–1948 gg.," Preduprezhdnie prestupnosti nesovershennoletnikh (Moscow, 1965), 231–234.
22 "Ob organizatsii spetsialnykh kamer narsuda po delam o nesovershennoletnikh," Postnovlenie Presiziuma Verkhovnogo suda RSFSR ot 3–4/IX 1935 g., SIu, 1935, no. 29, 24; Miakinnikova, "Kak rabotaet Saratovskii narsud po delam o nesovershennoletikh," ibid. no. 12, 7; A. Svidler, "Kak boriutsia s prestupnostiu nesovershennoletnikh v Kharkove," ibid., no. 8, 22–23; Bezrukova, "Borba s detskoi presupnostiu v Leningrade," SZ, 1936, no. 4, 13; Akimenko, "Nedochety borby s detskoi prestupnostiu v Rostov-na-Donu," SIu, 1937, no. 6, 43; K. Gurchenko, "Borba s detskoi prestupnostiu v Voronezhskoi oblasti," ibid., no. 10–11, 74–75;
23 V. Ginzburg, "Opyt narodnogo suda Kluzhskogo raiona po borbe s destkoi beznadzornostiu," ibid., no. 19, 18; Nemchenko, "O chem govoriat dela o nesovershennoletnikh prestupnikakh v Mariiskoi ASSR," ibid., no. 8, 19–21.

these convictions were canceled when appealed. The new law was also overused in the first two years. Authorities rushed cases to court, including many for petty thefts. School principals sought to rid themselves of difficult children by sending them to court. It was also common for courts to apply the edict to crimes other than those listed. The RSFSR Supreme Court sharply condemned this practice, refusing to allow convictions even for acts similar to those listed in the edict – such as robbery (as opposed to theft) or hooliganism (as opposed to assault). The USSR Supreme Court disagreed, insisting that the edict be given this minimal degree of elasticity. The RSFSR Supreme Court also encouraged judges to increase the use of educational measures in place of punishment, but the USSR Supreme Court declared the RSFSR Supreme Court's instruction mistaken. On the one hand, it was wrong "to counterpose educational measures with imprisonment, as if imprisonment were not educational." On the other hand, it was also "wrong to encourage liberalism on the periphery."[24]

The assignment of punishments to young offenders was no easy task. The favorite noncustodial sanction, corrective work, made little sense for convicts too young to hold jobs. At the same time, suspended sentences struck some observers as ineffective without some kind of supervision. Nonetheless, reluctant to send many delinquents to prison, judges continued to use both of these noncustodial alternatives in large numbers.[25] At the height of the campaign against juvenile delinquents, the last eight months of 1935, judges in the RSFSR limited custodial sentences to 59.4% of 16- and 17-year-olds, and 53.5% of persons between 12 and 15.[26] These rates did exceed the rate of imprisonment for adult convicts (around 45%), but the average length of the terms received by the juveniles remained well below the norms for adults. The typical sentence for a juvenile fell between one and two years, while the average sentence for adult offenders was at least a year higher. Sometimes, judges assigned young persons terms under a year, despite the fact that there were no longer any legal grounds for so doing.[27] Judges also gave out long terms to a small number of young offenders. Thus in 1936, 793 juveniles (under 18) received terms of five to ten years and 14 terms of ten years; the corresponding figures for 1937 were 965 and 11.

---

24 Tadevosian, "Zakon 7 apreliia 1935".
25 Depending on the location, either sanction could reach the 40–45% level. Starovoitov, "Oblastnaia prokuratura Kievshchiny v borbe s detskoi besprizorsnosti i prestupnosti," SZ, 1936, no. 4, 11–12; V. Tadevosian, "Prokuror i sledovatel po delam nesovershennoletnikh," SZ, 1937, no. 4, 25–27; F. Nakhimson, "Tri goda deistviia zakona o merakh borby s prestupnostiu nesovershennoletnikh," Slu, 1938, no. 8, 1–12.
26 GARF, f.9474sch, op.16s, d.79, 73. I am indebted to Gabor Rittersporn for the citation.
27 V. Tadevosian, "Borba s prestupleniiami nesovershennoletnikh," SZ, 1935, no. 11, 4–8.

But many of these sentences were reduced on appeal, often to terms under two years.[28]

Although most juveniles received relatively short sentences, their prospects remained grim. Convicts under 16 were meant to serve only in juvenile labor colonies, but there were few such colonies in operation (none at all in the Ukraine). As a result, many adolescents ended up in regular penal colonies alongside of adult offenders. However, with the exception of the small number of juveniles whose sentences after appeal remained at three years or more, the young offenders served their sentences in corrective-labor colonies close to the main urban centers and not in the remote labor camps of Gulag. Note that the same corrective-labor colonies also housed a substantial number of juveniles sentenced not by courts but by police bodies, such as the ordinary police *troiki* for criminal cases that operated in 1937 and 1938.[29]

In 1938 the struggle waged by legal officials to handle juvenile offenders in a sensible manner received a blow. The new Law on Court Organization, promulgated in connection with the 1936 Constitution, provided that all judges of the people's courts be elected by their district constituencies. This provision left no room for the appointment of specialized judges at the level of whole cities. The veteran juvenile court judge of Moscow, Comrade Makarova, proposed that electors in the capital city have the opportunity to vote for both a people's court judge in their district and a special citywide judge for juvenile cases. Her proposal was rejected, however, and the specialized chambers for juveniles were eliminated.[30] Almost at once, the city court of Moscow responded by establishing a special collegium for juvenile cases to hear these cases on appeal from the people's courts. One of the people's court judges in the city began grouping juvenile cases for hearings on particular days of the month. Narkomiust approved this innovation for replication by judges elsewhere. The agency also suggested that lay assessors for juvenile cases consist only of teachers.[31] All the same, the

---

28 Tadevosian, "Zakon 7 apreliia 1935"; GARF, f.8131sch, op.27s, d.533, 203. "Prezidium Verkhovnogo suda RSFSR o sudebnoi praktike po delam o nesovershennoletnikh prestupnikakh," *SIu*, 1936, no. 1, 24; Nakhimson, "Tri goda deistviia."

29 Rozovskii, "Kolonii dlia nesovershennoletnikh," *SIu*, 1937, no. 12, 32–33; no. 1, 24; Nakhimson, "Tri goda deistviia." Getty et al., "Victims of the Soviet Penal System," claims that 55% of juveniles passing through labor colonies in 1935–1940 were sentenced by the police (a much higher percentage than that for adults). On the ordinary police *troiki*, see Mikhail Shreider, *NKVD iznutri. Zapiski chekista* (Moscow, 1995), 74.

30 I. Budovnits, "V narodnom sude po delam o nesovershennoletnikh prestupnikakh," *SIu*, 1983, no. 8, 18–19; Faivush, "Iz istorii."

31 Gorvits, "Iz sudebnoi praktiki po delam nesovershennoletnikh," *SIu*, 1939, no. 7, 44–46; "Poriadok rassmotreniia del o prestupieniiakh nesovershennoletnikh," ibid., 1939, no. 17–18, 77–78.

spreading of juvenile cases to many different judges did not work well, and in March 1940 the Collegium of Narkomiust proposed to the Praesidium of the USSR Supreme Soviet that all juvenile cases be handled by special judges at the city and regional courts. In 1943 this suggestion was finally accepted, and juvenile chambers resumed operation in some cities. However, in 1948 the chambers were eliminated once again.[32]

The struggle by some legal officials to cushion the impact of the edict of April 7, 1935, received further rebuffs in 1940 and 1941. On the eve of World War II, Stalin issued three new decrees relating to juvenile crime, all of which extended the criminal responsibility of young persons. One decree added a new offense – causing a train accident – to the list of crimes for which responsibility at the age of 12 (perhaps news of a crash caused by an adolescent prank had reached Stalin's ear). Another decree clarified that, for all crimes not mentioned in the edict of April 7, criminal responsibility began at age 14. This decree closed a legal loophole. Since the demise of the juvenile affairs commissions, there had been no way to prosecute 14- to 16-year-olds for offenses not covered by the edict. The problem was that the commissions had had the exclusive right to deal directly with these offenders or refer them to the courts. Once the commissions had been abolished, police and educational officials should have stepped into the breach and assumed responsibility for referrals to court, but a joint directive of the top legal agencies in summer 1935 specifically forbade this. It read: "For crimes not mentioned in the edict children between 12 and 16 are not punished in criminal procedure." Finally, a third decree overruled a decision of the USSR Supreme Court to shield from prosecution under the edict children who committed offenses by accident or out of negligence. No, stated the Council of People's Commissars for Stalin, the Court had erred in trying to narrow the scope of the edict. For the crimes listed, criminal responsibility began at the age of 12, whether or not they were committed with intent.[33]

The implementation of Stalin's law on juvenile crime revealed how stubborn and resilient Soviet officials could prove when regime policies called for excessively harsh and inappropriate measures. As we have seen, investigators and judges joined with teachers and police to find

---

[32] D. Gorvits, "Rassmotrenie del o nesovershennoletnikh v Moskve," *SZ*, 1938, no. 12, 82–83; Faivush, "Iz istorii."

[33] Tadevosian, *Rassledovanie*, 43–51. Several cases were reported to the USSR Procuracy in July 1990 of children removing screws from railroad tracks or placing objects on them. GARF f.8131sch., op.27s, d.243, 131–132. Thanks to Gabor Rittersporn for this citation.

alternative solutions to conviction and punishment according to the new law. Joining in these efforts at least periodically were top legal officials, from Narkomiust and the USSR Supreme Court. Despite occassional rebuffs from Stalin and his circle, officials did succeed in limiting the potential damage that the law might have inflicted. Far more young persons might have faced trial and conviction, and the punishments imposed by judges could have been more severe.

Nonetheless, the edict on juvenile crime had its effects. Whereas before 1935 no persons under 14 faced criminal prosecution and a relatively small number of persons aged 14 and 15, after 1935 thousands of adolescents in these age groups were sent to court, and of these a substantial share received custodial sentences. By the standards of tsarist criminal justice, though, the number of adolescents receiving terms of imprisonment under the 1935 edict was not unusual. My analysis of official statistics shows that approximately the same number of offenders under 16 was incarcerated in 1940 as in 1914. The difference lay in the length of the terms. Whereas in 1914 most juveniles stayed in prisons for periods under three months (whether under sentence or awaiting trial), their counterparts in the late 1930s usually received terms of one or two years. Under Stalin some adolescents received even longer terms, but appellate courts usually reduced the sentences to the one- to two-year range.[34] The evidence on the treatment of the youngest offenders, those under 14, yields a similar story. Again, the overall number of 12- to 13-year-olds sent to cor-

---

[34] According to official data, 24,467 convictions of persons under sixteen were registered in the USSR in 1939. Just under half of the total convictions for that year (adults and juveniles combined) produced custodial sentences, including 45% of those for theft of personal property, the main offense committed by juveniles. If juveniles were imprisoned at the same rate as adults, one could infer that no more than 12,000 juvenile convicts were sent to prisons and colonies in 1939. If one takes the Russian figure of 53.5% (the percentage of convicts under 16 who received imprisonment in 1935), and applied it to the USSR data of 1939, one would get 13,094 imprisoned juveniles. Compare these figures with the data from one of the last years of the tsarist regime. In 1914, 14,800 persons under 16 served time in the penal institutions under the aegis of the Central Prison Administration (the prisons and arrest houses); still others, not included in these figures, served time in local prisons that received persons sentenced by the justice of the peace courts (*mirovve sudi*). GARF, f.9492sch, op.6s, d.14, 26, 30; GARF, f.9474, op.16s, d.79, 73 (per Gabor Rittersporn); Miakinnikova, "Kak rabotaet Saratovskii narsud," 7; Gurchenko, "Borba s detskoi presupnostiu"; Popov, "Gosudarstvennyi terror," 23; P.I. Liublinskii, *Borba s prestupnostiu v detskom i iunosheskom vozraste (sotsialno-pravovye ocherki)* (Moscow, 1923), 46–53.

Note that a further check has shown that the figure of 63.5% of juvenile convicts under 16 imprisoned in 1935 and the first half of 1936 – cited by Getty et al. – was incorrect. Getty et al., 1026–1027.

rectional institutions in 1940 approximated that of 1914, but they received longer terms.[35]

For some Soviet jurists in the 1940s this situation remained unacceptable. Especially intolerable was the prosecution of children under 14. The issue arose in a conference convened in 1940 by Narkomiust to discuss judicial practice in juvenile cases. After extended discussion of the many defects in the handling of these cases, one participant dared to ask the crucial question. Was it not time, five years after the edict of April 7, 1935, to consider raising the minimum age of criminal responsibility back to 14? Posing the question was none other than the Old Bolshevik Shmuel Fainblit, at the time an official in Narkomiust, formerly in the 1920s the procurator of the city of Moscow and close friend and associate of Aron Solts, known then as the "conscience of the party" on the legal front.[36] For the moment Fainblit's proposal gained no support from leadership circles, and even the draft USSR Criminal Code of 1946 retained 12 as the age of criminal responsibility. However, in the summer of 1947 the RSFSR Council of Ministers supported raising the age to 14 and the drafting commission changed its position to incorporate this change. As a result, the 1949 version of the draft USSR Criminal Code set the minimum age of criminal responsibility at 14.[37] In its submission the RSFSR Council of Ministers cited the small number of cases against 12- and 13-year-olds as grounds for the change. It is likely, though, that a key factor influencing the reversal by the drafting group was the promulgation of the decrees of June 4, 1947, that increased drastically the penalties for theft, the offense most commonly committed by juveniles.

[35] In 1946, a year with artificially high rates of crime due to an outbreak of homelessness (*bezprizornost*), 14.5% of juvenile convictions went to 12- and 13-year-olds. The tsarist norm was around 10%. A plausible figure for the late 1930s would be 12%. How many convictions of juveniles under 16 occurred annually in the late 1930s? The numbers varied, but the highest prewar year was 1939, when 24,474 under 16's were convicted of crimes. Twelve percent of 24,474 yields 2,936 children under 14 convicted in court. If 45% to 53.5% of them received sentences of imprisonment (cf. note 34), then between 1,321 and 1,571 spent time in prison. The number of children under 14 who passed through tsarist prisons in 1914 was 1,525. GARF, f.9492sch, op.6s, d.14, 26; Rittersporn, private communication; Liublinskii, *Borba s prestupnostiu*. Note that the calculations in notes 34 and 35 refer only to juveniles convicted of crimes by courts. According to Getty ("Victims," 1026), in the late 1930s more than 80,000 young persons spent time in penal institutions *without* convictions. Probably some of these were children of adult inmates, but many others were convicted by extrajudicial bodies such as the police *troiki*.

[36] "Soveshchanie o sudebnoi praktike po delam o nesovershennoletnikh," *Slu*, 1940, no. 6, 17–19. In the mid-1930s Aron Solts worked in the complaints department of the USSR Procuracy, but by 1938 he had been confined to a mental institution. Roy Medvedev, *Let History Judge* (New York, 1971), 217–218.

[37] GARF, f.9492, op.1, d.1962, (Otzyvy i predlozhenii po proektu UK SSSR), 5–6; ibid., d. 1946 (Ugolovnyi kodeks SSSR Proekt), Article 12.

The decision to raise the age of responsibility in the draft criminal code of 1949 had no direct impact, because that code was never promulgated. The actual elimination of criminal responsibility for juveniles under 14 had to wait until the post-Stalin era. Nonetheless, there are indications that in practice the prosecution of juveniles in general declined sharply after 1947, and it is likely that the youngest delinquents were among the prime beneficiaries. As I shall explain in Chapter 12, top legal officials instructed their subordinates to avoid prosecutions of juveniles under the new laws on theft, and most of them gladly complied. As a result, the number of adolescents under 16 convicted of criminal offenses in 1948 dropped by nearly two-thirds and remained for the rest of the Stalin era at a level under half of that of 1940.[38] The irony was that in legislating unusually severe punishments for theft, Stalin unwittingly undermined his earlier edict criminalizing juvenile delinquency. As far as judicial practice was concerned, the decriminalization of juvenile delinquency began in 1948, when the bulk of thefts by adolescents disappeared from the courts and no longer brought criminal sanctions.

The criminalization of abortion

On June 27, 1936, Stalin issued a decree banning all abortions other than to protect the health of the pregnant woman or prevent the birth of a child with an inherited disease. In so doing, Stalin reversed the Bolshevik policy since 1920 of permitting free abortions on request when performed by doctors in hospitals and returned Soviet law to its tsarist origins.[39] Before the Revolution Russian law had subjected abortionists to the threat of five or six years' imprisonment and women who aborted their fetuses with instruments to four to five years. Sporadic implementation, however, assured that the tsarist prohibitions affected few people (at the height eighty-three convictions were recorded in 1910).[40] In

---

[38] See Chapter 12, note 70; Popov, "Gosudarstvennyi terror," 23; GARF, f.9492, op.6s, d.14, 26.

[39] "O zapreshchenii abortov, uvelichenii materialnoi pomoshchi rozhdnitsam, ustavnolenii gosudarstvennoi pomoshchi mnogosemeinym, rasshirenii seti rodilnykh domov, detskikh iaslei i detskikh sadov, usilenii ugolovnogo nakazaniia za neplatezh alimentov i o nektorykh izmeneniiakh v zakonodatelstve o razvodakh," Postanovlenie TsIK i SNK SSSR ot 27 iiunia 1936, in Goliakov, Sbornik dokumentov, 390–393; L.A. and L.M. Vasilevskii, Abort kak sotsialnoe iavlenie (Moscow and Leningrad, 1924), 104–105. For English translations of both the directive legalizing abortion and the decree that criminalized it, see Rudolph Schlesinger, ed., Changing Attitudes in Soviet Russia: The Family in the USSR (London, 1949), 144–145.

[40] Vasilevskii, Abort, 21–22; M. Ravich, "Abort v istorii ugolovnogo prava," SIu, 1936, no. 34, 9–10; Elizabeth Waters, "From the Old Family to the New: Work, Marriage and Motherhood in Urban Soviet Russia, 1917–1931," unpublished doctoral dissertation (University of Birmingham, 1985), 251.

contrast, Stalin's decree was bound to produce many more prosecutions and convictions. By the mid-1930s the number of abortions performed each year in the USSR was a multiple of the 1914 rate; and far more abortions occurred in cities, where detection was easier than in the villages. Yet, like other extensions of the criminal law attempted by Stalin, the criminalization of abortion proved impossible to enforce as Stalin wanted, and it did not achieve its purpose. Not only legal officials, but also doctors and clients helped to undermine implementation of the ban on abortions.

Through the ban on abortion Stalin sought to raise the birthrate, and thereby remedy one of the negative consequences of his rule. Since 1927 the USSR had experienced a steady drop in the number of births to the point where population growth, especially among the Slavic peoples, was threatened. The reasons lay in Stalin's own policies of collectivization and deportations. On the one hand, these processes separated or broke up many families. On the other hand, they had set in motion mass migration to the cities, which reduced the housing available for families and forced a large number of women to enter the workforce. Increasingly, urban families, whether of working-class or white-collar status, found it impossible to handle more than a small family. The women from these families provided the majority of abortion patients and made abortion into a widespread and effective means of limiting the size of families.[41]

In pursuing a natalist policy, Stalin relied on more than the crude instrument of banning abortions. That measure came as part of a larger package. To begin, the law that banned abortions also promised financial assistance to women with large families; allocated some funds for the construction of new maternity homes, nurseries, and kindergartens; made divorces harder to arrange; and raised the penalties for nonpayment of alimony by divorced spouses. A companion law raised the penalties for employers who discriminated against pregnant women (by firing or refusing to hire them). Further, a secret directive of the Commissariat of Health ordered the withdrawal from sale of contraceptive devices.[42] But this package of measures – even if fully realized – could not remove the need or demand for abortions. Few women in cities were able or willing to raise more than one or two children (their

---

41 Moshe Lewin, *The Making of the Soviet System* (New York, 1983), chap. 9; Wendy Goldman, "Women, Abortion, and the State," in Barbara Evans Clements et al., eds., *Russia's Women: Accommodation, Resistance, Transformation* (Berkeley, Calif., 1991), 262–266.

42 "Ob ugolovnoi otvetstvennosti za otkaz v prieme zhenshchin na rabotu i za snizhenie im zarplaty po motivam beremennosti," Postanovlenie TsIK i SNK SSSR ot 5 oktiabria 1936 g.," in Goliakov, *Sbornik dokumentov*, 393; GARF, f.9474, op.1, d.109, 143.

counterparts in the villages might consider three). And for most Russian women, in the absence of contraceptives, abortion remained the only form of birth control.

Sudden and excessive though it was, Stalin's ban on abortions did not represent the first Soviet effort to limit abortions. The first two decades of Soviet power had witnessed a gradual accumulation of restrictions on abortion, most of which had the support of doctors as well as politicians. Moreover, the prosecution of underground abortionists, who continued their illegal trade under the Bolsheviks, far exceeded tsarist norms.

The 1920 legalization of abortion in hospitals happened only because radical doctors and lawyers assumed key posts in the new commissariats of health (Narkomzdrav) and justice (Narkomiust). Both of these groups had promoted decriminalization of abortions before the Revolution and gained approval for this goal at meetings of like-minded colleagues in 1913 and 1914.[43] In issuing the directive that legalized abortion, these Bolshevik officials put Soviet Russia ahead of all countries of Western Europe.[44] But they lacked broad support among fellow professionals. Liberal (as opposed to radical) lawyers had favored reducing punishments for abortion rather than legalization. Moreover, meetings of doctors in the provinces in 1920 opposed the legalization sponsored by the Commissariat of Health. Even the Bolshevik officials who decided to legalize abortion disapproved of the practice. The very directive that decriminalized abortion in hospitals declared that abortion was an evil and certain to decline once Soviet power ended the War and improved living conditions. The authors of the directive endorsed legalization only to enable women victimized by conditions left from the old society to obtain necessary abortions without damage to their health.[45]

Before the Revolution and during the Civil War, many women had relied on the services of the underground abortionists, typically old peasant women known as *babki*. Using crude methods and working in unsanitary conditions, the *babki* killed 4% of their patients (according to

---

[43] Vasilevskii, *Abort*, 81–105; Waters, "From the Old Family to the New," 251–256.
[44] Weimar Germany reportedly became the most lenient government in Western Europe when it reduced the crime of having an abortion from a felony to a misdemeanor. As a result, convicted women spent only a few months in jail, instead of longer periods. In 1922 more than 5,000 pregnant women and their accomplices had received the longer terms of imprisonment. See James Woycket, *Birth Control in Germany, 1871–1933* (London, 1988), 147–148; and Cornelia Usborne, *The Politics of the Body in Weimar Germany* (London, 1992), 174.
[45] Schlesinger, *Changing Attitudes*; Vasilevskii, *Abort*, 104–105; Waters, "From the Old Family to the New," 258; "O zapreshchenii abortov."

the decree of 1920) and gave nearly half extended periods of illness. At the same time as Bolsheviks legalized abortions by doctors in hospitals, they kept other kinds of abortions, especially by the *babki*, criminal. The 1922 RSFSR Criminal Code called for up to one year imprisonment for the performance of an abortion by anyone other than a doctor or in unsanitary conditions; and set a punishment of mandatory imprisonment of up to five years for persons who performed abortions as a trade or caused the death of a patient.

The attempt by Bolshevik officials to move abortions from the underground of the *babki* into the hands of doctors in hospitals had considerable success. To be sure, in remote parts of the countryside, there was little change, as women lacked transport to hospitals in the cities and relied upon traditional medicine for most illnesses. In urban centers, however, the share of abortions done in hospitals reached 70% in 1925, and, according to some reports, went even higher in the next few years. Soon, there was a problem of capacity. The demand for abortions in hospitals rose quickly, and the shortage of beds led to unacceptable delays. Already in 1924 the Commissariat of Health instructed hospitals to establish abortion committees to screen applications and assure that priority went to unwed mothers, the poor, and women deemed overburdened. To further relieve congestion in hospitals, the Commissariat legalized abortions by doctors in private clinics (in 1925).[46]

The rise in the number of abortions confirmed the worst fears of the more conservative doctors, and in the later 1920s they initiated a new discussion of abortion in journals and at meetings of gynecologists and obstetricians. While a minority of pragmatic doctors supported fighting abortion through the spread of contraceptives, the majority favored more restrictions.[47] The antiabortion sentiment prevailed and translated into practical measures. In 1926 the Commissariat of Health forbade abortions after the first months of pregnancy and within six months of a prior abortion. In 1933, it encouraged hospital review committees to refuse more applicants for abortions. And, in 1935, the agency reportedly introduced a ban on abortions for women pregnant for the first time.[48]

---

46 Waters, "From the Old Family to the New," 222–226; A. Avdeev, "Abort – demoklov mech nad kazhdoi semei . . . " in V.T. Mukomel, ed., *SSSR: Demograficheskii diagnoz* (Moscow, 1990), 314–344.
47 Ibid., 344; See also Susan Gross Solomon, "The Demographic Argument in Soviet Debates over the Legalization of Abortion in the 1920s," *Cahiers du Monde Russe et Sovietique*, 33:1 (1992), 59–82; Susan Gross Solomon, "The Soviet Legalization of Abortion in German Medical Discourse: A Study of the Use of Selective Perceptions in Cross-Cultural Scientific Relations," *Social Studies of Science*, 22:3 (1992), 455–487.
48 Avdeev, "Abort – demoklov mech," 345–346; David and Vera Mace, *The Soviet Family* (Garden City, N.Y. 1963), 246.

In the mid-1930s the legal agencies joined the Health Commissariat by reviving the prosecution of underground abortionists and making their punishments more severe. During NEP authorities had encouraged prosecution of underground abortionists and gained some cooperation from law enforcement. After all, legal alternatives were available. But during collectivization prosecutions against the *babki* had slackened off, so that by 1933 the number of convictions registered in the RSFSR stood at a quarter of that of 1929 (407 versus 1,629). In contrast, 1934 and 1935 saw a sharp increase in prosecutions of underground abortionists (the city of Leningrad recorded a doubling in the first half of 1935 over the same months of the previous year), and by the early months of 1936 the rate of convictions in the RSFSR as a whole exceeded that of 1929. At the same time, the punishments imposed on abortionists became more severe. In Leningrad, the share of custodial sanctions went from 19.6% in the first half of 1934 to 46% in the second half of the year. By 1935 the typical sentences for qualified abortion (performed as a trade or causing the death of the mother) shifted from the one- to three-year range to three to five years. Some contemporary observers argued that the rise in prosecutions mirrored an increase in the incidence of underground abortions.[49] But the sudden shift in sentencing practice suggests a change in enforcement of the law if not also in policy.

Other signs in 1935 of a new policy of fighting underground abortions included a circular of the RSFSR Procuracy and the prominence given to underground abortions in the national press. The circular asked regional procurators to step up prosecution of abortionists. Its authors gave special attention to a private letter of complaint received by the RSFSR Procuracy about the harm inflicted by "*babki*-murderers" in one rural district. The complainant registered disdain for the local procuracy office, which had neither uncovered the villains (instead, fellow villagers had denounced them to the district newspaper) nor reacted quickly to the signals.[50] A month later, *Izvestiia* published an article that laid out in graphic terms the plight of young pregnant women turned away from jobs by employers (current and potential) and ended up at the door of the abortionist. Similar articles appeared in the regional press.[51]

---

[49] A. Gertsenzon and N. Lapshina, "Zakon o zapreshchenii abort," *SZ*, 1936, no. 10, 26–31; Khutorskaia and Krasilnikov, "Borba s podpolnymi abortami," ibid., no. 4, 20–25; GARF, f.9474, op.1, d.113, 32–37.

[50] "O borbe s nezakonnymi abortami i s ukloneniam ot alimentov," Tsirkuliar NKIu RSFSR no. 69 ot 8 iuniia 1935 vsem krai (obl.) prokuroram, *SIu*, 1935, no. 20, 25.

[51] "U dverei abortariia," *Izvestiia*, 8 July 1935, 4; Khutorskaia and Krasilnikov, "Borba s podpolnymi abortami."

Neither creeping restrictions on abortions by health agencies nor the flurry of activity against underground abortionists prepared the Soviet public for Stalin's decision to ban abortions. The actual decree spelled trouble for everyone involved in abortions. It subjected doctors to one to two years' imprisonment for unauthorized abortions (where a hospital committee had not established pressing medical need). It set the term for nonmedical personnel performing abortions at not less than three years (eliminating the earlier distinction between the casual abortionist and persons doing abortions as a trade). The law also made persons who encouraged a woman to abort liable to two years' imprisonment, and any pregnant woman undergoing an abortion subject to public censure by the court, or, for a repeat conviction, a fine.[52]

Soviet leaders faced a challenge in selling the decree to the public. Stalin and Molotov justified the ban with the promise that now that socialism was built, good living conditions were on the way and that the regime would provide everything that mothers needed. The leaders also arranged for advance publication of a draft of the new law and the staging of a national discussion.

Most of the participants in the discussion lined up to support the law. But through the chorus of mindless praise – demonstrating in the words of one journal that "our country is a genuine democracy" – one can discern objections. Letters published in *Izvestiia* and *Pravda* mentioned that the current state of housing and daycare made it difficult if not impossible for some women to have children. Other commentators warned that careers would be destroyed in the making and children themselves harmed when they were doomed to be raised in families that resented their presence. Most jurists commenting on the law cautiously praised it, perhaps venturing to stress the importance of the promised services for women and children. Only a few lawyers spoke out against a law so clearly from Stalin's hand. Aron Solts was one of them. He accepted the law's main parameters but called for flexibility in its implementation, suggesting that commissions be empowered to approve abortions "when the complexities of life require it." Another critic was V.G. Tadevosian, the official in the USSR Procuracy in charge of juvenile crime. He warned that the new law was bound to increase the number of unsupervised and difficult children. Better, he asserted, to encourage births through the "colossal building of children's institutions" and "gradual measures to improve

---

[52] "O zapreshchenii."

life" (i.e., housing), rather than through "forced births." Tadevosian also foresaw an increase in underground abortions.[53]

Tadevosian was correct. The new law did lead inexorably to a massive increase in illegal underground abortions. This is not to say that some women did not accept the law's message. A minority of them – at least at the start – probably did decide to go through with pregnancies that they would otherwise have terminated. Both Soviet and Western experts agree that the ban did produce a temporary and, according to official data, substantial drop in the total number of abortions in the USSR, and a corresponding rise in the birthrate. At the same time, the underground abortion clinics expanded and grew in number, soon meeting the demand left by the virtual cessation of abortions in hospitals. By World War II the number of abortions had likely returned to the levels before June 1936.[54]

Naturally, there was also a rise in prosecutions against illegal practitioners of abortions. At the peak of the campaign, the first months of 1937, the rate of prosecution in the RSFSR had nearly doubled from the comparable period in 1936: from 1,374 convictions in the first half of 1936 to 1,228 in the first quarter of 1937.[55] During 1938–1940, the rate of prosecution declined. Even the highest level of prosecution, however, did not meet the expectations of the leadership. It was clear to all observers – including members of the USSR Supreme Court – that no more than a small fraction of abortionists were caught and prosecuted. A spokesman for the Commissariat of Health reported that most doctors who had operated legal private abortion clinics before the law stayed in business. To compensate for higher risk they raised prices – in Moscow from an average of 100 rubles per abortion to 700. The *babki* also continued their trade and were joined by more old women abortionists from the villages coming to meet the new demand.[56]

53 Wendy Goldman, *Women, the State, and the Family: Soviet Family Policy and Social Life, 1917–1930* (Cambridge, 1993); Schlesinger, *Changing Attitudes*, 251–279; A. Lisitsyn, "K zakonoproektu o zapreshchenii aborta . . . " *SIu*, 1936, no. 17, 1–2; A. Tadevosian "Zakonoproekt o zapreshchenii . . . " ibid., 3–4; A. Solts, "Abort i alimenty," ibid., 4–5; editorial, ibid., no. 18, 1; "Rabotniki iustitsii aktivno uchastvuiut v obsuzhdenii zakonoproekta," ibid., 2.

54 Avdeev, "Abort – demoklov mech," 346–347; Waters, "From the Old Family to the New," 306; GARF, f.9474, op.1, d.111, 93. According to the official records of *registered* abortions, the number of abortions performed in 1940 stood at 76% of the number in 1936. See GARF, f.9415, op.3, d.1396, 3. Thanks to Gabor Rittersporn for this reference.

55 GARF, f.9474, op.1, d.113, 32–37; V. Tadevosian, "Zakon 27 iiuniia 1936, g. v deistvii," *SZ*, 1937, no. 8, 43–47. In contrast to Russia, the Ukraine registered no increase in prosecutions against abortionists; GARF, f.9474, op.1, d.113, 48 ff.

56 GARF, f.9474, op.1, d.109, 139–140; A. Alimbek, "Zakon o zapreshchenii abortov v praktike narodnykh sudov g. Saratova," *SIu*, 1938, no. 12, 14–17.

Why was there so little increase in prosecutions even during the height of the campaign and why did the rate slacken soon thereafter? The answers lie in the failure of patients and doctors to cooperate with law enforcement and the disinterest, if not also passive resistance, on the part of legal officials.

Investigators from the Procuracy (who were responsible for the execution of the law on abortion) could not start cases against abortionists without the help of doctors and patients. Large numbers of women arrived at hospitals bleeding and suffering from incomplete or poorly performed abortions. Only if doctors or other medical personnel signaled these cases to the investigators could they begin action (unless the Procuracy assigned an investigator to full-time duty at each hospital – an impossibility, given the meager staff at procuracy offices). Most of the time, though, the efforts by investigators proved fruitless. For most of the women were unwilling to admit that they had gone to an abortionist let alone identify the person. Of hundreds of women who entered the hospitals of Voronezh in 1937 with profuse bleeding from abortions only six reported on the *babki* who had performed them. According to a member of the USSR Supreme Court the silence of the victims of botched abortions reflected "female solidarity" – something that the (presumably male) legal officials lacked the means to overcome.[57] Absent cooperation from the victims, doctors could not usually distinguish the work of abortionists from self-inflicted or even natural abortions. Moreover, doctors disliked meetings with investigators and arguing with patients, not to speak of the burden of attending court should an abortionist be uncovered. As a rule, most doctors limited their reports of suspected abortions to cases where the victim actually fingered the offender, where the victim died, or where the signs of outside intervention were obvious. The rest of the cases they classified as accidents or self-inflicted abortions, a category unmentioned in the law of June 1936. In Leningrad in 1940 doctors referred to the Procuracy just one of every forty incidents of suspected abortions.[58]

Investigators and procurators contributed to the meager enforcement of the ban on abortion. Overburdened with other kinds of cases, disinterested, if not also ambivalent about, investigation of abortions (which too often proved fruitless in any case), they gave abortion cases low priority. Sometimes, they failed to prosecute even with strong

---

[57] S. Kopelianskaia, "Borba s abortami," *SZ*, 1939, no. 8–9, 51–58; M. Averbakh, "Borba s nezakonnymi abortami v Voronezhskoi oblasti," ibid., 1940, no. 12, 62–64; GARF, f.9474, op.1, d.109, 97–98.

[58] I. Slepyshov, "Nepolnye aborty," *SZ*, 1940, no. 2, 53–54; M. Shargorodksii and D. Khurtorskaia, "Sudebnaia praktika po delam o podpolnykh abortakh," *SIu*, 1941, no. 20, 11–13 and no. 21, 7–9.

evidence. In the Ukraine one procurator refused to act against the husband and mother who forced a young woman to abort or the "auntie" who did the job. In Dneprepetrovsk a hospital reported five deaths to the procuracy office, but its staff failed to pursue the lead because the abortionist in question looked after the wives of a party organizer and a rural soviet chairman. In Gorlovki, the procurator was fired because his office investigated only 7% of the case materials sent from the hospitals. Many procuracy offices started investigations of materials sent from the hospitals but stopped cases without trials. A study of 163 stopped cases in Moscow reported the causes as "guilt not established" (23%), death of the victim (14.1%), disease (11.7%), and "because the abortion was the first and did not lead to bad results" (10.5%).[59]

With time investigators discovered a simple way out of their dilemma – to charge the woman for undergoing an abortion (what they called colloquially "self-abortion") and forget about the abortionists. This pattern, reported as dominant in Leningrad in 1939–1940, soon prevailed for much of the USSR. The benefit lay in the fact that investigators avoided unproductive searches for abortionists but at the same time recorded enough convictions under the abortion law to satisfy their bureaucratic superiors. As for the convicted women, they received a mere censure or a small fine – itself insignificant in comparison with what they paid the abortionist – so there was nothing to trouble the conscience of the investigators.[60] After World War II, investigators developed the practice of visiting hospitals to generate cases of "self-abortions" whenever they fell behind their general caseload quota. As a result, convictions for self-abortion numbered in the tens of thousands and outnumbered prosecution of abortionists tenfold.[61]

For their part, judges also managed to blunt the edge of the law banning abortions. The RSFSR Supreme Court warned judges in Russia to observe strictly the punishments stipulated in the law, but judges exercised their wonted discretion anyway. The law envisaged only imprisonment for convicted abortionists. Yet even during the campaign, 10% received noncustodial sanctions and by the later 1930s this

[59] V. Osenin, "Usilit borbu s prestupnymi abortami," SZ, 1941, no. 6, 28–32; S. Kolelianskaia, "Borba s prestupnymi abortami," ibid., no. 6, 32–25.

[60] Shargorodskii and Khutorskaia, "Sudebnaia praktika"; Iakovlev, "Borba s prestupnymi abortami," ibid., no. 5, 5–6. Whereas in 1937 the number of women convicted for self-abortion barely exceeded the number of persons convicted of performing abortions on others, in 1939 the former exceeded the latter by more than threefold. GARF, f.9492sch, op.6s, d.14, 15.

[61] Interviews. In the peak year of 1952 there were 64,865 convictions of women for "self-abortions," as opposed to 6,380 convictions of abortionists (also a high). GARF f.9492sch, op.6s, d.14, 15.

percentage increased. In Voronezh *Region* between 1937 and 1939 out of thirty-six convicted abortionists (all women), judges gave four suspended sentences, four terms of corrective work, and one two-year term of imprisonment. (Recall that the minimum sentence was three years.) Similarly, in the Ukraine in 1940 nearly one-quarter of convicted abortionists received noncustodial sanctions (10% suspended sentences and 14.4% corrective work).[62]

Difficulties in enforcing the ban on abortions occupied the attention of the USSR Supreme Court at its Plenary session in September 1937.[63] Much of the discussion focused on the problem of "self-inflicted abortions" (*samoaborty*). The law banning abortions called for application of censures and small fines to the women who underwent abortions, but it did not specify that this included abortions that women inflicted upon themselves. Yet, most women arriving in hospitals claimed to have performed the abortions, and there was usually no way that the doctors could disprove them. To make the ban more effective, the rapporteur at the Supreme Court suggested that all women whose abortions had involved an outside instrument deserved prosecution, regardless of who used it. (Recall that tsarist law punished women who used instruments for self-inflicted abortions.) The judge stressed, however, that he did not want the law extended to prosecutions against women who used iodine treatments or "jumped off the table" to achieve abortions. Commissar of Justice Krylenko objected even to the prosecution of women who used instruments, on the grounds that many chose to abort "because of difficult material conditions." The debate over prosecution for self-abortions came to an end after a bold intervention from a representative of the Health Commissariat. The problem, according to this doctor – who happened to be a woman – was that it was impossible to determine which abortions resulted from interventions and which were "natural." To reduce abortions, the doctor countered, the Commissariat of Health should change its policy on contraceptives. Since their withdrawal from the market the previous year, the Commissariat had built up a large supply. Making them available to the public would reduce the demand for abortions. After this statement the USSR Supreme Court

---

62 "O meropriiatiakh, vytekaiushchikh iz postanovlenii TsIK i SNK SSSR ot 27 iiuniia 1936," Postanovlenie Prezidiuma Verkhovnogo Suda RSFSR, *SIu*, 1936, no. 23, 20; GARF, f.9474, op.1, d.113, 32–37; Averbakh, "Borba s nezakonnymi abortami," N. Duzhanskii, "Borba s nezakonnymi abortami," *SIu*, 1941, no. 14, 16–17. A similar trend was observed in Leningrad, though observers attributed it to prosecutions of the "helpers" of abortionists; Shargodorskii and Khutorskaia, "Sudebnaia praktika," part two.

63 GARF, f.9474, op.1, d.109 (Stenogramma zasedaniia 58-ogo Plenuma Verkhovnogo Suda), 93–149.

decided – in its wisdom – to set aside the question of self-inflicted abortions.

By 1938 prosecutions for abortion in the USSR had started a three-year decline. Voronezh region recorded a drop of 50% from the level of 1937; and in the Ukraine, prosecutions against abortions dropped to a handful.[64] For one thing, the campaign had run its course. For another, the arrest of many procuracy officials during the Great Terror had lowered the capacity of that agency (for details see Chapter 7).

Soviet authorities did not give up completely on the abortion ban. In October and November 1940 the legal and health agencies issued new directives calling attention to the ban and insisting on faster prosecutions.[65] The pressure did generate additional convictions and the figures in 1941 rivaled 1937, but prosecution of abortion cases fell dramatically during the war.

The criminalization of abortion by Joseph Stalin proved to be a particularly ineffective extension of the criminal law, one that produced only negative results. Within a few years it was clear that there would be no lasting rise in the birthrate or drop in the rates of abortion. Instead, abortion went underground. For the doctors performing abortions this meant assuming the occupational risk of apprehension and prosecution that the *babki* had run all along; and some of both kinds of abortionists faced conviction and punishment. For their clients the shift to the underground meant higher prices for abortions and a greater risk of illness or death, not to speak of the unpleasantness of lying to doctors and investigators about the source of their abortions. For legal officials the ban on abortion supplied one more law that they chose not to implement, except in peculiar ways that suited their convenience.

The strengthening of punishment

The mid and late 1930s in the USSR witnessed a gradual and significant increase in the severity of punishments applied to ordinary criminals. Stemming from changes in judicial practice more than in law, the shift featured both a rise in the proportion of sentences to deprivation of freedom (imprisonment) and, more important, the use of longer terms of confinement than had been assigned to the same offenses in the 1920s.

---

[64] M. Averbakh, "Borba s nezakonnymi abortami," Kolelianskaia, "Borba s prestupnymi abortami."

[65] The directives stipulated that hospitals were to report suspicious cases within twenty four hours of the arrival of the women; the Procuracy was to decide on indictments within another twenty four hours; and judges had three days to hold a preliminary session and ten days in which to complete a trial (the minimum set by the USSR Supreme Court in 1937), Osenin, "Usilit borbu."

The trend toward more severe punishments was associated with particular policies, some of which involved Stalin. The trend may also have reflected the dictator's attitudes toward coercion and his use of harsh punishments for political offenders, often assigned extrajudicially.

Here we shall begin by delineating and explaining the main contours of the pattern of punishment for the decade of the 1930s. We shall then assess its meaning, especially the extent to which the increase in severity represented a return to traditional punishment of the tsarist era or alternatively a new degree of harshness.

To understand what happened to punishments in the mid-1930s one must start with a crucial policy shift of 1928–1929. On the eve of collectivization Soviet leaders decided to relieve the crisis of congestion in prisons and colonies once and for all by ordering judges to stop giving any terms of imprisonment for under one year. In place of short terms of imprisonment measured in months, judges were first instructed, later ordered, to assign noncustodial sanctions, especially the favorite sanction "compulsory work" (after 1933 "corrective work"). As I have explained elsewhere, judges disliked this directive, for they saw compulsory work at one's place of employment as nothing more than a fine, and knew that compulsory work at other locations was often not implemented.[66] Nonetheless, by 1930 most judges were awarding this sanction to most offenders convicted of ordinary theft, and hooliganism, as well as peasants who violated grain contracts and officials accused of negligence. Even more serious offenses sometimes resulted in noncustodial sentences; in 1932, one-quarter of murderers and one-third of sex offenders avoided confinement. In 1930, the high point of leniency in Soviet punishments assigned by courts, a mere 9.6% of sentences featured deprivation of freedom, and most of these were for periods under three years.[67]

The first departure from this pattern came with the adoption and implementation of the Law of August 7, 1932. As we saw in Chapter 4, this Law represented Stalin's answer to hungry peasants who tried to acquire or hold back grain needed for survival. After resisting the law for a short time, most judges gave in and produced a surge of long terms of imprisonment unprecedented in Soviet, or for that matter Russian, history. In the RSFSR alone, 22,400 persons were convicted in 1932, 103,400 in 1933, and 37,700 in 1934 – before the law declined into disuse.

---

[66] Peter H. Solomon, Jr., "Soviet Penal Policy, 1917–1934: A Reinterpretation," *Slavic Review*, 39:2 (June 1980), 195–217. See also M.D. Shargorodskii, *Nakazanie po sovetskomu ugolovnomu pravu* (Moscow, 1958), 83–4.

[67] Ibid., 74–84; A. Gertsenzon, "Klassovaia borba i perezhitki starogo byta," *SIu*, 1934, no. 1, 16–17.

Virtually all of these persons received long terms of imprisonment, usually in the five- to ten-year range.[68] Naturally, this spate of prosecutions influenced the overall data; the share of imprisonment in punishments jumped to 17% in 1932, to 29% in 1933, and slipped to 25.7% in 1934 (as prosecutions according to the Law slackened). The average length of terms went from 2.2 years in 1931, to 3.3 in 1932, to 4.6 in 1933, and back to 3.8 in 1934.[69] The Law of August 7, brutal as it was, represented a temporary politicization of theft, and its harsh contribution to the pattern of punishment did not last. Hidden in the data for this period was an increase in custodial sentences for other crimes (by my calculations the Law of August 7 accounted for about 8% of total convictions in 1933), and some of these were for sizable terms. In 1934 nearly half of all custodial sentences were for terms of three to five years, and these represented offenses other than Law of August 7. Note that a sentence of three years had special significance, since this meant the likelihood of serving in a camp operated by the OGPU (usually in a remote location) rather than a colony or prison of Narkomiust. The persons receiving terms of three to five years seem to have represented a cross section of more serious offenders, including persons convicted of serious official crimes, such as embezzlement in office and misuse of authority, as well as the more serious property offenses not handled under the Law of August 7. Not included in the expansion of middle-length terms of imprisonment were persons convicted of ordinary theft (most received noncustodial sanctions) and of hooliganism (only 12.8% received custodial sanctions in the first half of 1934).[70]

As of mid-1934 – apart from those persons (usually peasants) victimized under the Law of August 7, 1932 – most persons convicted in Soviet courts, especially of the common offenses of hooliganism and theft, still received noncustodial sanctions. The creeping return to imprisonment and its lengthening had focused thus far on relatively serious offenses that would have received imprisonment in the 1920s, though perhaps not for terms of the same length. One effect, though, of the longer sentences used under the Law of August 7 may have been a shift in penal values. A three-year term of confinement might have seemed more lenient than it did before.

---

68 Popov, "Gosudarstvennyi terror." The Law of August 7, 1932, also produced executions, 1,000 in 1932 alone, and at least that many in 1933, before the Instruction of May 8 signaled judges to cut back on applying the full force of the Law. See Ilin, "Kollektivizatsiia."

69 Shargoroskii, *Nakazanie*, 74–75; Ger P. van den Berg, *The Soviet System of Justice: Figures and Policy* (The Hague, 1985), 295, 307–308.

70 A. Shliapochnikov, "Prestupnost i repressii v SSSR (Kratskii obzor)," *Problemy ugolovnoi politiki*, 1 (1935), 75–100.

Nineteen hundred thirty-five marked a turning point in the share occupied by imprisonment in the sentences of Soviet judges. Imprisonment rose from 24.7% of punishments from courts in 1934 to 37% in 1935, and it would stay around the 40% mark for the next few years.[71] The change in 1935 reflected at least two developments, one temporary, the other of lasting import. The first was a new round of cases supplied by the political police. During 1935 in the wake of the Kirov murder, courts heard some 118,000 such cases, as opposed to 32,500 in 1934, many for anti-Soviet agititation and many resulting in long terms of confinement. As a result, the average term of imprisonment rose from 3.8 to 4.2 years. The courts heard roughly the same numbers of such cases in 1936.[72] Another change that influenced the level of imprisonment was a shift in regime policy toward hooliganism.

As we have seen earlier, 1932–1934 saw a substantial rise in incidents of hooliganism in Soviet cities and a shift toward more serious cases involving physical assaults and weapons. Many of the offenders were young workers, sometimes seasonal or temporary, who had migrated from the countryside and drank heavily for lack of other entertainment. Most often, their misdeeds were processed administratively, but many violations, including more serious ones that involved fights and weapons, came to the courts, and judges treated nearly half of them as "malicious hooliganism." Nonetheless, until mid-1934, sentences were mostly noncustodial.[73]

During 1934, however, authorities started reacting to this new threat. Hooliganism received special attention in the local press, and the leadership in the center responded with a new law against hooliganism on transport and a Komsomol edict directing that agency's activists to address the issue. In the last months of 1934 – perhaps in response to local directives – judges began giving more custodial sanctions. The big change occurred in early 1935.[74]

---

71 Van der Berg, *Soviet System of Justice*, 295, based on a variety of sources, including Gertsenzon, *Sovetskaia sudebnaia statistika* (Moscow, 1937), 203. Similar data for the RSFSR alone – a rise in imprisonment from 25.7% of sentences in 1934 to 36.3% in 1935 to 39.3% in 1936 to 44.6% in 1937 – is found in B. Mankovskii, "Voprosy ugolovnogo prava v periode perekhoda ot sotsializma k kommunizmu," *SGiP*, 1939, no. 3, 88–101. GARF, f.9474, op.1, d.104, 4.8, giving the share of custodial sentences in the RSFSR as 19.8% in the first half of 1934, 26% in the second; 33.0% in the first half of 1935, 38.8% in the second; and 38.19% in the first half of 1936.
72 Popov, "Gosudarstvennyi terror," 28; van den Berg, *Soviet System of Justice*, 307.
73 L. Vul, "Khuliganstvo v Moskve i borba s nim," *ZaSZ*, 1935, no. 8, 18–21; Shliapochnikov, "Prestupnost i repressia," 93.
74 Ibid., 94; A. Gertsenzon, "Organy iustitsii v borbe s khuliganstvom," *SZ*, 1935, no. 2, 14–19.

Perhaps in response to a secret party directive, perhaps on their own, political authorities in a number of cities initiated campaigns against hooliganism. The campaign became universal after a special directive of the RSFSR Supreme Court (Feb. 14, 1935); and in late March, Stalin added his voice with an edict raising penalties for malicious hooliganism to a maximum of five years and forbidding the possession of certain knives.[75]

The campaign was intense. In March the number of court cases for hooliganism in Moscow doubled, while the number of administrative sanctions rose by one and a half.[76] And, at the same time, custodial sanctions rose drastically to well over half of court convictions for hooliganism. During the campaign judges tended to overapply the charge of hooliganism and give excessive penalties. As a result, in 1935 the number of convictions for hooliganism rose 43.6%, and 42.4% of convicted hooligans received sentences of imprisonment in 1935.[77] And, while the number of hooliganism cases tapered off during 1936 (to more normal levels), the habit of using custodial sanctions did not go away.

During 1937 and 1938, the use of custodial sanctions for hooliganism climbed over the 50% mark, and according to one source, reached two-thirds of all convictions for hooliganism in courts in 1939. This was not due to any shift of cases out of the courts into administrative proceedings; the overall number of hooligans convicted in 1938 nearly returned to the high level of 1935. In fact, hooliganism was the only common crime *not* to register a major drop in court convictions in 1938. (In 1939 convictions for theft increased and for hooliganism decreased.)[78]

The other common offense that must have contributed to the trend toward more custodial sanctions was theft. Fragmentary data make it

---

[75] N. Aleksandrovskaia, "Prokuratura i pechat v borbe s khuliganstvom" *SZ*, 1935, no. 35, 33–36; Kurmanin, "Borba s khuliganstvom v Irkutske," ibid., no. 6, 46–47; Lagovier, "Sudebnye organy v borbe s khuliganstvom," *SIu*, 1935, no. 13, 9–10; E. Lvov, "Po khuliganam, banditam – besposhchadnyi udar," ibid., no. 14, 6; Goliakov, *Sbornik dokumentov*, 361.

[76] Vul, "Khuliganstvo v Moskve," 20.

[77] "Sudebnaia praktika po delam o khuliganstve," *SIu*, 1939, no. 12, 25–29. Also Glazkov, "Vernee i tverzhe udar po khuliganstvy," *SZ*, 1935, no. 5, 24–26; A. Kirzner, "Khuligastvo," ibid., no. 10, 48–50; Viach. Chernov, "O chem govorit sudebnaia praktika po delam o khuliganstve," *SIu*, 1934, no. 16, 6.

[78] B. Shaver, "Borba s khuliganstom i khuliganami," *SZ*, 1940, no. 1, 12–18; "Sudebnaia praktika po delam o khuliganstve," *SIu*, 1939, no. 2, 25, 29; Mankovskii, "Voprosy ugolovnogo prava," 91. GARF, f.9492sch, op.6s, d.14, 14; op.2s, d.42, 130. (On the drop in prosecutions for theft, see M. Krasnogorskaia, "Sudebnaia praktika po delam o khishcheniiakh sotsialisticheskoi sobstvennosti i rastratakh," *SIu*, 1940, no. 9, 1–6; and Mankovskii, "Voprosy ugolovnogo prava.")

impossible to delineate the trends, but my calculations indicate a small rise in the share of imprisonment between 1934 to 1939: for theft of personal property from the range of 10–15% to 20–25%; and for theft of state property from an estimated 35% to a reported figure of 43%.[79]

By 1939, then, some 45% of offenders received custodial sentences, and this figure no longer included any political offenders (whose cases were heard by NKVD tribunals and not included in court data). Two of every five persons convicted of stealing from the state went to prison, along with three of five persons convicted for hooliganism. Almost all of these offenders had been receiving noncustodial sanctions in the first part of the decade. To be sure, some of these offenders would have received terms of imprisonment in 1927, but then the terms would have numbered in months. Most of the sentences for these ordinary offenders in 1939 fell into the one- to three-year category.

Why did punishments for ordinary offenses increase between 1937 and 1939? It is interesting to speculate. One possibility is that, due to their loss of capacity during the Purge period (as many judges and procurators fell victim to terror), courts concentrated on more serious cases. The data suggest that this may well have happened with thefts in 1937–1938 and then with hooliganism in 1939.[80] Alternatively, the higher penalties may have reflected the Terror in other ways. Perhaps, some judges tried to protect themselves from criticism and falling victim to repression by producing the kind of sentencing statistics that no one could question. Perhaps, some of them received directives from

[79] Data from Leningrad Region and city show an increase from 9.0% of convictions in 1934 (first half) to 25.6% in 1935 (first half). This jump may have been extreme, but its upper limit probably represented the norm for other provinces, if not in 1935, at least by later in the decade. (Krasnilikov, "Borba s krazhei lichnogo imushchestva," SZ, 1936, no. 3, 19–22.) The small value of most items stolen and the litany of complaints later on about underestimation of this crime suggest that the rate could not have gone higher. According to Durmanov ("Krazha lichnogo imushchestva trudiashchikhsia," SZ, no. 5, 38–42), the rate of imprisonment for all kinds of theft (Article 162) in the RSFSR in the first half of 1934 was 21.3%. If the Leningrad figure for theft of personal property is combined with the Durmanov figure, the share of imprisonment for theft of state property becomes 32%. If one adds to this convictions according to the Law of August 7, 1932, that occurred in cities (about 30% of the total supplied by Popov in "Gosudarstvennyi terror") and would likely have reoccurred after the Famine-related offenses disappeared, one gets a new total of 35% custodial sentences for theft of state property. In 1939, according to I. Afanasev ("Usilit borbu s prestupnostiu," SZ, 1940, no. 10, 44–46), this figure reached 43.8%. The rise from about 35% to 43.8% may well have reflected the drop in prosecution of less serious thefts of state property (the 1938 and 1939 levels were 16–25% below that of 1937) and a corresponding increase in the seriousness of the cases in the pool. GARF, f.9492sch, op.6s, d.14, 14.

[80] Mankovskii, "Voprosy ugolovnogo prava," shows a drop in theft prosecutions but the level of hooliganism holding steady for the four-year period.

their local political masters, who, ever more responsible for the courts, also wanted irreproachable indicators. Then too, the scale of penal values used by judges may well have been influenced by the long terms of imprisonment that were being imposed on supposed political offenders, both by special collegia of the courts and extrajudicial bodies of the NKVD. Stalin contributed to the extension of the scale of sanctions by establishing in 1937 a new maximum term of imprisonment of 25 years, replacing the earlier limit of 10 years for some political crimes.[81]

For a number of years Stalin had indirectly encouraged the increasing severity of punishments by emphasizing as the purpose of punishment retribution and deterrence over reform and reeducation. While the laws of the 1920s referred to "corrective-labor" colonies and camps, laws in the 1930s deserted these euphemisms. The Law of August 7, 1932, called for confinement of the guilty in "concentration camps." The hooliganism decree of March 1935 would place malicious hooligans "in prison." The edict of April 7, 1935, calls for "locking up in prison" (*tiuremnoe zakliuchenie*) adults instigating juveniles to commit crimes, and the same phrase occurs three times in the 1936 law criminalizing abortion.[82] Similarly, drafts of a new criminal code in 1934 and late 1939 replaced the term "measures of social defense" with "punishment."[83] Also symbolic of the desertion of any reform orientation in punishment was the elimination of parole in 1938.[84]

The return of a substantial proportion of sentences in Soviet courts to terms of imprisonment, ranging usually from one to two and a half years, represented an increase in severity in comparison with the early 1930s and also with the 1920s. How, one might ask, does it compare with the punishments assigned by judges in the last years of tsarism? Did the new terms of imprisonment for hooligans and thieves represent a return to tradition or a new excess of Stalin?

It is difficult to make these comparisons, for it is necessary to take into account a variety of different kinds of courts that operated in prerevolutionary Russia, the broad administrative jurisdiction in the early Soviet period, and differences in the definition of crimes. But one can produce rough estimates. The hooliganism incidents of the mid and late 1930s that led to imprisonment usually involved fights (that is,

---

[81] Goliakov, *Sbornik dokumentov*, 396.

[82] Ibid., 335–336, 382–283, 390–392.

[83] Hiroshi Oda, "Criminal Law Reform in the Soviet Union under Stalin," in F.J.M. Feldbrugge, ed., *The Distinctiveness of Soviet Law* (Dordrecht, 1987), 77–95; A.A. Piontkovskii, *Staliniskaia konstitutsiia i proekt ugolovnogo kodeksa* (Moscow, 1947).

[84] Ibid., Solomon, *Soviet Criminologists*, 29. This classic incentive for prisoners to mend their ways was replaced by early release as a reward for extra hard labor (according to a system of labor-day counts).

elements of assault) and often weapons as well. While those assaults that caused bodily harm might in tsarist Russia end up in the district court (*okruzhnoi sud*) and bring substantial terms of imprisonment, most fights (especially where there was no serious injury) were heard in the lowest courts, such as the justice of the peace courts. There, the most typical punishment was imprisonment for one month, but sometimes, those who pleaded guilty got off with a fine, especially where local prisons were overcrowded.[85] While in the USSR some incidents of hooliganism with violence would draw fines from administrative commissions and others a sentence to compulsory work from a court, many, as we have seen, produced imprisonment for one or two years.

In prerevolutionary Russia, the most serious thefts (e.g., from a church) brought lengthy terms of confinement, but ordinary and petty thefts elicited mild responses, usually fines imposed by the lowest level courts, or, if not a fine, then prison terms measured in months.[86] Again, a sentence of one or two years of imprisonment for a simple theft at that time would have seemed high. To be sure, some of the petty thefts for which tsarist courts imposed fines would also in the late 1930s have led to noncustodial sanctions, some applied by courts, others in administrative hearings. But other nonserious thefts in the late 1930s resulted in a year or more of imprisonment.

The big problem in the late 1930s was the inconsistency of investigatory and judicial practice. Investigators and judges who were untrained in law and working under pressure, varied markedly in their qualification of particular incidents and the charges that they used. The bottom line was that in 1939 the chances of receiving one to two years' imprisonment for involvement in a drunken brawl in public were good; and it was possible, though less likely, to receive a similar term for a modest theft from the state. Neither of these outcomes was as common in prerevolutionary times.

At the same time, considerably more convicted offenders were receiving *long* terms of imprisonment in 1940 than had been the case in 1914 – far more than could be accounted for by changes in the structure or dynamics of crime itself. According to the records of the tsarist Ministry of Justice, in 1914 30,838 persons were serving terms of imprisonment or hard labor for terms of four or more years. Since these data describe offenders convicted over a number of years (some for sentences of eight, ten, or twelve years), one can assume that no more than

[85] *Obshchii obzor statisticheskikh svedenii o deiatelnosti sudebynykh ustanovlenii za 1914 god* (Petrograd, 1916), 6; *Svod zakonov ugolovnykh* (ed. N. Ozernetskovskii; 2nd ed., St. Petersburg, 1915), passim; conversation with Joan Neuberger, Oct. 16, 1992.

[86] Ibid.

6,000 received their sentences in 1914. Moreover, these data include political offenses. By contrast, in 1940 26,503 received new sentences of five years or more for nonpolitical offenses, and NKVD tribunals sentenced to terms of six or more years 22,033 persons and 43,684 to terms of three to five years.[87] By my reckoning, sentences of four years or more in 1940 constituted a multiple of at least 8 of those assigned in 1914.

In short, by the end of the 1930s the modal punishments for ordinary criminals in the USSR exceeded the norms of the last years of the tsars. However, as we shall see, Stalin had only begun to sharpen the sword of the criminal sanction. To begin, through an edict issued on August 10, 1940 (see Chapter 9), Stalin set a new minimum penalty of one year's imprisonment for both hooliganism and "petty theft at the enterprise." As a result of this edict and a general tightening of discipline due to the War, the share of custodial sentences went as high as 67% in the second part of 1941.[88] Even more dramatic were Stalin's draconian laws on theft issued June 4, 1947 (see Chapter 12). Through these postwar laws Stalin raised the severity of punishments in the USSR for non-political offenses to qualitatively new and excessive heights.

[87] *Otchet po glavnomu tiuremnomu upravleniiu za 1914 god*, chast 2: prilozheniia (Petrograd, 1915), 24–25; Popov, "Gosudarstvennyi terror," 23, 28; GARF, f.9474, op.1, d.4157, 201.

[88] Goliakov, *Sbornik dokumentov*, 407–408; M.I. Iakubovich, "O pravovoi prirode instituta uslovnogo osuzhdeniia," *SGiP*, 1946, no. 11–12, 55–59; Popov, "Gosudarstvennyi terror," 23. From 1943, judges were authorized to soften the force of the high levels of deprivation of freedom by using conditional sentences.

7 The Great Terror and criminal justice

Like the collectivization drive at the beginning of the decade, the Great Terror of 1937–1938 did much harm to the legal agencies and the administration of criminal justice. Many, but not most, legal officials had to play parts in the delivery of extralegal repression. Even worse, a large number of legal officials personally fell victim to purges and repression. As if this were not enough, Stalin and Vyshinskii also used the criminal law to legitimate their actions, developing within it a jurisprudence of terror. Needless to say, the handling of ordinary criminality suffered. The substantial drops in criminal convictions recorded in 1937–1938 reflected not changes in the behavior of offenders but the weakened capacity of the legal agencies. Likewise, the program started by Stalin and Vyshinskii in 1934 to develop effective and reliable criminal justice through centralized management and improved qualifications of its officials was rudely interrupted and its implementation delayed.

For all this, the direct consequences of the Terror for the agencies of justice proved to be short-lived, and by the eve of World War II they had made a substantial recovery. Procuracy and courts alike had returned to their usual patterns of operation, a strong dose of centralized management had been introduced, and plans resumed for the promotion of legal education.

A number of factors facilitated that recovery. One was the low level of cadres and performance prior to the Terror, which made many former legal officials expendable. Another was the existence of the program of reforming the justice agencies ready for revival after the storm of terror had subsided. A third reason for the recovery was the disengagement of the justice agencies after 1938 from the conduct of political prosecutions, especially of the escalated and contrived types. This disengagement marked for the first time in Soviet history a real division between the agencies and staff administering ordinary criminal justice

230

and those charged with the implementation of political policing and repression.

The origins of the separation stem from decisions taken at the end of collectivization. That battle had brought legal officials even at the lowest level into political repression, especially in the implementation of the Law of August 7, 1932. Soviet authorities started the process of separation by depriving courts below the regional level of the right to hear cases of state crimes and then focusing the work on these cases at higher courts in distinct panels. Introduced in 1934, the panels were known as the special collegia of the oblast and republican courts. These bodies did remove most, if not all, political cases from the judges working in the regular divisions of those courts as well as lower courts. The special collegia joined the military tribunals as the main judicial bodies for hearing political cases.[1]

Also hearing political cases during the 1930s were extrajudicial bodies, the various formations of the OGPU, and its successor the NKVD. Briefly, after the Civil War, Bolshevik leaders deprived the security police of the right to adjudicate. But a series of decrees in 1922 and 1924 restored these rights with regard to particular categories of cases, including not only political crimes, but also banditry. The most important tribunal of the OGPU was its Special Board, established in 1924. But it was joined during collectivization by the ubiquitous *troiki*, three-man panels for political cases that would be revived in large numbers in 1937.[2] This chapter examines the impact of the Terror on criminal justice. It deals first with the role of law and legal officials in political prosecutions and the fate of procuracy and court officials as victims of purge and repression. The chapter goes on to explain how the regime stopped the Terror and minimized its impact on criminal justice for the longer term.

---

[1] The Special Collegium was apparently based upon a Ukrainian forerunner, the "extraordinary session" of the territorial court that operated during the 1920s. See Ger P. van der Berg, *The Soviet System of Justice: Figures and Policy* (The Hague, 1985), pp. 18–19. In Smolensk before the Great Terror the Special Collegium of the regional court was treated as second-class. Due to cramped conditions in the courthouse, it was not given its own room and had to hear cases in the hall! It lacked the budget to pay its witnesses and, according to some members of the court, it served as a dumping ground for the court's more incompetent members, "who were not fit for work in the criminal or civil collegia." In the spring of 1937 members of the Special Collegium began complaining about their situation. One of them was called to Moscow for a conference of members of special collegia, whose tasks were starting to change because of the Terror. Smolensk Party Archive, WKP 103, 78–79, 85, 100.

[2] For an authoritative and detailed account of the history of extrajudicial tribunals of the Soviet security police, see "O vnesudebnykh organakh," *Izvestiia TsK KPSS*, 1989, no. 10, 80–82.

The role of justice officials in the terror

From early 1937 until the end of 1938 the USSR faced an outbreak of extralegal coercion of unprecedented proportions. No less than 1.33 million persons (today's official data) met with groundless arrest followed by mock trial and labor camp or execution.[3]

The repression of 1937–1938 did not start from nothing. Between late December 1934 (after the murder of Leningrad party boss and Politburo member Sergei Kirov) and early 1937, a "quiet terror" unfolded, striking persons previously expelled from the party (for the wrong social origins or factional connections), imagined double-dealers, Leningraders, and others. In 1935 and 1936 more than 500,000 persons were convicted by courts and police bodies in cases started by the security police. While many of these cases involved either nonpolitical offenses or the rounding up of "socially dangerous persons," no less than 100,000 persons each year were arrested (and presumably convicted) for counterrevolutionary crimes, including anti-Soviet agititation. Nearly half of the cases started by the security police in 1935–1936 were heard in courts, that is, the special collegia of the regional courts and the military tribunals.[4]

Some of the judges and procurators handling these cases had not learned to treat charges brought by the political police as sacrosanct and continued to review the evidence and exercise discretion (just as they had done in 1933–1934 with charges under the Law of August 7). Thus, during the wave of repression that followed the murder of Kirov, some judges on the special collegia gave suspended sentences or corrective work to persons convicted of "counterrevolutionary agitation." In late February 1935 the Praesidium of the USSR Supreme Court "categorically forbade" this leniency. But the chairman of neither the USSR nor the RSFSR Supreme Court was willing to have the special collegia abandon adjudication in political cases. In June 1935 Alexander Vinokurov, chairman of the USSR Supreme Court, directed judges to stay alert for groundless prosecutions and dismiss them "in order to preserve cadres for socialist construction." Cleverly, Vi-

3 V.P. Popov, "Gosudarstvennyi terror v sovetskoi Rossii, 1923–1953 gg." (istochniki i ikh interpretatsii), *Otechestvennye arkhivy*, 1992, no. 2, 28, supplies official data on political convictions in the USSR. For 1937: 790,665; and for 1938: 554,258. Of these, more than half were executed! 353,074 in 1937, and 328,618 in 1938. See also, J. Arch Getty, Gabor T. Rittersporn, and Viktor N. Zemskov, "Victims of the Soviet Penal System in the Pre-War Years: A First Approach on the Basis of Archival Evidence," *American Historical Review*, 98:4 (Oct. 1993), 1017–1049.

4 Robert C. Tucker, *Stalin in Power: The Revolution from Above, 1928–1941* (New York, 1990), 302–314; Popov, "Gosudarstvennyi terror," 28. According to GARF, f.9401, op.1, d.4157, 203 (per Gabor Rittersporn), in 1935 108,935 persons were arrested for counterrevolutionary crimes (Article 58), including 43,686 for anti-Soviet agitation.

nokurov tried to use Stalin's recent pronouncement "cadres decide everything" to stem the tide of NKVD sponsored repression. This bold move did not go unchallenged. After a complaint from Vyshinskii the party group at the Praesidium of the Central Executive Committee condemned Vinokurov's directive as politically harmful and arranged for its cancellation.[5] Later that same year the Praesidium of the RSFSR Supreme Court confirmed a decision of its Special Collegium to replace a death sentence with ten years' imprisonment in a case of a "confessed" counterrevolutionary agitator. The judges reasoned on legal grounds that without evidence of the existence of a terrorist group they could not apply the article in the criminal code (58-11) that authorized capital punishment. Their decision, however, prompted Procurator-General Vyshinskii to complain to the party Control Commission, whose deputy head Matvei Shkiriatov composed a deposition for Stalin. Presumably on the Leader's orders, the Commission ordered the firing of two members of the Special Collegium of the RSFSR Supreme Court and the censure of its chairman I.L. Bulat for, among other things, manifesting a "crude-bureaucratic attitude" in the case in question. The Commission also instructed Commissar of Justice Krylenko to "monitor" the work of the Special Collegium of the RSFSR Supreme Court.[6]

Notwithstanding the rebuffs suffered by the heads of the two Supreme Courts, Procurator-General Vyshinskii and Commissar of Justice Krylenko could not abide the growing power of the political police during 1935. In the first months of 1936 first Krylenko and then Vyshinskii registered complaints with Stalin about the misuse by NKVD officials of prosecutions for anti-Soviet agitation and propaganda. According to both complainants, a third of the charges concerned commonplace critical remarks, most often by ordinary persons ("toilers"), about an official, institution, or policy. In such situations criminal prosecutions represented "excesses" (according to Krylenko) and were "groundless" (according to Vyshinskii). While both urged Stalin to inform the NKVD of its errors, Vyshinskii also urged that with but few exceptions the special collegia of regional courts, and not the Special

5 Oleg V. Khlevniuk, *1937-i: Stalin, NKVD i sovetskoe obshchestvo* (Moscow, 1993), 63–66; N.V. Zhogin, "Ob izvrashcheniiakh Vyshinskogo v teorii sovetskogo prava i praktiki," *Sovetskoe gosudarstvo i pravo* (SGiP), 1965, no. 3, 25–26. The research for Zhogin's article was conducted by Igor Petrukhin (personal communication).
6 TsK VKP(b) – tov. Stalinu, I.V. ot Shkiriatova, "O gruboi politicheskoi oshibke Verkhovnogo Suda RSFSR, dopushcheveno pri rassmotrenii dela kontrerevolutionerki i terroristki byvsh. kniazny Gagarinoi V.A. i ee souchastnikov" (n.d.); "Zapiska iz protokola No. 32 zasedaniia komissii partiinogo kontrolia pri TsK VKP(b) ot 27 noiabria 1935;" I am grateful to J. Arch Getty for providing copies of these documents.

Board of the NKVD, hear these cases, on the grounds that the latter used overly simplified procedures.[7]

Meanwhile, away from the central stage, some judges in the provinces in 1936 continued to exercise their functions in political cases, stopping prosecutions at the special collegia and military tribunals or requalifying them to nonpolitical charges. For their part, some procurators, especially in the military procuracy, refused to approve the arrest orders composed by the security police. These actions prompted the chiefs of the provincial security police to complain to their superiors in Moscow about interference in their work by judges and procurators. NKVD officials in Azovo-Chernomorskii Territory, the North Caucasus Territory, Cheliabinsk Region, and the Republic of Uzbekistan supplied detailed reports on the "defects" in the work of the courts and procuracy "leading to the distortion of penal policy and distortion of revolutionary justice." The NKVD chiefs in Moscow forwarded the reports to the party Central Committee. In January 1937 Vyshinskii joined his colleagues in the political police in complaining about "mistakes and delays" in the work of the special collegia and suggested that Narkomiust review the makeup of these bodies, a task that the Commissar Krylenko promptly entrusted to the territorial and regional courts.[8]

The opposition to far-fetched political prosecutions on the part of even a small number of legal officials may explain the role and fate of legal officials in the Great Terror. On the one hand, the failure of judges on the special collegia and the military tribunals to cooperate fully with the security police may have led Stalin to rely on alternatives to the courts for the conduct of the Terror. Most of the nearly 800,000 political prosecutions of 1937 were handled not by courts but directly by the NKVD, including its revived *troiki*. Naturally, the courts that heard political cases could not by themselves have coped with a threefold increase in caseload, and some expansion in overall capacity to process political cases was necessary. Had the special collegia and military tribunals performed more reliably, those bodies might have been expanded. But in practice, various sources agree, their work contracted! According to one source, the caseload of those two bodies combined fell dramatically with the onset of the Great Terror – from 114,283 in 1936

---

7 GARF, f.8131, op.37, d.73, 228–235; d.71, 127–133; d.70, 163–166. A response by NKVD chief Iagoda to one of Vyshinskii's critical letters is found in d. 70, 138–142. Vyshinskii also sought to gain for the Procuracy the right to release persons placed in detention by NKVD officials. See d.70, 166.

8 RTsKhIDNI, f.17, op.120, d.171, 130–151, 170–190; Khlevniuk, *1937-i*, 65. A. Muranov and V. Zviagintsev, *Sud nad sudiami (osobaia papka Ulrikha)* (Kazan, 1993); GARF, f.5446sch., op.20a, d.854, 1–6ob.

to 39,694 in 1937.[9] On the other hand, the demonstration by some legal officials of a capacity for independent judgment in political cases may have marked all legal officials as suspect in the eyes of the leadership and increased the probability that large numbers of them would be repressed in 1937–1938.

The Great Terror itself consisted of three social processes – a campaign of vigilance, purges of targeted groups and individuals, and mass arrests. The Terror began in a low key in September 1936 with a purge directed at former party members whose connections with oppositions of the past made their loyalty suspect. To this ongoing enterprise was added in February 1937 the campaign of vigilance. Launched by Stalin and Molotov, the campaign warned citizens of the presence of traitors in their midst and rallied them to uncover and denounce on the slightest pretext their bosses, employees, rivals, or perfect strangers as wreckers or another kind of enemy. Then, in May–June 1937 Stalin started the well-known purge of current politicians and officials, the purge of the powerful. Sometimes by personal order, as often through the agency of local vigilantes responding to cues, the Leader engineered the firing and arrest as saboteurs of many leading party and governmental officials in the provinces and in the capital city. Finally, along with the campaign of vigilance and the purge of the powerful (as opposed to the earlier purge of the dispossessed) came in summer 1937 the launching of "mass operations." The Politburo (i.e., Stalin) directed party and NVKD officials in the regions to arrest large numbers of "former kulaks and criminals" (including any persons who had ever struggled against Soviet power) and supplied each region with numerical quotas (*limity*) for the numbers of persons to be arrested and imprisoned or shot. A second

---

9 Popov, "Gosudarstvennyi terror," 28. According to Popov's data, the political caseload of the special collegia and military tribunals rose in 1938 to 95,057. Ibid. This increase may have reflected the huge flow of new political cases (many accumulated from 1937) and the replacement of many judges on the special collegia and military tribunals, which presumably made those bodies more reliable. Gabor Rittersporn (private communication citing GARF, f.9401, op.1, d.4157, 202) contends that Popov missed some 45,060 persons sentenced by the special collegii in 1937. Adding these to Popov's figures would make the drop between 1936 and 1937 and increase between 1937 and 1938 less precipitous.

Note that another source, which does not include military tribunals, lists the political cases heard by courts at 59,325 for 1937 and 79,883 for 1938. The increase here came mainly through a doubling of caseload of the Military Collegium of the USSR Supreme Court. Caseloads at the regional level special collegia remained nearly constant from 1937 to 1938. (GARF, f.9492sch, op.6s, d.14, 9.) Yet another source (GARF, f.9492, op.6s, d.15, 7) lists the total caseload of the special collegia at 39,953 for 1937 and 53,911 for 1938, but these data include all criminal cases heard by these bodies, not just the political (counterrevolutionary) cases.

round of mass arrests, also with quotas, followed early in 1938. While the purge of the powerful was directed from the center, the selection of victims of the "mass operations" was left to lower level officials, who were encouraged to exceed their quotas. The stream of personal denunciations encouraged by the campaign of vigilance and the tortures imposed on individual arrestees contributed to both the purges and the mass operations. What united all aspects of the Terror was their contribution to Stalin's goal of destroying all persons (and categories of persons) who seemed to represent a potential danger to him or his regime, especially, recent evidence suggests, under the threat of war. Included in the Leader's view of a potential fifth column was not only a large part of the current political elite but also persons who had been the subject of deprivations or coercion earlier on.[10]

The law and legal officials played major parts in the legitimization of the Great Terror overall *and* in the conduct of the campaign of vigilance.[11]

Stalin and Vyshinskii went to some lengths to ensure that the conduct of purge and terror had the appearance of legality. To begin, they supplied a legal framework for the investigations and hearings conducted by the security police. Already in December 1934 (after Kirov's murder) a new law had empowered the police to use in cases of terrorism a drastically simplified procedure that gave the accused a mere twenty-four hours to acquaint himself with charges and evidence, provided for an *in camera* hearing without defense counsel, disallowed cassation appeals, and authorized immediate implementation of death sentences. In September 1937 another law extended most of these provisions to the common political charges of the time, wrecking, and subversion.[12] Even in the quick summary hearings of the security police

[10] The most persuasive, archive-based interpretation of the Great Terror, albeit in preliminary form, is Oleg Khlevnyuk, "The Objectives of the Great Terror, 1937–1938," in Julian Cooper et al., *Soviet History, 1917–1953: Essays in Honour of R.W. Davies* (London, 1995), 158–176. The traditional major accounts of the terror include Robert Conquest, *The Great Terror: Stalin's Purge of the 1930s* (London, 1968) – and, in an updating, *The Great Terror – A Reassessment* (Oxford, 1990) – and Roy Medvedev, *Let History Judge* (New York, 1971), chaps. 5–10. For newer interpretations and research, see J. Arch Getty, *Origins of the Great Purges* (Cambridge, 1985) and J. Arch Getty and Roberta T. Manning, eds., *Stalinist Terror: New Perspectives* (Cambridge, 1993).

[11] See Khlevniuk, "Rol Politbiuro v izmenenii karatelnoi politikii," 16–18; and Mikhail Shreider, *NKVD iznutri Zapiski chekista* (Moscow, 1995), 41ff.

[12] "O vnesesnii izmenenii v deistvuiushchie ugolovno-protsessualnye kodeksy soiuznykh respublik," Postanovlenie TsIK i SNK SSSR ot 1 dekabria 1934 g., Goliakov, *Sbornik dokumentov*, p. 347; "O vnesenii izmenenii v delstvuiushchie ugolovno-protsessualnye kodeksy soiuznykh respublik," Postanovlenie TsIK SSSR ot 14 sentiabria 1937, ibid., p. 396.

boards the prosecution had to support its charges but this task became increasingly easy to perform. In 1928 the USSR Supreme Court had eliminated the need to show counterrevolutionary intent in most political cases.[13] Then, in a lecture delivered in April 1936 (published in 1937) Vyshinskii started developing his theory of evidence that downgraded the importance of "objective proofs" and gave special weight to confessions, especially in cases of counterrevolutionary crime.[14]

Second, certain legal officials were required to work with the security police in its application of force against victims of purge or denunciation. Procurators, especially in the provinces, had to sanction the arrests planned or executed by the security police, for despite their sweeping powers, the security police lacked legal authority to make arrests. Like ordinary policemen they required the formal permission of the procurators. Needless to say, during the Great Terror most procurators did not dare to exercise their right to decide whether proposed arrests were justified. There were exceptions, bold procurators (including dozens in the military procuracy) who resisted arrests in contrived cases and personally suffered as a result.[15] As a rule, though, most procurators either rubber-stamped the arrest orders already compiled by the operatives (sometimes in the middle of the night) or provided the police with already signed blank arrest forms. When police officials forgot to obtain the sanction for an arrest, many regional procurators provided back-dated orders of arrest. To ensure that a procurator would be available at night to sign arrest forms, Vyshinskii gave permission to the procurator of Irkutsk Region to assign assistant procurators to night duty; the city of Stalingrad used the same procedure.[16]

Moreover, some judges also dealt with cases from the security police. As a result of the campaign of vigilance the special collegia of the

13 "O priamom i kosvennom umysle pri kontrrevoliutsionnom prestuplenii," Raz'ias-nenie 18 plenuma Verkhovnogo Suda SSSR ot 2 ianvaria 1928 g. For discussion of the effects of this directive, see *Sorok let sovetskogo prava, 1917–1957*, 2 (Leningrad, 1957), 486–487.

14 These propositions were derived from the notion that the task of a judge was to establish not absolute truth but maximum probability of truth. See A. Ia. Vyshinskii, "Problema otsenki dokazatelstv v sovetskom ugolovnom protsesse," *Problemy ugolovnoi politiki*, 4 (1937), 13–38. For insightful analysis of the jurisprudence of terror, see Robert Sharlet, "Stalinism and Soviet Legal Culture," in Robert C. Tucker, ed., *Stalinism: Essays in Historical Interpretation* (New York, 1977), esp. 163–168.

15 T.S. Panferov, ed., *Rasprava – prokurorskie sudby* (Moscow, 1990); I.P. Raskovel, "Protiv proizvola," in A.V. Afanasev, comp., *Oni ne molchali* (Moscow, 1991), 226–242.

16 Roy Medvedev, *Let History Judge*, 393; GARF, f.8131, op.14, d.23, 20–22. According to Gabor Rittersporn (private communication), in August 1937 the USSR Procuracy authorized waiving the procuratorial approval of arrests effected in "mass operations," that is, large-scale arrests to meet planned quotas.

regional (and republican) courts received new cases that by 1938 increased their loads and raised their status within the regional courts.[17] At the same time, military tribunals continued to hear cases of counter-revolutionary crimes, and from March 1937 the Military Collegium of the USSR Supreme Court began holding sessions on circuit in various provinces and republics. The Collegium dealt with charges of wrecking and terrorism, especially against persons included on lists provided by Ezhov and Vyshinskii, usually with indications of the recommended punishments.[18] Soon the productivity of the security police required further outlets, and an increasing proportion of these cases was processed directly by panels of the NKVD. These panels included the Special Board of the NKVD in Moscow and the *troiki* and *dvoiki* (three-person and two-person tribunals) organized by republican and regional branches of the agency. Regional procurators were expected to attend all sessions of the *troiki* before August 1937 in the capacity of prosecutor and from that date as members of the *troiki* hearing the case. In addition, procurators in the provinces received an order from Vyshinskii (on December 27, 1937) to use the *troiki* instead of the courts "when the evidence of guilt will not allow its use at trial," that is when it featured denunciations or false testimony from provocateurs.[19]

The most dramatic and best-known means adopted by Stalin for legitimating the Purge and Terror was the public show trial, a device already used successfully to justify the earlier campaign against bourgeois specialists. The three major show trials held in Moscow in August 1936, January 1937, and March 1938, featured former leading politicians as defendants and warranted detailed coverage in the national press. With Procurator-General Vyshinskii directing the proceedings, the accused confessed to the most heinous and elaborate conspiracies against the Soviet state. The judges of the Military Collegium of the USSR Supreme Court duly condemned them to shooting or long imprisonment. But these major show trials were just the tip of the iceberg. It was also necessary to explain how the enemies and traitors could have

[17] In spring 1937 members of the Special Collegium in Smolensk began demanding better treatment from the regional court in the form of quarters and funds to pay witnesses. WKP 103, 100, 130, 209.

[18] G. Ovcharenko and A. Cherniak, "Vernut verkhovenstvo zakonu: stranitsy istorii," (Beseda s. E. Skriplevym, V. Maslovym i N. Chistiakovym), *Pravda*, Sept. 1, 1989, 1; GARF, f.8131, op.14, d.4, 57.

[19] "O vnesudebnykh organakh"; Ovcharenko and Cherniak, "Vernut verkhovenstvo zakonu"; V.P. Maslov and N.F. Chistiakov, "Staliniskie repressii i sovetskaia iustitsia," *Kommunist*, 1990, no. 10, 107; idem, *Vopreki zakonu i spravedlivosti* (Moscow, 1990), 34. A former police chief from the period recalled the establishment in late 1937 of "special *troiki*" that did not include the procurator. See Shreider, *NKVD iznutri*, 70–71.

penetrated the most backwater province. Accordingly, during the second half of 1937 and much of 1938 a series of public trials was staged – with Politburo (read Stalin's) approval – throughout the republics, regions, and even districts of the USSR. To the dockets of the special collegia of the regional courts and the republican supreme courts came leading party and government officials of the regions and districts, and at the trials the procurator of the region or republic personally accused the defendants of wrecking the output of the kolkhozy, undermining the conduct of trade, or committing another act deleterious to the well-being of the country. Because these regional show trials were reported only in the regional and local newspapers, they have been overlooked by most Western observers. The Soviet historian Roy Medvedev, however, found references to trials in Leningrad Region, in North Ossetia, in the Far East, and in the cities of Kuibyshev, Voronezh, and Iaroslav; other sources refer to trials in Abkhaziia, Tbilisi, and Ivanovo regions. Solzhenitsyn described a trial that backfired when some of its defendants refused to confess and challenged their accusers. Archival sources indicate that the Politburo approved some seventy show trials in the regions.[20]

Apart from procurators, and judges on the Special Collegia, other legal officials had little to do with the activities of the security police or their legitimization. This does not mean, however, that these officials escaped involvement in the Terror, for the campaign of vigilance affected their work directly.

The campaign of vigilance, urging Soviet citizens to uncover the enemies and wreckers in their midst, began in the winter of 1937, after the second show trial (against former leaders of Soviet industry) and after the February meeting of the CPSU Central Committee. To be sure, the bases for the campaign had been laid beforehand. In March and April 1936 the Soviet public had heard about "saboteurs" who opposed the Stakhanovite movement and after the August 1936 show trial about "wreckers" in industry.[21] At the end of November a secret directive of

[20] Medvedev, *Let History Judge*, 236–238; Faina Baazova, *Prokazhennye* (Jerusalem: Biblioteka-Aliia, 1980), 7–8; Conquest, *The Great Terror*, 340–341; Aleksander Solzhenitsyn, *The Gulag Archipelago, 1918–1956*, 1–2 (New York, 1973), 419–431. Solzhenitsyn also asserted that the failure in the Ivanovo show trial led to the cessation of the practice of local show trials, but no other source confirms this point. See Solzhenitsyn, ibid. Sheila Fitzpatrick has analyzed some of these trials. See her "How the Mice Buried the Cat: Scenes from the Great Purges of 1937 in the Russian Provinces," *Russian Review*, 52 (July 1993), 299–320. On Politburo approval of regional show trials see Khlevnyuk, "The Objectives of the Great Terror," 163–166.

[21] On sabotage in the Stakhanovite campaign, see Donald Filtzer, *Soviet Workers and Stalinist Industrialization: The Formation of Modern Soviet Production Relations, 1928–1940* (Armonk, N.Y., 1986).

Procurator-General Vyshinskii had ordered procurators to review all cases of accidents, defective goods, and arson to bring out the "elements of counterrevolutionary wrecking." But in 1936 the administration of justice did not yet reflect this preoccupation with wrecking. A survey of criminal cases allocating responsibility for accidents stemming from violations of safety rules for 1936 revealed that the guilty did not usually receive a custodial sanction.[22]

In fact, the start of the campaign of vigilance had been delayed by the opposition of Sergo Ordzhonikidze to harassment of managers. Just as he had rushed to protect the bourgeois specialists in 1930–1931, so in 1936 the chief of the Commissariat of Heavy Industry defended his managers and engineers from Stalin's new impending onslaught. When he failed, Ordzhonikidze committed suicide. His death came shortly after the second show trial (against such leaders of Soviet industry and colleagues of Ordzhonikidze as Iuryi Piatakov) and on the eve of the Central Committee Plenum where the campaign of vigilance was launched.

The plan for the campaign of vigilance came from Stalin, who assigned and reviewed the drafts of speeches prepared for the Plenum. Originally, Ordzhonikidze had been assigned the speech on wrecking in heavy industry, and he used his draft to try to contain the campaign, arguing that enemies had been for the most part exposed and that the task had become destroying the consequences of wrecking. Stalin's critical comments on Ordzhonikidze's draft speech suggested that Ordzhonikidze would not have succeeded. After Ordzhonikidze's suicide, Viacheslav Molotov took over his role and gave the kind of report that Stalin wanted.[23]

Unlike the other speeches on wrecking (delivered by Kaganovich, Ezhov, and Andreev), Molotov's speech to the February Plenum received wide publicity and held special meaning for legal officials. Molotov explained to his audience that wrecking and wreckers often accounted for such phenomena as "accidents in factories, explosions in shops, breaks in gaslines, the widespread spoiling of machines, caveins of the walls of mines, attempts to discredit the Stakhanovite movement, widespread defective production, the creation of difficult living conditions for workers, and delays in the payment of salaries" – in short, just about anything that might bother a worker or an ordinary employee in an enterprise. Often, he went on, these matters reached the courts as cases of violations of safety rules or as crimes by officials, but much

[22] Zhogin, "Ob izvrashcheniiakh Vyshinskogo," 24.
[23] Khlevniuk, *1937-i* 15–18; Oleg Khlevniuk, *Stalin i Ordzhonikidze, Konflikty v Politbiuro v 30-e gody* (Moscow, 1993), 95–110.

more might lie beneath the surface. Nor should one tolerate small violations, Molotov explained, for often the small violations served as "preparation" for larger, more serious ones.[24] For legal officials Molotov's speech had immediate significance, for they were already dealing with many of these shortcomings through the application of ordinary criminal charges. In case any investigators or procurators failed to notice or heed Molotov's warnings, Procurator-General Vyshinskii repeated the message. In speeches to his subordinates, he emphasized the subtlety of the methods used by the traitors and wreckers and the need to press political charges against these enemies before they turned to larger misdeeds.[25]

During the spring and early summer of 1937 the pressure upon investigators, procurators, and judges to find, prosecute, and punish "wreckers" and "traitors" responsible for the catalogue of ills cited by Molotov mounted continuously. The central press and publishing houses filled the minds of their readers with tales of nasty deeds and villains. The local press attacked judges who had treated accident cases leniently in the past.[26] Finally, the top legal officials called for extensions of the net of political prosecutions. In this effort, Vyshinskii took the lead. He issued circulars "suggesting" that arson of state property be qualified as sabotage regardless of motive and that prosecutors should look for counterrevolutionary design in all cases connected with harvest campaigns. When some products were found in 1937 to be infected with ticks, Vyshinskii declared this the work of wreckers and insisted upon the death penalty for all convicted. (Apparently, some peasants added ticks to make their harvests unacceptable to the authorities.) Moreover, Vyshinskii also made it clear to regional procurators that a low rate of prosecutions for political offenses would be considered as a sign of poor performance.[27] It appears that Krylenko and Narkomiust were a little slower in promoting the campaign of vigilance than was Vyshinskii. At least, Narkomiust's instruction of early June dealing with cases of labor safety violations spoke in a bland, unhysterical tone about the need both for more severe punishments and for the use of more expertise in these cases. However, not long after Narkomiust called for a review of all cases from 1936 and

[24] Kh., "Shpiony, diversanty, vrediteli" (Obzor literatury) *SIu*, 1937, no. 15, 6–9. "Materialy fevralsko-martovskogo plenuma TsK VKP(b) 1937 soda," *Voprosy istorii*, 1993, no. 8, 3–26.

[25] Ibid.; "Aktiv prokuratury," *SZ*, 1937, no. 6, 96–101.

[26] Obozrevatel, "Vragi naroda i ikh posobniki v sudebnykh organakh," *SIu*, 1937, no. 15, 26–27; Kh., "Mestnaia pechat o rabote suda," ibid., 27–28; Vinokur, "Sudia, nedostoinnaia etogo zvaniia," ibid., 33–34.

[27] Zhogin, "Ob izvrashcheniiakh Vyshinskogo," 24–25. I am grateful to Gabor Rittersporn for information about the peasants' "tick trick."

the first half of 1937 in which regional courts had registered convictions for criminal negligence (Article 111) to check whether a charge of wrecking (Article 58/7) would not have been more appropriate.[28]

By the summer of 1937 it was hard for any justice official to withstand the pressure to join rank and lay political charges wherever possible. For, once the Purge itself went into high gear and judges and procurators themselves were registered among its victims, pursuing the vigilance campaign became a matter of life and death for Soviet legal officials. Escalating charges and punishments according to the dictates of the campaign became a necessary, though hardly sufficient, step for investigators, procurators, or judges who were to survive the Purge.

The vigilance campaign led to the laying of political charges, often "wrecking," in connection with mishaps and failures in the economy. We have seen – in Chapter 4 – that during the early 1930s it became standard practice to use *criminal* charges for such mishaps, both to provide scapegoats and deter repetitions in the future. As a rule, though, the resulting cases came under the category of "crimes of officials," and convictions often resulted in mild noncustodial sanctions. If intent could be shown, the charge might be abuse of office; otherwise, it would be "criminal negligence," one of the most common charges found in Soviet courtrooms in early and mid-1930s. Though in theory these charges were reserved for responsible officials, in practice they were used and misused against all sorts of lesser personages, down to technicians in factories and even individual kolkhozniki, in short against anyone who could be blamed for accidents, breakdowns of machines, and defective goods.[29]

From summer 1937 well into 1938 many, if not most, current cases involving accidents, defective goods, broken machines, or other problems of the economy were escalated from their usual status of "criminal negligence" to the more exalted one of "wrecking." The evidence is particularly clear with regard to accidents in rivers and harbors. An analysis of the statistics (however crude) for 1936 and for the first three-quarters of 1937 (including only the first part of the campaign of vigilance) revealed that although there had been no more than the usual number of accidents, the number of associated court cases had "increased significantly" (numbers not given). Moreover, the rate of convictions in these cases had risen from 63.9% to 80.1% and the sentences

---

28 *SIu*, 1937, no. 15, 50–51; ibid., 1937, no. 16, 50–51.
29 B.S. Utevskii, *Obshchee uchenie o dolzhnostnykh prestupleniiakh* (Moscow, 1948), esp. 244–281; Ya Gurevich, "Organy iustitsii TsChO na khlebzagotovitelnom fronte," *SIu* 1931, no. 9, 22–24; Iodkovskii and Lagovier, "Neobkhodim reshitelnyi perelom o praktike primenenia St. III U.K.," *SIu* 1936, no. 20, 8–10; "O sudebnoi praktike po delam o dolzhnostnykh prestuplenii (St st. 109, 110, 111 UK RSFSR)," *SIu* 1937, no. 6, 56.

had become more severe.[30] These data reveal nothing about the carelessness with which charges were laid, investigations and trials conducted, and convictions reached. A later review by the USSR Supreme Court stated that in many of the cases of accidents on the rivers, the violations of the safety rules had been slight and the consequences insignificant. As a result of these prosecutions, "a huge number of good captains and machinists were affected." The campaign of vigilance had damaged the Soviet merchant marine.[31]

There is no reason to assume that the situation in water transport differed from that on the railroads, on the farms, or in industry generally. The pressures upon local justice officials dealing with these realms were the same, and the latter seem to have pressed charges of wrecking wherever they could. In some procuracy offices, such as that of the Kalmyk Republic, procurators "forgot about the concept of ordinary official and economic crimes and treated every crime as wrecking." For, as one regional procurator explained, "when an individual district procurator suggested that there might not be wrecking in a particular case, he himself became an object of suspicion and lack of trust."[32] Procurators came under public scrutiny in this period. According to a procurator in Moscow many cases were started at the initiative of institutions and enterprises. As a result, "our district procurators became afraid, felt out of control, and left all the burden to investigators," who in turn had to handle forty to fifty cases at a time. (A high caseload before the campaign period was twenty.) The procurator of Omsk admitted that he did not bother checking cases of wrecking submitted by his investigators; he rubber-stamped all prosecutions and arrest orders submitted to him.[33]

Nor did judges stand in the way of the torrent of weak political cases that came before them. According to official sources, "individual judges, unworthy of the high title of Soviet judge – out of careerist motivations and because of fear – convicted the innocent without sufficient grounds, in order to make a show of vigilance."[34] When local procurators or judges failed to escalate charges, provincial level col-

---

[30] In 1937, 82.3% of convicts received imprisonment as opposed to 62.6% in 1936; and 43.8% received a term of three years or more, in place of 21.2% the previous year. "Dela ob avariakh na vodnom transporte," *SIu*, 1938, no. 10, 13–14. Data uncovered by Gabor Rittersporn from trade-union files (GARF, f.5451, op.9, d.4, 8–9) indicate that while safety conditions in industry overall did not change, there were more accidents in 1936 in some areas of transport and extracting industries.

[31] "Preniia po dokladu tov. A. Ia. Vyshinskogo," *SZ*, 1938, no. 6, 23; see also "V Narodnom Komissariate Iustitsii SSSR," *SIu*, 1938, no. 12, 22.

[32] "Preniia po dokladu," 18, 16.

[33] Ibid., 19, 18. See also GARF, f. 8131, op.15, d.3, 96–101.

[34] "Zadachi sudebnykh organov v svete ianvorskogo Plenuma TsK VKP(b)," *SIu*, 1938, no. 2–3, 4–5.

leagues often rectified the sitation. Thus, when a district procurator in Belorussia wanted to use charges of criminal negligence to deal with a shortage of 100 tons of potatoes, the republican procuracy overruled him, insisting instead on a charge of "economic counterrevolution." When a people's court convicted the new head of a pig farm with negligence resulting in the loss of 200 young hogs and sentenced him to six months' correctional work, the Supreme Court of Belorussia canceled the verdict and insisted upon a new trial for economic counterrevolution. The Special Collegium of the Smolensk regional court even established a panel to review cases from lower courts to find those that might be requalified as political.[35]

The escalation of charges from ordinary to political was not restricted to official and economic crimes. There were at least individual judges who failed to distinguish hooliganism from counterrevolutionary activity. One judge in Moscow escalated to a political charge a case involving criticism of Soviet leaders made in public by a drunken instructor at the district soviet building. Another judge saw counterrevolution in the breaking of a glass door by a doorman, also drunk, at the entrance to a building designated to serve as polling station in forthcoming elections to the Supreme Court. One investigator brought charges of terrorism against a member of a collective farm who, while drunk at a party, struck a guest who happened to be a Stakhanovite.[36]

In short, the campaign of vigilance forced many legal officials – most procurators and investigators and at least some regional court judges – to abandon evidentiary and procedural standards. Among legal officials only the people's court judges did not play an active part in the Terror, but they were well represented among its victims.

Justice as victim

During the second half of 1937 and the early months of 1938 the Great Purge struck justice officials with a vengeance. Close to half of all procurators and judges in the USSR lost their jobs and in most cases were

---

[35] "Vsebelorusskoe prokurorskoe soveshchanie," SZ, 1938, no. 7, 84. Out of 883 ordinary cases reviewed in Sept.-Oct. 1937, the panel requalified 105 as political. WKP 103, 209.

[36] "Preniia po dokladu," 21; WKP 103, 79. On occasion even the police politicized ordinary criminal cases. When a drunken youth unknowingly tangled with Aleksei Stakhanov himself (after the latter had evicted the youth from a pond where swimming was not allowed), the local police chief not only charged the lad with malicious hooliganism but also forwarded the case to an NKVD troika. The troika added a charge of "anti-Soviet agitation" and ordered the unfortunate hooligan executed. Nikolai Astafev, "Vysshaia mera po delu o khuliganstve," Zapiski kriminalistov, 2 (Moscow, 1993), 161–165.

arrested as well. By the start of 1938 procuracy agencies had already hired some two thousand new employees (investigators and procurators) and there remained a substantial number of vacancies.[37] Even in the spring of 1938 there were no procurators at all in parts of Moldavia, in seven districts of Georgia, in dozens of districts in Central Asia, in twenty of thirty-six districts in Chita region. In one district in Belorussia there had been no procurator, investigator, or judge for four months.[38] Among judges the situation was similar. As of early 1938, 51.4% of judges in the Kazakh Republic were new; half of those in the Turkmen Republic had less than a year's experience; and in one district of Moscow, only one of eight judges in place in June 1938 antedated the spring of 1937.

According to a report from Narkomiust, as of Jan. 1, 1939, 35.9% of people's court judges had served less than one year, and another 31.0% less than three years. And in 1938 alone, 40% of the members of regional and republican supreme courts were refilled.[39]

The temporary shortage of legal officials prompted the hearing of some nonpolitical criminal cases by *troiki* formed from ordinary police (*militseiskie troiki*). Since their establishment in 1935 the police *troiki* (as opposed to the better known special *troiki* for political cases established in 1937) had shouldered responsibility for processing cases of persons deemed to be "socially harmful." These included convicted criminals who had returned from confinement and renewed ties with known criminal elements; persons who neither worked nor had a permanent residence; professional beggars; and violators of the passport regime – all of whom were subject under Article 35 of the RSFSR Criminal Code to up to five years' imprisonment or banishment from the region. When in 1937 the shortage of legal officials rendered the courts incapable of handling their entire criminal caseload, it was easy to transfer other cases to the police *troiki*, and according to one informant, Ezhov himself gave the authorization.[40]

---

37 Ia. Gorbulev and R. Rakhunov, "Kadry," *SZ*, 1938, no. 1, 26–31.
38 "Preniia po dokladu," 14, 29, 37, 38; "Vsebelorusskoe prokurorskoe soveshchenie," 84.
39 "Rech deputata Burmasheva," *SZ*, 1938, no. 9, 63–64; "Prikaz narkom iustitsii v deistvii," *SIu*, 1938, no. 9, 6–8; interview with a former judge of a Moscow people's court appointed in 1938; GARF, f.5446, op.23a, d.312, 65–75. It should be noted that a small portion of the judges removed in 1937 lost their posts before the Purge during a review of credentials prior to nominations for the first election of judges.
40 GARF, f.8131sch, op.38, d.6, 62–64; Shreider, *NKVD iznutri*, 74. The performance of police *troiki* in 1935–1936 was marked by superficial investigations, arbitrary decisions after hearings that averaged three minutes, and many convictions without the required preference of the accused. GARF, f.8131sch., op.38, d.8, 1–4, 7–9, 25–26. According to a top-secret communication from NKVD chief Yagoda to Stalin and Molotov (dated Feb. 11, 1936), the police *troiki* (including the *troiki* of local administration) convicted 122,726 persons of ordinary, nonpolitical crimes in 1935. GARF, f.8131, op.37, d.70, 138.

The Purge also claimed many victims in the central legal agencies. In the last months of 1937 many of the Procuracy's leading officials were replaced; and similar purges struck Narkomiust at the beginning of 1938 and the USSR Supreme Court in the spring.[41]

First and foremost among the victims were procurators and judges who held line posts, or positions of authority. According to a deputy procurator-general of the post-Stalin period who examined the archives of the USSR Procuracy, 90% of regional procurators were purged, and his estimate is supported by contemporary data on promotions. As of January 1938, 400 procurators had been promoted to "responsible leading positions" in procuracy-investigatory organs, that is, to posts of procurator of a region, head of a department in a republican procuracy, or higher.[42]

In some regions of the RSFSR, according to the republican procurator, over 75% of district procurators lost their jobs and were replaced by young communists and *komsomol* members with neither knowledge of law or experience.[43] In most firings and arrests of procurators the Procurator-General Andrei Vyshinskii played a part. Already in the summer of 1936 he issued an order that none of his subordinates be fired without his preliminary sanction. Like many instructions this order was honored in the breach, and in June 1937 Vyshinkii repeated the message, "categorically forbidding" the firing of almost all procurators and investigators without his consent. As the purge became widespread even Vyshinskii recognized the need to bend his rule. "Where necessary," he explained, he would allow the permission of a republican procurator to substitute for his own, as long as he was informed later on.[44]

Many judges at people's and regional courts alike joined procurators as victims of purge, but it was particularly the chairmen and deputy chairmen of the regional courts who were most likely to fall.[45] The example of the Smolensk regional court (more to come) suggests that as soon as the leading political officials of a region were exposed, their

[41] Gorbulev and Rakhunov, "Kadry;" M.N. Rychkov, "Zadachi sudebnykh organov," *Slu* 1938, no. 2–3, 16–18; and see note 71. In the first half of 1938, Narkomiust RSFSR lost eight heads of departments, 11 inspectors, and 14 consultants. It also hired 6 new department chiefs, 24 inspectors, and 18 consultants, many to replace persons lost in 1937. As of September, 9 professional posts still lay vacant. TsGA, f.353, op.13, d.4 ("Soveshchanie u Narodnogo Komissara Iustitsii, RSFSR," 4 sent.1938 g.), 200.

[42] Zhogin, "Ob izvrashcheniiakh Vyshinskogo," 26; Gorbulev and Rakhunov, "Kadry."

[43] GARF, f.8131, op.15, d.3, 89.

[44] *Sbornik prikazov prokuratury SSSR* (2nd ed., expanded; Moscow, 1939), 231.

[45] In the RSFSR 769 people's court judges and members of the regional courts lost their jobs in the first half of 1938. "Soveshchanie u narodnogo komissara," 201. At least as many (if not more) fell victim in the second half of 1937.

colleagues in other governmental posts, including the justice agencies, fell under suspicion.[46]

Another category of justice official almost certain to be repressed comprised any and all whose actions impeded, intentionally or not, the vigilance campaign or the Purge. Making complaints about illegal methods of the NKVD led to the arrest of a group of procurators from Briansk and a military procurator for border troops in Siberia. The latter, according to Vyshinskii, deserved his fate because he lacked a "class nose [chute]." He was one of dozens of military procurators whose failure to participate in repression led to their arrest. Unwillingness to rubber-stamp arrest orders got other procurators into trouble. One who insisted on reviewing the political biography of the accused was denounced by political police for "unfounded delay of arrests." For refusing to sanction arrests, his colleague, the procurator of the city of Moscow, found himself arrested. Occasionally, procurators receiving arrest orders warned the persons under threat, a course of action described by the head of the USSR Supreme Court's Military Collegium Vasilii Ulrikh, as "direct treason."[47] Arrest and prosecution awaited the chief procurator of water transport, Remnev, who objected to the procedures used by the special boards, and Ivan Akulov, who had reportedly lost his job as procurator-general in 1935 because he had complained about abuse of power by the NKVD chief, Iagoda.[48] While some of the procurators repressed for obstructing terror and purge engaged in conscious resistance to these processes, others may simply have failed to read the new political signals in good time and experienced disorientation on account of the frequent changes in regime policies regarding the prosecution of particular categories of offender.

---

[46] WKP 103, passim; WKP 238, 302–305.

In the Far Eastern Territory the purge of one regional party secretary and his clique led to the firing (by the territorial procurator) of the procurator of the region. The procurator in question, described by the second secretary of the obkom as "a good lad," had always cooperated with his bosses, among other things stopping a case against one of their clients (the deputy chairman of the city soviet) and removing the file of the case to his apartment. The fired procurator managed to get work as an assistant in the procuracy of a neighboring region, but he was nonetheless scheduled for arrest. GARF, f.8131, op.14, d.4 (Protokol soveshchaniia aktiva kraevoi prokuratury), 43–52.

[47] Zhogin, "Ob izvrashcheniiakh Vyshinskogo," 26; L. Zaika, "V reabilitatsii otkazat," SZ, 1990, no. 2, 61–65; Maslov and Chistiakov, Vopreki zakonu, 32; Rasprava prokurorskie sudby, 50, 226; GARF, f.9474, op.1, d.119, 138.

[48] Zhogin, "Ob izvrashcheniiakh Vyshinskogo," 26; Medvedev, Let History Judge, 217. In 1935 Akulov was demoted from procurator-general to secretary of TSIK. He was arrested in 1937. Donald Barry, "Leaders of the Soviet Legal Professions," Canadian-American Slavic Studies, 6, no. 1 (Spring 1972), 73–92.

Judges who did not facilitate the work of the NKVD also suffered. For showing leniency or giving acquittals judges on military tribunals were often condemned as "enemies of the people." The head of the USSR Supreme Court's Special Collegium, Vasilii Ulrikh, kept a special file of such judges, whose names were supplied by the NKVD. Back in 1935 – as we have seen – Chairman of the USSR Supreme Court A.N. Vinokurov went so far as to issue a Directive Letter calling for an end to groundless prosecutions and for the preservation of cadres, which Vyshinskii protested. Later, in 1937, this "political error" served as a pretext for the removal of Vinokurov from his post.[49] Another veteran justice worker, the fiery Old Bolshevik Aron Solts, could not stomach Stalin's campaign of mass repression. Serving in the USSR Procuracy he demanded evidence in cases of political repression, including that of the father of the late writer Iuri Trifonov. Solts also tried to confront Stalin on the issue but was rebuffed, isolated, and removed from the party's Central Control Commission. In February 1938 he was fired from the Procuracy (allegedly on the grounds that he had told the senior Trifonov that it was necessary to replace the Stalinist leadership) and later confined to a mental hospital.[50]

Other categories of justice workers who suffered in the Purge comprised those deemed to be alien – whether through birth or political association – and persons who had proven incompetent in their jobs or were unpopular with their subordinates. Though vulnerable to attack, few of these officials would have suffered had not some other person taken the initiative and denounced them. There were, of course, many such denunciations, for through accusing another an individual might try to prove his own bona fides and protect himself. Denunciation also offered an opportunity to vent personal grudges or to further one's career.[51] A survey of accounts in local newspapers of meetings of the court and procuracy workers (June 1937) reported that everywhere officials were criticizing each other. Thus, in Omsk a senior people's court judge who later turned out to be a Trotskyite was "exposed" by his secretary for being rude to subordinates in the presence of visitors. In Khasski district the procurator tried to blame his subordinates for various problems, but the latter responded by bringing him to account, "revealing" him to have been a Trotskyite who had illegally stopped

---

49 Muranov and Zviagintsev, *Sud nad sudiami*, esp. 69–76. Zhogin, "Ob izvrashcheniiakh Vyshinskogo," 25–26; Khlevniuk, *1937-i*, 66.
50 Iurii Trifonov, "Otblesk Kostra," *Znamia*, 1965, no. 2, 142–177. GARF, f.8131sch., op.37, d.111, 2, 37.
51 This privatization of terror by using denunciation to serve personal interests was one of the characteristic features of the Stalinist variety of terror. See Jan T. Gross, "A Note on the Nature of Soviet Totalitarianism," *Soviet Studies*, 34, no. 3 (1982), 367–376.

cases of wrecking. In another procuracy office where an investigator tried to expose his boss, the district procurator responded with indignation. Interrupting the list of charges proffered by his subordinate, the procurator asserted, "I am the procurator and a communist, and I can do what I want. You have no right to criticize me here (among the nonparty members)."[52]

From the minutes of the meetings of the party organization at the Smolensk regional court comes the richest illustration of the dynamics of the Purge in justice. As one would expect, the four major figures at the court – its chairman, deputy chairman (who was also head of the criminal collegium), the head of the civil collegium, and the party secretary all fell victim during the second half of 1937. The first two of these, Chairman Andrianov and his deputy, Grachev, became the objects of detailed scrutiny and criticism by the court's own party organization, just as soon as the regional party boss Rumiantsev "and his gang" had been denounced and arrested. Searching for pretexts, party activists on the court brought a catalogue of charges against the court's leaders. Typically the charges were petty or reflected personal grievances. Grachev, the inquisition soon revealed, was disliked by his colleagues because of his "dictatorial style" and "rudeness to all." They objected in particular to his "order" to the people's court judges of the region to stop giving sentences of corrective work for a variety of crimes. Grachev claimed that in insisting that judges choose between a prison term or referral of a case to the rural lay court he had been implementing an instruction from the USSR Supreme Court, but his colleagues insisted that he was trying to improve his statistics on punishment. Grachev was also accused of failing to fire the chauffeur of the regional court, who allegedly beat people at the door of the courthouse! The seemingly ineffectual Chairman Andrianov drew blame for a variety of lesser shortcomings, including failure to obtain money for paying witnesses and to deal with malfeasance in the court's administration (e.g., a court administrator who failed to pay the secretaries and sold for his own profit a stove belonging to the court). He was also accused of failing to recognize and expose the defects of the "Rumianstev gang" including their drinking bouts, about which he should have known from his periodic visits to the state dacha for provincial bigshots. (Ironically only months before Andrianov had been criticized for not maintaining close relations with the city party committee, thereby depriving his subordinates of access to good apartments.) Neither the content of the charges nor the quality of the accused's explanations made any difference, and though the discussion of their alleged shortcomings

[52] "Aktivy sudebno-prokurorskikh rabotnikov na mestakh," *SZ*, 1937, no. 7, 93–97.

dragged on for months after they had lost their jobs, their expulsions from the party were inevitable.[53]

The court's party secretary, Panov, was so popular that his party colleagues refused to expel him; they limited themselves to censuring Panov for failing to uncover the wrongdoings of the "traitors and wreckers" Grachev and Andrianov. Nonetheless, later on in the fall, the regional party committee insisted that Panov be dismissed.[54] The story of Leiman, head of the regional court's civil collegium was different. Even before the Purge struck the court in June, Leiman had already received a party censure for a series of blunders that he had committed during a lecture to an evening course for notaries. Leiman had told his students, incorrectly so his accusers made out, that the new Stalin Constitution would allow prisoners to vote and that despite the minimum age of 18 provided in that Constitution new judges ought to be somewhat older. As if this were not enough, while illustrating a point, Leiman had accidentally let his hand touch a poster bearing Stalin's picture and left a mark! All the same, Leiman was not singled out for attention during the attack on the court's leaders, and he lasted in his post for most of the year. In December, the NKVD security police arrested him, thereby forcing the court's party organization to expel him after the fact. Leiman was not alone in this fate. During 1937 at least three other members of the regional court were arrested by the NKVD as Trotskyites without any involvement on the part of the court's party body.[55] To some extent, purge and terror were still distinctive phenomena.

In Smolensk, as elsewhere, more than the brass of the regional court suffered in the Purge, and the pretexts for dismissals (and possible arrest) varied widely. For example, a people's court judge named Vetrova was fired and excluded from the party in spring 1937 for failing to be quick enough in denouncing an acquaintance as a Trotskyite. For some reason Vetrova was restored to party and post in July, but in October the regional court's party committee decided to protest her restoration. Two members of the regional court itself lost their posts because of newly revealed defects in their personal histories – one for suspicious behavior during the Civil War and the other for an illegal border crossing in 1921 and fudging party documents early in his career. The court's party organization also expelled one of its judges for cause. The judge had met with the relative of an accused person and then proceeded to requalify the case and give an unusually lenient

53 WKP 103, 126–42, 174–84; WKP 238, 302–305.
54 WKP 103, 187, 195–196; WKP 238, 302–305.
55 WKP 103, 120–122, 146–147, 212.

sentence. Although the examiners could not prove bribery, they resolved that a person who gave the appearance of impropriety did not deserve to be a party member or a judge.[56]

The party organization of the Smolensk regional court had its core of active members who took the lead in making denunciations and launching attacks on those singled out for purging. Typical of these was a certain Selilovskii who despite his youth and inexperience led the inquisition of the court's leaders Andrianov and Grachev. It turned out that Selilovskii held personal grudges against both of them – against Andrianov because he had reprimanded Selilovsky for failing to attend lectures at the juridical courses and against Grachev for his refusal to supply Selilovskii with money for a trip. I am sorry to report that Selilovskii was rewarded for his "vigilance" and made the new secretary of the court's party organization after Panov was dismissed.[57]

With the exception of the "trials" of Andrianov and Grachev, the party organization of the Smolensk regional court did try to conduct serious investigations into charges leveled against its members and to arrive at fair dispositions. Because of this, there was always the chance that a person who had been denounced would survive. A case in point is that of Comrade Karpov, a member of the regional court since 1934 and a judge since 1921. While out on circuit in May of 1937 Karpov had stopped for a drink with a district procurator and in the course of conversation cited Lenin's comments about Stalin in his so-called Testament. Unaware that Stalin had referred to the document in a speech published in *Pravda* (in 1927), the procurator assumed that Karpov was expounding counterrevolutionary ideas and reported him to party authorities. After the submission of lengthy depositions to the district party committee and a series of discussions in the court's party organization, Karpov got off with a warning for "tactless behavior." This veteran judge survived 1937 without further incident until December, when an anonymous letter accused him of drinking and beating his wife.[58]

Not every judge on the Smolensk regional court fell victim to the Purge, but every one of them had to endure a period of extraordinary tension and fear that could easily affect his or her performance on the bench.[59] The records of the Purge in Smolensk suggest that there was no sure way a judge could protect himself. And, even though the party

---

[56] Ibid., 81–82, 87, 142, 188–189, 194, 198–199, 203–204.
[57] Ibid., 78, 134, 204b.
[58] Ibid., 98–99, 104–113, 207.
[59] In autumn 1937 an increasing number of judges fell under suspicion and were scheduled to have their credentials examined by their peers in 1938. But there is no record on their fate.

organization of the regional court tried to examine the merits of most allegations brought against its members, there are no indications that the political police of Smolensk (the UNKVD) did likewise.

The recovery and its explanation

The Great Terror and Purge of 1937–1938 were bound to leave a mark on the agencies of justice for some time to come. The Purge had decimated the staff of those agencies. While the majority of the victims were inexperienced and uneducated newcomers to the administration of justice who were easy to replace, a sizable minority did have either learning or experience (especially those from the central agencies). The Terror also had distorted the normal operations of justice agencies. As we have seen, it prompted legal officials to escalate ordinary cases into political ones, conduct groundless prosecutions, and convict with slight regard for the evidence. The Terror was also responsible for a general decline in standards at the legal agencies, as an overload of work, criminal and civil alike, fell into the hands of the new and inexperienced officials.[60] Especially affected was the Procuracy's responsibility for supervising the legality of public administration. At all levels procurators faced a torrent of complaints, many concerning illegal firings and other grievances related to the Terror and Purge.[61] Nevertheless, within just a few years, by the onset of World War II, the effects of the Purge and Terror were no longer apparent. At least in the provinces and localities the operations of justice agencies had returned to the admittedly low standards of operation of the pre-Purge period.

Two policies of the regime were responsible for keeping the effects of the Purge and Terror limited in duration. These were the regime's struggle to stop improper and escalated prosecutions by legal officials; and its effort to rebuild and strengthen the agencies of justice.

The first signals from the leaders that it was time to slow down the Purge and Terror came as early as January 1938. The January 1938

---

60 "Aktiv Narodnogo Komissariata Iustitsii Soiuza SSR," *SIu*, 1937, no. 8, 12; "Ob organizatsii rukovodstva narodnymi sudami," Prikaz NKIu SSSR ot 4 marta 1938 g. no. 21, in *Sbornik prikazov i instruktsii narodnogo komissariata iustitsii Soiza SSR* (Moscow, 1940), 53; "59 Plenum Verkhovnogo Suda SSSR: Praktika sudov po grazhdanskim delam" (26–29 Dek. 1927, g.), *SZ*, 1938, no. 2, 116–123; B. Boshko, "Sudebnaia praktika SSSR po alimentnym delam," *SZ*, 1938, no. 11, 50–54.

61 "Aktiv Prokuratury Soiuza," *SZ*, 1938, no. 2, 126–140; "Vsesiouznoe prokurorskoe soveshchanie," *SZ*, 1938, no. 6, 12–13. In May-June 1938 procurators were mobilized to address some of these complaints, see "O nadzore organov prokuratury za pravilnym razresheniiem zhalob na nezakonnoe uvolnenie i nezakonnyi otkaz v prieme na rabotu," Prikaz ot 28 maia 1938 no. 547, *Sbornik prikazov prokuratury*, 120–122.

Plenum of the Central Committee of the CPS condemned "careless, mass expulsions from the party, often leading to arrest," and blamed regional party officials for allowing them to occur.[62] In the light of the Plenum's resolutions the journal of Narkomiust told judges that they too must handle cases more carefully, avoid "formalism," and pay attention to the grounds for conviction. "Some judges," the editors chided, "have not conducted a Bolshevik fight with careerists and slanderers, who frighten, violate Soviet law, and provoke the just wrath of the slandered. . . . " In the same spirit a Procuracy order (*prikaz*) in January "suggested that the procurators of republics and regions check all cases under investigation in which the suspect was in detention to ensure that there were grounds for the charges."[63]

The initial consequences of these new signals for the practice of criminal justice were limited. With the Purge and Terror continuing through the spring (as political police contended with new quotas) procurators in the provinces and regions did not believe that it was safe to stop escalating charges and sending weak cases to court. A combination of inertia and fear maintained the momentum of groundless prosecutions, and few of the higher procurators seem to have been ready to stop it. However, in Moscow and Leningrad at least judges began returning badly prepared cases to the procuracy for supplementary investigations, and these cases included some with a political cast.[64]

Spring 1938 was the turning point for Soviet criminal justice, for it marked the beginning of the end of the campaign of vigilance. First, in April the USSR Procuracy instructed regional and republican procurators to get clearance from the USSR Procuracy before starting new political cases (Article 58); and at the same time to prosecute "slanderers," that is informers whose denunciations prove false. Then, in May the doyen of Soviet justice, Procurator-General Vyshinskii, convened a

---

62 "Ob oshibkakh partorganizatsii pri iskliuchenii kommunistov iz partii, o formalnobiurokraticheskom otnoshenii k apelliatsim iskliuchehnykh iz VKP(b) i o merakh po ustraneniiu etikh nedostatkov," Postanovlenie plenuma TsK VKP(b) ot 20 ianvaria 1938, *SIu*, 1938, no. 2–3, 1–5. According to a Soviet scholar with access to the party archives, this decree responded to complaints made by NKVD employees about Ezhov's illegal use of force and the execution of party members without investigation or trial. Boris Starkov, "Narkom Ezhov," in Getty and Manning, *Stalinist Terror*, 21–39.

63 "Zadachi sudebnykh organov v svete ianvarskogo Plenuma TsK VKP(b)," ibid., 4–5; cited in M. L'vovich, "Za bolshevistskuiu kontrol ispolneniia" *SZ*, 1938, no. 10, 15–18. For a similar cautionary directive issued February 25, 1938, see GARF, f.8131sch, op.28s, d.24, 6–8.

64 A. Murugov and I. Kaganovich, "God raboty na osnove iiunskogo prikaza," *SZ*, 1939, no. 7, 12–19; D. Brodskii and K. Viatkin, "O delakh, obrashchaemykh k dosledovaniiu," *SZ*, 1939, no. 2, 64–66.

meeting of republican and regional procurators that discussed and condemned many distortions of justice that had characterized the year of Purge and Terror. While Vyshinskii's speech concentrated on such bland matters as the current state of justice agencies, other participants raised the question of the escalation of charges and groundless prosecutions. This discussion prompted Vyshinskii himself to step into the fray and vilify the procurator of Omsk region Busorgin who had admitted to rubber-stamping indictments without reading them. After setting him up as a scapegoat, Vyshinskii called for the poor fellow's banishment from the meeting.[65]

Spelling out the new line announced at the conference, the USSR Procuracy issued on June 1 a major directive on the overhaul (*perestroika*) of its work. The directive told investigators and procurators in no uncertain terms "to quash all unfounded prosecutions that had been started" and "to cease this practice in the future." This order heralded a six-month transition period during which escalated and unfounded prosecutions did decline. Not, however, without a struggle! After all, legal officials had become accustomed to arresting and prosecuting suspects on the slightest pretext, often nothing more than a denunciation. How else could they "insure themselves" against the same fate? Breaking this habit called for more than mere directives. One way was for the central Procuracy to use its new screening authority. Between May and December the procurator-general received from procurators in the RSFSR 98,478 requests for permission to start new political cases. Of these his office cleared only 237.[66] In recognition of this fact, central Procuracy officials brought criminal charges against a handful of regional and district procurators for excesses that only months before would have earned praise. In July *Pravda* began reporting a series of trials of these former procurators, all of them heard at the RSFSR Supreme Court and resulting in terms of imprisonment. (In October the former procurator of Omsk was among them.)[67] At the same time, after a slow start in the spring, summer and fall witnessed

---

[65] "Aktiv Prokuratury Soiuza," *SZ*, 1938, no. 9, 119. "O reshitelnoi borbe s klevetnicheskimi obvineniami chestnykh liudei," Prikaz ot 5 apreliia 1938 g., no. 346, *Sbornik prikazov Prokuratury SSSR* (1939), 146; "Vsesoiuznoe prokurorskoe soveshchanie," 41–46.

[66] Murugov and Kaganovich. "God raboty," 12; GARF, f.9474, op.1, d.116, 114–115. The screening related mainly to Russia. The Ukrainian Procuracy presented only six requests, of which the procurator-general approved three.

[67] I. Iartsev, "Prokuror – samodur," *Pravda*, July 22, 1938, 6; "Prokuror – samodur," ibid., July 27, 1938, 6; I. Iartsev, "Prokuror – perestrakhovshchik," ibid., Aug. 2, 1938, 6; "Nebolshevistskaia pozitsiia riazanskogo prokurora," ibid., Sept. 21, 1939, 6; "Prestuplenie prokurora," ibid., Oct. 27, 1938, 6.

a series of well-publicized trials of "slanderers," at which officials of the Procuracy prosecuted informers rather than responded to their cues.[68]

There was external pressure as well. Procurators might have been reluctant to reconsider political cases already in progress, but they had little choice when party control commissions started reviewing appeals from Purge victims and insisted that prosecutions be dropped against persons they restored to the party. The need to stop bad prosecutions was underscored when in October 1938 the Criminal Collegium of RSFSR Supreme Court took a political case on appeal and converted the charge to an ordinary one, and then the USSR Supreme Court, hearing the same case at the request of Procurator-General Vyshinskii, canceled the conviction entirely.[69]

Despite all these efforts, the decline in escalated and unfounded prosecutions was gradual and incomplete. There were signs of change. In fall 1938 serious accidents in industry produced ordinary rather than political prosecutions. Judges applying more rigorous standards of evidence began returning fewer cases to the Procuracy for supplementary investigation.[70] Still, at the same time there were contradictory trends. In August 1938 a series of show trials was held at the regional court in

---

68 *Pravda* (1938) contained the following reports on cases against slanderers: I. Iartsev, "Klevetnik," April 6, 6; "Vinovniki uvolneniia pedagogov privlekaiutsia k otvestvennosti," April 7, 5; N. Kuzovkin, "Razoblachitel Gronskii," April 8, 6; "Klevetniki," Aug. 27, 2; "Klevetniki," Sept. 6, 5; "Klevetniki ostalis 'beznakannye,' " Nov. 24, 2; P. Lidov, "Klevetniki," Nov. 28, 6; K.M. Tabgalov, "Klevetniki," Dec. 3, 1; P. Maniulov, "Klevetniki," Dec. 27, 6. See also "Peregibshchik," *Izvestiia*, July 9, 1938, 4; and "Klevetniki," ibid., Sept. 6, 1938, 4.

69 Between February and August 1938 the party control commission in the Bashkir ASSR heard 1,308 appeals and restored 687 persons to the party, "many of whom had been victims of slanderers." Solodii, "Beznakazannye klevetniki." There are also signs that other party bodies joined in the effort to stop the momentum of prosecution. Delegates to a provincial party conference in Kursk condemned "the arbitrary actions of the police, court, and procuracy of Kursk *oblast*, who had committed crude violations of revolutionary legality." "Kurskaia oblastnaia partiinaia konferentsiia," *Pravda*, July 13, 1938, 2; I. Iartsev, "Neobosnovannyi prigovor," *Pravda*, Nov. 7, 1938, 6.

70 N. Mikhailovskii, "Prestupnoe otnoshenie k tekhnike bezopasnosti," *Pravda*, Oct. 16, 1938, 6, and Interview no. 524 of the Harvard Project on the Soviet Social System. On the unpublished material of the project, see Marjorie Mandelstam Balzer, "Guide to Materials from the Harvard Project on the Soviet Social System," Soviet Interview Project Working Paper no. 1 (Urbana-Champaign, Ill., Aug. 1980). In May 1939 judges returned less than half the number of cases to supplementary investigation than they had in May 1938. Murugov and Kaganovich, "God raboty," p. 13. Although the defects in many cases stemmed from the inexperience of the investigators more than from the pressures of the Terror, it is hard to disentangle the two. Even in the spring of 1939, the authors admitted, some cases were pursued because of the procurator's fear of refusing to prosecute and desire to play it safe (*perestrakhovka*).

the Donbass. In September and October *Pravda* reported cases of arson qualified as wrecking. And right to the end of the year "slanderers" continued to deliver denunciations and procurators to respond to them.[71]

It was unlikely that the mass terror could be curtailed and the justice agencies removed from it without decisive action by Stalin himself. As early as spring 1938, some of the Leader's colleagues in the Politburo began criticizing the effects of repression. Zhdanov and Andreev reportedly called Stalin's attention to the low quality of the cadres who replaced purged officials and the weakening of the country's economy and defense. In August, Mikoian and Kaganovich joined the chorus. But by this point Stalin himself had started to act. First, also in August, Stalin appointed his new protégé, Lavrentii Beriia, deputy head of the NKVD and, within the commissariat, chief of the administration of state security. The result was to isolate Ezhov (who already held a second ministerial post along with NKVD) and remove him from direct control of the political police. In September the NKVD itself was supposed to have lost much of its capacity for hearing political cases, when the *troiki* were transferred to the official jurisdiction of the Sovnarkom, a preserve of Molotov.[72] The crucial moment, though, came with the issuing of the decree of the Sovnarkom and Central Committee of the Communist party on November 17, 1938, "On Arrest, Procuracy Supervision, and the Conduct of Investigations."[73]

Signed by Stalin and Molotov, the secret decree of November 17 ordered an end to mass arrests and resettlements; the liquidation of all *troiki* (henceforth only courts or the Special Board of the USSR NKVD would hear cases); the revival of procuracy screening of arrest orders and the establishment of procuracy supervision of investigations con-

---

71 *Sotsialisticheskii Donbass* (Aug. 1, 1938) gave the transcript of the trial of a "right-Trotskyite" group of officials held responsible for a fire in a coal mine; and on August 4, the paper announced the discovery of another such group in two other coal trusts. I am indebted to Lewis Siegelbaum for providing this information. For cases of arson by traitors see N. Iartsev, "Diversanty-podzhigately," *Pravda*, Sept. 24, 1938, 6; N. Iartsev, "Podzhigateli," ibid., Oct. 10, 1938, 6. One slanderer in Kiev continued his denunciations to the end of 1938. "Klevetnik," *Pravda*, Feb. 4, 1939, 6. Note that further prosecutions of slanderers were reported in *Pravda* in March, April, and July of 1939.
72 Starkov, "Narkom Ezhov," 28–31; A. Antonov-Ovseenko, "Put naverkh," in *Beriia – konets karery* (Moscow, 1991), 60–63. According to his son, Georgii Malenkov turned Stalin against Ezhov in August 1938. See Andrei Malenkov, *O moem otse Georgii Malenkov* (Moscow, 1992), 33–35.
73 "Ob arestakh, prokurorskom nadzore i vedenii sledstviia," Postanovlenie Soveta Narodnykh Komissarov SSSR i TsK VKP(b) ot 17 noiabria 1938 g. No. P.4387, RTsKhIDNI, f.17, op.3, d.1003, and, as reprinted in *Istoricheskii arkhiv*, 1992, no. 1, 125–127.

ducted by all police (including security). The decree also laid the blame for the Terror squarely on the shoulders of its executors. The NKVD (in part because it was allegedly penetrated with enemies) had "consciously distorted Soviet laws," conducted "mass and groundless arrests," set aside investigatory work in favor of more simplified methods such as "mass arrest," and developed a "fixation" on the evidence supplied by the accused during interrogation. In focusing upon the excesses of those who implemented the Terror rather than upon its creator, Joseph Stalin, the decree of November 17, 1938, bore a striking similarity to the Instruction of May 8, 1933, that had called for the end of mass arrests associated with collectivization. (In fact, the 1938 decree refers to the earlier decree.)

A series of further measures from Stalin and his colleagues helped to implement the policy line announced in the decree of November 17 – that is, curtailing the Terror and removing the legal agencies from association with it. First, the special collegia of the regional and republican court were eliminated. This step further reduced the bodies available for adjudicating political cases, leaving the military tribunals and the Special Board of the NKVD to assume most of the responsibility for such cases.[74] Second, through the vehicle of a guiding decision of the USSR Supreme Court, the leadership set out new standards of evidence for the most commonly used categories of political crime during the campaign of vigilance. At its December 1938 Plenum (more about this meeting below) the Court overturned its earlier ruling of 1928 and henceforth required a showing of intent in cases of wrecking, sabotage, and attacks on transport. The new requirement made it difficult for a procurator to prove wrecking on the part of a person held responsible for an accident, unless the defendant could be convinced to confess to a political motivation. Since Vyshinskii's thesis on the sufficiency of confession as proof in political cases remained enshrined in Soviet jurisprudence, this ruling helped only those defendants who were strong enough to resist pressure from their interrogators.[75] Resisting pressure to confess might have been facilitated by a third measure from Stalin. According to a telegram sent by Stalin on January 10, 1939, to police

---

[74] Ger van den Berg, *The Soviet System of Justice: Figures and Policy* (The Hague, 1985), 19. Note that in Georgia the Special Collegium of the Supreme Court was still in operation in the first half of 1939. Faina Baazova, *Prokazhennye* (Jerusalem: Biblioteka-Aliia, 1980), 64. For an example of a political case heard at the Supreme Court of an autonomous republic (in 1941) and thrown out on appeal by the RSFSR Supreme Court (in 1942), see A. Avtorkhanov, *Memuary* (Frankfurt, 1983), 605–610.

[75] "O primenenii st. st. 58⁷, 58⁹, i 58¹⁴ UK RSFSR i sootvetstiuishchikh statei UK drugikh soiuznykh respublik," Postanovlenie Plenuma ot 31 dekabria 1938, in Goliakov, ed., *Sbornik deistvuiushchikh postanovlenii*, 5.

chiefs and party secretaries, "The application of physical force in the practice of the NKVD, permitted since 1937 by the Central Committee [sic!] has sped up the exposure of enemies of the people. The Central Committee thinks that this method must be applied from now on, as an exception, to clear and still dangerous enemies as the correct and expedient one." In other words, beatings to extract confessions were to be removed from routine practice of most investigators.[76] Finally, as a further protection for party members and officials another decree from Stalin and Molotov reestablished the system of party clearances for arrests of those persons.[77]

Police and legal officials understood from this package of measures that the mass terror was over, but Stalin underscored the message with his usual practice of supplying scapegoats. A large-scale purge of the purgers – that is of high- and middle-ranking officials of the NKVD – followed immediately. Along with this purge went the arrest and prosecution of a smaller number of legal officials for their participation in "mass groundless arrests." These included the procurators of Omsk region (not Busorgin, who had already been arrested, but his successor Iarchuk), of the Voroshilov railroad, of the regions of East-Kazakhstan and Smolensk. Smolensk's procurator, Terentev, was a classic victim of the shift in policy. Just a few weeks before the Plenum, the USSR Supreme Court began checking for unfounded prosecutions in political cases. It called for a review of one case heard earlier in the year by the special collegium of the Smolensk regional court, a case that had ended with the shooting of the accused. In an effort to ensure a consistent version of the facts, the procurator and head of the court made the mistake of sending identical telegrams to the Supreme Court. When the Court's review of the case led to its dismissal, the procurator and judge faced the charge of "operating a family circle." A circuit panel of the USSR Supreme Court gave the procurator of Smolensk region three years' imprisonment "for this offense and other excesses." His colleague, regional court chairman Andreev, got off lightly with a year of corrective work.[78]

In addition to adopting measures to stop mass terror and providing scapegoats for it, Stalin sought to restore public belief in the fairness of the Soviet government, and especially of its legal agencies. The vehicle Stalin used for this purpose was the USSR Supreme Court. The

[76] Maslov and Chistiakov, *Vopreki zakonu*, 23.

[77] "O poriadke soglasovaniia arestov," Postanovlenie Soveta Narodnykh Komissarov SSSR i TsK VKP(b) ot 1 dekabria 1938 goda No. P 4404, in "Postanovleniia Politbiuro."

[78] Medvedev, *Let History Judge*, 244; GARF f.9474, op.1, d.119 (Stenogramma Pervogo Plenuma Verkhovnogo Suda SSSR ot 25 dekabria 1938 goda), 117–121.

Court had resumed operations in the fall of 1938 (after suffering a thorough purge the previous spring). The new members of the Court had acquired through the Law on Court organization promulgated in August the unusual power to accept in supervisory review any criminal case directly from any court in the USSR.[79] At its first Plenum since reconstitution, in later December 1938, the Court began reviewing and reversing convictions in political cases.[80] Both the Plenum itself and the Court's involvement in rectifications received detailed coverage in the national press. Articles in *Izvestiia* emphasized the new power of the Court to reopen any case and the commitment of its chairman, Ivan Terentevich Goliakov, to address instances of incorrect prosecutions and pay attention to "living persons."[81] And, in the months that followed, the Court did review and reverse the convictions of "tens of thousands" (35,000–40,000) of persons convicted of counterrevolutionary crimes, especially by transport courts (which came under the direct subordination of the USSR Supreme Court) but also from other courts. Moreover, behind the scenes the NKVD also authorized internal reviews of political cases heard by its former *troiki*, but these reviews required the personal involvement of the NKVD's regional chiefs, and, as a result, the number of *troika* convicts released in 1939 and 1940 was not large, numbering, I estimate, no more than a few thousand. Naturally, these instances of reversal and rehabilitation involved only a small proportion of the cases of unfair and unfounded repression (very few, of those heard by the *troiki* of the security police), but they were sufficient to create in the Soviet public a widespread belief that a new era of legality had dawned. Because the repressions of the past were associated with Ezhov, many observers credited his successor, Beriia, with responsibility for the new era. He did not deserve it, for unfounded repressions continued on

[79] The new list of judges provided in "Ob izbrannii Verkhovnogo Suda SSSR," *Pravda*, Aug. 24, 1938, 2, contained only one of the ten members of the Supreme Court who had spoken at its Plenum of December 1937 or at its *aktiv* of March 1938. GARF, f.9474, op.1, d.111 (59 Plenum Verkhovnogo Suda SSSR); F. Kamenskii, "Na sobranii aktiva rabotnikov Verkhovnogo Suda SSSR," *SIu*, 1938, no. 5, 20–21. "Zakon o sudoustroistve SSSR, Soiuznykh i avtonomnykh respublik," *Pravda*, Aug. 24, 1938, 1–2, art. 63 and 64. Previously the Court had been limited to reviewing cases already heard at republican Supreme Courts and then only at the initiative of the USSR Procuracy.

[80] *Sbornik postanovlenii plenuma i opredelenii kollegii Verkhovnogo suda SSSR (1938 g. i pervoe polugodie 1939 g.)* (Moscow, 1940), passim; GARF, f.9474, op.1, d.119.

[81] "Sobranie aktiva rabotnikov Verkhovnogo suda SSSR," *Izvestiia*, Dec. 9, 1983, 3; Goliakov, "Revoliutsionnaia zakonnost nerushima," ibid., Dec. 22, 1938, 3; "Pervyi plenum Verkhovnogo suda SSSR," ibid., Dec. 27, 1938, 1; Dec. 28, 1939, 4; Dec. 29, 1938, 4; and Dec. 30, 1938, 3.

a selective basis and Beriia himself was their principal stage manager.[82]

One clue that contrived political prosecutions were likely to continue (although not on a mass basis) was the failure of Stalin and Vyshinskii to eliminate the jurisprudence of terror. To be sure, the Supreme Court's new requirement of a showing of intent in cases of wrecking and sabotage did put an end to the escalation of political cases deserving charges of negligence and malfeasance. But two provisions that gave a legal basis for patently unjust proceedings in political cases remained in the law. The edict of December 1, 1934 (the lex Kirov) ensured that cases of terrorism would be heard immediately by a judge sitting alone, and that sentences (including to death) would be implemented at once without any appellate review or application for pardon. The edict of September 14, 1937, established that for cases of wrecking and sabotage there would be no cassation review and shooting would be performed at once after the refusal of a petition for pardon. Since charges of wrecking and sabotage had been especially common during the Great Terror, this second law greatly facilitated the repression. At the Supreme Court Plenum of December 1938 that reviewed and rectified some unjustified prosecution, the judges discussed at length whether the edict of September 14, 1937, should be repealed. While some favored such a move, all spoke cautiously, sounding fearful of any appearance of leniency

---

82 Roi Medvedev, *K sudu istorii* (New York, 1974), 471, refers to "neskolko desiatkov tysiach chelovek" (a few tens of thousands). The English translator rendered this figure as "a few thousand" in *Let History Judge*, 247. The perception of a new fairness is noted in Alexander Uralov (Artorkhanov), *The Reign of Stalin* (London, 1953); Baazova, *Prokazkennye*, 110, 132; Harvard Project interviews, nos. 50, 306, 1,498.

According to the archival evidence, the political police through the Special Board and special collegia registered 63,889 convictions in 1939 and 71,806 in 1940. While a far cry from the levels of 1937 and 1938, these figures confirm that selective terror remained substantial. Popov, "Gosudarstvennyi terror," 28. Beriia's son claims that the selective terror was entirely the responsibility of the "hypocritical party leadership" and that his father always resisted repression. I know of no evidence to support this assertion. See Sergo Beriia, *Moi otets – Lavrentii Beriia* (Moscow, 1995), 74–89.

From December 26, 1939, until April 22, 1940, the regional chiefs of the NKVD had the right to reverse decisions of the former *troiki* and ask central NKVD officials to implement releases from the camps. As of April 23, 1940, the regional chiefs were allowed only to recommend such reversals to the Special Board of the NKVD in Moscow (a procedure already introduced in October 1939 for requests regarding simple reduction of punishments in *troika* cases). The only relevant data that I have encountered thus far concern decisions of the Special Board in the first three months of 1940 on requests regarding the review of decisions by *troiki* on the railroads (a special category of cases whose review already required central involvement). The Board ordered releases in eighty such cases (of the ninety-two brought to its attention). GARF, f.8131, op.37, d.136, 2–13.

toward enemies of the Soviet state. Even so, the majority disagreed and advised retaining the law.[83]

The man who did the most to implement Stalin's policy of selective rectifications and rehabilitations was Chairman of the USSR Supreme Court Ivan Terentevich Goliakov. As a veteran of military justice, including the Military Collegium of the USSR Supreme Court, Goliakov had played a part in the Terror, but more than most of his colleagues he found means of expiation.[84] The dedication of this quiet, erudite man to the correct application of the law and fair treatment of persons accused of crimes is evident both from his own writings and the testimony of lawyers who dealt with him on case appeals.[85] Goliakov did not deserve the mockery of Solzhenitsyn, who in *Gulag Archipelago* asked what Goliakov's famous collection of books (especially fiction) had done for his sense of morality. Much later – after retirement from the Court – Goliakov would write a book on law and courts in the fiction of Western Europe and Russia. Ironically, though, Goliakov's book collecting would help to get another judge into trouble. In 1946 a senior military court judge, F.L. Bereznoi, whose leniency had antagonized the NKVD but who had strong protection in Moscow (he was actually nominated for but declined a post on the Military Collegium of the USSR Supreme Court), made an official trip to Kharbin, Manchuria. On his return to the USSR, the police discovered that Berezhnoi had brought back a large number of books, including prerevolutionary Russian legal publications (such as Novotorzhskii's *What Is a Law-Based State?*, St. Petersburg, 1906). Using the books as a pretext the NKVD charged the judge with misuse of office, citing among other things his "mass purchase of for-

---

[83] Note 4, supra, and GARF, f.9474, op.1, d.119 (Stenogramma Pervogo Plenuma), 40, 85–85, 112, 125.

[84] Other members of the Military Collegium of the USSR Supreme Court who survived the Purge also received promotions. Along with Goliakov, other new chiefs of the Court who had served previously on the Military Collegium included I.T. Nikitchenko, the deputy chairman; P.A. Kameron, the head of the Criminal Collegium; and I.M. Zarianov, head of the Collegium for Railroad Cases. The new USSR Commissar of Justice, N.M. Rychkov, and the RSFSR Commissar of Justice, Ia.P. Dmitrev, both appointed in 1938, had also served on the Military Collegium of the USSR Supreme Court. See O.F. Suvenirov, "Voennaia kollegiia Verkhovnogo Suda SSSR (1937–1939)," *Voprosy istorii*, 1995, no. 4, 145–146.

[85] Baazova, *Prokazhennye*, 113–124; interviews with former Soviet lawyers in emigration conducted by the author between 1985 and 1987, many under the auspices of the Soviet Interview Project and supported by contract no. 701 from the National Council for Soviet and E.E. Research to the University of Illinois at Urbana-Champaign, James B. Millar, Principal Investigator. I. Goliakov, "Nekotorye voprosy nauki i sudebnaia praktika v resheniiakh Plenuma Verkhovnogo Suda SSSR," part one: *SIu*, 1940, no. 4, 1–5; part two: *SIu*, 1940, no. 5, 5–10; and I. Goliakov, "Sovetskii sud kak orudie vospitaniia," *SZ*, 1944, no. 2, 6–10; Solzhenitsyn, *Gulag Archipelago*, 1–2, 172.

bidden books and their illegal import through the border." The accused explained that he had bought many of the books for Supreme Court Chairman Goliakov, whom he had met at a reception a year earlier. Tried at the Military Collegium of the USSR Supreme Court itself (on an ordinary charge!) Berezhnoi received and served a three-year sentence, gaining rehabilitation in 1953.[86]

Ivan Goliakov was the right man for the task of restoring the prestige and public image of the pinnacle of the legal system and by implication the legal system itself. There are signs that he was chosen for this part by Vyshinskii, and it was clear at the first Plenum of the Supreme Court that Vyshinskii remained the politician in charge of judicial policy. When Goliakov asked for questions about the day's agenda, Vyshinskii answered for all with a "nyet" and Vyshinskii interrupted repeatedly throughout the session.[87] Although dependent upon Vyshinskii, and ultimately Stalin, for the policies pursued by his Court, Ivan Goliakov showed great enthusiasm for the program of restoring legality. He even went so far as to attempt its extension, by seeking permission for the Court to reconsider those political cases that its own military collegium had heard as a court of first instance. After enlisting support from Procurator-General Pankratev and Commissar of Justice Rychkov, Goliakov took the bold step of sending a letter (on December 3, 1939) directly to Stalin and Molotov. The letter informed the leaders that a spot check of cases heard by the military collegium had revealed "many erroneous accusations and convictions that deserved to be set aside," including instances of the qualification as counterrevolutionary crimes of actions that should have been designated crimes of officials. However, according to the Law on Court Organization the review of decisions of the Supreme Court's Military Collegium could be undertaken only by a plenary session of the Court, after a protest by the Court's chairman or the procurator-general. This group, Goliakov suggested, was "too large" for the review of many cases (it would be hard to make copies of the materials) and its use might lead to embarrassing divulging of secrets! Therefore, Goliakov requested permission to review these cases in a small group of three judges, consisting of himself, Deputy Chairman I.T. Nikitchenko, and the head of the Military Collegium, Vasilii Ulrikh, with the participation of Procurator-General Pankratev. In requesting the establishment of a simpler mechanism for reviewing cases from the Military Collegium, Goliakov was also asking for the right to review them in large numbers. Molotov took charge of the matter and asked the opinion of

86 Muranov and Zviagintsev, *Sud nad sudiamu*, 91–112.
87 GARF, f.8131, op.15, d.3, 118; f.9474, op.1, d.119, 10 and passim.

Lavrentii Beriia. The latter replied that it would be "inexpedient" to violate the law on court organization, and days later a meeting of top officials around Molotov turned down Goliakov's request. Vyshinskii was charged with reporting the decision to Goliakov, Pankratev, and Rychkov.[88]

Even Goliakov's initiative did not deal with the review of unfounded convictions perpetrated directly by the political police, a category that constituted more than 90% of political cases in 1937 and 1938. As we have seen, at the end of 1938 the NKVD did establish an internal procedure for such reviews, but it reached the tiniest fraction of wrongful convictions perpetrated by its *troiki*. In October 1939 a group of officials in the USSR Procuracy took up the cause of these innocent victims and wrote to Central Committee Secretary Andrei Zhdanov condemning the NKVD's internal review procedure as wholly inadequate, since hundreds of thousands of innocent persons convicted by the *troiki* remained in the camps. The procedure had failed, the writers alleged, because Ezhov's successor Beriia cared more about upholding the honor of his agency than doing justice and because Procurator-General Pankratev was too weak to stand up to Beriia and force the

---

[88] GARF, f.5446sch, op.230, d.303, 1–7. For a simplified version of the tale see P. Skomorokhov, "Iz istorii Verkhovnogo Suda SSSR," 1964, no. 2, 34–35. On the infamous role played in the Terror by the Military Collegium of the USSR Supreme Court under Vasilii Ulrikh, see Anton Antonov-Ovseyenko, *The Time of Stalin: A Portrait of a Tyranny* (New York, 1981), 150. There are signs that the USSR Supreme Court in plenary session did review at least a few cases from the Military Collegium at the request of political leaders. GARF, f.8131sch, op.27s, d.239, 45; d.542, 94–95.

This was not the only instance of an attempt by Ivan Goliakov to get cases of unjust convictions reviewed. A few months earlier he presented to Andrei Vyshinskii at the USSR Council of People's Commissars a draft edict on judicial practice in cases of anti-Soviet agitation that would encourage judges to review convictions. Goliakov sought Vyshinskii's consent to discussion and approval of the draft at the next plenary session of the court (Sept. 15). At first Vyshinskii agreed, sending Goliakov a note with the words "no objection"; but just a few days later he dispatched a second note explaining "that the Council of People's Commissars considered it inexpedient to discuss and adopt the edict." GARF, f.5446, op.23a, d.299, 1–33. In another attempt to restore justice, however, Goliakov took a more cautious posture. In August 1939, the RSFSR Minister of Justice, Ia.P. Dmitrev, proposed the review of cases of unjustified sentences to capital punishment that had already been implemented. In passing this proposal to Molotov, Goliakov opined that it might be unwise to undertake such reviews, as knowledge of "mistakes in the application of the death penalty could be used against the USSR." At the same time, though, Goliakov noted that an official at the Council of People's Commissars, Faingold, thought such reviews appropriate because formal rehabilitation could help family members of the deceased. Speaking on behalf of Molotov, Vyshinskii gave a qualified approval; yes, "you may review particular cases where there are signs of groundless application of the death penalty." GARF, f.5446, op.23a, d.296, 1–2.

issue. The complaining procurators begged Zhdanov to replace Pank-ratev.[89]

The efforts of this brave band of officials in the USSR Procuracy went for naught, for the author of the repressions of 1937–1938 had been not Ezhov but Stalin; and, in issuing the edict of November 17, 1938, Stalin had intended merely to stop mass terror and denunciations from below and to distribute blame, not to correct most of the injustices that the Terror had wreaked. Nine months later Stalin did replace Pankratev (see Chapter 9), but not with a successor ready to stand up to Beriia, who was, after all, Stalin's servant.[90] The rehabilitation of most victims of Stalinist repression had to wait for the tyrant's death.

Through this gamut of measures Stalin did succeed in turning off the mass terror. At the same time, he confined the continuing selective use of extralegal repression to bodies outside of the regular system of criminal justice. With the elimination of the special collegia of the regional and republican courts, Stalin removed political offenses not only from the hands of the judges of those courts but also from the investigators and procurators who served them. Most cases of state crimes came to be handled by either the military procuracy and military tribunals or the NKVD's investigators and Special Board. From 1939 until Stalin's death in 1953 the regular Procuracy and ordinary courts had minimal involvement in political cases.[91]

---

[89] "Pismo ot 28 oktiabria, 1939 ot prokurorov Prokuratury SSSR k tov. Zhdanovu," RTsKhIDNI, f.77, op.1, d.1949, II, 4, 40b, 5ob. This item was included in an exhibit held at the Library of Congress, Washington D.C., June 17–July 16, 1992, entitled "Revelations from the Russian Archives." I am grateful to Dr. Harold Leich of the Library of Congress for providing a copy.

[90] Donald Barry, "Leaders of the Soviet Legal Profession,"

[91] In some places the actual implementation of Stalin's edict on the elimination of the special collegia may have been delayed for a couple of years. At least one veteran legal official, who worked in a procuracy office at the end of the 1930s, recalled the existence of a special department in the Leningrad regional procuracy that prepared cases for closed hearings of the special collegium of the Leningrad regional court in 1939–1940. V.I. Terebilov, "Professiia – iurist," part one, SZ, 1991, no. 5, 61. In addition to the military tribunals, a small share of political cases (state crimes) was heard by the line courts, the courts in the labor camps, and the regional and supreme courts. GARF, f.9492, op.6s, d.14.8.

More than two dozen former investigators, procurators, and judges who worked in the legal agencies of the USSR between 1945 and 1953 agreed that the procuracy and courts, particularly at the lower and provincial levels, had almost no contact with the security police. Pressure and interventions came not from the NKVD but from party officials. See Peter H. Solomon, Jr., "Soviet Politicians and Criminal Prosecutions: The Logic of Party Interventions," in James Millar, ed., *Cracks in the Monolith* (Armonk, N.Y., 1992), 3–32.

The virtual separation of ordinary from political justice flowed from Stalin's policy – in place from 1934 – of promoting at one and the same time two different kinds of coercive power: traditional legal order and extralegal repression. Arguably, the utility of both instruments of rule gained from separation, but this was especially so for the legal order. Left to their own devices, the chiefs of the legal agencies were able to rebuild and resume the program of reform started before 1937.

One facet of rebuilding was the renewed emphasis by the central legal officials upon standards of evidence and procedure. Far more than at any earlier time in Soviet history, the journals of the Procuracy and Narkomiust devoted themselves to explaining the meaning of laws, establishing standards of performance, and holding up for emulation model investigators and judges who met them. Even more important, the courts, under the lead of the USSR Supreme Court, began requiring better standards of evidence. The ruling on the need to show intent in cases of wrecking was not an isolated act but the start of a trend. Thus, just months later the journal of the Procuracy told its readers that in cases of criminal negligence (the source of so many wrecking charges in 1937) it was now necessary to demonstrate a causal connection between the omissions of the accused and their supposedly harmful consequences.[92] In imposing these and other evidentiary standards, the Supreme Court did not act alone, for by 1939 the cassation appeals panels of other courts began to function again. At the end of 1939 Goliakov himself reported that instead of the rubber-stamping of "not so long ago" (when most cassation decisions read, "The guilt was demonstrated by the materials of the case and the punishment is appropriate"), the appeals panels of the republican supreme courts and the regional courts were now examining the evidence and often reaching "motivated decisions."[93] Apparently, the revival of standards by judges had an impact on the quality of investigations, for the percentage of cases returned to the Procuracy for supplementary investigation fell from 15.4% in May 1938 to 7.6% in May 1939. Investigators were still starting weak cases, but they were managing to stop many before trial (in Moscow in the first part of 1939, 27.6% of those started).[94]

The recovery of the administration of justice from the Terror and Purge required more than the promotion of new standards of evidence

---

[92] *SIu*, 1939, passim; *SZ*, 1939, passim; "O kvalifikatsii prestuplenii," *SZ*, 1939, no. 10–11, 15.

[93] Goliakov, "Nekotorye voprosy nauki i sudebnoi praktiki," part 1, 2.

[94] B. Lebedinskii, "Godovshchina prikaza Prokuratury Soiuza ot 1 iuniia 1938," *SZ*, 1939, no. 7, 7–11; Murugov and Kaganovich, "God raboty." GARF, f.5446, op.23a, d.318, 1–14 includes a report (mid-1939) on the continuation of old methods of investigation and an NKVD-Procuracy directive on the subject.

and procedure. That recovery called for the recruitment and training of a largely new cohort of legal officials – investigators, procurators, and judges – to replace predecessors eliminated in the Purge. The recovery also entailed the revival of the effort begun before the Terror to centralize the administration of justice, both to increase its efficiency and to counteract the ever-present influence of local political power. These processes form the subject of the next chapter, on the reconstruction of criminal justice.

8 The reconstruction of criminal justice

As the Purge in the legal agencies subsided, the top legal officials – apart from Vyshinskii mainly new faces – resumed the efforts of their predecessors to educate legal officials and centralize management of the justice agencies. Not surprisingly, it proved impossible to raise the quality of legal officials above the low levels of the mid-1930s. The Purge had left many vacancies in the procuracy and courts, and to fill them authorities had to turn (once again) to new recruits lacking even rudimentary training in law. In contrast, the centralization of power within the legal agencies was easier to accomplish, and in the years just prior to World War II the heads of the legal agencies established mechanisms of centralized administration. Centralization proved a mixed blessing. While it encouraged uniformity and efficiency in the work of the Procuracy and courts, it also introduced methods of evaluating the performance of legal officials that had counterproductive results. From the late 1930s quantitative indicators of performance served as the principal means of assessing individual officials, and those officials became preoccupied with findings ways of achieving the right indicators.

Centralization within legal agencies was also supposed to reduce the influence of local politicians in the administration of justice, but this goal was realized only in part. The assertion of priority in managing legal officials by the legal agencies helped to diminish the practices that developed during collectivization, such as the assignment of legal officials by local politicians to tasks unrelated to legal work. But the strengthening of the hands of the vertical master did not undermine the bases of the authority of the horizontal one. Party officials in the localities remained in a position to ask for and gain the cooperation of procuracy officials and judges alike, in both law enforcement policies (such as campaigns) and the disposition of individual cases.

This chapter examines the problem of personnel for the legal agencies and legal education prior to World War II; it analyzes centralization within the procuracy, courts, and Justice Commissariat and the practice of rule through quantitative indicators; and, finally, it inquires into the continuation of local influence in the administration of justice, before and after the War.

The problem of personnel

We saw in Chapter 7 how the Great Purge removed from the ranks of legal officials as many as half of their number. A high rate of turnover had afflicted the legal agencies even before the Purge, and during 1935–1936 the rate approached that experienced during the Purge itself. But there was a key difference. The Great Purge deprived the legal agencies of not only a large number of their officials but also their most experienced and accomplished ones. In the pre-Purge years most officials who left the legal agencies were new officials, including both those with weak records of performance and competent ones attracted to better jobs elsewhere in government. The Purge targeted a different group of legal officials, those already promoted into positions of authority and responsibility within the legal agencies. To gain appointment as the procurator of a district or chief judge of a city or region required both a display of ability and experience in more lowly posts. Persons promoted to positions of responsibility were also more likely to have received legal education than the others, and to have made a career in the legal agencies. In short, the Purge deprived the procuracy and courts of their most experienced and capable staff.

This loss could not have occurred at a more inopportune time. As we saw in Chapter 5, Stalin had decided in 1936 to encourage legal officials to acquire skills through legal education and to make careers in the legal agencies. The Purge set back the realization of both of these commitments and forced central legal officials to start anew the training of subordinates. Before this, legal authorities had to recruit new judges, procurators, and investigators and find ways to keep them on the job.

The recruitment of new legal personnel extended over the second half of 1938 and first half of 1939, and it followed old methods and criteria of selection. As a rule, local party officials (many of whom were also new to their jobs) located candidates, usually young party members, and forwarded their dossiers to the legal agencies. Either a Narkomiust official in a regional center (for judges) or an official in a republican procuracy office (for investigators and assistant procurators) would review and rubber-stamp the files. There was little more that the reviewers could do. Most aspirants to jobs in the Procuracy were applying for their first job and even would-be judges often lacked relevant work experience. The educational qualifications of both sets of recruits were low, representing on average elementary education. Any applicant already trained for the legal agencies in a one-year juridical school was accepted automatically for the post of investigator or assistant procurator. A careful scrutiny of the file of an applicant, according to one observer in the Procuracy, meant "seeing that the applicant's grandmother was correctly named." Interviews with applicants were usually not feasible.[1]

This pattern of recruitment assured that the quality of the new cohort of legal officials would remain uneven at best. Higher legal officials tried to shape the corps of investigators, procurators, and judges by firing or recalling those whose initial performance proved unsatisfactory. Moreover, as before, many of the better performers left their posts because of the lack of incentives to remain. Pay levels in the legal agencies remained lower than in other governmental bodies, even when gradations of pay to reward experience and rank were introduced. (In Kirov in 1939 an investigator received 10% less than a procurator; in Tula, 20% less; but in Saratov Region all procuracy officials at all levels received the same miserly sum of 675 rubles per month.)[2] To compensate, the central legal agencies established competitions for the "best judge" or "model investigator" and the winners received recognition and cash prizes, but neither proved sufficient to offset low pay and poor work conditions.[3]

The result was the return of high rates of turnover. Among investigators and assistant procurators, the annual proportion leaving their posts during 1939 varied from 25% to 50% depending on the region. Most of these young officials left during the first year and a half on the job. Turnover among judges averaged 28% in 1939 and recorded a

---

[1] F. Kudrin, "O podbore i rasstanovka kadrov," SZ, 1939, no. 10–11, 6061; idem, "Rabota s kadrami v Prokurature RSFSR," SZ, 1941, no. 6, 40–42; N.M. Rychkov, "Itogi XVII Vsesoiuznoi partiinnoi konferentsii i zadachi organov iustitsii," SIu, 1941, no. 9, 1–5.

[2] Kudrin, "Rabota s kadrami," Bashkeev and Nikitochkin, "K itogam soveshchaniia fevralskogo aktiva NKIu RSFSR," SIu, 1940, no. 6, 19–24; "Respublikanskoe soveshchanie sledstvennykh otdelov prokuratury ASSR, kraev i oblastei RSFSR," SZ, 1940, no. 7, 33–39.

[3] L. Sheinin, comp., "Dela i liudi," a regular column beginning in SZ, 1940, no. 3, 59–65; G. Ginzburg, "Entuziast," SIu, 1941, no. 1, 19–20 and others in the series "best court workers"; M. Grechukha, Moia rabota narodnym sudei (Moscow, 1940), and its introduction by I.T. Goliakov.

similar level in 1940, leading one commentator to remark that "almost all the judges have left their posts during the past three years."[4]

The high rates of turnover assured the continuation of the perennial shortage of personnel, which was aggravated further by the expansion in the number of posts for judges in 1939. Each of the legal agencies returned to the palliatives of the past. In 1939 Andrei Vyshinskii, still procurator-general, issued an order to local procuracy offices to recruit a new cohort of "socialist substitutes" – at least one or two for each district office, 10–15 for regional procuracy offices and 100 for the USSR Procuracy. At the same time, Narkomiust told its officials to organize for each judge a pool of three to five assessors to serve as backup judges whenever the regular judge went on holiday or sick leave. In practice, the "spare judges" were allowed to serve for many months at a time, despite a two-month limit in the directive. The spare judges enabled the regular judges to reduce their backlogs. The spares (who lacked any legal qualifications) also proved useful for difficult, controversial cases when "a judge does not want to spoil his relations with the district agencies."[5]

The only way to break the vicious cycle of weak recruitment and high rates of turnover was through the promotion of legal education for judges and procurators. Already in place since 1936 was the program for legal education, both the remedial variety to help current staff and higher legal education to supply better recruits for the future. Top legal officials continued during and after the Purge to implement both prongs of this program.

During 1938–1941 central officials of the Procuracy and Narkomiust paid special attention to secondary legal education for legal officials. This entailed, to begin, the revamping of the juridical schools and exten-

---

4 GARF(TsGA), f.353, op.13, d.29 (Stenogramma soveshchaniia aktiva Narkomiusta RSFSR ot 13/II–1940 g.), 2–5; ibid., d.45, (Stenogramma respublikanskogo soveshchaniia rukovodiashchikh rabotnikov iustitsii RSFSR i materialy k soveshchaniiu ot 9 apreliia 1941, tom 4) 57, 84; "Respublikanskoe soveshchanie sledstvennykh otdelov"; Kudrin, "Rabota s kadrami."
    Recruitment into the provincial bars of persons lacking higher legal education was by the late 1930s a common practice. Due in part to the shortage of new lawyers and the periodic attempts by Bolsheviks to change the political complexion of the bars, the admission of less qualified cadres changed the nature of legal representation. Whereas in the 1920s most advocates were jurists (often educated under the tsars), by 1938 only 53.3% of advocates had higher legal education. In 1939 this figure dropped to 37%. Huskey, Russian Lawyers and the Soviet State, 217–218.
5 Kozhevnikov, "Puti razvitiia sovetskoi prokuratury" (part two), 88; "Rabota s sotssovmestiteliami na vysshem stepeni," SZ, 1939, no. 5, 50–51; Sbornik prikazov i instruktsii narodnogo komissariata iustitsii Soiuza SSR, (Moscow, 1940), 30; A Vasnev, Narodnye sudy stolitsy (Moscow, 1939), 16; "Rech Narkomiusta SSSR N.M. Rychkova na soveshchanii aktiva NKIu RSFSR," SIu, 1941, no. 21, 3–4.

sion of their programs from one to two years. In the mid-1930s the judicial schools had provided preparation to many of the legal agencies' new recruits. As of 1938 more than one-third of judges, procurators, and investigators had studied at the schools, and they had become "the basic channel for adding cadres to the procuracy." Their quality, though, left much to be desired. Like the legal courses described in Chapter 5, the juridical schools lacked full-time teachers and textbooks and sometimes even a stable schedule or academic program. A conference of directors of the juridical schools held in mid-1938 resolved to rectify these shortcomings through lengthening the program to two years, which would include a seven-month apprenticeship in one of the agencies ("production practice"). The on-the-job component of the program would give its graduates experience in procuratorial or judicial work before they assumed posts from which they would be fired quickly if their performance proved substandard. As of 1940 there were 37 secondary juridical schools in the RSFSR with 4,225 registered students. All of their graduates were earmarked for work in the courts, Procuracy, notarial offices, or the regional defense bars (*advokatura*).[6]

Moreover, for those legal officials already on the job who lacked even secondary school legal preparation, the authorities now insisted on remedial training. As of October 1, 1938, secondary legal education *by correspondence* became obligatory, at least for judges and inspectors from Narkomiust, and the latter also received one day off per week for good performance at their studies, as well as travel expenses to attend the examinations. The obligation to obtain legal training produced large numbers of enrollments among legal officials (8,361 at the two-year secondary legal correspondence schools in 1940), but many of them did not keep up with their studies. Thus, three-quarters of the judges in Leningrad who lacked legal education enrolled in 1939, but of them three-quarters failed to do the written work and barely half turned up for the examinations. Less than a third of these judges gained promotion to the second year of study.[7]

The heads of Narkomiust also succeeded in the late 1930s in expanding higher legal education. Whereas in 1936, 2,490 persons were pursuing full-time university level studies in law, by 1938 the figure reached 4,000, and by 1940 nearly 5,000. These enrollments fell below the planned levels (of 7,000 by 1938 and 9,000 to 10,000 by 1940), but

6 P.P. "Vsesoiuznoe soveshchanie po voprosam iuridicheskogo obrazovaniia," *SZ*, 1938, no. 7, 99–101; *Sbornik prikazov*, 41–49.
7 Ibid., 46, 51; Kozlov, "Zaochnoe iuridicheskoe obrazovanie," *SIu*, 1940, no. 1, 12–14; "Srednoe zaochnoe obrazovanie," ibid., 1941, no. 24, 16–17; GARF, f.5446, op.25a, d.375, 65–69.

represented an achievement all the same.[8] The main obstacles to the expansion of higher legal education were physical. Shortages of dormitories and classrooms limited the intake of new students. Implementation of the expansion of higher legal education may also have suffered from the purge of most officials in Narkomiust responsible for higher legal education. All the same, in 1938, 816, in 1939, 1,150, and in 1940, 828 lawyers graduated from institutes and faculties in the USSR (as opposed to 250–300 per year in the mid-1930s and 390 in 1937). The establishment in 1939 of night divisions at some legal institutes made possible further expansion of higher legal education without new facilities.[9] Still, even a thousand new lawyers a year would not begin to meet the needs of the legal agencies. Only a portion of them would take posts in the courts and procuracy and they would fill only a fraction of the vacancies in the legal agencies.

The policy of expanding legal education also led to renewed discussion of its content. The denunciation in *Pravda* (January 1937) of Pashukanis and the antilaw strain prompted a rewriting of the textbooks in such fields as civil, labor, collective farm and public law, as well as legal theory and jurisprudence. Removing the influence of the nihilist perspective meant in most instances the revival of traditional legal doctrines and courses of study, and this process aroused little controversy.[10] Another issue divided jurists and that was the question of specialization within legal education. From 1930, after all higher legal education was concentrated in institutes under Narkomiust, students had been divided into separate streams preparing for work in the Procuracy and courts, police science, or the economy. Mimicking the pattern used in engineering institutes, each stream provided (at least on paper) a special program of courses that emphasized preparation for particular jobs. Moreover, all of the course programs deemphasized legal subjects of a general or academic nature, such as contemporary bourgeois law and history of state and law. Despite the streaming (which was sometimes more formal than real), the graduating lawyers often took posts other than those for which they had been trained. In 1937 formal streaming went out of fashion, and some general legal subjects returned to the curriculum. However, all the institutes remained under Narkomiust, and the general curriculum still stressed preparation for work in the Procuracy, courts,

---

8 I. Krastin, "Stalinskaia Konstitutsiia i zadachi pravovogo obrazovaniia," *SZ*, 1936, no. 11, 27–30; M. Granovskii, "Organizatsiia sudov v tretei piatiletkie," *SIu*, 1937, no. 12, 5–7; M.K. Gorshenin, "Vazhneishaia rabota Narkomiusta," *SIu*, 1938, no. 18; "Iuridicheskoe obrazovanie v SSSR," *SIu*, 1941, no. 16, 1–4.

9 Ibid.; *Sbornik prikazov*, 129–130; GARF, f.5446, op.25a, d.375, 65–69.

10 Sharlet, "Stalinism and Soviet Legal Culture," 170–178; A.F. Shebanov, *Iuridicheskie vysshie uchebnye zavedeniia* (Moscow, 1963), 65.

and defense bar (*advokatura*). At the end of 1940 a group of distinguished (and less distinguished) legal scholars proposed (in *Izvestiia*) that law faculties be established once again in universities with the mandate to prepare jurists of a broad profile, suitable for work in the economy and public administration. The students would receive "not only legal but also the economic, philosophical, and historical knowledge needed for successful work in the Soviet apparatus." The idea of producing a corps of broadly educated lawyers to improve public administration and the role of law in public life did not arouse objections. Already in December 1935 Andrei Vyshinksii had proposed to the party leadership the revival at law faculties of such subjects as the history of philosophy, political economy, Roman law, history of public law, constitutional law of capitalist countries, foreign languages, and Latin. The problem with the initiative of 1940 lay elsewhere. In promoting a new kind of university law training, the scholars had abandoned the existing network of institutes under Narkomiust. Those institutes were to continue preparing lawyers for the courts and procuracy and designing curriculum appropriate to that task.[11] The result of the proposed reform of legal education would have been two different kinds of lawyers – university graduates with a broad profile and graduates of the institutes with narrower training.

Objecting vigorously to this aspect of the proposal was another distinguished legal scholar, Professor Aleksei Gertsenzon, at the time the rector of the Moscow Juridical Institute, the most important in the Narkomiust system. Gertsenzon contended that not just the economy and government but also the courts and procuracy needed jurists of a broad profile. Such jurists would prove better lawyers wherever they chose to work. All Soviet jurists, Gertsenzon insisted, needed to study Marxist-Leninist philosophy, state (or public) law, and civil and criminal procedure of all kinds; and all should know the history of state and law and contemporary bourgeois law. The goal of Soviet legal education overall, and not just one particular stream, should be to produce "deeply and broadly educated, cultured specialists." The problem with his colleagues' proposal lay not in the idea of broadening legal education, but in limiting it to one group of lawyers.[12]

Before this particular round of debate over legal education could be resolved, World War II broke out and the discussion was put on hold. But the issues did not go away and would haunt the training of legal official-

---

11 "O iuridicheskikh fakultetakh" (Pismo v. redatitsiiu), *Izvestiia*, Dec. 7, 1990, 4. The signatories included: M.P. Trainin, M.A. Arzhenov, S.A. Golunskii, M.S. Strogovich, and eight others. GARF, f.8131sch, op.27s, d.58, 62–66.

12 A Gertsenzon, "Iuridicheskoe obrazovanie," *SIu*, 1941, no. 2, 10–11.

dom for decades to come. Although the proposed division of labor between university faculties and institutes was never adopted, the higher legal education received by most legal officials in the decades after World War II did differ in kind from that received by lawyers who worked as advocates and legal advisors in government and the economy.

As of June 1941, five years after the decision by the Soviet leadership to promote legal education, the results of the effort were modest. To be sure, more lawyers were graduating, and, had there been no war, their numbers would surely have increased further. Through the secondary juridical schools (day and correspondence), many legal officials were receiving basic training in legal skills. The high rates of turnover during and after the Purge, however, meant that the overall educational profile of legal officials changed only slightly. On the eve of the War, most legal officials still had not completed secondary school legal training. The 30% of judges who had done so replaced a similar group of judges from the mid-1930s who had finished the six-month courses in law.[13] Arguably, without the War, far more legal officials would have completed secondary training. But the War not only put a stop to the process of training legal officials, it also set it back. Many of the legal officials of 1941 did not return to their posts. Despite this setback, though, the leadership remained committed to developing legal officials with legal education. How the struggle was renewed forms the core of Chapter 10.

Centralization and rule by indicators

Centralization was one of the major purposes of the reorganization of the legal agencies approved by the Soviet leadership in 1936. That process gave each of the central legal agencies not only new functions but also increased authority over subordinate agencies and officials. Thus, the USSR Procuracy gained exclusive control over republican procuracies and through them lower level procuracy offices. The USSR Supreme Court obtained extraordinary appellate powers (in effect the right to hear on appeal almost any court case). And, with its functions concentrated on judicial administration, Narkomiust received encouragement to centralize and streamline its operations.

The years of Terror and Purge delayed the implementation of these changes. Only in 1938 and 1939 did the central legal agencies fully assume their new powers and fashion their instruments of rule. The most important of these instruments was management of personnel. In the legal agencies, just as in other parts of Soviet public administration,

---

13 GARF(TsGA), f.353, op.13, d.41, (Stenogramma respublikanskoi soveshchanii, tom. 1), 89.

decision making about the hiring, firing, and promotion shifted to central and republican agencies. However, the centralization of decisions about personnel was to have serious, unintended consequences.

The new centralized system of personnel management in the legal agencies emerged through a series of directives issued between 1936 and 1939. Already in 1936 the USSR Procuracy assumed responsibility for appointing the procurators of regions as well as republics and directed that procurators of cities and districts be appointed by republican procurators. In 1938 regulations further stipulated that republican procuracy officials appoint assistant procurators and investigators working in any procuracy office, even those of cities and districts, and inform the USSR Procuracy of these appointments. The addition of entry level posts to the hiring responsibilities of the central and republican procuracies meant little at the time, for the recruitment of new staff remained largely in the hands of local politicians. Far more important for higher Procuracy officials was their acquisition of the power to rule on promotions within the agency and on firings. According to a directive of June 1937, reaffirmed in April 1939, the firing of any procurator or investigator other than those working in a city, or district procuracy officials, required the preliminary approval of the procurator-general.[14]

For its part, Narkomiust also centralized personnel management and a good deal of operational decision making as well. Unlike the Procuracy, Narkomiust had obtained from the reorganization of the legal agencies a set of new functions, including responsibility for organizing the election of judges (including selection of the candidates), supervising judicial practice, and collecting judicial statistics. The execution of these functions, previously handled by the staff of regional courts, required a staff presence for Narkomiust at the provincial level, and in December 1938 Narkomiust RSFSR gained permission to establish field offices known as "administrations" (*upravleniia*) in the regions. Unlike their predecessors (the judicial departments of Narkomiust RSFSR that were abolished in 1923 and the staff of the regional courts that had handled judicial administration through 1938) the new provincial administrations of Narkomiust were *not* subordinated to provincial government. Like the regional procuracy offices, the provincial justice administrations answered only to their vertical superiors in Narkomiust RSFSR. The chiefs of Narkomiust RSFSR in Moscow appointed and fired the heads of the

---

14 "O poriadke naznacheniia, uvolneniia i peremeshcheniia prokurorskogo rabotnika," Prikaz 14 avgusta 1938 g., no. 1003 in *Sbornik prikazov prokuratury SSSR* (2nd ed., Moscow, 1939), 231–233; G. Roginskii, "Za bolshevistskuiu perestroiku raboty organov prouratury," *SZ*, 1938, no. 5, 20; F. Kudrin, "O podbore i rasstanovka kadrov," *SZ*, 1939, no. 10–11, 60–61.

provincial justice administrations. The republican commissariat also established a department for judicial agencies, which, along with the departments of cadres and educational institutions, exercised supervision over the provincial administrations.[15] The reorganized justice commissariats left much responsibility for both personnel and operations in the hands of the republican agencies, but the chiefs of the All-Union Justice Commissariat made sure that this responsibility did not mean autonomy or power. To establish its authority over the republican justice commissariats, Narkomiust SSSR ruled in August 1938 that the republican commissariats had to send their directives to the central body immediately after issuance. In February 1939 the central agency ordered republican commissariats to submit their directives *in advance* for preclearance by the All-Union Commissariat. In June 1939 the latter insisted that republican commissariats obtain "visas," that is permission in writing, from Narkomiust SSSR before circulating any directives.[16] Of course, the USSR Commissariat also retained and used the right to issue its own binding directives on almost any subject.

Through the Law on Court Organization of August 1938 the USSR Supreme Court gained effective power to review the casework of all lower courts. The Court began hearing a large volume of cases in supervision, many directly from the people's courts without prior consideration in cassation by a regional court. In anticipation of a large caseload, the newly constituted Court included forty-five judges; by 1945, it had expanded to sixty. Most of the appellate work was handled by three-judge panels working under one of the Collegia (civil, criminal, transport courts, and military tribunals).[17] In 1939–1940 the Supreme Court changed the sentences or verdicts or called for new trials in nearly all of the cases that it chose to review. As a result, its reputation for giving claimants a new chance became widespread. Sometimes, convicts themselves showed up at the door of the Court to present their appeals.[18]

The centralization of power in the legal agencies did not establish a clear division of labor among them. As in other areas of Soviet public

[15] Kozhevnikov, *Istoriia sovetskogo suda*, 310. "Polozhenie o Narodnom Komissariate Iustitsii SSSR" (Utv. 15 iuniia 1939) and "Polozhenie ob upravleniiakh Narodnogo Komissariata Iustitsii RSFSR" (utv. 1 iiuniia 1939), in G.N. Safonov, ed., *Spravochnik po zakonodatelstvu dlia sudebno-prokurorskikh rabotnikov* (Moscow, 1949), 1, 47–54. Aleksei Kazakov, "Organy sudebnogo upravleniia RSFSR v period s 1930 po 1970 gody," unpublished *kandidat* dissertation (Sverdlovsk Juridical Institute, 1984), 136ff.

[16] *Sbornik prikazov i instuktsii Narodnogo Komissariata Iustitsii SSSR*, (1940), 13–14.

[17] T.N. Dobrovolskaia, *Verkhovnyi sud SSSR* (Moscow, 1964), 44–50, 56.

[18] "Vsesoiuznoe soveshchanie prokurorov ugolovno-sudebnykh otdelov," *SZ*, 1940, no. 6, 50; *Sbornik deistvuiushchikh postanovlenii Plenuma i direktivnykh pisem Verkhovnogo Suda SSSR 1924–1944 gg.* (Moscow, 1946), 9.

administration so in the justice realm, agencies shared responsibilities and their functions overlapped.[19] For example, the power to examine case files, protest verdicts, and start appellate review of cases in supervision extended not only to republican and all-Union procurators and the heads of the corresponding Supreme Courts but also to the commissariats of justice. The latter rarely used this power, but their officials felt free to "signal" cases that they wanted reopened to the attention of procurators or judges. The fuzzy division of labor between the USSR Supreme Court and Narkomiust produced lasting tensions. In 1939 Narkomiust claimed the right to screen all instructions and circulars issued by the Supreme Court (as part of the agency's responsibility for judicial policy). Naturally, the Supreme Court objected. Even after new legislation clarified the situation, Narkomiust continued to issue instructions on matters falling within the Court's exclusive purview, such as how to qualify particular crimes and what sorts of procedures judges should use for handling particular kinds of cases. The dispute was revived in 1947 by a querulous member of the party's Central Revision Commission who also served as a deputy minister of justice (in 1946 commissariats were renamed ministries). The assertion by the Ministry of the right to issue directives on judicial practice was one of the "errors" that S. Dukelskii denounced in a letter to Stalin criticizing a recently published *Handbook for Judges*.[20]

The arguments over who had the right to issue directives on particular subjects or review the circulars of other agencies did not affect the key instrument of management used by the central and republican legal agencies over their subordinates. Central officials had at their disposal and used their new power to rule on promotions and firings and to give censures and award prizes as well. Making these decisions, though, required assessing the work of legal officials far away from Moscow and the republican centers.

How to make this assessment? Republican and central officials could ask their subordinates in provincial and local agencies to prepare written qualitative appraisals of the work of legal officials under their supervision. Mounting special checkup missions was also an option. In fact, the central and republican agencies used both of these methods. But there was also another approach, both easier to use and for most

---

19 Seweryn Bialer, *Stalin's Successors. Leadership, Stability and Change in the Soviet Union* (Cambridge, 1980), 16–17; Charles Fairbanks, "Bureaucratic Politics in the Soviet Union and the Ottoman Empire," *Comparative Strategy*, 6:3 (1987), 333–362; idem, "Jurisdictional Conflict and Cooperation in Soviet and American Bureaucracy," *Studies in Comparative Communism* 21:2 (Summer 1988), 153–174.
20 Kozhevnikov, *Istoriia sovetskogo suda*, 314–315, based upon archival sources. GARF, f.9492, op.2s, d.42, 243–247; f.9474, op.16s, d.311, 43–49.

supervisors and officials more reliable as well. It was using statistical data about case processing and outcomes to assess the work of justice officials.

Statistical data of this kind were readily available. In fact, Russia had a long tradition of collecting statistics on crime, punishment, and prosecutions. For decades, tsarist justice agencies had collected and even published voluminous statistical data that documented both the movement of cases and their dispositions. As a rule, tsarist statisticians arranged the data by province and by type of crime and offender. The Bolshevik officials who took over the legal agencies continued tsarist practices in the collection of statistics, barely modifying the forms.[21] Like their tsarist predecessors, the Bolshevik chiefs of the justice agencies used statistical data to monitor the performance of the justice agencies overall and in particular geographical districts. Thus, the republican Narkomiust compared the stability of sentences (the percentage of those appealed that were not overturned) of the judges of particular provinces; and the procuracy of Moscow Region compared how the investigators of particular districts fared in their rates of case completion. At the same time, Soviet officials added to the traditional concerns about the effectiveness of their subordinates' performance a new concern with the fulfillment of regime policies, especially those that led to law enforcement campaigns. Campaigns called for special reports, in which procuracy offices and courts had to demonstrate that they had generated enough cases, processed them quickly, and awarded harsh punishments. Moreover, Soviet leaders outdid tsarist officials in concern with the efficiency of the administration of justice. This concern reflected both the Bolshevik disdain for the bureaucratic tendencies of courts and Stalin's personal belief in the deterrent value of rapidly delivered punishments.

Although Soviet legal chieftains had relied on statistical indicators to assess the work of the procuracy and courts in particular districts, there is no indication that before the late 1930s they used those indicators for

---

[21] See, for example, *Otchet Keletskago okruzhnago suda za 1885–1889s.s.* (Keltsakh, 1890); *Svod statisticheskikh svedenii po delam ugolovnym proizvodiamshimsia v 1904 godu v sudebnykh uchrezhdeniiakh* (St. Petersburg, 1907); *Vsepoddanneishii otchet Ministra Iustitsii za 1914* (Petrograd, 1915); and *Sbornik statisticheskikh svedenii Ministerstva Iustitsii*, vyp. 13, "Svedeniia o lichnom sostave i o deiatelnosti subednykh ustanovlenii Evropeiski i Aziatskoi Rossii za 1914" (Petrograd, 1916).

For similar data for the Soviet period, see, for example, *Otchet Prokuratury RSFSR Prezidiumu VTsIK za 1926 g.* (Moscow, 1927); N.A. Cherliuchakevich, ed., *Prestupnost i repressia v RSFSR* (Moscow, 1930). A comprehensive guide to statistical publications in the Soviet period (which by the 1930s became sparse) is Ger P. van den Berg, *The Soviet System of Justice: Figures and Policy* (The Hague, 1984).

regular assessment of performance of individual legal officials.[22] This is not to say that indicators of performance for individuals were not kept or used by their immediate superiors in local and provincial agencies. In fact, it is likely that the statistical evaluation of the work of legal agencies in regions or districts rippled down. Thus, if a particular district procuracy office had a poor rate of completion of cases, its procurator would face criticism and proceed to check on the work of each of his investigators. The investigatory department of the regional procuracy that supervised those investigators might launch its own inquiry. In short, poor performance on statistical indicators by a group of officials might trigger the interest of supervisors in the indicators of individual officials. Still, for the regular assessment of performance of individual procuracy officials and judges by their immediate superiors, statistical indicators did not play a major role. As long as the evaluation of most officials was done by persons who knew them personally and could see their work firsthand, there was no need to rely upon statistical indicators. The centralization of decision making about promotions and firings (and awards and censures) changed this situation and led from 1939 to a heightened and exaggerated preoccupation with the statistical indicators of performance of *individual* legal officials.

The use of statistical indicators to assess and compare the performance of individual legal officials suggested new questions. Which indicators should be used, and in what rank order? Which criteria should take precedence when they come into conflict? Some of the goals of Soviet politicians for the justice agencies remained in permanent conflict. Avoiding mistakes and achieving high percentages of good decisions – for example, for investigators a low share of cases sent to court that did not require supplementary investigation or for judges a high percentage of verdicts and sentences not changed on appeal – called for deliberate, careful work. But the bureaucratic masters called also for efficiency, fast tempos of work by investigators and judges, and the avoidance of backlogs of cases. Campaigns exacerbated these conflicts, for generating extra cases and harsher penalties required to meet campaign quotas often meant violating other legal norms and laying the basis for changes by appellate courts. The actual rank order of different criteria of performance was often unclear, and frequently not even articulated. Moreover, the relative importance of particular

---

22 The legal journals of 1939–1941 contain sustained discussion of statistical assessment of the work of individual legal officials. Before then, the subject received occasional mention and only in the context of special measures. Thus, a contest for the best investigators in Moscow Region in 1934 focused on speed and rates of case completion as well as the percentage of cases returned to supplementary investigation. "V borbe za vysokoe kachestvo sledstviia," *Slu*, 1935, no. 33, 1–3.

indicators changed with time. Such a key indicator of performance of the late 1940s and 1950s as the rate of acquittal did not enter into the assessment of most procurators or judges before World War II.

Achieving the right indicators became a major concern in 1939–1940 of any legal official seeking to please his masters and pursue a career in the agencies. One way that legal officials received this message was through involvement in a series of competitions for "best judge" and "best investigator." Following instructions from central legal agencies, regional and local level supervisors organized these contests from late 1938 through 1940. In all of them the key, if not the only, basis for assessment was quantitative indicators of performance, and as a result the competitions helped publicize the centrality of good numbers for the well-regarded legal official. This point was reinforced in the profiles of model judges and investigators published in the legal journals and in the accounts of competitions. Winners of the contests for the "best" usually received cash prizes as well as recognition. The "best investigators" were scheduled to gather at a national conference in 1941. (The conference was put off because of the War, and convened only in 1950.)[23]

The quest for indicators influenced in major and counterproductive ways the conduct of procurators, investigators, and judges alike. For procurators involved in criminal work the most important criterion at that time was the number and percentage of appearances in court. Already in 1934 procuracy offices had received instructions from Vyshinskii to prosecute more cases in court. In October 1938, after nearly five years of slow progress on this issue, the procurator-general issued an order making participation by procurators mandatory at preliminary sessions, trials, and cassation hearings! Vyshinskii also ordered procuracy offices to oversee how local procurators implemented this directive.[24] The procurator of the city of Tagil reported that his scru-

23 *SIu*, 1938, no. 22, 1–5 contains accounts of the first competition among judges. Further discussion is contained in "Sotsialistcheskoe sorevnovanie nuzho rukovodit," ibid., no. 23–24, 4–5 and "O rabote sudebnykh organov predstavitelstnikh NKIu RSFSR po Moskve. Preimirovanie luchshikh sudebnykh rabotnikov Moskvy," ibid., 1939, no. 7, 46–47. On competitions among investigators and procurators see P.Ushnov, "Sotsialistichekoe sorevnovanie mezhdu Ivanovskoi i Kievenskoi gorodskimi prokuraturami," *SZ*, 1939, no. 5, 84; I. Lenov, "Ob uchete raboty sledovatelei," ibid., no. 6, 75–77; Dvornik, "Itogi sorevnovaniia sledovatelei Volodoskoi oblasti," *SZ*, 1940, no. 6, 54–55; and R. Rakhunov, "O rukovodstve sledstviem," ibid., 1940, no. 7, 14–17. For examples of a role model with good indicators see V. Berlezev, "Narodnyi sledovatel," ibid., 1939, no. 5, 69–71, and A. Krasenenko, "Narodnyi sudia A.M. Sukhova," *SIu*, 1939, no. 7, 51–53.
24 *Sbornik prikazov Prokuratury*, 251–253; "Vsesoiuznoe soveshchanie prokurorov," 40; A. Kokozalov, "Sudebnaia rabota prokuratury Krasnodarskogo kraia," *SZ*, 1939, no. 2, 61–63.

tineer, the deputy procurator of Smolensk Region, used to give informal warnings: "Keep in mind that we judge your work wholly on the basis of the number of times you appear in court." Not surprisingly, district procurators did increase their attendance in court – from 8.5% of trials in the first half of 1938 to 41.5% in the second half of 1939; and from 15% of cassation hearings to 89.7% in the same time periods. However, the performance of procurators in court was weak. According to one report, "The procurator says little or nothing . . . takes a passive role. Procurators need to learn to speak in court."[25]

Another standard used to evaluate procurators was the percentage of their trials that ended with a return to supplementary investigation. Unlike acquittals, which before World War II did not represent failures for procurators and investigators, returns for supplementary investigation did suggest to most observers that the procuracy officials had failed. In 1939, many of the cases returned came from the period of the Great Terror, when contrived and poorly investigated cases were common. But by 1940 this was no longer the case, and a high rate of returns spoke badly for the procurators who had been charged with screening cases produced by investigators and spotchecking those forwarded by police. In practice, procurators rarely performed either of these tasks. The rates of returns to supplementary investigations did decline during 1939 from 20% of cases at trial at the start of the year to 13% in the fourth quarter. But regional procurators responsible for supervising the work of procurators in court still felt on the defensive. At a conference in May 1940 they repeatedly blamed judges for sending back too many cases and spoiling their records! Much of the time, judges had good reasons to return cases, but sometimes they allowed their own needs or emotions to dictate their conduct. In Daghestan one judge used returns to supplementary investigation as a way to cut his backlog of cases and help his indicators. Another judge from the same district told the party committee, "The procurator put himself above me and I do not like it." Were this not the case, the judge conceded, he would not return so many cases![26]

The officials most deserving blame for high rates of returns to supplementary investigation were the investigators who prepared the cases. But investigators also had to contend with another criterion of evaluation, the percentage of cases stopped during the pretrial phase. Before World War II this criterion took priority over failures in court. A

25 M. Zolotov, "Zadachi ugolovno-sudebnykh otdelov," *SZ*, 1940, no. 6, 9–14; G. Sverdlov, "Nekotorye voprosy perestroiki," *SZ*, 1939, no. 1, 28–32.
26 M. Pankratev, "Nazrevshie voprosy sledstviia," *SZ*, 1939, no. 8–9, 11–17; Sverdlov, "Nekotorye voprosy perestroiki"; "Vsesoiunoe soveshchanie prokurorov," 40–43.

procuracy official supervising investigators in Azerbaizhan confided that his charges often sent weak cases to court to avoid having an overly high rate of cases stopped during the investigation! The point of this indicator was to make investigators think before they started cases. But many cases started with arrests by the police, and investigators were often not up to stopping these cases. Other cases started "under pressure from district organizations," for example cases of criminal negligence against kolkhoz chairmen. Sometimes, even higher procuracy officials ordered the launching of weak cases, reported an investigator from Leningrad. Without these extra pressures, the heads of regional procuracy departments of investigation agreed, most of the cases started by investigators in 1940 would have been justified. Despite the pressures, there were already a handful of model investigators, praised and awarded prizes, who managed to stop no cases at all for periods of months and present all of their cases to the courts.[27] It is likely that these investigators had the good fortune to deal only with particularly easy cases.

Investigators also faced regular assessments of the efficiency of their work – how fast they completed cases, how many they finished in a given period, and the size of their backlogs. In the fall of 1939 the procuracy of Molotovsk Region reported that while its best investigators completed twelve cases per month, a pair of slow investigators finished only nine between them. No mention was made of the complexity of the cases handled by the particular investigators in question or the quality of their work. The pressure upon investigators to move cases quickly led them to forward weekly prepared cases to the courts and to refer many cases belonging in their jurisdiction to police inquiries.[28]

For judges the most important indicators were tempos (speed of case processing and size of backlog) and stability of sentences (percentage of appealed decisions left unchanged by higher courts). As we have seen, undue attention to either efficiency or stability was bound to hurt a judge's achievement on the other scale, and authorities alternated between emphasizing one or the other. In 1938–1939 cutting backlogs of cases from the period of the Terror assumed top priority – according to one top legal official it was a "fixation" – and Narkomiust pressured its judges to conquer their backlogs. As a result, judges assigned lay assessors to preside over trials to help them get through the loads. By mid-1940, when the backlogs had been reduced, the Commissariat shifted the focus back to stability of sentence, which naturally had not im-

---

[27] "Respublikanskoe soveshchanie sledstvennykh otdelov prokuratury ASSR, kraev i oblastei RSFSR," SZ, 1940, no. 7, 22–41.
[28] Ibid.: Rakhunov, "O rukovosdststve sledstviiem," 14–17.

proved. In many places, the percentage of sentences changed upon appeal stood above 50% and the average for the USSR stood near 40% [15–20% of total convictions were appealed]. For the RSFSR the percentage of sentences left unchanged (when appealed) had moved from 58.7% in 1936 to 61.5% in 1940.[29] The number of sentences changed on appeal reflected the inexperience of trial judges, the pressure to move cases quickly, and the norms of performance for the judges sitting on cassation panels.

Trial judges looked best when fewer of their decisions were appealed, but they had little control of the process. Disgruntled accused and their advocates had an automatic right to cassation review and higher level procuracy officials charged with reviewing court work were bound to start a number of reviews. In addition, the procurators who had argued cases at trial had the right to appeal against acquittals and lenient sentences, but few of them bothered to do so. In the city of Kolomensk in 1940, however, the procuracy adopted a policy of reviewing twice a week all cases heard by the city courts in order to check for "incorrect sentences and decisions" and launch protests within the ten-day period. The judges of that city realized that this unusual action by the city procuracy threatened to harm their records on stability of sentences. Their creative response was to arrange that the court secretaries hold back some already decided cases as "still being filed" until the cassation term had passed. An observer described the secretaries' actions as reflecting "patriotism for their bailiwick."[30]

Apart from distorting the conduct of legal officials – even pitting one official against another – the emphasis on rule through indicators increased the importance of statistical and other reports. The more important reports became, the more reports the various levels of the legal agencies required, and paradoxically, the weaker the performance of subordinates in completing them. Even before the late 1930s there had been too many orders directed at lower officials and too many reports required, but the centralization of management in the judicial agencies and the new use of indicators to assess individual officials aggravated the situation. From the USSR and republican procuracies, complained the head of a regional procuracy's investigatory department, came "a stream of orders" and a call for "far too many reports . . . which, evidently, no one in the procuracy reads." In addition, the regional procu-

---

[29] *Sbornik prikazov i instruktsii Narodnogo Komissariata Iustitsii,* 133–136; K. Gorshenin, "Za vysokoe kachestvo raboty sudov," *SIu,* 1940, no. 8, 1–4; "Soveshchanie aktiva NKIu RSFSR," *SIu,* 1940, no. 23–24, 8–15.

[30] N. Shur, "Kak organizovan nadzor za sudami v Kolomenskoiprokurature," *SZ,* 1941, no. 4, 36–37.

racy offices issued their own orders. The office in Chkalovsk Region in 1940 produced 92 orders, which demanded 44 summary tabulations and reports, all of this above and beyond statistical accounting required by the USSR and republican procuracies. According to one count, city and district procuracy offices had to complete 138 reports a year, about one every two working days, and many of them involved duplication. Small wonder that some of these reports were not completed. When the Kirov regional procuracy called for supplementary monthly checks of cases investigated by the police, it got replies from 11 of 50 district procuracy offices, and even these were not completed properly.[31]

The situation in the courts was even worse. Both the all-Union and republican commissariats of justice bombarded regional justice chiefs with circulars (more than 300 between the two in 1940 and nearly twice the annual average in the late 1920s), which many of them proceeded to ignore. As of 1941, according to Commissar of Justice Rychkov, some directives went unnoticed; and no one in a given provincial administration office had heard of them. Some chiefs of justice administrations took an interest in the commissariat's orders only when their names or those of their subordinates were mentioned. Naturally, it was worse for judges at the people's court for they received directives from the regional justice administrations as well. In 1940 judges in Moscow received 502 orders, or two per working day. Many of these included requests for reports.[32]

Another result of the focus on indicators was that collection of statistical data came to dominate the process of supervising lower officials in the procuracy and courts, at the expense of instruction or help. Visits from the central Procuracy, according to a regional procuracy official in 1940, usually consisted of "statistics collection missions." The republican procuracy's investigation department sent out former investigators who pursued their tasks "bureaucratically." The inspectors dispatched from regional procuracy offices usually had such limited experience that they could do little more than collect statistical data for most aspects of procuracy work.[33]

The collection of statistics occupied an equally prominent place in the supervisory activities of Narkomiust. The bulk of staff in the provincial justice administration consisted of "inspectors" (*revizory*), whose sole duty was to tour people's courts throughout the province and inspect

31 "Respublikanskoe soveshchanie sledstvennykh otdelov," 22–29; S Farkin, "Nedochety v organizatsii raboty prokuratur Chkalovskoi obalsti," *SZ*, 1941, no. 3, 51–53.
32 "Rech Narkmoiusta SSSR N.M. Rychkova na soveshchanii aktiva NKIu RSFSR," *SIu*, 1941, no. 21, 5–9; "Iz zala sovehshchanii aktiva NKIu RSFSR," ibid., no. 17, 6.
33 "Respublikanskoe soveshchanie sledstvennykh otdelov," 24–25, 28–29.

them. Inspections required filling out forms, providing basic facts (location and facilities of the court), a description of the office of the court ("the work of the office does not correspond with the demands of directives"), and a portrait of the work of the judges. Inspectors were to gather statistical data and provide as well examples of incorrect application of the laws. As a rule, the inspectors arrived, completed their paperwork, and left. They neither conferred with the judges nor helped them. One reason was that the inspectors lacked qualifications. They were no better educated than the judges, and often worse; they did not know the decisions of the USSR Supreme Court that should have guided the judges; and they lacked experience on the job (the turnover rate among inspectors stood at 55% per year). It was hardly surprising that they focused upon paper-shuffling and for comic relief finding "the sensational, anecdotal mistakes."[34] Before 1939, when members of the regional courts used to take part in inspection trips to the people's court, the judges of the latter received more tutelage than after judicial administration shifted to Narkomiust.[35]

In sum, centralized management of the judicial agencies and in particular the careers of their officials made quantitative indicators of performance a principal instrument of rule for central legal officials. To be sure, this reliance on statistics had its critics. But in the plain words of a top official in the Russian Commissariat of Justice: "without statistics one cannot direct the work of judges."[36] Which statistics mattered most in the appraisal of particular officials would change more than once, and the conflict between measures of efficiency and quality of performance remain a constant theme. The mounting of campaigns would shift the emphasis sharply in one direction or another. But as long as the management of procuracy and courts remained in the hands of all-union and republican officials (well into the 1980s), statistical indicators of performance remained the primary tool for assessing individual legal officials.

At the same time, the question for good indicators would continue to shape the conduct of legal officials. Already before World War II, inves-

---

34 Sokolov, "Rol i zadachi revizora," *SIu*, 1941, no. 2, 4–5; "Rol i zadacha revizora: Obsuzhdaem statiu tov. Sokolova," ibid., no. 9, 9–11; "Rech Narkmoiusta SSSR," 5–6.
35 Kazakov, "Organy sudebnogo upravleniia RSFSR," esp. 149–152.
36 For an early and well-written critique of the reliance on statistics, see P.A., "Ucheti i otsenka raboty sledovatelei i raionnykh prokurorov v Moskovskoi oblastnoi prokuratury," *SZ*, 1939, no. 3, 92–94. The quotation is from "Soveshchaniie aktiva NKIu RSFSR," 9.
     After the War a deputy procurator-general gave this answer to critics of the overreliance upon quantitative indicators. "Of course there can be no quantity without quality. I would say that we need not quality in general but 'top-notch quantity' (*kachestvennoe kolichestvo*). Such is our task." GARF, f.8131, op.27, d.4034, 304.

tigators, procurators, and judges found ways to achieve this result that were counterproductive and often pitted officials of one agency against those of another. After the War, improvisations and conflicts stemming from the evaluation of performance would multiply, especially when a larger share of legal officials made careers in the legal agencies. Before the War, the question for indicators was tempered by the rapid turnover of legal officials.

The concern of legal officials with good indicators might also have been tempered had the other master, the party and government officials of the locality, paid little attention to them. But, as we shall see, the more involved local party secretaries became with supervising the justice agencies, the more they too came to value the indicators as measures of performance.

Local influence in the administration of justice

Reducing excessive influence of local politicians in the administration of justice became regime policy in the mid-1930s, and it supplied one reason for the centralization of authority within the legal agencies. Already under NEP procurators and judges had become dependent upon party chieftains and accustomed to honoring their requests. The decentralization of power that accompanied collectivization had strengthened the hands of local politicians vis-à-vis legal officials in their bailiwicks. In 1935 Soviet leaders took a first step toward weakening the leverage of local power over the justice agencies by shifting responsibility for the budgets of courts from local government to the governments of the provinces. Centralization of operations, including personnel management, within the legal agencies was supposed to advance this course of action and produce a new balance between the vertical and horizontal masters of legal officials.

The centralizing measures that we have examined in this chapter did change that balance. As the central legal agencies strengthened their leverage over subordinates, they emerged as the most important master for legal officials, the one most involved in the work of investigators, procurators, and judges on a regular (even daily) basis and the one requiring constant satisfaction. Nevertheless, the stronger hand of the legal agencies did not reduce the dependence of legal officials on local political power or remove them from its influence and direction. There were, to be sure, changes in the demands local politicians made of legal officials, but local power remained a second master to whom legal officials as a rule felt obliged to defer. This pattern reflected an underlying reality of Soviet public administration from the early 1930s well into the post-Stalin era. Hypercentralization might increase the bureaucratic disease of "departmentalism" (*vedomstvennost*), but never did it eliminate manifestations of its alter ego "localism" (*mestnichestvo*). Centralization merely reduced the prominence of localism and its importance relative to the service of departmental interests.

As of 1940, legal officials depended on the goodwill of local politicians for both the progress of their careers and the allocation of scarce resources relating to work and personal lives.

The new rules for making and confirming appointments to posts in the legal agencies and firing of legal officials did not remove party bosses from personnel management. For one thing, the actual recruitment of new staff for posts in the procuracy and forwarding of their candidacies to republican procuracy offices came mainly from the local party committees. With the exception of the graduates of juridical schools and legal institutions, which together produced a quarter of the new recruits, finding persons to serve as investigators and assistant procurators remained in the hands of local politicians, and many a job-seeker felt obliged for their help. Of course, the republican procuracy officials did not have to accept all of the nominations forwarded from the localities, but serious review of the files proved difficult. Most of the candidates lacked background legal work or many had not completed secondary school. Moreover, the demand for new staff was so acute that failing to accept a nominee might mean leaving a post vacant.[37] The simplest expedient for procuracy officials at the republican level was to accept the most nominations from below and quickly fire the poor performers, especially those who produced weak statistical indicators. A similar pattern obtained in the courts. Regional justice administrations routinely accepted the candidates for judgeships supplied by district party bosses and then proceeded to fire them (through recalls) at the first sign of difficulty.

The control of the careers of legal officials once on the job, including decisions about promotion and firing, was supposed to lie exclusively in the hands of the legal agencies. But local party bosses proved unwilling to play by the rules. When the actions of a judge or investigator displeased them, the bosses went ahead and fired the offending official, often without having received the required permission from higher levels of the Procuracy or Narkomiust. Central legal officials repeatedly denounced but could not stop this practice. Nor could the party's Central Committee, which at Stalin's orders denounced unauthorized removals of legal officials in a secret directive (June 25, 1932).[38] As a result,

---

[37] Ia. Gorbulev and R. Rakhunov, "Kadry," *SZ*, 1938, no. 1 26–31; "Vsebelorusskoe prokurorskoe soveshchanie," ibid., no. 7, 80–99.

[38] Kudrin, "O podbore"; *Pisma I.V. Stalina V.M. Molotova*, 243–244.

it was risky for a judge, procurator, or investigator to displease either of his or her masters – the bureaucratic superiors in the agencies or the political chieftains on the spot.

The other basis for dependence of legal officials on local politicians lay in the latter's control of the allocation of resources and benefits. As of the late 1930s, these did not usually include budgetary allocations, either for basic operations or special purposes. In 1935 the budgets of courts were shifted from the governments of districts and cities to those of provinces (procuracy budgets already came from their vertical superiors). In 1938 the USSR Procuracy supplied substantial supplementary allocations to its republican and *oblast* offices to pay for items that local procurators had previously received as lures from city and provincial bosses. These included typewriters, bicycles, and sometimes cars.[39] Even without budgetary dependence, local politicians still had much to offer judges and procurators. The resources of local governments still included the allocation of buildings for courts, procuracy offices, and juridical schools; the repair and maintenance of these buildings and allocation of fuel to heat them; and attending to the personal needs of legal officials such as apartments (moving the judge or procurator to the head of the line) and vacation packages. Local politicians could also select their favorite legal officials for honorific positions that brought privileges (such as deputy to a local soviet). These were all matters of cardinal importance to legal officials over whom local politicians had much leverage and officials in the legal agencies in Moscow almost none.[40]

Allocation of buildings is an example well documented in published sources from the late 1930s. Local politicians had the right to decide which institutions would occupy public buildings in their cities and they used this resource to suit their interests and needs. Thus, in June 1938 the "leading agencies" (i.e., party bosses) of the city of Voronezh decided to remove the juridical school from a conveniently located building in the center of town to make space for a new police station. They relocated the school to seven small, half-destroyed buildings twelve kilometers out of

[39] N.N. Belkovich and V.A. Shavrin, *Mestnoe khoziaistvo i mestnye biudzhety SSSR* (Moscow, 1938), 172; A Iodkovskii, "Bolshe vnimaniia narodnomu sudu," *Vlast sovetov*, 1936, no. 6, 23–24; "Vsesoiuznoe prokurorskoe soveshchanie," *SZ*, 1938, no. 6, 45; Peter H. Solomon, Jr., "Local Political Power and Soviet Criminal Justice, 1922–1941," *Soviet Studies*, 37:3 (July 1985), 309–310, 319.
[40] This list of lines of dependence comes mainly from interviews with former investigators, procurators, and judges, many conducted under the auspices of the Soviet Interview Project and others in Israel. Most of the informants began their careers only after World War II, but the few who worked in the late 1930s confirmed that the same bases of dependency operated then as later on.

the city that had once belonged to a state farm. These buildings lacked electricity, plumbing, and kitchens. There was no decent road leading to them and no bus service to accommodate the faculty, most of whom lived in the city. One might have expected that Narkomiust would have protested the decision, but the Commissariat's representative decided to make the best of a bad situation (he was in fact powerless) and try to build a model school "like a resort with clear air." Perhaps, he extracted the city's help with road repair, but for the reconstruction of the buildings Narkomiust had to allocate 100,000 rubles. The project took so long to complete that an entire school year was lost. The Commissariat of Justice had similar difficulties in protecting its schools elsewhere. The juridical school in Smolensk lost its dormitory at about the same time as the Voronezh school its quarters. Another juridical school, in Alma-Ata, faced eviction a year later, when its facilities were chosen to accommodate a school of journalism that reportedly did not need all the space.[41]

There is no reason to believe that Narkomiust had any more influence over the choice and maintenance of the buildings used for courts. The tales of poor facilities were legendary. In one courthouse a large hole in the ceiling forced judges to take "rainbreaks," suspending trials whenever heavy rains descended upon the proceedings.[42] Just to keep their courthouses in repair, judges cultivated their relationships with local potentates.

In short, judges and procuracy officials still needed the goodwill of local politicians, and this fact ensured that dependence would also continue. But what did this mean in practice? How did lines of dependence affect the work of legal officials?

The demands made by local politicians upon legal officials started to change in the late 1930s in a couple of respects. First, the practice of ordering legal officials to perform administrative tasks unrelated to their functions as investigators, procurators, and judges declined, because the special demands of the collectivization campaigns had become a thing of the past. Still, those procurators most closely tied to the local power structures who were fortunate enough to become members of the bureau of the district party committee (as opposed to merely members of the committee) remained vulnerable to requests to assume unlikely responsibilities. Second, party officials had been made more directly responsible for the performance of the legal agencies in their districts, especially their success in fighting crime. This responsibility encouraged local bosses to monitor the work of the procuracy and

---

41 Kirichenko and Dvoretsksii, "Kak NKIu RSFSR sozdaet 'obraztsovuiu' iuridicheskuiu shkolu," *SIu*, 1939, no. 8, 42–43; "Vernut shkole pomeshchenie," *SIu*, 1941, no. 1, 22.
42 G. Ginzburg, "Entusiast," *SIu*, 1941, no. 1, 19–20.

courts, and, on occasion, even to review the indicators of performance developed by the central legal agencies.[43] However, any significant convergence of interest among the two masters of legal officialdom came only after World War II, when most legal officials began making careers in the legal agencies and supervision of justice became the responsibility of particular party officials in the regions.

What did not change in the late 1930s or after the War was the intervention of local political chieftains in particular criminal cases. Local and regional level politicians regularly ordered procurators to refrain from some prosecutions (e.g., against managers) while directing them to pursue others (especially against kolkhoz chairmen). For their part, the procurators usually complied.[44] Likewise, the local political bosses continued trying to influence their judges, most often with success.[45] At the same time, some judges and procurators resisted the demands of local politicians and insisted upon defending what they saw, correctly or incorrectly, as their prerogatives. In the late 1930s, resistance by judges emerged with special force; in the immediate postwar years, local procurators made party screening of prosecutions an issue, through both resistance and complaints to their superiors in Moscow.

Ironically, some judges in the late 1930s used the guarantee of judicial independence set out in the 1936 Constitution as an excuse for resisting encroachments by politicians. This guarantee reinforced the long-standing view that direct interference in trials was unacceptable. It also encouraged some judges to attempt to cut off all contact with local party and government authorities, citing the Constitution in support! This understanding of the Constitution on the part of judges convinced top politicians and legal officials that they needed to spell out the proper relationship between legal agencies and political officials. After all, at least since 1936 party officials had been expected to actively supervise the administration of justice. While even regional party committees would not have specialized officials for these tasks until 1948, even before the War the secretaries of many party committees shouldered responsibility for the legal agencies and periodically examined their work.[46]

---

43 Solomon, "Local Political Power," 314–318; GARF, f.8131 sch, op.27s, d.4034, 127, 337–338; "Protokol No. 31 zasedaniia biuro Medynskogo RK VKP(b) ot 9/XI, 1934 goda," WKP 80, 184–185.
44 S. Golunskii, "Lenin o prokurature," SZ, 1939, no. 1, 8; G. Roginskii, "Za bolshevistskuiu perestroiku raboty organov prokuratury," SZ, 1938, no. 5, 20; "Respublikanskoe soveshchanie sledstvennykh otdelov," 22–23.
45 "V NKIu SSSR," SIu, 1937, no. 15, 23; GARF f.8131sch, op.29, d.11, 95–99.
46 The Smolensk archive shows district party committees reviewing the work of courts and procuracy as early as 1934 and on a regular basis starting in 1936. See WKP 80, 34–42; 48–54; 100–113; 140–143; 154–55; WKP 86, 157–163, 238–241.

Even before the new Constitution had been promulgated, Procurator-General Vyshinskii had tried to distinguish proper party supervision from improper interference in the work of the procuracy. While party officials were, in his view, obliged to check how well the procurator fulfilled the party line on the building of socialism or the class struggle, they had no right to get involved in the procuracy's operational work. Party officials were not to indicate their "point of view," "opinion," or "line" with regard to particular cases, persons, or actions or interfere in the operational work of the courts. This position had been endorsed by Stalin in a secret Central Committee directive in 1932, and underscored in a resolution approved by the Central Control Commission in 1933. In practice, though, the distinction between proper supervision and improper interference was hard to draw. To give an opinion in a case was wrong, but to fail to inquire about the progress of an important case was also a mistake. In reply to procurators in Kiev who had complained about interference by party officials, Vyshinskii explained: "Only a poor party secretary would simply let his procurators and judges do what they wanted." And only a lazy procurator, he went on, one who had not prepared his case, would have any difficulty winning over the party secretary with documents and evidence.[47]

Judges no less than procurators were expected to maintain close and mutually beneficial ties with the local politicians. No less an authority than the Commissar of Justice, N.M. Rychkov, explained in June 1940 that judges who avoided contact with local authorities misunderstood the Constitution's article on judicial independence. As a result, the judges had no chance to use "local experience" in deciding cases, and local government agencies could not have the benefit of court data in their work.[48] A few months later, an authoritative article put the same message in blunter terms. "One can hardly imagine a greater absurdity," wrote the author, "for a Soviet judge to imagine himself some special extraterrestrial person, a sort of deep thinker in flight, who has no ties to other institutions or organizations in the region." To fall into the sin of self-reliance was simply "misplaced conceit." To decide cases properly a judge had to have a deep understanding of his district and know all its peculiarities. Otherwise, how could he help the prevention of crime? The writer of this sermon then brought forward the example of one particular people's court judge in Moscow who had developed the right kind of relationship with his political confreres. It was not like the old days, reported Judge Saprykin, when the district authorities did

---

[47] Vyshinskii, *Sudoustroistvo*, 23; A. Ia. Vyshinskii, "Nashi zadachi," *ZaSZ*, 1935, no. 5, 6; *Pisma I.V. Stalina V.M. Molotova*, 243–244; RTsKhIDNI, f.613, op.1, d.151, 97.

[48] N.M. Rychkov, "Rabota suda sdelat otlichnoi," *SIu*, 1940, no. 6, 2–4.

not care about guiding the courts but were only interested in particular sentences. As late as 1936, he reported receiving "directive telephone calls" from the district party committee or soviet in which "they would simply dictate on the telephone the sentence that was useful to them." Moreover, the secretary of the district soviet used to summon the judge to discuss particular cases. But now, in 1940 – with the new Constitution firmly in place – these practices had ended (sic!), and in their place a new relationship had developed between judges and local politicians. Now "we help them with information on particular crimes (hooliganism here, juvenile delinquency there) and provide supplementary judgments . . . and they give us information relevant to our casework and help us with political tasks . . . including elections."[49]

This idyllic portrait did not typify the actual relationship between most judges and their political masters. Even this model relationship contained the seeds of what some observers would deem improper involvement with politicians. What sort of information could party and government officials provide judges that was "relevant to their casework"? It might consist of indications that certain crimes assumed priority for awhile and should be treated with particular care (read "severity"). In fact, it was becoming commonplace to involve judges in the fight against crime and expect their cooperation. Thus, another district party committee in Moscow held a meeting – at the initiative of the local procuracy and police chief – to discuss hooliganism and speculation and concluded with an instruction to judges to raise penalties for both offenses! A writer who described the meeting commented on what he saw as an impropriety – that the judges had not been in attendance. But he had no difficulty with the fact that politicians had given a directive to develop a pattern of sentencing that suited their policy preferences.[50] To be sure, such directives did not represent interference in particular cases, and may well have responded to authentic local needs, but directives to judges about sentencing showed how easily criminal policy could replace criminal law as the basis for sentencing and punishment.

The idea that judges were still expected to respond to the dictates of criminal policy (from any level of party and government, whether or not expressed through law) finds support in another paean of praise to a judge who established the right kind of relationship with district authorities. This particular people's court judge actually served as a member of his district executive committee and party committee, hon-

---

49 V.Kh., "Nezavisimost sudei i sviaz ikh s rukovodiashchimi organami raiona," *SIu*, 1940, no. 10, 1–8.
50 Ibid.

ors rarely bestowed on judges. He knew the party boss well, for the judge had once served as procurator of the same district. Naturally, this model judge took a leading role in addressing problems of the district. He took a tough line in cases regarding the delivery of potatoes from private plots; he cracked down on swindlers in cooperatives; he helped with a scam in timber felling. On average, he spent four days a month at the executive committee hearing reports and learning about what was important to government officials. In the previous two years he had not received a single direction from them about a particular case, but this was hardly surprising. For this particular judge had political antennae of such sensitivity that he would make the right decisions without prodding.[51]

As presented in the journal of Narkomiust in 1940, the model judge was expected to be so politically attuned that he would implement the policies of the party (center and local officials alike) without improper kinds of intervention. Judges of this kind were rare prizes and well protected by their politician friends. Most judges were less consistent and aggressive in conforming to the expectations of party bosses. One reason was that many of them, like their predecessors in earlier cohorts of Soviet judges, had not committed themselves to careers as judges. Lacking legal education, the typical Soviet judge had no reason to envisage a career in the justice realm; other, better posts in public administration might come his way.

In practice procurators had as much trouble maintaining a good relationship with local party chieftains as did judges. The performance of their procuratorial duties called for occasional prosecutions against important persons, and procurators faced periodic pressure from central authorities to confront the illegal actions of officials. Thus, in 1945 Central Committee Secretary Viacheslav Molotov called upon the procuracy to "bring order into the provinces" and criticized those procurators "who want to live with everyone, be good people, argue with no one, so that all will be satisfied."[52] At the same time, however, procurators had to deal with local party bosses, most of whom insisted upon not only having the chance to remove the party cards of members before prosecution but also to decide whether prosecutions would proceed. Did party bosses have the right to screen prosecutions of party members or members of a party *nomenklatura*? Technically not. Although authorized to supply procurators with written permission authorizing prosecutions against party members under their aegis, they were not supposed to offer opinions on the wisdom of particular prose-

[51] V. Subbotin, "Pravilno ponimaetsia nezavisimost sudei," *SIu*, 1940, no. 11, 7–9.
[52] GARF, f.8131sch, op.27s, d.2241, 185–187.

cutions. The removal of the party card was supposed to follow any reasonable request from the procuracy.

The realities of power in the provinces and localities made this distinction impossible to maintain, and many, if not most, party bosses appropriated the right to screen prosecutions, notwithstanding the rules. At the start of 1947 a regional level procurator sought clarification, after the first secretary of the regional party committee told him that for all prosecutions of Communists, for no matter what charge, he had to gain the consent of a party secretary at no lower than the district level. Repeated inquiries to the procurators-general and a query to the Central Committee led only to the officially correct answer, "that no permission from party agencies was needed for concrete cases."[53]

The conflicting expectations of procurators on the part of their vertical superiors and local party bosses assured that some procurators would anger the latter and become the centers of controversy. To begin, some procurators failed to ask for clearances before pursuing cases against officials. In June 1946 the Plastovskii city party bureau fired the procurator of the city for prosecuting the head of the city's financial department without permission of the city party committee, and the Cheliabinsk regional party committee approved the dismissal. In Krasnoiarsk a procurator was cited for conducting a search of the apartment of the chairman of the territory cooperative union and seizing material, all without permission of the secretary of the territorial committee. Both of these firings prompted appeals for help to higher levels of the procuracy. In each instance, the deputy procurator of the RSFSR launched a special investigation, and in the first one found no basis at all for the firing. The procurator had not even been involved in the investigation and the eventual conviction had been correct! As a result, the USSR procurator-general asked the Central Committee to review the decisions of the city and regional party committees.[54]

More common than the failure of procurators to ask for party approval of prosecutions was unwillingness on their part to live with the results. Direct disobedience of the orders of party bosses was risky. A district procurator in Mordovsk Region was fired by the regional party committee after he had disagreed with an attempt to dictate to him in concrete cases. The charge against him was "helping to sabotage the grain collection and effort to stop theft of socialist property." The repub-

---

[53] Solomon, "Soviet Politicians and Criminal Prosecutions," 8–9; GARF, f.8131s, op.27s, d.4034 (Vtoroe vsesoiznoe soveshchranie prokurorov respublik, kraev, oblastei i gorodov respublikanskogo podchineniia, Stenogramma, 5–15 apreliia 1948), 125–126.

[54] GARF, f.8131sch, op.27s, d.2821 (Spravka o faktakh osvobozdeniia ot dolzhnost rukovodiashchikh prokurorskikh rabotnikov, protivopostavliavshikh sebia partiinym organam . . .), 12.

lican party committee restored him to his post.[55] A more prudent approach for procurators seeking to resist the instructions of party secretaries was to appeal to higher levels of the procuracy or party structure. In 1948 a regional procurator reported starting prosecutions against four heads of machine tractor stations. When he went after a man called Pakas, he met a stone wall. The regional party secretary challenged him: "Whom do you want to prosecute? I won't give you Pakas." The procurator sent the case to the republican procuracy, and Georgii Safonov himself (the procurator-general) ordered the prosecution. But the party boss would not budge. "Do not pursue this case," was the message. "We do not know your Gorshenin and your Safonov." (At the time, Gorshenin was minister of justice.) The procurator took the cue and went after another MTS chief, but before he could act, the regional party committee sent the man to the higher party school in Moscow, thereby necessitating permission of the Central Committee of the party before prosecution.[56]

There were limits to what Procuracy officials in Moscow could do for their subordinates in faraway places. The procurator of Karaganda Region wrote the then Procurator-General Konstantin Gorshenin about his failure to gain permission to prosecute a group of district bosses, including the head of the agricultural department, the head and deputy head of the executive committee, and the first secretary of the district party committee. Three times the regional party committee discussed the matter and each time refused to allow prosecution; it even awarded prizes to two of the suspects. The procurator's appeal to Moscow did have results. It led to one suspect's exclusion from the prize list and approval of prosecutions against three of them. But to press charges against the party secretary, Gorshenin warned, required approval of the regional committee.[57]

One complaint by a district procurator to the procurator-general led to the dismissal of a district party secretary by the regional committee. The complaint dealt with interventions in a number of cases. One of them involved press workers who had faked the accounts to cover up the loss of 4,360 rubles. The district secretary called the procurator and investigator to his office more than once and used threats and inducements to stop the case. He brought in the judge as well. In another case, the same party secretary declared openly at the district committee that the procurator and investigator would be removed from their jobs if

55 GARF, f.8131sch, d.27s, d.2818, 21.
56 GARF, f.8131sch, op.27s, d.4037 (Vtoroe vsezoiunoe soveshchanie), 100.
57 GARF, f.8131sch, op.29s, d.11 (Soobshcheniia prokuratur o raznoglasiiakh s partiinymi organami v voprosakh privlechelniia chlenov partii k ugolovnoi otvetsvennosti), 50–53.

they broke with the local party establishment. The secretary supported his position with popular wisdom: "The law one can get around" (*zakon mozhno oboiti*) and "One must do what is ordered" (*nuzhno ispolniat kak govoriat*). Apparently, the crude approach of this party secretary to his legal officials led to his fall from grace.[58]

The archival records show that in the late 1940s district procurators regularly appealed to the regional party committee the refusals of district committees to sanction prosecutions, and that these appeals sometimes met with success.[59] But, as with all cases of resistance to the directions of local bosses, these initiatives bore risks. The outcomes depended upon the "distribution of forces," as well as on the facts of the case.

There was no clear formula of success for local procurators. Neither total compliance with the demands of party bosses in the localities nor insistence on complete autonomy met with approval of central authorities. In 1946 the procurator-general fired the procurator of Dnepropetrovsk region for "not showing sufficient strength and principles" in pursuing serious violations of legality by leading officials of the region. At the same time, he approved the firing of the procurator of Tomsk Region by the regional party committee for treating "the correct demands put by the committee . . . as incorrect attempts at interference in his functions as regional procurator." His sins included failing to discuss with the party committee the crime situation in the region and to inform it about violations of legality by regional organizations.[60]

Often, central Procuracy officials tried to help their subordinates deal with local politicians. In 1945, Procurator-General Gorshenin proposed to the political leadership that the "evaluation of the work of district procurators and right to remove them through party procedures [*v partiinom poriadke*]" be raised from the district to the regional party committee level (for regional procurators to the republican level and republican level to the all-Union level). It appears that this change did take place, but the examples given above suggest that this did not protect procurators from the wrath of their political counterparts. Moreover, the USSR Procuracy did take up many complaints from lower level procurators about their treatment by local political bosses. But there were limits to the patience of central officials. At the Second All-Union Conference of regional and republican procurators (held in April 1948), regional procurators regaled their masters with complaints about interference and mistreatment by party officials. The chiefs of the

---

58 Ibid., 100–122.
59 Ibid., 43–49; GARF, f.8131sch, op.27s, d.2821, 14.
60 Ibid., 9–10.

Procuracy, however, downplayed the problem. The complaints of provincial procurators, they insisted, exaggerated the difficulties in their relationship with party bosses.[61]

In the end, local procurators were left to find their own golden mean, a pattern of conduct that would satisfy both of their masters even though their demands sometimes conflicted. Most of the time, maximum feasible cooperation with local authorities sufficed. Trouble came when blatantly illegal activities by local officials came into the open.

Cooperating with local authorities most of the time had another advantage. Not only did it avoid conflict, it also conferred upon procurators the benefits that came with a close relationship to political power. These included, as we shall see, a readiness on the part of party officials to take the side of procurators in their disputes with judges and discipline those judges who made the work of procurators difficult. We shall examine the place of the procurator in the local power structure in Chapter 11. Despite their increased responsibility for monitoring the administration of justice, until 1948 most party officials in the localities paid only sporadic attention to the justice agencies – with one exception. The exceptional situation that brought local politicians into close, even daily contact with the Procuracy and courts was the mounting of campaigns. Law enforcement campaigns represented the quintessential form of criminal policy, an indication by leaders that particular kinds of crimes or offenders required not merely severe sanctions but also an aggressive or proactive form of law enforcement. Campaigns meant targeting and a goal-oriented style of operation, and Stalin favored them for many purposes other than criminal policy. As we shall see in Chapter 9, law enforcement campaigns would return to haunt the legal agencies and draw local politicians deeply into their work.

Conclusion

In the two and a half years between the end of the Great Terror in November 1938 and the outbreak of war in the USSR in June 1941, the chiefs of the legal agencies succeeded in reconstructing the administration of justice. With the help of local politicians they recruited replacements for the many judges, investigators, and procurators who fell victim to terror and purge and set out to provide the newcomers with remedial education in law. At the same time, the top legal officials implemented the centralization of power within the Procuracy and courts that Stalin and colleagues had mandated before the Terror. While this process gave the USSR Narkomiust and Procuracy in Moscow new

---

[61] GARF, f.8131sch, op.27s, d.2241, 185–187; d.4037, 131.

leverage over the conduct and careers of legal officials throughout the country, it did not succeed in reducing significantly the influence of local politicians upon the administration of justice.

In centralizing decision making about personnel and assuming responsibility for the performance of legal officials on the periphery, the legal chieftains began using statistical indicators to assess *individual* legal officials. This embracing of numbers to monitor and evaluate the work of individual investigators, procurators, and judges stemmed, on the one hand, from its utility to the legal chiefs, for whom numbers supplied an easy, "technocratic" way to respond to pressures from politicians to show good performance. On the other hand, the use of quantitative indicators to assess individual officials reflected the absence of alternatives, once the hypercentralization of the management of legal cadres had taken place. Supervisory officials lacked direct knowledge of their subordinates and were unprepared to rely upon qualitative reports of intermediate officials (because of their incompetence and self-interest). Whatever the mixture of causes, the new reliance on statistical indicators of performance of individual legal officials was an innovation that would continue for decades. We shall examine its further development in Chapter 11.

9 Preparing for war: the criminalization of labor infractions and related campaigns

Barely had Soviet legal officials time to recover from the whirlwind of Terror and Purge when Stalin imposed on them new burdens. In the summer of 1940 – to raise industrial productivity and prepare society for war – Stalin took two dramatic steps. He criminalized common labor infractions, quitting and shirking, and raised to new levels of severity the minimum penalties for hooliganism, petty theft at factories, and production of defective goods. Each of these measures led to a campaign that, taken together, made 1940 a year of campaigns for Soviet officials. But this was not all. One of Stalin's actions, the criminalization of unauthorized quitting and shirking (that is, missing or coming late to work) had a lasting impact on the work of Soviet judges. The prosecution of labor offenses increased caseloads dramatically and would preoccupy judges for years to come. During the campaign of 1940 these cases produced more than two-thirds of all criminal convictions in Soviet courts. Even in 1945 labor infractions constituted more than half of all criminal dispositions, and, as late as 1949, over 40%.[1]

The mounting of this set of campaigns in the summer and fall of 1940 harmed, if it did not undermine, the effort to strengthen the administration of justice described in the previous chapter. The pressure of earlier campaigns – during collectivization and the Terror – had forced legal officials to work more erratically than usual and show little regard for standards of evidence and procedure. The campaigns of 1940, in the main hysterical and politically managed, had these same effects. To accomplish the rapid conviction and punishment of large numbers of workers the leaders authorized simplified procedures, and judges went on to develop their own shortcuts as well. Standards of performance by

---

[1] GARF, f.9492sch, op.6s, d.14 (Statistika sudimosti) 11–16. See also V.P. Popov, "Gosudarstvennyi terror v sovetskoi Rossii, 1923–1953gg. (istochniki i ikh interpretatsii)," *Otechestvennye arkhivy*, 1992, no. 2, 23.

judges declined further when they themselves were threatened with reprisals. Judges who resisted implementing the draconian edict that criminalized quitting and shirking faced denunciation, firing, and even criminal prosecution. Even some judges who applied the edict met similar fates. For a time the mere failure to process cases of labor infractions quickly or award the maximum sentences prescribed in law could bring the sword of Damocles on a judge's head. As a result, judges became intimidated and for a time applied the edict of June 26, 1940, in a mood of panic. The contradiction between the effects of campaigns and the goal of developing consistency in the administration of justice reflected an underlying tension in the history of Soviet criminal justice that was never resolved during the Stalin years. However much Stalin came to appreciate the utility of a centralized and efficient criminal justice, he never abandoned the view of criminal law as a weapon that he as leader could use as he chose.

The war-inspired changes in Soviet criminal law also had long-term effects on the administration of justice, but those effects varied from one measure to another. The higher minimum punishments for already existing offenses – production of defective goods, hooliganism, and petty theft at factories – had a limited impact on practice – real, but much less than the changes in the law had threatened. The new penalties remained in law during and after the War, but changes in patterns of policing and sentencing circumscribed the use of those penalties, muting the impact of the decrees. This was not so, however, in the case of the new labor-related offenses. The use of the criminal sanctions to manage the labor force lasted throughout the War and proved so useful to Stalin that he found it hard to abandon. During the War further laws extended the prohibitions on quitting and shirking to students in trade schools and persons mobilized for work in construction; and agricultural workers who failed to fulfill their norms also faced convictions as shirkers. Taken with the original edict of June 26, 1940, that criminalized quitting and shirking, the degrees produced a labor draft, whose enforcement overwhelmed the courts and pushed judges toward shortcuts in procedures. After the War central legal officials struggled to get this group of "wartime decrees" rescinded and the work of the courts normalized, but, as we shall see in Chapter 12, they encountered resistance, particularly to changing the edict of June 26, 1940.

To understand Stalin's reluctance to remove the ban on quitting and shirking calls for an appreciation of the full meaning of the edict. Although described in the late 1940s as a "wartime decree," the edict of June 26, 1940, represented more than a response to the threat of war. It marked as well the culmination of a decade of conflict between the regime and its workforce.

This chapter examines the origins of the edict of June 26, 1940, the extraordinary campaign to implement it, the routinization of the edict's enforcement, and finally the other campaigns of 1940.

Criminalizing labor infractions: the origins of the edict of June 26, 1940

The edict of June 26, 1940, extended Soviet criminal law into labor discipline. First, the edict subjected any employee of a state firm who quit a regular job without permission to a term of imprisonment of two to four months. Such permission was made hard to obtain. Employers were "allowed and obliged" to approve applications from employees to leave their place of employment only on grounds of physical incapacity to perform any work at the enterprise (supported by a doctor's certificate), admission to higher education, or attainment of the age of retirement. As a result, most workers became bound to their enterprises, entering a state of conscription. Second, the same law also forbade managers to fire their workers for shirking (absenteeism or tardiness) – previously, such firing had been mandatory – lest workers miss work intentionally in order to get themselves dismissed. Instead, the edict provided a new way to handle truants. Any employee who shirked – that is, missed all or part of a day at work simply by arriving more than twenty minutes late – faced a punishment of one to six months' corrective work with a deduction from earnings of up to 25%. Finally, the edict threatened with criminal prosecution managers of enterprises who failed to report employees who violated the edict's provision.[2]

The criminalization of labor violations was part of the Soviet regime's preparation for war. Military conscription had already reduced the size of the labor force, and the threat of war made further shortfalls in industrial production unacceptable to the leadership. According to the memoir of a top industrial official, a number of the commissars running Soviet industry complained to Stalin – in the winter of 1940 – that they could not fulfill the high targets of the Third Five-year Plan due to the shortage of labor and its undisciplined character. They suggested that Stalin issue a decree to confront labor turnover and shirking. The leader at first resisted this suggestion, but then changed his mind

---

[2] "O perekhode na vosmichasovoi rabochii den, na semidnevnuiu rabochuiu nedeliu i o zapreshchenii samovolnogo ukhoda rabochikh i sluzhashchikh s predpriiatii i uchrezhdenii," Ukaz Prezidiuma Verkhovnogo Soveta SSSR ot 26 iiunia 1940 g., *SIu*, 1940, no. 11, 5–6 and abridged version in Goliakov, *Sbornik*, 405–406. For an insightful account of this law see O. Khlevniuk, "26 iiunia 1940 goda: illiuzii i realnosti administrirovaniia," *Kommunist* 1989, no. 9, 86–96.

and authorized the preparation of the new edict "in the Central Committee" and scheduled its discussion at an expanded meeting of the
Politburo attended by all commissars who were also members of the
Central Committee of the Bolshevik party. After approval by the Politburo, the draft edict reached the Praesidium of the Supreme Soviet "at
the initiative of the Trade-Union Council."[3]

The immediate pretext of the edict, though, does not explain its
content, nor why it lasted for many years after the end of World War II.
The criminalization of labor infractions was not, in fact, a bolt from the
blue. Rather, it represented the culmination of a decade-long struggle
between the Soviet regime and its industrial labor force. Until 1940 the
regime's efforts to discipline its unruly workers fell mainly into the
realms of labor and administrative law.

The struggle began with the industrialization drive of the late 1920s
and early 1930s. The rapid expansion of Soviet industry ended the
unemployment of the 1920s and created an unprecedented demand for
workers. As a result, many of them succeeded in disregarding disciplinary rules and moving repeatedly from one factory to another in search
of better salaries and living conditions. Soviet authorities responded
with the harsh labor law of November 15, 1932, a law that for the first
time obliged managers to take actions against their employees. Any of
the latter found to have missed work even for a single day faced automatic dismissal, loss of ration card, and eviction (with family) from
enterprise housing. Because of the shortage of labor, however, most
managers refused to fire more than a handful of workers and found
ways to circumvent the law. For such dereliction of duty some managers were convicted of criminal negligence. Although these scapegoats
were few in number, their prosecution for noncompliance with labor
laws set a precedent.[4]

The mid and late 1930s saw an intensification of the regime's struggle
to mold a productive workforce out of new peasant workers. In
1935–1936 Stalin chose to emphasize positive incentives. Personally
exceed your plan, he told Soviet workers, and you can gain recognition
as a Stakhanovite, a hero-worker subject to praise, publicity, and prizes.
To most Soviet workers, the so-called Stakhanovites were rate-breakers,
if not also tools of managers who created special conditions to facilitate

---

3 John Barber and Mark Harrison, *The Soviet Home Front, 1941–1945: A Social and Economic
History of World War II* (London and New York, 1991); B.L. Bannikov, "Zapiski nark-
oma," *Znamia*, 1988, no. 1, 148–150; "O perekhode."
4 Donald Filtzer, *Soviet Workers and Stalinist Industrialization. The Formation of Modern
Soviet Production Relations, 1928–1941* (Armonk, N.Y., 1986), 111–115. See also Solomon
M. Schwarz, *Labor in the Soviet Union* (New York, 1952), chap. 3.

their performances. As such, they deserved not praise but reprisals. Many Stakhanovite workers did experience harassment from bench-mates, and occasionally persecution and physical attack. From the political vantage point, though, Stakhanovites were a holy breed, and attacks upon them (even verbal) merited stern reactions. Procurators received instructions to prosecute all forms of "opposition to the Stak-hanovite movement" and qualify physical attacks on Stakhanovites as political crimes.[5]

In 1938 Stalin set in motion another crackdown on the workforce. Two years of Terror and Purge had worsened labor discipline by encouraging employees to attack their bosses and undermining respect for management. The timing proved unfortunate, since by the end of the Terror the threat of war in Europe was real.[6] Two new laws issued in December 1938 addressed the exacerbated problem of labor discipline and put the USSR on the path toward labor conscription. The new laws required employees to carry workbooks (in which all disciplinary measures would be recorded) and to give a month's notice before leaving a post. Moreover, they became subject to automatic dismissal and eviction from factory housing for arriving at work twenty minutes late three times in any one month or four times in two months. As with the almost forgotten law of 1932, enforcement of the new labor laws of December 1938 was compulsory. To underscore the point Procurator-General Vy-shinskii instructed procurators to charge with criminal negligence all managers who failed to implement the laws. Still, most of the latter avoided firing their workers. Some managers adopted ruses, such as firing and rehiring their employees without even starting eviction from factory residence. Other managers made the law work to their own advantage. One director of a factory protected his valuable workers while firing the expendable ones, regardless of the merits of their cases. When exposed, he lost his job and party card and faced prosecution in court. Another director claimed that the law did not apply to his enterprise (ship docks) because he had a shortage of workers. To help the campaign succeed, however, he made up statistics on the number of workers fired![7] When cases against managers who failed to fire offend-

[5] Ibid., chap. 7; "Organy iustitsii v borbe za Stakhanovskoe dvizhenie," *ZaSZ*, 1936, no. 3, 1–3; P. Kravstev, "Organy iustitsii Leningradskoi oblasti v borbe s protivodeistviem stakhanovskom dvizhenii," ibid., 1936, no. 6, 26–30;

[6] Lewis Siegelbaum, *Stakhanovism and the Politics of Productivity in the USSR, 1935–1941* (Cambridge, 1988), 260–267; Bannikov, "Zapiski narkoma."

[7] Filtzer, *Soviet Workers*, chap. 9; "Ob uchastii organov prokuratury v ukreplenii trudovoi ditsipliny," Prikaz Prokuratury SSSR No. 192 ot 31 dek. 1938, *SZ*, 1939, no. 1, 108–109; "O praktike primenenii zakona ot 8 dekabriia 1938 g.," Prikaz Prokuratury SSSR No. 102–103 ot 29 maia 1939, ibid., no. 7, 105–106.

ing workers did come to court, judges felt obliged to award custodial sentences but shrank from long terms. The USSR Supreme Court resolved their dilemma by granting them permission to ignore the one-year minimum term of imprisonment set out in the criminal code. Apparently, there were enough such prosecutions to make managers afraid, for some of them went to the opposite extreme. To protect themselves, they fired everyone whom they could, paying no heed to the explanations offered by their employees. As a result, some factories released hundreds of workers.[8]

Not only managers but also workers proved resourceful in finding ways to evade the December 1938 decrees. To avoid staying on the job for a month after giving notice (when a new post already beckoned), some workers earned immediate dismissal through intentional tardiness. This tactic made it clear that to limit movement of workers required a different approach to shirking.[9]

By mid-1939 the pressure to enforce the December 1938 laws on labor discipline had subsided, but the problems did not go away. The continuing presence of new young recruits in the labor force, the disrespect for superiors bred by the campaign of vigilance during the Terror, and traditions of labor culture that had developed during the 1930s still exercised powerful influences on the conduct of workers, affecting not only discipline but also productivity. Moreover, with the onset of a supply crisis in the second half of 1939 and first part of 1940, workers of all ages took to leaving the factory during their shifts to line up for scarce goods, thereby hurting production.[10] Yet, as World War II began in Europe, the need to raise productivity became paramount, if only to maintain current levels of production as part of the labor force left the factories for military service.

The solution, as we have seen, was to make both unauthorized quitting and shirking criminal offenses. Stalin took these steps at the request of his industrial commissars, but he was not striking out in an entirely new direction. There were precedents in Soviet history for conscripting

---

8 "O vozmoshnosti primeneniia lisheniia svobody na srok nizhe odnogo goda po delam ob uklonenii rukovoditelei predpriatii i uchrezhdenii ot provedenii mer po ukreplenii trudovoi ditsipliny," Postanovlenie plenuma Verkhovnogo Suda SSSR ot 4 maia 1939 g., *SZ*, 1939, no. 6, 121; N. Shlykov, "Ob izvrascheniiakh Postanovlenie SNK SSSR i TsK VKP(b) i VTsSPS ot 28 dek. 1938 goda," *SZ*, 1940, no. 1, 44–46.
9 Khlevniuk, "26 iiuniia 1940 goda," 88.
10 This process was described by Dr. Elena Osokina at a session of the Research Colloquium of the Stalin Era Research and Archives Project, University of Toronto, January 25, 1996. On the supply crisis of 1939–1941 and its sources, see E.A. Osokina, "Liudi i vlast v usloviiakh krizisa snabzhenii 1939–41," *Otechestvennaia istoriia*, 1995, no. 3, 16–32.

the workforce and using criminal sanctions against persons who breached labor discipline. The precedents come from an earlier time of emergency for the Bolshevik regime, the Civil War. At that time, the Bolsheviks used military conscription to recruit labor for their enterprises, and missing or leaving work could subject conscripted workers to a criminal charge of "labor desertion." The 1922 Criminal Code of the RSFSR actually retained this offense for persons subject to labor mobilization (with a penalty of corrective work), but when labor conscription ended, prosecutions ceased. The 1926 Criminal Code eliminated the offense of "labor desertion," but the idea of labor conscription policed by the criminal law did not die. Likewise, another legacy of the Civil War period was the notion that "tardiness" for work could merit a legal sanction. In 1920 the government of the RSFSR made it illegal for members of local executive committees (*ispolkomy*) to arrive more than fifteen minutes late to meetings and subjected the truants to disciplinary measures.[11]

In short, the decision to criminalize labor infractions taken in June 1940 represented a desperate response to problems of labor discipline that less punitive approaches had failed to address. The looming threat of war supplied both reason and justification for the severity. On the one hand, the need to maintain production with a smaller workforce supplied reason for the new policy; on the other hand, war had served to justify the conscription of labor earlier in Soviet history, if not also the history of other countries. When war did come, the edict of June 26, 1940, proved especially appropriate, and it was soon supplemented by a series of other laws extending the net of persons subject to new restrictions and standards of labor discipline. Still, the edict of June 26, 1940, represented more than a preparation for war; it was the regime's response to the failure of less stringent measures to produce a pliant and obedient workforce. At least Joseph Stalin did not forget this fact. As we shall see, he proved reluctant to repeal the edict, and found in the challenge of postwar reconstruction sufficient grounds for leaving in place a law that tyrannized the workforce.

The campaign

The implementation of the edict criminalizing labor infractions fell into three stages. The first month of the edict was marked by an ordinary campaign, which called for attention from legal officials but did not put them under unusual pressure. In late July Stalin converted the campaign into an intense and hysterical witchhunt. He insisted on a crack-

---

[11] Z.A. Vyshinskaia, *Prestupleniia v oblasti trudovykh otnoshenii* (Moscow, 1949), 17–47.

down not only against violators of the edict but also against their "shielders." These included managers who failed to report infractions and judges who failed to repress with sufficient vengeance or speed. Finally, after two months of frenetic repression of violators and "shielders" alike, authorities began warning against excesses and errors and the campaign waned. By early 1941, routine patterns of implementation had developed.

The life of the edict of June 26, 1940, began quietly. On the day after its promulgation Procurator-General Mikhail Pankratev and Commissar of Justice Nikolai Rychkov issued a joint instruction signaling to their subordinates that the new labor offenses should get high priority. The instruction asked them to process these cases rapidly, while still following usual procedures. Investigators from the Procuracy were expected to do thorough investigations (visit the factories, collect the facts, study the work records of the accused) but complete this process within three days of the initial report of an offense. Judges were to hold trials in cases of labor infractions within five days of receiving the dossiers from the procuracy. Where possible, judges were also to hold demonstration trials in the factories, with procurators in attendance![12] With hindsight it is clear that the instruction suffered from internal contradictions. It was impossible for legal officials to handle any sizable volume of cases of labor infractions so quickly and still observe the normal rules of evidence and procedure.

The edict of June 26 charged the managers of enterprises with responsibility for policing labor infractions. Upon discovering violations, factory officials were to signal the local procuracy office. Naturally, managers disliked this new responsibility. Many of them ignored the new law, and procurators responded by prosecuting some of them for failing to report their employees' misdeeds. The risk of a procuratorial response became sufficiently great that a sizable proportion of enterprise managers soon started reporting labor infractions. In the case of valuable workers, though, management often supplied references about good behavior and work records (so-and-so was a Stakhanovite). On occasion, managers even sent representatives of the factory to trial to help with the defense. At the same time, the trade-union organizations in many enterprises tried to soften the blows by bringing to light workers' explanations for instances of shirking and sometimes holding cases back from court.[13]

---

12 "Prikaz Narkomiusta SSR i Prokurora SSSR ot 27 iiunia 1940 No. 72/117," *SIu*, 1940, no. 11, 6–7.
13 Filtzer, *Soviet Workers*, 240–243; Samarin, "Borba s progulshchikami, letunami i pokroviteliami progulshchikov – boevaia zadacha prokuratury g. Moskvy," *SZ*, 1940, no. 9, 54–56, Khlevniuk; "26 iiuniia 1940 god," 90.

Likewise, legal officials sought to soften the blows, at least against workers whose offenses they deemed trivial. One procurator dismissed all cases of tardiness under three hours, reserving for the court only cases of persons who had missed at least half a day of work without an excuse. In another city the procurator refused to prosecute forty offenders who had no previous charges recorded during the year. Judges used all the measures available in their arsenal. Some judges acquitted any accused person with a reasonable excuse, such as oversleeping, not being used to the job, or having "to look after the cow." Other judges gave suspended sentences and sentences under the minimum in the edict (e.g., corrective work in cases of quitting, or for shirking corrective work in doses as small as ten days with a 2% garnishing of wages). For the bulk of offenders most judges did assign penalties within the range supplied by the edict but at the lower end of the scale. Thus, using their legal discretion, judges in the Kiev district of the city of Moscow gave 71% of shirkers in July 1940 a sentence of one to three months' corrective work with a deduction from wages of 5% to 15%. Generally, judges avoided the longer terms and higher rates of deduction for the simple reason that they saw no reason to act otherwise. A judge from Moscow region was to explain to his critics, "I gave mainly three months terms, thinking that this represented the penal policy of the day." Neither agency directives nor the press suggested that judges should have done otherwise. Overall, central newspapers such as *Trud* and *Izvestiia* gave the edict spotty coverage, and even *Pravda*'s fuller exposure slackened in mid-July.[14]

Resistance to the edict on the part of managers, trade-union officials, and judges was matched by more general disdain for the edict among the workers themselves. As a rule, they kept their attitudes hidden, but at the demonstration trials held in factories during the first weeks of the campaign, those feelings surfaced. At many of these trials, according to both trade-union and party officials, the audience moved quickly to the support of accused shirkers or quitters, and sometimes in a demonstrative way. At a trial held at the automobile factory in Gorkii, where defense counsel had made a fine speech, the listeners broke out into shouts when the procurator asked for the maximum penalty of six months' corrective work. The accused was an illiterate woman who had overslept after a late visit from relatives and come to work late for the first time in her life. At another trial, this time held in a textile factory in

---

14 "Besposhchadno karat progulshchikov, letunov i ikh pokrovitelei," *SZ*, 1940, no. 9, 1–5; S. Egiazarov, "Za vypolnenie ukaza 26 iiunia na zheleznodorozhnom transporte," ibid., 23–25. Filtzer, *Soviet Workers*, 243–246; GARF, f.9492, op.1, d.56, 65; *Pravda, Izvestiia, Trud* for July 1940, passim.

Yaroslavl, a woman accused of illegal quitting cried so hard that the audience took her part. When the court sentenced her to three months in prison, a crowd of "three hundred workers of both sexes followed her out of the factory, objecting to the sentence and accompanying her to prison with expressions of indignation." Public reaction to the edict on labor infractions was sufficiently hostile that the demonstration trials backfired. Rather than spreading the message that the regime had intended, they served as outlets for the resentment of workers against the harsh and unfair edict.[15]

Workers frustrated the realization of the edict in another way. Ever watchful for loopholes in the law, workers who needed or wanted to quit a job without a justifiable excuse looked for ways to get themselves fired. The ploy of the recent past, that is arriving late to work, no longer served this purpose, for tardiness now led to sentences of corrective work (that is deductions from pay) rather than to firing. But there were other ways to bring about removal from the job. It was standard practice to fire workers who stole items of small value from their place of employment or committed rowdy acts on the premises. All of a sudden, within days of the edict, workers began leaving the factory "brandishing a salami" or handing directly to the factory guards items that they had stolen. Other workers got drunk and raised a debauche on the shop floor. There were reports of workers striking deals – "I will steal, you will report me; you will show revolutionary vigilance, and I will leave the factory." Acts of these sorts did get most of their perpetrators fired and enabled them to move on to new jobs without facing threat of prosecution for unauthorized quitting.[16]

Despite the resistance, the actual implementation of the edict was reasonable by any objective standard. Official statistics revealed that over 100,000 cases had been started in the first month, and that of these the procuracy had sent 85,000 to the courts. Of the 85,000 cases the courts had already heard some 51,000. But these figures represented neither the scope nor the pace of implementation that the leadership had come to desire.[17]

The routine and unenthusiastic conduct of the campaign to implement the edict on labor infractions and the new ruses developed by workers to evade its consequences infuriated Stalin, so much that he decided to make the edict a centerpiece of discussions at the Plenum of

15 Khlevniuk, "26 iiunia 1940 goda," 90; RTsKhIDNI, f.17, op.2, d.671 (Plenum TsK VKP(b), 29–31 iiuliia 1940. Stenograficheskii otchet. Doklad Malenkova), 60.
16 Ibid., 98; RTsKhIDNI, f.17, op.2, d.673 (Plenum TsK VKP(b), 29–31 iiuliia 1940. Stenograficheskii otchet. Prenie po dokladu Malenkova), 7.
17 Ibid., 27, 62.

the Central Committee convened to meet July 29, 1940.[18] Only once before had the execution of the criminal law received attention at a Plenum (the Law of August 7, 1932, at the January 1933 Plenum), and never such extended or intense discussion.[19] Secretary Malenkov delivered a long report on the subject, in whose delivery Stalin also took part.

Malenkov began by observing that in one month of the edict of June 26, 1940, work discipline had improved negligibly and that there had been little increase in production (despite both the longer work shifts and the threat of prosecution for shirking). The reason for this unsatisfactory result, he insisted, lay in the failure of all officials – party secretaries, managers, and legal officials alike – to make the edict work. Regional party officials had failed to pursue the edict – held insufficient discussions with district party staff, failed to pressure judges, allowed demonstration trials that backfired. Directors of factories "chattered about discipline but did little about it," while their superiors in the commissariats just issued formal directives. Procurators dragged out proceedings by demanding too much data from the factory staff, and judges processed cases slowly and failed to give the maximum sentences. In the future, Malenkov warned, all of these officials would be held personally responsible for seeing the edict fulfilled. To underscore the point he singled out one particular official, USSR Procurator-General Pankratev, for immediate reprisal.[20]

Pankratev served as a classic scapegoat. At the Plenum he was pilloried by Malenkov, Stalin, and Kaganovich, and finally fired from his post "for not coping with his responsibilities and guaranteeing fulfillment of the edict."[21] His primary sin, according to his accusers, was having issued the joint directive of June 27 authorizing demonstration trials, "which in practice were so poorly organized as to discredit the edict." To be sure, Minister of Justice Rychkov had also signed the directive, but, as Malenkov put it "he is ashamed of this . . . and he issued a new directive on the 25th of July canceling the demonstration trials." Rychkov had admitted that the demonstration

[18] Among the signs of haste in arranging the Plenum's discussion of the labor infractions was the preparation by the USSR Procuracy of two memoranda on cases of hooliganism in factories during the first month of the edict on labor infractions. The memoranda were unusually sloppy and consisted of seemingly random examples that the authors managed to find in a matter of hours. GARF, f.8131sch, op.27s, d.157, 50–58.

[19] RTsKhIDNI, f.17, op.2, d.514, vyp.2, 3–21.

[20] Ibid., d.671, 50–112.

[21] Ibid. GARF, f.8131sch, op.27s, d.157, 35–36ob ("O kontrole nad provedeniiem v zhizn Ukaza Prezidiuma VS SSSR ot 26 iiuniia 1940 'O perekhode na vosmichasovoi rabochii den . . .'" Postanovlenie Plenuma TsK VKP(b) ot 31 iiuliia 1940). See also the veiled reference to the reasons for the firing of Pankratev in "Osvobozheniie tov. Pankratova, M.I., ot obiazannostei Prokurora SSSR," *Trud*, Aug. 5, 1940, 3.

trials had been "a crude mistake that undermined the edict." Pankratev was also accused of giving a liberal speech at the Council of People's Commissars and issuing another incorrect directive regarding shirking by police officials, but the demonstration trials remained the main pretext for the attack. As Stalin concluded in one of his dialogues with Malenkov, "He (Pankratev) did not arm his people in the localities, he disorganized them." "Yes," said Malenkov, "he disorganized them." Stalin: "Disorganized."[22] Minister of Justice Rychkov also faced an inquisition at the Plenum, but it was clear that he was scripted to be spared. Rychkov had proved more cooperative with the leadership. While both officials conceded fault, Pankratev insisted on defending himself, even at the Plenum. "I admit," he told the audience, "to underestimating the importance of the edict and making mistakes, but not to . . . taking a fundamentally incorrect position." Rychkov claimed that his big mistake was issuing the directive on demonstration trials "without consulting the Council of People's Commissars or Central Committee." But in the Council, he explained, "we had been criticized the last time [we came for a clearance], because we brought up so many petty questions." Although Rychkov was spared, the Plenum succeeded in terrorizing him, and he proved a most faithful executor of the frenetic hysteria that was to follow.[23]

Some of the regional party secretaries attending the Plenum also rose in self-defense. Comrade Kuznetsov from Leningrad offered the lame excuse for inaction that "we thought that the mere issuance of the edict would be enough, that it would automatically reduce shirking." He went on to blame the Procuracy in Leningrad for mismanaging the case flow. According to Kuznetsov, the procurator of Leningrad discouraged factories from starting too many cases. At trade-union meetings he declared that since Shvernik, the national trade-union leader, had cited 34% as the normal rate of shirking Leningrad should have that very rate. To achieve it, he ordered the return of many cases to factories for the imposition of disciplinary warnings instead of criminal prosecution. Kuznetsov also reported the practice of "focusing on the smaller factories so as not to discredit the large ones."[24]

---

22 RTsKhIDNI, f.17, op.2, d.671, 82–93; d.673, 27–36. The choice of Pankratev rather than Rychkov as the prime scapegoat for the weak enforcement of the June decree may have reflected the former's reputation as a weak administrator. A group of officials in the USSR Procuracy sent an anonymous letter to Central Committee Secretary Zhdanov in October 1939 complaining of Pankratev's inability to both stand up to Beriia on illegalities perpetrated by NKVD officials and to secure pay raises for procuracy staff. RTsKhIDNI, f.77, op.1 d. 194a, 4–5ob.

23 Ibid., f.17, op.2, d.673, 58–70.

24 Ibid., 39–53.

Besides casting blame, the Plenum also addressed some of the short-comings in the implementation of the edict. To begin, it confirmed the telegram sent by Rychkov banning both demonstration trials and any trials held during working hours. Malenkov presented an example of a recent case of shirking on the part of workers who came thirty minutes late, where seventeen hours of working time were lost in the processing of the case, from investigation through trial. Stalin deemed this "the organization of shirking."[25] The result of the ban was that judges would hold many trials for labor infractions at night. Second, the Plenum addressed the question of thefts and rowdy conduct staged for the purpose of getting fired. After airing the issue, Malenkov suggested changing the criminal law to require one year of prison for all persons convicted of petty theft or hooliganism at an enterprise. Former Procurator-General Vyshinskii (now deputy head of the Council) interjected that the new punishment should not be limited to hooliganism at factories alone but should apply to hooliganism in general. After all, he pointed out, it was just as easy to do mischief outside the factory gates as inside its walls. Vyshinskii's suggestion carried the day. The resolution of the Plenum called for the new mandatory one year in prison for petty theft at factories and hooliganism everywhere, and the decree of August 10, 1940, brought these sanctions into the criminal law.[26]

The Plenum of the Central Committee of July 29–31 marked a turning point in the campaign to implement the edict. The Plenum itself, its secret resolution, and the *Pravda* editorial that followed made it clear that Stalin and his colleagues were insisting on a new kind of campaign. Particularly evil, according to *Pravda*, were "the harmful antistate practices" of managers who failed to report all of their shirkers and judges who did not apply the full force of the law. Both were ordered to end their manifestations of "rotten liberalism" and "petty-bourgeois sentimentality" or face punishment themselves. At the same time, the leaders promised, legal procedures for cases of labor infractions would be simplified and tempos of case processing raised.[27] Immediately after the Plenum the procurator-general ordered procurators to skip preliminary investigations in cases of labor infractions. It was enough to review materials submitted by the factories and send the case files to court. Within days the Council of People's Commissars eliminated even perfunctory screening of case files by the procurators. Henceforth, factory

25 GARF, f.8131sch, op.27s, d.157, 35–360b; RTsKhIDNI, f.17, op.2, d.671, 79, 101–103.
26 Ibid., 95-103; RTsKhIDNI, f.17, op.2, d.673, 70–72; GARF, f.8131sch, op.27s, d.157, 36–36ob; Goliakov, *Sbornik dokumentov*, 407–408.
27 GARF, f.8131sch, op.27s, d.157, 35–36ob; "Pokrovitelstvo progulshchikam – prestuplenie protiv gosduarstva," *Pravda*, Aug. 5, 1940, 1; "Bespochshadno karat."

officials bore sole responsibility for reporting instances of shirking directly to the court. No later than twenty-four hours after discovering an offense, they had to supply the court with a short statement and the work record of the accused.[28] The procuracy's role in the enforcement of the edict was reduced to finding and prosecuting managers who failed to initiate cases against their employees. In the month that followed procurators generated hundreds of new prosecutions against managers.[29] The leadership also announced a short-cut for trials of labor infractions. Judges were to hear cases of illegal quitting and shirking *alone*, without the help of lay assessors. Some judges damned this simplification as "a violation of the socialist tradition of court organization."[30]

The task of limiting the discretion of judges and pushing them to give more severe sentences fell to the USSR Supreme Court and Narkomiust. The Court instructed judges that for cases of labor violations it was impermissible to award suspended sentences or terms under the minimum set out in the edict; that they should ignore good biographies and work records (even designations as Stakhanovites); and that for shirking they should award only terms of four to six months' corrective work with deductions of 25%. Sentences of one to three months with lower levels of deduction from wages, the Court told judges, represented unacceptable deviations from policy, even though they remained legal according to the text of the edict. (The edict itself was not changed.) Judges also had to shoulder added responsibility for the implementation of their sentences. Often, the actual attachment to the earnings of a shirker waited for weeks while sentences were typed and delivered to the bureaus of corrective labor and the bureaus communicated their orders to the factories. A Narkomiust directive told judges to ensure that such delays did not occur.[31]

Narkomiust's main method for bringing judges into line was a witch-hunt! This process began with a telegram-order from Commissar Rychkov dated July 29, 1940, that is the first day of the Central Committee Plenum. The order warned that judges who failed to organize hearings

---

28 *SIu*, 1940, no. 13; 5; A. Volin, "Prokuratura RSFSR v borbe za Ukaz 26 iiuniia," *SZ*, 1940, no. 9, 9–14; "Besposhchadno karat"; "O poriadke napravleniia v sud del o progulakh . . . " Post.SNK SSSR ot 21 avgusta 1940, no. 1502, *SIu*, 1940, no. 14, 5–6.

29 Samarin, "Borba s progulshchikami"; L. Iachanin, "Moshchnyi rychag v borbe za pobedy kommunizma," *SZ*, 1940, no. 9, 14–17.

30 "O rassmotrenii narodnymi sudami del o progulakh . . . bez uchastiia narodnykh zasedatelei," Ukaz Prezidiuma Verkhovnogo Soveta SSSR ot 10 avgusta, 1940, g., *SIu*, 1940, no. 14, 5; B. Arsenev, "Protsessualnye osobennosti rassmotreniia del o progulakh i samovolnom ukhode s raboty," *SIu*, 1941, no. 2, 508.

31 "O nedostatkakh sudebnoi praktiki po delam o samovolnom ukhode . . . " Postanovlenie Plenuma Verkhovnogo Suda ot 15 avgusta 1940, *SIu*, 1940, no. 13, 6–8.

properly (quickly and without calling witnesses during the day) or allowed distortions in their sentences (anything less than the upper range allowed in the law) would be held responsible "up to and including prosecution at trial." The chiefs of the administration of Narkomiust at the regional level would be held accountable for the performance of their judges and inspectors.[32]

The attack on the judges started at once – from the top down. On August 2, Narkomiust SSSR ordered the firing of a Moscow judge for giving a conditional sentence to a shirker. On August 6, after a review of the work of judges in parts of Moscow, the Commissar fired three more of them and sent two to trial for "mistakes" in the scheduling of cases and sentencing. The head of the city's justice administration received notice that he too would be fired if judges in Moscow did not change their ways. On August 9, the Collegium of Narkomiust discussed a report on the implementation of the edict in Kalinin region, and the Commissar fired and sent to trial four judges and the head of the justice administration himself for "red-tape" and "distortions." On August 16, the Collegium met again, in a session for which the stenographic report was preserved. This meeting reviewed the practice of judges in Moscow Region, the city of Moscow, and the republic of Belorussia. The result was the firing of four people's court judges, three members of the regional court, the head of court administration for the republic of Belorussia, and the Belorussian commissar of justice. The sins of the commissar, apart from "actually not working at all," included personal opposition at a meeting of officials in the Belorussian Narkomiust to a proposed extension of the law on labor infractions to cover seasonal and day workers. Officials responsible for the peat and construction industries in Belorussia, where many employees were not permanent, had sought the extension. The justice commissar of the republic not only refused to cooperate but promised "to convict all judges who supported accusations against these persons." During the month of August, warnings and censures also came from Narkomiust in Moscow to the justice commissars of the Ukraine, Uzbekistan, and Azerbaizhan, as well as a number of their assistants.[33]

Thus far I have mentioned only some of the firings of judges and judicial officials initiated by the USSR Commissariat of Justice and one republican commissariat. Dozens more judges fell victim to initiatives of other republican commissariats, and some to those of local party officials. Some procurators also paid for alleged sins, such as the one who refused to prosecute tardiness under three hours, one who dis-

[32] "V Narodnom komissariate iustitsii SSSR," SIu, 1940, no. 13, 9–11.
[33] Ibid.; GARF, f.9492, op.1, d.56, 65, 99, 111–114.

missed cases of shirkers who had good work records, and one who simply held back one case for a month.[34]

One thing is clear. The repression of dozens of legal officials represented classic scapegoating. As often as not, the offenders had both cooperated with the law and followed current instructions on its implementation. Frequently, the reprisals came after the rules or policy toward labor cases had changed, and typically the legal officials selected for repression had performed no differently from their colleagues. Let us examine the stories of two judges subjected to inquiries at the meeting of Narkomiust's Collegium on August 16.

The first was Judge Brodskii, from a rural district within Moscow Region. Like other judges Brodskii had begun by awarding most shirkers terms of up to three months' corrective work (71% of his sentences). An inspector also discovered that Brodskii had acquitted a worker accused of arriving an hour late, solely because he was a pensioner. The judge who had made these "mistakes" had started working in the courts in July of 1939. Already a veteran official of the Communist Youth League (Komsomol), he got an "excellent" in the preparatory course for judges in the region, "largely because he had completed 700 cases (instead of the usual 400) in a three-month period." Young Brodskii was puzzled by his fate, but proved eager to make amends. "It feels strange," he admitted, "to be accounted a politically backward person, after all my time as a Communist Youth official." He went on to explain to the Collegium that he had been on leave until July 15, and many of these cases in question had been heard by his replacement, a lay assessor! Still, he admitted, it was clear that "I did not understand the political significance of the edict." After the inspector's visit, however, Brodskii had changed his ways, moving cases more quickly and giving more severe punishments. To ensure that his sentences were implemented, "I have now become a courier and personally carry the sentences to the corrective-labor bureau." As for his past sins, Brodskii added that at least he had never given a suspended sentence to a shirker (despite good character references supplied by employers); and he had been advised by the procurator, evidently erroneously, that pensioners were not subject to the edict. With this defense Brodskii won over Commissar of Justice Rychkov. Since Brodskii had been on leave and his work had improved, it was enough to give him a warning. How-

---

[34] "NKIu i sudebnye organy RSFSR v borbe za provedenie v zhizn ukaza Prez. Verkh.soveta SSSR ot 26 iiuniia 1940 g.," *SIu*, 1940, no. 114, 1–5; S. Shvarts, "Razgrom suda v SSSR," *Sotsialisticheskii vestnik*, May 22, 1941, 123–127; Boris A. Konstantinovsky, *Soviet Law in Action. The Recollected Cases of a Soviet Lawyer* (Cambridge, 1953), 10.

ever, no such reprieve awaited Judge Butskaia from the Krasnopresen-
skii district of the city of Moscow.

Butskaia's conduct in July did not differ from that of Brodskii, but
unlike the latter she had failed to mend her ways. In August, according
to her accusers, even after the telegram order of July 29, Butskaia had
continued to give 76% of shirkers short terms of corrective work with
deductions of a mere 10% from their wages. Nor had Judge Butskaia
observed the simplified rules of procedure. She had continued to hear
cases with lay assessors and as late as August 13 was still calling
witnesses to appear in court during working hours. Butskaia also gave
acquittals that did not withstand political scrutiny. Thus, she let off one
truant who had missed work due to the arrival of his brother from the
Finnish front. Especially offensive to her accusers was Butskaia's award
of a mild sentence (one month corrective work at 10% deduction) to an
employee who had missed three days of work due to an attack of
chronic colitis. He had phoned the clinic requesting a home visit by a
doctor, but the clinic would not confirm the call. In her sentence Butskaia had described his plight "lovingly," but her attentiveness proved
misguided when the same man missed two more days of work two
weeks later due to a drinking bout!

Like Brodskii and most other people's court judges of the day, Butskaia had assumed her post in 1939. Formerly a secretary at a court, she
had been promoted by party officials to her new post. Before August 13,
she explained to the Collegium, her work had never received criticism.
At the end of July, in fact, a "comrade from the city party committee"
(the *gorkom*) had checked her cases and told her that he had no comments about her sentences or tempo of work. The procurator who made
weekly checks also had no comments. Then suddenly on August 13 an
inspector from Narkomiust had arrived and seized the files of only the
twenty-nine cases with the most lenient dispositions. The man with
colitis, she explained, had a perfect work record and a medical
certificate confirming his condition; only his personal situation had
prevented hospitalization. Moreover, Butskaia added, his case was decided not by her alone but by "the whole court," that is, a panel including two lay assessors. Many of the other cases of acquittals or mild
sentences involved students from the technical schools who had just
started their first summer jobs and had arrived only twenty-five minutes late. As far as the change in the policy of Narkomiust was concerned, Butskaia claimed that she had never seen the telegram order of
July 29 nor had she heard of it!

All of Butskaia's explanations went for naught. Commissar Rychkov
would hear none of them. After joining in the ridicule of this decent but
politically naive woman, he supported both the firing of Butskaia and

her prosecution for negligence. It made no difference that the problem of tardiness on the part of students doing production practice was a general one (about which the representative of the Moscow city court had complained at the same session of the Collegium), nor that Butskaia had not seen the order of Narkomiust. The head of the Moscow regional judicial administration observed that there was no reason for a judge to wait for instructions from the Commissariat when the newspapers reflected the change in policy. "Every people's court judge," he explained, "must read the newspaper, at least the section on the work of the courts." (In August *Pravda* ran a daily column on the campaign.) The official had no doubt that judges were obliged to follow the penal policy of the day. To be sure, with the recent emphasis on judicial independence, some judges had become lax and paid less heed to policy. In so doing, they "misunderstood their independence." Judge Butskaia had to learn the hard way.[35]

Judges Brodskii and Butskaia were among a half-dozen judges who had to face inquisition at the hands of the collegium of Narkomiust SSSR. While few of their colleagues had to undergo that particular ordeal, dozens (if not hundreds), along with higher court judges and judicial administrators, fell victim to similar actions taken by officials at other levels in the hierarchy of Narkomiust, all of whom had to demonstrate their bona fides. During August, the collegium of Narkomiust devoted seven meetings to reviewing how republican justice commissariats implemented the edict of June 26, and it expected those republican bodies to have performed their own inspections of judges. At the same time, Narkomiust dispatched commissions to make inspections on the spot. The inspection commissions had a simple mandate: collect data, select judges and officials for reprisals, and identify cases that could be used against them.[36]

Republican justice commissariats went through similar exercises. In early August, for example, thirty top officials of the RSFSR Narkomiust were sent to the provinces to meet with the heads of the regional justice administrations and launch reviews of how courts handled the edict. The Collegium of RSFSR Narkomiust proceeded to discuss judicial practice with the edict for Rostov (on August 9), for Gorkii (on August 14), and for the whole of Russia (on August 19). In the final days of the month officials from the Commissariat held meetings with judges in Moscow, Yaroslavl, Rostov, Novosiribsk, Saratov, and Kazan.[37]

---

[35] GARF, f.9492, op.1, d.56, 57–70 (Protokol no. 29 3asedaniia Kollegii Narkomiusta ot 16 augusta 1940 8.).

[36] "V Narodnom komissariate iustitsii SSSR;" GARF, f.9492, op.1, d.56, 48–50, 71–77.

[37] "NKIu i sudebnye organy RSFSR."

Local party officials also joined in promoting the edict. District party secretaries and their staff warned or fired factory managers for sloppy implementation of the edict and removed party cards from workers convicted of shirking. In many cities party officials made judges report to meetings of the *aktiv* on their handling of the edict. The *aktiv* meetings "explained the 'facts of political work' to the judges," and in one instance fired a judge because of one acquittal![38]

Not surprisingly, all of this pressure on judges had an effect. During the peak of the campaign (from early August to late September) most legal officials complied with its demands. Punishments for shirking increased markedly. Whereas in July 38% of truants received corrective work in terms of three months or more, in August 64% suffered that fate; by the first half of October, 78%. Where sentences did not meet the new norms, procurators often initiated reviews. In the Ukraine procurators reportedly reviewed all cases of shirking and protested more than a thousand verdicts. Of cases heard in supervision by the RSFSR Supreme Court, 57% were remanded to lower courts because of lenient sentences.[39]

In response to the pressures of the campaign most judges also stepped up their tempos of case processing. It proved hard to try all cases of quitting and shirking within five days of receiving the files from the factories, and judges varied their responses. In Zaporozhe, for example, 45% of cases were outside the five-day limit. In Belorussia, one judge found it simpler to change the dates recorded for the arrival of cases (this fakery cost him his job!). The more common practice was to schedule trials within the limits and face the consequences. Often, key players like the accused or a witness failed to receive notice and did not appear in court. Some judges reacted to this development by putting the trials off for later dates, comfortable in the assumption that once having scheduled a case within the time limit, they had complied with the rules. Other judges, however, chose to protect themselves from censure by hearing the cases without the accused, even though this step violated procedural law. The verdicts in these cases were bound to be reviewed in cassation and were more likely to be dis-

38 "Sobranie partiinogo aktiva," *Pravda*, Aug. 14, 1940, 3; I. Riabov, "Sudia Komarkov i drugie," ibid., Aug. 19, 1940, 4; "Sobranie partiinogo aktiva Erevana," ibid.; "Sobranie partiinogo aktiva," ibid., Aug. 21, 1940, 3; Konstantinovsky, *Soviet Law in Action.*
39 P. Nadezhin, "Sudebnyi nadzor po Ukazu 26 iiuniiá 1940 g.," *SZ*, 1941, no. 2, 11–14; Iachenin, "Moshchnyi rychag;" L. Gromov, "Sudebnaia praktika RSFSR po delam o progulakh i samovolnom ukhode," *SIu*, 1941, no. 24–25, 9–10;

missed or overruled than verdicts from trials that had been conducted properly.[40]

From campaign to routine implementation

Law enforcement campaigns do not last long, for they involve mobilization and targeting of scarce resources and they distort the normal operations of police and legal officials, not to speak of their bureaucratic and political masters. The fate of the law or policy around which a campaign is organized, however, remains an open question. To be sure, the enforcement of no policy or law can remain at the level of the campaign, once resources have been moved away from the target of the moment. But the routinization of enforcement can take a variety of forms. Some campaigns leave little enforcement in their wake (for example, the defective goods campaign of 1933), while other ones (such as the campaign against abortionists in 1936) succeed in entrenching a new crime or punishment and leaving behind a meaningful, if modest, level of routine enforcement. Three factors seem to explain the difference – whether postcampaign enforcement is feasible; whether relevant actors or enforcers face sufficiently strong incentives to overcome any inclination to avoid or resist enforcement; and whether the larger context supplies additional rationale for enforcement.

In the case of the edict of June 26, 1940, criminalizing labor infractions, all of these factors came into play, and after the campaign ended, a considerable amount of enforcement continued. In addition, as we shall see, Stalin and his subordinates went out of their way to tell legal officials to stop only the excesses of the campaign and not enforcement in general. Here we examine the winding down of the campaign through signals in the press, judicial policy of the USSR Supreme Court, and the new jurisprudence on the edict supplied by legal scholars. Then, we analyze postcampaign patterns of enforcement – during and after World War II – and try to explain the successful routinization of the edict.

The slackening of the campaign started with changes in press coverage. Already in mid-September columns on quitting and shirking became less regular, as *Pravda*'s legal reporters gave more attention to the new laws on hooliganism and defective goods, and legal affairs got less coverage overall.[41] Equally important, when the press did deal with the

---

[40] Nadezhin, "Sudebnyi nadzor"; "V Maloi Vishne progulshchikov ne sudiat," *Izvestiia*, Sept. 29, 1990, 3; "V Narkomiuste SSSR," *Slu*, 1940, no. 19–20, 5; M. Avdeeva, "Sudebnaia praktika po delam o melkikh krazhakh na proizvodstve," part one, ibid., no. 10, 3–6.

[41] *Pravda*, Sept.-October 1940, passim.

edict, it was more likely to criticize excessive and foolish prosecutions than promote its enforcement. On September 29, for example, *Pravda* reported the tale of a teachers' conference in Daghestan. In the opening speech the local commissar of education called for an end to tardiness among teachers in his autonomous republic. The speech inspired one of his subordinates to compile a list of seventeen delegates who had arrived late at the conference and send it to the court! The official who made the list went on to threaten the judge: "Convict these miscreants or we will get you convicted as a 'protector of slackards.' " The "pliant judge," as *Pravda*'s correspondent put it, did convict fourteen of the persons charged (one of the acquitted had not even been a delegate, just a local teacher who had dropped in out of curiosity). The Supreme Court of the republic overturned the convictions on the ground that notices of the time of the meeting had not been delivered nor had sufficient time been allowed for the arrival of delegates from distant places. Most interesting for readers of *Pravda*, though, was the reaction of the bureau of the regional party committee. After reviewing the saga, this body censured the first secretary of the district party committee (who allegedly knew what had happened and bore responsibility for the prosecution and conviction); had the trial judge fired and given a party censure; and arranged that the educational official who had initiated the case be not only fired but also charged with a criminal offense.[42]

Less than two weeks later *Pravda* printed another cautionary tale of excessive enforcement of the edict on labor discipline. This article bore the title "Slanderers and Reinsurers" – terms that knowledgeable readers would recognize as signals for the end of the campaign. (Recall how these same epithets were used in the second part of 1938 to turn off the campaign of vigilance associated with the Great Terror.) In this particular instance, two employees of a transport office (also, as it happened, in Daghestan) had denounced their boss as a truant. The deposition stated that the director had left his office at 1:35 P.M. supposedly to visit the warehouse, but had, according to reliable sources, gone home and returned to work only at 2:45. The director explained to the court that he had gone home for lunch, to be sure later than usual because he had first to attend to pressing business. This valid explanation led the procurator to investigate the origins of the denunciation. He learned that its source was none other than the party secretary at the transport office. Not only had the secretary dictated the denunciation for others to sign, but he had organized a team of snoopers that followed the director and

---

[42] P. Iurzin, "Unter-Prishibeevy iz Kakhita," *Pravda*, Sept. 26, 1940, 2.

recorded the times of his movements. For these machinations the "slanderer" was fired and "purged from the party."[43]

In mid-October central press coverage of the edict on labor discipline all but ceased. When another story appeared in *Pravda* in December, it dealt with misuse of the edict by officials pursuing a personal vendetta. The campaign was over, and the new task was to enforce it in a balanced way.[44]

Even before the signals in the press, the USSR Supreme Court began sending the same message. At the height of the campaign Chairman Goliakov wrote in *Izvestiia*, warning that even in cases of labor infractions judges were obliged to observe trial procedures.[45] Moreover, in appellate decisions taken in August the USSR Supreme Court represented a force of moderation. However, the delay in publication of the Court's decisions assured that they became known to other judges only in the fall, after the campaign had run its course.

Some of the decisions taken by the USSR Supreme Court between August and November confirmed government prohibitions against lenient sentences, the use of suspended sentences, and treating good work records as mitigating circumstances. But other rulings rejected unfair or silly convictions rendered by trial judges during the campaign. Some of these rulings clarified when tardiness or shirking was justified and did not constitute a crime. According to the USSR Supreme Court, judges had no right to ignore medical certificates or penalize persons who left work to visit clinics. They had been wrong to convict an old man who lived alone and was too sick to go to the clinic, a doctor who

---

[43] P. Iurzin, "Klevetniki i perestrakhovshchiki," ibid., Oct. 9, 1940, 2.

[44] "Konets odnogo 'khrometrazha'," *Izvestiia*, Dec. 17, 1940, 4. In this seeming parody from real life, the chiefs of a trust office decide to check on how the head of the planning section used his work time. Two employees were assigned to sit with the top planner in his office and clock his movements. They recorded how the planner had shuffled papers and made notes from 8:00 until 8:26; and then paid a visit to the director of the trust. Only two of the ten minutes spent with the director involved work! Throughout the morning the sleuths determined that the planner had wasted time in conversations and taken smoking breaks. After three days of this sort of observation, the findings were published in a local newspaper (*Altai Trud*) and then forwarded to the court. The trial judge decided that the planner had shirked and sentenced him to five months' corrective work with a 20% deduction. (A ruling of the USSR Supreme Court had extended shirking to include wasting more than twenty minutes a day of work time.) Not surprisingly, though, the territorial court decided to stop this silly conviction, but one of the appeals court judges wrote a dissenting opinion claiming that the planner really was a truant. The RSFSR Supreme Court not only agreed to stop the case but ordered the prosecution of the timekeepers for distorting the Law of June 26 and themselves wasting work time while timing the movements of the planner.

[45] I. Goliakov, "O tekhnike sudebnogo protsesse i kachestve prigovora," *Izvestiia*, Aug. 16, 1940, 3.

arrived late at a clinic because of other medical work at the institute, and a nurse who had arrived late one morning after having spent the previous two nights caring for a sick child.[46]

The need to look after children was one of the most acceptable excuses for truancy and even quitting. The Supreme Court overturned a whole series of convictions of women juggling the demands of work and family. Thus, the Criminal Collegium quashed the case of a woman electrician who stayed home from her factory job because her child had a stomachache. Since the child could not be left unattended, it was clear, the court ruled, that no crime had been committed. Nor was it right to convict for illegal quitting a statistician who returned six weeks late from maternity leave. The delay had been occasioned by illness of the new baby and the mother's fulfillment of doctor's orders to take the child to the country and continue breastfeeding. All the same, the employer had refused to grant a petition for extended leave; a trial court had convicted the woman; and the Supreme Court of Armenia had sustained the conviction! Similarly, it was left to the Criminal Collegium of the USSR Supreme Court to overrule conviction of a woman forced to stop work by the unexpected departure of her housekeeper, leaving her alone with two small children. As it happened, the woman had only just begun the job in question, and for the one month's trial period had the right to quit. But the management had refused her request and ignored complaints from the trade union. Instead the employer pressed the case in court, the judge convicted, and the cassation panel of the Dnepropetrovsk regional court confirmed.[47]

Although these decisions corrected particular injustices perpetrated by lower courts, they did not offer judges guidelines on the application of the edict. To fill this void, Chairman of the USSR Supreme Court Goliakov invited juridical analysis of the 1940 law. Legal scholars Zinaida Vyshinskaia (the daughter of Andrei Vyshinskii) and Vladimir Menshagin responded with a pithy essay synthesizing the scattered interpretations of the government and higher courts on such matters as the meaning of truancy (e.g., it did include coming back late from lunch by twenty minutes and doing no work on the job for twenty minutes); the valid grounds for arriving late to work, eliminating criminal responsibility (physical incapacity, an accident on transport, a fire, helping a sick family member, helping an accident victim); the meaning of "guilt"

---

[46] "Sudebno-nadzornaia praktika prokurora soiuza," *SZ*, 1940, no. 11, 64–68; "Postanovleniia Plenuma Verkhovnogo Suda SSSR po otdelnym delam," *SIu*, 1940, no. 16, 39; "V Sudebno-Nadzornoi Kollegii po ugolovnym delam Verkhovnogo suda SSSR," ibid., no. 19–20, 37–43; "Sudebnaia praktika," ibid., 1941, no. 1, 24–30.

[47] Ibid., "Sudebnaia-nadzornaia praktika;" "V Sudebnoi kollegii."

(if a worker oversleeps because his roommate moved the hands of the clock, he is not guilty); and the scope of the law (it does not apply to students, soldiers, or members of collective farms).[48]

The signals in the press, interpretations of the Supreme Court, and new jurisprudence had the desired effect. In late 1940 the campaign to implement the edict of June 26, 1940, petered out and enforcement started moving onto a normal footing. The rates of prosecution began declining at once. In Belorussia prosecutions for truancy in October registered half the level of August. In the RSFSR cases started in the fourth quarter stood at 70% of the third quarter's level, and in the first part of 1941 the rate dropped more.[49] Nonetheless, overall statistical data for the USSR indicate that prosecution and conviction for illegal quitting and shirking remained common and that enforcement did not cease. Convictions for quitting in 1941 stood at 51% of the annual rate for 1940 and for shirking at 54.6%, but these figures represented more than the lower rates of enforcement per se. They also reflected the loss to the Germans in summer 1941 of a portion of the Soviet workforce and the mobilization of a sizable part of those workers most prone to prosecution for shirking and quitting. The bulk of offenders had consisted of young and inexperienced workers (often recent arrivals from the country), and the draft of summer and fall 1941 of men between 23 and 38 must have affected some of them. The decline in prosecutions for shirking continued at a gradual rate in 1942 and 1943, as more and more younger men were drafted and industry was staffed increasingly by women. Nineteen hundred forty-three registered a major drop in prosecutions for quitting, perhaps because of reduced capacity of law enforcement.[50]

Soviet commentators greeted the decline in prosecutions in early 1941 as a sign that labor discipline had actually improved. No doubt some workers did take more care to arrive on time, but the bulk of cases

---

48 Z. Vyshinskaia and V. Menshagin, "Ugolovnaia otvetsvennost za progul bez uvzhatelnoi prichiny i samovolnyi ukhod s raboty," *SZ*, 1940, no. 12, 7–13; I. Goliakov, "Borba za ditsipliny i zadachi nauki prava," *SGiP*, 1941, no. 1, 12–25. A provincial procurator criticized the Vyshinskaia and Menshagin study for requiring proof that a truant had actually slept on the job or been drunk for twenty whole minutes before allowing a qualification for "shirking." The fact of being found in such a state should be sufficient, opined the procurator. Safronov, "O primeneniiakh Ukaza 26 iiuniia 1940," *SZ*, 1941, no. 6, 67–68.

49 V. Ginzburg, "Prokuratura Belorusskoi SSR v borbe za vypolnenie Ukaza 26 iiuniia 1940 g.," *SZ*, 1941, no. 1, 32–33; A. Volin, "God borby organov Prokuratury RSFSR za vypolnenie Ukaza 26 iiuniia 1940 g.," ibid., no. 6, 9–11.

50 GARF, f.9492sch, op.6s, d.14, 11, 16; Barber and Harrison, *Soviet Home Front*, 216; "Tshchatelno, gluboko izuchaete kazhdoe delo po ukazu 26 iiuniia." *SIu*, 1940, no. 23–24, 30–32.

of truancy and shirking stemmed not from carelessness, family problems, or "watches going slow" (before the War Soviet watches were of poor quality) but from drunkenness.[51] It is hard to imagine that the threat of prosecution would have deterred and reformed unruly young workers prone to drinking.

A more plausible explanation for the decline in prosecutions was a decrease in the reporting of breaches by enterprise managers. Few of them enjoyed acting as Stalin's policemen and they cooperated with the edict only under threat of reprisals. The reprisals that managers feared depended upon procurators engaged in supervision of factories (a part of "general supervision" of the legality of public administration). City and district procuracy offices lacked the staff to inspect factories with any regularity, and even the departments of general supervision in regional procuracy offices could visit no more than a small share of the factories for which they were responsible.[52] The more factories they visited, the less thorough their inspections could be, and procurators were supposed to check for defective goods, violations of safety rules, and financial irregularities as well as the implementation of the edict of quitting and shirking. With the campaign concluded, many regional procurators chose to focus on just a few major factories, to which they paid repeated visits and where they organized "assistance groups." The procuracy of Rostov region claimed to have received eleven hundred signals of omissions by the management of enterprise from its roster of 2,000 assistants (that is, employees recruited to inform). Only sixty-three of these signals led to prosecutions. The scrutineers of the implementation of the edict in the central procuracy (who received reports from below) confirmed that the focus on major factories was common practice. They claimed to have little knowledge of the fate of the edict in "factories of republican and local subordination."[53]

---

51 K. Gorshenin, "Ukaz v deistvii," *Izvestiia*, July 26, 1940, 3; "Tshchatelno, gluboko izuchaete"; Ginzburg, "Prokuratura Belorusskoi SSR."
52 According to official counts, procuracy officials inspected over 50,000 factories in the second half of 1940 and over 40,000 in the first quarter of 1941. (P. Kudriavtsev, "Iz praktiki nadzora za vypoleniem Ukaza 26 iiuniia 1940 g.," *SZ*, 1941, no. 6, 12–15.) If there had been 500 procurators working on general supervision in the USSR at that time, this would have meant a load of 200 factories per procuracy official in 1940 and 320 in 1941. The average visit would have consisted of one day, during which time the officials would have been expected to check for defective goods production, violations of financial discipline, and breaches of labor safety, as well as the state of labor discipline. Even officials of experience and skills would have had difficulty doing all of these jobs well, but fully half of procuracy officials performing general supervision were new and inexperienced.
53 Kudriavtsev, "Iz praktiki nadzora;" Volin, "God borby"; "Republikanskoe soveshchanie prokurorov po obshchemu nadzora," *SZ*, 1941, no. 5, 34–38.

As the pressure subsided, judges also found ways to mute the harshness of the edict of June 26, 1940. Even at the height of the campaign more than 20% of their sentences fell outside the norms; with the pressure off, this share increased. Moreover, judges started to acquit more persons accused of labor infractions. By 1941 the rate of acquittals in these cases averaged 25%, more than double the rate for other offenses. Many of these acquittals reflected the failure of factory officials to provide the documents on their employees' misdeeds. According to procurators, judges relished finding technical excuses.[54]

All the same, prosecutions for shirking and quitting continued in large numbers. Even with the reduced rates of enforcement, in each of 1943, 1944, and 1945, more than a million convictions were registered (mostly for shirking); and in 1945, convictions according to the edict still represented 51.1% of all criminal convictions in the USSR.[55] How can one explain the successful routinization of the edict of June 26, 1940?

The edict of June 26 outlived its campaign for three reasons. First, after the simplifications introduced by the leadership after the first month the edict became easy to enforce. Factory staff could supply judges with materials of the cases, and judges process them quickly. To be sure, quitters who left town or went into hiding could and did escape conviction, and factory officials chose to overlook many shirkers. But, enforcement of the edict was feasible. Second, at least for some managers and judges the consequences of failing to enforce the edict remained serious. The managers at least of larger and strategic factories still faced prosecution for failing to comply (as did managers of any factory who fell into conflicts with local political bosses). And, in punishing shirkers and quitters, judges had to meet the expectations of their superiors and maintain the appropriate indicators. Third, and most important, the outbreak of War gave the edict a new rationale. The country went onto emergency footing as most physically capable men were drafted and women entered the factories in large numbers. The whole civilian or "home" front was mobilized to join the defense of the country, and in this context the edict made sense. At the same time, a series of further edicts extended the demand for work discipline to collective farmworkers, construction workers, and students in trade schools. Once the War was over, though, the edict of June 26, 1940, had a checkered existence. Prosecutions for shirking dropped steadily in the postwar period, as managers saw less reason to comply and justice officials lobbied behind the scenes for the decriminalization of shirking. (Partial decriminaliza-

---

[54] Ginzburg, "Prokuratura Belorusskoi SSR"; Volin, "God borby."
[55] GARF, f.9492sch, op. 6s, d.14 (Statistika sudimosti) and my calculations. See also Popov, "Gosudarstvennyi terror," 23.

tion came in 1951 and is discussed in Chapter 12.) Prosecutions for
illegal quitting did make a revival in the late 1940s, but this reflected
both the interest of managers in retaining workers at a time of severe
shortage and the regime's policy of keeping the labor force in place
during the postwar reconstruction.[56]

The legacy of the criminalization of labor infractions for the administration of justice was not a happy one. Simplified procedures were
necessary for legal officials to handle the new caseload, but they hurt
the larger effort to strengthen the regularity and fairness of judicial
decisions. Moreover, in extending the criminal sanction beyond its normal uses, the edict generated erratic and inconsistent enforcement, after
as well as during the campaign. Once the pressure of the campaign had
ended, many managers ignored the law or found ways to evade it while
others, especially in closely watched enterprises, even overprosecuted.
How the courts handled these cases proved equally inconsistent, as
some judges punished to the hilt while others mitigated the edict's
severity. The edict of June 26, 1940, demonstrated that the Stalin program for improving the administration of justice did not deter the
leader from pursuing a criminal policy detrimental to that goal.

Another question is whether the criminalization of shirking and
quitting led to a reduction in these phenomena. There is no way to
know for the Stalinist leadership took this as a matter of faith and never
tried to determine the impact of the edict on labor discipline.[57]

The other campaigns

The criminalization of labor infractions was only part of Stalin's program to raise industrial productivity in preparation for war. In the same
summer of 1940, the leader issued two further edicts, one that raised
punishment for the production of defective or substandard goods (from
"up to five years" imprisonment to "five to eight years") and the other,
as we have seen, setting new minimum punishments of one year in
prison for petty theft in factories and for hooliganism.[58] Each of these
three changes generated its own campaign, and authorities found it
difficult to manage them along with the campaign to punish quitters

56 See the edicts of Dec. 28, 1940, Dec. 26, 1941, and Feb. 13, 1942, in Goliakov, *Sbornik dokumentov*, 410, 417–18; GARF f.9492sch, op.6s, d.14.
57 Khlevniuk, "26 iiuniia 1940 goda," 94.
58 "Ob otvetstvennosti za vypusk nedobrokachestvennoi ili nekomplektnoi produktsii i za nesobliudenie obizatelnykh standartov promyshlennymi predpriatiami," Ukaz Prez. Verkh. Soveta SSSR ot 10 iiulia 1940 g., in Goliakov, *Sbornik dokumentov*, 406; "Ob ugolovnoi otvetstvennosti za melkie krazhi na proizvodstve i za khuliganstvo," Ukaz Prez. Verkh. Soveta SSSR ot 10 Avgusta 1940 g., ibid., 407–408.

and shirkers. More striking, though, was the leaders' failure to ensure that the changes introduced by these edicts had lasting effect. In the case of the edict on defective goods, this was understandable. The opponents of prosecution of managers for defective goods production were so powerful that even the campaign to promote this edict proved a failure. Arguably, serious prosecution for this offense was not feasible. The higher punishments prescribed for petty theft and hooliganism, however, might well have had important lasting effects, had the enforcers of that edict – factory managers, police, and judges alike – not muted its impact in the course of implementation. Here was an instance – not the first one that we have encountered – in which the enforcers of a law shaped, even distorted, its impact, as they adjusted it to their own sense of fair play. Higher authorities had failed to supply reason or incentive for them to act otherwise.

The previous law on defective goods (from 1934) had produced few cases (as we saw in Chapter 4), and more of them had collapsed at trial. By 1939 that law was rarely enforced.[59] The edict of July 10, 1940, challenged procurators to develop cases of production of defective goods against managers at the same time as they came under pressure to prosecute managers who had failed to report quitting and shirking by their employees. Under the circumstances, the procurators delivered few cases of defective goods to the courts, and even these cases lacked proper evidence.[60] Moreover, in 1940, judges were insisting upon clear demonstration of the causal links between the production of substandard goods and the actions or omissions of the officials charged. As a result, judges acquitted many of the accused "for lack of proof" or "because the amount of the defects in the goods was small," and they returned other cases for supplementary investigations "to establish objective connections." In so doing, trial judges at the regional courts were following the guidelines supplied by the USSR Supreme Court in 1939 that demanded high standards of proof in cases of economic and state crimes – guidelines that had helped to reduce the flow of inflated and weak charges from the purge period.[61] Trial judges were also responding to the concerns of provincial party bosses to ensure the protection of their clients. One wonders how often the legal justifications supplied by judges for acquittals masked deference to their patrons or local political masters.

---

[59] "O praktike primenenii zakona ot 8 dekabriia 1933 g.," *SZ*, 1939, no. 7, 105–106.
[60] "Vazhneishie zadachi organov prokuratury," *SZ*, 1940, no. 10, 1–6; K. L'vov, "Organy prokuratury v borbe s vypuskom nedobrokachestvennoi . . . produktsii," ibid., 6–9; "Ukaz 10 iiuliia 1940 g.," ibid., no. 12, 14–18.
[61] "O kvalifikatsii prestuplenii," *SZ*, 1939, no. 10–11, 15.

For judges to frustrate policymakers by applying the letter of the law made delicious irony. To a politically attuned member of the USSR Supreme Court who reviewed judicial practice in these cases it made no sense. Why was it, the scrutineer wondered, that trial judges worried so much about objective proof and causal connection? If the goods were defective, they were defective, and managers had to bear responsibility and blame. It was as simple as that. Could not judges understand the spirit and intent of Stalin's new law?[62]

The campaign against defective goods limped on until the outbreak of World War II. Although it produced a handful of celebrated cases against officials in important factories (such as the Moscow cable company), most prosecutions focused on managers of local industry, especially food. Few of these cases ended in convictions.[63] During and after the War, prosecutions of managers for defective goods became rare. Although feasible, such cases were difficult for procuracy investigators to prepare and often politically risky as well. Unless local party bosses sanctioned the prosecutions, they could not be pursued without procuracy officials themselves risking trouble. Like the earlier laws on defective goods, the edict of 1940 had largely symbolic meaning.

The edict of August 10, 1940, setting a minimum term of one year's imprisonment for petty theft in factories and for hooliganism, was designed to stop workers from using those acts to get fired from jobs that they wanted to quit. Reinforcing the edict on labor infractions, the new edict on petty theft and hooliganism demanded a sharp increase in repression. In the previous year, less than two-thirds of convictions for hooliganism had produced custodial sanctions (the average for the previous four years was 62.9%). Of persons convicted of ordinary (not petty) theft of state property during 1937–1940, 60.7% had received terms of imprisonment. The figure for persons convicted of theft of personal property was 45%.[64] Moreover, the bulk of less serious incidents of hooliganism and theft had not led to criminal prosecution at all. Since 1928 *petty* hooliganism had constituted an administrative rather than a criminal offense and been subject to a fine imposed in administrative proceeding. The same had applied to any theft valued

---

[62] "Borba s vypuskom nedobrokachestvennoi produktsii/Besedy s sudebnymi rabotnikami," *SIu*, 1941, no. 7, 3–6.

[63] L'vov, "Organy prokuratury"; "Vypusk nestandartnoi produktsii," *SIu*, 1941, no. 3, 23–24.

[64] "Sudebnaia praktika po delam o khuliganstve," *SIu*, 1939, no. 12, 25–29; "Statisticheskee dannye," 30–31; GARF(TsGA) f.353, op.13, d.4 (Stenogramma respublikanskogo soveshchaniia rukovodiashchikh rabotnikov iustitsiiu RSFSR i materialy k soveshchaniiu ot 9 aprela 1941), 47–70.

under fifteen rubles. As a result, the new edict threatened not only more severe punishments but also a flood of criminal prosecutions where they had not previously occurred. To ensure that judges delivered the severe minimum sentences against all persons convicted, the USSR Supreme Court immediately forbade judges from giving sentences below the minimum and suspended sentences to either hooligans or petty thieves.[65]

To speed up conviction of these miscreants, Stalin also ordered simplified inquiries and rapid processing of cases. For hooliganism cases pretrial inquiries by the police (always less thorough than investigations) were to be replaced by the compiling of a short protocol (with the names and addresses of the person arrested, the victim and any witnesses). Police were to forward the protocols directly to the courts, and trials were to be held within *two* days (in large cities at a special courtroom). By analogy, factory guards who apprehended an employee with stolen goods were to prepare a similar protocol and trial was to follow within two days.[66] Here too was a situation of considerable irony. These new regulations established the kind of simplified procedures that Nikolai Krylenko had repeatedly advocated and for whose advocacy he had been denounced and repressed. Yet not two years after Krylenko's physical demise Stalin and Vyshinskii introduced simplified procedures (for hooliganism, petty theft in factories, and the labor infractions) without fanfare or ideological spin, simply to implement Stalin's latest repressive urge.

Prosecution of each of the offenses targeted in the August edict began with a campaign. For a couple of months factory authorities generated a rash of prosecutions against pilferers. The quality of the evidence supplied was shoddy and the rate of acquittals in these cases double the normal levels. As in other campaigns, judges were disoriented by the pressure and acted in inconsistent ways. Thus, while some judges convicted accused persons for trifles (for example, the case of a worker who used sheets of paper from his factory to wrap his cold feet under his socks), other judges padded their conviction rates under the new law by qualifying more serious incidents as "petty" theft. Predictably, after two months the rate of prosecution for petty theft dropped precipitously, as

---

[65] See Chapter 2; V. Tadevosian, "Ukaz 10 avgusta 1940 i nashi zadachi," *SZ*, 1940, no. 9, 26–28. *Sbornik deistvuiushchikh postanovlenii Plenuma i direktivnykh pisem Verkhovnogo Suda SSSR 1924–1944 gg.* (Moscow, 1946), 8.

[66] "O poriadke napravleniia v sudy i sudebnom rassmotrenii del o khuliganstve," Prikaz NKIusta SSSR, NKVD SSSR i Prokuratury SSSR No. 111/786/200 ot 6 sent.1940, *SIu*, 1940, No. 17–18, 4; Postanovlenie SNK SSSR No. 1679, "O poriadke rassmotreniia del o krazhakh na predpriiatiiakh i uchrezhdeniiakh," ot 13 sent. 1940, ibid., 3.

the campaign subsided and many factories ceased delivering their pilferers to court.[67]

Factory management and judges alike soon developed their own
ways of enforcing the edict on petty theft in factories. Often factory
officials gave warnings or reprimands for the first, even second offenses, and sent only the repeaters to court. As a result, during the War
years convictions for petty theft averaged only 60,000 per year (about
7% of the total for crimes other than labor infractions). Moreover, from
mid-War if not earlier judges resumed sentencing petty thieves to both
suspended sentences and corrective work (as a sentence below the
minimum), even though the edict required imprisonment and the Supreme Court had forbade any softening of its provisions. It was easy to
rationalize such conduct, since the other parts of the article on theft in
the Russian criminal code (Article 162) had not been adjusted to Stalin's
demand for prison terms for petty theft in factories, and persons guilty
of more serious thefts still received noncustodial sanctions. By 1944
noncustodial sanctions for petty theft in factories had become widespread; they were awarded to 42% of convicts in Moscow, 63% in
Vladimir region, and 68% in Kostroma region.[68] In fact, punishments
for all kinds of theft, including petty, had reverted to prewar levels and
would remain there until the issuance of the draconian edicts of June 4,
1947 (see Chapter 12). It appears that judges took this line of action on
their own, without open encouragement from judicial officials in the
center. However, the absence of criticism on their part suggests a kind
of tacit approval. Apart from a natural inclination to revert to normal
standards in sentencing, judges may have reacted to the feminization of

---

[67] Z. Ioffe, "Putaniki iz Dnepropetrovskogo oblastnogo suda," *Slu*, 1941, no. 19, 22; P.
Nadezhzhin, "Ukaz 10 avgusta v deistvii," *SZ*, 1941, no. 3, 26–28; M. Avdeeva, "Sudebnaia praktika po delam o melkikh krazhakh na proizvodstve," in 2 parts: *Slu*, 1941,
no. 10, 3–6 and ibid., no. 11, 7–9; Kozhevnikov, "Puti razvitii sovetskoi prokuratury,"
102.

[68] I. Sapozhnikov, "Borba s khishcheniiami na predpriiatiakh tekstilnoi promyshlennosti," *SZ*, 1945, no. 3, 25–28; GARF, f. 9492sch, op.6s, d.14.

Compare Article 162, part e, "petty theft, independent of its size, committed at a
factory or institution" – which merited one year of prison "unless its character called
for a more serious punishment" – with Article 162, g, "theft committed by a private
person from state or public warehouses, railroad cars, ships and other storage sites or
in places of public use, using technical means or by agreement with other persons, or
more than once, and equally committed without these conditions by a person with
special access to these warehouses or assigned to guard them or during a fire, flood, or
other public disaster" – which called for deprivation of freedom up to two years *or
corrective work for a term up to one year*. *Ugolovnyi kodeks RSFSR* (Moscow, 1948), 82.
(Note that this edition prints the edicts of June 4, 1947, separately. It does not incorporate them into the code, even though they took precedence over Article 162.)

the industrial labor force. From 1942 women held over 50% of industrial jobs; and as of 1944 they represented 43% of all persons convicted of ordinary (not petty) theft of state property.[69]

Judges may also have taken into account the general mood of liberalization during the later part of the War. But their failure to impose more serious sentences after the War, until the theft laws of 1947 made the offense "petty theft in factories" obsolete, suggests that they were dancing to their own tune.

Stiffer enforcement of the prohibition against petty theft in factories and stiffer punishments were feasible, but neither factory officials nor judges were inclined to deliver them. Many managers preferred not to lose workers to the prisons, and at least some judges shunned assigning to petty thieves harsher sentences than they were giving to ordinary ones. In the absence of pressing reasons to comply with the edict the enforcers of petty theft in the factories adjusted law to practice rather than the other way around.

The campaign against hooliganism of late summer and fall 1940 had more dramatic effects than the campaign against petty theft in factories. The rate of prosecution for hooliganism increased three- or fourfold (producing a yearly total for 1940 as a whole nearly double that of 1939).[70] There were good reasons why the prosecution of hooliganism proved so responsive to the pressures of a campaign. For one thing, the enforcers of the law were not disinterested amateurs (like factory security or management) but the police themselves. For another, hooliganism – that is "mischievous conduct accompanied by clear disrespect for society" – overlapped with both other offenses in the criminal code and a number of administrative infractions. Thus, hooliganism could easily encompass incidents subject to qualification as "delivering insults" or "inflicting minor bodily blows" (if not assault itself), and judicial policy was inconsistent.[71] In 1939 the USSR Supreme Court issued an explanation (after lengthy discussion at a plenary session) warning against the misuse of the charge of hooliganism in situations where personal conflicts were played out in public places. As a result of the Court's ruling, the number of prosecutions for hooliganism in the USSR dropped by one-third during 1939. During the hooliganism campaign of 1940 police and judges alike chose to ignore the Supreme

---

[69] Barber and Harrison, *The Soviet Home Front, 1941–1945*, 216. GARF, f. 9492sch., op.6s, d.14, 19.

[70] Ibid., d.14, 14.

[71] R. Eidovitskii, "Praktika provedeniia v zhizn Ukazov 26 iuniia i 10 avgusta v Voronezhskoi oblasti," *SZ*, 1940, no. 12, 48–49; "Soveshchanie aktiva NKIu RSFSR," *SIu*, 1940, no. 23–15; Ianovskii, "Usilit borby s khuliganstvom," *SZ*, 1940, no. 5, 58–60.

bected by their superiors. Those expectations could change,
he postwar period when top judicial officials themselves
br the decriminalization of shirking, they relaxed their demand
application of the edict's provisions on shirking. But neither
lopment nor the partial decriminalization of shirking in 1951
pter 12) deprives the edict of its place in the history of Soviet
justice as one of the most dramatic attempts to use the criminal
new purposes, thereby increasing and extending the net of
on. The impact of the edict on the courts outlasted the threat
osed for the average worker.

Court directive, and returned to qualifying personal attacks as hooliganism.[72]

The crime of hooliganism could also be confused with the administrative offenses of petty hooliganism and public drunkenness, misdeeds that produced summary convictions and sometimes police fines on the spot. In the rush to meet campaign quotas, police prosecuted as crimes incidents that they would previously have treated as administrative violations or even ignored. Thus, in Moscow, police brought charges of hooliganism for refusing to pay a fine on a tram, jumping off a moving train, walking down a street drunk, singing a song on the street, and throwing water on the floor of a cafeteria.[73] But police conduct was far from consistent, and many patrolmen and police chiefs continued to exercise personal discretion. Thus, police refused to pursue potential cases on such grounds as "lack of harmful consequences," that the miscreant had "no criminal record," or that "he was a party member and drunk."[74]

In the rush of the campaign, police also made many errors. They qualified as ordinary hooliganism incidents that deserved the charge of malicious hooliganism. Often, they failed to supply judges with evidence, for example writing on the protocol that the accused had "uttered uncensored obscenities" and then appearing in court as the only witnesses.[75] Trial judges reacted unpredictably, sometimes acquitting for lack of evidence, other times convicting the accused and leaving appeals judges the task of overruling their decisions.[76]

Narkomiust began signaling the end of the hooliganism campaign in early 1941, and the rate of hooliganism convictions dropped quickly.[77] Almost every person convicted of hooliganism during the campaign received a term of imprisonment (96.7% in the RSFSR fourth quarter of 1940 versus 63.9% in the first half of 1940) and this pattern appears to

[72] K. Cherniavskii and B. Kleiner, "Usilit borbu s khuliganstvom," *SZ*, 1952, no. 4, 35–38. Official statistics for the USSR recorded a drop in court convictions for bodily blows (ordinary and light) of 12,000 between 1939 and 1940 – a figure that can account for 13% of the rise in convictions for hooligans in 1940. GARF, f.9492, op.6s, d.14, 16.

[73] "Soveshchanie aktiva NKIu RSFSR," 11; I. Afanasev, "Oshibki v rabote po vypolneniiu Ukaza 10 avgusta 1940 g.," *SZ*, 1940, no. 12, 53–55; M. Isaev, "Sudebnaia praktika po delam o khuliganstve," part 1: *SIu*, 1941, no. 12, 4–6; part 2: ibid., no. 13.

[74] I. Kaganovich, "Borba s khuliganstvom v Moskve," *SZ*, 1940 no. 10, 14–19.

[75] E. Boitsov, "Nadzor prokurora za vypolnenii Ukaza 10 avgusta 1940 g.," *SZ*, 1941, no. 2, 14–16; Afanaev, "Oshibki v rabote"; "V sudebnykh organakh Moskvy," *SIu*, 1941, no. 6, 17.

[76] O. Britkevich and S. Lifshits, "Sudebnye dela o khuliganstve," *SIu*, 1941, no. 18–19; "Soveshchanie aktiva NKIu RSFSR."

[77] Isaev, "Sudebnaia praktika po delam o khuliganstve," part two; "Khuliganstvo menshchaetsia," *SIu*, 1941, no. 8, 16.

have continued in 1941. However, by 1942 enforcement of hooliganism had returned to prewar norms.[78]

First of all, the year 1942 registered an extraordinary drop in the number of cases of hooliganism. The annual figure for 1942 stood at 17% of that for 1941; and it would drop further in 1943, before starting a slow climb through the postwar years. One reason was demographic. Together, the loss of territories to German invaders and the mobilization of young men to the front removed from the jurisdiction of civilian police and courts in the USSR a large share of the persons who had engaged in rowdy, drunken conduct in public. Moreover, with many in this age cohort killed during the War, it would take some years for hooliganism cases to return to their prewar share of criminal caseload. Another reason for the drop in hooliganism cases was the return in police and judicial practice of the charge of "light bodily blows" in place of hooliganism. Trends in official statistics and postwar criticism of the enforcement of hooliganism provisions indicate that this shift occurred.[79]

Second, once the pressure was off, judges shied away from awarding terms of prison to almost every person whom they convicted of hooliganism. Using the familiar resources provided by the criminal code – suspended sentences and sentences below the legal limit – judges in Sverdlovsk region in 1945 assigned noncustodial sanctions to 43% of persons convicted of ordinary hooliganism and 12% of those convicted of serious (or qualified) hooliganism. Combined, these figures yield an overall rate of imprisonment of 67%. Data for the USSR as a whole suggest that the level of imprisonment for hooliganism found in Sverdlovsk typified the USSR as a whole from 1942 on.[80] After World War II sentencing for hooliganism became more severe, producing an average rate of imprisonment for 1946–1952 of 86.7%. There were, however, far

[78] GARF, f.353, op.13, d.4, 70.

[79] GARF, f. 9492sch. op.6s, d.14, 14–16; Barber and Harrison, *The Soviet Home Front*, chap. 9; Cherniavksii and Kleiner, "Usilit borby." In 1942 convictions for minor assault stood at 41% of the 1941 level, while convictions for hooliganism had fallen to 17%. (My calculations based on "Statistika sudimosti.")

[80] My calculation assumes that one-third of convictions were for the more serious form of hooliganism (Article 74, part two). GARF, f.353, op.13, d.580 (Protokol oblastnogo soveshchaniia narodnykh sudei Sverdlovskoi oblasti, sostoiavsheevsia 23–27 ianvaria 1946 g. v Sverdlovske), 13. GARF, f. 9492sch. op.6s, d.14, 31, reports an average for 1940–1945 of 84.5% imprisonment for hooliganism convictions. If one assumes that sentencing during 1941 remained at the level of 95% custodial sentences that was reached at the end of 1940, and subtracts out the first seven months of 1940, when the rate of imprisonment stood at 64%, then the average for 1942–1945 would stand at 68–69% imprisonment. These assumptions and calculations leave room for a more gradual drop in the share of custodial sanctions during 1941.

---

fewer such convicts than there had bee[...] to the continuing shortfall of young me[...] increased their use of alternative charge[...] delivering insults. Under pressure to gi[...] hooligans, police and judges reacted by [...] less serious incidents with charges that a[...] custodial response.[82]

The readiness of police and judges to s[...] punishment for hooliganism, especially th[...] understandable. They could have acted othe[...] young men to prison, but such a response [...] sense of the gravity of many incidents, espe[...] time offenders which did not have serious[...] political leaders nor top judicial officials sho[...] adjustment in practice, and judges could rea[...] approval. The shortage of young men in warti[...] may have justified the tendency by law enforcei[...] lenience toward some young troublemakers.

It is worth noting the contrast between the l[...] edict on hooliganism and petty theft in factories[...] ting and shirking, both of them products of sum[...] judges used their discretion in charging and sen[...] effects of the former, but they could not prevent the[...] pain on many persons not normally affected by [...] adding significantly to the work of the courts. Both[...] charged with enforcing the edict of June 26, 1940, a[...] the edict, at least its provisions relating to shirking,[...] around it, but many of them complied with it all the[...] of reprisal at least for managers of important factorie[...] and the development of a separate and detailed syst[...] and reporting data on cases of shirking and quitting kep[...] able to reprisals should they fail to deliver the convictio[...]

[81] The number of convictions for hooliganism averaged 73,000 per ye[...] compared with 152,621 and 140,167, recorded respectively in 1938 an[...] 9492sch, op.6s, d.14, 14, 21–22, 31.

[82] Whereas between 1946 and 1950 the rate of convictions for hooliganisn[...] constant (rising from 69,789 to 71,907), convictions for light bodily blov[...] (from 39,299 to 58,700) and for insults (and slander) more than doublec[...] to 55,802). Ibid., 14–16.

[83] One may discount convenience as a reason for the tendency of police to u[...] charges. Prosecution of charges of "light bodily blows" and "delivering[...] quired more paperwork than did prosecution of hooliganism using the[...] procedures.

334   C[...]

ments ex[...] and in t[...] pressed f[...] for stern[...] this dev[...] (see Cha[...] crimina[...] law for[...] repress[...] that it [...]

PART IV

The Stalinist synthesis

10 Molding legal officials for careers: the effects of education for service

Since 1936 Stalin had pursued a policy of encouraging legal officials to acquire legal education and make careers in the legal agencies. This process was interrupted first by the Great Purge and then by World War II, as large numbers of officials left their posts and were replaced by newcomers. As a result, in 1945 the educational profile of procurators, investigators, and judges did not differ from that in 1936. In the first year after the War the legal agencies resumed their efforts to involve legal officials in educational programs, but Stalin and his colleagues lost patience with the slow pace of change. In October 1946 they announced a new program for making legal officials into jurists. A resolution of the Central Committee of the CPSU obliged all legal officials who lacked higher legal education to enroll in secondary or higher education, usually by correspondence. The resolution also provided for an expansion of full-time day legal education, at both levels, to provide a "stream of young specialists" ready for absorption into the legal agencies.[1]

By Stalin's death in March 1953 this program had yielded significant results. Nearly one-third of legal officials had completed higher legal education and most of the rest secondary level training in law. By 1956 nearly half of legal officials had higher legal education; and by the mid-1960s the recruitment of nonlawyers was rare.[2]

On one level, the legacy of Stalin's program to educate legal officials is clear. In the USSR after his death the administration of justice was performed by jurists. The question is what kind of jurists? Officials of the courts and the procuracy remained overwhelmingly members of the

[1] RTsKhIDNI, f.17, op.116, d. 227 (O rasshirenii i ulushchenii iuridicheskogo obrazovaniia v strane), 4–8, and op.118, d.644, 98–102.
[2] A. Mishutin, "Postoianno ulushchit podbor, rasstanovku, i vospitanie prokurursko-sledvennykh kadrov," ibid., 1956, no. 1, 7–16; "Pravilno organizovat rabotu po podboru i vospitanie narodnykh sudei," *SIu*, 1957, no. 8, 3–6; GARF, f.8131, op.28, d.1383, 1.29.

party and upwardly mobile representatives of the working and peasant classes. The education that they received gave them some knowledge of the law, and, I shall argue, increased capacity to observe procedural and evidentiary rules. But legal education through correspondence – the education received by most legal officials – did not draw them into a legal profession (along with other kinds of jurists). Nor did this education instill in them a commitment to the legal process or legality that might enable them to resist bureaucratic and political pressures at work. In fact, to the extent that newly acquired legal education encouraged investigators, procurators, and judges to make careers in the legal agencies, that education helped to produce a more pliant and conformist corps of officials. In short, the expansion of legal education for officials of the procuracy and court contributed more to the bureaucratization than to the professionalization of Soviet legal officials.

This chapter begins by examining the new program of legal education and its place in the careers of legal officials. It goes on to consider the relationship between legal education and the observance of procedural rules. I shall argue that, while legal education did bring a decline in procedural mistakes, it did not eliminate the penchant of legal officials in the USSR to find and use shortcuts. In the absence of a strong commitment to legality, shortcuts, informal practices, and even abuses (such as forced confessions) represented a natural response to political and bureaucratic pressures. In the next chapter we shall examine how those pressures evolved in the postwar period and shaped the administration of criminal justice in the USSR for many years after Stalin.

Education for service

World War II produced yet another crisis in legal cadres. Many of the young investigators and judges appointed in 1939–1941 to fill vacancies left by the Purge had left for the front and most of them had not returned to their posts. Procuracy and courts alike had to recruit new staff and drew, out of necessity, upon demobilized members of the armed forces, especially soldiers who had joined the Communist party during the War. Largely from simple backgrounds and with education interrupted by the War, most of the recruits lacked legal training and many had not even completed secondary school.[3] To be sure, the new cohort of legal officials did not differ in its profile from earlier ones, but its low quality disappointed central legal officials and politicians. Since 1936 they had promoted education for legal officials and planned the expansion of higher legal education as well.

3 Interviews.

After the War the legal agencies resumed the promotion of legal training for their officials. In December 1945, for example, Narkomiust issued a directive to regional procuracy offices and the judicial administrations to identify which of their officials failed to study properly. Many had registered for legal correspondence education but had neither studied nor showed up for the exams. Later in the month, Narkomiust representatives explained at a meeting of the directors of the juridical schools, a large number of the correspondence students (*zaochniki*) would be kicked out of school and many would then lose their posts as well. In addition to clearing the dead souls out of the registers of the correspondence schools, Narkomiust officials promised to schedule the exams at another time of the year. Many students had failed to appear for September exams because they coincided with the harvest campaigns! In addition, the procurator-general directed regional procuracy offices to summon their subordinates to the exams with special documents (*otnoshennii*) signed by the regional procurator and the director of the juridical school, and required that each procuracy employee who failed to appear provide a written explanation to the department of cadres of the regional procuracy.[4]

Even these special measures proved insufficient to convince many legal officials to take their education seriously. All too common among judges and procuracy officials was a disdain for legal education. A consultant on correspondence education to the Sverdlovsk justice administration reported in 1946 that many judges in his region had a bad attitude toward studying. "Why do I need to study? It is not I alone who does not study, but all of us do not study." Such was the typical response to his questions. This attitude – even more than the difficulties of the War – he believed, accounted for the slow pace of legal training of legal officials.[5]

Only pressure from the top, it appeared, could jump start the development of legal education and move it off its sluggish path. Early in summer 1946 Stalin and his colleagues decided to act, and the result was the Central Committee resolution of October 5, 1946. No doubt their decision was prompted in part by the simple desire to have educated legal officials, a goal that they had adopted ten years earlier. At the same time, the urgency of the push to educate legal officials after World War II suggested some additional concern on the part of Soviet leaders. It may well be that Stalin and the other leaders of the Great Power that the Soviet Union had become found the performance of the

4 GARF (TSGA), f.353, op.13, d.580 (Protokol oblastnogo soveshchaniia narodnykh sudei Sverdlovskoi oblasti, sostoiavshegosia 23–27 ianvaria 1946 g. v g. Sverdlovske), 63–65.
5 Ibid., 77.

justice agencies embarrassing. If this were the case, the conversion of legal officials from semicompetent amateurs to educated professionals was necessary not only to improve the actual administration of justice but also to make it presentable to the outside world. Appearances always mattered to Stalin, but never more than in the postwar years, when the USSR assumed its new role in world affairs.

At the order of Secretary Andrei Zhdanov, five staff members of the Central Committee administrations for propaganda and cadres conducted an inquiry into the state of legal education, and on August 5, 1946, they delivered to Zhdanov a report and a draft resolution of the Central Committee. The rapporteurs stressed the extreme shortage of lawyers for both the legal agencies and public administration and noted that lawyers represented the only educational specialty that did not yield more graduates than in tsarist times. To address this deficiency the draft resolution that they compiled called for a major expansion of higher legal education, to be aided by the opening of new law faculties and publishing of textbooks, and the establishment of a one-year apprenticeship for graduates of higher legal education in the courts and procuracy. On August 28 the Orgburo of the CPSU reviewed the draft resolution and formed an editorial commission, whose members included the heads of the legal agencies as well as members of the original inquiry. Zhdanov's main charge to the editorial commission was to make the resolution more specific – for example, to specify which posts in the legal agencies should require higher legal education right away. Reporting back to the Orgburo one week later, the commission offered a strikingly different draft. Although little of the substance changed, the tone of the resolution was sharpened so that it read like an important, rather than a routine, document. For the first time, the resolution called raising the educational standards of legal officials a "top priority" (*vazhneishaia zadacha*) for both the Ministry of Justice (the Commissariat of Justice renamed) and the Ministry of Higher Education. Following Zhdanov's directions, the resolution included a detailed list of positions to which only persons with higher legal education (or, on occasion, secondary legal preparation and long experience in the legal agencies) could be appointed. The resolution no longer "suggested," it now "obliged" the Ministry of Higher Education and the legal research institutions to produce textbooks on demand. And, the resolution blamed Minister of Justice Rychkov for past failures to transform legal education.[6]

The commission's version of the resolution, with minor changes, was approved a month later at another meeting of the Orgburo. While the resolution remained unpublished, a detailed summary did appear in

6 RTsKhIDNI, f.17, op.117, d.636, 92–101; op.116, d.274, 2; d.644, 105–114.

the journal of the USSR Procuracy and Ministry of Justice. The resolution's importance was underscored by the frequent and urgent checks on its implementation conducted by Central Committee officials in the months and years to come.[7]

The Central Committee resolution of October 5, 1946, called, first of all, for a dramatic increase in the production of jurists, in part to work in the courts and procuracy. The intake of students into higher legal education was set to rise to 6,000 per year, nearly triple the level of 1946 and well above the record enrollment of 1937. Even if some failed to complete their studies, far more lawyers would graduate in 1951 than the 749 of 1946 and the prewar high of 800. Some of these students would study at five new law faculties. More would pursue their degrees through the enlarged network of legal correspondence centers. The resolution envisaged a comparable expansion of the secondary legal schools, whose two-year programs prepared high school graduates for jobs in the procuracy and courts. In particular, secondary legal education by correspondence gained extra support. Finally, the resolution established new remedial courses for legal officials who could get released from their jobs temporarily. To train teachers of law the decree authorized an increase in the number of graduate students studying law and a crash program in the writing and publishing of textbooks.[8]

In addition to ordering the expansion of legal education (and the involvement of all legal officials in it), the resolution of the Central Committee called for an improvement in its quality. The decree spoke of the need to prepare "jurists of a broad profile and jurists specializing in international relations and the structure of Soviet government and public administration." These brave words parroted the views of those legal scholars who before the War had promoted broad-gauged legal education (see Chapter 8) and to a degree the position taken in 1944 by Ivan Goliakov, Chairman of the USSR Supreme Court. To be a good judge with the capacity for independent action, wrote Goliakov, required not only knowledge of the law in the narrow sense but also having (in the words of Koni, the prerevolutionary judge and scholar) "a wise and deep education, including acquaintance with the history of art and literature." Of all people Goliakov had a right to call for humanistic education; he himself knew Russian and world literature well. Later on, he would write a series of articles and a book on repre-

[7] Ibid., f.17, op.116, d.277, 4–8; d.283, 88; d.291, 61–64; d.293, 10; op.117, d.691, 65–71. The published summary appeared as "O rasshirenii i ulushchenii iuridicheskogo obrazovaniia v strane," V TsK KPSS, SZ 1946, no. 11–12, 13–14.
[8] RTsKhIDNI, f.17, op.116, d.277, 4–8; "O rasshirenii i ulushchenii;" "Za rasshirenie i ulushchenie iuridicheskogo obrazovaniia," SZ, 1946, no. 12, 15–18.

sentations of courts and judges in European and Russian literature. Goliakov was not alone in citing the words of Koni. At a conference of judges in Sverdlovsk, Narkomiust official G.Z. Anashkin (a future member of the USSR Supreme Court) quoted the same passage in support of a broad legal education.[9]

While a broad, and even humanistic, legal education had its proponents, most of the top legal officials still preferred a more practically oriented training, legal education designed to remedy the deficiencies in the technical skills of legal officials. By and large, legal education of that narrow profile was the education that those legal officials would obtain. As we shall see, most legal officials, and particularly those who stayed on and made careers in the procuracy and the courts, gained their education in the secondary judicial schools and the correspondence programs (both at the secondary and higher levels). Both of these supplied the vocational education preferred by most higher legal officials (Goliakov and Anashkin excepted).

The resolution of the Central Committee made legal education a "top" priority for the legal agencies, and their leaders obliged officials at lower levels to ensure the fulfilment of the new policy. In conjunction with the Central Committee staff, leading officials of the Procuracy and Ministry of Justice drew up a plan for the education of their officials. The goal was to ensure that in four to five years all judges, procurators, and investigators working at the regional level and higher, along with district procurators and people's court judges in the capital cities of republics and regions, would have completed higher legal education – or, at the very least, juridical preparation combined with long practical experience. (This realistic fall-back was not included in all the drafts of the resolution!) The rest of legal officialdom was to have achieved no less than completion of a secondary juridical school or a nine-month retraining course.[10]

Realizing the plan for educating legal officials was no simple matter. Typically, local politicians did not want to release their legal officials to attend school full-time. Many procuracy officials and judges still did not want to take correspondence courses after work, and once enrolled, ignored their reading assignments. More than a quarter failed to obtain promotion to the next year of the program. To overcome such inertia required a battery of supervisors in the cadres' departments of regional

9 I. Goliakov, "Sovetskii sud kak orudie vospitaniia," *SZ*, 1944, no. 2, 6–10; Goliakov, "Sud i zakonnost v khudozhestvennoi literature," in 4 parts: *SZ*, 1949, no. 3, 26–34; no. 4, 32–39; no. 7, 32–37; no. 9, 34–39.
10 "Aktiv rabotnikov iustitsii," ibid., 1947, no. 2, 7–12; "V Ministerstve iustitsii," ibid., no. 4, 28.

procuracy offices and justice administrations to monitor the recruitment
of students for the secondary legal schools, the enrollment of legal
officials in correspondence courses, and the progress of both sets of
students. In 1949 the Ministry of Justice ordered all judges to enroll in
the appropriate program or lose their jobs.[11]

Meeting the timetable for acquisition of legal education set out in the
plan proved impossible. But the officials of the cadres' departments did
succeed in enrolling most legal officials in some kind of legal education,
and within a few years producing a corps of legal officials who at least
on paper had received legal training. Thus, in academic year 1949–1950
– three years after the Central Committee decree – 48,193 students were
enrolled in higher and secondary legal education, three and a half times
the level of 1940. Of these, more than 32,000 were pursuing higher
eduction (11,772 full-time day students; 21,000 by correspondence), a
figure more than six times that of 1940. In spring 1949, nearly 4,000
lawyers had graduated (2,153 from full-time education, 1,828 from correspondence), and over 3,000 persons completed secondary legal education. Almost all of the latter went on to do higher education.[12]

Not all of these graduates ended up working in the legal agencies.
(Only one-third of graduates of full-time higher legal education in 1949
started working as legal officials.) But the educational profile of legal
officialdom started to change. Whereas in 1948 only 21.4% of judges had
legal training (6.2% higher, 15.2% secondary), in 1951 the figure had
risen to 57.6% (20.2% higher; 37.4% secondary). An analogous shift took
place among procuracy officials. In rural Vitebsk region only 28% of
investigators and procurators had legal education (including secondary) in 1946; in 1952 that figure had tripled to 85.1% (40.5% higher,
44.6% secondary).[13]

These data suggest that the procuracy improved its educational
profile faster than the courts. The reason was that the courts could not
hire many of the graduates of juridical schools and law faculties because
of their age. To stand for election as a judge required attainment of the

[11] GARF, f.8131, op.28, d.242b (Protokol vsesoiuznogo soveshchanii zamestitelei prokurorov soiuznykh respublik po kadram i nachalnikov otdelov kadrov . . . 30 noiabr – 9 dekabria 1950, v Moskve), passim; GARF, f.9396, op.2, d.293 (Godovoi otchet o rabote VIuZI za 1948/49 uchebnyi god); GARF, f.9492, op.1, d.198 (Nastavlenie o rabote s kadrami narodnykh sudei), 347–358.
[12] GARF, f.9492, op.1, d.218 (Stenogramma soveshchanii zamestiteli ministrov iustitsii po kadram soiuznykh i avtonomnykh respublik i zamestiteli nachalnikov upravlenii ministerstva iustitisii po kadram, 18 po 21 sentiabria 1950), 1.49–52; f.9396, op.2, d.293, 14–22; f.9396, op.2, d.403 (Otchet o rabote Glavnogo upravleniia iuridicheskikh vuzov, 1949–1950), 22.
[13] GARF, f.9492, op.1, d.243 (Ob itogakh vyborov narodnykh sudov . . . v Dek. 1951); GARF, f.8131, op.28, d.1092, 112–115.

age of 23 and some work experience as well. The allocation of the graduates of schools and faculties paid no attention to age, and the court simply had to refuse many of the graduates allocated to them. This situation prompted Minister of Justice Konstantin Gorshenin to appeal twice to secretaries of the Central Committee of the CPSU to have the whole contingent of graduates of full-time higher education in 1949 sent to the courts. The Procuracy, Gorshenin contended, could take the leavings. This was the only way, according to the minister of justice, that his ministry could avoid doing worse than the Procuracy in fulfilling its plan for legal education pursuant to the Central Committee decree.[14] Gorshenin had a point, and he would repeat his appeal later on, but the politicians refused to act. The secretaries turned down the appeal, and procuracy officials continued to have a higher educational profile than judges until the mid-1950s. Ironically, in February 1947, when Gorshenin headed the USSR Procuracy (before his transfer to minister of justice), he had asked for preferential treatment of the Procuracy – specifically that the Central Committee direct local party officials to recruit for the agency "the best persons from the party and Soviet *aktiv*" and among party members with higher legal education not currently working in the Procuracy or courts. In fact, as a result of Procurator Gorshenin's initiative, the Central Committee did require republican and regional party committees to recruit 450 "leading party and soviet officials" for work as procurators of cities.[15]

Overall, though, when measured in quantitative terms, the campaign to educate legal officials pursued in the late 1940s and 1950s proved an overwhelming success. Whatever the differences between the Procuracy and courts, the staff of both agencies did acquire degrees testifying to the completion of secondary or higher legal education. The problem was the *quality* of that education. Not only was the education received by most officials narrow and simplified, but also it failed to instill in them an attachment to the legal process.

To begin, despite the urging of Goliakov and the Central Committee's support for new courses on Soviet state law and international law, the curriculum even in the best daytime faculties of law remained narrow. The undergraduate students devoted most of their time to subjects needed for practical work, especially criminal and civil law and procedure. They encountered little philosophy or history. Jurisprudence they studied through the lens of Marxism-Leninism. While history of political thought was taught at the best faculties, it did not become a standard subject. As late as 1955 there were no textbooks for

14 GARF, f.9492, op.1, d.169, 79–82; op.2s, d.67, 335–338.
15 RTsKhIDNI, f.17, op.117, d.697, 115–121; d.709, 56–59; op.116, d.300, 10.

Soviet state law, international law, history of political thought, and governments of bourgeois countries.[16]

Second, the textbooks for the core course in law presented the material in a simplified and descriptive way that neither emphasized controversy nor stimulated argument. To be sure, professors prepared a new set of texts in the late 1940s and early 1950s in an attempt to accommodate the new demand, but these books represented collective efforts, which were reviewed and vetoed by committees and by officials in the ministries of higher education and justice, if not also by staff of the Central Committee. As a result, most of the textbooks – in the words of a critic writing in 1956 – "had a descriptive character and suffered from verbosity and often dogmatism."[17]

The narrow curriculum and bland texts did not prevent good teachers from introducing their students to controversial issues, the history of particular branches of law, theoretical and comparative perspectives, or the nuances of legal reasoning. The best professors at the established daytime faculties (Moscow and Leningrad universities, for example), many of whom had received their education before the Revolution or in the 1920s from prerevolutionary mentors, overcame the limitations of course design and textbooks.[18] Some became legends. Most students of law in the postwar USSR never encountered such teachers. There were few qualified teachers of law – let alone erudite or inspiring ones – to staff the new and expanded faculties and institutes. Graduate training in law had slowed to a trickle in the 1930s. The Central Committee decree of 1946 did support its revival and the training of a new generation of law teachers as quickly as possible. In the meantime, many instructors lacked advanced degrees, and some had themselves received meager training.[19]

[16] A.F. Shebanov, "Ulushchit podgotovku iuridicheskikh kadrov," *SGiP*, 1955, no.1, 10–19; "Za ulushchenie iuridicheskogo obrazovaniia v SSSR," ibid., 1956, no. 8, 3–12; A.F. Shebanov, *Iuridicheskie vysshie uchebnye zavedeniia* (Moscow, 1963), 72 ff.; G.G. "Obsuzhdenie maketa uchebnika po istorii politicheskogo uchenii," *SGiP*, 1954, no. 5, 125–129.

[17] GARF, f.9492, op.1, d.169, 11. 130–136; "Za ulushcheniie iuridicheskogo obrazovaniie v SSSR," *SGiP*, 1956, no. 8, 3–12.

[18] Interviews; personal experience as student at law faculty, Moscow State University, 1968–1969. Moscow University differed from most faculties and institutes in the quality of the term papers (*diplomnaia rabota*) written by students in fourth and fifth years. While at most places, students wrote boring, repetitive papers "largely copied from textbooks," at Moscow University there was a variety of interesting topics (in the words of a critic), such as "Presidential Power in the USA." See "Za ulushchenie iuridicheskogo obrazovaniia."

[19] "O rasshirenii i ulushchenii iuridicheskogo obrazovaniia"; Shebanov, *Iuridicheskie vyshyie*, 75 ff. According to Shebanov, in 1948 38% of instructors in higher legal education had advanced degrees (kandidat or doktor nauk); by 1953 this figure had risen to 60.7%.

Most legal officials, however, did not have the benefit of regular instruction even from untrained or inexperienced teachers. For most of the investigators, procurators, and judges studied law by correspondence. Some took the university level courses offered by the All-Union Legal Correspondence Institute, a body based in Moscow that directed a network of regionally based branches. Other officials, who lacked secondary school education, pursued secondary legal education by correspondence.

The virtue of correspondence education lay in making legal education available to countless officials working in provincial cities and rural areas who otherwise could not have received it. The drawback was that they had to study mostly on their own, memorizing the material presented in textbooks rather than discussing or going beyond it. The Institute's organizers understood these limitations and tried to counteract them. In theory, the Institute provided its students with not only a study plan and textbooks but also the opportunity to travel twice a year to the nearest branch of the Institute and spend ten days meeting with instructors. The value of these short sessions of face-to-face instruction was limited by the paucity of qualified teachers (most were local practitioners), the shortage of textbooks, and the absence of facilities such as lecture halls and dormitories. The branches of the All-Union Legal Correspondence Institute had modest quarters. The Kiev branch had a room in the regional court building; the Odessa branch a room in the apartment of its director. The library of the Odessa branch had sixty titles, not all in multiple copies, and textbooks were scarce.[20] The underlying problem was that the enrollment of thousands of legal officials in correspondence education came without warning or preparation. The sudden expansion of legal education by correspondence was an instance of a Stalinist *shturmovshchina* (storming). In its sacrifice of quality for quantity and speed, it resembled the expansion of technical education in the early 1930s.[21]

Secondary legal education by correspondence provided such minimal training that already in 1948 critics called for its disbanding. (This happened only in 1956.) Some of the students, though working as judges or procuracy officials, lacked sufficient general education to handle the program. Unprepared for independent study, they needed much help from teachers whom they met on occasional visits to the schools. But some of the teachers were as unprepared as the students. In the Mordovsk ASSR civil procedure was taught by a practitioner

20 GARF, f.9396, op.2, d.293; f.9492, op.1, d.218, 154; f.8131, op.28, d.242b, 34–39, 142.
21 See Kendall E. Bailes, *Technology and Society under Lenin and Stalin: Origins of the Soviet Technical Intelligentsia, 1917–1941* (Princeton, N.J., 1978), part 3.

who was himself in the second year of the All-Union Correspondence Institute and had not yet passed the examination in the subject. The schools also faced organizational difficulties. In Alma-Ata the secondary juridical school had no records on which students were enrolled in which courses and with what exams to their credit.[22]

Emigré jurists from the USSR who taught in the correspondence programs – higher and secondary – remained highly critical of their graduates. According to my informants, most of the graduates were war veterans with party cards but little education. Some had learned to speak well, but they knew little law. This fact was reflected in their grades. Despite pressure to pass most students in order to fulfill the plan, teachers of correspondence legal education still failed 20% and gave another 30% grades of "C." Even so, supervisors from the Institute in Moscow berated teachers for showing too much "liberalism." Legal officials themselves enjoyed anecdotes at the expense of their less knowledgeable colleagues. For example, a district procurator from Zaporozhe Region had no answer in response to the examiner's question, "What is a juridical person?" When the examiners pressed on and asked the examinee whether he was a juridical person, he stopped, "looked at his shoulder pads (where the insignia of ranks were placed) and replied " 'No, I am not yet a juridical person.' " "Is the Procurator-General of the USSR a juridical person?" "Oh, most certainly!"[23]

The weakest students aside, the correspondence programs did give Soviet legal officials already working in the Procuracy and courts a mediocre command of the technical core of Soviet law, sufficient to improve their capacity to observe legal rules. But, I shall argue below, it did not instill in most of them commitment to a legal ethos.

There was, of course, another potential source of better educated cadres for the legal agencies – that is, the graduates of full-time legal studies. These included students of higher legal education at the law faculties and institutes, some of which provided superior education. Forty percent of graduates of full-time higher education in law received their initial assignments of three years to posts in the Procuracy and courts.[24] In addition all of the graduates of the full-time secondary juridical schools were available for assignments in the Procuracy and courts. Although their

[22] A. Raiter, "Zaochnoe srednoe iuridicheskoe obrazovanie netselesoobrazno," *SZ*, 1947, no. 7, 19–20; G. Rusakov, "Iuridicheskie shkoly i kursy pered uchebnym godom," *SZ* 1947, No. 9, 7–9; V. Vetiutnev, "Serezny nedostatki zaochnogo iuridicheskogo obrazovaniia v Alma-Atinskoi iuridicheskoi shkole," ibid., 1948, no. 11, 49–50.

[23] Interviews; "Protokol vsesoiuznogo soveshchaniia . . . po kadram," 39; GARF, f.9396, op.2, d.293, 40–42, f.8131sch, op.27s, d.4038, 24.

[24] GARF, f.9396, op.2, d.403, 22.

training was at the secondary school level, they often learned aspects of law better than officials who had completed higher legal education through correspondence. In recognition of the superiority of all full-time day study, the graduates of higher and secondary level programs were known as "young specialists."

Many of the young specialists who took posts in the legal agencies did not stay and make careers. One reason was mistreatment by provincial and local authorities. Despite referrals from the Ministry of Justice or the Procuracy, regional authorities often failed to give the graduates assignments. Once given jobs, the latter often could not find apartments. One young specialist sent to the procuracy in Stalingrad reportedly slept with his family on benches in the park for two weeks. Aware of the hassles that awaited young specialists on assignment, officials of the Ministry of Justice issued a series of directives ordering cadre officials in the provinces to assure the graduates both jobs and living space.[25] Even after assuming posts in the legal agencies, young specialists often found the milieu hostile to them. In many localities authorities preferred to recruit as legal officials persons connected to their own patronage networks rather than the outsiders sent by Moscow. In fact, local authorities took advantage of incidents of improper conduct (e.g., drinking) to fire young specialists. Only in places where finding replacements of any kind was difficult (e.g., Omsk) did the local bosses tolerate misdeeds of the young specialists. The young specialists also left their assigned posts for a variety of personal reasons. Some did not adjust to life in the provinces (a veteran procurator in Tiumen described them as "just children" unprepared for the harsh climate and ethnic conflicts). Others left for better paying jobs as advocates or jurisconsults; and some out of frustration with the compromises that bureaucratic and political realities required.[26]

The statistics on turnover reflected the strains between the young lawyers sent from the cities and the local politicians. In 1949, 15% of all procuracy officials left their posts (down from 19% in 1947), but of the young specialists in the procuracy 36% departed. Officially, nearly half of the latter were fired for poor performance or misdeeds (more than the norm for procuracy officials as a whole); the rest left of their own choice.[27]

---

25 GARF, f.9492, op.1, d.218, 49–52; f.8131, op.28, d.2426, 112ff; "Ob itogakh raspredelenii molodykh spetsialistiv (iuristov) . . . ," Prikaz ministerstva iustitsii ot 6 sent. 1947 g., no. 20, *Sbornik prikazov i instruktsii Ministerstva iustitsii SSSR 1936–1948 gg.* (Moscow, 1949), 111.
26 GARF, f.8131, op.28, d.1093b, 200, 216; op.27, d.4038, 24.
27 GARF, f.8131, op.28, d.242b, 6; d.1092, 107–111, op.27s, d.4038, 32–34.

The expansion of full-time higher legal education had surprisingly little impact upon the makeup of officials of the Procuracy and the courts. Sixty percent of graduates in the early 1950s took jobs elsewhere, and of the 40% who started in the legal agencies more than a third left their posts within three years. Thus, of the approximately 850 jurists who entered the Procuracy and courts in 1949, some 500 remained in 1952. Compared with the many thousands of officials already working in the legal agencies and receiving education by correspondence, this represented a small share.[28]

For the generation of officials in the Procuracy and courts who began work between 1939 and 1955, the officials who embodied the transition from the prewar experiment with administration of justice by uneducated political trustees to the administration of justice by jurists – the modal form of education was by correspondence. This fact underscores the importance of the impact that legal education by correspondence exercised on those who pursued it.

Education by correspondence did give legal officials a grasp, however tenuous, of the technical core of Soviet law. It also gave them a credential that encouraged them to pursue careers in the legal agencies. But this kind of legal education did not make most of them into adherents of a legal ethos or make them identify as jurists rather than as officials. By a legal ethos I mean a set of attitudes that would provide a basis for self-definition as jurists. Such an ethos might include (1) a belief in the "autonomy and scientific nature of the law" (at least as a desideratum); and (2) a respect for legal rules and procedures (if not also placing their observance ahead of the achievement of intended results). Put more succinctly, a legal ethos implies commitment to the legal process as something distinct from (if not also superior to) other forms of governance.[29] Critics of legal education in the United States have complained of an excessive emphasis on the autonomy of legal reasoning that encourages future lawyers to ignore the political and ethical dimensions of the legal problems.[30] But for the development

---

[28] Extrapolated from the 1949 data in GARF, f.9396, op.2, d.293 (*godovoi otchet*).

[29] My definition of "legal ethos" draws on William Wagner, *Marriage, Property and Law in Late Imperial Russia* (Oxford, 1994), chap. 1, esp. 29–32.

[30] Karl Klare, "The Law-School Curriculum in the 1980s: What's Left?" *Journal of Legal Education*, 32 (1982), 336–343; Stephen Halpern, "On the Politics and Pathology of Legal Education," ibid., 383–394; Gerald P. Lopez, "Training Future Lawyers to Work with the Politically and Socially Subordinated: Anti-Generic Legal Education," *West Virginia Law Review*, 91, no. 7 (Fall 1988–1989), 305–387; Howard Lesnick, "Infinity in a Grain of Sand: The World of Law and Lawyering as Portrayed in the Clinical Teaching Implicit in the Law School Curriculum," *UCLA Law Review*, 37 (Aug. 1990), 1157–1191.

of law in nineteenth-century Russia and its detachment from the traditional subordination of law to politics the emergence of a legal ethos among legal officials had proved essential. The Judicial Reform of 1864 owed its origins to the emergence of such attitudes among a corps of elite government officials and the realization of that reform, with all its tensions and conflicts, reflected a strong commitment on the part of some Russian legal officials to principles of law.[31] Significant improvement in the administration of justice in the USSR under Stalin and after would require a similar change in attitudes.

Legal education does not automatically generate among law students a strong commitment to legal process. At least three factors increase the likelihood of this result, but none of these was present in the USSR in the late 1940s and 1950s. The first was a predisposition toward a belief in the autonomy of law and priority of legal rules stemming from prior experience in home and school. Although widespread in Western Europe and North America, in Russia such a predisposition was likely to be limited to the children of Western-oriented intelligentsia families. A second factor bearing upon the development of a legal ethos was the existence of a legal profession that transcended the different kinds of jobs lawyers performed and gave them a common professional identity. Although such a legal profession existed in the Anglo-American world, in the USSR, as in Western Europe, there was no single legal profession. Graduates of Soviet law faculties pursued a set of parallel legal careers (prosecutor, judge, advocate, jurisconsult). When Soviet jurists changed posts, they usually moved away from the legal agencies not toward them; a person did not become a judge after working as an advocate, but vice versa. Those who made careers in the Procuracy or courts usually identified as legal officials rather than as jurists who happened to work in government. As in many European countries so also in Russia, there was no national organization to which all jurists belonged and which might help to shape and maintain a professional identity.[32]

A third factor facilitating the acquisition of a legal ethos was the provision to all jurists of a common legal education at an early age and

---

31 Wagner, "Marriage, Property and the Struggle for Legal Order," 31–32; Richard S. Wortman, *The Development of a Russian Legal Consciousness* (Chicago, 1976), 244–250.

32 On legal professions in Europe, see John Merryman, *The Civil Law Tradition* (Stanford Calif., 1960), chap. 15; Henry Ehrmann, *Comparative Legal Cultures* (Englewood Cliffs, N.J., 1976), chap. 4; and Richard Abel, "Lawyers in the Civil World," in Richard Abel and Philip Lewis, eds., *Lawyers in Society, Vol. 2: The Civil Law World* (Berkeley, Calif., 1988), 1–53.

before they started on particular legal careers.[33] In Western Europe, the study of law for all jurists began in the undergraduate university years. German commentators assumed that this uniform education supplied a basis for the coherence of the "legal profession" in that country, by creating *"einheitsiurist."* The content of legal education in Western European countries was not ideal. In Germany, critics say, it was narrow and dogmatic in style; in France, so broad as to resemble political science. In both countries, many law students did not become lawyers. But all who pursued legal careers did experience a common education at an early age before starting work.[34] Moreover, the study of law for these students was a full-time activity. However dry and dull the textbooks, in lectures and seminars the professors at least had the opportunity to communicate admiration, if not also enthusiasm, for the traditions of law. Moreover, sustained interaction with peers interested in law might help develop the students' respect for legal reasoning and procedures.

Correspondence education, the dominant mode of legal education in the USSR between 1945 and 1960, deprived its recipients of both the opportunity to study law before adulthood and sustained contact with teachers and fellow students. Even worse, this education guaranteed that most Soviet investigators, procurators, and judges studied law only *after* they had started careers in the legal agencies. Inevitably work roles superseded education in the shaping of attitudes and values. Finally, the impact of legal education was further reduced by its narrow vocational character; only the best day faculties offered much breadth. In short, through correspondence education legal officials were unlikely to develop a strong commitment to law and legal process.

It is instructive to compare the experiences in the legal agencies of legal officials pursuing correspondence education with that of the "young specialists," especially those who had received higher legal education at full-time day programs of the law faculties and institutes. The latter, according to the testimony of former Soviet legal officials, were much more likely than other legal officials to dislike the bureaucratic and political pressures that dominated the work of the legal agencies. They were also more likely to resist those pressures while on the job and more likely to leave posts in the legal agencies for

---

[33] Studies of the socialization of students in American law schools, which offered postgraduate education to young adults after the completion of university, found that this training in law came too late to influence the students' attitudes toward civil rights or to cultivate in them a sense of social responsibility. See Murray Schwartz, "The Realities and Limits of Legal Education," *Journal of Legal Education*, 32 (1987), 543–568.

[34] Erhard Blankenburg and Ulrike Schulz, "German Advocates: A Highly Regulated Profession," in *Lawyers in Society*, 124–159; Ronald Sokol, "Reforming the French Legal Profession," *International Lawyers*, 26:4 (Winter 1992), esp. 1033–1036.

other kinds of legal work.[35] The conflict of culture between the bulk of legal officials who attained their credentials through correspondence courses and the young specialists who joined the legal agencies after full-time legal education was reinforced by differences in social class. At least some of the young specialists, particularly those who had completed higher legal education, came from educated families. In contrast, most legal officials educated on the job hailed from humbler origins, and for them posts in the legal agencies represented social advancement.

The reliance on correspondence education to train legal officials in postwar USSR had a practical and economic basis. Circumstances forced authorities to recruit another cohort of uneducated legal officials, and it was easier to give them training in law after work than to triple or quadruple the capacity of full-time legal education. But top legal officials were by and large satisfied with this approach and did not want their agencies staffed by graduates of full-time higher legal education. According to a Ministry of Education official, the Procuracy and Justice Ministry often preferred graduates of the secondary juridical schools to the better educated graduates of the regular law faculties. The school graduates, unlike the university-trained lawyers, were "adult persons, possessing rich experience and extensive involvement in work and public life, mainly members and candidate members of the Communist party."[36] In other words, the graduates of the secondary schools made up for their lesser expertise by a readiness to put loyalty and deference to the established modes of operation ahead of attachment to principles or the legal process.

Though political maturity remained the prime quality that politicians and top legal officials valued in legal officialdom, they also wanted their subordinates to have technical expertise. Recognizing the inherent weakness of correspondence education, they decided in 1954 to develop night programs at many law faculties and institutes. The night programs for higher legal education attracted persons working in the legal agencies (who had finished secondary legal education through correspondence) and policemen aspiring to become investigators or judges. By the 1960s a substantial portion of the cadres in the procuracy and courts were studying at night rather than through correspondence. Graduates of the night programs did attain better technical legal skills than their counterparts who studied through correspondence, but they did not develop attachment to a legal ethos and remained officials of their agencies more than jurists.[37]

---

[35] Interviews.   [36] Shebanov, 79.   [37] Ibid., 85; interviews.

If the heads of the legal agencies had been dissatisfied with the education received by their officials through night study or correspondence, they might have pressed for the expansion of full-time day programs. But there is no evidence that they did so. In contrast to the expanding night and correspondence programs, the number of students graduating from day faculties remained constant at 2,000 per year.[38] If anything, the gap between the programs of full-time law students and the others increased in the post-Stalin years. For in response to renewed criticism of the narrow applied character of legal education, the Ministry of Higher Education supported new courses that broadened the program. But the improvements in the curriculum came mainly in the full-time day programs, attended by future advocates, jurisconsults, and government officials. The correspondence and night faculties that trained legal officials continued to emphasize the technical core of the law.

The spread in the late 1940s and early 1950s of higher legal education through correspondence did have a positive result. As its promoters had hoped, even a rudimentary legal education encouraged legal officials to make careers in the Procuracy and courts. Before World II, the uneducated political trustees in the legal agencies usually lasted only a few years before moving on to other kinds of work. If they had talent, they gained promotion to governmental posts outside of the world of justice; if they performed poorly, they were fired. The acquisition of basic legal education gave most officials the skills that they needed to continue in their jobs with the Procuracy and courts, and it gave them credentials. Most important, with degrees in law in hand, the investigators, procurators, and judges were marked as specialists in the administration of justice. Fewer were tempted to desert the legal agencies for work unrelated to law, though many continued to leave for better paying legal work as jurisconsults or advocates. In addition, the relative normalcy of the decade after World War II (which had no purges or wars to disrupt careers in the making) made it easier for legal officials to stay at their posts. With their new credentials and identification with the legal agencies, many did just that. To be sure, the rates of turnover among procuracy and court workers remained high, as one-quarter to one-third of new appointees (including many of the young specialists) left within a few years. But for those who stayed, extended careers became the norm. The proportion of officials with long tenure increased steadily. Thus, the share of officials in the procuracy whose work experience in the legal agencies

38 Ibid., 81.

exceeded ten years increased from 31.3% in 1954 to 48.2% in 1958 to 55.4% in 1965.[39]

The shift from casual short-term employment in the legal agencies to careers in the Procuracy and courts was bound to influence the conduct of legal officials in the USSR. As career officials, they became more sensitive to the expectations of their superiors and more keen to conform to the standards of evaluation imposed upon them. At the same time, as we shall see in Chapter 11, those expectations became more stringent, in ways that served bureaucratic and political convenience more than the interests of fairness.

Simplification and shortcuts

Despite its shortcomings the legal education acquired by Soviet legal officials in the late 1940s and early 1950s did influence their performance. One aspect of the administration of justice particularly subject to change was the observance of procedural rules. As we saw in earlier chapters, the criminal procedure law adopted by the Bolsheviks had proved too complicated for the uneducated legal officials to execute, and in the 1920s the urge to simplify procedures gained official support because of the mismatch between the capabilities of officials and the

---

[39] These data were based on tables compiled by Yoram Gorlicki from GARF, f.8131, op.28, d.1481, 1.1; d.3941, 1.2; and d.5051, 1.29. For a fuller picture, see the following brief table:

Procuracy officials by years working in procuracy/justice

	1954	1958	1965
Under 3	29.5%	12.4%	19.1%
3–10	40.2	39.4	25.5
10+	31.3	48.2	55.4

Source: Extracted and calculated from tables compiled by Yoram Gorlicki from GARF f.8131, op.28, d.1481, 1.1; d.3941, 1.2; d.5051, 1.29.

It would appear that some judges also began staying in their posts for longer periods. For the rate of turnover of judges in between elections (every three years) declined markedly. Between the 1948 and 1951 elections 24.4% of judges left or were recalled; between the 1951 and 1954 elections only 10.5%. (In 1948, 1951, and 1954, the election years, about one-third of judgeships gained new occupants.) GARF, f.9492sch, op.6s, d.15, 25.

demands of the law. In the mid-1930s Stalin and Vyshinskii rejected the simplifications promoted by Krylenko and insisted that in ordinary (as opposed to political) cases all rules of evidence and procedure be observed. However, many legal officials lacked the capacity to do so.

By the late 1940s the policy of promoting the observance of procedural norms and rejecting simplification had been firmly established for all criminal cases except labor infractions (for which, as we have seen, special simplified procedures had been established). In 1939–1940 and again in 1946–1949 the leadership set legal scholars to work preparing a new, detailed all-Union code of criminal procedure, a code designed to refine and extend criminal procedure rather than to simplify it (as the Krylenko draft codes had done). In the course of drafting, scholars promoted increased protection of the accused through such reforms as early admission to case proceedings of defense counsel (at the end, if not even the start, of the preliminary investigation).[40] The draft code of criminal procedure, however, was never promulgated. Not only did Soviet leaders support the strengthening of procedural norms, but judges on appellate courts insisted on their observance by trial court judges. Even small, technical errors by the latter led to the rehearing of many cases.[41]

The strong support for formal legality in ordinary criminal cases contrasts with the continuation of the "jurisprudence of terror" in political cases. The law continued to permit drastically simplified procedures in cases of sabotage and wrecking, but after the elimination in 1939 of the special collegia of the republican and regional courts, political prosecutions occurred only at tribunals of the security police and selected military tribunals. Vyshinskii's encouragement of confessions in political cases continued to have official support.[42] Yet, as I will explain, the impact of Vyshinskii's ideas about confession on ordinary criminal justice was limited by the separation of political and ordinary justice. What mattered for the Procuracy and the courts was the emphasis placed by the leadership on rules of evidence and procedure.

[40] *Trudy pervoi nauchnoi sessii Vsesoiuznogo instituta iuridicheskikh nauk, 27 iavariia – 3 fevralia 1939* (Ed. I.T. Goliakov, Moscow, 1939), 229–230; M.S. Strogovich, "K podotovke proekta Ugolovno-protsessualnogo kodeksa SSSR," *SZ*, 1946, no. 7–8, 6–10; M. Cheltsov, "Usilit garantii pravilnogo razresheniia del v novom U.P.K.," ibid., no. 10, 10–11; L. Povolotskii, "K proektu UPK SSSR," ibid., no. 11–12, 43–44; I. Ivanov, "Predlozheniie po UPK," ibid., 1947, no. 1, 1920.

[41] GARF (TsGA), f.353, op.13, d.134 (Stenogramma oblastnogo soveshchanii narodnykh sudei, 30–31 inavariia i 1 fev. 1950, Rostov-na-Donu), 94ob and 95.

[42] See Chapter 8. For evidence of continuing support for Vyshinskii's ideas, consider the awarding in 1946 to his book on theory of evidence the Stalin prize first class. See A. Ia. Vyshinskii, *Teoriia sudebnykh dokazatelstv v sovetskom prave* (3rd ed., Moscow, 1950), 2.

The combination of official support for procedure and the acquisition of legal education by most judges, investigators, and procurators should have led to an improvement in the observance of legal rules. I shall argue that this did take place. During the late 1940s and the 1950s the frequency of mistakes due to ignorance, incompetence, sloppiness, and disregard for the rules did decrease. What did not slacken, however, was the penchant of judges and investigators alike to resort to informal practices and shortcuts that suited their convenience or facilitated their work. To be sure, shortcuts and informal practices play a part in all systems of criminal justice. The nature of the shortcuts, however, varies with the country and the legal tradition. The implications of informal practices for the fairness of the administration of justice in the USSR, a country where legal process was not well entrenched, were more grave than those of comparable practices in Western countries.

The evidence of improvement in the observation of rules of procedure is strongest for judges. As of the late 1940s, judges at criminal trials still made a variety of procedural errors, any of which could lead to the upsetting of their verdicts by higher courts. These mistakes included failing to observe the preconditions for holding a trial – such as conducting proceedings in the language of the accused, having the accused present at the trial, or ensuring that the accused was represented by counsel whenever a procurator appeared to argue the case. Absent any of these conditions, judges should have put off the trial, but out of ignorance or desire to complete trials within the required time period, some judges held trials in violation of these rules. Judges also violated the rules for the conduct of trials, by failing to consider requests for the calling of witnesses, to give the accused a final word, or to announce the time period for launching an appeal. Moreover, judges often prepared the sentence protocol in a cursory way that deprived appellate judges of the chance to review decisions properly – by omitting information on the nature of the crime, the involvement of the accused, or reasons for the verdict. Judges also failed to sign the protocols (sometimes they blamed the typists).[43]

The cancellation of verdicts and return of cases for retrial by appellate courts were often due to these kinds of procedural errors. Overall, procedural irregularities accounted for 60% of all verdicts changed on

---

[43] A. Volin, "Strogo sobliudat zakonnost v rabote sudov," SZ, 1950, no. 1, 5–12; GARF (TsGA), f.353, op.13, d.134, 95–96; d.150 (Stenogramma mezhoblastnogo soveshchaniia zamestitelei predsedatelei verkhovnykh sudov ASSR, kraevykh i oblastnykh sudov, 25 aprelia 1951 g., Rostov-na-Donu), 26–29; TsGAOR goroda Moskvy, f.819, op.1, d.33 (Protokoly operativnykh soveshchanii pri predsedatelei moskovskogo gorsuda za 1950), 11A–12.

appeal in the late 1940s. Some of these changes responded to shortcuts employed by judges in hearing cases of shirking (see below), but many related to the kinds of mistakes just described.[44]

Official statistics on the movement of cases supports the proposition that procedural mistakes declined in the late 1940s and early 1950s. To begin, the percentage of verdicts from the people's court left standing in cassation appeals rose. In 1946 that figure stood at 65.5% for all crimes other than labor infractions; in 1952 it reached 78.8%. These figures contrasted with the prewar average of 60.5% (for the years 1937–1939, when many appeals involved excesses from the Terror). Note that until 1954 most of the changes made in cassation consisted of cancellation of verdicts (often with directions for retrial or even supplementary investigation) and not merely of changes in sentence. Cancellations were more likely to reflect serious errors in procedure or handling of evidence and were correspondingly less sensitive to fluctuations in penal policy. Moreover, the inference from these data that the quality of judicial work improved gains further support from the fact that the actual percentage of cases appealed declined during this period: from 37.1% in 1946 to 30.6% in 1952 (again excluding the labor related cases), even though the average severity of punishment increased (not through a larger share of custodial sentences but through longer terms).[45] Naturally a decline in the percentage of verdicts upset in cassation could have reflected changes in the appellate process itself, such as a policy of discouraging judges to change verdicts on appeal. To my knowledge, though, no such changes occurred before Stalin's death. Only after 1956 did judges hearing appeals in cassation become responsible for the conduct of the subordinate judges whose cases they reviewed. That conflict of interest would lead in the 1960s to a decline in the number and percentage of changed verdicts and a corresponding increase in the rate of stability of sentences (close to the 90% range).[46]

It is more difficult to document improvements in the observance of procedural rules by investigators. One reason is the investigators faced less pressure than judges to observe the letter of the law. Most of their work occurred during the pretrial stage of criminal proceedings, and was therefore largely hidden from public view. Since defense counsel lacked access to pretrial events (such as searches, questioning of the

---

[44] GARF (TsGA), f.353, op.13, d.150, 32ob, ff.

[45] GARF (TsGA), f.9492, op.6s, d.15 (Tablitsy sravnitelnyth statistichnykh dannykh), 18, 16; V.N. Kudriavtsev, ed., *Effektivnost pravosudiia i problem ustraneniiu sudebnykh oshibok* (Moscow, 1975), in two volumes: vol. 1, 9, 145–146, 181. These pages fall into the sections of the book written by Igor Petrukhin.

[46] Ibid., 205; Peter H. Solomon, Jr., "The Case of the Vanishing Acquittal," *Soviet Studies*, 39:4 (Oct. 1987), 531–555.

accused, and interviews with witnesses and experts), many irregularities never came to light. Not surprisingly, discussions at procuracy conferences of ways to improve the work of investigators paid little attention to the observance of procedural forms or the care with which paperwork was completed.[47]

At the same time, however, investigators did face increasing pressure to produce cases that would succeed in court. Avoiding such "failures" as acquittals or returns of cases for supplementary investigation became, as we shall see in Chapter 11, a preoccupation for investigators, and to the extent that failure to comply with procedural rules detracted from the quality of the evidence supplied to the court, procedure mattered. Thus, if new, inexperienced investigators in the procuracy failed to compile properly the protocols of a witness interrogation or present their conclusions about the evidence in a convincing way, the judge, at preliminary hearing or trial, might return the cases for supplementary investigation. This result often led to criticism or censure of the investigator.

In the postwar years the rates of returns to supplementary investigation (and of acquittals as well) dropped significantly. In 1949–1952, judges at people's courts returned 4.1% of their cases and at regional and republican supreme courts, 14.9%; the corresponding figures for 1953–1956 were 2.3% and 9.2%. Moreover, whereas appellate courts returned for new investigations in 1946–1952, 6% of the cases that they reviewed, in 1953–1956, the figure had dropped to 2.7%.[48] It is likely that these declines in returns to supplementary investigation did reflect improvements in the technical side of investigation including increased observance of the rules of evidence and procedure, but the data reflected other factors as well. In Chapter 11, we shall explain why judges cooperated with the needs of investigators for low rates of acquittals and returns to supplementary investigation.

Although the acquisition of legal education led to a decline in procedural errors by legal officials, it did not stop the pursuit of shortcuts or informal practices. Shortcuts that suited the convenience of legal officials persisted, whatever their relation to procedural rules, and they made up a part of the work of both judges and investigators.

---

[47] *Rabota luchshikh sledovatelei. Materialy uchebno-metodicheskoi konferentsii luchshikh sledstvennykh rabotnikov organov prokuratury:* Sbornik 1 (Moscow, 1951); Sbornik 2 (Moscow, 1951); Sbornik 3 (Moscow, 1953); Sbornik 4 (Moscow, 1954).

[48] GARF, f.9492sch, op.6s, d.14, 12, 13, 18. Rates of acquittals for all crimes dropped from 9.9% in 1946 to 7.5% in 1952 to 4.6% in 1956. The decline was steeper once labor infractions and cases of personal accusations (insults) were removed. Thus for theft of state property, acquittals went from 7.4% in 1946 to 4.1% in 1952 to 2.0% in 1956. Ibid., 14–15.

In the late Stalin years judges in the USSR regularly used shortcuts in cases of shirking. Admittedly, as we saw in Chapter 9, the political leadership had authorized a simplified set of procedures. Judges were to hear these cases alone, without the help of lay assessors and without involvement of police or procuracy officials. According to the rules, judges were expected to review the short protocols submitted by factory management and to do so in the presence of the accused but outside of work time. Some courts, though, had such a large volume of these cases that night sessions and trials at lunch hour (held at the factories) proved insufficient to mount even short trials. Small wonder that judges indulged in their own unauthorized forms of simplification. Many judges began hearing these cases "in bundles" (*pachkami*), and they commonly put off writing up their decisions. Some judges did the paperwork at home in the evening (when they did not have night sessions). After all, most judges did not have offices in the simple buildings that served as courthouses.[49] These practices declined in July 1951 when most forms of shirking were decriminalized (see Chapter 12).

Another shortcut, even more widespread in the late 1940s than the informal means of handling cases of shirking, was the use of "replacement judges." Already in 1939 the city of Moscow had designated a hundred lay assessors to serve as replacements for judges who were on vacation or ill. To cut backlogs and keep cases moving, other cities had followed the same course. During World War II, when many judges left for the army, the practice expanded, forcing the USSR Ministry of Justice to regularize it. The Ministry ordered local governments to stop appointing assessors at short notice to fill in for a few days and to stop opening extra temporary courtrooms to reduce backlogs. Instead, each people's court judge should receive from the pool of assessors one or two assigned replacements, who, after confirmation by the local executive committee, would prepare for eventual work at trial.[50] These sensible rules were largely ignored. A Ministry of Justice letter in 1948 reported that replacement judges were being recruited not only from assessors but also court secretaries and bailiffs, and were assigned, without confirmation by city governments or preparation, to run extra courtrooms simply to reduce backlogs. In Kiev Region not just assessors and officials of the courts but all sorts of officials served as replacement

---

[49] See Chapter 19, notes 18 and 19. GARF, f.9492, op.1, d.179, 243; d.157, 168–175 (Postanovlenie Kollegii Ministerstva Iustitsii SSSR ot 15 oktaibria 1947, "O faktakh grubogo narushenii Ukaza ot 26 iuniia 1940 goda v narodnykh sudakh Kemerovskoi oblasti).

[50] A. Vasnev, *Narodnye sudy stolitsy* (Moscow, 1939), 16; "O poriadke vozlozheniia na narodnykh zasedatelei ispolneniia obiazannostei narodnogo sudi," Prikaz Ministerstua iustitiia ot 19 sent. 1943 g., no. 72, *Sbornik prikazov i instruktsii*, 15–17.

judges. In 1953 in the Ukraine more than a thousand replacement judges worked regularly, each hearing six to ten cases a month.[51]

Lacking legal preparation, the replacement judges made many more errors than the regular judges and had a greater share of their sentences overturned. Top legal officials recognized this fact. In 1951 USSR Supreme Court Chairman Anatolii Volin called for the elimination of all kinds of substitute judges.[52] But the practice persisted into the post-Stalin period because replacement judges enabled the regular judges (and local politicians responsible for their work) to meet the statistical norms on backlogs of cases and length of time cases waited before trial.[53]

The use of replacements contradicted the regime's current policy of promoting the administration of justice by persons with legal education and harkened back to a time when almost any party member could serve as a judge. The replacements also resembled the "socialist substitutes" who had worked alongside regular judges in the 1930s. However, the contrast between the substitutes and regular judges at that time was not great, since even the latter had minimal legal training. By the late 1940s, when most judges were acquiring legal education of a kind, the differences between the regular judge and the "replacement" became meaningful.

Even more than judges, investigators used shortcuts and informal practices. Working outside public scrutiny, they could shape their work routines to suit their convenience. Some of the dubious practices of the investigators will receive attention in Chapter 11, when we explore how legal officials adjusted their conduct in the face of new criteria of evaluation. These practices included the artificial generation of criminal cases (prosecutions) to fill quotas and the delay of the official start of pretrial investigations in order to avoid violating the time limits for investigations. One serious shortcut by investigators will be discussed here, and that is the reliance upon confession of the accused and failure to gather other incriminating evidence.

In mid-December 1938, at the height of the reaction to the Great Terror, Commissar of Justice Rychkov and USSR Supreme Court Chairman Goliakov instructed their subordinates "as a rule not to accept cases based exclusively on the confession of the accused." However,

---

51 "Ob ustranenii narushenii ustanovlennogo zakonom o sudoustroistve SSSR . . . proiadka zameshchenii narodnogo sudi v sluchae vremennogo ego otsutstviia," Direktivnoe pismo ot 7 iuliia 1948 g., No. D-36, ibid., 17–19; f.9492, op.1, d.287, 159.

52 GARF, f.9492, op.1, d.243. (Stenogramma vsesoiuznogo soveshchaniia rabotnikov iustitsii, 3–5 iuliia 1951), 7; d.241, 14; d. 179, 346–347; d.218, 61.

53 According to Yoram Gorlizki, as of the mid-50s replacement judges were used mainly in remote places, where no regular judges could cover for another's summer holiday. (Personal conversation.)

within a month the head of the Council of People's Commissars, Molotov, forced the legal chiefs to reverse this directive, on the grounds that according to article 319 of the Russian Code of Criminal Procedure confession of the accused constituted a valid form of evidence, to be considered in the context of all of the circumstances of the case.[54]

All the same, the failure to provide judges with evidence apart from the confession of the accused could have bad consequences. Should the accused change his mind and at trial recant the confession made during the pretrial phase, the case against him could collapse.[55] Judges on the city court of Moscow complained in 1950 that they often faced this situation and that it produced many of the acquittals and returns to supplementary investigations ordered by them. The fault for such collapsed cases, the judges insisted, lay with the investigators. Former Soviet investigators in emigration interviewed by me agreed that they were expected to come into court with more than a confession in hand. They insisted that none of them personally had relied on confessions, but admitted that some of their colleagues had been less virtuous. Archival sources agreed. In 1948 USSR Supreme Court Chairman Goliakov reminded responsible procuracy officials of the difficulties of convicting on the basis of confession alone and called for an end to the "harmful practice of seeking confessions as the main thing." A procuracy report in 1950 confirmed that "many investigators think that, having obtained a confession, their obligations are over."[56]

The value that investigators placed on confessions assured that there would be occasional attempts to extract them by force. Officials of the Procuracy, though, were rarely involved in these illegal actions. A review of crimes by procuracy officials in 1947 noted only a few instances, and former investigators and assistant procurators of the period confirmed that procuracy officials had little to do with confessions.[57] Most attempts to extract confession were the work of the *police*. Procuracy inquiries into police violations provide vivid examples of forced confessions, as well as of illegal arrests and violations of the laws on search and seizure. In Novosibirsk, police arrested four persons for one murder and then extracted "by illegal means" confessions to twenty other murders and thefts that had occurred in the past two years. The police in Kuznetskii District of Kemerovo Region had threatened an accused with a gun and wounded him with a knife to get an admission

54 GARF, f.8131, op.37, d.139, 67, 73.
55 Supreme Court Chairman Goliakov emphasizes this fact in "Vsesoiuznoe soveshchanie rukovodiashchikh rabotnikov prokuratury," part one, *SZ*, 1948, no. 6, 39.
56 TsGAOR goroda Moskvy, f.819, op.1, d.33, 70–71A; interviews; GARF, f.8131sch, op.27s, d.4034, 384–385; op.29s, d.108, 30.
57 Ibid., op.27s, d.3503, 256.

of guilt. To extract a confession police in Tyrnovsk district of the Moldavian Republic "systematically beat" six men, took away their clothes and placed them in a cold room.[58] A review of violations by police prepared by the RSFSR Procuracy in 1950 noted an increase in such complaints (dozens each year) and stressed that the incidents occurred in all parts of Russia. They almost always involved beatings.[59]

The presence of forced confessions in some ordinary criminal cases calls for explanation. Neither the use of forced confessions in *political* cases nor the doctrine of Vyshinskii approving that practice gave police or legal officials license to extend it to ordinary criminal cases. In the years after the Great Terror the realms of law and terror became increasingly compartmentalized. Most legal officials, and one suspects police as well, had no relationship with the security police. (The main exception was procurators, who had to sign arrest orders on behalf of the security police.)[60] Moreover, the writings of Andrei Vyshinskii drew a sharp distinction between ordinary and political prosecutions. To be sure, in his book *The Theory of Judicial Evidence in Soviet Law* Vyshinskii developed a variety of notions that facilitated prosecutions in ordinary criminal cases. These included the rejection of the concept of absolute truth in favor of "maximal probability"; the extension of guilt to anyone loosely involved in a crime; the shifting of the burden of proof to the accused when the latter was caught in possession of stolen goods. But Vyshinskii was best known for his proposition that in cases of anti-Soviet, counterrevolutionary organizations and groups, confessions by the accused "inevitably assume the character and significance of fundamental, vital, and decisive evidence."[61] Vyshinskii's book on evidence appeared for the first time in 1941 and again in expanded editions in 1946 and 1950. The 1946 version, the winner of a Stalin prize, was described by one of its reviewers (sometime colleague of Vyshinskii, Mikhail Strogovich) as "without exaggeration . . . the best known, most read and studied juridical work . . . " and "a reference book for all investigators and procurators." Moreover, Vyshinskii's main ideas were absorbed from his treatise into the textbooks on criminal procedure published during the late 1940s and early 1950s. Although Vyshinskii himself no longer worked in the Procuracy, he retained immense authority in the administration of justice.[62]

58 Ibid., op.27s, d.457, 2–17; op.28s, d.452, 40–55; op.29s, d.466, 137–138. See also RTsKhIDNI, f.17, op.117, d.653, 167–170; op.116, d.280, p.211; op.117, d.693.64–71, op.116, d.293, p. 339.
59 Ibid., op.29s, d.466, 136–153; op.27s, d.4034, 174.
60 Interviews. See also Kudriavtsev, *Effektivnost pravosudiia*, 183.
61 Vyshinskii, *Teoriia sudebnykh dokazatelstv*, 264.
62 M.S. Strogovich, "Review of *Teoriia sudebnykh dokazatelstv* . . . " *SZ*, 1946, no. 11–12, 54–57.

Did Vyshinskii's approval of the search for confession in political cases influence the conduct of investigators in ordinary ones? Perhaps, to a degree. But Andrei Vyshinskii himself made a point of stressing that his doctrine on confessions applied *only* to political cases. In non-political cases, Vyshinskii wrote, investigations should *not* be organized around the obtaining of confessions. The reason was obvious. In ordinary cases when confessions were the main or only evidence, Vyshinskii warned, the case could collapse, especially if the accused retracted his confession. In interviews, former investigators and procurators from the period recalled this distinction without prompting, and insisted that Vyshinskii's ideas about confession had applied only to political cases.[63]

Vyshinskii's limiting of the value of confessions to political cases represented an advance over tsarist law. Article 316 of the Collection of Criminal Laws, issued in 1845 and lasting in force to 1917, declared that confession was "the best evidence in the world [*v svete*]."[64]

If neither the Terror nor Vyshinskii's jurisprudence explains the occurrence of forced confessions in ordinary criminal cases in the late 1940s, why did they occur? The simplest answer is that forced confessions served the needs of the police and the convenience of investigators. For police the obtaining of confessions, even by force, represented a quick and easy solution to the crime at hand, for which they could take credit. For investigators the confessions already obtained by the police helped them complete investigations within the short time frames set by their superiors and move cases to trial. Moreover, the absence of meaningful restraints on police – especially cultural ones – facilitated the pursuit of self-interest by police and investigators. My emphasis upon bureaucratic pressure and legal culture to explain abuses in policing and criminal investigation in the late Stalin years gains support from the subsequent history of Soviet criminal justice. In 1953 Stalin's successors stopped the extrajudicial processing of political cases. In the early 1960s they authorized the denunciation of Vyshinskii's jurisprudence.[65] Nonetheless, forced confessions continued to occur in some ordinary criminal cases. If anything, the bureaucratic pressures on police and investigators to achieve

63 Vyshinsky, *Teoriia sudebnykh dokazatelstv*, 263; interviews.
64 M.A. Cheltsov-Bebutov, *Ocherki po istorii suda i ugolovngo protsessa v rabovladelcheskikh, feodalnykh i burzhuazhykh gosudarstvakh* (Moscow, 1957), 740.
65 D. Karev, "Likvidirovat posledstviia kulta lichnosti v sovetskoi pravovoi nuake," *SZ*, 1962, no. 2, 54–62; "Do kontsa likvidirovat vrednye posledstviia kulta lichnosti v sovetskoi iurisprudentsii," *SGiP*, 1962, no. 4, 3–16; N.V. Zhogin, "Ob izrashcheniiakh Vyshinskogo v teorii sovetksogo prava i praktike," ibid., 1965, no. 3, 22–31.

the appearance of success increased; and the legal culture that permitted abuses also continued.[66]

The attainment by Soviet legal officials in the late 1940s and early
1950s of legal education – secondary or higher, usually by correspondence – contributed to the development of a trained and competent
body of legal officials capable of observing the norms of criminal procedure. Already by Stalin's death, the average quality of investigatory
and judicial work had improved. But legal education of this kind did
not, and could not, eliminate the penchant of law enforcement officials
to seek and find shortcuts that made their work easier. And, the limitations of an education designed not to create a legal profession but to
give legal skills and credentials to officialdom hindered the spread of a
legal culture that might discourage abuses in investigations.

Conclusion

The program of legal education for legal officials developed in the late
1940s fulfilled the expectations of the Soviet political leaders who endorsed and promoted it. Judges, investigators, and procurators acquired skills and technical expertise sufficient to improve their
performance but did not develop an attachment to a legal ethos or the
values of a legal profession. Like their tsarist predecessors, Soviet leaders did not favor the emergence of a legal "profession" in a Western or
especially Anglo-American sense. Not only did they choose not to train
most future legal officials at full-time day faculties of law, but they
continued to keep any and all lawyers from organizing beyond the
regional level. Even the advocates, a select and elite group of practicing
lawyers, had no national organization until 1989.

For Stalin and colleagues the challenge lay in finding a way to establish and staff modern legal institutions to serve the state without creating a legal profession. After all, even a carefully regulated and licensed
legal profession could acquire a modicum of autonomy and power – a
development incompatible with the Soviet brand of authoritarianism.
On a larger plane the Soviet leadership had just faced, for the second
time, a characteristic dilemma of legal modernization – its inherent
connection with various kinds of autonomy, including that of a legal
profession.[67] After the Revolution Bolshevik leaders had chosen to
avoid tainting their courts and procuracy offices with potential legal
professionals by hiring political trustees lacking legal education. In the

---

[66] Peter H. Solomon, Jr., "Gorbachev, Judicial Reform and Soviet History," in Albert
Schmidt, ed., *The Impact of Perestroika on Soviet Law* (Dordrecht, 1990), 15–22.
[67] See Unger, *Law in Modern Society*.

long run, though, their performance failed to meet expectations, and the Stalinist leadership recognized the importance of legal education and careers for both the performance and loyalty of legal officials. In choosing to provide legal education by correspondence or at night to persons already working in the legal agencies, Stalin found a way, perhaps unknowingly, to educate legal officials for service and make them better bureaucrats rather than lawyers in office.

The acquisition of legal education represented part of the conversion of jobs in the legal agencies into careers. As a larger share of investigators and judges became career officials – a trend already clear in the 1950s – so they became more sensitive to the demands of their bureaucratic and political superiors. The content of those demands, that is what new careerists in the legal agencies had to do to please their masters, gained definition for the most part in the years before Stalin's death. That story forms the subject of the next chapter.

11 The dynamics of Stalinist justice: bureaucratic and political pressures on legal officials

Shortly before World War II the legal agencies in the USSR underwent a centralization of power and authority that placed much of decision making about personnel and operations in the hands of republican and central authorities. With this centralization came reliance on statistical indicators to monitor and assess the performance of legal officials. After the War, the influence of formal assessment upon procurators, investigators, and judges grew markedly when the bulk of them enrolled in legal correspondence education in preparation for careers in the agencies. A new long-term perspective, with aspirations for promotion and rewards, gave evaluation of performance by superiors greater import. As career officials, investigators, procurators, and judges were bound to become more sensitive to the expectations of their superiors.

In 1948–1949, those expectations underwent a dramatic change. No longer preoccupied mainly with the efficiency of the administration of justice, the top legal officials shifted their focus to its substance or quality, and in particular to eliminating "mistakes" that led to acquittals and verdicts or sentences overturned on appeal. Moreover, in an effort to confront what they now called "unfounded prosecutions" and "unfounded convictions," the chiefs of the legal agencies adopted a stubborn and uncompromising approach. Their goal was nothing less than the elimination of alleged symptoms of imperfection such as acquittals and reversals on appeal. For some four years, mid-1948 through 1951, the chiefs of the legal agencies conducted a campaign for perfection in the work of their subordinates.

The pressure exerted upon legal officials for new standards of performance – measured by such statistical indicators as frequency of acquittals and the percentage of sentences that held up on appeal – received further support from party officials in the regions and localities. Of course, the other master of legal officialdom lost none of its interest in the cooperation of judges and procuracy officials with its own particular needs. At the same time, as party officials at the regional committees assumed more responsibility for the performance of the legal agencies, they paid attention to how well the latter met the new standards of performance set in the center. At least for a time, party officials in the regions and localities joined in the campaign for perfection – perhaps because it had support from top party leaders.

The quest for perfection in the administration of justice and the avoidance of "unfounded prosecutions and convictions" had devastating consequences. They included, on the one hand, exacerbation of conflicts between the procuracy and the courts and between different levels within the justice agencies; and, on the other hand, a series of adjustments in the practice of investigation, prosecution, and adjudication. While some of these adjustments represented harmless shortcuts, others constituted serious distortions of the conduct of prosecutions and trials. The distortions outlasted the Stalin era by decades.

Chapter 11 examines the bureaucratic and political pressures that impinged on Soviet legal officials in the last years of Stalin's rule. The chapter begins with analysis of the new expectations of central officials and their implications for rank-and-file legal officials. It goes on to explain how local politicians came to share the expectations of central legal officials and why judges in particular listened responsively; to document conflicts between the legal agencies and the compromise solutions or distortions invented by legal officials; and, finally, to consider the role of the top party leadership in shaping the dynamics of mature Stalinist justice, including the quest for perfection.

Perfecting the administration of justice

The first sign of pressure upon legal officials throughout the USSR to achieve new levels of performance came in a speech delivered by Deputy USSR Procurator-General Konstantin Mokichev at the second All-Union Conference of Leading Procuracy Officials, which convened in April 1948. "In the country of victorious socialism," Mokichev asserted, "legality is the basic factor of state power," and "in such a country there must be no place for unfounded prosecutions. With all decisiveness we must eliminate these cases." Moreover, "with each groundless prosecution and conviction we discredit ourselves, first of all as an agency supervising legality." By unfounded prosecutions and convictions Mokichev meant any case that ended in an acquittal – either at trial or on appeal – or was stopped by the procuracy after a return for supplementary investigation. To reduce and eventually eliminate these events meant treating "each instance from a political vantage point," that is, "as an extraordinary happening of great political import."[1]

Mokichev was not the first official to use the terms "groundless prosecutions" and "groundless convictions" to describe cases that ended in acquittal at trial on appeal. This language was already visible in documents prepared by Central Committee officials in 1946–1947, and even before the War in reports prepared for the Central Control Commission.[2] Nor was this the first time that the Procuracy had sought a reduction in weakly prepared cases that ended in acquittals. At the end of 1943 Procurator-General Safonov had initiated a secret review of acquittals from courts in selected regions, a review that found that most acquittals had been correct and resulted from weak cases. More striking were the actions of the justice ministers of Belorussia and Ukraine, both of whom wrote during 1947 or early 1948 to their respective republican central committees complaining about groundless prosecutions, the first in May and the latter in the turn of the year. Party leaders in the Ukrainian Republic responded by highlighting the issue in a secret, edict on socialist legality issued January 28, 1948. The edict called upon the Procuracy to "investigate every instance of groundless prosecution and illegal detention and punish the persons responsible for these crude violations of the rights of citizens." The Ukrainian edict explained that groundless prosecutions (and arrests) were especially common in the Western regions of the republic, which had joined the USSR only at the end of World War II and in 1946–1947 undergone seizures of private property, including collectivization of agriculture. At least in Ukraine, and perhaps also in Belorussia, the issue of unjustified prosecutions gained a place on the political agenda earlier than in Russia and the USSR as a whole because of the need to tame the police vigilantes who had been executing socialist transformation. In another time and place Stalin and Molotov's Instruction of May 8, 1933, had responded to the same challenge.[3]

Forerunners aside, Konstantin Mokichev was the first top legal official in the USSR to describe acquittals as "groundless prosecutions" in a *published* statement and the first to call for the *elimination* of the weakly prepared cases that led to acquittals. At first glance, the exhor-

---

1 "Vsesoiuznoe soveshchanie rukovodiashchikh rabotnikov Prokuratury," part one: SZ, 1948, no. 6, 38; GARF, f.8131sch, op.27s, d.4034 (Stenogramma vsesoiuznogo soveshchaniia prokurorskikh rabotnikov, 5–15 apreliia, 1948; tom 1), 297–318, esp. 300–302.
2 RTsKhIDNI, f.17, op.117, d.681, 58–65; d.764, 104–105, GARF f.8131, op.27s, d.157, 18. One also finds the term "illegal convictions."
3 RTsKhIDNI, f.17, op.136, d.70, 33, 43; Tsentralnyi Derzhavnyi Arkhiv Gromadskikh Ob'ednan Ukraini, f.1, op.6, d.1169, 16–30, esp. 28 (quotation) and 21. Thanks to Viktor Maniichuk for retrieving this document.

tations of Mokichev seem praiseworthy. If he had merely urged investigators and procurators to exercise more care in the choice of cases that they sent to trial and how they prepared them, and the rhetoric mere hyperbole, then Mokichev's words would have done no harm. But this was not the case. The speech of the deputy procurator-general foreshadowed a campaign to drastically reduce the number and percentage of both acquittals and returns for supplementary investigation – at trial and on appeal – and as a result make the administration of criminal justice in the USSR appear not just fair but flawless.

In the months following Molkichev's speech the USSR Procuracy seems to have taken no further action on acquittals. The USSR Ministry of Justice limited itself to ordering its republican ministries to study the phenomenon in general and in particular regions and districts, including Moscow city and region.[4] In contrast to the union level officials, the RSFSR Minister of Justice I. Basavin developed a whole program for confronting "groundless prosecutions and convictions." After reporting to the Central Committee on the numbers of acquittals and launching his own studies of the problem on July 28, 1948, Basavin issued a directive to judges and justice officials in the Russian Federation. In the directive Basavin called for much the same measures as had the Central Committee in the Ukraine. He "suggested" that

1. with each instance of an acquittal or return to supplementary investigation in a case that had been investigated by the district procuracy, the *judge* (sic!) inform the regional procuracy office for a "determination of responsibility";
2. in each instance of an acquittal or quashing of a conviction on appeal, the regional court inform the regional justice administration, so that it could take "appropriate measures," including, when necessary, a review of the trial judge's conduct by a disciplinary college of the Ministry of Justice.
3. the justice administration and regional courts conduct studies of groundless prosecutions and convictions and together with the procuracy hold meetings to plan further measures.[5]

Basavin's directive – through read only by judges and judicial officials in the RSFSR – contained the essential ingredient of the broader campaign against acquittals that unfolded in 1949–1951 – namely, the element of personal responsibility. If a trial ended in an acquittal, then

---

[4] GARF, f.9492, op.1, d.174, 62–63; GARF (TsGA), f.353sch, op.16s, d.72, 155.
[5] GARF (TsGA), f.353sch, op.16s, d.70, 42–47; d.72, 34–37, 91–95, 155–206.

those who had prepared and approved the case (the investigator and procurator) should not have sent it to trial. If a sentence were changed on appeal, then the trial judge had made the wrong choice. According to the directive, all legal officials who made these "mistakes" had to be held to account!

Wherever implemented, the Basavin directive promised to exert pressure on both judges and officials of the procuracy and even pit one against another. Such a conflict emerged in the Chuvash autonomous republic. Following the directive, the republic's minister of justice, Alekseev, ordered a study of "groundless prosecutions and convictions" for the first ten months of 1948. The resulting report revealed substantial numbers of both and blamed weak investigation by procuracy officials for both acquittals rendered at trial and the convictions overturned on appeal. Alekseev passed the report to the party committee of the republic and waited three months without a reply. Thereupon, he sent the report with a personal letter of complaint directly to Secretary of the Central Committee, Georgii M. Malenkov. Inquiries from the top led to the discovery that the procurator of the Chuvash ASSR had supplied his superiors in the RSFSR Procuracy with falsified data. The procurator had allegedly "created the appearance of normality (*blagopoluchie*)" by reporting a mere 32 acquittals in cases investigated by the procuracy during 1948, instead of the more than 300 acquittals registered by the republic's justice officials. As a result, the Central Committee and the USSR Procuracy fired this veteran official, despite his good work record in the past, and the Chuvash party officials added a censure. The bureau of the regional party committee also devoted a session to "groundless prosecutions and convictions" (in April 1949), and in a resolution directed the new procurator to check "every fact of groundless prosecution of citizens."[6]

As the drama in the Chuvash Republic unfolded, justice officials in other parts of the USSR began paying attention to acquittals. On February 18, 1949, the USSR minister of justice – reportedly "at the initiative of the USSR Procuracy" – instructed republican ministers of justice to direct all people's court judges "to inform regional procuracy offices about every case reaching trial from the district procuracy that is either stopped in preparatory session or ends in an acquittal," indicating exactly which officials in the police and procuracy had composed the accusation and which had confirmed it. This instruction extended the July 1948 directive of the RSFSR Ministry of Justice (the Basavin directive) to the other republics of the USSR. Moreover, in March and April the Central Committee received reports on groundless prosecutions

6 RTsKhIDNI, f.17, op.136, d.70, 3–9, 10–20.

and convictions from the justice ministries of the RSFSR, Ukraine, and Belorussia and the Supreme Courts of Belorussia, Uzbekistan, and the Mordovian ASSR.[7] What sent the campaign into high gear, however, was the decisive action taken by the procurator-general of the USSR.

In a secret directive (Order No. 61s of April 4, 1949) Procurator-General Grigorii N. Safonov instructed regional procuracy offices throughout the USSR to establish "operational control" over every instance of an acquittal or stopped case. District procuracy offices were to mount an inquiry, while the investigatory department or department for supervision of the police in the regional procuracy did the same. If those checking the case from the regional procuracy thought the acquittal justified, they were to identify the person(s) at fault – the investigator and assistant procurator – and raise the question of responsibility. If they found the acquittal unjustified, they were to send the case to the department of supervision of the courts in the regional procuracy for the launching of an appeal and, again, consideration of reprisals against the judge who rendered the decision and the procurator who failed to protest it. For their part, the heads of the departments of courts in the regional procuracy were to keep exact records of all stopped cases and acquittals using special cards and statistical forms.[8] Lest any procuracy official fail to recognize the seriousness of the first order on acquittals, Procurator-General Safonov issued a follow-up order in December 1949, condemning the allegedly high rate of acquittals and stopped cases in the city of Moscow and punishing those held responsible. Served up as scapegoats were the procurator of the city (who received a censure), some of his subordinates (who were warned), and the procurator of the district within the city that had the highest rate of "unfounded prosecutions." The latter was fired for "antigovernmental practices."[9]

The USSR Procuracy acted in 1949 as if the rate of acquittals in the USSR had reached some new crisis level. But this was not the case. In 1948, courts acquitted just over 10% of the accused brought before them, the same rate as the average for the past decade. (In the 1920s and early 1930s rates of acquittal had stood even higher, and in the late tsarist period had averaged one-third of all cases.)[10] To be sure, the 1948 rate represented a rise over 1947's anomalously low level of 6.3%. (The level of cases stopped was also low that year.) The return to normal levels of

7 GARF, f.9492sch, op.1s, d.558, 7; GARF (TsGA), f.353, op.16s, d.713, 13; RTsKhIDNI, f.17, op.136, d.70, 1–2, 21–80.
8 GARF, f.8131sch, op.28s, d.597, 31–34 (Prikaz Generalnogo Prokurora No. 61s ot 4 apreliia 1949 "Ob usilenii borby s faktami neosnovatelnogo privlecheniia k sudebnoi otvetsvennosti").
9 GARF, f.8131sch, op.28s, d.597, 133–135.
10 GARF, f.9492sch, op.6s, d.15, 12–13.

acquittal in 1948 stemmed at least in part from intensified pressure on investigators to avoid stopping cases before trial. In any event, top procuracy officials like Mokichev and Safonov never mentioned this statistical event. Moreover, most acquittals in 1948 and 1949 came about for normal reasons. In some cases, especially those handled directly by the police without preliminary investigation by a procuracy investigator, the trial revealed that no crime had been committed. In a larger share of acquittals the problem was evidentiary. Sometimes, the accused retracted a confession that the investigator or police had failed to support with corroborating evidence; more often, witnesses changed their testimony. Although better work by police and investigators might have prevented some acquittals, it would not have stopped many of them.[11]

The preoccupation of the Soviet authorities with "unfounded prosecutions and convictions" stemmed not from a change in the practice of the procuracy or courts but from a new intolerance toward imperfections in the administration of justice. The origins of and reasons for this posture present a special problem of interpretation, to which I shall return at the end of the chapter.

The implementation of the campaign against acquittals assumed high priority in the work of regional procuracy officials. To ensure that these offices did inquire into every acquittal as ordered, they had to submit quarterly reports to higher procuracy authorities (in the RSFSR to republican procuracy). Although the initial reports in 1949 revealed difficulties in compiling the data, let alone doing the checks, most regional procuracies did produce scorecards on individual procurators and investigators in the district and delivered censures and warnings to those with the worst records. The pressure from the USSR and RSFSR procuracies to monitor and reduce acquittals continued unabated for three years, long enough to make the avoidance of acquittals a habit.[12] The reports for 1951 showed improvements in the performance of regional procuracy officials in confronting acquittals. The procuracy of Smolensk Region had checked the work of 28 of 44 district procuracy offices and hearing reports in open sessions from 8 of their procurators and 16 investigators. The department of court supervision of the regional procuracy claimed to have checked every acquittal and sent 79 letters to district procurators concerning particular acquittals. The office also sent three communiqués to the regional justice administration complaining about judges who gave unjustified acquittals. The procurator of Smolensk Region gave censures, warnings, or transfers to district and

11 GARF, f.9492sch., op.6s, d.15, 12–15; f.8131, op.29, d.108, 28–30; (TsGA), f.461s, op.8s, d.219, 13; f.8131sch, op.27s, d.5179, 4.
12 GARF (TsGA), f.461, op.8s, d.1733, d.1953, d.219.

city procurators with especially high rates of acquittal in 1951, and fired the leader, a district procurator with 13 acquittals (8.7% of his cases). The struggle against "unfounded prosecutions" in Smolensk proved especially successful; the rate of acquittal reportedly dropped from 6.6% in 1950 to 2.7% in 1951.[13]

The procuracy's campaign against acquittals during 1949–1951 had the full support of regional *party* officials. As we have seen, the Chuvash party committee tackled the issue in April 1949. In July party secretaries in Sverdlovsk Region issued a resolution about procuracy investigations that focused on unfounded prosecutions. Pursuant to this resolution, the head of the Administrative Organs Department prepared a study of unfounded prosecution arrests in the region (December 1950), hosted a meeting of legal officials on the subject (March 1951), and collected further reports during the year from the legal agencies of Sverdlovsk.[14] As of July 1950, 31 regional party committee *biuros* had discussed the problem of unfounded prosecutions. Moreover, during 1949 and the first part of 1950 a series of regional party committees (e.g., Gorkii, Irkutsk, Kursk, Orlovskii, Rostov, Mariiskii ASSR) ordered or helped to arrange conferences of procurators and judges, with party secretaries themselves often in attendance. In late 1950 and 1951, many other party committees (including Daghestan and Novosibirsk) followed suit. One of the first of these conferences took place in Orlovsk Region in March 1950. Following instructions from the party committee the regional procurator organized a conference of procurators, judges, investigators, police chiefs, and advocates (225 persons in all). The themes of the conferences were "criminal investigation, groundless prosecutions, and unfounded convictions of citizens." The head of the regional party committee missed the event in favor of participation in the sowing campaign, but on his return issued a decree on the subject of groundless prosecutions and convictions.[15]

The involvement of so many regional party committees in the campaign against unfounded prosecutions suggests direction from the Central Committee of the CPSU. In fact, in May 1950 the Administrative Organs Department prepared for Central Committee Secretary Ponomarenko a draft resolution of the Central Committee "On measures for the elimination of groundless prosecutions and convictions of

13 GARF (TsGA), f.461s, op.8s, d.219, 1–18.
14 Partiinnyi arkhiv Sverdlovksogo obkoma KPSS, f.4, op.47, d.259, 115–130; op.49, d.251, 14–20; 105–107; 112–117; 118–127. I am grateful to James Harris for locating and arranging photocopies of these materials.
15 GARF (TsGA), f.353sch, op.16s, d.110, 11–13; f.461, op.8s, d.1828, 1–9, 17–29; 30–66, 82–86.

citizens," which included a "suggestion" to regional party officials to increase their supervision of the work of the legal agencies. The draft edict was composed after the receipt by the Central Committee of an anonymous complaint about the failure of the USSR Procuracy to take sufficiently strong measures against groundless prosecutions. The complaint led first to the preparation of a memorandum for Ponomarenko and then to the draft resolution.[16] I do not know whether the resolution was adopted, but it is clear that even before its composition many regional party secretaries had taken action.

The intense pressure on investigators and procurators to avoid acquittals represented only a part of the campaign for perfection in the administration of justice. Legal officials also faced analogous demands (and sanctions) to avoid returns to supplementary investigation and arrests of persons not later sentenced to imprisonment. Demands for better performance on the traditional measures of efficiency, such as meeting caseload quotas and mandatory time periods, also increased, and judges, as well as procuracy officials, faced pressure to achieve new standards of performance. In the centralized system of management that had entered the legal agencies before World War II, statistics were kept on how individual officials met these standards. With most legal officials making careers in the legal agencies, they had to take these demands seriously.

The pressure to reach new levels of performance was bound to produce distortions in the administration of justice, for there were limits to the possibilities for improvement. The legal officials remained the same people working with the same constraints of time and resources and in the same environments. To be sure, as the RSFSR minister of justice put it at a conference in 1951, "Statistics is an art, not a science"; and officials did not resist the temptation to construct the right kind of data, and as we have seen, occasionally fake them.[17] But there were limits to the art of statistics. The bottom line was that strong pressure upon procuracy officials might result in additional pressure upon judges.

We shall now examine how each of the legal officials – investigators, procurators, and judges – adjusted to the campaign for perfection – first in the efficiency of performance and then in its substance.

Investigators, procurators, and judges did find ways to improve efficiency but often through manipulation and distortion. Investigators,

---

[16] RTsKhIDNI, f.17, op.136, d.166, 322–329. For the text of the anonymous letter see ibid., op.118, d.720, 91–95ob.

[17] GARF (TsGA), f.353, op.13, d.138, 47; "Ob ukreplenii otchetnoi ditsipliny i povyshenii kachestva operativnykh statiticheskikh otchetov," Prikaz Gen. Prok. SSSR ot 19 avgusta 1956 g., no. 107, *Sbornik deistvuiushchikh prikazov i instruktsii Generalnogo Prokurora SSSR* (Moscow, 1948), 297–298.

for example, had to fulfill norms of productivity set by the All-Union Procuracy by completing investigations of a specified number of cases per month. This demand led investigators to prefer "easy" cases. A star investigator praised at a conference of the best investigators in 1950 noted that he had handled only two "hard" cases in the previous year (by "hard" he meant lasting more than two months). This situation enabled him to complete 44 cases in the first six months of 1950 and produce an average of 7.3 cases per month, thereby bettering his 1949 rate of 4.5.[18] Naturally, the easier cases were also less likely to produce returns for supplementary investigation or be stopped before trial for lack of evidence.

At the same time, some investigators got stuck with more hard cases than others and found themselves falling behind on their totals. To avoid a shortfall and get some extra "ticks" (*palochki*) onto their records, investigators found a way to add easy cases quickly. When faced with a shortage of cases completed at the end of a month or quarter, they would approach the local hospital and collect evidence to start cases of "self-performed abortions." This was a safe and easy charge that called for no active investigation. The hospitals identified women who suffered bleeding from botched abortions performed by the underground "babas." To protect the abortionist the victims would insist that they had done the abortions themselves and as a result receive a small fine. One investigator managed to include cases of self-inflicted abortions on his records even when they were diverted to comrades' courts and ended with warnings.[19]

Investigators also had to reduce the percentage of cases that they stopped during investigation for lack of suspect or evidence. The response to this demand was simple. Investigators began delaying the formal start of investigations until after they had done enough inquiries to be sure that they had enough evidence. Already in 1950 the head of the investigatory department of the RSFSR Procuracy observed that delays of one to two months were becoming commonplace. A directive of 1954 described the practice as a "preinvestigation," developed to ensure that investigators would create the appearance of success in their work.[20]

---

18 *Rabota luchshikh sledovatelei. Materialy uchebno-metodicheskoi konferentsii luchshikh sled-stvennykh rabotnikov organov prokuratury.* Sbornik 1 (Moscow, 1951), 63; GARF, f.8131, op.28, d.1383 (Materialy uchebno-metodicheskoi konferentsii sledstvennykh rabotnikov strany, 8 iuniia–13 iuniia 1953), 24–25.
19 Ibid., 58–59; interviews.
20 *Rabota luchshikh sledovatelei* (1), 76; "O poriadke razresheniia pervichnykh materialov i soobshchenii o sovershennykh prestupleniiakh," Ukazanie Gen. Prok. SSSR ot 19 iiunia 1954 g. no. 3/114, "*Sbornik deistvuiushchikh prikazov,*" 33–34.

Procurators also confronted new demands to demonstrate productivity. For one thing, the prewar pressure to increase their appearances at trials continued and produced results. In 1946 a procurator (usually an assistant procurator) appeared in almost half of all trials (as opposed to 10% in 1937), and in 81% of serious trials. By 1948, according to the procurator of Irkutsk, the norms for all cases had reached 80%.[21] But quantity still took precedence over quality. Typically, procurators merely confirmed the written accusation in an opening speech and did little more. They failed to supervise legality in the courtroom (most complaints about procedural violations issued from the defense), and they limited their appeals in cassation to complaints about leniency on the part of the judge – including verdicts of acquittal. As of 1948, assistant procurators still avoided reviewing the results of trials that they had not attended.[22]

Efficiency and productivity also played a prominent part in the assessment of the work of judges. Size of backlogs, number of cases completed per month, and the length of delays in hearing cases figured among the indicators of a judge's performance.[23] Meeting expectations on these counts required many judges to work long hours into the night. It also led to shortcuts, such as setting aside paper work until the completion of a series of trials, and an aversion to putting off scheduled trials when the prerequisites were not met. The accused, his lawyer, or a key witness might fail to appear, but rescheduling the trial might hurt the judge's record of productivity.

The pressure on legal officials to achieve high standards of efficiency and productivity was real, but it took second place to the new concerns of top legal officials about the substance of performance. By 1950 the most important indicators for investigators (and all procuracy officials supervising them) became the rates of acquittals and returns to supplementary investigation; for procurators, the frequency of "bad arrests"; and for judges, the "stability of sentences." The effort to meet these substantive criteria of performance had tragic consequences for the delivery of justice in the USSR.

We have already examined how the chiefs of the Procuracy cracked down on acquittals in 1949, making each instance the object of special

[21] K. Mokichev, "Sudebno-nadzornaia rabota Prokatury," SZ, 1947, no. 5, 18; GARF, f.8131, op.27, d.4034, 37.

[22] "Soveshchanie nachalnikov ugolovno-sudebnykh otdelov prokuratur soiuznykh i respublik, ASSR, kraev, i oblastei," SZ, 1948, no. 3, 24–28. When in the early 1950s, the USSR Procuracy introduced mandatory reviews of case files when the procurator had not attended trial, attendance increased. Interviews.

[23] S. Fainblit, "Pokazateli otsenki kachestva raboty narodnykh sudov," SZ, 1948, no. 5, 25–28; Spravochnik narodnogo sudi (Moscow, 1946), 98–100.

inquiry and a potential source of trouble for the investigators and procurators involved in the case. At the same time, the Procuracy's leaders continued treating returns for supplementary investigation as another sign of failure for investigators. The Procuracy had targeted this particular form of defective work in 1948, prompting some city procurators to check all of the returns in their bailiwicks. Lest local procurators turn their attention away from returns, the procurator-general issued a "telegram-directive" in November 1949 denouncing high rates of returns, and returns figured prominently in the selection of the "best investigators" – a contest revived from the prewar years.[24] At the first annual conference of the "best" investigators convened by the All-Union Procuracy in 1950 the stars boasted of having reduced their personal rates of returns to supplementary investigation to zero; for a whole year none of their cases had been returned by the courts.[25] In at least some instances, the "best" investigators had benefited from support of their offices (e.g., were given only cases that seemed to have strong evidence), in order to produce "winners" in the competition.

At the same conference (in 1950) the chiefs of the investigatory departments described the methods they had adopted for dealing with returns and acquittals. In Dnepropetrovsk Region the department asked city and district procuracy offices to supply monthly lists of cases returned for supplementary investigations with details of each case and explanations from the investigator. For each acquittal not protested by the procurator, the latter had to send a personal explanation to the same department. The procurator of Chernigovsk Region reported that for each return he required the investigator to present an explanation in person at the regional procuracy office! The same procurator also asked his regional court to send over all cases that it heard on appeal and decided to return to local procuracy offices for supplementary investigation. As a result of his efforts, the procurator reported, Chernigovsk Region went from having only three districts with no returns in 1948 to nine in 1949 to 15 (of 40 districts) in 1950.[26]

These efforts notwithstanding, Deputy Procurator-General Mokichev repeated his stinging words of two years before. "It is no secret . . . ," he declaimed at the conference, "that we still have cases of unfounded prosecution. One should remember that the burden of responsibility for this lies first of all on the procurators and investigators – for investigations that prove defective, where an acquittal is granted or the case is returned for supplementary investigation. . . . " Meeting this responsi-

[24] GARF, f.8131sch, op.27s, d.4037, 43, 54, 65; op.28s, d.817, 12, 15–17, d.1383, 24–25.
[25] *Rabota luchshikh sledovatelei* (1), 49, 57.
[26] Ibid., 30–36; 60–61.

bility, Mokichev continued, was nothing less than a political require-ment.

> We must approach the evaluation of indicators of our work from the position of strictly state interests. We are obliged to recognize that every act of a procurator or investigator is an act of political meaning. These acts must not discredit the procuracy agencies and they must not discredit the authority in whose name we act. We are rightly considered to represent the Soviet state, since we act in the name of the state.[27]

Procurators shared the investigators' concern with curtailing acquit-tals and returns. To begin, as the administrative superiors of the inves-tigators, the procurators bore responsibility for their performance. Moreover, procurators had a concern of their own that was intimately related to the fate of cases in court. Procurators needed to avoid "bad arrests," that is, the detention before trial of suspects or accused persons whom judges failed to convict or sentence to confinement. Procurators, or assistant procurators acting in their names, had to sanction all pre-trial detentions lasting more than three days. When the person held was not convicted or, though convicted, sentenced to a noncustodial sanc-tion, the arrest was deemed to have been "unjustified." For an accused person to sit for months in prison awaiting trial, only to be acquitted, was a grueling experience; for the authorities, it was embarrassing, and to some also unjust. A related problem was the failure of investigators (and police) to observe the legal rules governing pretrial detention – including various clearances – and apply to higher level procurators for extensions after the initial two-month period had expired. In 1943, the procurator-general issued an order (No. 20s) insisting that investigators and procurators rectify these defects.[28] This order followed earlier di-rectives of the Procuracy and the party leadership (in 1933, 1935, and 1938) to keep arrests under control.[29]

The crackdown on "unjustified arrests" started in 1945 with the issuing by the central Procuracy of a new order (No. 172s). Focusing upon the failures of the procuracy office in Briansk region, the 1945 order censured procurators there for the arrest of persons later acquit-ted or sentenced to corrective work. The order went on to establish for the first time regular collection of data on persons released from deten-tion, including the grounds for their releases – when their cases had

---

[27] Ibid., 6.
[28] GARF (TsGA), f.353, op.13, d.134, 91, 93–93ob; GARF, f.8131, op.28s, d.155, 33–36.
[29] See GARF f.353sch, op.16s, d.13, 44–46; RTsKhIDNI, f.17, op.3, d.1003, 85–86.

been stopped during investigation, when detention was canceled before trial, when release followed acquittal or stopping of the case by the court, and when judges imposed noncustodial sentences. The new forms for recording these data also called for the identification in each instance of the procurator who had sanctioned the arrest, so that he (rarely she) could be held responsible for what turned out to have been an "unjustified arrest."

A year later the procurator-general issued a follow-up order condemning "bad arrests" in Kursk region and highlighting censures and firings of procuracy officials there. Starting in 1947 republican procuracy offices had to compile special reports on the fulfillment of rules on arrests. The Belorussian one depicted the continuation of "bad arrests" and the censure of more district procurators. Finally, in 1949, the USSR Procuracy issued yet another order, this time criticizing the handling of pretrial detention in Saratov region, again with censures and warnings.[30] Coming in the stream of directives about unjustified prosecutions, the 1949 order delivered extra punch, and in practice the review and criticism of acquittals and bad arrests were often merged. Arguably, procuracy offices could cut down "bad arrests" by holding fewer persons before trial, and some offices did just that, especially in cases where the evidence was weak. (As a result, police chiefs sometimes complained to local party officials about the procurator's failure to cooperate in the "fight against crime.") But as long as cases came apart in court, there would be "unjustified arrests." A report for the USSR as a whole in 1949 revealed a total of 31,068 such detentions: 16.9% where the cases had been stopped; 34.8% because of acquittals; and 48.3% that ended with noncustodial sanctions.[31]

For their part, judges also experienced strong pressure to avoid giving acquittals. This came in part from demands that judges achieve ever higher rates of "stability of sentences" and in part from the efforts of local party officials to rid their legal agencies of "unfounded prosecutions."

Stability of sentence referred to the percentage of a judge's verdicts and sentences upheld on appeal by the higher courts. For purposes of this calculation a change in sentence or verdict signaled an error on the part of the judge. Stability of sentence had served as a measure of judicial performance since the 1920s; and it had assumed a position of special prominence just before World War II. In the 1920s and first half of the 1930s, the years of the experiment with uneducated political

---

30 GARF, f.8131sch, op.28, d.235, 111–116 (Prikaz Prokuratury SSSR no. 172s ot 1 avgusta 1945); d.282, 100–103; op.27s, d.3871, 6–12; op.28, d.597, 82–85.

31 GARF (TsGA), f.353, op.13, d.150, 29ob, 70; GARF, f.8131sch, op.29s, d.108, 36.

trustees as judges, the chiefs of the agencies expected that a substantial share of sentences would be changed. Appellate reviews provided the needed corrective for the rawness of the judges. By the late 1930s that tolerant attitude had vanished, and authorities wanted trial judges to decide cases correctly. As we have seen, the spread of legal training helped to reduce obvious procedural mistakes, and the average rates of stability of sentences did improve. Before World War II around 60% of the appealed sentences of people's court judges remained unchanged (e.g., 57.3% in 1927, 58.7% in 1936, and 61.8% in 1940). In 1951 the rate was 74.7%, and in 1952, 78.2%.[32] The stability of sentences of regional court judges went from an average of 75.7% during the war years to 81.7% in the postwar period (1946–1952). The percentage of decisions of trial courts that produced appeals in cassation stayed constant throughout.[33]

In 1948 the USSR Ministry of Justice launched a drive for perfection in the work of judges analogous to the one that was occurring in the Procuracy. The Ministry's Collegium ordered a study of judges who had succeeded in working for months without a single verdict or sentence changed. Some of these judges received recognition as "the best judges," and rewards as well. Supervisors in the Ukraine boasted of an increase in the number of such judges. Moreover, chairmen of regional courts reportedly assessed the work of people's court judges on the basis of minuscule changes in their rates of sentences changed (e.g., from 82% to 84%).[34]

To achieve a good record in sentencing required that trial judges not only apply the law correctly (to deter appeals from the defense) but also follow the political line in judicial policy. In the late Stalin years this meant avoiding punishments more lenient than the norm – especially for serious offenses and cases related to current campaign priorities (such as theft). The reason was simple. In the USSR procurators had the right to appeal sentences, and for their own protection many procurators who argued cases in court felt obliged to appeal sentences or verdicts that appeared lenient even when there was no justification. For their part, appellate judges also were inclined to change some lenient verdicts, so as to conform to the "line" in their own work. For trial

---

32 Radus-Zenkovich, "Sudebnaia sistema," part 2; "Soveshchaniia aktiva NKIu RSFSR" (1940); GARF, f.9492, op.6s, d.15, 17.

33 In 1937–1940, 36.4% of sentences and convictions of people's courts were appealed; in 1941–1945 (not counting labor offenses), 33.5% and in 1946–1952 (also minus labor offenses), 35.6%. In the postwar period, 58.7% of decisions of regional courts were appealed, as opposed to 55.5% during the War. Ibid., 16.

34 GARF, f.8131, op.26, d.12, 101; f.9492, op.1, d.179, 71–72; GARF (TsGA) f.353, op.13, d.150, 111.

judges, there was no simple way to ensure success. When they punished harshly petty offenders, juveniles, or others who claimed extenuating circumstances, trial judges ran the risk of canceled sentences and returns for new trials. Moreover, some appellate judges proved inconsistent, even arbitrary, in their conduct, frustrating the trial judges subject to their reviews.[35] Still, most judges found that it was better to err on the side of severity.

Another deterrent to awarding lenient punishments was possible suspicion of bribe-taking. A postwar crackdown on corruption in the administration of justice led to the conviction for bribe-taking of dozens of judges, including some in high places. Convicted in 1948 and 1949 were members of the Latvian, Georgian, Russian, and USSR Supreme Courts, as well as members of military courts in Moscow (including the Military Collegium of the USSR Supreme Court). The most dramatic set of cases concerned bribery in the courts of Moscow – its city court, the RSFSR Supreme Court, and the USSR Supreme Court. The investigation led one deputy chairman of the USSR Supreme Court, A. P. Solodilov, to commit suicide. It led as well to the removal of Ivan Goliakov from the post of chairman for "failing to cope with his responsibilities and overlooking the criminal activity of employees of the Supreme Court" and Vasilii Ulrikh from the posts of deputy chairman and head of the Military Collegium for leading "an amoral life style." While Ulrikh stayed on as a member of the Supreme Court, Goliakov moved to full-time employment as a scholar and teacher.[36] All the same, in 1949,

---

[35] V. Krutskikh, "Povysit kachestvo kassatsionnykh i chastnykh protsessov," *SZ*, 1956, no. 2, 26–31.

[36] Apart from missing the corruption scandal from which he took his fall, Goliakov had long irritated his superiors in the Central Committee apparatus. At least in the years after the War, 1945–1948, he stood above the fray, leaving the operations of the court to his subordinates and devoting considerable time to other work as head of a research institute, teacher, and scholar. The party officials charged with justifying his removal wrote of his "spinelessness, and lack of organizational ability" and complained that he had "not once in ten years brought for consideration by the Central Committee one issue arising from the practice of the Supreme Court." (To some observers this would deserve praise!) Evidently, Goliakov did not fit the bureaucratic mold of a high justice official that by the late 1940s suited the political leadership.

The amoral lifestyle of Ulrikh consisted allegedly of long-standing drunkenness and living with a woman alcoholic who took morphine. Meanwhile, Ulrikh's wife had interfered in cases on behalf of interested parties, and the judge himself gave too lenient sentences after the removal of the death penalty.

The unfortunate Solidilov, the deputy chairman of the USSR Supreme Court who committed suicide, had, according to his accusers, not only taken bribes on a regular basis but also engaged in the worst kind of sexual harassment, forcing both petitioners to and female staff of the Court into "intimate relations." RTsKhIDNI, f.17, op.118, d.96, 131–141.

charges were laid against 247 persons including 27 judges, 22 court staff, and 27 advocates.[37] To avoid embarrassment and protect the reputation of Soviet courts, the chiefs of the legal agencies recommended to Secretary Malenkov the use of special closed sessions for these cases. The hearings would proceed without the participation of the sides (prosecution and defense) – that is, following the procedure used in the tribunals of the political police.[38]

Not surprisingly, with corruption exposed even in the higher courts, authorities in Moscow believed that they had seen only the tip of the iceberg. They assumed that many other judges and legal officials were acting in a similar manner and going undetected. To root out corruption among the judiciary, the chiefs in the Ministry of Justice instructed inspectors to stay alert for symptoms of bribery – such as the systematic awarding of acquittals, punishments below the legal limit, and requalifications of charges to ones bringing lighter penalties. According to a study prepared by the Ministry, the inspectors performed this assignment in a perfunctory way. Rather than investigate, they would write that "such and such a judge did not understand the political significance of the law on theft," and repeat the formula from one inspection to the next. To the author of the Ministry's report, this diagnosis made no sense. With all the propaganda about these laws (he was referring to the laws of June 4, 1947, that drastically increased penalties for theft – see Chapter 12), it was impossible for a judge to underestimate their political significance. "Either the judge is a total [sploshnoi] idiot . . . or someone who consciously commits crimes out of mercenary motives."[39] Although most inspections did not uncover bribery, judges still had reason to worry about lenient dispositions. Most prosecutions launched against judges used lenient sentences as a pretext, and local authorities sometimes pressed bribery charges against judges whom they disliked. Thus, between 1945 and 1947 twelve judges in Azerbaizhan faced prosecution for bribe-taking, all because of their "liberalism." The evidence was so weak that all but three were acquitted or delivered to supplementary investigation. But even the judges who won their cases

[37] GARF, f.9492sch, op.1s, d.578, 54; op.2s, d.44, 112–115; d.58, 237; f.8131sch, op.27, d.4044, 7, 173.

[38] GARF, f.9492sch, op.2s, d.58, 140–141. One Moscow city court judge convicted of taking bribes insisted that he had been wronged and complained incessantly to the political leaders. Even after his release in the amnesty of March 1953 (after Stalin's death), A.V. Vasnev sought Khrushchev's help with his petition for rehabilitation. However, a review of his case conducted by staff of the Central Committee later in 1953 concluded that Vasnev's complaint was groundless. RTsKhIDNI, f.17, op.136, d.70, 124–136.

[39] GARF, f.9492, op.1, d.169, 181–185 (quotation on 184ob); d.515, 287–294; d.242, 102–105.

spent months in prison awaiting trial and lost their jobs. Similar experiences befell the head of the Arkhangelsk regional courts in 1948 and a people's court judge in Cheliabinsk region in 1949.[40]

To achieve the required stability of sentences, judges had to avoid lenient outcomes, in particular acquittals that were not easy to justify. Cutting back even justified acquittals became necessary for judges after they became black marks in the Procuracy in 1948 and 1949. One reason was that the colleges for judicial discipline established in the region in 1948 "regularly misused their powers and punished judges for . . . giving acquittals or light punishments." (Note that in July 1948 the RSFSR Minister of Justice had advocated this use or "misuse" of the disciplinary colleges.)[41] The more fundamental and lasting reason was the need to keep good relations with the local procurator and the party bosses, who typically joined their procurator in fighting acquittals. When a judge gave more than the occasional acquittal or acquitted in an important case, the procurator would often complain to the party secretary. Such requests usually led to inquiries by the party officials, often to the judge in question having to report to the party committee and sometimes to disciplinary measures.[42] To understand the responsiveness of judges to the needs of the procuracy to avoid unfounded prosecutions requires an appreciation of the relationship among procurators, judges, and party officials at the local level.

Local politicians and the administration of justice

Why did the party chieftains in most cities and districts discourage judges from giving acquittals? Why did local politicians care about "unfounded prosecutions"?

One reason was that the party bosses worked closely with the procurators. As the most important justice official in the locale, the procurator usually had a membership in the district party committee and sometimes also its bureau. He had almost daily business at the committee and knew its secretaries well. He drank with them, used the same government dachas, and went on the same hunting parties. In short, he was a member of the local ruling clique. None of this could be said of the numerous people's court judges who worked in a locality. Hardly any of them had a personal relationship with the party bosses.[43]

[40] GARF, f.9492, op.1, d.514, 143–153; op.2s, d.58, 115–135, 149–150.
[41] Ibid., op.1, d.197, 81–13, 129–140; f.353s, op.16s, d.70, 47.
[42] GARF, f.8131, op.29, d.108, 42; GARF (TsGA), f.461s, op.8s, 2185, 35–36; d.2048, 169–171; f.353, op.13, d.134, 57; interviews.
[43] Interviews. See Solomon, "Soviet Politicians and Criminal Prosecutions."

A second reason for party bosses to cooperate with the procurator in discouraging acquittals was the logic of exchange. Party bosses asked and expected the cooperation of procurators on many matters, including the stopping of prosecutions of important party members in the locality. We saw in Chapter 8 that despite pressures on the procurators this cooperation did not come automatically. Some procurators resisted encroachments by party officials and appealed to higher levels of procuratorial or political authority in order to pursue prosecutions against the will of local party officials. One way that party secretaries could reward procurators for cooperation was helping them do their own jobs, by chastising judges who gave too many acquittals.

A third reason why local party bosses joined in the discouragement of acquittals was the responsibility they had assumed for the performance of the justice agencies in their regions. The origins of this involvement dated back to the mid-1930s, when party officials in some regions began to scrutinize the work of the justice agencies (see Chapter 5). By the late 1930s, many court and procuracy officials were reporting on their work to meetings of local party committees as well, and regional party secretaries issued their own instructions to procurators and judges. The responsibility of party officials at lower levels for the administration of justice grew with the establishment in 1948 of departments of administrative organs at the regional party committees and the designation of particular secretaries at the city and district committees to monitor the legal agencies.[44]

In the late 1940s and early 1950s the responsibility of party officials for the administration of justice focused, as before, on the management of cadres – that is, the recruitment, discipline, advancement, and firing of legal officials. The assessment of particular judges, procurators, and investigators by party officials included their performance on the job, and party officials often used for this purpose the criteria of evaluation developed by the legal agencies, including rates of acquittals and "bad arrests." As we have seen, in 1949 and 1950 some regional party committees or their bureaus even issued their own decrees on combatting "unfounded prosecution." The adoption by local party bodies of operational goals and standards was common in other areas of public administration (such as industry). At the same time, there is reason to suppose that the party leadership in Moscow had encouraged party officials to support the struggle against unfounded prosecution. Naturally, this did not mean that party officials in the localities stopped pursuing their

---

[44] GARF, f.9492, op.1, d.243, 5–6; GARF (TsGA), f.353, op.13, d.134, 8, 23ob, 91ff.; d.150, 13ob, 21, 38ob; Amy Knight, *The KGB: Police and Politics in the Soviet Union* (Boston, 1988), 129.

own interests, for example intervening to protect the managers in their bailiwicks from prosecution or punishment. At a conference in 1950 a number of judges chastised for leniency in particular cases blamed the need to respond to local pressures. At the same time, however, many party bosses did expect that the legal officials of their regions would satisfy their superiors in the legal agencies and cut down on acquittals and bad arrests.[45]

The next question is why judges paid heed to the interests of party bosses in keeping the level of acquittals low. The answer is straightforward. In the years after World War II, as before, judges remained dependent upon the good will of party bosses in their districts for both the progress of their careers and the conditions of work and life. In fact, as more judges acquired legal education and made judging a career, they found themselves in a position where they had to please the party chief. Renomination for election as a judge (after the War, elections came every three years) required the consent of the party secretary. The latter could also initiate a recall before the expiry of term. According to the rules, any "firing" of judges required the consent of supervisory officials in the Ministry of Justice's provincial administrations (and in the case of the release of "young specialists" the consent of the cadre's department of the USSR Ministry of Justice). But local bosses often acted on their own, ignoring the rules on clearances. Moreover, local party officials could expose judges to party discipline, adding censures or warnings to their party records when they failed to meet expectations.[46] Party officials even went so far as to join procurators in the fabrication of charges of bribe-taking and other misdeeds.

Take, for example, the case of a people's court judge from Tirasopol in Moldavia, who complained to Stalin about his treatment by the procuracy and party officials. Whenever the procurator disliked a verdict (especially in cases where he had not appeared), he told the district party secretary, who without checking or understanding law, called in the judge in question and cursed him out, even though the Supreme Court of the republic left the sentence in place. The particular judge had dared to give acquittals, "even when the procurator said he wanted a conviction." These incidents led to discussions at the city committees and persecution of the judge in the form of fabricated charges for drunkenness, bribe-taking, and contact with criminal elements. The party and procuracy officials arranged for various citizens to admit to

45 GARF (TsGA), f.461s, op.8s, d.1828, 8; d.1829, 169; f.353, op.13, d.150, 8, 21; d.134, 42, 57, 91ff; interviews.
46 "Soveshchanie ministrov iustitsii soiuznykh respublik," SZ, 1946, no. 9, 26; "V Ministerstve iustitsii SSSR," SZ, 1948, no. 1, 29; GARF, f.9492, op.1, d.181, 100–101.

offering bribes. Then the city party committee met to scold the judge (with four procurators in attendance) and give a censure. Six weeks later the same committees heard the procurator complain about court delays in cases of arrested suspect and as a result the judge received another censure. The judge who experienced all this trouble was an educated man, a graduate of the Moscow Juridical Institute in 1940. In September 1947 he complained to the Moldavian Ministry of Justice, and a lengthy review by the Central Committee of the Communist party of Moldavia led to his transfer to another district and a lighter load. But, reportedly the persecution of this judge did not stop.[47]

Judges also depended upon the goodwill of party bosses for conditions of life and work. The acquisition of an apartment required a dispensation of favor by local authorities, as did the provision of a vacation in a resort. (One judge complained that each year her court with six judges got only one vacation trip, which they had to give to a secretary or cleaning lady.) Moreover, the acquisition and maintenance of buildings, telephone lines, fuel, and means of transport often required help. In earlier chapters we have recorded examples of dismal conditions of many courthouses (and procuracy headquarters as well). In the last years of Stalin the situation did not improve. Disgraceful conditions were reported for Sakhalin, Novosibirsk, and Rostov; in Moscow itself in 1949 one in six court districts had no quarters at all, while others had poor ones (such as a basement shared with a notary office).[48] In Omsk and Sakhalin the judges depended on horses not only for their own travel but to haul fuel to heat the court building. Typewriters remained in short supply. "Though we live in the century of mechanized writing," said the procurator of Omsk, "we continue to use 'medieval methods' of 'scribes' and 'copiers.' " Often courts could not obtain fuel without the help of local politicians. A judge from Rostov region reported in 1950 that while his district party committee had helped him get the front door of the courthouse repaired, it had left him off the list for coal. After repeated entreaties, the party bosses did manage to obtain some coal for the court, but it was the wrong kind "not usable in our building," so as a result the judges stopped hearing cases until spring.[49]

The physical conditions in the courts were so poor that in 1946 Council of People's Commissars Chairman Molotov issued a decree requiring local governments to provide accommodations and furniture. But implementation was spotty, and physical conditions remained an

[47] GARF, f.9492sch, op.2s, d.50, 119–166.
[48] GARF, f.9492, op.1, d.179, 120–124, 186–187; d.514, 27–52; d.196, 59–60.
[49] GARF, f.8131, op.28, d.1093b, 204–207; GARF (TsGA) f.353, op.13, d.134, 15–17.

object of conflict. Take, for example, the situation of Judge Loseva from a district in Rostov Region. Loseva started working as a judge at the age of 16, directly upon graduation from secondary school in 1947. The district party committee, she complained, treated her as a young girl, not helping her in her work, but cursing and dictating how to judge and whom – "although I paid no attention." On her own initiative, Loseva fixed up her court building, making it, she claimed, "the best court-house in the area." The judge must have succeeded, for the district political authorities started commandeering the court's building for classes, meetings, and an agricultural exhibition, effectively converting it into a club. The judge complained first to the regional justice administration then to the district party secretaries itself, and finally to the administrative department of the Ukrainian Central Committee. The latter ordered the district prosecutors to stop all noncourt functions in the building, but this victory proved to be pyrrhic. The party bosses managed to make life so unpleasant for Loseva that she left to work in another district.[50]

For judges, it was impossible to pursue a career and work in tolerable conditions without maintaining good relations with local politicians. To do so obliged judges to follow bureaucratic and political directives about sentencing, produce good indicators of performance, and cooperate with particular requests regarding sentencing and the resolution of civil conflicts. The discreet telephone call indicating the need to punish "a bit on the mild side" or "with force" usually sufficed, and failure to comply could lead to trouble. Interventions in civil cases often focused upon that scarce and valuable commodity, the apartment. A district party secretary in Sverdlovsk region ordered a judge to have an apartment vacated at once, threatening that if the order were not fulfilled "your behavior will be discussed at the party bureau (*raikombiuro*). Report in three hours."[51] For judges, following criminal policy could mean giving more severe punishments than usual, and this might happen because of a local initiative. Some district party committees insisted that during the initial campaign following the 1947 laws on theft judges give the maximum sentences allowed by law. Finally, judges were expected not only to achieve good indicators themselves but to help their colleagues in the procuracy do the same. Thus, one district party secretary threatened to fire any judge who gave an acquittal! A more typical response to judges who gave acquittals was a discussion at a party meeting, followed by a censure or warning, and perhaps reprisals

---

[50] GARF, f.9492, op.1, d.196, 39–60; GARF (TsGA) f.353, op.13, d.134, 15–17.
[51] Solomon, "Soviet Politicians and Criminal Prosecutions," interviews; GARF, f.9492, op.1, d.179, 100 ff.

such as refusing to repair the courthouse or supply a vacation package.[52]

The dynamics of the situation of judges should now be clear. Dependent upon local party bosses, judges had to meet their expectations, and party bosses expected judges to avoid acquittals and other signs of leniency, not only to please the procurators with whom they consorted but also because they too shared responsibility for the performance of the justice agencies. Good performance by the procuracy and courts meant securing convictions at trial, not producing failures in court, such as acquittals and returns to supplementary investigation. There could be few, if any, "unfounded prosecutions or convictions," especially the sort that produced unjustified arrests.

Conflict and compromise: coping with demands for perfection

In the late 1940s and early 1950s the achievement of good statistical indicators preoccupied legal officials, shaping their outlook and conduct. Unfortunately, the quest for perfection also led to conflicts among groups of officials. One source of conflict was differences over the relative importance of particular indicators, especially when the pursuit of one indicator conflicted with the attainment of another. An even more common source of conflict was the dependence of one set of officials for the achievement of its indicators upon the conduct of another set of officials. We shall illustrate both kinds of conflicts and then detail the means developed by judges for avoiding them.

Which mattered more – that judges deliver sentences implementing current criminal policy, that is the "line" regarding the choice and severity of sanctions, or the attainment by those same judges of a high rate of stability of sentences? A conference of deputy chairmen of regional courts held in 1950 revealed that officials of the Ministry of Justice cared more about the former and trial court judges about the latter.

The conflict emerged when officials of the Ministry of Justice criticized the people's court judges of a particular region for excessive leniency, especially for their use of punishments below the legal limit (Article 51) and suspended sentences (Article 53). These measures had become in 1949–1950 dispositions of choice for judges wishing to mitigate the excessive severity of the 1947 laws on theft, particularly as applied to women and juveniles. Started by trial judges, the practices

---

[52] Solomon, "The Case of the Vanishing Acquittal," 537; interviews; GARF (TsGA), f.353, op.13, d.134, 8.

had received approval from higher courts including the USSR Supreme Court. At the conference, individual people's court judges claimed that they had followed the lead of the RSFSR Supreme Court, which had earlier on changed or canceled more severe sentences delivered by them for these categories of offenders.[53]

RSFSR Minister of Justice Fedor Beliaev responded by explaining why most judges should not follow the RSFSR Supreme Court! That court, Beliaev claimed, differed from trial courts. To begin, it heard cases mainly in supervision, "a few years after the trial, when punishments had been partly served and taken into account." Its role was to join the commission on amnesty in demonstrating "the humanism of our Soviet country." This was the "political function" of the RSFSR Supreme Court, and in performing it, the minister stressed, the court received periodic guidance from the "directive agencies" (i.e., party officials). On the other hand, trial judges also had to take account of the political situation in their own locales. If hooliganism were on the decline in the province or city, "you could apply suspended sentences widely and no one would complain." But if the opposite were so, judges would have to send most hooligans to prison. In short, Beliaev concluded, "the court is a flexible party mechanism and therefore one cannot say, do as the Supreme Court does."[54] In this nakedly political analysis of Soviet courts, the RSFSR minister of justice was telling his judges: unless there is some special reason for leniency, punish severely and let the higher courts, especially the Supreme Court of the Federation, soften the blow, in accordance with political instructions.

Beliaev's advice did not satisfy many of the judges at the conference. For if the use of suspended sentences and sentences below the legal limit were left to the Supreme Court to introduce by changing the sentence from the trial, the trial judge's record of performance would be hurt. In the measurement of the judge's record on stability of sentences, the case would be registered as a verdict that was not left in force, and for the trial judge it would constitute "defective goods" (*brak*), even though the judge had made no real mistake. There would be, in short, a conflict between the demand to achieve stability of sentences and the policy of avoiding leniency, if higher courts were left to modify sentences in the direction of leniency. At least some trial judges were unwilling to accept this situation. A judge from North Ossetia expressed his resentment. "Why should the Supreme Court of the Federation have the right to think (*myslit*) and we do not?"[55]

53 GARF (TsGA), f.353 op.13, d.150, 16–18.
54 Ibid., 19–20.
55 Ibid., 91ob, 99, and 54 (quotation).

Conflicts among legal officials also stemmed from the dependence of one set of officials upon another for the achievement of good indicators. The pressure to "eliminate unfounded prosecutions" brought these conflicts into the open, pitting trial judges against appellate court judges and officials of the procuracy against judges.

In launching the campaign against unfounded prosecutions, the top legal officials intended to press investigators and prosecutors to improve their work and send to court only cases that had firm evidence. But procuracy officials could not afford to stop too many cases during investigation (this would hurt their records), and no matter how hard they tried, they could not work perfectly. The rates of acquittal at trial did decline somewhat in 1949 and 1950, but partly because judges – cooperating with the needs of procurators – convicted offenders that they should have acquitted. Naturally, many of these cases then arrived at the door of the cassation panels of the regional courts, and their judges were forced to render acquittals on appeal! In reaction to the increase in acquittals at this later stage, the Ministry of Justice of USSR and RSFSR issued directives declaring that "the prosecution and conviction of persons later acquitted was intolerable." Top party authorities in the center probably stood behind this move, for the regional party committee of Arkhangelsk also issued a decree on the subject, stating that "unfounded convictions of citizens" represented an "antigovernment practice." Under pressure from the ministries and the party bosses, regional court judges readily referred the criticism to the people's court judges below. The chairman of the Arkhangelsk regional court reported that in 1949 his court had acquitted 434 persons convicted by lower courts, of whom 173 were sitting in prison. This was "simply embarrassing," he said. "The person is not guilty but sits in prison."[56]

As of the early 1950s appellate judges did not yet face direct pressure to reduce the number of sentences that they changed on appeal. This would come only in 1956 when higher court judges came to be evaluated on the basis of the stability of sentences of the judges whose courts they supervised.[57] All the same, to deflect criticism that might come their way, regional court judges were quick to blame trial court judges for failing to acquit when appropriate. Too often, an appellate judge explained, our trial courts "judge people on the basis of supposition (*predpolozhenie*) when unshakable evidence is absent."[58] But what could

56 GARF (TsGA), f.353, op.13, d.134.
57 Solomon, "The Case of the Vanishing Acquittal."
58 GARF (TsGA), f.353, op.13, d.150, 92.

the trial judges do, when procurators and party bosses would not tolerate acquittals?

Naturally, the pressure on judges to avoid acquittals led judicial officials to blame their counterparts in the procuracy. At an operational meeting of the Moscow city court in 1950, one of the judges went so far as to state a bitter, but rarely articulated, truth: "People's court judges reach incorrect convictions, because they are to a certain degree dependent upon the procurator." When the justice administration of Rostov region launched an inquiry into the acquittals rendered by its appeals court, it discovered that the overwhelming majority had been correct and that the cases "had been sent to court illegally." In other words, the procuracy deserved the blame rather than the trial court judges.[59]

Conflict between judges and procurators happened in many localities. Some procurators believed that they could get judges to do whatever they wanted. In one district in Rostov province, a procurator sent a theft case to court and shepherded it through the preliminary session. When the case finally reached trial, the procurator called up the judge. "You know, you should stop the case against that boy." The judge replied, "Then why did you send it to court?" "Because the regional procurator wanted the prosecution." In this instance, the judge took umbrage and replied icily that he had to hear the case and could not guarantee how it would end, but he did promise to write a complaint about the procurator and his shenanigans.[60] The judge in question, however, was unusually brave, one of those principled persons who probably did not stay a judge for long.

To help the Procuracy monitor the work of district level procuracy officials, the RSFSR Ministry of Justice (in 1948) and the USSR Ministry of Justice (in 1949) directed people's court judges to report all acquittals directly to the regional procuracy. Most of the judges, however, proved unwilling to make the reports "for fear of spoiling their relations with the (local) procurator."[61] In the fourth quarter of 1949 judges reported only 20 of 430 acquittals rendered in Moscow region and 5 of 182 in Kiev Region. Some procurators complained to their regional party committees about the failure of judges to report acquittals. Even so, the regional procuracy offices could not check all of the cases reported to them. In the fourth quarter of 1949 they checked 2,613 of 9,815 reported acquittals (for the USSR as a whole). The problem lay in part with the refusal

59 TsGAOR goroda Moskvy, f.819, op.1, d.33 (Protokoly operativnykh soveshchanii pri predsedatelei Moskovskogo gorodskogo suda za 1950), 6ob; GARF (TsGA), f.353, op.13, d.150, 70.
60 GARF (TsGA), f.353, op.13, d.134, 136–137.
61 TsGAOR goroda Moskvy, f.819, op.1, d.33, 60b; GARF (TsGA) f.353, op.13, d.150, 32ob.

of procurators in departments for supervising police or investigations to help procurators in the department for supervising the courts.[62]

How were judges in the USSR to deal with the pressures that they faced from all sides? How could they cut back on the awarding of acquittals and not at the same time spoil their sentencing records when higher instances changed their verdicts? To put the question in a nutshell, was there a way to dispose of weak cases that reached trial without leaving behind an "unfounded prosecution" or an "unfounded conviction"? In the early 1950s Soviet judges found at least two substitutes for acquittals that had this effect.[63]

The first substitute for acquittals was returning cases for supplementary investigation. Once the case was back in the hands of the investigator, he could stop the case quietly for lack of evidence. To be sure, returns to supplementary investigation also embarrassed procuracy officials, and for that reason judges could not return all cases that fell apart in court. Some procurators complained about judges who returned cases to protect themselves (*perestrakhovka*).[64] But returns did not represent the calamity for investigators and procurators that acquittals did. Returns did not constitute blatant instances of unfounded prosecutions and did not automatically lead to investigations from superiors. There was, however, one further problem with the returns. If the accused in a case stopped during supplementary investigation were already in custody, the procurator could face censure for approving a "bad arrest."

The second substitute for acquittals was conviction of a charge less serious than the one used in the indictment and the passing of the most lenient sentence that proved convenient. If the defendant had been at liberty before the trial, the judge would choose a noncustodial sanction; if the defendant had awaited trial in prison, the judge would sentence him to the time already served, thereby justifying the pretrial detention and sparing the procurator responsibility for the arrest. These so-called compromise decisions had the double virtue of keeping the number of returns to supplementary investigation down to a reasonable level and avoiding "bad arrests." A charge used regularly for compromise decisions was criminal negligence (Article 111 of the RSFSR Criminal Code of 1926). Rarely did this charge form the basis of a prosecution in the late Stalin years; instead it served as a residual charge, ready as a replacement for more serious offenses like theft of state property or

---

[62] GARF, f.8131sch, op.29s, d.108, 35–58.
[63] This discussion of substitutes is based upon Solomon, "The Case of the Vanishing Acquittal."
[64] GARF (TsGA), op.6s, d.15 (Tablitsy), 12–15.

misuse of official position, which were harder to prove. After all, if goods disappeared from a warehouse, the official in charge must have been negligent, whether or not his actions had any bearing on their absence.

Other charges could also serve as the basis for compromise decisions, and sometimes investigators initiated compromises. Consider this example. In a town in southern Russia the police discovered a man from Kiev selling handkerchiefs at the market and promptly arrested him for speculation. Without hesitation the procurator approved the arrest and ordered an investigator to start proceedings. Later on, though, the accused informed the investigator that his wife had knitted the handkerchiefs, and a visit to the couple's modest quarters in Kiev confirmed that this was so. The case was spoiled. The man could not be convicted of speculation because he had not purchased goods and resold them. He had merely sold the product of his wife's work, an action that was legal. But he was already in prison, and releasing him without a conviction would embarrass the procurator. The investigator found an exit by reducing the charge to "engaging in a forbidden trade." Formally the charge covered the situation and the judge cooperated by sentencing the accused to time served, as it happened a month and a half. The investigator conceded that an acquittal would have been more appropriate, but, he explained, "the man had already sat, and I had to maneuver somehow."[65]

With the help of returns to supplementary investigation and compromise decisions judges in the USSR did reduce substantially the rate of acquittals. The rate for all crimes dropped from 9.9% in 1946 to 7.5% in 1952, but these figures included less serious offenses like shirking, failure by collective farmers to fulfill their labor-day quotas, and personal accusations (insults), which did not involve preliminary investigations and whose quality of case preparation was lower than the norm. The decrease in acquittals for "real" crimes was sharper: theft of personal property fell from 5.7% in 1946 to 2.7% in 1952 and of state property from 4.1% to 2.0%; speculation fell from 9.9% to 5.5%; criminal negligence and misusing one's position from 6.6% to 3.2%; and hooliganism from 11.5% to 2.6%. By 1956 the overall rate stood at 4.6% and the rate for the particular crimes just listed varied from 1.2 to 2.6%.[66] At the same time, by using substitutes that did not cause major harm to the accused, the judges assured that the defense would not appeal the decisions to higher courts. This meant fewer verdicts changed into acquittals on appeal, better sentencing records, and fewer "groundless

---

[65] Interviews.   [66] GARF, f.9492, op.6s, d.15 (Tablitsy), 12–15.

convictions."[67] As I have explained elsewhere, the pressure to avoid acquittals at trial and on appeal increased in the 1960s, 1970s, and early 1980s. As a result, the substitutes for acquittals that developed in the late 1940s and early 1950s lasted for decades, to the point where legal officials in the USSR accepted their use as natural and had for the most part forgotten why they had emerged.[68]

The leadership, justice administration, and the quest for perfection

It is reasonable to suppose that the top party leaders including Stalin were complicit in the drive for perfection in the administration of justice, if they did not serve as its source. I have no proof, say in the form of an actual resolution of the Central Committee or decision of the Politburo, nor do I expect to uncover one. The absence of mention of such a resolution or decision in the May 1950 *draft* resolution of the Central Committee on unfounded prosecutions and convictions suggests that it was to have been the first on the subject. But there is a good deal of evidence, direct and indirect, to support the proposition that the party leadership approved and encouraged the policy of combatting acquittals.

To begin, some of the top leaders had opportunities to know about the campaign against unfounded prosecutions and convictions. In 1949, Malenkov's office received a series of materials relating to the Chuvash affair, including the original letter from the local justice minister and a special summary report on the incident prepared for him in June by staff of the Department of Administrative Organs. In 1950 Ponomarenko received the anonymous complaint about the work of the procuracy on unfounded prosecutions and set in motion the study of the issue and the drafting of a resolution. Moreover, in 1948 the RSFSR minister of justice sent two letters on unjustified prosecutions to the Central Committee and probably his directive as well (since the Central Committee supervised RSFSR as well as USSR ministries); and in 1949 the Administrative Organs Department of the Central Committee received a series of reports on the issue from various republican ministries of justice.[69]

---

[67] Even with the new use of returns to supplementary investigation as a substitute for acquittals, the rate and number of returns also dropped: from 5.6% of criminal trials in 1948 to 4.0% in 1950 to 3.6% in 1952 to 2.8% in 1954. My calculations based on data in ibid., 12.

[68] Solomon, "The Case of the Vanishing Acquittal."

[69] RTsKhIDNI, f.17, op.136, d.70, 1–80.

Another indication of likely high-level involvement is the character of the struggle against unfounded prosecutions and convictions. The active campaign period of three years was unusually long, and the concern with acquittals retained high priority for decades thereafter. Moreover, provincial and local party officials joined in the campaign of 1949–1951, not only by pressuring judges individually but also by issuing resolutions of their own. As a rule, resolutions issued by provincial party committees responded to concerns expressed by higher party officials.

Apart from the particulars of the struggle against acquittals, the normal pattern of activity of Central Committee secretaries and their relationship with ministerial leaders supplies further grounds for suspecting involvement in that struggle. At least in the late 1940s, top party officials treated ministerial leaders as their direct subordinates and engaged in a good deal of micromanagement. The minister of justice and the procurator-general were expected to gain approval of Central Committee secretaries for a wide variety of measures relating to routine as well as important issues. An archival file of correspondence between the USSR minister of justice and party secretaries (for 1948) showed the minister seeking consent from his political superiors to close a branch of the water courts (courts organized along rivers and in harbors); to change the requirements for admission to the juridical schools; to start two new journals, *Sovetskii sud* and *Sovetskaia advokatura* (permission not granted); to reprint a brochure on the election of judges; to issue a *festschrift* in honor of Andrei Vyshinskii; and even to clear a speech that the minister was to present to a conference of judges. Other issues handled by Central Committee secretaries in 1947 and 1949 included a request for a new building for the USSR Supreme Court, salary raises for judges, and alleged mistakes in the recently issued *Handbook for Judges*.[70] Especially revealing was the scandal that erupted when Procurator-General Safonov arranged to hold a conference (the All-Union Methodological Conference of Best Investigators) *without prior clearance* from the Central Committee. Officials in the Department of Administrative Organs learned about the conference by chance only a day before it opened (in October 1948), and on their own initiative summoned the main rapporteurs to check over their reports. (The party officials found the theses of a report on "Criminal Investigations in the USA" insufficiently critical!) Treating Safonov's failure to clear the conference as a breach of discipline, staff of the Department complained to secretaries

---

[70] GARF, f.949, op.1, d.169 (Initsiativnye i informatsionnye pisma v TsK VKP(b), fev.-dek., 1948), passim; f.9474sch, op.16s, d.322, 87–97; d.311, 24–29; f.9492sch, op.2s, d.58, 180–182.

Malenkov and Kuznetsov; and the Secretariat voted on a resolution "to inform the Procurator-General of the USSR Comrade Safonov, G.N., that holding the conference on investigators without permission of the Central Committee of the CPSU was intolerable." In a later "conversation" at the Department of Administrative Organs, Safonov admitted that he had erred.[71] Two years earlier the then Minister of Justice Rychkov had received a similar rebuke from the Secretariat of the Central Committee in failing to obtain the required clearances for appointments of twelve chairmen of military tribunals.[72]

In addition to holding a veto power over even small initiatives of the minister of justice and procurator-general, the secretaries of the CPSU also served as a court of final appeal with regard to both administrative issues and court cases. Much like the tsar in earlier times, they received and responded to petitions from aggrieved and desperate citizens.

One such person was a young judge working in a town in Belorussia, who decided, as a last resort, to write to Stalin personally about the horrible conditions in which he had to work. When the Germans retreated in 1944, the people's court reopened, but operated in a private apartment with two unequipped rooms, one of which had icons hanging on the wall that the owner refused to remove. In August 1947, the owner suddenly decided to kick the court out of his apartment! The regional government assigned to the court on a temporary basis an unused wooden house belonging to the highway department of the republican Ministry of Internal Affairs. Within three days a ministry official came asking the judge to leave, on the grounds that the ministry planned to demolish the building. The regional executive committee did nothing for the judge and soon the ministry began stripping the building, taking away what it could and leaving the court to function "in dust and sand." The building was far from convenient. Located on the outskirts of town, five kilometers from the office of the procuracy and ten from the police headquarters, it lacked a telephone and proximity to public transport. It was at this moment that the judge wrote his

---

[71] "Sekretrariam TsK VKP(b) tov. Malenkovu, G.M., tov. Kuznetsovu, A.A., ot Zam. Zav. Administrativnvm Otdelam TsK VKP(b) Bakakina i Zav. sektorom Administrativnogo Otdela TsK VKP(b) Lopukhova (16 oktriabiia 1948 g.)"; "V tekhsekretariata TsK VKP(b) ot zav. sektorom Administrativnogo Otdela Tsk VKP(b) Lopukhova i instruktora Administrativnogo Otdela Tsk VKP(b) Iakimenkov (12 fevralia 1949 g.)"; "O sozyve t. Safonova, G.N., Vsesoiuznoi metodicheskoi konferetnsii luchshikh sledstvennykh rabotnikov organov Prokuratury SSSS," Postanovlenie Sekretariata TsK VKP(b) – na golosovanie. Note that the Ministry of Justice also held a conference in October 1948 but sought and obtained clearance from the Department of Administrative Organs. RTsKhIDNI, f.17, op.118, d.189, 102–108.

[72] RTsKhIDNI, f.117, op.116, d.283, 295.

appeal to Stalin. Whether or not Stalin ever saw the letter, the appeal to the top produced some results. The responsible secretary sent the letter over to the USSR Ministry of Justice for action and a report. The USSR Ministry in turn pressured the Belorussian Ministry of Justice. As a result, the latter made a special provision of 50,000 rubles just for fixing up the building for use as a courthouse. How the saga ended, I cannot tell. The last report in the archive file indicated that months after the budgetary allocation the repairs had not begun, because the supply of materials and labor for reconstructing the building depended upon cooperation from the nearby city soviet.[73]

The problem of grossly inadequate buildings plagued not only lower courts on the periphery, but also the top courts in Moscow. In the late 1940s the RSFSR Supreme Court occupied two middle floors of the building of the republican Ministry of Justice. The eight panels of the court had at their disposal only two courtrooms, and six of them heard cases in small offices. The USSR Supreme Court occupied similar quarters in the building of the USSR Procuracy, and all of that court's collegia heard cases in small rooms, while lawyers, procurators, petitioners, and witnesses were left milling about in the hall. Judges on both of these Supreme Courts lacked office space and not surprisingly worked on case files and opinions at home, a practice for which they were repeatedly rebuked. Ironically, the corruption of scandal of 1948 helped the USSR Supreme Court out of this morass. That court's new Chairman, Anatolii Volin, in a top secret report addressed directly to Comrade Stalin, pressed the leadership to hand over the building at 13 Vorovsky Street, the elegant former mansion of a rich Moscow merchant then occupied by the Moscow regional court and the Moscow Administration of Justice. Appealing cleverly to Stalin's concern with appearances, Volin warned that the Supreme Court's existing quarters "discredited the USSR Supreme Court as the highest judicial organ and undermined the authority of Soviet justice." Volin's effort was rewarded, for in due course the Court did obtain that fine building and occupied it up to the collapse of the USSR in 1991.[74]

Not only did the top party leaders intervene over the heads of government officials in appeals about administrative issues, they also received appeals about the outcomes of criminal cases. Although party secretaries took care not to intervene in ways that might be perceived as improper, their responses could affect the outcomes of the cases. For

---

[73] GARF, f.9492, op.1, d.169, 103–112.
[74] RTsKhIDNI, f.17, op.118, d.34, 62–70; d.96, 131–141, d.184, 38–59; op.117, d.650, 136–137; op.116, d.279, P310, d.355, P4, d.369, P15, d.384, P3, op.3, d.1072, P91.

example, in November 1952 the party bureau of a shoe factory in Kuznetsk wrote directly to Aleksei Kosygin, at the time a candidate member of the expanded Praesidium of the CPSU. The letter complained about the sentencing of the factory's director to five years in prison for producing defective goods. In a careful way the appeal described the circumstances of the case and the persons involved and argued that the verdict and sentence were simply wrong. The party bureau of the factory asked Kosygin "before it is too late (and cassation has been concluded) that you involve yourself (*vmeshaetsia*) in this case and help to establish an objective and fair resolution. . . . " Kosygin sent the petition for investigation to both Minister of Justice Gorshenin and Procurator-General Safonov.[75]

Another appeal to the political center concerned the fate of the head of the business department at the Kherson provincial court after he was caught speculating. The official in question was a close friend of the chief judge and his deputy; in fact the latter had provided the car used by the accused to drive around the city selling vegetables, flour, and fruit at high prices. When the court official was apprehended, his friends did not fail him. They arranged for a trial behind closed doors and a sentence of only six months' corrective labor, suspended at that. All might have ended happily had not other employees of the court taken offense and written to "secretary of the Central Committee" Lavrentii Beriia (he was actually a Deputy Head of the Council of People's Commissars). The latter asked the minister of justice to check on the matter and report in a day.[76]

The party leadership even took part in the review of sentences from courts. In 1947 there was still a commission of the Politburo on court cases (*sudebnym delam*). Chaired by the head of the Praesidium of the Supreme Soviet, candidate member of the Politburo N.M. Shvernik, and including M.F. Shkiriatov (Central Control Commission), V.S. Abakumov (Security), and K.P. Gorshenin (Procuracy), the Commission met on a weekly basis. In its session of May 6, 1947, it reviewed 76 cases decided by the Military Collegium of the USSR Supreme Court; the head of the Collegium, Vasilii Ulrikh, served as rapporteur. Most of the cases involved the death penalty. It is unclear whether the commission had duties other than reviewing cases from the military trials and sentences of capital punishment. Needless to say, the records of the

[75] Ibid., d.267, 63–67 (Khodotaistvo ot sekretaria partbiuro partorganizatsii Kuznetskoi obuvnoi fabriki, V. Moskaev, k chlenu Politburo VKP(b) tov. Kosyginy, Aleksei Nikolaevich, 6/XI-52.)

[76] Ibid., 18–19 (Pismo ot rabotnikov Khersonskogo oblsuda Sekretariu TsK VKP(b) tov. Beriiu, L.P., 2/III-52).

Politburo commission on court cases were classified as top secret, as was the existence of the commission.[77]

Finally, as part of their regular duties, Central Committee secretaries had at least the opportunity to review normative acts issued by ministerial and government agencies. The policy of discouraging acquittals was realized, as we have seen, in secret orders and directives of the USSR Procuracy, and the RSFSR and USSR Ministries of Justice.[78] I do not know whether such orders and directives required advance screening by officials of the Central Committee (that is, staff serving the secretaries), but the latter should have known about their contents. The issuing of important instructions and orders often followed meetings of the collegia, which were sometimes attended by Central Committee staff and whose protocols were likely delivered to them. Moreover, as we shall see in Chapter 12, the resolutions of the USSR Supreme Court, which, as public directives, had the authority of law, received detailed consideration by officials of the Central Committee during their preparation. One assumes that copies of ministerial orders were filed in the departments of the Central Committee.

It is clear, then, that in the late 1940s the top party leaders, like their counterparts at middle and lower levels of the administrative hierarchy, treated the administration of justice like other areas of public administration and involved themselves in the work of the courts and procuracy. If they took part in decisions about routine administrative issues, reviews of appeals in criminal cases, and the preparation of resolutions of the USSR Supreme Court, then they were almost certainly involved in the drive against unfounded prosecutions. We have seen that at least on occasion secretaries Malenkov and Ponomarenko dealt with the issue. What remains unknown is whether the party leaders were merely complicit in the struggle for perfection in the administration of justice, responding to initiatives from the legal agencies such as the procuracy, or themselves acted as its initiator. A plausible case can be made either way.

Although in 1948 the RSFSR Ministry of Justice introduced the first measures to reduce acquittals, by mid-1949 the policy had become the preserve of the Procuracy, promoted by it and ultimately serving its interests. Once "unfounded prosecutions" had become an issue in justice politics, the Procuracy's leaders were put on the spot. Blame for prosecutions that ended in acquittals fell squarely on the shoulders of procuracy officials, and the heads of that agency wanted to minimize

[77] "Protokol no. 18 zasedaniia komissii Politburo Tsk VKP(b) po sudebnym delam ot 6 maia 1947 goda."

[78] GARF (TsGA) f.353, op.13, d.134, 91ff.

harm to the prestige of their agency. Since its founding as a separate body in 1933, the chiefs of the USSR Procuracy had built it into the most powerful of the legal agencies. Under the leadership of Andrei Vyshinskii the agency accumulated key functions – exclusive control of pretrial investigations (1928); the right to supervise the legality of proceedings at trial (1933); and the task of monitoring the legality of public administration as a whole (1936), including the work of other ministries. When Vyshinskii left the Procuracy just before the War, his agency dominated the legal realm. Less able and well-connected successors followed him as procurator-general, but they remained committed to maintaining the power and prestige of the agency. When groundless prosecutions and convictions emerged as an issue in 1948, Deputy Procurator-General Mokichev focused upon their consequences for the Procuracy, "With each groundless prosecution and conviction we discredit ourselves, first of all as an agency supervising legality."[79] He repeated the same words about "discrediting" the agency in 1950. To ensure that the spotlight on unfounded prosecutions did not harm their agency, the chiefs of the Procuracy may themselves have promoted the intense campaign against acquittals pursued from April 1949.

At the same time, there were reasons why Stalin, Zhdanov, or Malenkov might have sought the appearance of an administration of justice that worked flawlessly. One was the position of the Soviet Union in the world order. Rivalry with the United States in the Cold War and the new role of the USSR as a model for allies in Eastern Europe made it important for the Soviet government to have the best public face. Soviet ideologists of the day described the USSR as having built socialist government, a higher form that the "people's democracies" in Eastern Europe could only try to emulate. In this context the reputation of Soviet criminal justice had special import, because of the damage done to the reputation of Soviet government by the Great Terror. Abroad, the USSR was known for the "unfounded prosecutions and convictions" delivered in the tribunals of the NKVD. While after the War the political police pursued repression in relative secrecy, the more visible activity of Soviet courts could signal to the outside world that the USSR now met its standards. Stalin and other leaders might have hoped that a decline in "unfounded prosecutions and convictions" in ordinary criminal cases would enhance the reputation of Soviet government abroad. There were precedents for this line of thinking. The promulgation of the Constitution of 1936 was meant in part to convey the message of normal legal order to the outside world; and the policy of educating legal

---

[79] "Vsesoiuznoe soveshchanie rukovodiashchikh rabotnikov"; GARF, f.8131, op.7, d.40134, 301; *Rabota luchshikh sledovatelei* (1), 6.

officials, especially in its 1946 iteration, also reflected embarrassment of the leaders with the amateurish and sloppy work of the justice agencies.

Second, Soviet leaders may also have been concerned that the reputation of their government at home could be tainted by foreign propaganda about their repressive tendencies. In a speech in 1948 the chairman of the USSR Supreme Court, Ivan Goliakov, referred to the challenge of ideological struggle with the capitalist world and noted the importance of countering Western "legal ideology" with an administration of justice that delivered an educational message to the Soviet public.[80]

Finally, there was the possibility that some members of the leadership wanted to combat not only the appearance of an inefficient and sometimes unfair administration of justice but also its reality. That is, they may have believed that fighting what they called groundless prosecutions and arrests and making investigators and procurators responsible for the persons whom they delivered to trial or put into detention would reduce the number of persons needlessly exposed to these experiences and thereby serve the cause of justice. There seems to have been an undercurrent of this kind of thinking in the crackdown against pretrial detention of persons against whom cases were weak, a development that predated the campaign against acquittals by three to four years. However, for Soviet leaders to believe that the stigmatization of acquittals could have such a good effect requires a peculiar mindset that deserves explanation here.

How, a reader might ask, could Soviet leaders have been so naive as to think that the virtual elimination of acquittals could signal a well-functioning and fair administration of justice? From the vantage point of the Anglo-American legal tradition, where the trial is meant to serve as a locus of conflict between the two sides, this proposition sounds strange. But in the Civil Law tradition, to which the USSR belonged, the trial represented not the place for a contest but rather the final stage of a common search for truth. If investigators and prosecutors have performed their tasks properly in the pretrial phase – and have had the right to stop cases where the evidence proved insufficient – then there should be few acquittals at trial. In this context, then, acquittals might plausibly be understood as signs of "mistakes" in judgment by the officials responsible for pretrial investigation. The same kind of rhetoric came to be used in the USSR in connection with changes in verdicts introduced at the appellate courts. When a higher court reversed the decision of a lower one, this meant that the lower court judge had erred or committed a "judicial mistake." Though strange to Anglo-American

---

[80] GARF, f.8131, op.27s, d.4034, 389.

ears, this kind of language was used in the USSR of the 1970s by jurists of all political stripes, including reformers.[81]

In addition to the notion of "mistakes" in the administration of justice, the mindset that facilitated the stigmatization of acquittals included a habit of promoting courses of action through *blame*. As I have argued elsewhere, Stalinist political style featured a "culture of blame."[82] Singling out scapegoats became for Stalin a mechanism for announcing and entrenching new politics, especially the start and termination of campaigns. And with the multiple and overlapping accountability of Soviet officialism, there were plenty of candidates for blame. As we have seen, the campaign against "unfounded prosecutions" and "unfounded convictions" entrenched personal responsibility for "mistakes" as a key and lasting tool for the management of legal officials in the USSR.

The turn against acquittals, then, derived from an unfortunate combination of the legacy of the inquisitorial tradition in criminal justice and Stalinist political style. These were the enabling factors that made the campaign for perfection in Soviet criminal justice an explicable, though hardly inevitable, development.

Conclusion

The campaign for perfection in the administration of justice represented the culmination of the larger process of developing for Soviet justice a corps of reliable legal officials and shaping their conduct through monitoring and evaluation. Along with the centralization of power in the legal agencies, the reliance on statistical indicators, and the development of careers in the agencies with education for service, the stigmatization of such mistakes as acquittals completed the course of the bureaucratization of Soviet criminal justice. To be sure, this process did not stop with Stalin's death but reached its culmination a decade or so later. But by the tyrant's death the foundations of a system of criminal justice well primed to serve its political masters had been fully laid.

However good the intentions of Soviet leaders may have been in deciding to fight "unfounded prosecutions and convictions," the consequences of that struggle proved unfortunate. No legal official could achieve perfect results by natural means, and the pressure to produce perfection, in the form of rates of conviction and stability of sentence,

---

[81] Kudriavtsev, *Effektivnost pravosudiia*.

[82] For more detail, see Peter H. Solomon, Jr., "The Bureaucratization of Criminal Justice under Stalin," in Peter H. Solomon, Jr., ed., *Reforming Justice in Russia, 1864–1994: Power, Culture, and the Limits of Legal Order* (Armonk, N.Y., 1997).

led to the distortions in the administration of justice described in this chapter, including the various substitutes for acquittals. These distortions have been described by Soviet commentators in recent years as representing an "accusatory deviation." That this bias entered ordinary criminal justice in the years after World War II is clear. Exactly how and why remains something of a riddle.

12 The Distortion and limits of criminal policy

We have seen how in the years right after World War II the Soviet leadership successfully promoted education for legal officials and supported a crackdown on such "imperfections" in their performance as acquittals and bad arrests. Both of these actions represented part of the effort to fashion a more compliant and responsive body of investigators, judges, and procurators. At the same time as these initiatives were being pursued, important developments were also occurring in the way Stalin and his colleagues used the criminal law and its administration. From the early 1930s Stalin had taken a keen interest in not only repression by the political police but also the milder, more routine, and visible forms of coercion. From 1932 on, most, if not all, changes in Soviet criminal law received Stalin's personal stamp of approval. This pattern would continue after World War II until the tyrant's death in March 1953.

The main development in criminal policy during the postwar years was the emergence in full form of a set of distortions, all of which reflected Stalin's inclinations. These included (1) the enhanced significance of administrative regulations as supplements to and substitutes for law (including the conversion of resolutions, or guiding explanations, of the USSR Supreme Court into quasi-laws); (2) the hiding of some norms of the criminal law from public view through the use of secret regulations and laws; and (3) the enacting for nonpolitical offenses of punishments of unusual severity. In developing these features of criminal policy, Stalin showed little originality; all had less extreme precedents in the criminal law of the tsars before 1864. But this fact did not diminish their impact. These anachronistic developments interrupted progress made in the interim toward the development of modern legal order. While each of these distortions first entered Soviet criminal justice in the 1930s, it assumed full and excessive form only after World War II.

The cardinal moment in Soviet criminal policy after the War was the issuing by Stalin on June 4, 1947, of a pair of decrees on theft.[1] As we shall see, these decrees drastically raised punishments for theft, to the point where officials refused to apply the decrees to many offenders. Judges found loopholes to soften the blows against teenagers, women, and petty thieves, and police and other enforcers of the law cut back on prosecutions against many perpetrators. The resistance to executing the decrees on theft joined earlier resistance to Stalinist excesses in criminal policy as an illustration of the limits of the criminal sanction.

This chapter starts with an examination of Stalin's primacy in the determination of the criminal law, using as an example the decrees of June 4, 1947. The chapter goes on to illustrate the various distortions introduced by the leader – excessive reliance on regulations, secrecy (and concern with appearances), and severity of sanctions. Finally, the chapter analyzes in detail the implementation of and resistance to the theft decrees.

Stalin and criminal law

Almost from the start of his ascendancy to the status of dictator, Stalin monopolized criminal law. Not only did he use the law as a tool for the pursuit of political goals (already evident during collectivization), but also he made the criminal law his personal domain. From the mid-1930s most changes in the criminal law represented either his personal initiative (e.g., the criminalization of abortion) or his reshaping of the initiatives of others (e.g., the criminalization of juvenile delinquency and labor infractions). As a rule, changes in the criminal law bore the mark of Stalin's hand in both language and content. After World War II this pattern became universal. All changes in the criminal law were Stalin's. At the same time, the number and frequency of changes declined precipitously. During the 1920s, a community of justice officials and politicians had struggled openly over the criminal law and changed it regularly. By the second half of the 1930s, however, such changes had become infrequent and after the War rare.

Apart from the infamous theft decrees of 1947, only a handful of changes was registered in criminal law during the postwar period. They included decrees that raised the punishment for rape and for home-brewing, that criminalized even small breaches of the rules on state

---

[1] "Ob ugolovnoi otvetsvennosti za khishchenie gosudarstvennogo i obshchestvennogo imushchestva," Ukaz Prezidiuma Verkhovnogo Soveta SSSR ot 4 iiunia 1947 g.; and "Ob usilenii okhrany lichnoi sobstvennosti grazhdan," Ukaz Prezidiuma Verkhovnogo Soveta SSSR ot 4 iuniia 1947 g., both in Goliakov, *Sbornik dokumentov*, 430–431.

secrets, and that first repealed and three years later revived the death penalty. The initiative for every one of these changes seems to have come from the top. Some of them originated in personal reactions of Stalin and his colleagues to chance events that came to their notice. Thus, the decision to raise the punishment for rape allegedly followed Stalin's learning that the daughter of a Central Committee official had fallen victim to a sexual attack; and the decision to extend the reach of the criminal law for violations of the rules of state secrets followed a scandal in which Western governments and press became privy to information about promising medical research being conducted in the USSR (the Kliueva-Roskina affair). Why Stalin chose to repeal the death penalty in May 1947 I have yet to determine (the propaganda value at a time when harsh laws on theft were about to be issued is one hypothesis). But it is clear that the leadership took a direct interest in capital punishment. There remained a special commission attached to the Politburo that reviewed all sentences to capital punishment and reversed some of them.[2]

Stalin's personal dominance of the criminal law limited the opportunities of even his lieutenants in the legal realm to shape the law. The procurator-general, minister of justice, and head of the Supreme Court were willing to ask for correctives in past policies, especially in the form of regulations (even secret ones) governing the enforcement of the law, and sometimes changes in the law itself. When they sensed the slightest possibility of the controversial, however, they offered their initiatives in jointly signed letters or memoranda, thereby sharing responsibility lest Stalin or a member of his circle be angered by the suggestion.

In the later Stalin years there remained one vehicle for broader consideration and discussion of the criminal law and procedure – the drafting of new USSR Codes of Criminal Law and Procedure. The Stalin Constitution of 1936 had shifted criminal law and procedure into all-Union jurisdiction; but the drafting and discussions of 1938 to 1941 had been interrupted by the German attack. The process of making new codes resumed when, with leadership approval, a new governmental commission convened in June 1946. In ninety-two meetings over a period of a year and a half, the commission and its two subcommissions

---

2 Goliakov, *Sbornik dokumentov*, 429–435, interview with Dr. Aleksandr Shtromas, May 18, 1974; personal communication from Nikolai Krementsov on the Kliueva-Roskin affair (Nov. 1993) and V.D. Esakov and E.S. Levina, "Delo 'KR' (Iz istorii gonenii na sovetskuiu intelligentsiia," *Kentavr*, 1994, no.2, 54–69 and no.3, 96–118, "Protokol No. 18 zasedaniia Komissii Politbiuro TsK VKP(b) po sudebnym delam ot 6 maia 1947 goda." Note that from October 1945 all death sentences were rendered by courts; the Special Board of the NKVD was restricted to maximum sentences of eight years' imprisonment. GARF, f.9401sch, op.2, d.99, 400–401.

produced new draft codes, and the drafters included in their handiwork a number of changes in the law. Thus, the 1947 draft criminal code called for, inter alia, the removal of the principle of analogy, and the revival of parole (eliminated from the law in 1939). The draft also narrowed the definition of "shirking" (*progul*) to one full day away from the job, thereby eliminating prosecutions for tardy arrival at work or back from lunch.[3] The writing of the draft criminal code involved wide, behind-the-scenes consultation. Versions were circulated during summer 1947 to republican ministers of justice, councils of ministers, supreme courts, police ministries, research institutes, law faculties, and colleges of advocates, most of which replied with letters or memoranda. Collected in two large archival volumes, some comments sought clarification of terms, but others advocated substantial changes in the law. Thus, in separate memos a group of three professors and the RSFSR Council of Ministers recommended that the minimum age of juvenile responsibility be raised from 12 to 14. In its brief the RSFSR Council of Ministers supplied data indicating the small number of convictions of children aged 12–13: in 1945, 4,996, and in 1947, 4,432 (83% for theft). The drafters accepted this particular proposal, and the early 1949 version of the draft criminal code set the minimum age of criminal responsibility at 14. On the other hand, this version of the code eliminated the revival of parole despite the bureaucratic support for this step.[4]

In the interim the draft criminal code had gone to the top leadership. In July 1948 the government commission sent the latest version to three secretaries of the Central Committee, Suslov, Kuznetsov, and Zhdanov, in each case with an explanatory memorandum addressed directly to Stalin.[5]

Early in 1949, the draft criminal code reached the USSR Supreme Soviet, and the Commission on Legislative Suggestions established a subcommittee to review it. The subcommittee, however, disagreed with the draft on a number of important points and decided to circulate its own report entitled "Basic Discussion Points in the Draft Criminal Code." Among the fifteen points included were: the issue of parole (the subcommittee wanted it revived after all); the issue of analogy (the

---

[3] Peter H. Solomon, Jr., *Soviet Criminologists and Criminal Policy: Specialists in Policy-Making* (New York and London, 1978), 21; GARF, f.9492, op.1, d.1959 (Protokoly pravitelstvennoi kommisii po podgotovke proektov UK i UPK SSSR), esp. 78–80, 113, 119.

[4] GARF, f.9492, op.1, d.1962 (Otzyvy i predlozheniia po proektu UK SSSR, I), 5–6, 49; d.1963 (Otzyvy i predlozheniia, II), 60, 161, 198, 209; d.1946 (Ugolovnyi kodeks SSSR, Proekt, 1949); f.9492sch, op.2s, d.45 (Perepiska po proekty Ugolovnogo Kodeksa SSSR), 1–3; d.49 168–169.

[5] GARF, f.9492, op.1, d.169, 119–121.

subcommittee was divided); the draft criminal codes's limiting of negligent crime to offenses specifically mentioned in the code (the subcommittee thought this would disarm the state); and the proposal included
in the draft that Article 51, which enabled judges to sentence below the
limits for particular crimes, be itself limited to one-half of the minimum
sentence (the subcommission thought this inappropriate). The report
was circulated at least to republican governments, and the response of
one (the government of Latvia) revealed yet another set of positions on
the issues.[6] Ultimately, this draft USSR criminal code – like its prewar
predecessor – died stillborn. The failure to promulgate the code
reflected the inability of legal and political officials to resolve their
differences. Its ultimate demise, however, stemmed from the willingness of Stalin to live without a new code. For him the new code may
have seemed unnecessary, since he had resolved the most pressing
issues of criminal policy through decrees, especially the pair of decrees
of June 4, 1947. More likely, with his capacity for work reduced by ill
health, the Stalin of 1950–1953 may have lost interest in a new criminal
code, preferring to deal with more pressing issues and political intrigues.

In their final, draconian form the 1947 decrees on theft were Stalin's
personal creations, but these decrees had their origin in proposals for
modest increases in punishments for theft that many law enforcement
officials were ready to support. After the War the USSR experienced a
surge in cases of theft; 1946 registered 23% more convictions (of theft of
all kinds) than did 1945. Some of the new cases involved juvenile
offenders, representatives of the wave of homeless children left by the
War. Others reflected a rise in thefts of grain committed by hungry
peasants in war-devastated rural areas. But most of the thefts lacked
these special qualities.[7] Admittedly, the increase in convictions for theft
did not exceed the fluctuations in levels recorded in early years, but it
was sufficient to worry the leadership and open up the question of
punishment. To political leaders and legal officials alike the penalties
available to judges in Russia provided blunt instruments for stemming
the rise in theft. To be sure, judges still had at their disposal the Law of
August 7, 1932 (discussed in Chapter 4), which called for terms of
imprisonment of ten years and even the death penalty for theft of state

---

[6] GARF, f.7523sch, op.65s, d.243, (Osnovnye diskussionye voprosy proekta UK SSSR),
1–20.
[7] GARF, f.9492sch, op.6s, d.14, 14; V. Tadeovsian, "Borba za likvidatsiiu detskoi prestupnosti v SSSR k desiatiletiiu zakona 7 apreliia 1935g.," SZ, 1945, no. 5, 5–12; GARF,
f.8131sch, op.28s, d.291; V.F. Zima, "Golod v Rossii 1946–1947 godov," Otechestvennaia
istoriia, 1993, no. 1, 35–52.

and socialist property. But since 1935 the Supreme Court had confined the use of this law to serious cases of large-scale theft and even after a wartime revival of the law, prosecutions numbered annually in the thousands (in 1946, 4,546).[8] Most thefts were not large-scale and did not fall under the Law of August 7, 1932. For ordinary theft legal officials had to rely upon Article 162 of the RSFSR Criminal Code of 1926. This article set as the maximum sentence for qualified theft of private property (committed by a repeat offender, or with preliminary agreement, or using technical measures) at one year of prison and for qualified theft of state property at two years (five years if the guilty party's job provided special access to the stolen goods). First-time offenders who stole from persons or organizations (the state) could receive at most three months in prison or as likely a noncustodial sanction (corrective work), as long as their thefts were small and nonviolent. There was one exception. From mid-August 1940 petty theft in factories (see Chapter 9) required a full year of confinement, that is, a penalty greater than that imposed for ordinary theft of state property.[9] In practice, since 1943 nearly half of persons convicted for petty theft in factories had received noncustodial sanctions. Offenders convicted of stealing private property in Russia in 1946 were likely to receive terms of imprisonment (three-quarters of them did), most for terms under one year. In the Ukrainian republic, the criminal code allowed harsher punishments for theft, and as a result in 1946 nearly half of those convicted of theft of personal property received terms of one to two years.[10]

Already in April 1946 the heads of the Commissariat of Justice, Procuracy, Supreme Court, and NKVD had prepared for Stalin a draft decree raising penalties for theft in modest amounts to a maximum of three years' confinement for regular theft, five years for qualified, and eight for theft of state property. This draft was the outcome of six months of communications among the legal and political chiefs that had started with a memo from Procurator-General Gorshenin to Molotov in November 1945 suggesting that the RSFSR align its punishments for theft with those of other republics. The draft decree of April 1946 was set aside, and no more heard on the subject of punishment for theft until the next year. On January 21, 1947, the legal chiefs sent another joint memorandum, this time to Stalin as well as Molotov, calling for similar increases in punishment for thefts in the RSFSR. The memorandum

8 GARF, f.9492sch, op.2s, d.42, 24–29.
9 Goliakov, *Sbornik dokumentov*, 284–285, 407–408.
10 GARF, f.9492, op.1, d.516 (Spravka o sudebnoi praktike po delam o melkikh krazhakh na predpriiatiiakh i v uchrezhdeniiakh i poriadke rassmotrenii etikh del v narodnykh sudakh), 89–97. GARF, f.9492, op.2s, d.42, 24–29; GARF, f.9492, op.2s, d.44, 27–29, (Molotovu ot Zam Miniust SSSR Rubicheva, 15 IV 1947), 27–29.

provided data on the rise of theft in 1946 and how the punishments applied in the RSFSR compared with those used in other republics, and a draft decree accompanied the memo. Taken on its face, the memorandum of January 1947 represented an initiative of the heads of the legal agencies, but similar memoranda were often prepared on demand to give political leaders justification for their initiatives (for example, in the case of the decree on punishments for rape issued in 1949).[11] It is possible that the renewed initiative for an increase in punishments for theft came from Stalin himself.

Whether prepared on instruction of the Central Committee or at the initiative of the legal chiefs, the January draft of a new decree on theft called for modest and sensible changes in the law. The draft did not distinguish thefts of personal and state property; while raising penalties for more serious forms of theft, it also expanded judicial discretion, giving judges the tools for handling minor as well as major offenses. Basic theft of all kinds could bring imprisonment of as much as three years (instead of the previous limit of one year) or as little as three months, and the noncustodial sanction, corrective work, remained available. Qualified theft (e.g., by a recidivist, in a group) called for a term of two to seven years, thereby replacing the old maximum of one year with a minimum of two years.[12] Had this version of the theft decree become law, the sentences for all but the least serious thefts would on average have doubled, and the response to the small thefts remained unchanged.

The first 1947 version of a draft decree on theft was bound to appeal to judges, and those judges exposed to it readily lent their support. In March 1947 a conference of two dozen judges of the city of Moscow praised the draft. Some reported that in their courtrooms members of the public had objected to the leniency of one-year terms of imprisonment and that thieves themselves declared brazenly, "You will see me in a year; you cannot give me any more." One judge told how a habitual thief detained for trial in one theft admitted to committing four other thefts in recent months. Asked why he made the admission, he replied that he would still get one year! According to the conference report, the judges approved not only the option of longer terms of prison but also the discretion that the draft law afforded them.[13]

Throughout March a commission of top legal officials refined the draft decree, assembling supporting documents and the opinions of

---

11 GARF, f.5446sch, op.49s, d.3403, 1–52; f.8131sch, op.27s, d.3405, 92–96; f.9492sch. op.2s, d.50, 374–378 and 390; RTsKhIDNI, f.17, op.117, d.697, 127–131.

12 Ibid.

13 GARF, f.9492, op.1, d.514 (Spravka o vystuplenii sudei i sudebnykh rabotnikov na soveshchanii Ministerstva Iustitsii SSSR 15 marta 1947), 256–260.

interested agencies. At the beginning of April it forwarded an official draft to the party leadership. The first official draft differed from the January 1947 proposal in distinguishing theft of state property from theft of personal property and stipulating higher penalties for the latter. Thus, ordinary theft of state property called for imprisonment of six months to four years, as opposed to three months to three years for ordinary theft of personal property; qualified theft of state property through three to ten years in prison, as opposed to two to six years for qualified theft of personal property; and theft of state property in especially large amounts, ten to twenty years. In all probability, these changes followed instructions from the leadership. A meeting of the Orgburo on April 16 reviewed the draft (already slightly revised) and returned it to the commission for further changes, including raising the penalty for petty theft in factories from one year to one to five years![14]

In May Joseph Stalin reviewed the draft decree on theft and reportedly lost his temper. Despite his earlier instructions, he alleged, the chiefs of the legal agencies had proved unable to remove from the draft decree all elements of leniency. Only Stalin knew how to handle thieves, and this justified his decision to discard completely the draft decree prepared by legal chiefs over the past months. In its stead the dictator reportedly dictated in rough a new pair of theft decrees (one for personal, the other for state property) with entirely different numbers. Stalin's draft decrees made three years' imprisonment the minimum penalty for theft of personal property, rather than the maximum (now set at six years); a repeat theft required six to ten years. Theft of state property would draw not a maximum of four years but a minimum of five and maximum of ten, and even more when committed by an organized group. But this was not the end of the story. No more than a day or two before proclamation (perhaps even at the time of signing), Stalin changed the theft decrees one more time. With a quick stroke of the pen he drastically reduced judicial discretion by raising the minimum sentence for theft of personal property from three to five years, leaving judges to choose between five and six years, and raised the minimum punishment for theft of state property from six to seven years.[15] Instead of providing judges with the tools for distinguishing petty offenders from veteran thieves, and habitual petty thieves from

[14] GARF, f.8131sch, op.27s, d.3405, 105; f.9492sch, op.2s, d.42, 2429; f.9492, op.1, d.514 (Proekt ukaza ob ugolovnoi otvetsvennosti za pokhishchenie imushchestua grazhdan), 261–262; RTsKhIDNI, f.17, op.117, d.733, 15–22; op.121, d.612, 35–43.
[15] Interviews; GARF, f.9492, op.1, d.1959 (Protokol no. 60 Pravitelstvennoi Komissii po podgotovke proektov UK i UPK SSSR, 31 maia 1947, no. 61 . . . 2 iuniia 1947), 176–179; "Ob ugolovnoi otvetsvennosti za khishchenie"; "Ob usileniie okhrany lichnoi sobstvennosti."

dangerous offenders, Stalin commanded his judges to give all persons who stole at least five or six years' imprisonment and any person who stole a second time (or in a group) between ten to twenty-five years.

Perhaps to cushion the blow and gain good publicity at home and abroad, Stalin also ordered (in late May) the elimination of the death penalty from Soviet criminal law. Terms of twenty-five years' imprisonment replaced capital punishment wherever it appeared in the criminal code. The prohibition on the death penalty lasted only three years. In 1950 Stalin revived its use for political crimes. In 1951 and 1952 the Central Committee received letters from a regional court judge and a senior investigator urging the extensions of the death penalty to murder, but the return of capital punishment for nonpolitical offenses came only after Stalin's death.[16]

Not only were the theft decrees extraordinarily harsh and restrictive, but they also raised difficult interpretative issues. In his arrogance Stalin eliminated some of the traditional distinctions among types of theft and replaced them with his own improvisations. We shall see how legal officials dealt with the severity and the imprecision of the decrees later in this chapter. (See Table 12.1 on the development of theft decrees.)

Regulations for laws

In the later 1930s and the 1940s, when the criminal law in the USSR expressed only Stalin's will, certain kinds of regulations also assumed the status of criminal law. These included both resolutions issued in the name of the Council of People's Commissars (*Sovnarkom*) and its successor the Council of Ministers (*Sovmin*), and the guiding explanation of the USSR Supreme Court. In addition, the Procuracy and Ministry of Justice continued issuing directives on criminal matters, often, though not always, signaling the attention of legal officials to particular resolutions of the Council of People's Commissars. Many of these regulations criminalized acts (by targeting particular misdeeds for prosecution or refining what the law meant) or set the punishments to be used by judges, thereby narrowing the scope of judicial discretion supplied in the criminal code.

In itself, the issuing by the central legal agencies of directives and instructions relating to criminal law and procedure was nothing new. In the 1920s, Narkomiust and the RSFSR Supreme Court had continued the tsarist bureaucratic tradition of ruling officialdom by decree. Likewise, in the late 1920s and early 1930s, at the height of Krylenko's

---

[16] Goliakov, *Sbornik dokumentov*, 429–430; RTsKhIDNI, f.17, op.3, d.1079, p.207; op.136, d.298, 207–210; d.440, 168–174.

Table 12.1. *Development of 1947 theft decrees**

Types of theft	1926 Code amended in 1932 & 1940	January 1947 proposals	Stages		
			April 1947 official drafts (3)	May 1947 Stalin's first version	Decrees of June 4, 1947
1. Personal property	Up to 3 months' deprivation of freedom (or corrective work)	3 months to 3 years (or corrective work)	Up to 3 years	3–6 years	5–6 years
2. Personal property, qualified[a]	1 year	2–7 years	2 (3) to 6 (8) years	6–10 years	6–10 years
3. State property	3 months	3 months to 3 years (1–5 years)	Up to 4 years	5–10 years	7–10 years
4. State property qualified[a]	2 years (5 years if special access)	2–7 years	3 (5) to 10 years	10–20 years	10–25 years
5. Petty theft at factory	1 year	1 year	1 year (1–5 years)	5 years	7 years
6. State property in large amounts	10 years or death	10 years or death	10–20 years or death	10–20 years	10–25 years
7. Robbery	Up to 5 years	5–10 years	5–10 years	10–15 years	10–15 years
8. Robbery qualified[a]	5–10 years	10–20 years	10–20 years or death	15–20 years or death	15–25 years

* *Source:* Based on *Ugolovnyi kodeks RSFSR* (Moscow, 1948) and citations in notes 11, 14, and 15.
[a] Qualified theft includes a repeat offense and an offense committed with preliminary agreement.

influence on legal policy, regulations had substituted for laws as the vehicle for the establishment of a whole series of simplifications in criminal procedure, as well as directing legal officials about the current priorities of the regime in prosecution and sentencing. For a while, the idea of the actual replacement of law with regulations had official support. But in the process of creating order and reviving the authority of government after collectivization Stalin and Vyshinskii turned away from the abandonment of laws. Within a few years they not only re-stored the official status of the law, but also gave the world the image of the USSR as a government on a constitutional footing.

From the mid-1930s the core of criminal and criminal procedure law was defined once again in the respective codes. However, the impor-tance of regulations did not decline, despite the denunciation and purg-ing of Krylenko and the legal nihilists. For the most part, the justice agencies did cease issuing regulations that substituted for laws, but the agency that directed the economy of the USSR, the Council of People's Commissars, started issuing a stream of resolutions that affected the criminal law. Here are some examples. In April 1938 a resolution (in this case issued jointly with the Bolshevik party's Central Committee) di-rected legal officials to treat the embezzlement of kolkhoz funds as an especially serious crime and qualify it under the Law of August 7 or as "wrecking" (Article 58.7). In like manner resolutions of the Council defined criminal violations of the rules on the cutting of timber and the punishments to be used by judges. A new version of Article 85 of the RSFSR Criminal Code issued in October 1936 had set the minimum value of the felled timber that would qualify as a crime, designated commerce in illegal timber as a serious offense, and provided guide-lines for punishment. But the actual specification of the particular of-fenses that were illegal came in a joint decree of the Council of People's Commissars and Central Committee issued on April 2, 1937, and was given expanded form in a 1939 Instruction of Narkomiust, the Procu-racy, and the Chief Administration of Forest Protection, approved by the Council. In 1943 the Council added a further order that classified forests in the USSR into three types and then laid out a set of fines to be imposed for illegal felling of particular amounts of timber from the forests of each group. Judges hearing cases of charges relating to timber violations (Article 85) were expected to rely upon all of these resolutions and orders of the Council of People's Commissars; they were reprinted in the 1948 collection of regulations of the Ministry of Justice.[17] This particular collection included as well a whole series of ministry orders

---

[17] *Sbornik prikazov i instruktsii Ministerstva iustitsii SSSR 1936–1948 g.* (Moscow, 1949), 170–178.

based upon Council resolutions, all of which defined particular offenses. Examples from the postwar period included a directive letter on how to deal with theft in consumer cooperatives and another directive letter alerting judges to the fact that an edict of the Council of Ministers (1948) required managers and kolkhoz chairmen to sue for return of lost property in cases of significant thefts.[18]

The refinement and extension of the criminal law through resolutions of the Council of People's Commissars made it difficult even for legal officials to know the content of the law, let alone members of the public who might be affected by it. Many resolutions of the Council and, from 1946 the Council of Ministers – if they were not secret – were published in the "Collection of Resolutions (*Sobranie Postanovlenii*), but this publication was not easily accessible to most legal officials (it was not part of the libraries of courthouses or procuracy offices). During the 1930s and 1940s there were few if any editions of the republican criminal codes with detailed commentaries. (Even the editions of the 1930s usually neglected relevant resolutions of the Council of Ministers; the authors relied almost exclusively upon resolutions of the USSR Supreme Court.) The relevant parties were unaware of resolutions of the Council of People's Commissars. In 1947 a top official of the RSFSR Ministry of Justice proposed that the USSR Supreme Court clarify whether kolkhoz peasants who failed to perform timber-felling duties for which they had contracted with the timber authorities were subject to prosecution under the edict of June 26, 1940, for absenteeism or shirking. The official did not know that the Council of People's Commissars had issued an edict on this very question in 1946.[19] (Possibly the USSR Procuracy and Ministry of Justice had failed to issue their own directives calling the edict to the attention of their officials.)

The examples cited here of the use of Council of People's Commissars resolutions to refine and extend the criminal law represent only a portion of this phenomenon. Its actual breadth is difficult to gauge because of the many layers of secrecy and specialization. Thus, all Council orders relating to the military-industrial complex in the USSR were secret, and there is no reason to assume that the criminal law did not regulate the conduct of the employees of those agencies. (For persons working in secret installations around the USSR a secret network of courts was established known as the "special courts.")[20] By all ac-

[18] Ibid., 157–160.
[19] GARF, f.9492, op.1, d.157, 125ff.
[20] Yuri Luryi, "Special Courts in the USSR: A Comment," *Review of Socialist Law*, 8 (1962), 251–257; Richard Buxbaum and Kathryn Hendley, eds., *The Soviet Sobranie of Laws. Problems of Codification and Non-Publication*, Research Series of International Area Studies, no. 78 (Berkeley, Calif., 1991).

counts, the practice of specifying particular criminal offenses and punishments in resolutions of the Council of Ministers continued after Stalin's death.[21]

The targeting of offenses in resolutions reflected the desire of the managers of the directed economy to use the criminal sanction for their purposes. The practice also suited Stalin, who preferred to keep laws as vehicles for communicating with the broad public. For Stalin the deterrent and symbolic dimensions of law – the dramatic part – also mattered.

By the postwar period the chiefs of the legal agencies realized that most refinements of the criminal law had to be resolved not in the law itself but in regulations, either of the Council of Ministers or their own agencies. But these officials, and their political masters too, recognized that some important shadings of the law required public articulation by an authoritative body. Neither resolutions of the Council of Ministers nor orders of the agencies (Procuracy and Ministry of Justice) reached a broad public. But the "guiding explanations" or resolutions of the USSR Supreme Court were different. Published openly and distributed broadly within legal circles, the "guiding explanations" represented statements of policy issued in the name of the Court rather than decisions in particular cases.

From at least 1940 Supreme Court resolutions did not represent merely the positions of the top judges on particular issues. On the contrary. Before the formal approval of any guiding explanation by a plenary session of the Supreme Court, a draft of the explanation was circulated among the top officials of all the legal agencies and to staff of the Central Committee of the Communist party.[22] Discussions extended for months, sometimes years. Often, the initiative for a new guiding explanation came not from the Court itself but the Ministry of Justice. Thus, in 1947, after receiving repeated inquiries from judges about the application of the law on absenteeism to kolkhoz peasants working on contract in timber felling, officials in the Ministry prepared a draft edict and sent it to the Court. (A new, repeat edict of the Council of Ministers

---

[21] "Opiat ob instruktsiiakh: Beseda oborzrevatelia Iu. Feofanova s A. Pigolkinym i S. Poleninoi," *Izvestiia*, Sept. 23, 1987, 3; V. Gulier et al., "O verkhovenstve zakona i stikhii podzakonnykh aktov," ibid., Feb. 26, 1989, 2.

[22] See the letter from Supreme Court Chairman Goliakov to Central Committee Secretary Malenkov (Dec. 6, 1940) requesting approval of a draft resolution of the Supreme Court Plenum that had already been "visa-ed" by Narkomiust, the Procuracy, and the Supreme Court itself. GARF, f.8474, op.16s, d.162, 157. For a sanitized version of the process of composing guiding explanations (resolutions) of the USSR Supreme Court, see M.M. Isaev, *Voprosy ugolovnogo prava i ugolovnogo protessa v sudebnoi praktike Verkhovnogo Suda SSSR* (Moscow, 1948), 28–31.

preempted the Court's draft resolution and made Supreme Court Chairman Ivan Goliakov question the need for comment by the Court.) Similarly, in 1950 the Minister of Justice, Konstantin Gorshenin, sent a letter to Supreme Court Chairman Anatolii Volin proposing a guiding explanation on the application of fines to women who had undergone illegal abortions (the issue was whether to count prior abortions for which there had been no conviction). Again, the minister supplied a draft directive which the Court's Plenum approved late in the year.[23] Finally, the preparation of the Supreme Court's 1952 explanation on the theft laws of 1947 (more below) followed a long and tortuous course. The initial draft was composed in 1949, but set aside. An operational session composed of eight members of the Court (of seventy-two) and four consultants met in September 1951 to refine the draft and sent it out for comments. By March 1952 the Court had received detailed analyses and reactions from the procurator-general of the USSR, the procurator of the RSFSR, the ministers of justice of the two governments, and the chairman of the RSFSR Supreme Court.[24]

The status of resolutions of the USSR Supreme Court gained recognition from legal scholars in a debate held at the Institute of Law of the USSR Academy of Sciences in 1946. The question was whether or not the Court's guiding explanations constituted legal norms or the equivalent of laws. The contestants disagreed, one (Isaev) claiming that they did, another (Strogovich) that they did not, and a third (Makinskaia) saying that it depended on whether the court was striking out into new ground.[25] The middle position made sense, for in the last years of Stalin at least some of the Court's resolutions covered matters that in the 1920s would have called for changes in the law. To give a few examples. A guiding explanation of the Court issued in 1942 determined that despite a decree imposing criminal responsibility for failure to respond to the agricultural draft on all persons who were not students, the Court decided to exempt as well 14- to 16-year-olds who did *not* attend school. Similarly, in 1949, a resolution of the USSR Supreme Court set out the punishments for repeat instances of absenteeism (this was not the first statement of the court on this subject). Finally, in 1950 a brief explanation of the court established that cases of ordinary hooliganism (Article 74.1) were to have a full preliminary investigation and be tried according to general procedures. This decision effectively repealed the special

---

23 GARF, f.9492 op.1, d.157, 125ff; f.9474, op.10, d.79 (Protokoly zasedanii Biuro Verkhovnogo Suda SSSR za 1950).

24 Ibid., d.65 (Materialy – proekt postanovleniia Plenuma Verkhovnogo Suda SSSR, protokol operativnogo soveshchaniia, zakliucheniia, dokladnye zapiski, statii – o sudebnoi praktike po primeneniiu Ukaza ot 4 iuniia 1947 g.), esp. 10, 30, 47ff., 84–86.

25 "V sektore sudebnogo prava Instituta prava AN SSSR," *SGiP*, 1946, no. 10, 41–43.

simplified procedures for cases of hooliganism used since August 1940 – composition by the police of a short protocol followed by a quick trial within two days.[26] To be sure, that simplified procedure had not been introduced in a law or decree but rather by joint order of Narkomiust SSSR, the USSR Procuracy, and NKVD SSSR! Even in 1940, Stalin and his colleagues hadn't bothered to amend the Criminal Procedure Code for such a basic change in the rules of procedure.

The fact that scholars could even imagine that Supreme Court guiding explanations might be tantamount to laws indicated that the Court's resolution had gained special status. At the minimum, they were understood by contemporaries as statements of policy. Consider how RSFSR Minister of Justice Fedor Beliaev characterized resolutions of the USSR Supreme Court at a conference of judges held in 1951. In a direct manner, Beliaev told his charges, "decisions of the Plenum of the (USSR) Supreme Court represent the party line. . . . They are approved, just as the directives of the ministries of justice of the Union and the Federation are also approved," if not by the leaders then by an "apparatus that decides which directives meet party demands." Later the Minister continued, "I have said a few times already that an edict of the Plenum of the Supreme Court is a canonical text, an approved text. All that is written there is obligatory for us, no matter who signed it. . . . They were given the task and they signed!"[27] So much for the authority of the court and the law. To this RSFSR minister of justice it was the word of the party bosses that counted.

Secret regulations and laws

During the rule of Stalin an increasing share of legal norms came to be expressed in the form of secret or restricted regulations and laws. By the 1940s, the reach of secret rules had extended from political to ordinary, nonpolitical, criminal law. No doubt the development of the secret dimension in Soviet law suited the convenience of Soviet officials; hypercentralization and strict lines of subordination within the agencies bred

26 "O nedopustimosti privlecheniia k ugolovnoi otvetstvennosti podrostkov do 16 let za uklonenie ot mobilizatsii na selskokhozaistvennye raboty i za samovolnyi ukhod mobilizovannykh s etikh rabot," Postanovlenie Verkhovnogo Suda SSSR no. 16/M/18/u ot 8 otiabria 1942 g., *Sudebraia praktika Verkhovnogo Suda SSSR*, 1942, no. 11, 5–6; "O poriadke opredeleniia nakazaniia za povtornyi progul bez uvazhatelnykh prichin," Postanovlenie Plenuma ot 22 iiunia 1949 g., no. 9/4/u, ibid., 1949, no. 9, 1–2; "O poriadke rassmotreniia sudami del o khuliganstve," Postanovlenie Plenuma ot 3 fevralia 1950 g., no. 3/4/u, ibid., 1950 no. 4, 1.

27 GARF, f.353, op.13, d.150 (Stenogramma mezhoblastnogo soveshchaniia zamestiteli predsedatelei . . . oblastnykh sudov. 25 apreliia 1951), 48ob, 49ob.

secrecy. At the same time, secret laws reflected the fetish with secrecy that the paranoid leader nourished over the years. Stalin's concern with secrecy found expression in the way Soviet criminal law treated the release of classified data. In 1943 a law made even the accidental loss of such information a criminal offense (before that time only the transfer, or theft, or collection of data for the purpose of transfer constituted crimes). More dramatically, in 1947 a new Stalin law increased the sanctions for all breaches of the rules on "state secrets," including accidental losses. According to the law, an official who accidentally released classified data (if he were not subject to charges of spying) could still be sentenced to eight to twelve years' imprisonment. Stalin also approved a new, detailed list of the types of information to be defined as state secrets, a list that extended the definition to include economic, trade, and scientific data and any information deemed secret by the Council of Ministers.[28]

Already in the 1930s a sizable part of the regulations issued by the Council of People's Commissars and the commissariats of the USSR and republics stayed out of public view. By the 1940s this share had increased. One may distinguish three categories of unpublished regulations: (1) those classed as secret or top secret; (2) those designated "for internal use" or "not for dissemination"; and (3) those technically open to the public but so narrowly distributed as to be unavailable to most persons. In the 1930s and the 1940s resolutions of the Council fell into all three categories. Those marked "secret" or "for internal use" were distributed by lists and placed, if at all, in specially restricted library collections. The decrees classed as open were published in the *Sobranie Postanovlenii Pravitelstva SSSR* (Collection of Resolutions of the Government of the USSR), an official publication available mainly in law libraries, and reprinted in handbooks and anthologies prepared for the use of officials.

The restricted circulation of the regulations of the legal agencies developed gradually. In the 1920s almost all of the directives and instructions of Narkomiust and other legal agencies were published in both journals and special collections. In the early 1930s directives relating to the administration of penal institutions and the implementation of the Law of August 7, 1932, were secret. The establishment of the USSR Procuracy in 1933 extended the quantity of secret directives. From the start nearly half of the orders and directives of the USSR Procuracy were secret and only a portion of the open ones were published in a journal. Between 1933 and 1953 the USSR Procuracy published only one open collection of its directives (in 1939), and all its future collections of nonsecret directives (e.g., in 1957 and 1966) were marked "for internal

---

[28] Goliakov, *Sbornik dokumentov*, 423–424, 431–433.

use only."[29] At the same time, Narkomiust also restricted more of its instructions, publishing fewer in journals, and limiting itself to two open collections of directives (1940 and 1948). The postwar period witnessed a stark increase in the secrecy of regulations of the justice agencies. The journals ceased publishing the exact texts of any regulations.[30] Moreover, some two-thirds of the orders and instructions of the USSR Procuracy were marked "secret."[31]

Even with good access to formerly secret archival collections it is difficult to chart the penetration of secrecy into Soviet criminal law. Here are broad outlines of the story. As might be expected, in the 1930s there was a substantial body of secret regulations concerning political prosecutions and the prosecution of important people. We have already encountered the resolution of the Sovnarkom and the Central Committee of May 8, 1933, that is, Stalin and Molotov's "letter" that called a halt to mass arrests associated with the final collectivization drive, and a similar joint resolution of November 17, 1938, that provided the mechanisms for stopping the Terror and Purge. In the interim there were at least two other such joint resolutions (all secret) dealing with arrests and investigation in political cases and the clearances for the arrest of important persons. As part of the winding down of the Great Terror yet another secret joint resolution (December 1, 1938) established a more stringent system of clearances for the arrest of important persons.[32] Moreover, the files reveal that Procurator-General Vyshinskii issued numerous secret orders in connection with the Terror and Purge, and management of labor camps, and police. But I have not encountered *secret* resolutions or agency orders in the 1930s relating wholly to the definition or prosecution of *ordinary* crimes.

By the 1940s, however, secrecy had entered ordinary criminal law, as the nature of crimes and punishments came to be defined in not only secret resolutions of the Council of Ministers (already discussed) but

---

29 *Sbornik prikazov prokuratury SSSR deistvuiushchikh na 1. dek. 1938* 2nd ed. (Moscow 1939); *Sbornik deistvuiushchikh prikazov i instruktsii generalnogo prokurora SSSR* (Moscow, 1958, "dlia sluzhebnogo polzovaniia").

30 *Sbornik prikazov i instruktsii Ministerstva iustitsii SSSR* (Moscow, 1939); *Sbornik prikazov i instruktsi Ministerstva Iustitsii SSSR, 1936–1948 gg.* (Moscow, 1949); *Sotsialisticheskaia zakonnost*, passim.

31 This inference is based upon comparison of files in the open (for limited access) and the secret parts of GARF, fond 8131 (Prokuratura SSSR).

32 "Instruktsiia vsem partiino-sovetskim rabotnikam i vsem organam OGPU, suda i prokuratury," WKP 178, 135–136; and GARF, f.353s, op.16s, 1; "Ob arestakh, prokururskom nadzore i vedenii sledstviia," Postanovlenie Sovnarkoma SSSR i TsK VKP(b) ot 17 noiabria 1938, no. P.4387, *Istoricheskii arkhiv*, 1992, no. 1, 125–128; "O poriadke soglasovaniia arestov," Postanovlenie Sovnarkoma SSSR i TsK VKP(b) ot 1 dekabria 1938 goda, no. p. 4404, replacing a similar decree of June 17, 1935.

already in secret decrees of the Praesidium of the USSR Supreme Soviet, the equivalent of laws. Apart from a 1949 decree of the Praesidium on criminal responsibility of officials for overloading airplanes IL-12 and LI-2 with passengers and freight (probably in response to a crash), the Praesidium's secret decrees in the realm of criminal law concerned two subjects, the early release of prisoners and refinements in the laws governing prosecutions for labor infractions.[33]

Until World War II most early releases of whole categories of inmates from corrective labor institutions came through amnesties, which were announced in openly published laws. Although tied to an occasion, such as the celebration of an anniversary of the Revolution, amnesties served the function of relieving custodial institutions of excess population. The frequency and scope of amnesties reflected the needs of penal administration.[34] There was one major exception. The single largest early release of prisoners resulted not from an amnesty but from the secret Instruction of May 8, 1933, issued by Stalin and Molotov to reduce by 400,000 the persons placed in custody during the grain collection campaign of winter 1932–1933. The need to keep the famine secret justified this special handling of the releases.

During the first year of World War II the Soviet leadership once again decided to release a variety of categories of persons from confinement not in openly proclaimed amnesty but through secret decrees. Covered by the decrees were persons whose labor could help the war effort (those convicted of quitting jobs in factories and juveniles sentenced to less than two years) and persons whose nonproductive status represented a burden to the penal institutions (pregnant women, women with young children, invalids, and old men).[35] The War itself supplied ample reason to keep these releases secret. The enemy could not be informed that the Soviet Union found it necessary to return prisoners to staff its factories behind the front.

Near the end of the War, in January 1945, pregnant women and women with small children benefited from yet another secret release. The reason for secrecy this time was avoiding informing the world that Soviet prisons contained so many women of this kind. Not many months later, at the War's conclusion, a traditional public amnesty for prisoners was issued, one that covered inter alia all persons sentenced to terms of imprisonment under three years, but the amnesty did not mention pregnant women, their children, or juvenile offenders.[36] In fact,

---

[33] GARF, f.7523sch, op.65s, d.358.

[34] P.S. Romashkin, *Amnistiia i pomilovanie v SSSR* (Moscow, 1959).

[35] GARF, f.7523sch, op.65s, d.97 and d.105.

[36] GARF, f.7523sch, op.65s, d.107; Goliakov, *Sbornik dokmentov*, 426–427.

the habit of keeping secret decrees that targeted for release these categories of inmates continued until Stalin's death. The major releases of women (August 16, 1947, April 22, 1949) and juveniles (September 26, 1950) came once again through secret decrees of the Praesidium of the Supreme Soviet. These amnesties were occasioned by the arrival in the camps of women with children and juveniles convicted under the theft decrees of June 1947.[37]

The other secret decrees of the Praesidium related to a subject familiar to the reader from Chapter 9 – the definition and handling of the crime of "shirking," an offense that included unjustified absence from work and tardiness. To begin, a chain of decrees and resolutions, mostly unpublished and secret, addressed the extension of the edict of June 26, 1940, to collective farmers (kolkhozniki). The story begins with the issuing on February 15, 1942, of an unpublished decree of the Praesidium of the Supreme Soviet, making able-bodied collective farm members liable to criminal prosecution for failing during a whole agricultural cycle to perform the required number of labor-days. This decree was quickly superseded by a published joint resolution of the Council of People's Commissars and the Central Committee (April 13, 1942), which gave the details of criminal liability already specified in the unpublished decree.[38] But two days later, on April 15, 1942, the Council issued another secret decree extending the liability for failure to fulfill labor-day quotas to kolkhozniki who had voluntarily taken jobs in industry. The implementation of this decree produced sharp disagreements. Was it possible to punish a person for working for the government? If so, how? Should a sentence of corrective work be served by the offender at the kolkhoz or the factory where the kolkhoznik was employed? This last question put the RSFSR Ministry of Justice and RSFSR Supreme Court into direct conflict as late as 1950, a conflict resolved in a resolution of the Council of Ministers and the Central Committee (April 12, 1951). This was no minor, technical issue, for in some rural districts charges according to the secret decree of April 15, 1942, were among the most common prosecutions.[39] Unpublished, or at least obscure, laws added yet one more dimension to the liability of kolkhozniki. A pair of resolutions of the

---

[37] GARF, f.7523sch, op.65s, d.346, 366, 363. For an account of these releases of children and pregnant women, see V.F. Zima, "Golod i prestupnost v SSSR (1946–1947 gg.)," unpublished paper (1993), 15–20. The initiative for the release of mothers and pregnant women is found in a note from A. Abramova to Zhdanov in May 1948. RTsKhIDNI, f.17, op.121, d.642, 1–7. For controversy over the implementation of the amnesty see ibid. op.136, d.166, 299–301.

[38] *Sovetskoe pravo v period velikoi otechestvennoi voiny chast 1; Grazhdanskoe pravo – Trudovoe pravo* (Moscow, 1948), 226–230.

[39] GARF, f.353, op.13, d.150, 4–5, 129.

Council of Ministers (in 1946 and 1947) made all peasants liable to charges of shirking if they failed to fulfill contracts for timber felling.[40] This meant that a kolkhoz member who signed a contract for timber felling faced a double bind – criminal liability for failing to meet his obligations both to the kolkhoz and to the timber agency. Finally in 1948 kolkhozniki who persistently refused to work at their collective farms became subject to not only court-applied fines for shirking but also severe punishments applied through mere administrative decisions. In a pair of unpublished decrees of the Praesidium of the USSR Supreme Soviet (February 11 and June 2, 1948) the leadership endorsed a proposal from Nikita Khrushchev to entrust kolkhoz general meetings, first in the Ukraine and then in the USSR as a whole, with the power to banish to outlying places for eight years members who did not work and led an "antisocial, parasitical way of life." Unlike the OGPU's banishment power in 1935–1936, the authority granted to kolkhoz meetings in 1948 was not covered by the criminal code or introduced into the criminal law, but it entailed the application of serious punishments for actions or omissions of a nonpolitical character.[41]

Another important secret law relating to labor violations was the decree of the Praesidium of the Supreme Soviet of July 14, 1951, that decriminalized most forms of shirking (*progul*). Although this decree eliminated nearly three-quarters of criminal prosecutions for shirking generated under the law of June 26, 1940, and more than a fifth of prosecutions overall, the decree bore the mark "not for publication."[42]

The reader will recall from Chapter 9 the difficulties faced by Soviet authorities in enforcing the law of June 26, 1940. Only by threatening factory managers and judges with prosecution were political leaders able to secure compliance. In the postwar years, long after the campaign for the implementation of the law, enforcement had become erratic. There were some districts and cities where prosecutions for shirking were no longer common, but in many other places they had reached levels that overwhelmed the courts. Typically, the degree of enforcement varied as well from factory to factory within particular cities. (In

---

[40] GARF, f.9492, op.1, d.157, 125ff.
[41] RTsKhIDNI, f.17, op.121, d.673, 51–53, 78–79. It is striking how Khrushchev's 1948 initiative regarding "parasites" on the kolkhozy prefigures his larger attack on the nonemployed in the late 1950s when he was First Secretary of the CPSU.
[42] For the text of the decree and related regulations and documents on their origins see GARF, f.5446sch, op.59s, d.7056. See also GARF, f.9492, op.1, d.61 (Spravka proverki del o prestupleniiakh, predusmotrennye Ukazom Prezidiuma Verkhovnogo Soveta SSSR ot 14/VII-51g.), "O zamene sudebnoi otvetsvennosti rabochikh i sluzhashchikh za progul . . . ," 18–26. The data are derived from GARF, f.9492sch, op.6s, d.14 (Statistika sudimosti), 11, 12.

Murmansk Region, where 20% of the labor force was prosecuted for shirking in 1945–1946, leading officials in two factories were themselves sent to court for "groundless referrals to court of workers and staff.")[43] Unfair as this pattern of enforcement was, it did not prompt justice officials to action. What made them press for reform was the amount of court time expended on cases of shirking. In the mining city of Kemerovo, for example, in 1947 cases of "shirking" represented 73% of all criminal cases heard at the people's courts. To manage the caseload, some judges cut corners, hearing cases of shirking in "batches" (*pachkami*) and not bothering to compile protocols or sentences. The judges just announced their decisions and fixed up the paperwork later on. Often, they heard these cases not in the courts but in the mines and factories, and the hearings bore little resemblance to trials. (As a result, many verdicts were overturned on appeal.)[44]

Although the situation in Kemerovo represented an extreme (the example was cited repeatedly), the Siberian city was not the only place where the provisions on shirking had produced an unmanageable caseload. The deputy minister of justice of the Ukraine reported in April 1948 that in recent months more than 100,000 cases of shirking had been started in the Ukraine, creating a massive backlog. "We have communicated four times to the USSR Ministry of Justice," he complained "but we get discussions rather than action." In fact, the fault did not lie with the Ministry. More than a month before, Minister of Justice Gorshenin had written to Stalin and Molotov proposing the transfer to comrades' courts of all cases of shirking under one day.[45] Three years later the USSR minister of justice advised the audience at another conference of judicial officials that action was finally coming, and in July 1951 the Praesidium of the Supreme Soviet issued a secret decree eliminating from the criminal law all instances of shirking that did not result in lengthy absences (measured in days) or repeat offenses. All ordinary instances of shirking were to be treated as administrative (rather than criminal) offenses, and heard, where possible, by comrades' courts.[46]

Moreover, the new law indicated that to qualify even as an administrative offense, an act of shirking had to consist of one full day away from work or drunk on the job. Henceforth, mere tardy arrival at work or return from lunch would no longer count as shirking, representing

43 Interviews; GARF, f.9492, op.1, d.530 (Protokol operativnogo soveshchanii narsudei g. Kharkova ot 15 aprelia 1947 goda), 247; RTsKhIDNI, f.17, op.122, d.257, 4–7.
44 GARF, f.9492, op.1, d.157 (O faktakh grubogo narusheniia Ukaza ot 26 iiuniia 1940 goda v narodnykh sudakh Kemerovskoi oblasti) d.179, 243.
45 GARF, f.9492, op.1, d.181 (Protokol zasedaniia aktiva rabotnikov iustitsii 23–26 apreliia 1948), 52; op.2s, d.578, 66–75.
46 GARF, f.9492, op.1, d.243, 219; *Sorok let sovetskogo prava* (Leningrad, 1957), 2, 337–338.

instead only a minor disciplinary matter. This narrowing of the definition of shirking was prefigured by jurists working on the draft USSR Criminal Code. Already in November 1948 they had planned to decriminalize tardiness and absenteeism not exceeding one day. The adoption of this idea through a secret edict required some dissemination in order to be implemented. The change in the definition of shirking was introduced in 1951 into the "Rules of Internal Labor Order" (adopted first in 1941), which was approved by the Council of Ministers and distributed to enterprises and trade unions. But no changes relating either to the definition of shirking or the limitations on criminal prosecution were introduced into the RSFSR Criminal Code or given publicity. Minister of Justice Gorshenin complained in a note to Central Committee Secretary Malenkov that it was important to find ways to propagandize the edict despite the stamp "without publication in the press"; but Malenkov seems to have ignored this request.[47]

The secret decree of July 14, 1951, had dramatic effects on the work of many courts. In the city of Moscow cases of shirking dropped sevenfold in the second part of 1951; Rostov on the Don experienced a similar decrease. A study of labor infractions in Rostov noted, however, that the number of administrative convictions (by courts or local soviets) did not rise, and that, while comrades' courts did hear some cases, as a rule factory administrators now handled shirking on their own. The report from Moscow also noted a drop in cases of illegal quitting (the other part of the law of June 26, 1940), even though the new edict did not decriminalize that offense.[48]

The decree of July 14, 1951, bore a strong resemblance to two laws of the 1920s, which had transferred to administrative jurisdiction whole categories of petty crimes in order to reduce congestion in the courts (see Chapter 2). But there was a difference. The laws that decriminalized offenses in the 1920s came in amendments to the RSFSR Criminal Code. The decriminalization of lesser forms of shirking came in a decree that was secret, unpublished, and unmentioned in published materials. The decree of July 14, 1951, received *no mention* (let alone publication) in the

[47] Ibid.; GARF, f.9492, op.1, d.1959, 78; f.9492sch, op.2s, d.78 (ot Gorshenina k Malenkovu), 55; Harold Berman was told by legal scholars in Moscow about the decriminalization of shirking. See *Justice in the USSR* (Cambridge, 1963), 149.
[48] GARF, f.9492, op.1, d.594 (O rezultatakh izuchenii del po ukazu "O zamene sudebnoi otvetsvennosti rabochikh i sluzhashchikh za progul"), 1–15; d.61 (Spravka proverki del . . . "O zamene sudebnoi otvestvennosti"), 18–26; d.2796 (Protokol kustovogo soveshchaniia . . . zam. nachalnikov UMIU kraev i oblastei po sudebnoi rabote i po kadram ot 29/VII-1952), 38. The decrease in cases of illegal quitting proved temporary; in 1952 their number returned to a level close to that of 1950. GARF, f.9492, op.6s, d.14, 11.

official record of the USSR Supreme Soviet whose Praesidum had issued it; in the central press (*Izvestiia* or *Trud*); in the labor journals
(*Professionalnye soiuzy, V pomoshch profsoiuznomu aktivu*); and in a large
collection of laws relating to labor published in 1953 and marked "for
internal use."[49] Perhaps, Stalin did not want to tell his workers that
shirking would be treated less seriously than before. Perhaps, the Soviet
leadership believed that changes in the scope of an offense, the types of
sanctions applied and modes of its imposition were technical matters,
about which only trade-union and legal officials needed to know.

Severity of punishment for nonpolitical crimes

Legislation of severe punishments for crimes not defined as political
came relatively late in Stalin's reign. Such laws appeared only in the
years *after* the Great Terror and especially after World War II. There
were other developments, to be sure, that increased the severity of
punishments actually applied to thieves and other ordinary offenders
and prepared Soviet society for new levels of brutality imposed by the
state.

Even under Lenin, the Soviet regime provided for severe punishments for what it defined as political crimes (as had the tsarist regime
before), and Stalin periodically extended the concept of political crime
to embrace offenses normally understood as nonpolitical. Thus, during
collectivization Stalin made the theft of socialist and state property into
a political offense. Through the law of August 7, 1932, peasants who
stole grain became subject to long terms of imprisonment and even the
death penalty. But this elevation of theft into a political offense proved
temporary; as soon as the battle over the countryside was completed,
Stalin restricted the use of the Law of August 7 to a small category of
the most serious forms of theft. During the Great Terror itself police
and prosecutors were encouraged to qualify as political offenses actions or inactions by managers that would at earlier times merit such
charges as misuse of authority or criminal negligence. Again, this pattern turned out to represent a *temporary politicization* of an offense,
rather than a commitment to impose severe punishments on a long-
term basis.

---

[49] I could find no references to the law decriminalizing absenteeism (shirking) in *Vedomo-
sti Verkhovnogo Soveta SSSR* for 1951; in *Izvestiia*, and *Trud* for July 1951; in *V pomoshch
profsoiuznomu aktivu* and *Professionalnye soiuzy* for 1951; or in the authoritative collection of labor law for internal use, G. Aleksandrov et al., ed., *Zakonodatelstvo o trude.
Kommentarii zakonodatelstvu o trude SSSR i kodeksa zakonov truda RSFSR* (Moscow, 1953).
On page 69 this collection contains the cryptic remark "responsibility for absenteeism
without good reasons is regulated specially."

At the same time, during the decade of the 1930s, the sentences meted out by judges for ordinary crimes became increasingly severe. In the middle and later years of the decade, with encouragement from their bureaucratic and political masters, judges used their legal discretion and gave more sentences of imprisonment and less of noncustodial sanctions (e.g., for hooliganism); and the terms of imprisonment for some crimes started to increase. By and large, though, this trend represented the return to traditional punishments for ordinary crimes rather than qualitatively new levels of severity. The emphasis on noncustodial sanctions in the 1920s, followed by the ban on short-term imprisonment in 1928, had produced in the early 1930s a deviation from normal patterns of punishment in Russia, which many judges themselves found strange. The policy of revived harshness of sentences for ordinary crime in the mid- and late 1930s required no changes in legislation. Using the discretion already built into the 1926 criminal code, judges were able to give more (or longer) terms of imprisonment.[50] In addition, the elimination of parole in 1939 gave all sentences to imprisonment a sharper edge.[51]

Nineteen hundred and forty represented the turning point, the year in which Stalin first legislated unusually severe punishments for ordinary offenses. To be sure, in introducing a five- to eight-year term for managers responsible for producing defective goods (up from five years), the law referred to the crime as "antigovernmental," suggesting a weak form of politicization. But the imposition of a minimum sentence of one-year imprisonment for both petty theft in factories and hooliganism represented a qualitatively new incursion into the realm of severity. Not only did this decree significantly reduce the use of noncustodial sanctions, but it also forced judges to impose a full year of custody for minor breaches.[52] As we have seen, this decree was a part of Stalin's desperate attempt to raise the output of industrial production on the eve of World War II. The targets of the decree were workers who stole from their enterprises or staged drunken brawls in order to get themselves fired, thereby evading criminal responsibility for unauthorized quitting.

The full expression of Stalin's readiness to use severe punishments for ordinary crimes came only after World War II. The most important example was the decrees on theft, which, as we have seen, called for minimum terms of five or six years and maximums well into the double

---

[50] See Solomon, "Soviet Penal Policy;" M.D. Shargorodskii, *Nakazanie po sovetskomu ugolovnomu pravu* (Moscow, 1958).

[51] On labor-day accounts as a substitute for parole from 1953, see Solomon, *Soviet Criminologists*, 42–45.

[52] Goliakov, *Sbornik dokumentov*, 406.

digits. There were other examples of severity. The penalty for making homebrew for purpose of sale was raised from a maximum of one-year imprisonment to a term of six to seven years. The penalty for ordinary rape increased from "up to five years" to "ten to fifteen years" and for rape of a minor from "up to eight years" to "fifteen to twenty years." The penalties for the mere loss of classified documents were on the same order. Curiously, the punishment for premeditated murder remained at "up to ten years," despite the suggestion of Minister of Justice Gorshenin in July 1949 (and again in Dec. 1950) that it be raised to ten to twenty years (and twenty to twenty-five years when committed in a group). An analogous initiative from Procurator-General Safonov on the penalties for offering and taking bribes also remained still-born.[53]

It is difficult to appreciate just how draconian these new guidelines for punishment were. From the realm of political justice under Stalin we are all too familiar with punishments numbering ten, fifteen, or twenty years. But, it is important to realize that such punishments were something wholly new for nonpolitical offenses (or offenses not temporarily politicized), and that the new severity broke not only with previous Soviet experience but also with the punishments found in tsarist criminal law in the last few decades before the Revolution. Take theft as an example. To be sure, tsarist law relied almost exclusively on custodial sanctions, providing even for the most minor breaches terms of confinement numbering in months. But for most serious thefts, the terms of imprisonment were under four years; and the typical theft qualified for a sentence in the one- to two-year range. According to criminal statistics of the Ministry of Justice, for 1899–1903, only 3.9% of convictions for theft brought a sentence of over four years (that is, exile with or without hard labor).[54] To find parallels for Stalin's new harshness in Russian history, one must go back to at least the early nineteenth century, if not earlier. I know of no such levels of punishment for theft in twentieth-century Europe.

Muting the laws on theft: judges and others

Stalin's decision to suppress theft through draconian punishment met the same fate as his earlier attempts to extend the scope of the criminal

53 Ibid., 431–435, RTsKhIDNI, f.17, op.118, d.456, 132–135; GARF, f.5446sch, op.80a, d.8023, 72–80; op.51a, d.5339, 1–59. The original draft edict on rape (August 1949) prepared by the chiefs of the legal agencies at the request of the secretariat called for "five to ten years" for ordinary rape. The change was probably Stalin's doing and may have reflected the rape of the daughter of a Central Committee official. RTsKhIDNI, f.17, op.118, d.117, 29–30; op.116, d.373, p.47; op.3, d.1073, 299.
54 Fridman, *Prestuplenie i nakazanie po ulozheniiu o nakazaniiakh* (Moscow, 1912), 67–72 and *Itogi russkoi ugolovnoi statistiki za 20 let (1874–1894 gg.)* (St. Petersburg, 1899), 95–96.

law. To legal officials and other enforcers, the prosecution of managers for producing defective goods, workers for breaches of labor discipline, women for having abortions, and children for delinquent acts was in varying degrees wrong or inconvenient. The implementation of these extensions of the criminal law was checked by the unwillingness of relevant actors to report wrongdoers, initiate prosecutions, or impose the designated sanctions. The theft decrees of 1947 did not create new offenses, but they changed fundamentally the reaction of state authority to familiar ones. In so doing, the decrees aroused the same reactions as had the earlier extensions of the criminal law. Judges sought and sooner or later found ways of avoiding the excessively harsh penalties required by the law, at least for the lesser offenders, and many of those responsible for starting theft cases avoided prosecution. Behind this resistance to the new harshness in the law lay a familiar blend of conscience and convenience. Officials everywhere found it wrong to imprison children for their pranks and poor women for their acts of desperation. At the same time, few factory managers could afford to have their pilfering workers locked away for years, and few local politicians were willing to have key managers removed from their posts.

As we saw earlier in this chapter, the two decrees on theft promulgated on June 4, 1947, introduced minimum penalties of five and six years' imprisonment and specified terms of ten to twenty-five years for the various forms of qualified theft, such as a repeat offense or theft committed in an organized group. The decrees contrasted starkly with previous law and practice. In 1946 nearly one-quarter of persons convicted of theft received noncustodial sanctions, and the majority of the rest terms in prison of *one year* for theft of personal property and of two to three years for theft of state property.[55] To be sure, the Law of August 7, 1932, had set imprisonment of ten years as the minimum for theft of state property and established on paper capital punishment as a normal response to this crime. As we saw in Chapter 4, however, few judges were willing to use the death penalty for any but the most serious incidents and within two years the use of the law itself had been limited by the Supreme Court to those events. Both the criminal law and the practice of the courts before June 1947 reflected a basic reality, that most thefts perpetrated in the USSR involved small values, perhaps not small enough to qualify as "petty theft" but small all the same.

The campaign to implement the new decrees on theft assured a substantial increase in cases, especially of small-scale thefts. Prominent

[55] GARF f.9492sch, op.6s, d.14, 30–31. See also f.9492, op.1, d.179, 443.

among them were thefts in the countryside, especially from kolkhozy. The campaign ended in September and by October a long-term drop in cases had begun. But theft prosecutions for the whole of 1947 rose by 47% for state property and 76% for personal property. The police generated most of the new cases, and too often procurators proved unwilling to risk stopping cases.[56] As a result, judges were put on the spot and forced to confront large numbers of accused whose crimes did not deserve the penalties required by the decrees.

The challenge posed by Stalin's theft decrees divided Soviet judges. Some of them tried to soften the blow. In the words of one of their supervisors, "Judges at all levels used every sort of loophole to avoid the punishments set by the law." In the first months some judges ignored the new laws and relied instead on the article of the criminal code (Article 162) that the laws were meant to replace. Although the USSR Supreme Court denounced this practice, it did not cease. Judges also made use of their prize tools of judicial discretion, the articles in the code authorizing sentences below the limit set for particular offenses (Article 51) and suspended sentences (Article 53).[57] As soon as Stalin's new laws were announced, some judges queried higher judicial officials about using Articles 51 and 53, displaying to one observer their disloyalty (negosudarstvennyi podkhod).[58] Despite strong discouragement from superiors, some judges used these articles even during the campaign period, although not in a large percentage of cases. In Russia, suspended sentences and sentences below the limit figured in 3% of convictions during the second half of 1947 and the awarding of even 5% to 7% singled out particular judges for criticism. (In other republics the averages reached 7% and 9%.) Another common practice of judges in the first months of the new theft laws was to classify serious thefts as ordinary ones, thereby avoiding the extremely long terms of imprisonment set for qualified theft. The judges did this by excluding from the ranks of repeat offenders accused persons whose first theft had not been prosecuted; and by treating as "organized groups" only those persons who had committed thefts together prior to the ones currently on trial.[59]

56 GARF f.9492sch, op.6s, d.14, 14. Between June and December 1947 police investigated 87% of cases of theft of personal property and 61.4% of thefts of state/social property. GARF, f.8131, op.27s, d.4036, 50.
57 GARF, f.9492, op.1, d.183 (Stenogramma soveshchaniia aktiva rabotnikov Ministerstv iustitsii SSSR ot 26–28 oktiabria 1948 g.) 5; d.179 (Stenogramma vsesoiuznogo soveshchaniia predsedatelei . . . oblastnykh sudov), 443–468.
58 Ibid., 458.
59 Ibid., 443–468, 534; I. Perlov, "Ustranit nedostatki borby s khishcheniiami sotsialisticheskoi sobstvennosti," SZ 1948, no. 1, 9–13.

In contrast to the resistant judges who tried to blunt the edge of the new laws stood many other judges who, recognizing the political meaning of the laws, joined zealously in their application. Some of the cautious judges applied the new laws on theft so literally as to draw criticism from their superiors. Some treated every theft committed by two or more persons as "theft by an organized group;" some convicted children for stealing "mere trifles."[60] In rural areas of the Ukraine and Kazakhstan, police started large numbers of cases against persons who had stolen a kilo of meat or grain, and, given the chance, judges imposed harsh sentences. While some of these judges willingly applied the harsh laws, others sought to protect themselves from censure. The instinct of judges for self-protection had roots in experience. Some of the judges who had resisted the application of Stalin's edict against shirkers (in 1940) had lost their jobs. In fact, similar scapegoating did occur with the decrees on theft as well. In 1948 a small number of higher court judges were fired for tolerating leniency on the part of people's court judges in the application of the decrees.[61]

From the start the chiefs of the legal agencies tried to balance condemnation of liberalism on the part of particular judges and districts with clarifications of controversial issues. Some of the clarifications curbed outrageous consequences of the laws, but not all. Thus, in August 1947 the USSR Supreme Court affirmed that the theft decrees of June 4 had rendered obsolete the August 10, 1940, edict that had established one year of prison as punishment for petty theft in factories. (Although the leaders had intended this result, they had not bothered to repeal the Law of August 10.) Likewise, in March 1948 the USSR Supreme Court told judges to treat as repeat offenders accused persons whose previous thefts had not resulted in conviction, but in December 1949 the Court reversed itself.[62] Still, on two major issues the USSR Supreme Court and other legal agencies did strike a balance. These

---

[60] Ibid., "O primenenii ukazov ot 4 iunia 1947 g. v otnoshenii nesovershennoletnikh," Rukovodiashchee postanovlenie Plenuma Verkhovnogo Suda SSSR ot 17 fevralia 1948 g., reprinted in M.M. Isaev, *Voprosy ugolovnogo prava i ugolovnogo protsessa v sudebnoi praktike Verkhovnogo suda SSSR* (Moscow, 1948), 113–115.

[61] "For distortions of the decrees of June 4, 1947, and weakening of the struggle against crime," the chairman of the Supreme Court of the Ukraine, one of his associates, and the chairman of the Supreme Court of Azerbaizhan were fired. GARF, f.9492, op.1, d.183, 43.

[62] GARF, f.7583, op.65, d.384; "O primenenii ukazov ot 4 iiuniia 1947. . . . " Rukovodiashchee postanovleniie Plenuma Verkhovnogo Suda SSSR ot 16 dekabriia 1949 g., reported in A. Piontkovskii, "Osnovnye voprosy praktiki primeneniia ukaza 4 iiuniia 1947, "Ob ugolovnoi otvetsvennosti za khishchenie gosudarstvennogo i obshchestvenogo imushchestva," SZ, 1951, no. 1, 20.

were the prosecution of juvenile offenders, and the definition of an "organized group."

The new theft laws posed a serious threat to young offenders. According to the law of April 5, 1935 (see Chapter 6) criminal responsibility for theft began at the age of 12. Moreover, the War and postwar periods had witnessed a substantial increase in thefts by juveniles, partly a result of the new wave of homeless children produced by the War. To confront these problems, authorities established new orphanages and juvenile labor colonies, commissions to confront the problems of children, special juvenile courts in large cities, and groups for juvenile cases within procuracy offices. Top legal officials introduced rules requiring that cases with juveniles have preliminary investigations and representation of the accused by defense counsel.[63] All the same, in 1946 theft convictions of juveniles (under 18) numbered 30,358, that is 73% of all crimes committed by them, and in 3,679 cases the convicted were children of 12 or 13.[64]

The theft laws of 1947 were bound to affect the sentences of young offenders, and in the first months many juvenile thieves did receive long terms of imprisonment. When trial judges showed leniency, cassation panels tended to reverse their decisions. But higher authorities moved quickly to intervene. On September 17 the first secretary of the Komsomol, N. Mikhailov, sent a letter to Central Committee secretaries Zhdanov, Kuznetsov, and Suslov complaining about the prosecution under the 1947 theft laws of 12- to 16-year-olds (in June-July, 410 in the city of Moscow and 729 in Moscow Region) and calling for a Supreme Court Directive to check this misuse of the laws. The secretaries of the CPSU responded in late October by establishing a commission to study the matter.[65] Already in November, though, top legal officials started discouraging the prosecutions of children under the laws. First, in an appellate decision rendered in November 1947 the USSR Supreme Court signaled that long terms were not appropriate for mere delinquents. In late July 1947 a Moscow court had given a 13-year-old boy a suspended sentence of five years for stealing from a neighbor's room in a communal apartment two jars of jam and a piece of bread. The Moscow city court had overruled the suspension, insisting that the lad receive five years of real imprisonment. The USSR Supreme Court reversed again, supporting the original sus-

63 Tadevosian, "Borba za likvisdatsiiu;" GARF, f.9492, op.1, d.515, 77.
64 GARF, f.9492, op.1, d.1960, 195–198; f.9492sch, op.6s, d.14, 26. Juvenile delinquents needing confinement were to be sent to juvenile colonies of the MVD *without* convictions for crimes.
65 RTsKhIDNI, f.17, op.117, d.952, 3–9.

pended sentence (on the grounds that the boy attended school and as a rule behaved). Second, almost simultaneously USSR Minister of Justice Rychkov sent a secret directive to all judges condemning the use of the new laws for any person under 16, especially when the theft involved trifles. He reminded judges that according to a Council of People's Commissars decree of 1943 they were obliged to stop such cases and remand the offending children to their parents or guardians. Finally, in February 1948 the USSR Supreme Court reinforced Rychkov's position. In a guiding explanation (as Mikhailov had requested) the Court declared that the theft laws of 1947 were directed against "criminal elements who do not want to work honestly," and not against children who steal to make mischief. The Court recalled the same decree of the Council of People's Commissars, as had the Minister of Justice, and directed judges to use Article 51 (sentences below the legal limit) in all juvenile cases where they did not stop the proceedings. Through its directive the USSR Supreme Court signaled a policy (with backing from political authorities) of removing juvenile offenders from the full force of the theft laws of June 1947.[66]

The question of the meaning of the phrase "organized group (gang)," however, proved to be more controversial. The definition of this term mattered, since theft committed by organized groups called for especially severe punishments. To help explain the term and other difficult aspects of the new laws, the editors of *Sotsialisticheskaia zakonnost* invited a contribution from Professor Durmanov of Moscow University's law faculty and a member of the commission drafting the USSR criminal code. In his article Durmanov chose an especially narrow construction of the term "organized group (gang)." For him, the term meant only a "stable, organized group," and stability implied some prior engagement by the group in criminal activity. The mere commission of a theft by two or more persons sharing criminal intent was insufficient, Durmanov argued, to establish the presence of a "stable group." This narrow interpretation promised to shield many offenders who stole in groups from the higher terms of imprisonment set for qualified forms of theft.[67] Durmanov's interpretation might have prevailed, had his article not come to the attention of top politicians. But it did, and a scandal ensued. On orders from the Central Committee of the CPSU,

---

[66] Case of T., announced November 19, 1947, text reported in Isaev, *Voprosy ugolovnogo prava*, 115–117; GARF, f.9492, op.1, d.158 (Pismo Ministra Iustitsii Rychkova ministram institsii soiuznykh respublik ot 18X1 1947), 103–106; "O primenenii ukazov ot 4 iiunia v 1947 g. v otnoshenii nesovershennoletnikh."

[67] N.D. Durmanov, "Nakazuemost khishcheniia gosudarstvennogo i obshchestvennogo imushchestva, krazhi lichnogo imushchestva i razboia po ukazam ot 4 iiuniia 1947 g.," *SZ*, 1947, no. 10, 3–8.

the top legal officials (the USSR minister of justice, the procurator-general of the USSR, and the chairman of the USSR Supreme Court) convened a special meeting and issued an unusual (if not unique) joint decree denouncing the errors in Professor Durmanov's article. The chairman of the USSR Supreme Court, Goliakov, also wrote a special article criticizing Durmanov's creative jurisprudence. Though bearing the brunt of verbal abuse, Professor Durmanov lost neither his job nor his freedom.[68]

A few months later, in March 1948, the USSR Supreme Court issued its own authoritative definition of an organized group (gang). It meant "a group of two or more persons, organized in advance to commit one or more crimes . . . " Although the Court rejected Durmanov's requirement of stability (that the group have committed previous crimes), the Court rejected the opposite loose view of a group as any two persons who tried to commit a crime. The Court insisted that an element of "advance organization" be present. This term remained subject to interpretation, but it did give trial judges a way to avoid the severe punishments for theft by an organized group. Not all trial court judges, however, made use of this opportunity. Especially after the reprimand of Professor Durmanov, many judges proved unwilling to make fine distinctions, and often appellate courts (including the USSR Supreme Court) had to reduce sentences of judges who had misinterpreted the meaning of organized group.[69]

Judges and judicial officials did not act alone in their attempts to limit the impact of Stalin's severe laws on theft. Police, procurators, factory administrators, and others in a position to initiate prosecutions all played their parts eventually by refusing to start cases. The official statistics tell a tale of a massive drop in prosecutions for theft, starting late in 1947 and continuing steadily through 1951. To be sure, the decrease in theft cases followed the huge surge that had occurred during the campaign to implement the new laws in 1947. That surge, however, proved short-lived; prosecution levels for 1948 not only wiped out the increase but fell to levels below 1946 (95% for theft of state property; 86.6% for theft of personal property). By 1951 prosecu-

---

68 "Postanovlenie soveshchaniia Ministra iustitsii SSSR, Generalnogo Prokurora SSSR, i Predsedatelia Verkhovnogo Suda SSSR po povodu stati prof. N. Durmanova, 'Nakazuemost khishchenii . . .' pomeshchannoi v zhurnale, Sotsialistcheskaia zakonnost, no. 10 za 1947 g.," ibid., no. 11, 19; I.T. Goliakov, "Protiv izvrashchenii smysla ukazov ot 4 iiuniia 1947 g.," ibid., 21–23.

69 "O primenenii ukazov ot 4 iiuniia 1947" (19 marta 1948). A judge from the Bashkir autonomous republic reported confusion over Durmanov's interpretation of "organized group." Better, the judge opined, to leave it at any "group." GARF, f.9492, op.1, d.179 (Stenogramma Vsesoiuznogo soveshchanii predsedatelei), 164–165.

tions for theft of state property stood at 61.6% of the 1946 level; and for theft of personal property at 48%.[70]

It is possible that the decline in theft prosecutions derived in part from a drop in actual thefts; the threat of harsh punishment could have deterred potential offenders. But the evidence indicates that *most* of the decline in prosecutions stemmed from changes in societal and bureaucratic reactions to particular kinds of theft.

First of all, the bulk of thefts perpetrated by juvenile offenders no longer led to prosecutions at all, as police and procuracy investigators began shielding children and even teenagers from the theft laws. For juveniles the levels of prosecution fell sharply. Prosecutions of 12- to 15-year-olds in 1948 stood at 38% of the 1946 levels; and of 16- to 17-year-olds at 53%. The prosecutions of the older age group would drop another 40% by 1952.[71]

Second, the management in many factories stopped reporting cases of theft by employees, especially when they did not involve items of

---

[70] The raw data on theft prosecutions were as follows:

	Theft of State Property	Theft of Personal Property
1946	263,085	135,282
1947	387,697	246,512
1948	251,553	117,144
1949	221,534	84,678
1950	196,518	68,055
1951	162,226	64,901
1952	180,485	68,758

Source: GARF, f.9492sch, op.6s, d.14, 14–15.
See also, GARF, f.9492, op.1, d.242, 63–65; d.183, 99; "Za iskorenenie khishchenii sotsialisticheskoi i lichnoi sobstvennosti," *SZ*, 1949, no. 6, 1–5.

---

[71] The official data on theft convictions for juveniles read as follows:

	Aged 12–15		Aged 16–17	
	State property	Personal property	State property	Personal property
1946	10,171	11,760	25,712	28,684
1947	9,896	13,905	30,349	36,827
1948	3,510	4,910	13,933	15,406
1952	3,818	4,217	6,914	10,820

Source: GARF, f.9492, op.6s, d.14, 26.

value. Thus, the Starotagilskii metallurgical factory produced 18 cases of petty theft in 1947 before the new laws were issued and none in the seven months thereafter. Another factory in Niznyi Tagil generated 48 cases in the five months before the laws and just 2 cases in the months that followed. According to a high official of the RSFSR Ministry of Justice, the cessation of prosecutions for petty theft in factories became widespread. Even when managers reported cases, police and procuracy officials frequently dropped them.[72] If the latter did not want to do so on their own, they received encouragement from judges. The chairman of the Ivanovskii regional court complained at a conference in 1948 that his court was receiving a lot of factory theft cases that should not have been prosecuted. His colleague at the regional court of Kostroma faced a similar problem in 1950. A surge of petty theft cases had entered the people's courts in his region, so that in the second quarter judges there had awarded a record 34% noncustodial sentences. The regional court's chief considered instructing his judges to drop cases of small value, but had been advised against it. Instead, he tried to stop such cases by organizing two interagency meetings, with police and procurators, and then personally informing the first secretary of the regional party committee and asking him to influence not only procuracy officials but also the directors of enterprises.[73]

Third, in addition to thefts by juveniles and thefts in factories, two other categories of small thefts registered substantial decreases from 1948 – rural thefts and thefts by women. The decrease in prosecutions of theft in the countryside followed an initial surge there. During the first two and a half months of the implementation of the new theft decrees theft at collective farms represented 50% of cases rather than its usual share of 32%. The disproportionate increase in prosecutions for theft in kolkhozy reflected a resumption on the part of police of the campaign against theft of grain (and waste spoilage) launched in August 1946 that had produced inflated levels of rural prosecutions in the last months of 1946. That campaign had come against the background of a shortage of grain in some parts of the country. To prevent prosecution of starving peasants, procurators had screened out and stopped nearly half of the cases started by the police.[74] In the repetition during

72 Perlov, "Ustranit nedostatki," 9–10.
73 GARF, f.9492, op.1, d.179 (Stenogramma Vsesoiuznogo soveshchaniia predsedatelei) 537; GARF, f.353, op.13, d.138 (Stenogramma mezhoblastnogo soveshchaniia nachalnikov upravleniia Ministerstva Iustitsii RSFSR i predsedatelei oblastnykh i gorodskikh sudov, 28 noiabria–1 dekabria 1950), 89–90, 99.
74 GARF, f.8131sch, op.28s, d.398, 187; f.9492sch, op.6s, d.14, 27; GARF, f.8138sch, op.28s, d.291 ("Materialy operativnogo soveshchaniia ot 11/XI 1946 o rabote organov prokuratury po borbe s khishcheniiami, razbazarivaniem i porchei zerna," esp. 48–66. Some of

summer 1947, procurators also screened cases – the procurator of one region in the Ukraine claimed to have stopped 60% of cases of rural theft – but many such cases still reached the courts. Later on, the police were blamed for excesses and the message delivered to rural authorities that the new theft decrees were not meant for use against petty pilferers of grain. Official data for cases of grain theft for the USSR fell accordingly: from 48,742 in third quarter 1947 and 30,381 in the fourth quarter to 14,416 and 12,225 in the first two quarters of 1948.[75]

At the same time, thefts by women dropped at a greater rate than those of thefts by men. Whereas in 1946 prosecutions against women made up 35.8% of cases of theft of state property and 21.9% of cases of theft of personal property, in 1952 those same shares had fallen to 20.7% and 16.1% respectively. These decreases resulted first from the general practice of restraint in the prosecution of petty thefts (in which the female share had been disproportionately higher). But it also reflected the realization by legal authorities, if not also employers, of the social costs of prosecuting women under the edicts. In the postwar era there were many single mothers, including war widows, struggling to support a family on one salary. Convictions of such women for small thefts were regularly reversed on appeal, and the amnesty commissions of republican governments waived the punishments of many whose convictions were not reversed. When it became clear that prosecutions against war widows would not succeed and police were chastised for pursuing them, a decrease was bound to ensue.[76]

Fourth, one further category of stealing fell out of the purview of the harsh Stalin laws, namely thefts by officials. Enterprise managers continued to be prosecuted for misappropriating funds (sometimes called "temporary borrowing") and party authorities to give clearances for prosecution. But charges came almost invariably under Article 109 of the RSFSR Criminal Code, "abuse of official position," rather than under the laws on theft. Instead of the long terms of prison required by the 1947 theft laws, Article 109 called for a minimum term of six months'

---

the prosecutions in late 1946–early 1947 were directed against kolkhoz chairmen who gave grain to their members and failed to meet delivery quotas. In June 1947 the Central Committee called a halt to these prosecutions and ordered a review of convictions already registered. Zima, "Golod i prestupnost v SSSR (1946–1947 gg.)," 6–12.

[75] GARF, f.8131sch, op.27s, d.4036, 38–40; 74–75, 98; "Iz prigororov raionnykh narsudov o privlechenii k ugolovnoi otvetstvennosti kolkhoznikov po Ukazu 1947 g.," *Sovetskie arkhivy*, 1990, no. 3, 55–60; GARF, f.9492, op.2s, d.50 (Spravka o rabote sudebnykh organov po primeneniiu Ukaza), 232. Note that cases of grain theft fell 75% from 1947 III to 1948 II, whereas cases of theft of personal property fell by 64%.

[76] GARF, f.9492, op.6s, d.14, 20, 24; f.9427, op.10, d.106, 80–88; f.8131sch, op.275, d.4036 (Vsesoiuznoe soveshchanie prokurorov), 98.

imprisonment.[77] The use of Article 109 to protect officials from more serious charges was not new. Long before June 1947, charges under Article 109 had served as substitutes for charges of large-scale theft under the Law of August 7, 1932.[78] As a rule, the protection of economic officials from long sentences had the support of local party chieftains, and judges dependent on them found it hard to resist. Once a people's court judge in Rostov objected to the charge of abuse of authority in such a case and returned the file to the procuracy for requalification as theft. But the regional procurator, to whom the district procurator had turned for help, refused to cooperate with the judge's request. Instead, the regional procurator proposed, they should declare an amnesty and stop the case. After all, the procurator contended, the participants in the case were party members and war veterans. The stubborn judge, however, did not accept this "compromise" and returned the case once again to the procuracy.[79]

Central legal officials never condoned the practice of protecting managers from theft prosecutions by substituting the charge of abuse of authority. Repeatedly, the chiefs of the legal agencies criticized the practice. In 1952, after a few years of discussion, the USSR Supreme Court issued a resolution reiterating the point. These pious statements had little effect, for the protection of managers stemmed from their powerful patrons, provincial and local politicians, who had means to compel the cooperation of legal officials.[80]

Avoiding prosecutions for theft represented an invisible and effective way of muting Stalin's theft decrees. Still, many theft prosecutions continued to occur and judges faced the unenviable task of imposing the harsh penalties required by the law. As we saw previously, some judges did find ways of working around the law, but during the campaign (June through Oct. 1947), they had little room to maneuver. Once the pressure of the campaign had subsided, and the signals from the USSR Supreme Court supplied support, judges at the trial level increased the use of sanctions not authorized by the decrees. In the third quarter of 1950, for example, judges in six regions of the RSFSR

77 GARF, f.9492, op.1, d.242, 65–66; Piontkovskii, "Osnovnye voprosy," 10–14; GARF, f.9492, op.1, d.2796, 37.
78 I.T. Goliakov, "Rech t. Stalina ot 9 fevralia 1946 g. i nashi zadachi," SZ, 1946, no. 3, 4–5.
79 GARF, f.353, op.13, d.134 (Stenogramma oblastnogo soveshchaniia narodnykh sudei), 72.
80 Piontkovskii, "Osnovnye voprosy"; GARF, f.9492, op.1, d.242, 63–66. "O sudebnoi praktike po primeneniiu ukaza Prezisiuma Verkhovnogo Soveta SSSR ot 4 iiuniia 1947 'Ob ugolovnoi otvetstvennosti za khishchenie gosudarstvennogo i obshchestvennogo imushchestva,' " "Rukovodiashchee ukazanie Plenuma Verhovnogo Suda SSSR ot 6 maia 1952," Sudebnaia praktika Verkhovnogo Suda, 1952, no. 6, 1–5.

awarded an average of 20% suspended sentences and sentences below the limit. This leniency came when many incidents of small theft no longer resulted in prosecution. The conduct of those judges was not anomalous. In 1951 in the RSFSR judges used suspended sentences and sentences below the legal limit (including corrective work) in 22.8% of sentences (in the first half of the year) and 25% (in the second half); in the first half of 1952 the figure reached 27.4% before dropping in the second half to 23%.[81]

Moreover, judges at the appellate levels also reduced the sentences of trial courts in a significant number of cases. This practice began in 1947 before the judges at trials felt safe to show leniency. The cassation panels of the regional courts regularly lowered sentences in theft cases, "usually without grounds" according to one official in the Ministry of Justice. Both Supreme Courts – of the RSFSR and USSR – lowered sentences in theft cases down to noncustodial, especially when the amounts stolen were small or the accused a deserving person, that is, a mother with children, a war veteran, an adolescent, or a pensioner. While the USSR Supreme Court did so sporadically, judges complained at conferences in 1951 and 1952 that they could not follow the cues of the RSFSR Supreme Court and prevent the latter from changing many of their decisions. Finally, when appellate courts failed to change harsh sentences, the praesidia of republican supreme soviets sometimes stepped into the breach. In Kazakhstan the Praesidium's amnesty department gave dispensations to persons convicted of stealing small amounts of food.[82]

In addition to judges and the enforcers of the decrees on theft, central legal officials also bore responsibility for the scope of their application. The chiefs of the Procuracy, Ministry of Justice, and Supreme Court were well aware that most thefts were small and many sentences under the decrees savage. But they were caught between the demands of the leaders for strict execution of the decrees and their own recognition of the need for flexibility. More than once, though, the legal chiefs overcame their hesitation and found the courage to address the leadership.

[81] GARF, f.353, op.13, d.138 (Stenogramma mezhoblastnogo soveshchaniia nachalnikov), 111; GARF, f.9492sch, op.6s, d.4 (Osnovnye dannye o rabote sudov po ugolovnym delam za 1951 g.), 49–50; GARF f.9492sch, op.6s, d.6, 50–51. Note that the rates of the use of suspended sentences and sentences below the legal limit for theft convictions for the USSR as a whole were lower than those for the RSFSR, falling in the 18–21% range for 1951 and 1952. These rates reflected the practice of judges in the Ukraine, where judges used these measures of leniency in only 8–10% of cases in 1951.
[82] Perlov, "Ustranit nedostatki;" GARF, f.9474, op.10, d.106, 80–88; f.353, op.13, d.150, 16–18, 51, 91ob; f.813sch, op.27s, d.4036, 98.

In the summer of 1948 they offered two ways of removing petty thefts from the full force of the decrees – endorsement of the use of Articles 51 and 53 (sentences below the legal limit and suspended sentences) and the revival of the edict of August 10, 1940 (which called for one-year imprisonment for petty theft in factories). In a letter to Central Committee Secretary Zhdanov on June 10, 1948 (two and a half months before his death), Supreme Court Chairman Goliakov suggested that a resolution of the Supreme Court's Plenum endorse the use of Articles 51 and 53 for petty thefts committed by pregnant women, women with small children, adolescents, and invalids. These were all categories of persons likely to benefit eventually from reversals on appeal, pardons, and as we shall see, amnesties; and they represented nonproductive forces in the camps. But Stalin and his associates did not agree with the suggestion. They may even have gone further and rejected entirely the use of Articles 51 and 53. For, in 1949, officials of the Ministry of Justice prepared a draft resolution for the USSR Supreme Court that included a blanket condemnation of the use of these articles for thieves. The circulation of this draft resolution took an unusually long time, and it is possible that some of the legal chiefs delayed its realization. The actual resolution was issued by the Court only in May 1952, and it did, inter alia, discourage judges from using suspended sentences and sentences below the minimum.[83]

The other, even more promising means of removing petty thefts from the scope of the June decrees was a revival of another Stalin law, the edict of August 10, 1940, that had established one year imprisonment as the punishment for petty theft in factories. Although that penalty seemed severe at the time, it looked mild in comparison to the six year minimum supplied by the June decree on theft of state property. The idea of reviving the August edict began in the Ministry of Justice and was developed and advanced by the Praesidium of the Supreme Soviet. In June 1948 a high official of the Praesidium delivered to the chief of that body, Nikolai Shvernik, a set of proposals that featured decriminalization of all first-time thefts under fifty rubles and subjection of repeat offenders to the decree of August 10. Shvernik proved unprepared to support the idea of partial decriminalization but he readily supported revival of the August decree. In a letter to Stalin and the Politburo (dated August 5, 1948) Shvernik challenged the legality of the resolution of the USSR Supreme Court of August 22, 1947, that had rendered inoperative both the edict of August 10 and Article 162 of the

[83] GARF, f.9474, op.16s, d.322 (Zhdanovu ot Goliakova, 10 iiuniia 1948), 20–22; op.10, d.79 (Materialy proekta postanovlenii Plenuma Verkhvonogo Suda); "O sudebnoi praktike po primeneniiu ukazov" (1952).

RSFSR Criminal Code. Shvernik now claimed that the Court's resolution (issued almost certainly with the approval of party leaders) "willfully cancelled legislative acts," and therefore should be set aside. He noted the support of the Ministry of Justice and the receipt by the Praesidium of many requests for pardons from relatives of convicts sitting six or seven years for minor thefts.[84] However well formulated, the proposals of Shvernik and the Ministry received no response.

Two years later (in October 1950) the heads of the three legal agencies tried again. In a letter to Central Committee Secretary Malenkov, the minister of justice, procurator-general, and chairman of the Supreme Court urged the revival of the edict of August 10 for petty thefts, especially by juveniles and women with small children; and they supplied a draft resolution of the USSR Supreme Court on the application of the August 10 decree to all persons convicted of petty theft of state property for the first time. In 1951 the legal chiefs repeated the same proposal. For their part the subcommittee of the Committee on Legislative Proposals of the USSR Supreme Soviet established in 1949 to review the draft USSR Criminal Code also proposed changing the law on theft so that first convictions for insignificant amounts would bring one to three years (for state property) and two months to one year or even corrective work (for theft of personal property). Needless to say, none of these proposals was realized.[85]

While the chiefs of the legal agencies struggled unsuccessfully to gain Stalin's consent for a revival of the edict of August 10, 1940, they also took steps to help some of the most deserving victims of those decrees. As we have seen, there was already a precedent for giving special dispensation to juveniles, pregnant women, and women with small children. These categories of persons had benefited from special releases during and soon after the War. During 1948 and 1949, heads of the legal agencies, along with counterparts in the apparatus of the Praesidium of the Supreme Soviet, pressed for and obtained secret decrees releasing from confinement many inmates in these categories, a substantial proportion of whom had been convicted under the theft decrees. A memo from the heads of the legal agencies to Stalin (dated February 17, 1949), noted that as of January 1, 1949, out of 503,000 women in places of confinement, 9,300 were pregnant, 23,700 had small children with them and another 40,000 had small children at home. The

84 GARF, f.7523sch, op.65s, d.346, 9–11; d.384 (I.V. Stalinu ot N. Shvernika, 5 avgusta 1948); the same letter is found in RTsKhIDNI, f.17, op.118, d.147, 68–70. See also V. Zima, "Golod i prestupnost v SSSR (1946–1947 gg.)," 4–6.

85 GARF, f.9492sch, op.2s, d.68, 346–349; d.78, 13; f.7523sch, op.65s, d.243 (Osnovnye diskussionye voprosy proekta UK SSSR), 9; RTsKhIDNI, f.17, op.119, d.159, 108–113; op. 121, d.642, 27–30, 32–35, 37–39.

proposal was to release all of them. The decree of April 22, 1949, authorized just that, and as of January 1950, 55,557 women had been released (along with 15,990 children). It also emerged that 13,000 convicted women had lied about having children under 7 back home, and many had relatives send fictitious documents.[86]

The initiative for a release of juveniles in confinement came in a joint letter to Shvernik from Minister of Justice Gorshenin and Chairman of the Supreme Court Volin (Feb. 18, 1949). The letter noted the decline of juvenile crime, reflected in a drop in the annual intake of juvenile colonies from 59,659 in 1947 to 12,519 in 1949; their total population on January 1, 1949, stood at 37,280. The actual decree (Sept. 26, 1950) authorized the release of all inmates under 18 convicted for the first time and held in confinement for not less than one year (as well as persons over 18 convicted of crimes convicted before the age of 16 and held not less than two years). Excluded were persons guilty of intentional murder, rape, robbery, and especially large thefts; and for repeat crimes those released faced higher punishments than those set in law. This condition had been part of all secret releases since 1941.[87]

The struggle to protect petty thieves from long terms of prison represented only a step toward the normalization of punishments for theft. As long as Stalin lived, it proved impossible for even the heads of the legal agencies to realize this goal. The decrees on theft were Stalin's own creations, which he was not only unprepared to discard but also ready to reaffirm. In July 1952 the USSR Supreme Court issued on behalf of the regime the long-delayed resolution calling for stricter implementation of the theft decrees. The resolution instructed judges to stop prosecuting managers for abuse of authority instead of theft and cut back on suspended sentences and sentences below the legal limit. Stalin's death, however, on March 5, 1953, opened the door for the eventual undoing of the Stalin decrees on theft. On April 27, 1953, Minister of Justice Gorshenin took the lead and sent Chairman of the Council of Ministers Malenkov a memorandum that called for lowering punishments for theft of personal property to one to six years' imprisonment (instead of six to twenty) and theft of state property to one to seven and eight to twenty for especially large amounts (these in place of seven to twenty-five years). In another communiqué, dated August 22, 1953, this time to

---

[86] GARF, f.9474sch, op.16s, d.322 (Zhdanovu ot Goliakova), 20–22; f.7523sch, op.65s, d.346 (Zhdanovu ot Abramova), 1–7; f.9492sch, op.2s, d.58 (Malenkovu ot Kuznetsova i Gorshenina, 9 Fev.1949), 59–60; ibid. (Stalinu ot Kruglova, Gorshenina, Safonova, Volina), 108–111; f.7523sch, op.65s, d.366 (Lopokhovu ot Kozlova), 1.

[87] GARF, f.9492sch, op.2s, d.55 (Shverniku ot Gorshenina i Volina, 18 fev. 1949), 43–46; f.7523sch, op.65, d.363, 2–3.

Khrushchev and Malenkov, the heads of four legal agencies (including the MVD) called for the elimination of criminal responsibility for petty theft. This measure did enter Soviet criminal law in 1955, but the more general readjustment of punishments for theft came only with the completion of criminal codes in 1960. For the first post-Stalin years softening the effects of the theft decrees came through future expansion in the use of suspended sentences (Article 53) and sentences below the limit (Article 51), finally approved by the USSR Supreme Court in 1954.[88]

In detailing the extraordinary efforts of legal officials to soften the blows delivered by the Stalin decrees on theft, I do not want to underestimate the decrees' impact. In spite of the drop in theft prosecutions and the partial revival of judicial discretion (Articles 51 and 53), the decrees imposed outlandish punishments on many offenders and made the administration of criminal justice in the USSR less fair. During the initial campaign, when the numbers of prosecutions rose sharply and most judges felt compelled to apply the letter of the decrees, hundreds of thousands of persons received long terms of imprisonment for stealing items of little value. After the campaign had subsided and legal officials found ways to mute the impact of the decrees, the most egregious injustices diminished. Many petty thefts, including most committed by juveniles and employees of enterprises, either were not prosecuted or resulted in lower punishments than the law dictated. Nevertheless, instances of injustice did not disappear. A stream of cases of minor thefts still resulted in long terms of imprisonment. Moreover, the theft decrees continued to deliver blows against persons who had committed real thefts of moderate value. It would be comforting to imagine that the bulk of those locked away for years were hardened professional criminals, but this does not appear to have been the case. In 1950, for example, 18.7% of those convicted of theft of personal property had a previous conviction registered for the same offense (29.1% for any offense); of those convicted of theft of state property, only 3.6% had a previous conviction for that offense (8.1% for any offense). Most of the persons convicted of both kinds of theft, therefore, were first-time offenders; and most of them did have to endure long terms of imprisonment. Of those convicted for theft of state property between June 1947 and December 1952, 91.8% received custodial sentences and the average term stood at 8.7 years! In the year and a half before Stalin's theft decrees, 73.9% of persons convicted of stealing state

88 "O sudebnoi praktike po primeneniiu ukaza . . . ot 4 iiunii 1947 . . . ukazania Plenuma Verkhovnogo Suda ot 6 maia 1952," GARF, f.9492sch, op.2s, d.93, 105–116, 61–66; Yoram Gorlizki, "De-Stalinization and the Politics of Russian Criminal Justice, 1953–1964," unpublished D.Phil. thesis, University of Oxford, 1992, 87–93.

property had received custodial sentences, and the average length stood at 3.2 years.[89]

There was another way in which the theft decrees made the administration of justice in the USSR less fair. Not only did the decrees impose excessively severe punishments, but they also fostered inconsistency in the response of authorities to thefts. The problem derived from the effort to reduce the impact of the decrees. The main way of softening the blow was making exceptions for either individual offenders or the other categories of offenders. While the protection of any offender from excessive punishment deserves praise, the method of designating exceptions was bound to foster uneven implementation of the decrees and make the delivery of justice in the USSR even more inconsistent than before. Depending on the time, the district, the agent of authority who encountered the act, and the judge, a person accused of stealing items of moderate value might go free *or* feel the full force of Stalin's decrees, a sentence of six or more years in a labor camp. This situation was bound to make members of the public sense the arbitrary quality in the administration of criminal justice and distrust the law. The root cause of these unfortunate developments lay in Stalin's insistence on punishments for thefts of all kinds that exceeded those deemed appropriate by the public and the enforcers alike.

Afterword

The draconian edicts of June 1947 imposed such severe punishments for theft as to prompt their enforcers to try to limit the use and impact of the decrees. Their effort showed, once again, that the criminal sanction has limits even in authoritarian states. Note that the struggle of legal officials, police, and others to soften the blow of the theft decrees occurred before the combination of the expansion of legal officials making careers in the agencies and the pressure to meet standards of perfection left their mark. Overall, the legal officials charged with implementing the decrees in 1947 through 1949 were more like their predecessors than the new cohort of legal officials in the making. Still, the means used by those officials to blunt the impact of the decrees were ones that even the most conformist, bureaucratically oriented legal officials could choose without risking the wrath of their superiors. To be sure, some judges did impose lenient sentences, for which they were often chastised. But far more common was the avoidance of laying charges (especially for juveniles and petty thieves) and the prosecution of offenders on alternative charges (for managers, criminal negligence). These were ap-

---

[89] GARF, f.9492, op.6s, d.14, 20, 24, 30.

proaches that legal officials could use without jeopardizing the assessments of their performance. If in the post-Stalin years, when the mechanisms of assuring the conformity of legal officials were more fully developed, the leaders had extended the criminal sanction in unpopular ways or introduced punishments disproportionate to their crimes, officials could still have reduced their impact. As it was, Stalin's successors lacked his flair for the sensational and never did test the reach or severity of the criminal law as their former master had.

The three distortions in criminal policy of the high Stalin years – the use of regulations as substitutes for laws, excessive secrecy, and unusually severe punishments – were all associated with the leader, Joseph Stalin. At least the first two of these had long afterlives, as Stalin's successors found the convenience of stigmatizing misdeeds through regulations and secret directives too attractive to avoid entirely. Under Khrushchev the leadership did repeal most of the draconian punishments (including, eventually, the theft decrees of June 1947) and eliminated the most hated extensions of the criminal law (such as its application to unauthorized quitting and performance of abortions). Gradually, though, during the Brezhnev years punishments became harsh once again, more in practice than in law, and the USSR kept its high place in the world rankings for severity of punishment. But punishments in the post-Stalin period never reached the excessive levels of the late 1940s. Never again would Soviet citizens have to face anything like the theft decrees of 1947.

Conclusion and Implications

The criminal law and its administration that took shape and matured in the USSR under Stalin present a classic example of an authoritarian approach to law. Stalin treated the criminal law in a nakedly instrumental way, as a political resource whose use required consent of neither the public nor the officials charged with its implementation. At the same time, the work of investigators, procurators, and judges was subordinated to political leaders at all levels of the administrative hierarchy and subject to their direction.

These basic traits of Soviet criminal justice were already present under Lenin and during the period of the New Economic Policy – that is, before Stalin and Stalinist politics had left their mark. Bolshevik leaders fashioned Soviet criminal law to suit their vision and adapted it incessantly to reflect their immediate needs. To administer their law, they relied on political trustees, ordinary members of the party, and effectively subordinated them to local party officials. But the strength and utility of the criminal law as an instrument of rule was weakened and partially obscured by novelties in the Bolshevik approach to law. In the early years of Soviet power the readiness of the Bolsheviks to openly apply terror to their enemies lowered the prestige of the law. Revolutionary fervor also contributed to the popularity of antilaw views, which were reflected in the commitment of some Bolshevik jurists to maximum flexibility in the application of the law and the simplification of legal procedures. In like manner, socialist convictions led Bolshevik politicians to turn against lawyers and staff the justice agencies with amateurs and use a variety of lay courts and lay participants in the work of the regular courts. Despite their membership in the party, these amateur judges and procuracy officials who were not pursuing careers in the administration of justice proved difficult to direct and manage from the center. Moreover the performance of these officials fell to such a low level as to breed disrespect for Soviet justice.

447

In time Joseph Stalin addressed most of these contradictions and deficiencies in Soviet criminal justice and succeeded by the end of his life in making criminal law a reliable tool for Soviet rulers. It was Stalin who rejected the antilaw perspective and made it illegitimate. It was Stalin who deserted many of the revolutionary and socialist features of Bolshevik justice. It was Stalin who supported new ways and means of making justice officials loyal and compliant and bringing them under the Leader's direction. And, it was Stalin who, as Leader, found new and rediscovered old uses of the criminal law and stamped it with the qualities of his personality. In short, the hand of Stalin weighed heavily in the development of Soviet criminal justice.

At the core of Stalin's quest to enhance the utility of criminal law lay the centralization of power in the justice realm. The weak leverage of the central legal agencies over local legal officials, especially as compared to that of local politicians, reflected a basic problem in Soviet government that in the mid-1930s Stalin sought to rectify. Joining him in his quest were a number of legal officials, most notably Andrei Vyshinskii, who shared and understood Stalin's desire to make the criminal law an instrument of central power.

Before the late 1930s central legal officials had difficulty directing the work of local procurators, investigators, and judges. One reason was the practice of using as legal officials uneducated amateurs. Without legal education to give them an esoteric skill and corporate identity, few legal officials made the administration of justice a career. Many of those who performed well gained promotion up and out of the legal realm into other, better paying and more prestigious posts in public administration. To receive a new post outside of justice called for the patronage of local politicians not central legal officials. Only those legal officials who sought promotions in the legal agencies needed to satisfy both masters. At the same time, the management of the administration of justice in the 1920s and early 1930s was decentralized. Legal agencies existed no higher than the republican level; and by the era of collectivization local authorities had gained control of the budgets of courts and responsibility for the physical conditions of court and procuracy offices alike. Under these conditions it proved difficult for central legal officials to get their local counterparts to comply with directives that did not suit the interests of the latter or their local masters.

The centralization of power within the justice realm began with the establishment in 1933 of the USSR Procuracy, the agency that from 1934 to 1939 belonged to Andrei Vyshinskii. It went further with the reorganization of the legal agencies approved in 1936 and implemented in 1938, which gave the USSR Supreme Court and the new USSR Commissariat of Justice major powers over local courts and judges. Reinforcing these organizational changes were the centralization of the management of personnel within the legal agencies (in 1939–1941) and, in the late 1940s, the adoption of new methods and criteria for evaluating the work of legal officials.

The strengthening of the central legal agencies would have had minimal impact upon judges and procuracy officials were it not for another major change approved by Stalin, the abandonment of the "experiment" with uneducated cadres in the legal realm and the adoption of a new approach to the legal officialdom. The new approach, endorsed fully by the leadership right after World War II, was to make the roles of judge, procurator, and investigator into careers. The initial recruitment of these officials would still emphasize political qualities (membership or candidate membership in the Communist party), but legal officials would also be expected to obtain, sooner or later, higher legal education and with this credential to serve in the legal agencies for the long haul. In the postwar years most Soviet legal officials started work at their posts without the required education and pursued legal education (secondary and higher) through correspondence courses. This pattern of education left much to be desired, minimizing as it did the identification of its recipients as jurists and their attachment to legal values. But it did enable most legal officials to obtain the technical knowledge and credentials that their masters required. As a result, a much larger share of them chose to make careers in the legal agencies, thereby giving their superiors new leverage for influencing their conduct. Gaining promotion within the procuracy and courts required meeting the expectations of higher legal officials, and in the late 1940s the latter made their expectations all too clear. These included a display of perfection in attaining the right statistical indicators of performance relating to both the efficiency and substance of work. The pressure to meet these standards had unfortunate consequences for the process of adjudication and contributed to the development of an accusatorial bias in Soviet criminal justice. The sharp decline of acquittals, both at trial and on appeal, was just one of the results.

The establishment of central authority in the legal realm did not undermine the power of local politicians vis-à-vis legal officials. Judges and procuracy officials alike remained dependent upon local power for conditions of work and necessities of life, not to speak of support in the development of their new legal careers. The renomination of judges, for example, still required clearance from party officials, as well as from representatives of the Ministry of Justice. Successful work as a procurator still required maintaining good relationship with the party secretary. Party officials expected to have their occasional requests fulfilled, but at the same time, at least in the early 1950s, supported the efforts of central legal officials to develop new standards of performance among procurators, investigators, and judges. The organization of departments of administrative organs at the regional party committees in the late 1940s seems to have increased the responsibility of party officials for the performance of legal agencies and at least for a time encouraged them to support the criteria of assessment used by central legal officials.

Stalin's death in March 1953 did not mark an end to the bureaucratization of Soviet legal officials or their increasing responsiveness to the demands of superiors in the legal agencies. The acquisition of higher legal education by legal officials continued, and within a few years the recruitment of new judges and investigators shifted to persons who had already obtained this goal. The percentage of legal officials making careers in the administration also rose, and the system of assessing the work of legal officials became entrenched. And, as a result, legal officials became more rather than less likely to conform with the desires of their bureaucratic superiors. In this sense, at least, the realization of Stalinist criminal justice came only after the tyrant's death. But this is a story for telling in other places.

While Stalin and his colleagues struggled to make the criminal law a more effective instrument of rule, they used it in ways that were new and different from what had come before. From 1929 until 1953 Stalin's criminal policy – and it is clear that it was Stalin's – was characterized by major and unusual extensions of the criminal sanction, increasingly severe punishments, reliance on secret laws and directives, and, after 1938, the separation of political cases from ordinary criminal justice. All of these changes departed from the Bolshevik mode. The criminal law of Russia in the 1920s had eliminated more offenders from the reach of the criminal law than it added, provided for what most observers saw as lenient punishments for nonpolitical offenders (from 1928 emphasizing noncustodial sanctions), produced few secret normative acts, and included regular courts in hearing a sizable portion of political crimes. During collectivization Stalin politicized criminal justice by mobilizing legal officials to go out to the villages and target offenses relating to grain procurement and the formation of kolkhozy. In the process, new offenses were devised, some through the law (e.g., killing one's own horse or cow), others through directives (e.g., failure by a kolkhoz chairman to deliver grain); the lowest courts, the people's courts, came to hear political cases; and punishments for theft of grain became excessive, especially during the campaign of 1932–1933.

But it was mainly after collectivization that Stalin's criminal policy began to assume its characteristic mold. First, the criminal law played an increased role in the management of the state economy, as new laws and directives made officials into scapegoats for the production of defective goods and industrial accidents. Stalin also extended the reach of the criminal law in traditional ways, recriminalizing the performance of abortions and crimes committed by young adolescents. In so doing, Stalin abandoned progressive features of Bolshevik criminal law. In criminalizing labor infractions (truancy, absenteeism, and unauthorized quitting) Stalin struck new ground, extending the criminal sanction in an innovative, though not necessarily productive, way. Second, under Stalin the punishments delivered by Soviet judges became more severe – first, in the mid and late 1930s through judicial practice, and then, more decisively, through changes in the criminal law – especially the introduction in 1940 of mandatory imprisonment for hooliganism and petty theft in factories and the draconian decrees on theft of June 1947. Third, from the early 1930s secret party and government decrees, instructions, and directives of the central legal agencies played an increasing part in the specification of what actions were criminal and which offenses were to assume priority in the practice of investigators and procurators. After World War II, secret laws shaped particular areas of criminal prosecution. Finally, after the conclusion of the Great Terror the processing of political cases, real or manufactured, was concentrated outside of the regular courts in the military tribunals and the agencies of the political police.

Many of Stalin's extensions of the criminal law and his introduction of harsh punishments for particular offenses contradicted the values of legal officials and their understanding of what was fair or appropriate. In fact, both judges and other would-be enforcers of these changes in the law resisted their implementation. The pattern of resistance by judges to what they saw as misguided directives started in the late 1920s, when judges refused for a time to substitute noncustodial sentences of corrective work for short terms of imprisonment (especially for persons convicted of hooliganism). Only an absolute ban on prison terms under one year and the threat of being fired convinced Soviet judges in 1929 that they should award sentences that they found so lenient as to be meaningless. In the 1930s, however, it was no longer leniency but the excessive severity and overreach of the criminal law that led judges to resist the policies of Soviet rulers. The decrees on theft of public property (1932), on juvenile crime (1935), abortion (1936), labor infractions (1940), and theft in general (1947) all aroused substantial resistance by judges. Judges in Stalin's Russia often succeeded in softening the blows, either through the requalification of charges or through the use of their special resources, Article 51 – punishment "below the legal limit" set for a particular offense – and Article 53 – suspended sentence. There was some irony here. Articles 51 and 53 reflected the belief of Bolshevik leaders that judges should have sufficient discretion in individual cases to follow the dictates of "revolutionary consciousness," especially when they contradicted the letter of the law. No one anticipated that these repositories of judicial discretion would become instruments in the hands of Soviet judges for wholesale resistance to implementing decrees issued by their rulers.

Not only judges but also the officials charged with implementing Stalin's initiatives in criminal policy failed to cooperate with his purposes. Local party officials blocked the prosecution of managers for producing defective goods; doctors failed to report incidents of suspected abortion; the police dealt with many juvenile wrongdoers informally or through administrative measures, shielding them from prosecutions; factory directors concealed many instances of shirking and absenteeism; and, after 1947, police and factory directors alike treated most lesser thefts as not worthy of criminal prosecution. To be sure, Stalin's henchmen marked the most important changes in the criminal law with campaigns, and during the campaign period succeeded in gaining compliance from enforcers, especially when they made scapegoats out of those who resisted (e.g., factory managers and judges with the labor infractions of 1940). But none of the campaigns lasted long, and both judges and other actors soon found ways to adjust enforcement and adjudication away from the excesses decreed by Stalin and in the direction of their own values and sense of societal norms.

Officials in the central legal agencies often shared the inclinations of their subordinates, but had to perform their duty and conduct the campaigns. When the campaigns had concluded, however, officials of the USSR Ministry of Justice, the USSR Supreme Court, and the USSR Procuracy often helped to produce compromise positions, new official stances on the implementation of laws with which judges and other lower officials could live. Although these compromises must have had the consent of some top party officials, it is uncertain whether Stalin knew about all of them. There were also moments when a top legal official resisted a harsh or extended decree of Stalin's. Most notable were the actions of Aron Solts, Old Bolshevik, "conscience of the party," who as head of Rabkrin's legal department led the resistance to the Law of August 7, 1932, and later voiced objections to the decree on abortion. Ivan Goliakov, chairman of the USSR Supreme Court from 1938 to 1948, deserves credit for trying in 1939 to extend the process of rehabilitation.

While the capacity and willingness of judges to resist what they perceived as improper crimes and punishments lasted throughout the Stalin period, it did not continue much beyond it. Once work in the procuracy and courts became for most legal officials a career and the central agencies joined local party officials in shaping those careers, legal officials had to comply with central directives. By all accounts, Soviet legal officials in the post-Stalin years did comply more with the demands of central legal officials than had their predecessors and displayed a more conformist bent. Admittedly, post-Stalin legal officials did not have to confront a steady stream of decrees extending the criminal law in unacceptable ways. In fact, most of the extensions of the criminal law introduced by Stalin were rescinded within three or four years of his death (e.g., abortion was decriminalized; the age of juvenile responsibility raised; labor infractions decriminalized; punishments for theft lowered, eventually). But post-Stalin officials also faced challenges to their values, whether in the increasing pressure to avoid acquittals (especially at the appellate level) or in the designation of the death penalty for large-scale economic crimes. Arguably, they were less able to resist these impositions on the part of their rulers.

Herein lies a paradox. Despite the tyranny and the presence of extrajudicial terror, judges and other legal officials had more possibility of resisting direction of superiors and exercising discretion in the Stalin years than they did in the Khrushchev and Brezhnev periods. This was true not only of the revolutionary generation of judges or those of the collectivization era, but also of the judges who came to their posts after the Great Terror and after World War II. The willingness of judges in the post-Purge years to resist, for example, the criminalization of tardiness in 1940 or the severe sanctions for theft in 1947 underscores the point. As long as careers were not at stake, many judges in the USSR were ready to resist orders that violated their sense of fair play. Only when the potential loss of post in a legal agency came to matter did judges adopt a more uniformly compliant cast.

The history of criminal justice under Stalin reveals that it took most (if not all) of the dictator's tenure for the Stalinist system of criminal justice to reach its full expression. Each of the main features of that system – an effective mechanism for ensuring the conformity of legal officials' conduct with the interests of their superiors; a criminal law that was extended, severe, partly secret, and influenced by bureaucratic regulations; delivery of justice marked by an accusatory bias – reached its apogee only in the late 1940s and early 1950s. The Stalinist mold of criminal justice proved to have lasting significance, for it persisted for decades after the death of the tyrant. Although jurists and politicians tried more than once to reform it, each of these core features of Stalinist criminal justice remained alive in the 1980s and became an object of concern for *perestroika* era reformers. The story of Soviet criminal justice after Stalin has its own subtleties and nuances, and it deserves extended treatment in other places.[1]

This account of the development of criminal justice under Stalin differs in significant ways from the conventional wisdom about criminal justice under Lenin and Stalin. In addition, my analysis has implications for the study of Stalinism in general and the comparative history and sociology of criminal justice.

Apart from dealing with issues not previously addressed (e.g., collectivization and criminal justice; the implementation of the criminalization of abortion and labor infractions; the bureaucratization of criminal justice and development of mechanisms of compliance for legal officials), this study calls for four modifications in previous interpretations of the history of Soviet criminal law and its administration.

The first concerns the importance of the antilaw or nihilist current in Soviet thought after the Bolshevik Revolution. Earlier writers, such as Harold Berman and Eugene Kamenka, who emphasized ideology as a driving force in the development of Soviet law, seem to have exaggerated the importance of the antilaw view, at least for the actual administration of justice.[2] My research suggests that the antilaw approach was never the prime shaper of action in Soviet criminal justice. Even during the Civil War, arguably the heyday of the antilaw perspective, the building of legal institutions and drafting of criminal and criminal procedures codes was based on instrumental more than nihilist premises. Once the old law and institutions had been destroyed – and this took only months – the shapers of Soviet justice emphasized the creation of norms and institutions to serve the new regime rather than the undermining of law. In the NEP years the emergence of more stable law and legal institutions, with many elements of tradition, offended some Bolshevik jurists and politicians and produced in its stead a persistent critique of Soviet justice. But this critique, based on antilaw Marxist premises, fell largely outside of the actual administration of justice and

---

[1] Yoram Gorlizki and Todd Foglesong are conducting serious inquiry on post-Stalin Soviet criminal justice. See Gorlizki, "De-Stalinization and the Politics of Russian Criminal Justice, 1953–1964" (unpublished D.Phil. thesis, University of Oxford, 1992) and Foglesong, "The Politics of Judicial Independence and Impartiality: Russian Criminal Justice, 1981–1992" (unpublished Ph.D. dissertation, University of Toronto, 1995).

[2] Harold Berman, *Justice in the USSR* (Revised ed., Cambridge, Mass., 1963); Eugene Kamenka, "The Soviet View of Law," *Problems of Communism* (March-April 1965). In "Stalinism and Soviet Legal Culture" [in Robert Tucker, ed., *Stalinism: Essays in Historical Interpretation* (New York, 1977), 155–179], Robert Sharlet demonstrates the devastating impact that nihilist doctrine had upon the *teaching* of law in the USSR until the late 1930s.

represented a minority view among jurists. Even during the period of Nikolai Krylenko's dominance at the Commissariat of Justice (1928–1933), when Krylenko preached simplification of legal procedure on the way to its elimination, he was unable to garner bureaucratic support for any of his draft criminal and criminal procedure codes. To be sure, in 1929–1931 Krylenko did issue a variety of ministerial regulations that introduced simplification of criminal procedure through the back door, but these regulations represented more a reaction to events than to their instigator. The main influence on the conduct of legal officials during collectivization was the orders of local party bosses mobilizing them to work in campaigns. Narkomiust's directives fit well with the demands of the times by approving patterns of conduct that would have occurred without its intervention. By mid-1932 the propagation of antilaw views had gone out of political fashion. From Stalin's new doctrine on strengthening the state under socialism and the June 1932 decree on revolutionary legality, leaders of the nihilist jurisprudence knew that times had changed; even Pashukanis began modifying his public statements. As Eugene Huskey has argued convincingly, the former representatives of the antilaw perspective were on the defensive throughout the mid-1930s, partially discredited and open to criticism from their rivals.[3] Their purge in 1937 represented an anticlimax that symbolized Stalin's commitment to the restoration of law as an instrument of rule. The purge was unnecessary for overcoming the influence of the theory of legal nihilism, except in legal education.

A second modification concerns the significance of party membership of legal officials. Observers have commonly suggested that the recruitment of judges and procurators from the ranks of party members ensured their loyalty and subservience to the regime.[4] Our story indicates, however, that securing loyalty and compliance from legal officials was more complicated. The mere recruitment of political trustees proved insufficient to secure obedience of legal officials, especially to directions from the central legal agencies and orders of which the officials disapproved. The Bolshevik formula of fostering loyal and pliant legal officials did emphasize the recruitment of "our people" (nashi liudi), unspoiled by the culture of legal professionalism. This first generation of legal officials paid heed to the voices of local political

---

[3] Eugene Huskey, *Russian Lawyers and the Soviet State* (Princeton, 1988), 173–185; Huskey, "Vyshinskii, Krylenko, and the Shaping of Soviet Legal Order," *Slavic Review* 46:3/4 (Fall/Winter 1987), 414–428; Huskey, "From Legal Nihilism to Pravovoe Gosudarstvo: Soviet Legal Development, 1917–1990," in Donald Barry, ed., *Toward the "Rule of Law" in Russia? Political and Legal Reform in the Transition Period* (Armonk N.Y., 1992), 23–42.

[4] Samuel Kucherov, *The Organs of Soviet Administration of Justice: Their History and Operations* (Leiden, 1970), xvi.

masters, but ultimately proved unmanageable even for them. For legal officials not making careers in the agencies were ready first to resist what they saw as unjust directives and, then under threat of reprisals, to overreact and commit excesses. It is not surprising that Stalin and his advisors chose ultimately to reject the Bolshevik formula and replace it. The new Stalinist formula did not abandon the criterion of party membership; procurators and judges at least were still expected to become members of the party. The change lay, first, in the requirement that all legal officials obtain higher legal education, a change that encouraged them to make careers in the procuracy and courts, *and*, second, the development of a centrally managed system of evaluating the work of these officials. The monitoring and use in career development of quantitative indicators of the quality of performance supplied strong incentives for legal officials to follow the directions of their masters, especially of politicians and officials in the central government and party agencies.

A third point of difference between this book and previous studies of Soviet criminal justice concerns the meaning of the difficulty faced by the Stalinist leadership in obtaining adequate enforcement of their initiatives in criminal policy. For Gabor Rittersporn the conduct of legal officials in failing to implement laws and instructions represented indiscipline and lack of control in the party-state. To Rittersporn this indiscipline derived partly from incompetence and partly from uncertainty about the criteria by which their work was to be judged. At the same time, though, it came to reflect an administrative culture shaped by those officials, which in turn limited what the rulers could actually achieve. Thus, legal officials in the 1930s (and even in the late 1940s) were, in Rittersporn's view, inherently unmanageable, ready to make the implementation of any directive problematic. On the other hand, the Russian historian Oleg Khlevniuk viewed the activity of legal officials in refusing to implement laws (such as the Law of August 7, 1932, or the decree of June 4, 1947) as signs of opposition to excessive aspects of Stalin's policies *and* symptoms of broader societal resistance to them. When judges avoided full enforcement of the law, they were, in Khlevniuk's view, stepping out of their roles as legal officials and reflecting instead their understanding of justice that derived from their membership in society.[5]

---

5 Gabor Tamas Rittersporn, "Soviet Officialdom and Political Evolution: Judiciary Apparatus and Penal Policy in the 1930s," *Theory and Society*, 13 (1984), 211–237; Rittersporn, *Stalinist Simplifications and Soviet Complications: Social Tensions and Political Conflicts in the USSR, 1933–1953* (Chur, Switzerland, 1991), 277. Oleg Khlevniuk, *1937-i: Stalin, NKVD i sovetskoe obshchestvo* (Moscow, 1992), 23–24, 63ff.

Both of these interpretations contain elements of truth. While I agree with Gabor Rittersporn that for a variety of reasons Soviet legal officials were hard to manage, I concur with Oleg Khlevniuk that the actions of judges and other would-be enforcers of overly extended or harsh Stalinist laws represented conscious resistance, not just stubbornness or lack of discipline. However, I am unsure to what extent the resistance of legal officials had societal roots. While there is evidence of societal disdain for some of Stalin's laws, the actions of legal officials may be seen as falling squarely within the fulfillment of their jobs. The administration of criminal justice always involves the exercise of discretion, and this was especially so in the USSR, where by design revolutionary consciousness of judges was supposed to shape judicial decisions. At the same time, the resistance of doctors to the abortion decree and factory managers to the law on shirking does suggest societal resistance, and when the actions of legal officials are considered in this context, there are grounds for speaking of society acting apart from, if not against, the state.

Not only in the Soviet Union but also in the Western world the enforcement of criminal law is subject to limits that stem from the mindsets of the law's enforcers. The underenforcement of Stalinist criminal law and resistance of legal officials, overt and covert, to its realization, demonstrates the limits of the criminal sanction – a problem, it turns out, even for authoritarian rulers. We shall return to the relevance of Soviet experience for Western thinking on this issue.

Finally, there is the old and vexing question of the relationship between law and terror in Stalin's Russia. The literature contains two different interpretations of this issue: the view (probably most widespread in popular culture) that the Terror overwhelmed the administration of criminal justice; and the view (perhaps more honored by specialists) that the realms of law and force were distinct and self-contained.[6] My study suggests that both of these views are partially correct, but for different time periods. The image of terror, or the extrajudicial application of repression by representatives of the political police, as influencing the administration of criminal justice applies best to the years of collectivization. Legal officials who served on the campaign trail sweeping into the villages to take grain, bankrupt private peasants, and pressure rural officials, worked under similar political pressures as their OGPU colleagues. And, especially in 1932–1933, they acted as if the substance of repression that they imposed took precedence over its

---

6 Peter Juviler, *Revolutionary Law and Order* (New York, 1976), 53–58, exemplifies the view of terror infecting and harming the administration of justice; while Berman, *Justice in the USSR*, esp. 7–9, exemplifies the opposing view, that law and terror became separate domains in Stalin's USSR.

legal basis or form. To a lesser extent, legal officials who participated in the Great Terror (mainly procurators) replicated the pattern. But after 1938 the separation of law and terror became the norm. Harold Berman was right to argue that Stalin possessed and used two distinct forms of repression – law and force. In fact, the evidence of compartmentalization of these two realms in the late Stalin years was striking even to an observer who expected it. But there remained an important connection between law and terror all the same.

The legal agencies had to pay a price for their separation from the world of terror, and that price was the burden of demonstrating to the world that the Soviet government operated an acceptable administration of justice. Developing and maintaining the reputation of the USSR as a normal state was one reason for revival of the authority of law in the mid-1930s. In the post–World War II period the rulers of Russia gave even more weight to the appearance of normal legality in their country. From this preoccupation with appearances came at least two consequences. The first was the expansion of secrecy in government, to cover up extralegal coercion and to prevent diffusion of information that might embarrass the regime. This included public mention of corruption in the courts, including the USSR Supreme Court, the trial of whose corrupt members was kept secret. Second, the leadership's concern about the appearance of legality in the Soviet order also provided a rationale, if not a motive, for the pursuit of perfection in the administration of justice as manifested in the policy of avoiding "groundless prosecutions" and "groundless convictions." As we have seen, these efforts referred not to any muzzling of the capacity of the political police to lay contrived charges, but rather to the push for criminal investigations so perfect as to make acquittals and supplementary investigations obsolete and for adjudication so sound as to make changes on appeal rare. Yet, perfection of this kind proved in practice impossible, and the drive against unfounded prosecutions and convictions led to a sharp decline in acquittals and in reversals on appeal. From the concern with appearances the "accusatorial bias" of Soviet criminal justice gained much of its force.

The history of criminal justice under Stalin also has implications for the study and understanding of the Stalinist experience more broadly. It speaks to two debates among Western historians of the Stalin era: about the roots of the tyranny and about the structure of power under the dictator.

How did Russia come to be ruled by a willful autocrat wielding terror? Some Western scholars have contended that Stalinism was the probable, if not inevitable, outgrowth of the political order established by Lenin. Others have insisted that Leninist politics in its NEP version could have led to a different outcome. The latter emphasized the distinctiveness of Stalinism and treated the onset of Stalin's collectivization as a sharp break in the political history of the USSR. Still other scholars in the West have found roots of Stalinism in the pre-Soviet Russian past, in the traditions of autocracy and police state under the tsars.[7]

Our account of criminal justice under Stalin lends some support to the evolutionary view of Stalinism, but it provides even more grounds for stressing the break between Bolshevik and Stalinist practices. As we have seen, the fundamental traits of Soviet justice – the subordination of legal officials to politicians and the primacy of the instrumental role of criminal law – were well developed before the Stalin era. Yet, the most distinctive elements of the administration of justice under Stalin came only during the tenure of the tyrant and at that only gradually. These included the broad extensions of the criminal sanction and severity of punishments for ordinary crimes; the rejections of the antilaw perspective; the rejection of progressive elements in criminal policy and revival of traditionalism; the centralization of power in the legal agencies and successful quest for means of exacting compliance with and execution of central directives; and the use of law to demonstrate the normalcy of the Soviet state and the push for perfection in the performance of the legal agencies. Arguably, the critical turning point in the development of Soviet criminal justice came not at the beginning of the Stalin era (in 1928–1929) but rather in 1935–1936, when Stalin and his colleagues committed themselves to strengthening the criminal law as an instrument of rule by centralizing power in the legal agencies and educating their officials for careers. Only with the implementation of these measures, a process that took fifteen years, did Stalinist criminal justice come into being.

The connection of criminal justice under Stalin to the administration of justice in tsarist Russia is an intriguing question, but thus far too little scholarship has been attempted to offer more than tentative statements. I would venture that, while one can find striking forerunners for Stalinist criminal justice in tsarist experience, the Stalinist mold differed in ways that made it qualitatively different. The revival of traditional crimes, such as abortion and offenses by juveniles, was one aspect of Stalin's criminal policy. Moreover, the Soviet (Bolshevik and Stalinist) urge to subordinate the administration of justice to political direction reflected the Russian authoritarian tradition. However, it would be

---

[7] Stephen F. Cohen, "Bolshevism and Stalinism," in Tucker, *Stalinism*, 3–29; Robert C. Tucker, "Sovietology and Russian History," *Post-Soviet Affairs*, 8:3 (July-Sept. 1992), 175–196. See also Giuseppe Boffa, *The Stalin Phenomenon* (Ithaca, N.Y., and London, 1992), passim.

hard to speak of a direct line of influence because in post-1864 Russia the traditional subordination of justice to political direction was broken to a considerable extent, at least at the level of the circuit court (*okruzhnoi sud*) and above. There judges had lifetime appointments and acted impartially in most civil and criminal matters alike. To be sure, they faced restrictions on their autonomy. The shift of political cases to the Senate and important cases in areas of civil unrest to military tribunals; the limitations on jury trials; the restriction of prosecutions against government officials stand as examples; so too does the provision in the last years of the century of new means of disciplining and transferring judges who failed to meet the expectations of either the ministry of justice or provincial governors. But on the whole the movement for judicial counterreform seems to have been checked, and Russia made a start at developing autonomous and impartial administration of justice.[8] The Bolsheviks proved unwilling to allow the continuation of judicial autonomy, not to speak of power, and the Soviet leadership under Stalin created mechanisms for fostering the compliance of legal officials with central directives that would have made officials of the late tsarist ministry of justice envious.

A second area of dispute among Western historians of the USSR under Stalin concerns the power and capacity of the dictator. The traditional view portrayed Stalin ruling Russia through a disciplined party, centralized bureaucracy subordinated to it, and a political police that kept officialdom in check. But a variety of more recent studies have brought to light the difficulties Stalin faced in managing party and government officials alike. Among others, the work of Arch Getty and Gabor Rittersporn documented the difficulties encountered by the Stalinist leadership in securing the compliance of local officials with their directives and how much those officials continued to shape administrative practice even after the Purge that was meant to subdue them. Rittersporn even questioned the degree of bureaucratization where administrative practice tended to subvert hierarchical relationships.[9]

[8] William Wagner, "Tsarist Legal Policies at the End of the Nineteenth Century: A Study in Inconsistencies," *Slavonic and East European Review*, 54:3 (July 1976), 371–394; Wagner, *Marriage, Property and Law in Late Imperial Russia*, chap. 1; Theodore Taranovski, "The Aborted Counter-Reform: Muraviev Commission and the Judicial Statutes of 1864," *Jahrbucher für Geschichte Osteuropas* 29 (1981), 161–184; *Padenie Tsarskogo rezhima. Stenografcheskii otchet doprosov i pokazanii, dannykh v 1917g. v Chrezvychainoi Sledstvennoi Kommissi Vremennogo Pravitelstva.* II (Leningrad-Moscow, 1925), 337–439 (dopros I.G. Shchelgovitova).
[9] Examples of the traditional view include Carl Friedrich and Zbigniew Brzezinski, *Totalitarian Dictatorship and Autocracy* (Cambridge, Mass., 1953), and Merle Fainsod, *How Russia Is Ruled* (Cambridge, Mass., 1953), whose arguments, often in bowdlerized

Reconciling good evidence about the limits of governance under Stalin with the traditional portrait of Stalin as a despot wielding terror proved difficult for some scholars. Some fastened on one phenomenon and tried to deny the other one, thereby dividing the field of Soviet history into traditionalists and revisionists, and generating controversy.[10] Yet, to other scholars the personal dictatorship and the weakness of central authority vis-à-vis lower levels of government and political power represented two real and compatible aspects of politics under Stalin. In *The Origins of the Stalinist Political System* Graeme Gill made a strong case for inclusion of both of these features in a revised standard version of government under Stalin. A personal dictatorship, he wrote, does not mean that Stalin himself decided all questions, only that he "did decide whatever questions he chose to decide, and whenever he intervened in an issue, that intervention was decisive." At the same time, Gill continued, Stalin lacked the capacity to provide regular supervision of governance at levels below the national. This did not suggest that the leadership could not address "intransigence or opposition" from particular localities when it chose to do so, but it could not intervene on an ongoing basis. As a result, politicians in the regions and districts had considerable autonomy in practice.[11]

My account of criminal justice under Stalin supports the synthesis of traditional and revisionist insights about Stalinist government advanced by Graeme Gill. At least until the late 1930s (if not the late 1940s) the central legal agencies exercised less leverage over the conduct and careers of legal officials than did local political bosses. Local power loomed large in the administration of justice, especially but not only during collectivization, and as a result the central legal agencies had difficulty gaining compliance with their directives. At the same time, the leader Joseph Stalin emerges in this story as a classic dictator,

form, became conventional wisdom. (Note that Fainsod always gave play to the nonfulfillment of directives by officials in the USSR. In fact, he claimed that their main contribution to policies came in reshaping decisions from the top in the course of implementation.) Examples of the new perspective include Arch Getty, *Origins of the Great Purges* (Cambridge, 1985), and his "State and Society," as well as Gabor Tamas Rittersporn, *Stalinist Simplifications and Soviet Complications. Social Tensions and Political Conflicts in the USSR, 1933–1953* (Chur, Switzerland, 1991).

10 For the controversy unleashed, see discussion in the *Russian Review*, 45:2 (1986), 357–409; 46:4 (1987), 375–431; and two overviews of the debate: Jane Burbank, "Controversies over Stalinism: Searching for a Soviet Society," *Politics and Society* (Sept. 1991), 325–340, and Vladimir Andrle, "Demons and Devils' Advocates: Problems in Historical Writing on the Stalin Era" in Nick Lampert and Gabor T. Rittersporn, eds., *Stalinism: Its Nature and Aftermath: Essays in Honour of Moshe Lewin* (London, 1992), 25–47.

11 Graeme Gill, *The Origins of the Stalinist Political System* (Cambridge, 1990), esp. 1–8.

capable of directing criminal policy and dominating decision making about it. From August 1932, at least, every change in the criminal law bore the mark of his hand. Still, the decision to extend the criminal law to a new offense or to raise punishments did not lead to automatic implementation, especially when the changes offended the persons charged with their realization. For much of his reign, the dictator Stalin lacked a strong state, one that combined centralization of power with effective penetration into local administration and society. Stalin knew it, and from the mid-1930s did all he could to remedy the situation.

Not only does this study lend support to the synthetic view of Stalinism advanced by Gill, but it also reinforces the argument that the Stalinist state did not emerge full blown but developed gradually, reaching its apogee near the end of the Leader's life. Not until the end of Stalin's reign did he have at his disposal highly centralized legal agencies with the means of managing local legal officials. I would suggest that this was no anomaly. On a broader scale, it took most of Stalin's life for him to create institutions that resembled the strong state that we have traditionally associated with his dictatorship.

One further caution. The achievement of a highly centralized state with leverage over its subordinates does not mean that officials in the center had achieved "full control." The operation of powerful central agencies generates informal mechanisms by officials, adjustments, evasions, techniques for coping with central demands. Just as Joseph Berliner's study of industrial administration in the 1940s and 1950s revealed informal dimensions, so our study of the administration of criminal justice showed a variety of adjustments and means of coping with central directives that had unexpected consequences for policy goals.[12] These included substitutes for acquittals, the widespread use by judges of suspended sentences and sentences below the legal limits, reliance of investigators upon confessions in some cases, failure by the police to register cases without suspects, and the generation of cases by investigators solely to fill quotas. Even in the most centralized system of criminal justice administration, practitioners manage to shape its contours in significant ways.

Finally, I would like to draw out some of the implications of the history of criminal justice under Stalin for comparative studies of criminal justice. I address three issues: the limits of the criminal sanction, the use of nonprofessional legal officials, and criminal justice under authoritarian regimes.

In Western democracies, scholars have argued, the criminal sanction is not a resource that governments can use in an unlimited or indis-

---

12 Joseph Berliner, *Factory and Manager in the USSR* (Cambridge, Mass., 1957).

criminate way. The criminal sanction had limits, so Herbert Packer explained, and its overuse and misuse led to serious costs. As the ultimate threat and unique coercive response of democratic governments to the conduct of their constituents, the criminal sanction could even lose its effectiveness. Overuse, especially for trivial matters, could "debase the currency." "The more indiscriminate we are in treating conduct as criminal, the less stigma resides in the mere fact of conviction." A second limitation on the use of the criminal law lay in the capacity of a government to enforce it. Packer found that laws that were enforced only sporadically produced more harm than good. They decreased public respect for law, led to improper methods of enforcement, encouraged arbitrary use of discretion, and often alienated the victims of crime as well. Finally, to take the extreme case, when used indiscriminately and coercively, the criminal law could threaten the freedom that in a democracy at least it was meant to protect.[13]

My study suggests that much of this now conventional wisdom about the limits of the criminal sanction applies to authoritarian as well as democratic rulers. To begin, Soviet experience demonstrates that indiscriminate and coercive use of the criminal law approaching naked repression discredits both the law and the regime that sponsors it. During the collectivization campaign Soviet legal officials reduced the use of legal procedures to the point where their actions resembled those of other agents of police and local power. As a result the authority and status of law was called into question, and much effort expended later on to restore the law to its normal footing. Less obviously, this account of the history of criminal justice under Stalin reveals that in an authoritarian regime the criminal sanction was also limited by capacity for enforcement. When Stalin tried to use the criminal law for purposes and in ways not accepted by its enforcers (legal officials, police, and others) or call for penalties that struck them as too severe, the result was evasion, resistance, and inconsistent enforcement. These consequences followed Stalin's extensions of the criminal law (e.g., to the policing of defective goods production and the regulation of the labor force); his recriminalization of old offenses (abortion and juvenile delinquency); and his mandating of the sharp increases in punishment for theft (in 1932 and in 1947). The point is that even a dictator whose authority is not limited by institutional checks faces limitations on his power stemming from the capacity of his government to enforce his decisions. Within Sovietological writing Merle Fainsod emphasized the capacity of officials to reshape the policies of Soviet rulers through implementation. His point applies with special force to the criminal law, whose

[13] Herbert Packer, *The Limits of the Criminal Sanction* (Stanford, Calif., 1968), part 3.

enforcement everywhere seems to require congruence between the values of the enforcers and the norms that they are asked to enforce.[14]

The use of laypersons, that is, persons who lack legal education, as judges in the lowest courts has received the endorsement of scholars who have studied their performance. By and large, in Western countries, nonlawyer judges serve *only* in the lowest courts that hear minor disputes and adjudicate lesser criminal and administrative offenses; often they work part-time, are not paid, and sometimes serve in panels. Often, they lack the power to sentence offenders to prison. After examining nonprofessional judges in a number of U.S. jurisdictions, Doris Marie Provine concluded that the performance of the amateurs displayed a standard no lower than that of their confreres who had legal education and worked full-time. In a comparison of the sentencing practices of educated full-time stipendiary magistrates and part-time voluntary lay magistrates working in the courts of England, Shari Diamond discovered that the lay judges paid more attention to the particulars of each case and tended to give somewhat lighter sentences than their more jaded, but also educated colleagues. In both England and the United States, the persons who served as nonprofessional judges usually had a decent level of general education (including a high school degree and usually some postsecondary education as well).[15]

The Soviet experience in using both nonprofessional judges demonstrates the limits of their utility – in general and in particular for authoritarian rulers. An unfortunate combination of ideology and need drove Bolshevik rulers to recruit as judges – and prosecutors and investigators – persons who not only lacked legal education but had little general education as well. Many Soviet legal officials in the first decades of Soviet power had completed primary school or less. As a result, they lacked the elementary degree of literacy and standards of logical thinking needed to perform their assigned duties. Moreover, their attachment to the norms of law and legal procedure was low, a fact that had mixed consequences. On the one hand, they responded all too readily to the demands of local politicians, even when they contradicted the law or central directives. On the other hand, nonprofessional legal officials stood ready to act on their own conscience when the law or central directives violated their moral sensibility. In this regard, Soviet judges

---

14 Fainsod, *How Russia Is Ruled.*
15 Doris Marie Provine, *Judging Credentials. Nonlawyer Judges and the Politics of Professionalism* (Chicago and London, 1986); Shari Seidman Diamond, "Revising Images of Public Punitiveness: Sentencing by Law and Professional English Magistrates," *Law and Social Inquiry*, 15:2 (Spring 1990), 191–221. See also Stanley Anderson, "Lay Judges and Jurors in Denmark," *American Journal of Comparative Law*, 38 (1990), 839–864.

resembled nonprofessional judges elsewhere, who tended in the direction of leniency.[16] As a whole, though, the conduct of Soviet judges proved inconsistent, at times erratic. Moreover, the weak performance of nonprofessional judges in the USSR mattered more than it might elsewhere. For, unlike nonprofessional judges in Europe and North America, Soviet judges worked full-time, heard cases as individuals (or in panels with members of the public, the lay assessors, who knew even less about the law than the judges), adjudicated a full range of serious criminal cases (not just misdemeanors), and applied an arsenal of punishments that included long terms of prison and, at least for regional court judges, the death penalty. The discrepancy between the serious crimes and punishments with which they dealt and the capabilities of nonprofessional judges and investigators worked to discredit the administration of justice in the USSR.

From the standpoint of authoritarian rulers like Stalin, the Soviet brand of amateur legal official proved to be a special disaster. Like any dictator Stalin sought officials whom he could direct and control. But uneducated legal officials, who lacked professional identity as well as competence, tended not to make careers in the legal agencies, and, as a result, proved less manageable than professional judges and prosecutors. Mere membership in the Bolshevik party, as we have noted, and even belonging to its most trusted group (the various *nomenklatury*), did not by itself produce the desired responsiveness. A similar logic applied to the lay judges, the volunteers who staffed the comrades' courts and rural social courts of the 1930s. Andrei Vyshinskii understood this point, and in the mid-1930s castigated the lay courts as incompetent and irrelevant, at the very time that he was promoting higher education for full-time legal officials.

There is an ironic twist here. While in democratic countries, the professionalization of legal administration leads mainly to improved handling of cases (along with, perhaps, a slight increase in punitiveness), the professionalization of the administration of justice in authoritarian countries has the added consequence of making legal officials more open to direction by their superiors (which may also produce harsher punishments). Put another way, in authoritarian countries like the USSR, nonprofessional and lay judges, although contributing to uneven execution of the law, may have supplied less biased adjudication than their better educated professional peers of the next generation.

Although most countries in the modern world have authoritarian regimes (or at least highly imperfect democratic ones), there has been

---

[16] But the leniency of Soviet judges did not reflect one of the common sources of the "lay leniency effect," namely part-time work as a judge. See Diamond, 215.

little analysis, not to speak of theory, about criminal justice in nondemocratic settings. In 1991 Sir Leon Radzinowicz set out a list of features of what he called the "authoritarian model of criminal justice." Each of its sixteen items represented the reverse of a component of a fully democratic criminal justice. The items included, for example: imprecise definitions of crimes, weak enforcement of evidentiary standards, judges and prosecutors pursuing the wishes of rulers, punishments traditional and harsh, the use of extrajudicial tribunals, and secrecy.[17] More recently, Adam Podgorecki tried to distinguish what made law in a country "totalitarian." For Podgorecki the essence of "totalitarian" law lay in the combination of a pretense to observance of legal forms (including the design of constitutions as facades) with the reality of the law's service to political power and wholly instrumental character. Features of totalitarian law included: subservient judges acting as agents of the regime; legal norms whose validity depended upon current political interpretations and sociopolitical practices; a "whimsicality" or capriciousness about the law in action and even unpredictability by design; and the regular use of both secret decrees and harsh punishments. Since this portrait of "totalitarian" law was drawn from Soviet and Eastern European Communist experience, its resemblance to late Stalinist justice is hardly surprising. To be sure, Podgorecki did recognize that in the real world many regimes fell between the extremes of democracy and totalitarianism and that as a result their law and legal institutions also constituted midpoints along a spectrum. But the author did not explore in detail the nature of these variants.[18]

The challenge of developing a theory of criminal justice in nondemocratic settings is too large to be met in a few pages of the conclusion to this book. But there are a number of insights coming from the Soviet/Stalinist experience that deserve consideration in the elaboration of a formal theory. I start with the differences between authoritarian and democratic regimes. In authoritarian governments political power tends to be more concentrated and less accountable, especially to soci-

---

[17] Sir Leon Radzinowicz, "Penal Regressions," *Cambridge Law Journal*, 50:3 (Nov. 1991), 422–444.

[18] Podgorecki advanced the interesting notion of "dotted democracy," a democratic order with pockets of totalitarian practices. The latter included total institutions such as prisons and mental institutions. Adam Podgorecki, "Totalitarian Law: Basic Concepts and Issues," in *Totalitarian and Post-Totalitarian Law*, edited by Adam Podgorecki and Vittorio Olgiati, (Aldershott, U. K., 1996). See also C. Neal Tate and Stacia L. Haynie, "Authoritarianism and the Functions of Courts: A Time Sense Analysis of the Philippine Supreme Court, 1961–1987," *Law and Society Review*, 27:4 (1993), 707–739; and Mark J. Osiel, "Dialogue with Dictators: Judicial Resistance in Argentina and Brazil," *Law and Social Inquiry*, 20:2 (Spring 1995), 481–560.

ety, than it is in democratic governments. In addition, in authoritarian settings political power commonly serves a narrow set of value commitments that relate to the interests of the rulers. The net result is that in authoritarian governments the instrumental role of law – to a degree universal for all regimes – tends to be more prominent and less tempered or checked either by structural design or legal/political culture. As Roberto Unger stressed in discussing what he called "bureaucratic law," the principal limitation of the use of law in authoritarian settings stems from the tension between maximizing the instrumental aspirations of rulers and the observation of forms and procedures of the law sufficient to maintain legitimacy for the law and its administration.[19]

Because of this tension many authoritarian regimes have sought to ensure that at least a share of adjudication is conducted by bodies perceived by their citizenry to be impartial or at least not unduly under the control of the regime. However, the rulers may fashion means of ensuring that legal officials consistently administer the law in ways that further the regime's interests. It is useful for analysis to distinguish the handling of politically sensitive cases from the management of ordinary criminal cases.

For authoritarian rulers to ensure desirable outcomes in politically important cases, they must either facilitate the penetration of political power into the legal order or compartmentalize political justice, separating it from the adjudication of ordinary criminal cases. Stalin used both of these techniques, though at different times. During collectivization local politicians succeeded in mobilizing legal officials to pursue the aims of the regime. As a result, ordinary judges, procurators, and investigators administered the law against the declared enemies of the regime, according to political direction. After collectivization rank-and-file investigators and judges were for the most part removed from political cases (now restricted to Article 58), as these were directed to the special collegia of the regional courts and the NKVD tribunals. These were the main vehicles for conducting the Great Terror. After 1938, political cases were concentrated only in certain military tribunals and bodies of the NKVD; ordinary courts even at the regional level played little or no role in their adjudication.

The politicization of the activity of the regular courts, which happened during Soviet collectivization, seems to occur especially at times of revolutionary change, when administration can mean mobilization and the discipline of law seem obsolete. On the other hand, the model of compartmentalization of political justice, through the creation of a separate set of institutions and actors following different rules from

---

[19] Roberto Unger, *Law in Modern Society* (New York, 1976), 48–76.

those mandated for ordinary cases, appears to be the option favored by rulers in periods of stability and order. It is, therefore, the more permanent solution and the one that most authoritarian regimes have employed. Regimes as varied as those of tsarist Russia, Franco's Spain, and even Nazi Germany prosecuted and repressed their political enemies through distinct and reliable tribunals and left the handling of ordinary criminal cases to courts and officials largely unaffected by the pressures and expectations faced by the political tribunals.[20] When in late 1938 Stalin opted unambiguously for compartmentalization, he was following a well-trodden path. I am not suggesting that all countries that separate political from ordinary justice produce the same results. Even among the countries mentioned here one can observe differences in the scope of political justice, its fairness (e.g. the balance between real adjudication and contrived or manufactured prosecutions), and the degree of compartmentalization and influence of political justice on the handling of ordinary criminal cases.

The management of ordinary criminal justice is also likely to reflect the aspirations of authoritarian rulers. Characteristic of these regimes, I would suggest, but not limited to them, is the effort to create career tracks and incentive structures that enable the regime to manage legal officials – in the words of Martin Shapiro, "systems of judicial recruitment, training, organization and promotion that ensure that the judge . . . (while) relatively neutral as between two purely private parties . . . will be the absolutely faithful servant of the regime on all legal matters touching its interests."[21] The centralized management of the careers of legal officials, with a clear (though at times contradictory) set of expectations for those desiring promotion, became by the early 1950s a key feature of Stalinist criminal justice. Lasting through the post-Stalin decades, this system of management turned out to be the critical ingredient in the conversion of legal officials into a troupe of loyal and conforming servants of the Soviet regime. This development may be understood as the bureaucratization of Soviet criminal justice (something Gabor Rittersporn found absent in the 1930s), but it was a process that was not complete at the time of Stalin's death. In fact, it is possible

---

[20] Wagner, "Tsarist Legal Policies"; Jose J. Toharia, "Judicial Independence in an Authoritarian Regime," *Law and Society Review*, 9:3 (1975), 475–496; Ernst Fraenkel, *The Dual State: A Contribution to the Theory of Dictatorship* (London, 1941); and Sharlet, "Stalinism and Soviet Legal Culture." For an alternative, but not-well supported view of judges under the Nazis, see Ingo Muller, *Hitler's Justice: The Courts of the Third Reich* (Cambridge, Mass., 1991). Critical reviews of Muller's book include those by Donald Kommers (*Review of Politics*, 54:4, Summer 1992) and Walter Weyrauch (*American Journal of Comparative Law*, 40:1, Winter 1992).

[21] Martin Shapiro, *Courts: A Comparative and Political Analysis* (Chicago, 1981), 32.

that the bureaucratization of criminal justice in post-Stalin Russia was never completed, or at least that it took on forms that were inconsistent with Western (i.e., Weberian) theories of bureaucracy. For one thing, the patrimonial element in Soviet administration of justice, expressed through the intervention of local politicians, continued in the post-Stalin years, despite efforts of Khrushchev to combat it. Still, the effect of the bureaucratization of Soviet criminal justice, whatever its peculiarities, was to create and in the long run maximize the accountability of Soviet legal officials not to the public or the values of objectivity and fairness but to the interests and policies of their bureaucratic and political masters.

It would seem that a thoroughly bureaucratized administration of criminal justice would serve the interests of authoritarian rulers in general and characterize their regimes (as long as their countries had reached the level of political development where judicial roles were separate from administrative ones and there were resources to create judicial bureaucracy). There is, though, a reverse side of the coin. The bureaucratization of criminal justice also poses a threat in democratic countries, where a similar focus of accountability contradicts democratic values and institutions. Although the image of criminal justice as a "self-perpetuating bureaucracy . . . a self-contained machine deliberately cut off from wider influences and reliable reassessments" applies to most authoritarian governments, it also reflects tendencies that appear in democratic ones as well.[22] Especially agencies of the police seem, even in Western democracies, to veer in the direction of self-absorption. In the Anglo-American world at least, judges may be immune from this process, but in the inquisitorial countries of Continental Europe the matter is less clear.

There are a variety of spectra along which systems of criminal justice range and that correspond to the nature of the political regime in which they are set. Developing a clearer portrait of the variables that define these spectra, and of authoritarian criminal justice in general, is needed if only to provide a baseline for assessing how criminal justice in a given country reflects or embodies transition from authoritarianism toward democracy. One hopes that other scholars will join in meeting this challenge.

[22] Radzinowicz, "Penal Regressions," 428.

Bibliography

1. **Archival sources (Abbreviations and fond numbers are given in parentheses.)**

   Gosudarstvennyi Arkhiv Rossiskoi Federatsii (GARF), formerly *Tsentralnyi Arkhiv Oktiabrskoi Revoliutsii* (TsGAOR).
   Ministerstvo Iustitsii SSSR (9492 and 9492sch)
   Ministerstvo Vysshykh Uchebnykh Zavedeniia SSSR (9396)
   Narodnyi Komissariat Raboche-Krestianskoi Inspektsii (373)
   Prezidium Verkhovnogo Soveta SSSR (7528sch)
   Prokuratura SSSR (8131 and 8131sch)
   Verkhovnyi Sud SSSR (9474 and 9474sch)
   Gosudarstvennyi Arkhiv Rossiiskoi Federatsii (GARF TsGA), formerly Tsentralnyi Gosudarstvennyi Arkhiv RSFSR (TsGA).
   Narodnyi Komissariat Iustitsii RSFSR (353 and 353s)
   Prokuratura RSFSR (461s)
   Partiinyi arkhiv Sverdlovskogo obkoma KPSS
   Oblastnoi komitet KPSS (4)
   Rossiiskii Tsentr Khraneniia i Izucheniia Dokumentov Noveishei istorii (RTsKhIDNI), formerly *Tsentralnyi Partiinnyi Arkhiv* (TsPA)
   Tsentralnyi Komitet KPSS (17)
   Tsentralnaia Kontrolnaia Komissia VKP(b) (613)
   The Smolensk Party Archive (files identified by WKP numbers)
   Tsentralnyi Gosdudarstvennyi Arkhiv Goroda Moskvy
   Moskovskii Gorodskoi Sud (819)
   Tsentralnyi Derzhavnyi Arkhiv Gromadskikh Ob'ednan Ukraini
   Politbiuro Ukrainy (1)

2. **Official publications**

For guidance in the use of official publications of the Soviet government, see Peter H. Solomon, Jr., "Laws and Administrative Acts: Sources and Finding Aids," in *A Researcher's Guide to Sources in Soviet Social History in the 1930s,* edited by Sheila Fitzpatrick and Lynne Viola. Armonk, N.Y., and London, 1990, 146–152.

God raboty pravitelstva RSFSR. Materialy k otchetu pravitelstva za 1917–1928. Moscow, 1929.

Goliakov, I.T., ed. *Sbornik dokumentov po istorii ugolovnogo zakonodatelstva SSSR i RSFSR 1917–1952 gg.* Moscow, 1953. This collection was compiled by A.A. Gertsenzon.

Golunskii, A.S., ed. *Istoriia zakonodatelstva SSSR i RSFSR po ugolovnom protsessu i organizatsii suda.* Moscow, 1955.

Instruktsii po sostavleniiu operativnykh statisticheskikh otchetov o rabote organov prokuratury v 1948 godu. Moscow and Leningrad, 1948.

"Materialy fevralsko-martovskogo plenuma TsK VKP(b) 1937 goda." *Voprosy istorii,* 1992, no. 2–3, 4–5, 6–7, 8–9, 10, 11–12, 1993; no. 2, 5, 6, 7, 8, 9; 1994, no. 1, 2, 6, 8, 10; 1995, no. 1, 2, 3, 4, 5, 6, 7, 8.

Narodnyi Komissariat Iustsitsii. *Otchet k vserossiikomu s'ezdu sovetov.* Moscow, 1921.

Obshchii obzor statisticheskikh svedenii o deiatelnosti sudebnykh ustanovlenii za 1914 god. Petrograd, 1916.

Otchet Prokuratury RSFSR Prezidiumu VTsIK za 1926 g. Moscow, 1927.

Piatnadtsatyi s'ezd VKP(b). Dekabr 1927 god. Stenograficheskii otchet. 2 volumes. Moscow, 1961.

Postanovleniia i raz'iasneniia Verkhovnogo Suda SSSR, 40–44 plenuma. Moscow, 1933.

Postanovleniia Plenuma Verkhovnogo Suda SSSR po delam o narusheniiakh Ukaza Prezidiuma Verhkovnogo Soveta SSSR ot 26 iiuniia 1940 goda. Moscow, 1940.

Safonov, G., ed. *Spravochnik po zakonodatelstvu dlia sudebno-prokurorskikh rabotnikov.* 3 volumes. Moscow, 1949.

Sostav rukovodiashchikh rabotnikov i spetsialistov soiuza SSR. Moscow, 1936.

Sbornik deistvuiushchikh postanovlenii Plenuma i direktivnykh pisem Verkhovnogo Suda SSSR 1924–1944 gg. Moscow, 1946.

Sbornik deistvuiushchikh prikazov i instruktsii Generalnogo Prokurora SSSR. Moscow, 1958.

Sbornik postanovlenii plenuma i opredelenii kollegii Verkhovnogo Suda SSSR (1938 i pervoe polugodie 1939 g.). Moscow, 1940.

Sbornik postanovlenii, raz'iasnenii i direktiv Verkhovnogo Suda SSSR deist vuiushchikh na 1 aprelia 1935 g. Moscow, 1935.

Sbornik prikazov i instruktsii Narodnogo Komissariat Iustitsii Soiuza SSR. Moscow, 1940.

Sbornik prikazov i instruktsii Ministerstva Iustitsii SSSR 1936–1948 gg. Moscow, 1949.

Sbornik prikazov prokuratury SSSR. 2nd ed., expanded. Moscow, 1939.

Sbornik raz'iasnenii Verkhovnogo Suda RSFSR. 1st ed. (Moscow, 1930); 2nd ed. (Moscow, 1931); 3rd ed. (Moscow, 1932); 4th ed. (Moscow, 1935).

Sbornik tsirkuliarov Narkomiusta RSFSR za 1922–1925. Moscow, 1926.

Sbornik tsirkuliarov Narkomiusta RSFSR za 1922–1926 gg. Moscow, 1927.

Sbornik tsirkuliarov Narkomiusta RSFSR deistvuiushchikh na 1 iiuniia 1931 g. Moscow, 1931.

Sbornik tsirkuliarov i raz'iasnenii Narkomiusta RSFSR deistvuiushchikh na 1 maia 1934 g. Moscow, 1934.

Sbornik zakonov SSSR i ukazov Prezidiuma Verkhovnogo Soveta SSSR (1938-noiabr 1958 g.). Moscow, 1959.

Svod zakonov ugolovnykh. Edited by N. Ozernetskovskii. 2nd ed. St. Petersburg, 1915.

Ugolovno-protsessualnyi kodeks RSFSR. Moscow, 1952.

Ugolovnyi kodeks RSFSR. Moscow, 1948.

3. Periodicals (journals and newspapers)

All published in Moscow, unless otherwise indicated. Articles that appeared in these journals are not listed separately in Part 4 of this bibliography. For citations, see the footnotes. For a characterization of the most important of these journals, see Peter H. Solomon, Jr., "Legal Journals and Soviet Social History," in *A Researcher's Guide to Sources on Soviet Social History in the 1930s,* edited by Sheila Fitzpatrick and Lynne Viola. Armonk, N.Y., and London, 1990, 189–201.

Administrativnyi vestnik, 1925–1930.
Biulleten Kalininskoi oblastnoi prokuratury (Kalinin), 1935–1936.
Biulleten TsKK-RKI, 1927–1930.
Bolshevik, 1929–1952.
Ezhenedelnik sovetskoi iustitsii (ESIu), 1922–1929.
Izvestiia, 1929–1953.
Izvestiia TsK VKP(b), 1920–1929.
Kommunist, 1953–1960.
Kontrol mass (Voronezh), 1930–1932.
Krestianskii iurist, 1928–1935. In 1932 the title changed to *Derevenskii iurist.*
Materialy Narkomiusta, 1918–1922.
Molot (Rostov), 1931–1936.
Partiinaia rabota (Samara), 1933.
Partiinoe stroitelstvo, 1934–1941.
Partiinyi rabotnik (Saratov), 1933–1936.
Partiinyi rabotnik severnogo kavkaza, 1932–1933.
Pravda, 1923–1953.
Pravo i zhizn, 1922–1929.
Problemy prestupnosti, 1926–1929.
Problemy sotsialisticheskogo prava, 1937–1939.
Problemy ugolovnoi politiki, 1935–1937.
Proletarskii sud, 1922–1930.
Proletarskoe revoliutsiia i pravo, 1918–1921.
Put sovetov (Rostov), 1930–1932.
Rabochii sud (Leningrad), 1924–1929.
Revoliutsiia prava, 1927–1929.

Revoliutsiine pravo (Kiev), 1932–1933.
Sbornik po voprosam okhrany detstva, 1934–1937.
Sotsialisticheskaia zakonnost (SZ), 1933–1956. From 1933 to 1935 published as *Za sotsialisticheskuiu zakonnost*.
Sovetskaia iustitsiia (SIu), 1930–1941; 1957.
Sovetskoe gosudarstvo i pravo (SGiP), 1930–1960. Called *Sovetskoe gosudarstvo i revoliutsiia prava* from 1930 to 1932 and *Sovetskoe gosudarstvo* from 1932 to 1938.
Sovetskoe stroitelstvo, 1926–1937.
Sud idet (Leningrad), 1929–1931.
Sudebnaia praktika Verkhovnogo Suda RSFSR, 1928–1931.
Sudebnaia praktika Verkhovnogo Suda SSSR, 1942, 1953.
Trud, 1939–1941, 1951–1952.
V razvernutoe sotsialisticheskoe nastuplenie (Sverdlovsk), 1932–1933.
Vestnik sovetskoi iustitsii (Kharkov), 1923–1929.
Vlast sovetov, 1919–1938.
Za tempy, kachestvo, proverku, 1931–1933.

4.   Books and selected articles in Russian

Afanasev, A.V., compiler. *Oni ne molchali*. Moscow, 1991.
Alkedeev, A. *Na strazhe zakonnosti (Stanovlenie i razvitie prokuratury Kazakhskoi SSR)*. Alma-Ata, 1981.
Asknazii, F.M., and N.V. Marshalova, compilers. *Sovetskoe ugolovnoe pravo. Bibliografiia. 1917–1960*. Moscow, 1961.
Avdeev, A. "Abort – demoklov mech nad kazhdoi semei . . . " in *SSSR: Demograficheskii diagnoz*, edited by V.T. Mukomel. Moscow, 1990, 314–344.
Avtorkhanov, A. *Memuary*. Frankfurt, 1983.
Baazova, Faina. *Prokazhennye*. Jerusalem: Biblioteka Alia, 1980.
Bannikov, B.I. "Zapiski narkoma." *Znamia*, 1988, no. 1, 130–160.
Beriia – konets karera. Moscow, 1991.
Berkhin, I.B. "K istorii razrabotki konstitutsii SSSR 1936 g." In *Stroitetstvo sovetskogo gosudarstva*. Moscow, 1972, 63–80.
Braginskii, M.M., and N. Lagovier. *Revoliutsionnaia zakonnost i prokurorskii nadzor v selskokhoziaistvennykh politicheskikh kampaniiakh*. Moscow, 1993.
Bukov, V. *Sud i obshchestvo v sovetskoi Rossii: u istokov totalitarianizma*. Moscow, 1992.
Cheltsov-Bebutov, M.A. *Ocherki po istorii suda i ugolovnogo protsessa v rabovladelsheskikh, feodalnykh i burzhuaznykh gosudarstvakh*. Moscow, 1957.
Cherliuchakevich, N.A., ed. *Prestupnost i repressiia v RSFSR*. Moscow, 1930.
Danilov, V.P. ed. *Ocherki istorii kollektivizatsii selskogo khoziaistva v soiuznykh respublikakh*. Moscow, 1963.
Dobrovolskaia, T.N. *Oblastnoi (kraevoi) sud*. Moscow, 1958.
Verkhovnyi sud SSSR. Moscow, 1964.
Esakov, V.D., and E.S. Levina, "Delo 'KR' (Iz istorii gonenii na sovetskuiu intelligentsiia," *Kentavr*, 1994, no. 2 54–69, and no. 3, 96–118.

Ezhegodnik sovetskogo stroitelstva i prava. Moscow, 1931.

Faivush, B.I. "Iz istorii spetsializirovannykh sudebnykh organov po delam nesovershennoletnikh v 1935–1948 gg." In *Preduprezhdenie prestupnosti nesovershennoletnikh.* Moscow, 1965.

Gernet, M.N. *Prestupnost za granitsei i v SSSR.* Moscow, 1931.

Gertsenzon, A.A. *Borba s prestupnostiu v. RSFSR.* Moscow, 1928.

Gertsenzon, A.A., et al. *Gosudarstvennye prestupleniia (Ugolovnoe pravo, Osobenennaia chast).* Moscow, 1938.

Grechukha, M. *Moia rabota narodnym sudei.* Moscow, 1940.

Ikonnikov, S.N. *Sozdanie i deiatelnost ob'edinennykh organov TsKK-RKI v 1923–1934 gg.* Moscow, 1971.

Isaev, M.M. *Voprosy ugolovnogo prava i ugolovnogo protsessa v sudebnoi praktike Verkhovnogo Suda SSSR.* Moscow, 1948.

Iuridicheskii kalendar na 1923. Moscow, 1923.

Iuridicheskii kalendar na 1929. Moscow, 1929.

Kabanov, V.V. "Iz istorii sozdanii Konstitutsii SSSR 1936 goda." *Istoriia SSSR,* 1976, no. 6, 116–127.

Kazantsev, Sergei M. *Istoriia tsarskoi prokuratury.* St. Petersburg, 1993.

Khlevniuk, Oleg V. "26 iuniia 1940 goda: illiuzi i realnosti administrirovaniia." *Kommunist,* 1989, no. 9, 86–96.

1937-i: Stalin, NKVD i sovetskoe obshchestvo. Moscow, 1992.

Stalin i Ordzhonikidze: Konflikty v Politburo v 30e gody. Moscow, 1993.

Khlevniuk, Oleg. V., et al., comp., *Stalinskoe Politbiuro v 30-e gody Sbornik dokumentov.* Moscow, 1995.

Kosheleva, L., et al., comp. *Pisma I.V. Stalina V.M. Molotovu, 1925–1936 gg. Sbornik dokumentov.* Moscow, 1995.

Kositsyn, A.P. ed. *Istoriia sovetskogo gosduarstva i prava.* 3 vol. Moscow, 1968–1970.

Kozhevnikov, M.V. *Istoriia sovetskogo suda, 1917–1956.* Moscow, 1957.

"Puti razvitiia sovetskoi prokuratury," in three parts. Part three: *Uchenye zapiski MGU,* vpy. 147, Trudy iuridicheskogo fakulteta, kn. 5 (1950), 17–45.

Krylenko, Nikolai V. *Sudoustroistvo RSFSR (lektsii po teorii i istorii sudoustroistva).* Moscow, 1923.

Krylenko, N.V., ed. *Sovetskaia ugolovnaia repressia.* Moscow, 1934.

Kudriavtsev, V.N., ed. *Effektivnost pravosudiia i problem ustraneniiu sudebnykh oshibok.* 2 volumes. Moscow, 1975.

Kufaev, V.I. *Iunye pravonarushiteli.* 2nd ed., expanded. Moscow, 1922.

Kuritsyn, V.M. *Perekhod k NEPu i revoliutsionnaia zakonnost.* Moscow, 1972.

Kurskii, D.M. *Izbrannye stati i rechi.* Moscow, 1948.

Lagovier, N. *Narodnye zasedateli.* Moscow and Leningrad, 1926.

Lagovier, N., and A. Rodzianskii. *Dela rabselkorovskie.* Moscow, 1929.

Liublinskii, P.I. *Borba s prestupnostiu v detskom i iunosheskom vozraste (sotsialno-pravovye ocherki).* Moscow, 1923.

Mankovskii, B.S., and V. Undrevich, eds. *Klassovaia borba i prestupnost na sovremennom etape.* 2 volumes. Leningrad, 1933.

Maslov, V., and N. Chistiakov. "Staliniskie repressi i sovetskaia iustitsiia." *Kommunist,* 1990, no. 10,

Maslov, V.P., and N.F. Chistiakov. *Vopreki zakonu i spravedlivosti*. Moscow, 1990.

Mulukaev, R.S., and A.Ia. Malygin. *Sovetskaia militsiia: etapy razvitiia*. Moscow, 1985.

Muranov, A., and Y. Zviagintsev. *Sud nad sudiami (osobaia papka Ulrikha)*. Kazan, 1993.

Na strazhe sovetskikh zakonov. Moscow, 1972.

Nakhimson, F.L., et al., eds. *Sud i prokuratura na okhrane proizvodstva i truda*. Moscow, 1931.

Ocherki po istorii iuridicheskikh nauchnykh uchrezhdenii v SSSR. Moscow, 1976.

Organy iustitsii na novom etape (5oe soveshchanie rukovodiashchikh rabotnikov iustitsii, iiun 1931). Moscow, 1931.

Padenie Tsarskogo rezhima. Stenograficheskii otchet doprosov i pokazanii, dannykh v 1917 g. v Chrezvychainoi Sledstvennoi Kommissii Vremenogo Pravitelstva. 2 volumes. Leningrad-Moscow, 1925.

Panferov, T.S., ed. *Rasprava. Prokurorskie sudby*. Moscow, 1991.

Petukhov, G.E. *Sovetskii sud i stanovlenie revoliutsionnoi zakonnosti v gosudarstvennom upravlenii*. Kiev and Odessa, 1982.

Piontkovskii, A.A. *Staliniskaia konstitutsiia i proekt ugolovnogo kodeksa*. Moscow, 1947.

Polianskii, N.N. *Ocherk razvitiia sovetskoi nauki ugolovnogo protsessa*. Moscow, 1960.

Popov, V.P. "Gosudarstvennyi terror v sovetskoi Rossii, 1923–1953 (Istochniki i ikh interpetatsii)." *Otechestvennye arkhivy*, 1992, no. 2, 20–31.

Portnov, V.P., and M.M. Slavin. *Stanovlenie pravosudiia Sovetskoi Rossii (1917–1922 gg.)*. Moscow, 1990.

Rabota luchshikh slevodatelei. Materialy uchebno-metodicheskoe konferentsii luchshikh sledstvennykh rabotnikov organov prokuratury. 4 sborniki: Sbornik 1 (Moscow, 1951); Sbornik 2 (Moscow, 1951); Sbornik 3 (Moscow, 1953); Sbornik 4 (Moscow, 1954).

Romashkin, P.S. *Amnistiia i pomilovanie s SSSR*. Moscow, 1959.

Shargorodskii, M.D. *Nakazanie po sovetskomu ugolovnomu pravu*. Moscow, 1958.

Shebanov, A.F. *Iuridicheskie vysshie uchebnye zavedeniia*. Moscow, 1963.

Sheinin, P.P., ed. *Nastolnaia kniga sledovatelia*. Moscow, 1949.

Shirvindt, E.G. *Administrativnye organy v novykh usloviiakh*. Moscow, 1930.
    Klassovaia borba i prestupnost. Moscow, 1930.

Shreider, Mikhail. *NKVD iznutri – zapiski chekista*. Moscow, 1995.

Shvekov, G.V. *Pervyi sovetskii ugolovnyi kodeks*. Moscow, 1957.

Smirnov, L.N. ed. *Verkhovnyi Sud SSSR*. Moscow, 1974.
    Vysshyi sudebnyi organ SSSR. Moscow, 1984.

Solts, A., and S. Fainblit. *Revoliutsionnaia zakonnost i nasha karatelnaia politika*. Moscow, 1925.

Sorok let sovetskogo prava. 2 volumes, Leningrad, 1957.

Spravochnik narodnogo sudi. Moscow, 1946.

Stalin, Iosif. *Voprosy Leninizma*. 11th ed. Moscow, 1952.

Stuchka, Petr. *Dvenatdtsat let borby za revolutsionno-marksistkuiu teoriiu prava*. Moscow, 1931.

Trudy pervoi nauchnoi sessii Vsesoiuznogo instituta iuridicheskikh nauk, 27 ianvariia – 3 fevralia 1939. Edited by I.T. Goliakov. Moscow, 1939.

Utevskii, B.S. *Obshchee uchenie o dolzhnostnykh prestupleniiakh.* Moscow, 1948.

Vospominaniia iurista. Moscow, 1989.

Vasilevskii, L.A., and L.M. *Abort kak sotsialnoe iavlenie.* Moscow and Leningrad, 1924.

Vasnev, A. *Narodnye sudy stolitsy.* Moscow, 1939.

Vilenskii, B.V. *Sudebnaia reforma i kontrreforma v Rossii.* Saratov, 1969.

Volodarskii, P.G. *Sotsialisticheskoe sovmestitelstvo v organakh iustitsii.* Moscow, 1934.

Voprosy sovetskoi kriminalistiki. Leningrad, 1933.

Vyshinskaia, Z.A. *Prestupleniia v oblasti trudovykh otnoshenii.* Moscow, 1949.

Vyshinskii, A. Ia. *Revoliutsionnaia zakonnost na sovremennon etape.* Moscow, 1932. *Sudoustroistvo v SSSR.* 3rd ed. Moscow, 1936. *Teoriia sudebnykh dokazatelstv v sovetskom prave.* 3rd ed. Moscow, 1950.

Zima, V.F. "Golod v Rossii 1946–1947 godov." *Otechestvennaia istoriia,* 1993, no. 1, 35–52.

5. Books and articles in English

Barber, John, and Mark Harrison. *The Soviet Home Front, 1941–1945: A Social and Economic History of World War II.* London and New York, 1991.

Barry, Donald, ed. *Toward the "Rule of Law" in Russia? Political and Legal Reform in the Transition Period.* Armonk, N.Y., 1992.

Beirne, Piers, and Robert Sharlet, eds. *Pashukanis: Selected Writings on Marxism and Law.* London., 1980.

Berman, Harold. *Justice in the USSR.* Revised ed. Cambridge, Mass., 1963.

Boffa, Giuseppe. *The Stalin Phenomenon.* Ithaca, N.Y., and London, 1992.

Brower, Daniel. "The Smolensk Scandal and the End of NEP." *Slavic Review,* 45:4 (Winter 1986), 689–706.

Burbank, Jane. "Controversies over Stalinism: Searching for a Soviet Society." *Politics and Society* (Sept. 1991), 325–340.
"Lenin and the Law in Revolutionary Russia." *Slavic Review,* 54:1 (Spring 1995), 23–44.

Buxbaum, Richard, and Kathryn Hendley, eds. *The Soviet Sobranie of Laws. Problems of Codification and Non-Publication.* Berkeley, Calif.: International Area Studies Research Series, 1991.

Carr, Edward Hallett. *Socialism in One Country, 1924–1926.* 2 vol. London, 1959. *Foundations of a Planned Economy 1926–1929.* 3 volumes. London, 1971.

Conquest, Robert. *The Great Terror: Stalin's Purge of the 1930s.* London, 1968 *The Great Terror – A Reassessment.* Oxford, 1990. *The Harvest of Sorrow. Soviet Collectivization and the Terror-Famine.* Oxford, 1986.

Davies, R.W. *The Socialist Offensive: The Collectivization of Soviet Agriculture.* Cambridge, 1980.

Fainsod, Merle. *Smolensk under Soviet Rule.* New York, 1958.

How Russia Is Ruled. Cambridge, Mass., 1953, and Rev. ed., Cambridge, Mass., 1963.

Filtzer, Donald. *Soviet Workers and Stalinist Industrialization: The Formation of Modern Soviet Production Relations, 1928–1940*. Armonk, N.Y., 1986.

Fitzpatrick, Sheila. *Stalin's Peasants. Resistance and Survival in the Russian Village after Collectivization*. Oxford, 1994.

Fraenkel, Ernst. *The Dual State: A Contribution to the Theory of Dictatorship*. London, 1941.

Getty, T. Arch. "State and Society under Stalin." *Slavic Review*, 50:1 (Spring 1991), 18–35.

Getty, J. Arch, and Robert T. Manning, eds. *Stalinist Terror: New Perspectives*. Cambridge, 1993.

Getty, J. Arch, Gabor T. Rittersporn, and Viktor N. Zemskov. "Victims of the Soviet Penal System in the Pre-War Years: A First Approach on the Basis of Archival Evidence." *American Historical Review*, 98:4 (Oct. 1993), 1017–1049.

Gill, Graeme. *The Origins of the Stalinist Political System*. Cambridge, 1993.

Goldman, Wendy. "Women, Abortion, and the State," in *Russia's Women: Accommodation, Resistance, Transformation*, Barbara Evans Clements, et al., eds. Berkeley, Calif. 1991.

Goldman, Wendy Z. *Women, the State and Revolution. Soviet Family Policy and Social Life, 1917–1936*. Cambridge, 1993.

Hazard, John N. *Settling Disputes in Soviet Society*. New York, 1960.

Huskey, Eugene. *Russian Lawyers and the Soviet State: The Origins and Development of the Soviet Bar, 1917–1939*. Princeton, N.J., 1986.

"Vyshinskii, Krylenko, and the Shaping of the Soviet Legal Order." *Slavic Review*, 46:3–4 (Fall-Winter 1987), 414–428.

Jaworskyj, Michael, ed. *Soviet Political Thought. An Anthology*. Baltimore, 1967.

Juviler, Peter. *Revolutionary Law and Order*. New York, 1976.

"Contradictions of Revolution: Juvenile Crime and Rehabilitation," in Abbott Gleason et al., eds., *Bolshevik Culture: Experiment and Order in the Russian Revolution*, Bloomington, Ind., 1985.

Kamenka, Eugene. "The Soviet View of Law." *Problems of Communism*, March-April, 1965.

Konstantinovsky, Boris. *Soviet Law in Action. The Recollected Case of a Soviet Lawyer*. Cambridge, Mass., 1953.

Knight, Amy. *The KGB. Police and Politics in the Soviet Union*. Boston, 1988.

Beria. Stalin's First Lieutenant. Princeton, N.J., 1993.

Kravchenko, Victor. *I Chose Freedom. The Personal and Political Life of a Soviet Official*. New York, 1946.

Kucherov, Samuel. *Courts, Lawyers, and Trials under the Last Three Tsars*. New York, 1953.

The Organs of Soviet Administration of Justice: Their History and Operation. Leiden, 1970.

Lampert, Nick, and Gabor Rittersporn, eds. *Stalinism: Its Nature and Aftermath. Essays in Honour of Moshe Lewin*. London, 1992.

Lapenna, Ivo. "Lenin, Law and Legality," in *Lenin: The Man, the Theorist, the*

Leader, edited by Leonard Schapiro and Peter Reddaway, New York, 1967, 235–264.

Leggett, George. *The Cheka: Lenin's Political Police*. Oxford, 1981.

Lewin, Moshe. *The Making of the Soviet System: Essays in the Social History of Interwar Russia*. New York, 1985.

Luryi, Yuri. "Special Courts in the USSR: A Comment." *Review of Socialist Law*, 8 (1972), 251–257.

Medvedev, Roy. *Let History Judge*. New York, 1971.

Morgan, Glenn. *Soviet Administrative Legality. The Role of the Attorney General's Office*. Stanford, Calif., 1962.

Oda, Hiroshi. "Revolutionary Legality in the USSR, 1928–1930." *Review of Socialist Law*, 6:2 (1980), 141–151.

"The Communist Party of the Soviet Union and the Procuracy on the Eve of the Revolution from Above," in *Ruling Communist Parties and Their Status under Law*, edited by Dietrich André Loeber. Dordrecht, 1986.

Orlov, Alexander [Lev Feldbin]. *The Secret History of Stalin's Crimes*. New York, 1953.

Packer, Herbert. *The Limits of the Criminal Sanction*. Stanford, Calif., 1968.

Podgorecki, Adam. "Totalitarian Law: Basic Concepts and Issues," in *Totalitarian and Post-Totalitarian Law*, edited by Adam Podgorecki and Vittorio Olgiati. Aldershott, U. K., 1996.

Provine, Doris Marie. *Judging Credentials: Nonlawyer Judges and the Politics of Professionalism*. Chicago and London, 1986.

Radzinowicz, [Sir] Leon. "Penal Regressions," *Cambridge Law Journal*, 50:3 (Nov. 1991), 422–444.

Radzinowicz, Leon, and Roger Hood. *The Emergence of Penal Policy in Victorian and Edwardian England*. Oxford, 1990.

Rittersporn, Gabor Tamas. *Stalinist Simplifications and Soviet Complications: Social Tensions and Political Conflicts in the USSR: 1933–1953*. Chur, Switzerland, 1991.

"Soviet Officialdom and Political Evolution: Judiciary Apparatus and Penal Policy in the 1930s." *Theory and Society*, 13 (1984), 211–237.

Schlesinger, Rudolph, ed. *Changing Attitudes in Soviet Russia: The Family in the USSR*. London, 1949.

Schwarz, Solomon M. *Labor in the Soviet Union*. New York, 1952.

Sharlet, Robert. "Stalinism and Soviet Legal Culture," in *Stalinism: Essays in Historical Interpretation*, edited by Robert Tucker, New York, 1977.

Sharlet, Robert, and Piers Beirne. "In Search of Vyshinsky: The Paradox of Law and Terror." *International Journal of the Sociology of Law*, 12 (1984), 153–177. Reprinted in *Revolution in Law: Contributions to the Development of Soviet Legal Theory, 1917–1938*. Armonk, N.Y., and London, 1990.

Shapiro, Martin. *Courts: A Comparative and Political Analysis*. Chicago, 1981.

Siegelbaum, Lewis. *Stakhanovism and the Politics of Productivity in the USSR, 1935–1941*. Cambridge, 1988.

Siegelbaum, Lewis H. "Defining and Ignoring Labor Discipline in the Early Soviet Period: The Comrades-Disciplinary Courts, 1918–1922." *Slavic Review*, 51:4 (Winter 1992), 705–730.

Siegelbaum, Lewis, and William Rosenberg, eds. *Social Dimensions of Soviet Industrialization*. Bloomington, Ind., 1992.

Solomon, Peter H., Jr. *Soviet Criminologists and Criminal Policy, Specialists in Policy-making*. New York and London, 1978.

"Soviet Penal Policy, 1917–1934: A Reinterpretation." *Slavic Review*, 39:2 (June 1980), 195–217.

"Criminalization and Decriminalization in Soviet Criminal Policy, 1917–1941." *Law and Society Review*, 16:1 (1981–1982), 9–44.

"Local Political Power and Soviet Criminal Justice, 1922–1941." *Soviet Studies*, 37:3 (July 1985), 305–329.

"The USSR Supreme Court: History, Functions and Future Prospects." *American Journal of Comparative Law*, 38:1 (1990).

Taranovski, Theodore. "The Aborted Counter-Reform: The Muraviev Commission and the Judicial Statutes of 1864." *Jahrbucher fur geschichte Osteuropas*, 29 (1981), 161–184.

Timasheff, Nicholas. *The Great Retreat. The Growth and Decline of Communism in Russia*. New York, 1946.

Timasheff, N.S. "The Impact of the Penal Law of Imperial Russia on Soviet Penal Law." *American Slavic and East European Review*, 10:4 (1953).

Toharia, Jose J. "Judicial Independence in an Authoritarian Regime." *Law and Society Review*, 9:3 (1975), 475–496.

Tucker, Robert C. *Stalin in Power: The Revolution from Above, 1928–1941*. New York and London, 1990.

Unger, Roberto. *Law in Modern Society*. New York, 1976.

Vaksberg, Arkady. *Stalin's Prosecutor. The Life of Andrei Vyshinsky*. New York, 1990.

van den Berg, Ger. *The Soviet System of Justice: Figures and Policy*. The Hague, 1984.

Viola, Lynne. *The Best Sons of the Fatherland*. Oxford, 1986.

Wagner, William. *Marriage, Property and Law in Late Imperial Russia*. Oxford, 1994.

"Tsarist Legal Policies at the End of the Nineteenth Century: A Study in Inconsistencies." *Slavonic and East European Review*, 54:3 (July 1976), 371–394.

Wimberg, Ellen, "Socialism, Democratism and Criticism: The Soviet Press and the National Discussion of the 1936 Draft Constitution." *Soviet Studies*, 44:2 (1992), 313–332.

Wortman, Richard S. *The Development of a Russian Legal Consciousness*. Chicago, 1976.

Yaney, George. *The Systematization of Russian Government*. Urbana, Ill., 1973.

Zelitch, Judah. *Soviet Administration of Criminal Law*. Philadelphia, 1931.

Zile, Zigurds. *Ideas and Forces in Soviet Legal History. A Reader in Soviet State and Law*. Oxford, 1992.

6. Unpublished

Foglesong, Todd. "The Politics of Judicial Independence and Impartiality: Russian Criminal Justice, 1981–1992." Unpublished doctoral dissertation, University of Toronto, 1995.

Gorlizki, Yoram. "De-Stalinization and the Politics of Russian Criminal Justice, 1953–1964." Unpublished D.Phil. thesis, University of Oxford, 1992.

Kazakov, Aleksei. "Organy sudebnogo upravleniia RSFSR v period s 1930 po 1970 gody." Unpublished Kandidat dissertation, Sverdlovsk Juridical Institute, 1984.

Khlevniuk, Oleg. "Rol Politbiuro v izmenenii karatelnoi politike v 1930-e gody." Paper prepared for the conference "Reforming Justice in Russia, 1864–1994: An Historical Perspective." Toronto, March-April 1995.

Waters, Elizabeth. "From the Old Family to the New: Work, Marriage and Motherhood in Urban Soviet Russia, 1917–1931." Unpublished doctoral dissertation, University of Birmingham, 1985.

Weissman, Neil. "The Soviet Campaign against Hooliganism in the 1920s." Paper delivered at the 1986 meeting of the American Historical Association.

Zima, V.F. "Golod i prestupnost v SSSR (1945–1947 gg.)," unpublished paper, 1993.

7. Interviews

Interviews used in this book fall into three categories:

A) In 1985 I conducted some twenty interviews in Israel with former Soviet legal officials and advocates, most of whom had worked during the Stalin period.

B) Between 1985 and 1987, my research assistant Gennady Ozernoi and I conducted more than thirty interviews with former Soviet legal officials and advocates living in the United States and Canada, many of whom began their careers in the Stalin years. These interviews were supported by contract No. 701 from the National Council for Soviet and East European Research to the University of Illinois at Urbana-Champaign, James R. Millar, Principal Investigator. Any analysis or interpretation drawn from these interviews is that of the author, and not necessarily of the sponsors.

C) Between 1990 and 1993 I conducted a number of interviews in Moscow with former Soviet legal officials and other informants. These included: Vladimir Terebilov, a procurator and justice official in the Stalin period, later USSR Minister of Justice and then Chairman of the USSR Supreme Court; Nikolai Chistiakov, an administrator for military courts in the late Stalin period and from 1935 to 1958 an instructor in the Administrative Organs Department of the Central Committee of the CPSU; Sergei Borodin, a member of the RSFSR Supreme Court in the early and mid-1950s; Arkady Vaksberg, veteran legal journalist and biographer of Vyshinskii; Vsevolod Kuritsyn, historian of Soviet legal institutions; and A.R. Ratinov, long-time student of Soviet legal culture.

To protect my informants, especially the emigre jurists, most of whom spoke on condition of anonymity, I have not indicated the source of particular comments, but refer only to "interviews." As a rule, I cite interviews only when more than one informant supported the same point.

Index

Abakumov, V. S., 398
abortion: fines for women undergoing, 417; legalization by Bolsheviks, 213–4; self-performed, 375; underground after ban, 217, 128–9; underground before ban, 213–5; in Weimar Germany, 213n
abortion, decree banning: discussion in press, 216–7; origins and content, 211–5; prosecutions, 217–21; punishment, 219–20; resistance by doctors, 218; under enforcement, 218–21
abortionists, underground, *see babki*
Abramova, A., 422n
absenteeism, criminalization of, 301; *see also* labor infractions; shirking
abuse of position, charge as substitute for theft, 437–8; *see also* crimes of officials
accidents: as basis for political prosecution, 240–3; criminal responsibility for, 138–42, 143–4; depoliticization of, 255
accusatory deviation, 403; *see also* acquittals, stigmatized
acquittals: campaign against, 372–4, 383, 385, 390–2; origins of stigmatization, 394–402; party officials discouraging, 383–5, 387; program confronting, 369–70; rates, 51–2, 135, 358n, 371–2, 393–4; stigmatized, 367–8; substitutes for, 392–4
adversary process, Krylenko's attack on, 71–4
advocates: lacking higher legal education, 270n; and pretrial investigation, 355, 357–8; role under attack, 73–4
age of criminal responsibility, *see* criminal responsibility, age of; juvenile crime edict
airplane, crime of overloading, 421
Akulov, Ivan, 105n, 145, 161, 163; losing

post as Procurator–General, 247; All-Union Legal Academy, 188
amnesties: during War and post-War period, 421–2, 441–2; of kolhozniki and rural officials, 128–9; to relieve overcrowded prisons, 67, 421; *see also* Instruction of May, 8, 1933
analogy, principle of: call for removal from criminal code, 407; in criminal code of 1922, 31–2; history in Russia, 31
Anashkin, G. Z., 342
Andreev, A. A., 240, 256
Andreev (of Smolensk), 258
Andrianov (of Smolensk), 249–51
Anglo-American Legal Tradition, 401–2
antilaw view, 18, 25–7, 186; during collectivization, 87–8; as less influential than assumed, 454–5; repudiation of, 156, 194
Antipov, 178
anti-Soviet agitation, 232; increase in 1935, 224
Antonov-Saratovskii, Anton, 181–2
appeals, avoidance during collectivization, 100–1; *see also* cassation review; supervisory review
appearances, fixation on, 458; and 1946 Resolution on Legal Education, 339–40; and Stalin Constitution, 191–2
arrests: groundless during collectivization, 121, 125, 127–8; struggle against groundless, 378–9, 392–3; resolution (Nov. 1938) on, 256–7; screening of, 128
Article 51 (of 1926 RSFSR criminal code), *see* sentencing below the limit
Article 53, *see* suspended sentences
Article 58, *see* political crimes
Article 61, *see* grain quotas, failure to fulfil
Article 111, *see* criminal negligence
Article 162, *see* theft
arson, as form of peasant resistance, 83

Series list, continued